TWENTIETH-CENTURY LATIN AMERICAN POETRY

The Texas Pan American Series

TWENTIETH-CENTURY LATIN AMERICAN POETRY

A BILINGUAL ANTHOLOGY

Edited by Stephen Tapscott

 UNIVERSITY OF TEXAS PRESS, AUSTIN

LIBRARY OF CONGRESS CATALOGING-IN-PUBLICATION DATA

Twentieth-century Latin American poetry : a bilingual anthology /
edited by Stephen Tapscott.
        p.   cm. — (The Texas Pan American series)
    Portuguese or Spanish originals with English translations.
    Includes bibliographic references and index.
    ISBN 0-292-78138-5 (cloth). — ISBN 0-292-78140-7 (pbk.)
    1. Latin American poetry—20th century.   2. Latin American
poetry—20th century—Translations into English.   I. Tapscott,
Stephen, 1948–   . II. Series.
PQ7087.E5T94   1996
861—dc20   95-40288

THIS ANTHOLOGY IS DEDICATED

—to those poets, translators, critics, and editors whose work it collects,

—to Andrew Rosing, and

—to Mary Tapscott

CONTENTS

PREFACE

This collection is weighted slightly toward values of representativeness and toward lyric forms. I have tried to choose poems, excellent on their own terms, that also represent some of the major patterns or stages of each author's development and that embody some of the terms and tendencies of the literary movements or moments in which the poems were written. This principle of representative selection allows me to include the most famous set pieces of individual writers and of various schools and movements (by and large, the selections do not differ significantly from those found in anthologies published exclusively in Spanish or Portuguese). I hope my choices also provide some context for those major and famous poems: within the individual career, within the intertextual conversation of poems and poets and movements, and within social and literary histories, including (in the translations) some North American traditions.

Nevertheless, I have never been particularly interested in the "Greatest Hits" approach to literary anthologies. Accordingly, I have preferred to offer several major and representative poems by each author included in the following pages. Because of limits of space, this decision to try to include more than one or two poems by each poet has meant that many excellent poets who deserve to be included are not, and that some fine poems here assume the extra pressure of serving as synecdoches, indicating not only the worth of a particular piece but also something of the richness of tradition around and behind it. I regret not being able to include more works by writers in exile or in the "Hispanic diaspora" (e.g., Chicano and Chicana poems, migrant worker songs, and poems by Hispanic writers living in the United States), more poems by politically engaged Nicaraguan and Salvadoran women, poems in indigenous languages (representing therefore different ethnic and class groups), more experimental poems and more poems in multisemic language combinations, more poems that challenge the hegemony of traditional Latin American gender roles—to cite only a few examples. I hope the biographical notes will indicate the clusters of association that surround and underlie those poems in this anthology which do represent the foregoing tendencies.

Limitations of space have resulted also in a preference for lyric forms as a principle of choice. I do believe that lyric forms are the most important mode of the Latin American poetic tradition. Assembling this collection, I found that in many cases to include a single longer epic or lyric sequence would demand the exclusion of so many important shorter lyrics that I reluctantly decided in most cases to favor the autonomous lyric examples. By rights, many poems of "epic" or of "lyrical epic" proportions—often poems that question the very dominance of the lyric structure or of the lyric voice—could have been included in an anthology that aspires to be comprehensive. These have had to be omitted or accounted for in other ways. In some cases, I simply believe that, however excellent the translation, a mere taste of a lyrical-narrative poem like João Cabral de Melo Neto's *Morte e vida severina / The Death and Life of a Severino* or Ferreira Gullar's *Poema sujo / Dirty Poem* would misrepresent the poem's true continuous energies. Much as I would like to have included samples from poems like these, I decided against such a distortion. In other cases, though, I have offered somewhat shorter poems to serve as exempla of the methods and arguments of the larger poem—not as substitutions, but as indicators. I hope that after having read William Carlos Williams' version of Octavio Paz' "Himno entre ruinas" / "Hymn among the Ruins," for instance, a reader will want to seek out Paz' systemic longer poem *Piedra de sol / Sunstone*. In still other cases, I *have* included edited samples from the longer poems (e.g., Vicente Huidobro's *Altazor*, Raul Bopp's *Cobra Norato / Black Snake*, and José Gorostiza's *Muerte sin fin / Death without End*), because I think the individual sections stand alone well enough. Fortunately, excellent bilingual editions of most of the book-length poems are available.

Pablo Neruda's poem sequence *Alturas de Macchu Picchu / The Heights of Macchu Picchu* presents a special case, in part because some critics would claim that this poem is itself part of a longer sequence, Neruda's survey of Latin American history in his *Canto general*, and so is fully comprehensible only in that larger context. As a compromise, this anthology offers pivotal sections by different English-language translators, in order both to sketch in the conceptual "plot" of *Macchu Picchu* and to point the reader toward different possibilities for a systematic interpretation of that essential poem, embedded in the translators' choices. Translation is an act of interpretation as well of rendering, a process of simultaneous transgression and appropriation, of encounter and respect. As I hope this set of choices about Neruda's poem sequence shows, the verb "to translate" (whether in Spanish or Portuguese or English) comes from the Greek word for "to transport," to lead or carry something substantive across a border.

I am grateful, first and primarily, to Victor Tulli, now of the University of Pennsylvania, whose brilliant lucidity and orderliness and energy helped make this book

cohere. Victor's work was sponsored largely by MIT's Undergraduate Research Opportunities Program (UROP), research which offers unique experiences for undergraduates at the university. Not only did the help I received from UROP make this project easier, but in profound ways the project would not have been possible without that help. Robert Noecker offered help early in the project; near the project's conclusion the program sponsored also some dedicated and energetic assistance, in the persons of Lukasz Weber and Chris Perry. I had not thought the young capable of such saintly patience. Some of the funds for production of this book were provided by the MIT Fund for Faculty Development, the Dean's Fund, and the Provost's Fund. The reference staff of the Humanities Library at MIT have been unfailingly helpful. My thanks also to the administrators and librarians of Balliol College, Oxford; to the custodians of the Widener Collection at Harvard (especially the Woodberry Poetry Room); to the Cornell University Graduate Library; and to the Poetry Room of the 92nd Street YMHA/YWHA in New York. And especially to my home at MIT, the literature faculty: to our chair, Peter Donaldson; our administrators, Monica Kearney, Eve Diana, and Janet Sahlstrom; our staff, Chris Pomiecko and Briony Keith. I would also like to thank Charles Purrenhage for his indefatigable and good-humored help in textual editing and design. Nancy Christoph of Cornell University and Sean Barrett of MIT offered sound and friendly advice about the critical assumptions of this project, and about my prose style. Michael Surman in Oxford offered organizational and moral support exactly when needed, and to the required degree. Mariusz Przybytek in Poland helped, laughed, and reminded me, at strategic moments, that I was in this enterprise for the joy of it.

Many of the poets represented here offered the rights to reprint their works for free, or for reduced fees, as the permission acknowledgments attest. Friends and other translators donated their energies generously; in many cases I have been able to repay them only with my thanks (and in one case with a bottle of Laphroig single-malt whiskey, as suggested, sent precariously through the U.S. mails). I am glad for the opportunity to thank them publicly.

S. T.
CAMBRIDGE, MASS.

A NOTE ON THE POEM DATES

For each poem or selection in this anthology, the date of first publication is shown at the end of the original-language version. If the date of first publication is significantly different from the date of composition, then the date of composition is given first, followed by the date of first publication (e.g., 1958/1964 or 26 octubre 1937/1939).

TWENTIETH-CENTURY LATIN AMERICAN POETRY

INTRODUCTION

This introductory chapter addresses the needs of the general reader—and of the intermediate student—who may already recognize some of the poems that follow. First-time readers might want to bypass the criticism and head straight for the poems, to enjoy a first encounter with them. Advanced readers and students will likely want to return to poems they already know, to discover new pleasures and connections for themselves. Some intermediate readers, though, in order to orient themselves for further discoveries, might welcome a map of the terrain with which they are already somewhat familiar.

The focus of this mapping essay is chiefly historical and textual. In it, I treat the "literary" as a category of activity within Latin American societies that is distinguished from other linguistic and social enterprises. I do so even though such a distinction is not always easy to draw crisply, and even though some Latin American writers have questioned whether such defining borders are appropriate ways to describe either the cultural role of poetic discourse in Latin America or the Latin American reader's experience of the poems. Often more partisan and yet more popular, more verbally dense and yet more emotionally accessible, more lyrical and yet more self-conscious, more ideologically freighted and yet often more sensuous than North American counterparts, poetry in Latin American societies has often filled cultural roles that differ from those of poetry in the intellectual and imaginative life of North America or Western Europe.

To a North American reader, the status of poems in Latin America can seem paradoxical. The poems seem more lyrically effusive but more publicly important than our poems, richer with metaphors and their connective energy, and yet at the same time more publicly responsible and revered, more attended to. Obviously, the social and cultural position of the poet in Latin America has differed also—sometimes because of the diverse ways those societies have associated their high cultures and popular cultures. When Latin American countries nominate their writers to be diplomats, international attachés, or makers and administrators of public policy, we in North America still register a mild surprise at the level of respect for creative writers and at the public familiarity with (and official tolerance of) their works.

The phenomenon involves not only writers as cultural personalities (although such iconography of course flourishes in Latin America as in the United States), but also the force of specific poems. These poems matter to their audiences in different ways than the poems of North American traditions matter to their literate audiences. The function or effect of the poem is culturally different, and the audience itself is often demographically different, as well. The statistical rate of literacy is technically higher in the United States than in other American countries, and yet in Chile even schoolchildren know, often from musical settings, sections of Pablo Neruda's poem "Manuel Rodríguez." Admittedly, the example of Neruda's popularity is an extreme case; he even ran, briefly, for the presidency of Chile. And yet the influence of the poets of the New Song movement in Chilean politics during the 1970s—immensely popular poets and singers, including Víctor Jara and Violeta Parra, whose politics reinforced Neruda's—suggests that Neruda may be the extreme example that proves the rule.

Years ago, I heard pivotal images from Neruda's "Ode to a Watermelon" while accidentally eavesdropping on a boy in Santiago who murmured the lines to a tray of melon slices he was selling on the veranda surrounding the city's fish market:

> Es la fruta del árbol de la sed.
> Es la ballena verde del verano...
>
> It is the fruit of the tree of thirst.
> It is the green whale of summer...

I did not recognize the lines. The boy did not seem moonstruck or drugged, nor especially bookish. I thought at the time that the child was a prodigious natural poet, or that some Latin American peoples have a special verbal affect (or some experience of the socialization of metaphorical language) which shapes them in that astoundingly lyrical way. Some time later I came across the lines in a collection of Neruda's poems, but I suspect that my first assumptions could still be partially accurate.

The chief advantage of the sequential, historical method of this introduction is that it sets these poems in contexts that might not be familiar to North American readers, contexts of Latin American cultural history and of the literary traditions of the "other" America. That sense of "otherness"—our apprehension of those traditions as innately foreign, often figuratively "feminized" in contradistinction to our tradition of "strong" poetics—has rendered these Latin American traditions subject to a certain kind of appropriation by translation. We take what we need from these writings as complements to our own traditions, or as ratifications of our own ambitions. In the 1960s, for instance, we translated the political Neruda because we needed an image of a popular political poet. In the process, we tended to ignore the historical contexts in which Neruda wrote (the Spanish Civil War, the CIA-supported undermining of the Chilean economy) and therefore missed the ways in which the populist power of Neruda's "simple" poems work in relation to a specific audience, a specific set of cultural forms, specific linguistic and literary traditions. Simi-

larly, we theorize about César Vallejo's "deep images," implicitly universalizing his work, but in the process we may miss the ways in which even in exile Vallejo remained deeply aware of his peculiar position as a Latin American Vanguardist writer with Indian and mestizo roots. Or we read Latin American women writers as protofeminist, even though the historical and cultural terms on which they discuss gendered social differences are related more directly to traditions of Latin American machismo, Catholicism, and nondemocratic nationalisms. The women poets of Latin America often address more directly the paradox of a literary tradition of machismo in a poetic tradition of refined, *raro* sensibility than they deal with what we would consider "feminist" themes.

The advantage of attending to such historical contexts is that it allows us to read the poets on their own historical terms. I hope that these translations, chosen both for their excellence as poems and for their historical signficance within our own tradition, can also shed light on the story of relations between the North and South. I hope we can more clearly see that "other" in its complex relations to us, and also see Latin America as autonomous in its "otherness," different in its traditions of literature as in its constructed gender relations, its economics, its metaphysical assumptions, its social and political procedures.

I think these advantages outweigh the disadvantages of the method, but we might as well acknowledge promptly the occasional disadvantages, both for this anthology and for this introduction. The historical patterns that this introduction and this collection trace will not explain the beauty and power of the individual poems, and I want to be clear that the linear method of the present introduction is by no means the only road to the interior of these poems, these poets, or this field. Some poems, and the shape of the careers of some writers, respond to historical contextualization more informatively than others. I accept that limitation, as I accept also three further unavoidable disadvantages of this method.

First, and most overtly, the historical method risks underestimating the odd, the unique: the uncategorized poet or the lightning-bolt poem. Too, the method presents occasional incongruous shifts of sequence in the anthology. This collection is arranged in order of the authors' dates of birth, and the resulting pattern can sometimes obscure the influence of "younger" poets on "older" poets. The elegaic portrait of Carlos Drummond de Andrade (b. 1902) by Manuel Bandeira (b. 1886) appears before Drummond's earliest poems in the sequence; similarly, some of the late poems by Neruda (b. 1904) were influenced by works of Nicanor Parra (b. 1914) which do not appear until later in the collection. Against such possibilities of omission or of anomaly, I can suggest only: reread the poems.

The second disadvantage of this method is that it can seem to obscure distinctions of state and nation in favor of continent-wide, sometimes totalizing, insights. Again, I am willing to work within this limitation, for two reasons. For one thing, distinctions of national boundaries are often less important in Latin American intellectual history than regional coherences (the Andean countries, Mesoamerica, Amazonia, the plains of the Río de la Plata, and so on). Also, despite the nationalistic urgencies of some of these poems, many of the important movements of Latin American writing in this century have been continent-wide and inclusive. In the cases of Modernism and New World–ism, for instance, countries that shared a religion, a common linguistic tradition, and similar colonial structures discovered terms of broad literary commonality. (I should mention also that fine anthologies based on national coherences and on thematic cohesions such as gender and race are already widely available, some in bilingual editions.)

The third limitation of this historical method is that, as the editor plots out latitudes and clusters and watersheds, monumental mountains in the distance remain unremarked, above the landscape and transcending the method of the map. This method, that is to say, will prove more helpful in sketching out tendencies and patterns than in explaining the rising syntheses that the best poets of the tradition accomplish. The present introduction does not explain how the brooding interiority of Vallejo's metaphors speaks so personally and powerfully to many individuals of widely differing aesthetic orientations. Historical explanations (the influence of Surrealist Vanguard movements, the pressures of the Spanish Civil War and of poverty and exile, the verbal lucidity and austerity of the Indianist and *sencillismo* ("simple-ism") traditions Vallejo obviously revered) cannot account for the ways Vallejo assimilates those tendencies and reintegrates them, making his voice private and singular and yet emotionally accessible. Nor can the historical method account for the transforming power of Neruda's evolutions: from the rangy Surrealism of his early love poems, through the meditative grandeur of his epic sequences in *Canto general*, through the Marxist-influenced tenderness of his later poems. Neruda's personalism confidently assimilates different aesthetics, modulating them into inflections of his own, uniquely recognizable voice. Historiography cannot entirely ac-

count for voice, nor therefore for effects of some of the most brilliant poems of this tradition, which for several generations since Modernism has depended largely on the power of the illusion of a speaking voice. Nor do I claim to do so in this introduction.

Thus, the limits of the historical method define the limits of my discussion here of several major writers, including Vallejo and Neruda, Gabriela Mistral, Nicolás Guillén, and Octavio Paz. Readers who are looking for other modes of information should read critical/biographical accounts of those individual poets. Better, one should reread the poems. This introduction is primarily for those intermediate readers and students, in the pause between reading and rereading the poems, for whom some historical contextualization might bring the shape of these luminous but blurry objects into clearer focus.

A POETRY OF IDENTITY: THE IDENTITY OF POETRY

A fertile myth, a pattern involving identity as a product and as a process in several modes, has informed much of Latin America's poetry. Questions of cultural and personal identity helped to define the underlying terms for the first generations of Modernist poets in Latin America. Further, the very history of responses and challenges to such questions has become in many cases a received body of themes and forms—a quasi-narrative "myth"—that serves the function of a tradition for subsequent generations of late Modern, post-Modern, Vanguardist, and contemporary writers. The traditions of Latin American literature, therefore, have often seemed paradoxical and provisional. Latin American poetry is grounded less in a stable relation between text and literate audience than in an uneasy set of questions about the very possibility of such a relation. The concern (whether in a satirical or a naturalistic mode) is less to define cultural forms than it is to define the very culture that such a poetry might address. Accordingly, Latin American poetry is less self-conscious about the illumination or reformation of society and more innately self-conscious about the challenge of poetry's verbal reality as a potentiating social form in itself. What other societies experience as Modern tensions of structural power, personal alienation, and the relation between writing and social organization, Latin American poetry from the start has tended to experience more directly as a self-reflexive thematic about the authority of writing itself.

It is true enough, but not the whole story, to say that poetry occupies a different position in Latin America than in other cultures that strongly experienced Romanticism. It is true also that at the ground of Latin American poetics clusters a set of key questions: (1) about the identity of Latin America as a collective cultural enterprise, or as an energy the poem springs from or speaks toward; (2) about the identity or function of the artist in such a complex and changing context; and (3) about the identity and structuring energy of the poetic enterprise itself. These three related modes of the myth of identity in Latin American poetry are the three chronological focal points of our discussion.

I. THE IDENTITY OF THE LATIN AMERICAN CONTEXT

The idea of America preceded the European settlement of the Americas. In an enduringly influential way, "America" was a project of European intellectual and political history. Conceiving of humanity as the locus of historical truth, understanding the human individual as a subject both within and aspiring beyond historical contingencies, the Renaissance on the European continent and in England wrote its ideals beyond the circumscriptions of local history. For intellectual and economic reasons, the Renaissance often conceptualized "America" as a fresh start beyond history, an El Dorado or a potential Utopia or a Virgin Land. America as an experiential place mattered chiefly as the locus of chronicles of imagination and daring, an epic landscape that demanded an equally epic scope of mind and word. In fact, the epic tendencies of lyrical prose accounts of the American experience, especially in Spanish and Portuguese writing, often allowed their authors to acknowledge the nobility of the Native American civilizations and the harshness of the conquistadores.

Among others, Bartolomé de Las Casas (in the Caribbean and Cuba, 1552), Garcilaso de la Vega (in Peru, 1605), and Bernal Díaz del Castillo (in Mexico, pub. 1632) recorded the conquest and exploitation of the Inca and Aztec civilizations in Homeric terms of respect for a noble enemy. Alternating scenes of historical battle with scenes of divine marvels and magic, Alonso de Ercilla dramatized both the Conquest and the courageous resistance of the native peoples of Chile, in his influential *Araucana* (1569–1589). Meanwhile, English models began to project Virginia in terms of lucrative real-estate possibilities (Thomas Hariot, 1588) and the New World as a staging ground for extended internecine European struggles, as in Shakespeare's *The Tempest* (1611). The Andean civilizations left no written literatures, and the literary traditions of the Mesoamerican

cultures, as Las Casas shows, were deliberately eradicated by the European conquerors. Both the process and the product of writing became associated in the emergent Latin American societies with European socioeconomic structures and, therefore, with Continental models of intellectual production.

Not surprisingly, from the time of the Spanish Golden Age, the predominant representations of Latin American reality tended to be filtered through Continental lenses. The mannered, ornate figurations of Luis de Góngora y Argote (1561–1627) imprinted themselves on colonial writing in both Spanish and Portuguese; Gongorism manifests itself as the American Baroque style. Its characteristics are its complex virtuosity, its rhetorical conceits and inversions, its mythological allusions and neoclassical artifice, its gallantry and velvety phrasemaking in the service of complex metaphors, its luxury and courtliness and oddly impersonal embellishments. On these terms, this Baroque style influences even the sonnets and ballads of the most passionate and mystical colonial poets of America, including Sor Juana Inés de la Cruz (1648–1695) in Mexico. On political terms, this received style affirmed cultural continuities between Europe and its colonies. Neoclassical satires leavened the exchanges occasionally, and, later, pre-Romantic theorists (Chateaubriand, Rousseau) effectively encouraged attention to an image of the Indian presence in the Americas.

For several centuries, a combination of factors reinforced imperial hegemony and the dominance of the Baroque forms that bespoke it. The Catholic Church's resistance to linear concepts of historical "progress," the association of aristocracy and literacy and privilege in the colonies, the economic-strategic advantages to Spain and Portugal from continued control of their empires: all these factors helped to ensure that the political and literary domination of the Americas would continue. Some twentieth-century writers, like José Lezama Lima in Cuba, have seen an essential tension of Latin American experience registered in the Baroque's combination of repressed eroticism and compensatory excesses. In this sense, Lezama Lima argues, the Baroque, not Modernism, is Latin America's first representative, indigenous style. This account has the advantage of explaining, to some degree, the enduring fascination of imagery and metaphor for Latin American poetics: the Image appeals to the Latin American experience of displacement, of the repressed desire and compensation that writing, as a form of identity formation, comes to represent in these changeable social contexts.

It is no coincidence that the gradual loosening of

colonial ties between the European empires and their Latin American colonies, under pressure from practical creole dissatisfactions with the administration of the colonies, was accompanied by shifts in received standard literary styles. Literacy and literature—especially poetry—remained largely the privilege of aristocratic classes (and of men), but the Wars of Independence (ca. 1810–1825) inaugurated an era of Romantic self-assertion. The campaigns of Simón Bolívar (in the northern sections of South America) and of José de San Martín (in the south) began to separate the colonies from the parent countries and opened the floodgates of early Romantic liberation in emotional, social, and political realms of experience. Ironically, the era of Bolívar began in Napoleonic Romanticism, when Napoleon laid claim to the throne of Spain and therefore loosened Spanish control of the colonies. The moment of opportunity crystallized when Napoleon was challenged in Europe; its high point coincided with Bolívar's late Romantic dream of a Latin American federation under a single constitution and governor. (In exile on Elba, Napoleon even considered invading Latin America as a new field of empire.) A reluctant dictator, by the 1820s Bolívar conceived of the South American continent as a single constituent entity, a vast and ethnically diverse fatherland ("magna patria") larger than the sum of its parts. For better or worse, Bolívar's dream of an organic Latin American unity, an organized hemisphere with a common historical destiny overriding its differences, would remain an attractive ambition, or at least a fertile metaphor, for many later writers and theorists.

Within a generation of Bolívar, however, that dream of unity fractured into a series of smaller conflicting ambitions, as the newly emergent nations of the continent tested the stability of republican democracy and the integrity of their new territorial borders (in the bloody War of the Triple Alliance against Paraguay, 1865–1870, for instance, and in the War of the Pacific, 1879–1884). Pressures of economic imbalance within the new democracies, not to mention external imperialistic challenges from foreign powers like the United States, seemed to demand strong assertions of social and personal autonomy—leading eventually toward caudillo dictatorships in several countries (like those of Juan Manuel de Rosas in Argentina, Antonio López de Santa Anna in Mexico, José Gaspar Rodríguez de Francia in Paraguay, Gabriel García Moreno in Ecuador). With some adjustments, many of the assumptions and forms of early European Romanticism were made to fit the demands of this new political configuration.

Romanticism empowered an aesthetic of ego and assertive autonomy; of anguish and personal turmoil manifested through social rebelliousness and through fierce fidelity to local experience; of heroic youthful liberalism (and sometimes hedonism); of sensibility to the landscape, especially to meditative vistas, the sublime, and the exotic; of compassion for disenfranchised classes and races of people. In its early stages, Latin American Romanticism's emphasis on autonomy encouraged nationalist rebellions. In its later stages, it strengthened autocratic dictators and, subsequently, several generations of liberal resisters to the caudillo regimes. As a set of tropes and forms and themes, Romanticism in Latin America introduced poets to the power of the local and to the vagaries of articulate public selfhood.

Although the Romantic movement impressed itself strongly across the continent, it had the effect of defining and consolidating different local structures, even to the point of allying Romantic poets with divergent nationalist and regionalist ideals. In the rich delta of the Río de la Plata, Argentine and Uruguayan writers postulated the myth of the gaucho as a liberalizing, rugged, Romantic personification of the historical moment, the spirit of a resolutely particular place. In Peru and Ecuador and Bolivia, Romantic writers asserted the historical novelty of mestizo consciousness, in which European habits of mind are grafted onto Incan racial memories: an integrated consciousness, new to human history and exotically strange even to itself. (The Peruvian José Santos Chocano revives the concept later, peeling away the exotic element and blending in a didactic tone, in his theories of *mundonovismo*, or New World–ism.) In Mexico and Chile, parallel Romantic impulses asserted the tumultuous truth of the "new" realities of landscape and consciousness in the New World, and that assertion diffracted variously into Indianism (with some sentimental distortions), *costumbrismo* poems of manner and local color (with some naturalistic emphases), and passionate nationalist braggadocio. In Brazil, Romantic poets eased the former colony out of the stream of Portuguese influence, challenged the evil of slavery (which was not finally abolished until 1888), and embued the poem with a personal, even Parnassian, elegance.

Despite its diverse applications in different areas of Latin America, Romanticism reoriented literary language in one large influential shift. Turning *away from* Spain and Portugal as political allies and as sources of literary influence, Latin American writing gradually turned *toward* France. As the example of Rubén Darío will demonstrate, late Romantics and early Modernists in Latin America adapted from their French models not only novel forms and tones, but also a set of attitudes toward the relation of the poem to its place. What began as Romanticism's tendency to reinforce liberation movements and patriotic resistance gradually modulated into a tendency to reinforce a more stringent independence, even isolation, within the poem's linguistically open, nacreously elegant "space." Some second-generation Romantics and early Modernists (like José Martí, José Asunción Silva, and Manuel Gutiérrez Náreja) did find in older indigenous forms (ballads, tales, and folk songs), and in English and North American popular art, models for the simplicity and clarity to which they aspired in their social poems. Nevertheless, despite the admiration and enduring affection that many people felt for Martí as a cultural figure (apologist for Cuban liberation from Spain and from the United States, martyr to the Revolution), Martí's sense of a potentially useful local literary tradition was only rarely shared among poets of Latin America. An attention to the scope and influence of French models, especially to the Parnassians and the Symbolist poets, was far more common.

The question of the political identity of the emergent American nation-states, therefore, dominated much of the discourse of several generations of Romantics in Latin America: from the youthful enthusiasms of Esteban Echeverría in Argentina and the sensibility of José María Heredia in Cuba (during the 1830s), through the prose polemics of Domingo Faustino Sarmiento in Argentina and of Juan Montalvo in Ecuador, to the "Men of the '80s" in Argentina, including Sarmiento's enemy José Hernández in his popular gaucho epic of 1879, *Martín Fierro*, which was to influence Jorge Luis Borges so strongly. The individuating impulses of various nationalistic political movements even lent momentum to the work of the "first Modern generation," especially Martí, Nájera, and Silva.

In this sense, then, it is reasonable to see the first wave of Modernism in Latin America as paradoxically both a stylistic rupture with the Romantic tradition and a conceptual continuity with the Romantic commitment to liberation. (As the example of the young Argentine Romantics suggests, the liberalism of early Romanticism did force many writers and intellectuals into opposition against certain dictators, and even into exile.) As the second generation of Modernists matured, however, the luster of the pure Romantic example was to fade, for several reasons. Aesthetically, the Romantic ode became a received standard form, its manner slightly academic and with a taint of arriviste mediocrity. Politically, Romanticism lost its early Pan-American grandeur. The early Romantics' optimism about the United States

as a potential political ally and as a model of the virtues of enlightened utilitarianism faded in the glare of realpolitik. As the vehicle for nationalist squabbles, Romantic emotionalism became too closely associated with self-serving local interests and with an opportunistic personalism on the part of manipulative politicians (a tendency that would survive in the cults of personality surrounding later Latin American autocrats like Perón and Castro). Culturally, by the end of the nineteenth century, Romanticism had compromised itself by falling into a pattern of collusion among intellectuals, poets, and dictators in several countries. (The Modernist revolution by no means ended this pattern, of course, as the careers of some important Modernist writers illustrate. Chocano, for instance, was willingly co-opted by the bloody dictator Manuel Estrada Cabrera of Guatemala. For that matter, in his travels Rubén Darío himself enjoyed the hospitality of some of the continent's worst dictators, including, at the end, Estrada Cabrera. By some accounts of Brazilian literary history, the controversies and the aesthetic insouciance of the first generation of Brazilian Modernists were encouraged by the owners of the coffee plantations, as a tactic to divert public energies from land-reform movements. And as late as the mid-1930s Chocano and Leopoldo Lugones were publicly arguing that fascist authoritarianism would be a more appropriate ordering principle for Latin American states than liberal democracy.)

By the late nineteenth century, the Romantic movement, asserting autonomy and a somewhat pious public emotionalism, had largely played itself out. The stage was set for a new set of questions about a Latin American literary and cultural identity—questions based less on the issue of the identity of Latin America and more on the issue of the identity of the Latin American individual, as revealed or invented or transformed through the poem. The Spanish-American War of 1898, which marked the final dissolution of the Spanish empire in the Americas, punctuated also a cultural, aesthetic, and moral shift. Freed from Spanish political domination, writers and other intellectuals came to identify the influence of Spain—hierarchic, grounded in the Catholicism of the Counter-Reformation, residually resistant to scientific progress, capitalist enterprise, and free speech—as stultifying. Movements toward "modernity" rushed in to take the place that the Spanish influence had vacated. The United States seemed for a while to offer models—Protestant discipline, prosperity, democratic freedoms—but admiration for the United States was quickly enough compromised by an imperial sense of Manifest Destiny and gunboat diplomacy. On aesthetic terms, the other option to the influence of Spain seemed to be: find other modes of a cosmopolitan "European" identity in the New World. Rubén Darío discovered French literary models, and Latin American Modernism was born.

2. THE IDENTITY OF THE LATIN AMERICAN POET

Modernism and Rubén Darío

In this context, the efflorescence of Latin American Modernism can seem to be both a repudiation of the bombastic sentiment of late Romanticism and yet also a dialectical turn of Romantic feeling back on itself, on formal terms. Theorists like José Ortega y Gasset and Enrique Anderson Imbert have measured the momentum of change in Latin American writing by distinguishing "generations" of change (late Romantics, first-generation Modernists, second-generation Modernists, post-Modernists, Vanguardists, and so on). Although sometimes these distinctions can seem arbitrary, the relative measurement this method offers can be useful. By this standard, Modernism can be read in part as a response to Latin America's new prosperity and stability, from the 1880s until early in the twentieth century, and in part as a dialectical, generational reaction against the excesses of the late Romantics. Or conversely, the late Romantics and first-generation Modernists can be said to have made possible the consolidation of Modernist values between the 1870s and World War I. (To use the vocabulary of Anderson Imbert's famous formulation: by constituting an obstacle that required Modernist writers to "clean house," the example of the Romantics helped the Modernists to define their own purposes dialectically.) Literary and cultural historians differ, therefore, both when they account for the origin of Modernism (continuity? rupture? wholly new direction?) and when they describe the scope of the Modernist moment.

Modernism, Federico de Onís argues, may have been part of a "crisis" in Western culture, a precipitation of new social forms in politics, religion, the arts, science, and domestic life. In this sense, also, Juan Ramón Jiménez reads the Modernist literary movement as participating in a general upheaval of values at the end of the nineteenth century. Other critics find in Latin American Modernism an expression of some enduring characteristics of Latin American identity and experience (emerging racial and class combinations in a new aesthetic

inclination, in contradiction to Anglo-Saxon utilitarian values, as José Enrique Rodó writes in *Ariel*, 1900: a pressure of spirit over technique, of indigenism over imperialism, and so on). The genius of *modernismo*, according to this reading, is that it articulated the characteristics of an identity that had been waiting to be expressed—and by expressing them, inscribed them into the world's conscience. Accordingly, by this account, pure Latin American Modernism defines, or realizes, a new combination of ancient and twentieth-century energies, a new consciousness that has wider applicability insofar as the emergent identity of this "American" character stands metonymically for more general human experience in the twentieth century, either freshly integrated or representatively conflicted.

Whether we think Modernism represents a specific literary movement or a general cultural condition, the track of a historical period or a recurrent attitude toward human experience, depends largely on the nature of the questions we ask of Modernist texts. (Of course, similar questions have been asked of Romanticism: historical movement or recurrent impulse in Western consciousness?) Both the focused and the generalizing explanations do accurately describe systematic patterns in Latin America's experience of Modernism: paradoxically, the first account fits with respect to textual causes, the second with respect to ideological and historical effects. Although the Modernist literary movement in Spanish America may have begun as a response to social conditions, it quickly became an effective cause in its own right.

For our purposes, a relatively neutral description might be best. In Latin America, *modernismo* was a primarily literary movement, manifested chiefly through poems and critical prose, in the last decades of the nineteenth century and the first decade of the twentieth. Insofar as it followed several generations of Romantic practice, which had come to be associated with nationalistic and public aims, Modernism both challenged Romantic tenets and refined Romantic practices. Modernism had the effect of shifting attention away from propagandistic sentiment and naively realistic representation, and toward experimental European, especially French, literary models. Asserting the need—even the responsibility—of the writer to present a verbal landscape of exoticism, elegance, and precision from the perspective of an "ivory tower" (in a poem of 1905 Rubén Darío adapts Sainte-Beuve's phrase), it pulled Latin American writing out of the Spanish and Portuguese mainstream and yet asserted another version of the utopianism, verbalism, and elegance that had always been part of the Hispanic legacy to Latin American language and identity. Modernism was a cosmopolitan, erudite movement of individuation and imaginative withdrawal. Its writers often saw themselves as alienated, sensitive *raros* who, by sketching lush internal landscapes, articulated the inner life of individuals in a culture challenged by materialistic and imperialistic forces.

Although its motivating force was aesthetic and individuating, Modernism had a unifying effect on Latin American intellectual life. Modernism was the first Latin American literary movement that spoke through and for Latin American writers identified *as* Latin Americans, citizens neither of a colony nor of separate emergent nations. It was the first movement to reverse the current of literary influence. Although its chief predecessors were French, by choice, *modernismo* was the first intellectually autonomous literary movement to influence Spanish and Portuguese writers in Europe. Sometimes it was received enthusiastically, as in the cases of Jiménez and Antonio Machado; sometimes hesitantly, as in the case of Miguel de Unamuno. Modernism began in— and also shaped—a period of liberalism, constructive positivism, industrialization, international capitalization, and Yankee imperialism. It ended in the Mexican Revolution and the rubble of World War I. Its chief proponent was Rubén Darío, whose career defined and summarized these tendencies.

The chief characteristics of the *modernista* poem are its mysterious clarity, as of an object viewed by moonlight or phosphorescence; its openness to rhythmic experimentation and new metrical forms; its passionate formalism, bordering on aestheticism but surprisingly willing to celebrate the uniqueness of Latin American landscapes, wildlife, tangled history, and racial diversity; its musicality, shaping through melodic lines a Wagnerian "pleasure landscape" of swans and lilies, Titans and princesses, gold and jewelry and languorous kisses; its eroticism, hedonism, verbal precision, and apparent frivolity; its cosmopolitan, transhistorical, and mythological references; its simultaneous coldness and "sincerity" (Darío's term); its aristocratic, occult disdain for "propaganda" and yet its nostalgia, melancholy, and compassion. And the clearest exempla of the *modernista* text are the poems of Rubén Darío.

The arc of Modernism is the shape of the influence of Darío. His development characterizes the movement—from the appearance of *Ismaelillo* (1882) and, more important, *Azul...* (Valparaíso, 1888), through the defining moment of "El cisne" ("The Swan") and *Prosas profanas* (1896), and into his later, overtly political declarations. Darío personified many of the complexities of the movement. Although he advocated French models,

from his earliest years he steeped himself in the works of classical Spanish writers: Garcilaso, San Juan de la Cruz, Góngora, Gustavo Adolfo Bécquer. Although his private life was often disheveled and alcoholic, he celebrated the serene "inner kingdom" the Modernist poem postulates. Although internationalist in outlook and dandyish in aspect, he was often mestizo in manner (and perhaps racially part Indian, too, as Vallejo suggests later—or part Afro-Peruvian, as Paz speculates). On one occasion, Unamuno laughed that under Darío's fancy sombrero he could see Indian feathers poking out. Darío gracefully turned the joke: "I take a quill like this one from under my hat, to write with!" One of the reasons for the wide appeal of Modernism in Latin America was that Darío, who was born in Nicaragua (not until then a locus of intense literary activity), deliberately spoke to and for a wider audience, perhaps even because of his obscure origins. One of the reasons for the inclusiveness of the movement was that Darío, whose parents had separated when he was three years old and who was raised by an aunt, seldom felt at home in any one place but traveled widely as a journalist, cultural attaché, and lecturer. And one of the reasons for Modernism's dissemination of interest in international models was that Darío himself, who discovered the French experimentalists only while he was living in Chile (1886–1888), later traveled widely in Europe and the Americas and personally transmitted much of his own passion for the French Parnassians and Symbolists to friends—Julio Herrera y Reissig, Ricardo Jaimes Freyre, Amado Nervo, and others.

The formal models that interested Darío shifted over time. Many poems in the first edition of *Azul...* obviously owe some of their clarity and metrical carefulness to the linguistic finesse—the "floating dream" effects—of the Parnassian work of Leconte de Lisle and Théophile Gautier. Within several years, in the pieces collected in the second edition of *Azul...* (1890) and in *Prosas profanas* (1896), the influence of the Symbolist poets shows up more strongly, as in the Baudelairean suggestiveness of "El cisne" and in the Verlaine-inspired music of "Era un aire suave...." (José Enrique Rodó's famous skepticism toward Darío's poems on the grounds of *Azul*'s preciosity appeared in Rodó's preface to the second, more Symbolist, edition of Darío's book. In this sense, the criticism was already slightly out of date when it appeared.) *Cantos de vida y esperanza* (1905) registers Darío's almost complete turn toward the subjectivity, figuration, and deeper mysticism of the fully Symbolist poets, especially toward his friend Verlaine's commitment to personal feeling mediated by sensuous musical symbols.

Throughout the range of his formal changes, however, Darío's strongest influence was and has continued to be one of liberation. The example of his wide appropriations of diverse metrical forms opened new fields of possibility for other writers. Darío virtually reinvented the sonnet, for instance, in the 1890s; he reintroduced the rhythms of the traditional ballad and the madrigal (1905); he was proud of having made the eleven-syllable accentual line a flexible vehicle of internal harmony for Spanish-language poems; when he used the fourteen-syllable Alexandrine line, especially in his later political works, Darío provided a lasting model of inclusiveness for Latin American poems with political and social arguments. (The obvious ideological analogy to Darío's inclusive line would seem to be Whitman's free-verse line of Jackson-era expansiveness, but Darío's intellectual antecedent, as he maintained, was the classical French example.)

For all his own adaptations of different metrical forms, Darío influenced Modernist experimentation chiefly because he offered a range of open choice more than a proscriptive model of what was *not* permissible. One way to measure Darío's influence is to watch the wide track of his friendships. Although he enthusiastically wrote criticism and travel accounts for journals (especially for the magisterial *La Nación* in Buenos Aires), and although he sponsored periodicals (like Jaimes Freyre's *Revista de América*, 1894), Darío founded no "school." The concept of association he preferred, typically, was that of a "brotherhood." Darío wrote the poems that defined the Modernist era (the date of his death in 1916 is sometimes given as the end of the Modernist period); other writers consolidated the style and the school of *rubéndarismo*. A dedicated and intense friend of many other writers, Darío in his literary associations encouraged others to accept the Modernist premise of the pursuit of their own (sometimes idiosyncratic) aspirations. In Buenos Aires (1894–1898) Darío promoted both the Argentine Leopoldo Lugones in his Symbolist individuation and the Bolivian Jaimes Freyre in his Parnassian elegance. In nearby Montevideo, despite Darío's own "mental Gallicism," the influence of Darío encouraged Herrera y Reissig in his sympathetic idealization of Uruguayan village life. In Paris and Madrid (1902–1905) Darío's example helped to confirm the Mexican poet Amado Nervo in his mystical pantheism; and yet Darío's later relations with the Peruvian José Santos Chocano helped Chocano, despite his outspoken resistance to French influences, to define his own tenets of Indianism and New World–ism. Many similarities link these colleagues of Darío as a "brotherhood" in a specific evolving historical moment, and yet what is re-

markable is that the mature works of these associates represent significantly different applications of Darío's Modernist commitment to personal aesthetic beauty and formalism. "Mi literatura es mía en mí" (My literature is mine and mine alone), Darío proclaimed, and he offered a range of similarly personal *modernista* permissions and possibilities to other writers.

Modernist Patterns and the Case of Brazil

Descriptions of Modernist poems can make their poised formality sound static. What continually surprises me as a reader, however, and what I believe the Modernist movement bequeathed to later generations, is a quality of sustained tension, as of a motion that closes its ring but continues to circle in place. I hear this quality of dynamic tension in the most famous *modernista* poems and also in later works, even some by writers who resist the Modernist formal example.

Consider the following features of the Modernist dynamic, already suggested in part by the preceding sketch of Darío's career:

- Darío's balance between eroticism and solitude ("Era un aire suave…") influences poets from José María Eguren through Alfonsina Storni, early Neruda through later Vallejo and Xavier Villaurrutia, to Eunice Odio and Alejandra Pizarnik.

- The tension between European (philosophical, literary) models and local (physical) loyalty (an issue that had arisen, for instance, in Martí's "Dos patrias") informs Darío's "Nicaraguan" poems and echoes through poems by writers as diverse as Lugones, Vicente Huidobro, Borges, and Nicanor Parra. Related to this tension is a question of identity that uses metaphors of the conflict between Christianity (transcendence) and paganism (pleasure). For literal examples, see the sequence of poems that includes Ramón López Velarde's "Domingos de provincia," Mário de Andrade's "Domingo," Jorge Carrera Andrade's "Domingo," sections of José Gorostiza's *Muerte sin fin*, even Vallejo's "Fué Domingo en las claras orejas de mi burro" and Ernesto Cardenal's "Oración por Marilyn Monroe."

- Similarly, the tension between strangeness and clarity pervading Darío's work in both a stylistic and a moral dilemma (see "Yo persigo una forma…") influences poems by other Modernists and post-Modernists (e.g., Lugones), Vanguardists and Ultraists (e.g., early Vallejo), and becomes an overt thematic in works of sexual ambivalence by Storni, Mistral, Villaurrutia, and others.

- What begins as a tension between control and passion, fixity and flight, in Darío's earliest work subsequently carries through as a formal and ethical question. One might simply follow the swans and nesting birds of Darío and Enrique González Martínez through Chocano's condor ("El sueño del cóndor"), Carlos Pellicer's doves ("Grupos de palomas"), Gorostiza's fireflies ("Luciérnagas"), and Adélia Prado's pelican ("O pelicano"). Similarly, the image of water recurs as a register of tensions between identity conceived as stable and singular versus identity conceived as aggregative or collective: follow the rain and the watersheds from Martí and Darío through the post-Modern streams of Lugones, Storni ("Yo en el fondo del mar"), Juana de Ibarbourou ("Noche de lluvia"), Mistral's sense of the "flow" of organic life ("Una palabra"), Vallejo in Paris ("Piedra negra sobre una piedra blanca"), Neruda in Asia ("Galope muerto"), Raul Bopp in the Amazon (*Cobra Norato*, sections VI and XI), Borges on the beach ("El mar"), Pablo Antonio Cuadra in the isthmus ("Caballos en el lago"), and João Cabral de Melo Neto in a liminal space, overhearing the sea and the canefield in dialogue ("O canavial e o mar," "O mar e o canavial"). (The influence of Darío on Bopp, Cabral de Melo Neto, Prado, and other Brazilians is certainly less direct than it is on the other writers here, but the continuity of metaphors is significant.)

- The quasi-narrative tension between Modernist elegance and compassionate awareness of tragedy, a tension that permeates Darío's "Sonatina," sets the terms of both a tonal and a moral challenge for later writers. See, for instance, the implied narratives underlying Jorge de Lima's "Essa negra Fulô," Guillén's "Pequeña oda a un negro boxeador cubano," Vallejo's poems of the Spanish Civil War (*España, aparta de mí este cáliz*), or Enrique Lihn's "Recuerdos de matrimonio"—to choose examples almost at random. This pattern of setting lyric intensity against an implied narrative is pervasive in Latin American poetry.

- The pattern, adumbrated by the Modernist brotherhood, of exploring the tension between culture (historical and verbal) and nature (renewable in an unarticulated, continuous present tense) is likewise pervasive. One could simply track the thematic—as it turns from a question of cultural identity, through a question of personal identity, to issues of semiotics—in a sequence of poems involving a myth or situation of "return": Julio Herrera y Reissig's "El regreso," Ramón López Velarde's "El retorno maléfico," Jaimes Freyre's "Aeternum vale," Manuel Bandeira's re-creation of place in "Evocação do Recife," Rosario Castellanos' psychological reconstructions in "El retorno," Olga Orozco's story of failed repetition in "Miss Havisham," and, of course, Neruda's triumphant return to South America in *Alturas de Macchu Picchu*.

- The case of Neruda's *Macchu Picchu* suggests also how the Modernist tension of culture, nature, and prodigal return lifts into ideological discourse, as later writers take the Modernist question and set a myth of a lost Utopian unity, often a pre-Columbian Eden (see Alfonso Reyes), against a European historicity or against a myth of a future-oriented or transhistorical integration (see, variously, Cardenal, Lezama Lima, and Heberto Padilla).

- The question of the poem as a possible mode of knowledge, of occult intuition versus historical location, underlies poems like Darío's "A Roosevelt" and becomes overtly the theme of poems by Borges, Ricardo Molinari, Mistral, Carlos Germán Belli, and others. As these examples suggest, Darío's philosophical questions of the status of writing (see "Yo persigo una forma...") are foregrounded, later, by experimental poets in terms of writing as a mode either of knowing or of feeling and, still later, in tensions between authority (power, even authorship) and subversion within the field of the poem itself as a controlled or resistant model.

- The question of the status of language as sign or semantic revelation in tension against its function as symbol or as agent of concealment is, of course, at the heart of the *modernistas*' Symbolist program. To recognize that tension in the Modernist poem is to infer a continuity forward even through the Vanguardists and the *Contemporáneos* poets toward the Constructionists and Concretists. It recurs in literary arguments (Lezama Lima's assertion that the Baroque is a pattern of repression and compensation) through the amazingly recurrent Latin American fascination with the Image.

A fascination with the tension of the Image, as vehicle of both revelation and concealment, cerebration and sensuality, artifice and desire, ornament and essence, is perhaps the single greatest Modernist inheritance pervading Latin American poetry since Darío. And this set of tensions—valences that the *modernista* poem works to hold together—reflects many of the tensions of an integrated Latin American cultural identity, as well. Regarded as qualities of the poem, these

Modernist tensions reflect many of the central thematics of Latin American poetry since the opening of the twentieth century, and they register much of the legacy of Modernism for subsequent generations.

Lists tend toward reduction. Items in a list (poems, for instance) tend to collapse into the collective common denominator of the sequence. I acknowledge the implied reductionism of my long list of some of the characteristic continuities and tensions of the *rubéndarista*/Modernist impulse in Latin American poetry. I accept, hesitantly, that risk of reductiveness, because I think it is important to register the pervasiveness and endurance of Darío's Modernist influence, across the continent. If Spanish American Modernism had a capital city, it was probably Buenos Aires, but the movement's influence, like the restless peregrinations of Darío himself, spread out in a consolidating web across the literary classes of the new nations, and the Modernist poets recognized and cultivated the interrelatedness of their movement.

Brazil, a continent within a continent, was the exception. Modernism in Brazil differed in major ways from the integral force that went by the same name in other parts of Latin America. Literary history has tended to describe Brazilian Modernism as a series of phases and moments (like the Week of Modern Art in São Paulo, February 1922, which celebrated the centennial of Brazil's independence with events announcing radically new forms of aesthetic liberation; see Oswald de Andrade). Brazilian Modernism had no "Darío" who personified the historical moment, no central summarizing leader. What is called Modernism in Brazil was neither formalist nor French nor exotically elegant (those values had been served by the generations of Parnassian poets and Symbolists, like João da Cruz e Sousa). Rather, Brazilian Modernism exalted free-verse liberties; it built on models of Italian Futurism; it experimented in local and regional idiolects. Its locus was not the oneiric, otherworldly space of the *modernista* imagination with its sense of writerliness, but the verbal, self-consciously linguistic space of the poem *an sich*, as the writer aspired to the illusion of speech. Its analogies were not abstractly musical but were derived from the spoken and plastic arts (popular songs, Cubist painting, monumental sculpture). An urban and urbane movement, throughout the 1920s Brazilian Modernism did center in a capital city (São Paulo), where the Andrades and, later, Lima and Bandeira lived (although they all aspired to a nationally inclusive diction). With time, other regional centers asserted their own gravities (Belo Horizonte in

Minas Gerais attracted Carlos Drummond de Andrade, and Rio de Janeiro with its more cerebral intellectual tradition was home to writers including Cecília Meireles).

A differing sense of the form and diction of the poem sprang from the political assumptions underlying the Modernist movement in Brazil, especially as a second wave of writers, after the movement's exuberant and fervid *paulista* founders, reinstated and restated those earlier aesthetic assumptions. Spanish American Modernism had often defined itself *against* nationalistic rhetoric; it was elegant and sometimes elitist; it valued the liminal isolation of the visionary poet; and it had an oddly internationalizing effect on the Spanish American consciousness. By contrast, Brazilian Modernism was outspokenly nationalistic; it was often democratic and demotic; it took its initial tone from the witty insouciance, the Futurist speed and scientism and collage, of Oswald and Mário de Andrade; it aspired to be not internationalizing but localizing, to project an integrative literature for an emergent Luso-American character—in the words of Mário de Andrade, "to make Brazilians 100% Brazilian, to nationalize a nation that is as yet so lacking in national characteristics."

In some senses, what Spanish America called "Modernism," Brazil had experienced as "Symbolism." What Brazil experienced as "Modernism," post-Darío Spanish America would work through under the name of post-Modernism. (And as Gordon Brotherston points out, the terms of César Vallejo's individuation from *modernista* traditions surprisingly resemble some of the major terms of Brazilian Modernism: Vallejo's guarded admiration of Darío, his resistance to strident Americanism like that of Chocano, his disappointment with Latin American poetry's dependency on European poetics.) Indeed, the poems of the Brazilian Modernists may feel somewhat closer to us as contemporary readers of English: their tone and free-verse rhythms, their political overtness and confessional personalism, are discoveries that Anglo-American writers and Spanish American writers alike made later than Brazilian writers.

Post-Modernism and Vanguardism

A sonnet by Enrique González Martínez from 1911 takes its referent from Darío's famous poem "El cisne" even while it challenges the hegemonic influence of Spanish American Modernism:

> Tuércele el cuello al cisne de engañoso plumaje
> que da su nota blanca al azul de la fuente;
>
> Wring the swan's neck who with deceiving plumage
> inscribes his whiteness on the azure stream;

When González Martínez advocates twisting the "swan's neck," he articulates an inevitable and perhaps Oedipal reaction against the domination, and some of the excesses, of the *rubéndarista* mode of Modernism. In some senses he is articulating also the rebellious ideals of the Mexican Revolution (1910–1920). After thirty-two years of the dictatorship-presidency of Porfirio Díaz, with its autocratic emphasis on conservative positivism, property, and enforced order (important characteristics of Latin American Romanticism), a liberal-aristocratic movement (viz., Modernism) replaced it, but in its idealism the new government of Francisco Madero (1911–1913) proved as oblivious to people's pragmatic needs as Modernism, in its way, had been. A revolution of the masses erupted. It was consolidated through systematic changes in the economics, land use, social structures, and cultural attitudes of modern Mexico.

The literary pattern, post-Modernism, recapitulates the political pattern, the Revolution. (I should add, however, that there are some important qualifications to this analogy: Modernism had not had the galvanizing effects in Mexico that it had elsewhere, in part because Mexico had a strong liberal tradition of political resistance through its Romantic and Modern generations. Terms of continuity between idealistic Romanticism and revolutionary post-Modernism are a bit clearer in Mexico than in other countries.) Post-Modernism remains important in Latin American literary history both because of the defining poems of its own moment and because it opened toward a still more liberating experimental wave—the Ultraist or Vanguardist movement—that until recently was the major legacy of original energy in Latin American poetics.

In literary terms, post-Modernism is revolutionary, twisting the neck of the language. Repudiating the aestheticism of the Modernists as autocratic, melancholic, and often morbid, early post-Modernist writers proposed instead a poetry of personal conscience, verbal directness, and (later) Social Realism. What González Martínez anticipated in 1911, a poet like Ramón López Velarde in Mexico soon realizes in poems of provincial tenderness and sinuous lucidity. In Argentina, Lugones celebrates his homeland as a nation-state that is both the literal refuge of immigrants and a quasi-magical landscape. The richness of pre-Columbian history, the flavors and concepts that Indian languages carry into Latin American Spanish and Portuguese, the harsh conditions of contemporary Indian experience, and the Indian component in Latin American consciousness became concerns of public policy in Mexico, powered by the cosmic optimism of José Vasconcelos. This energy became poetic material for Mexican writers like Alfonso Reyes (in poems and essays), fed the imagination of intellectuals like Pedro Henríquez Ureña and José Carlos Mariátegui (in history), and was obliquely influential for poets outside Mexico, including Alfonso Cortés, José Lezama Lima, and César Vallejo. Post-Modernist attentions to regional and class concerns opened the way for an African presence (*poesía negra*) in poems by Luis Palés Matos in Puerto Rico and Nicolás Guillén in Cuba, as well as those of Jorge de Lima in Brazil. (The *negrista* poets continued long past early post-Modernism, assimilating energies from later Vanguardist and indigenous movements, from the internationalist Négritude theorists, and from the Harlem Renaissance. In this sense, the *negrista* poems are influenced by, but not defined by, post-Modernism.)

If some of these early post-Modern values recall Romantic themes and techniques, that similarity is no coincidence. The post-Modernist revolution opened the emotional windows of Latin American poetry, transforming Darío's "sincerity" into a self-conscious and often autobiographical neo-Romantic authenticity. Latin American post-Modernism in the years just before and after World War I, moreover, reflects tendencies of the culture on a scale larger than the personal. Many Latin American intellectuals and writers softened their attitudes toward Spain and Spanish cultural models as sources of patrimony. Concomitantly hardening their attitude toward the United States (in the face of North American attempts to consolidate the U.S. economic and political presence in the Americas), writers were disinclined to participate in Pan-American or European affairs. This attitude intensified during World War I, although the Spanish Civil War later caused many Latin American intellectuals to return to an internationalist perspective, with a great sympathy for the Spanish Republic.

Throughout Spanish America from 1910 on, the populist momentum of literary post-Modernism had four important effects on the social forms of Latin American literature. First, because of the new emphasis on social concerns, the realistic prose narrative, building on a base of French naturalism, grew in complexity and stature. As it developed in irony and structural self-consciousness, Latin American fiction advanced toward the explosion of writing and reader interest in the 1960s that would become known as the "Boom." Second, realizing that the effective elitism of Modernist verse had been reinforced by low rates of literacy and by minimal systems for producing and distributing texts, many writers began to address those conditions constructively, by working for governmental programs of educational reform, for instance, and by promoting the establishment of major, centralized book-publishing houses and wider systems of distribution and marketing, including innovative small magazines for poems and essays. Third, the dissolution of Modernism's cultural dominance resulted in a diffusion of competing "schools" of poetry. Fourth, and most important, post-Modern attitudes of rebelliousness, populism, and responsibility coincided with the emergence of several waves of talented women writers. These last two phenomena, which proved more influential than post-Modernism itself, deserve elaboration.

Combined with the second effect (the opening of more effective systems of producing and distributing literary texts), the third of these four sociological phenomena produced a polysemous welter of schools, tendencies, and isms. Converging from different perspectives, both Octavio Paz and Roberto González Echevarría claim that Latin American writing has been strongly shaped by this tendency toward discourse through essays and manifestoes. Inheriting a Spanish intellectual framework that lacked the independent critical tradition of, say, Germany or France, Hispanic intellectual culture has often worked out its questions of authority and change through a myth of writing—making little distinction between literary and political activities—and through a class-based discourse of manifestoes and reviews, continuing the important tradition of Sarmiento, from the prose sections of his *Facundo* (1845), through Rodó's *Ariel* (1900), toward Roberto Fernández Retamar's *Calibán* (1968) and beyond.

Two examples of this tendency toward diversification—"Creationism" and "Ultraism"—will illustrate. These examples also suggest how the liberating intellectual energies of post-Modernism opened into the wider stream of Vanguardism. When Vicente Huidobro returned from Paris to Chile in 1916, he was heady with the yeasty brew of French experimentation, especially the syntactical fractures of the Cubists and Gertrude Stein and the typographical/syntactical novelties of Apollinaire. Combining those elements with the North American self-reliance of Emerson, whom he had revered for years, Huidobro announced the arrival of a Vanguardist "Creationism" in South America. Huidobro had written manifestoes earlier, but his return to Buenos Aires marked the avant-garde "Americanization" of many of these concerns. (The shift in thematic techniques begins to suggest also an incremental shift from post-

Modernism to Vanguardism, although the line is difficult to draw precisely. Poets like González Martínez, López Velarde, and Reyes are certainly "post-Modernists," even though they may shift direction later; poets like Huidobro, Borges, Neruda, Vallejo, Cuadra, and the early Paz are certainly "Vanguardists," even if they did begin in some cases as Hispanic "post-Modernists.") Sidestepping the questions of social responsibility that had occupied many in the first wave of Hispanic post-Modernists, Huidobro maintained that the three duties of the poet were simply "to create, to create, and to create." From 1917 through the 1920s, he trumpeted theories that described chiefly his own ambition, an art of transformation that included "nothing anecdotal or descriptive." As the generator of a "pure creation," the poet should "make a poem as nature makes a tree." In an important sense, Huidobro alone is the only truly Creationist writer—as befits, perhaps, a "movement" so dedicated to the privileged uniqueness of the poet—and yet the legacy of the Vanguardist movement continues far beyond the late post-Modernist movement and beyond Huidobro's example.

For all the partisan energy Huidobro expended to explain the importance and distinction of Creationism, finally the effects of that "movement" do not differ much from the effects of related Vanguardist tendencies. "Ultraism," for instance, was the name the young Jorge Luis Borges gave to the movement he almost single-handedly brought to Argentina from Spain, circa 1921. Borges' avant-garde rediscovery of the Spanish language as a vehicle for literary experimentation manifested itself chiefly in a commitment to "the greatest independence" for the metaphor as a "primordial" mode of knowledge and connotation. Borges' early poems are the chief examples in Latin America of the effect of "Ultraism" (a movement which was known by that name only in Spain and Argentina). The period during and just after Borges' "Ultraist" stage is the period of Borges' best poems. As he vividly reinvents Buenos Aires and the pampas as resonant oneiric metaphors outside the field of traditional cause and effect, Borges in those early poems is also developing some of the Surrealist techniques which will be the vehicle of his later major work in fiction.

Like the designation "Creationism," the name "Ultraism" serves a double function in literary history, indicating both the local particular (the emergence of an Argentine and Uruguayan avant-garde movement, known variously as Ultraism, *martínfierrismo*, and Florida) and the historical generality ("Here is our motto: Ultra, in which all advanced tendencies will fit"). Within a few years, Borges will come to regard his Ultraist insistence on surreal or arbitrary images as rather immature, a striving after spectacular effects; but in the work of a poet like Ricardo Molinari, for instance, the evidence of Ultraist influence, tempered by a more focused social conscience, is clear. Mexican post-Modernism had opened the poet's political eyes, and the technical experimentation of the Ultraist/Vanguardist movements opened the poems' forms. From the late 1920s until the late 1960s, the terms of this evolving Vanguardist synthesis were for the most part the dominant terms of Latin American poetics.

In their focus on the transforming and subconscious power of the verbal metaphor, Creationism and Ultraism realigned some of the emphases of the received literary tradition. Post-Modernism had discovered in the poems of Herrera y Reissig, for instance, Modern antecedents for the autonomy of the startling "Surrealist" metaphor. Rereading the late poems of Herrera y Reissig in these terms, the Vanguardists retrospectively defined a continuous line of influence from Modernism to subsequent Vanguardist poets like Molinari in Buenos Aires and Gorostiza, Pellicer, and Villaurrutia in Mexico. This tangled continuity makes it difficult to distinguish specifically among post-Modernist, Vanguardist, and even some post-Vanguardist work. The strength of the writer's commitment to metaphor as a mode of knowledge often becomes the defining criterion of such (arbitrary) classification. Because of Latin American poetry's continuous fascination with the Image, however, even that criterion seems somewhat porous. Further, Vanguardism in Latin America often contained a localizing, grounding energy of place. Blending nationalist energies and representative forms of indigenous cultures with European theories (Surrealism, Futurism, Dada), writers like the *negrista* poets of the Caribbean, the Nicaraguan *vanguardia* poets, and the nativist *orcopatas* poets of the Andes integrate European influences with local concerns, fusing those energies into the mysterious, quasi-autonomous dominant Image, beyond Darío's example.

Perhaps because of Latin American poetry's enduring engagement with the perceptions of place and with fictional landscapes, and perhaps because of the poetic culture's already rich tradition of dense images, a systematic Surrealism grounded in Freudian theories of the unconscious never took strong root in Latin American poetics. The Vanguardist liberation of the metaphor, however, has often had the effect of an indigenous Surrealism, albeit one grounded on a notion of metaphor—and on a linguistic tradition of the Image as a

function of normative speech—significantly different from that of French theories of Surrealism. For instance, it is possible to read some of Neruda's early poems, or the mature poems of Jorge Carrera Andrade and Mario Benedetti, or Vallejo's early experiments and later "deep images," as forms of Surrealism mediated or domesticated by the influence of Ultraism.

Major writers like Vallejo and Neruda, however, put their Vanguardist or Surrealist energies to different uses. Vallejo disrupts conventional syntax and word formation (*Trilce*, 1922), demystifies personal lyrical emotion (*Poemas humanos*, 1939), condenses. His Surrealism locates and individuates, shaping a diction for uniquely intimate private selves: the orphan, the exile, the survivors allied by the force of their solitudes. By contrast, Neruda's Vanguardist super-Realism optimistically expands and conjoins. Neruda "explains a few things." Especially after his *Residencias* (1933, 1935, 1947), the complex surreal image helps Neruda to project a public figure of revolutionary possibilities, a self who exclaims these images derived from common things in new combinations. (About the second *Residencia*, Amado Alonso made the early observation, in 1940, that Neruda's surreal metaphors were deliberately a new form of Gongorism, rehabilitating a recurrent and important Latin American tradition.)

Crucially important, as noted above, was the emergence of remarkable women writers and women's writing. In the new, post-Modernist dispensation, writers like Juana de Ibarbourou and Sara de Ibáñez in Uruguay, Alfonsina Storni in Argentina, and Gabriela Mistral in Chile—largely excluded from the Modernist "brotherhood"—passionately articulated the experience of women in traditional Latin American societies. (While she belongs in this group for other reasons, the Uruguayan Delmira Agustini did maintain a stronger loyalty to Darío's formal example, and in this sense ought to be classified as a "late Modernist" writer, perhaps, as much as a "post-Modernist.") In Brazil, Cecília Meireles returns to a Symbolist, even hermetic, "feminized" image as the energy source of lyricism. In each case, a socially reformist impulse—sometimes satirical, sometimes tragic—at first tended to make these writers define themselves as "woman poets" and implicitly as "post-Modernists." This tension between gender and male-defined literary traditions within the single identity of the Latin American woman writer continues throughout women's poetry during the rest of the century.

Motivated at first by a kind of gender-based regionalism, these writers, each in her own way, began by consciously "limiting" themselves to socially "female" concerns. Each of these poets, too, would later experience a kind of transvaluation, by which the designation "woman poet" came to seem less restrictive and more potentially universal, either because the writer learned to celebrate the experience of Hispanic women or because she gradually expanded the inclusive implications of the poem and of the act of writing, often shifting toward "Vanguardist" concepts of form. The most accomplished and celebrated female writer of Latin America in the first half of the twentieth century, Gabriela Mistral, aspired to a complex universality grounded solidly on the emotional facts of female and maternal experience. In her later poems, especially, Mistral's tenderness and counsel circle outward to include the voices of peasants, the urban working poor, and other disenfranchised people, reaching archetypal commonality on the basis of shared emotional experience. Paul Valéry recognizes the universalizing force of Mistral's female, often maternal, identification: "While so many poets have praised, celebrated, damned or called upon death . . . few seem to have meditated on that transcendental act par excellence, the production of the living being by the living being."

To some readers at the end of our century, especially to contemporary women readers, the strategies of these poets can sometimes seem reductive, deliberately limited to themes of female experience and to shorter lyric forms. If so, we should probably try to recontextualize these poets historically, to recover the boldness of their poems of female sexual energy and social experience in a political culture of machismo, a philosophical culture of transcendence, and a literary culture of *raro* Modernism. Despite their individual differences, these women writers tend to be associated in a cluster, in which critics sometimes hear a *sencillismo* tendency (from *sencillo*, "simple"), suggesting a loose association of these writers and some male poets. Beginning in Modernism and neo-Romantic sincerity, through their thematic innovations these writers in effect forged their own terms, autonomous and emotional and lucid and rich in images, inventing a different mode of Vanguardism by making themselves a vanguard.

The revolutionary, optimistic, resiliently Realist energy of the early post-Modernist movement was an energy of declaration. Inevitably, it came into conflict with more cosmopolitan, neo-Modernist aesthetic energies. In Mexico, the cosmopolitan side of the dialogue is represented by the provocative *Contemporáneos* group, centered around Mexico City. Taking their name from the review *Contemporáneos* (1928–1931), the "group" defined itself by a shared sense of the intellectual's deepest cultural responsibility to a West European intellectual tradition. Within that porous description, the movement influenced writers as diverse as Carlos Pellicer, Jaime Torres Bodet, Xavier Villaurrutia, and even Efraín Huerta and Eunice Odio. The *Contemporáneos* writers were aristocratic, Bohemian, learned, occasionally effete in their refinements. Because their primary commitment was aesthetic, the literary politics of the *Contemporáneos* group—especially their resistance to social protest writing, to noisy nationalist aesthetics, to Hispanic macho postures—were not so much programmatic commitments as prose positions in response to contemporary questions. Many of the group were excellent critics, and all were poets. The form of the meditative lyric seems flexibly congruent with their organic, visionary tones—from the speculative sensibility of Pellicer, through the charged nocturnal melancholy and homoeroticism of Villaurrutia, through the harsher indignation of Huerta.

Although the careers of some *Contemporáneos* poets, like that of Torres Bodet, testify to a sense of the intellectual's social responsibility, their occasional escapism or calculated indifference to political realities led them into conflict on the one hand with overt Social Realists and with the poets of *estridentismo* ("Stridentism," a Mexican form of socialist Futurism) and on the other hand with socially engaged humanist intellectuals like the young Octavio Paz. For this reason, the *Contemporáneos* generation can seem transitional, a group whose values register a set of aesthetic ideals more than a body of systematic principles. In a sense, they revivified the Modernist tradition by stripping Modernism of some of its residual elegant affectations and by returning Latin American poetry to its origins in a larger Western humanist tradition.

Because they resemble the Anglo-American Modernist generations in outlook, in politics, and in their attention to the Image (insofar as Anglo-American Modernism built on Ezra Pound's early Imagism and Vorticism), the *Contemporáneos* poets illustrate how much of what Latin America experienced as late post-Modernist or later Vanguardist energies, Britain and North America experienced under the name of "Modernism." The defining difference, once again, involves a question of the status of the Image, not only in the poem but in the discourse of the culture itself. One reason that the density and ubiquity of the Image in Modernist, post-Modernist, and Vanguardist Latin American poems strikes North American readers as surprisingly rich (and sometimes overripe) has to do, I suspect, with the comparative lack of metaphor—as ornamentation or as essential mode of argument—in our own conversation and in our public discourse. When Pound asserted the clean Image as the central, structuring energy mode of the "Modern" poem, his claim seemed new and counterintuitive. Of course, Pound was fighting against a Victorian sense of the Image as poetic ornament, but at the same time his Imagist claims challenged a popular pattern of factuality in our Anglo-American use of language. Pound's Modern concept of the Image is transgressive, revolutionary—and yet it led him to underestimate the import of the experiments of his old friend William Carlos Williams, who set out to use the factuality and idioms of North American speech as raw materials for the North American poem. In a different way, the emphasis on the Image that pervades Latin American poems from Romanticism through Modernism, post-Modernism, and Vanguardism makes those poems build on more common Latin American modes of conversation and of argument by metaphor. It is not surprising, therefore, that Latin American poetry became structurally self-conscious about the energy and movement of the Image earlier than North American poetry. If the values of the *Contemporáneos* group most approximate those of the North American Modernist generation, what North American poetry feels as the pressure of its structurally self-conscious and recent "post-Modernism" is a set of issues that Latin American poetry has been addressing since the Vanguardists. Their "Modernists" were like our "Symbolists," their "post-Modernists" like our "Modernists," their "Vangardism" more like our "post-Modernism."

I hope it's clear, then, that the movements that went by the names "post-Modernist" and "avant-garde" in Spanish Latin America differed significantly from North American movements known by similar names. (Typically, "post-Modernism" is not post-Modern.) What Hispanic Latin America registered as full Modernism, North Americans experienced as late nineteenth-century Symbolism and then as very early Modernism (e.g., Ezra Pound as Imagist, Wallace Stevens in mid-career). What Latin Americans call "post-Modernism" corresponds more nearly with the High Modernism of William Carlos Williams, Marianne Moore, Pound in mid-career, the Joyce of *Dubliners* and *Ulysses*, even some Auden. That Hispanic movement modulates into Vanguardism, which Anglo-Americans experienced largely as a second generation of Modernism (beginning with the later Joyce, Gertrude Stein, Pound of the *Cantos*, H.D.—leading toward poets like Robert Duncan, Denise Levertov, the Beats, the Black Mountain school).

Complicating matters further, some Latin American writers have occasionally used the term "post-Modern" to describe tendencies in their cultural traditions which *do* approximate our post-Modern aesthetics, although the contemporary term is as overdetermined in Latin American parlance as it is in ours. Our contemporary literary post-Modernism is rather like a belated version of Hispanic Vanguardism—and yet it *is* related to what in the Brazilian tradition is called "post-Modernism" and the "Vanguard."

In Brazil, the movement known as "post-Modernism" occurred in response to the momentum of Brazil's own, historically different "Modernist" energy. The generation of Brazilian Modernists more closely resembles one cluster of North American Modernists—not the internationalists Pound and Eliot, but the "local" William Carlos Williams, the regionalist Robinson Jeffers, Pound the early theorist and translator. Modernism in Brazil had addressed itself to questions of national identity, ethnic justice, formalism, and regional identity—questions that were to become the substance of the *post*-Modernist revolution elsewhere in Latin America. What Brazilians felt as post-Modernist energies were in effect more Vanguardist and experimental.

Owing to different social conditions, the responses of the Brazilian post-Modernists to political pressures likewise differed from those of the revolutionary Spanish American post-Modernists. Brazilian writers had the autocratic excesses of Getúlio Vargas (1930–1945) to come to terms with (the situation was complicated because many Modernist writers had been involved with the Vargas regime's social policies). Given the international political context and the tradition of social commentary in Brazilian writing, Brazilian post-Modernists also had more overt ideological questions to address—immediate questions about communism and capitalism, fascism and democracy. Writers like João Cabral de Melo Neto, Henriqueta Lisboa, and the "Generation of '45" later advocated a more internationalist orientation, and Carlos Drummond de Andrade wrote poems of angry anxiety about the effects of World War II.

These writers' sense of poetry's essential energy pointed their poems toward sculptural and written forms; the Spanish-language post-Modernists, by contrast, had preferred visual forms (like the murals of Diego Rivera) and the spoken voice. In their affirmation of poetry's public energies, however, the Brazilian post-Modernists' sense of social responsibility resembled the humanism of Spanish-language post-Modernists, some years earlier. And, more than in other societies, in Brazil the residual force of its Modernism continued to be felt, through a continuing interest in the Symbolist figurations of Modernists like Meireles and through vigorous defenses of Modernist values by writers like Oswald de Andrade. That influential rearguard form of Vanguardism lasted well into the 1950s and affected later Brazilian writers more directly than, say, the residual example of *rubéndarismo* continued its direct influence on writers in Spanish Latin America. For clear examples of Brazilian post-Modernism, on Brazilian terms, look to the poems of Cabral de Melo Neto and Drummond de Andrade. Finally, Brazil experienced a "Vanguardia" movement unlike that of Spanish American Vanguardism. Its best evidence here is in the work of the Constructivists and the Concretist poets (see Appendix).

3. THE IDENTITY OF THE LATIN AMERICAN POEM

The example of Brazil, and the dissimilarity between Hispanic and North American post-Modernism, have necessarily led us a bit forward toward contemporary poetics. We need now to return to the Hispanic mainstream, some years earlier, to see how late post-Modernism and early Vanguardism emerged and spread through other Latin American countries, from the 1930s toward the present. From this point on, the retrospective "map" of literary history seems more like a wide mural, a field of incipient, contemporaneous "pluralities" (to use one of Octavio Paz' tropes to describe the recent range of Latin American poetries). To follow the unique combination of experimentalism and social conscience that the dominant track of Vanguardism represents in these traditions, we need to go back at least as far as the Spanish Civil War.

For Hispanic Vanguardist writers and intellectuals after the first wave of post-Modernism, the defining international moment was not the Mexican Revolution or World War I, but the Spanish Civil War (1936–1939). That struggle attracted and compelled poets: Vallejo, for instance, addressed the suffering of his linguistic motherland with compassion (*España, aparta de mí este cáliz*, 1940). The civil war drove some of the most sympathetic and politically committed Latin Americans back home: when Neruda returned from Spain to South America in 1938, conscious of the dialectical shifts of history, he discovered the stony Incan ruins of Macchu Picchu waiting for him, a metaphor of Latin American epic history (*Alturas de Macchu Picchu*, 1947). As the early testing ground of the conflicts of fascism, socialism, and liberal democracy, the war demanded a clarification of values: in his early poems, Octavio Paz defined his leftist politics even while he began his lifelong philosophical investigation of poetic identity in the face of intransigent materiality. The war sent Spanish poets for the first time to the Americas, reversing the flow of influence: Luis Cernuda moved to Mexico and Juan Ramón Jiménez to Cuba, where he absorbed a *rubéndarista* sense of the moral urgency of the poem's internal structure, in a realization that later helped Jiménez to shape his poetry of pure essence (*poesía pura*).

The Spanish Civil War coincided with a high tide of Vanguardism in Latin America. To the rebellious energy of Vanguardist experimentation, a consciousness of the war and of the global economic depression added an element of moral gravity. The war seemed to demand a realistic, even despairing, self-awareness of verbal art in a world in which poetry usually (at least by Anglo-American standards) makes nothing happen. In various ways, the Spanish experiences and the Spanish Civil War poems of Vallejo and Neruda, Paz and Jiménez, highlight the fact of human cruelty and begin to question the function of poetry in the face of barbarism, materialism, and cyclical conflict. The results in Vanguardist poems were often currents of cynicism, nihilism, rebellious absurdism. (Because of his commitment to the Hegelian struggle, which he infused with associative super-Realist images, Neruda himself is sometimes called a "post-Vanguardist," as is Carrera Andrade.) That questioning of the nature of the poetic artifact and of the implications of the poem's process recurs with increasing self-consciousness throughout the rest of the century. Vanguardism refocused the attention of the poem on human speech. In the process, it called into question the tenuous nature of the speech act in poetry, with its transactions, shifting contexts, and decay of information.

The terms remain the same, but the arena in which they are contested changes, from the social world to the text of the poem itself considered self-consciously as a microcosmic "field" where competing forces contend. The terms of late Vanguardism and of subsequent movements are recognizable from the earlier history of Latin American poetics, traceable to Sarmiento's account of the conflict between "civilization and barbarism" in Latin America and traceable also to the tensions that had informed Darío's Modernist image. More recently, the choices manifest themselves metaphorically in a tension between the jungle and the city, between regionalism and cosmopolitanism, between collectivism (often associated with Indianism) and individualism (often associated with a European philosophical tradition). The familiar Modernist tension of public communicability versus hermetic suggestiveness reappears as a choice between a poetry of social engagement and a poetry of introspection, even as a choice between Marx and Freud.

Such tensions are manifest in an increased attention to the dynamics of Latin American literary history, as in revaluations of the figure of Darío himself: compare the tradition following César Vallejo's cosmic-mestizo reading of Darío ("to be a poet of America, the American sensibility was enough for Darío") and Octavio Paz' later reading of Darío (as Gordon Brotherston explains it) as a poet of personal eros whose example helps Paz come to terms with the Spanish elements of his own ("pluralistic") Latin American identity. By the 1950s, under pressure from the transcultural influence of North American capitalism, the tension reappears as a choice between a local sense of form (cultivating, for instance, the heritage of folk songs and oral traditions) and an international (read: North American) cultural perspective (welcoming Yankee cultural forms, jazz, comic books, Coca-Cola); or as a choice between Third World affiliations (often demanding guerrilla tactics) and a sense of continuity with the intellectual traditions of Western Europe (often equated with alienation and a closed sense of form); or as a choice between "impure poetry" (Neruda) and "pure poetry" (Jiménez, Florit).

As time passes, the terms revaluate. Although for decades Neruda's example seemed a model of self-confident generosity and solidarity with the international working class, by the early 1960s Nicanor Parra hears a Romantic egotism in Neruda's optimistic personalism. Parra proposes instead an "antipoetry" of bleaker vision, prosier rhythms, and starker, Surrealist deadpan humor. Neruda's later poems, image piled apostrophically on image, are held together by the force of Neruda's dominant will. Especially after the Chilean coup of the colonels in 1973, Parra questions such simple, centralized authorial power. Formally, Parra knits together his later poems with almost cynical threads of associated clichés, distortions of ordinary speech, and writhing common sense.

By the 1980s a deconstructionist paradigm sometimes defines the terms of conflict. In a matrix of cultural codes, of mixed determinants of class, gender, and discourses of power, two concepts of poetry contend: one that defines the poem as the representational illusion of the spoken voice claiming a cohesive linguistic presence through the fiction of an author or a speaker, and another that defines the poem as a written artifact, deferring its referents and substituting a sui generis linguistic space in which semiotic markers sparkle. Eventually, the question of the status of linguistic referentiality

versus the indeterminacy of any signifier challenges the integrity of the lyric poem and the authority of the poet-as-author. This tension carries special force for a Latin American tradition that had not always trusted a strong distinction between aesthetic and social realms of experience, a tradition in which the poet has been a public and honored figure even while his or her poems echoed from an "ivory tower."

The terms shift modes, but they continue in dialectical cycles. One major reordering in Latin American poetry since the Spanish Civil War has been a change in the arena of discussion, as poets and movements of poetry shift attention from questions of the cultural identity of Latin America or of the Latin American individual to questions about the nature, the propriety, the internally shaping forces, and the power configurations of the poem itself, and thus to questions about the implications of the recurrent power of poetry in Latin American cultures.

I describe these dynamic choices as a conflict over conceptual terms, within new arenas of concern about the nature of poetry itself, in part because I hesitate to characterize recent poets reductively, making them personify fixed factional positions. (Nothing embarrasses an anthology more than an out-of-date tone of up-to-dateness, and in any case I prefer to believe, with most working writers, that their best poems are always just about to be written.) True, sometimes historical circumstances and personal choices do set poets into telling juxtapositions. In contemporary Nicaragua, for instance, the political poems of the Catholic Sandinista poet Ernesto Cardenal and the poems of politically engaged women writers stand in contrast to the meditative, "sportive" poems of Pablo Antonio Cuadra (even though Cuadra began as a member of the Vanguardist movement that had challenged the complacency of Darío's influence in Nicaraguan poetry). However, attempts therefore to characterize Cuadra, a brave and personally generous man and the editor of the liberal newspaper *La Prensa*, as a reactionary poet in contradistinction to other Nicaraguan writers seem to me inaccurate and unfair, the result of an overactive sense of the geometry of literary politics.

There is a similar tendency toward argument by geometry, sometimes, among accounts of contemporary Latin American women poets and poets of color: a factitious dualism sets artificial terms of distinction for such writers. This rhetorical pattern occasionally has the effect of defining Latin American women poets, for instance, by their common victimization. Although the criticism of the dominant cultural forms (machismo, conservative Catholicism, transnational capitalism, and so on) may be valid, the terms of these contemporary representations of Latin American writers sometimes seem imported from discourse about gender, race, class, and psychosocial forms in North America. (The tendency has meant, incidentally, that many more outspoken leftist poets of Latin America have been well translated into English than poets of other inclinations. This phenomenon has skewed our perception of Latin American poetry from a strictly accurate picture of the field, and yet has enriched our own poetries by introducing tones of autobiography and of political witness that our Modernist generations had not valued. I am intrigued by the submerged stories that this anthology tells about the needs and interests of North Americans—namely, who chooses to translate which Latin Americans, which poems they choose, and how and when and why they translate as they do.) In their original cultural contexts, many of the finest Latin American women writers since the 1950s are more likely to define their own ambitions in different dialectical terms: Olga Orozco in deeply internal terms of psycholinguistic identity, Alejandra Pizarnik in terms related to *Contemporáneos* concepts of choice and personal destiny, Rosario Castellanos in terms of the complex intersection of gender and race in a mixed culture, Nancy Morejón in terms of the social dynamics of Castro's Cuba, and so on.

TOWARD THE TWENTY-FIRST CENTURY

The example of Octavio Paz looms overhead at the close of the present century, as other poetic angels—Vallejo and Neruda, Mistral and Guillén—had floated above in earlier decades. Although culturally he has become an institutionalized presence in Mexico (often admired but sometimes resented), the example of Paz' career of self-evolution seems an appropriately inconclusive and forward-looking conclusion to this survey. From his early leftist poems, through his meditations on the fusion of Indian and European components in the Mexican identity, through his Asian-inspired minimalism and his deconstructions of modes of consciousness externalized in the lyric poem, Octavio Paz has come to represent a paradigm of integrity within restless change.

I conclude with the example of Paz not as an endpoint but as a signpost—or as a crossroads signaling several intersecting (and divergent) paths. Arguably, most of Paz' best poems were written by the late 1970s, and yet his example figures, for me, something of the wide-

ness and "plurality" of possibility in recent Latin American aesthetics. As a poet of political conscience, Paz introduces a line of a different kind of political awareness among new poets, like those who flourished during the recent period of Central American revolutions: a line continued in the declarative intelligence of poets like Roque Dalton, Ernesto Cardenal, and Claribel Alegría. As a poet of disciplined experimentalism and philosophical speculation, Paz introduces a line of lyrically meditative poets of free-verse clarity and conceptual complexity. Poets like Rojas, Belli, Lihn, Pizarnik, Prado, and Zurita have given Latin American poetics new directions beyond Vanguardist formalism. As a poet of local fidelities, Paz stands for a cluster of regional and culturally identified writers (e.g., Teillier, Aridjis). As a figure of international stature actively engaged with global intellectual and political movements, Paz can be seen to introduce a series of writers similarly committed to addressing transnational questions within the lyric (e.g., Zaid, Gelman, Cisneros, Armand). As an internationalist, Paz is a voice of displacement and identity that echoes through the voices of poets of disenfranchisement and exile (e.g., Agosín, Padilla). This representative character of the figure of Paz is helpful even though he is not necessarily a direct influence on all these newer poets, and even though within the politics of national and international poetry he is not necessarily in the same political or aesthetic camps with them. I end with the example of the polyvalent Octavio Paz not as a terminus or final achievement but as a focal point of integrity within change, a point of consolidation from which to look both backward and forward.

When in 1950 he sounded the encomium that in their poetry Latin Americans have become "the contemporaries of all men," Paz himself was cannily looking backward and forward at the same time. Back, toward a series of visions of Latin American identity, recalling the colonial epics of the continent's potential, Bolívar's consolidating Romantic dreams, Darío's unifying Modernist power, José Vasconselos' post-Modern revolutionary ideal of a Latin American "collective soul" of social justice. And ahead, toward the tense ideological and psychological choices of contemporary poets who address global questions on Latin American terms. In Paz' account, the "open solitude" that is the determining characteristic of his Latin American consciousness (and of Latin American poetics) registers a general condition of the twentieth century—representative of Latin America and eloquently articulated in these poems, but not exclusive to Latin America. Paz' metaphor of an "open solitude" to describe the Latin American consciousness seems deliberately to recall the historical debate about Modernism and its significance. Was that Latin American node of activity chiefly a defining textual vehicle, or was *modernismo* a transformative cultural energy in itself? Was it a literary movement or a new mode of culture? Did Latin American Modernism announce a new race of people, embodying a novel and integrated mestizo consciousness, on the world's stage?

In this sense, Paz' reading of Latin American aesthetic history stresses again the centrality of Latin American poetry in its largest effects and in its sternest integrative paradoxes. Paz' theory helps to explain the curious phenomenon of these poems: that they speak so specifically to their historical moment and yet so generally and generously and powerfully to the rest of us.

José Martí

CUBA
1853–1895

As lecturer, guerrilla leader, theoretician, and poet José Martí was the intellectual leader of the struggle for Cuban independence from Spain. A dedicated and prolific public figure during his life, since his death Martí has become a model (both in Latin America's poetics and in its cultural politics) of the engaged life and of heroic martyrdom. Born in Cuba of impoverished Spanish parents, Martí spent part of his childhood in Spain. After the family's return to Cuba, Martí committed himself to the cause of independence. At age seventeen, he was sentenced to six years in prison because of his political work. After he had served two years at hard labor in the San Lázaro mines near Havana, Martí's sentence was commuted, and he went into exile. He lived outside Cuba—in Guatemala, Uruguay, Spain, Argentina, Mexico, and the United States—for much of the rest of his life.

In his poems, most of which were published after his death, Martí internalizes the terms of the political struggle and enacts them, verbally, in an early Modernist mode. Because of his politics and because of his aesthetic resistance to French models, Martí stands slightly apart from the other *modernistas*. However, the sweet exoticism of his poems and the attention he pays to the formal exactitude of Spanish versification ally him, as a first-generation Modernist, with Darío and others. At the same time, his poems often aspire to a simplicity resembling that of folk songs. The major books of poems Martí published during his life were *Ismaelillo* (1882), a bouquet of parental affection addressed from exile to his young son, and *Versos sencillos* (*Simple Verses*, 1891), which contains some of the most moving and famous patriotic poems of Latin America. Although emotionally and domestically his life was often anguished, and even though he was often physically in pain owing to the aftereffects of diseases he had contracted in the Cuban prison quarries, Martí subsumed his spiritual grief and physical suffering into elegant, suggestive forms. "Pain," he explained, "purifies and prepares." An incisive correspondent and a rousing lecturer, a journalist, and a pamphleteer, through his nonfiction work Martí also energized written prose style in Spanish. He was killed in Cuba during a guerrilla action in the abortive revolt of 1895, one month after his return to Cuba and three years before the final war of Cuban liberation from Spain.

Sueño despierto

Yo sueño con los ojos
Abiertos, y de día
Y noche siempre sueño.
Y sobre las espumas
Del ancho mar revuelto,
Y por entre las crespas
Arenas del desierto,
Y del león pujante,
Monarca de mi pecho,
Montado alegremente
Sobre el sumiso cuello,—
¡Un niño que me llama
Flotando siempre veo!

1882

I Dream Awake

I dream with open eyes
Both night and day;
I always dream.
And on the spindrift
Of the wide rough sea,
And on the rolling
Desert sands,
And joyously astride
The humble neck
Of a mighty lion,
Monarch of my heart,
I always see a floating child
Calling to me!

trans. Elinor Randall

Contra el verso retórico...

Contra el verso retórico y ornado
El verso natural. Acá un torrente:
Aquí una piedra seca. Allá un dorado
Pájaro, que en las ramas verdes brilla,
Como una marañuela entre esmeraldas—
Acá la huella fétida y viscosa
De un gusano: los ojos, dos burbujas
De fango, pardo el vientre, craso, inmundo.
Por sobre el árbol, más arriba, sola
En el cielo de acero una segura
Estrella: y a los pies el horno,
El horno a cuyo ardor la tierra cuece—
Llamas, llamas que luchan, con abiertos
Huecos como ojos, lenguas como brazos,
Savia como de hombre, punta aguda
Cual de espada: ¡la espada de la vida
Que incendio a incendio gana al fin, la tierra!
Trepa: viene de adentro: ruge: aborta.
Empieza el hombre en fuego y para en ala.
Y a su paso triunfal, los maculados,
Los viles, los cobardes, los vencidos,
Como serpientes, como gozques, como
Cocodrilos de doble dentadura,
De acá, de allá, del árbol que le ampara,
Del suelo que le tiene, del arroyo
Donde apaga la sed, del yunque mismo
Donde se forja el pan, le ladran y echan
El diente al pie, al rostro el polvo y lodo,
Cuanto cegarle puede en su camino.
Él, de un golpe de ala, barre el mundo
Y sube por la atmósfera encendida
Muerto como hombre y como sol sereno.
Así ha de ser la noble poesía:
Así como la vida: estrella y gozque;
La cueva dentellada por el fuego,
El pino en cuyas ramas olorosas
A la luz de la luna canta un nido
Canta un nido a lumbre de la luna.

1891

The Opposite of Ornate and Rhetorical Poetry

The opposite of ornate and rhetorical poetry
Is natural poetry. Here a torrent,
There an arid stone, here a golden
Bird that gleams among the verdant branches
Like a nasturtium among emeralds.
There the fetid viscous traces
Of a worm, its eyes two bubbles
Of mire, its belly brownish, gross and filthy.
Above the tree, far higher and alone
In a steel-gray sky, a constant
Star; and down below the star a furnace,
A furnace in whose fires the earth is cooking—
And flames, the flames that struggle, with open
Holes for eyes, their tongues like arms,
Their sap like a man's blood, their sharpened
Points like swords: the swords of life that finally,
From fire to fire, acquire the earth!
The fire climbs, comes from within; it howls, aborts.
Man starts in fire and stops in wings.
At his triumphant step the sullied
And vile, the cowards, the defeated—
Like snakes or mongrels, like
Crocodiles with powerful teeth,
From here, from there, from trees that shelter him,
From lands that hold him, the brooks
That slake his thirst, the very anvil
Where his bread is forged—they bark at him,
Nip at his feet, throw mud and dust in his face,
And all that blinds him on his journey.
But beating his wings he sweeps the world
And rises through the fiery air
Dead as a man, but like a sun serene.
This is what noble poetry should be:
Just as is life: both star and mongrel:
A cave serrated by fire,
A pine tree in whose fragrant branches
A nest of birds sings in the moonlight:
Birds singing in the moonlight.

trans. Elinor Randall

Versos sencillos

I

Yo soy un hombre sincero
De donde crece la palma,
Y antes de morirme quiero
Echar mis versos del alma.

Simple Verses

I

I am an honest man
From where the palms grow;
Before I die I want my soul
To shed its poetry.

Yo vengo de todas partes,
Y hacia todas partes voy:
Arte soy entre las artes,
En los montes, monte soy.

Yo sé los nombres extraños
De las yerbas y las flores,
Y de mortales engaños,
Y de sublimes dolores.

Yo he visto en la noche oscura
Llover sobre mi cabeza
Los rayos de lumbre pura
De la divina belleza.

Alas nacer vi en los hombros
De las mujeres hermosas:
Y salir de los escombros,
Volando las mariposas.

He visto vivir a un hombre
Con el puñal al costado,
Sin decir jamás el nombre
De aquella que lo ha matado

Rápida, como un reflejo,
Dos veces vi el alma, dos:
Cuando murió el pobre viejo,
Cuando ella me dijo adiós.

Temblé una vez—en la reja,
A la entrada de la viña,—
Cuando la bárbara abeja
Picó en la frente a mi niña.

Gocé una vez, de tal suerte
Que gocé cual nunca:—cuando
La sentencia de mi muerte
Leyó el alcaide llorando.

Oigo un suspiro, a través
De las tierras y la mar,
Y no es un suspiro,—es
Que mi hijo va a despertar.

Si dicen que del joyero
Tome la joya mejor,
Tomo a un amigo sincero
Y pongo a un lado el amor.

Yo he visto al águila herida
Volar al azul sereno

I come from everywhere,
To everywhere I'm bound:
An art among the arts,
A mountain among mountains.

I know the unfamiliar names
Of grasses and of flowers,
Of fatal deceptions
And exalted sorrows.

On darkest nights I've seen
Rays of the purest splendor
Raining upon my head
From heavenly beauty.

I've seen wings sprout
From handsomest women's shoulders,
Seen butterflies fly out
Of rubbish heaps.

I've seen a man who lives
With a dagger at his side,
Never uttering the name
Of his murderess.

Twice, quick as a wink, I've seen
The soul: once when a poor
Old man succumbed, once when
She said goodbye.

Once I shook with anger
At the vineyard's iron gate
When a savage bee attacked
My daughter's forehead.

Once I rejoiced as I
Had never done before,
When the warden, weeping, read
My sentence of death.

I hear a sigh across
The land and sea; it is
No sigh: it is my son
Waking from sleep.

If I am said to take
A jeweler's finest gem,
I take an honest friend,
Put love aside.

I've seen a wounded eagle
Fly to the tranquil blue,

Y morir en su guarida
La víbora del veneno.

Yo sé bien que cuando el mundo
Cede, lívido, al descanso,
Sobre el silencio profundo
Murmura el arroyo manso.

Yo he puesto la mano osada,
De horror y júbilo yerta,
Sobre la estrella apagada
Que cayó frente a mi puerta.

Oculto en mi pecho bravo
La pena que me lo hiere:
El hijo de un pueblo esclavo
Vive por él, calla y muere.

Todo es hermoso y constante,
Todo es música y razón,
Y todo, como el diamante,
Antes que luz es carbón.

Yo sé que el necio se entierra
Con gran lujo y con gran llanto—
Y que no hay fruta en la tierra
Como la del camposanto.

Callo, y entiendo, y me quito
La pompa del rimador:
Cuelgo de un árbol marchito
Mi muceta de doctor.

IX

Quiero, a la sombra de una ala,
Contar este cuento en flor:
La niña de Guatemala,
La que se murió de amor.

Eran de lirios los ramos,
Y las orlas de reseda
Y de jazmín: la enterramos
En una caja de seda.

...Ella dio al desmemoriado
una almohadilla de olor:
Él volvió, volvió casado:
Ella se murió de amor.

Iban cargándola en andas
Obispos y embajadores:

And seen a snake die in its
Hole, of venom.

Well do I know that when
The livid world yields to repose,
The gentle brook will ripple on
In deepest silence.

I've laid a daring hand,
Rigid from joy and horror,
Upon the burnt-out star that fell
Before my door.

My manly heart conceals
The pain it suffers; sons of
A land enslaved live for it
Silently, and die.

All is permanence and beauty,
And all is melody and reason,
And all, like diamonds rather
Than light, is coal.

I know that fools are buried
Splendidly, with floods of tears,
And that no fruit on earth
Is like the graveyard's.

I understand, keep still,
Cast off the versifier's pomp,
And hang my doctoral robes upon
A withered tree.

IX

In the shadow of a wing
I wish to tell this flowered tale
Of the girl from Guatemala
Who died of love.

The wreaths were of lilies
And jasmine and mignonette;
We laid the girl to rest
In a silken casket.

...She gave a little scented pillow
To the forgetful one, and he
Returned, returned now wedded.
She died of love.

Ambassadors and bishops
Carried her bier, and there were

Detrás iba el pueblo en tandas,
Todo cargado de flores.

...Ella, por volverlo a ver,
Salió a verlo al mirador:
Él volvió con su mujer:
Ella se murió de amor.

Como de bronce candente
Al beso de despedida
Era su frente ¡la frente
Que más he amado en mi vida!

...Se entró de tarde en el río,
La sacó muerta el doctor:
Dicen que murió de frío:
Yo sé que murió de amor.

Allí, en la bóveda helada,
La pusieron en dos bancos:
Besé su mano afilada,
Besé sus zapatos blancos.

Callado, al oscurecer,
Me llamó el enterrador:
¡Nunca más he vuelto a ver
A la que murió de amor!

X

El alma trémula y sola
Padece al anochecer:
Hay baile; vamos a ver
La bailarina española.

Han hecho bien en quitar
El banderón de la acera;
Porque si está la bandera,
No sé, yo no puedo entrar.

Ya llega la bailarina:
Soberbia y pálida llega:
¿Cómo dicen que es gallega?
Pues dicen mal: es divina.

Lleva un sombrero torero
Y una capa carmesí:
¡Lo mismo que un alelí
Que se pusiese en sombrero!

Se ve, de paso, la ceja,
Ceja de mora traidora:

Relays of people following,
All with flowers.

...Wishing to see him again,
She went out on the belvedere;
He returned with his wife;
She died of love.

Her brow was like molten bronze
At his parting kiss,
The brow I loved the best
In all my life!

...At dusk she entered the river;
The doctor pulled out her body.
They say she died of cold; I know
She died of love.

They laid her out on two benches
There in the frigid vault;
I kissed her slender hand
And her white shoes.

Softly, when evening fell,
The gravedigger bid me come.
Never again did I see that girl
Who died of love.

X

The lonely trembling soul can ache
When night is on the way;
There is a dance: let's go
To see the Spanish dancer.

It's good they took away
The big flag from the sidewalk,
For should it still be there
I doubt if I could enter.

The dancer is arriving now,
Haughty and pale of face;
Why say she is Galician?
Not so; she is divine.

She wears a matador's hat
And a cape of brightest red;
She's like a gilliflower
That had put on a hat!

We notice her brows in passing,
The brows of a traitorous Mooress,

Y la mirada, de mora:
Y como nieve la oreja.

Preludian, bajan la luz,
Y sale en bata y mantón,
La virgen de la Asunción
Bailando un baile andaluz.

Alza, retando, la frente;
Crúzase al hombro la manta:
En arco el brazo levanta:
Mueve despacio el pie ardiente.

Repica con los tacones
El tablado zalamera,
Como si la tabla fuera
Tablado de corazones.

Y va el convite creciendo
En las llamas de los ojos,
Y el mantón de flecos rojos
Se va en el aire meciendo.

Súbito, de un salto arranca:
Húrtase, se quiebra, gira:
Abre en dos la cachemira,
Ofrece la bata blanca.

El cuerpo cede y ondea;
La boca abierta provoca;
Es una rosa la boca:
Lentamente taconea.

Recoge, de un débil giro,
El manto de flecos rojos:
Se va, cerrando los ojos,
Se va, como en un suspiro...

Baila muy bien la española;
Es blanco y rojo el mantón:
¡Vuelve, fosca, a su rincón
El alma trémula y sola!

XXXVI

Ya sé: de carne se puede
Hacer una flor: se puede,
Con el poder del cariño,
Hacer un cielo,—¡y un niño!

De carne se hace también
El alacrán: y también
El gusano de la rosa,
Y la lechuza espantosa.

The glance of a Moorish lady,
The ears like driven snow.

A musical flourish, lights dim;
The Virgin of the Assumption
Appears in shawl and gown
In a dance of Andalusia.

She raises her head in challenge,
Draws round her shoulders her shawl,
She arches her arms above her,
Moves slowly her ardent feet.

Fawning, she taps on the stage
With the heels of her shoes as if
The flooring beneath her feet
Were a flooring composed of hearts.

The festive mood is increasing
In the fire of her eyes,
As she waves her red-dotted shawl
Round and round in the air.

She starts with a sudden leap,
Draws back, whirls round, and dips;
She opens her cashmere shawl,
Revealing a snow-white gown.

Her body yields and undulates,
She parts her provocative lips,
Those lips so like a rose,
And leisurely taps her heels.

Feebly turning, she gathers up
Her shawl that is dotted with red,
Then shuts her eyes and departs,
Departs as if in a sigh...

The Spanish girl dances well;
Her shawl is scarlet and white;
The lonely trembling soul returns
In a sullen mood to its corner!

XXXVI

I know: from flesh
A flower can be made;
From the power of love,
A sky—and a child!

From flesh a scorpion
Is also made; the worm
On a rose, as well,
And the awesome owl.

1891   trans. Elinor Randall

Dos patrias

Dos patrias tengo yo: Cuba y la noche.
¿O son una las dos? No bien retira
Su majestad el sol, con largos velos
Y un clavel en la mano, silenciosa
Cuba cual viuda triste me aparece.
¡Yo sé cuál es ese clavel sangriento
Que en la mano le tiembla! Está vacío
Mi pecho, destrozado está y vacío
En donde estaba el corazón. Ya es hora
De empezar a morir. La noche es buena
Para decir adiós. La luz estorba
Y la palabra humana. El universo
Habla mejor que el hombre.
          Cual bandera
Que invita a batallar, la llama roja
De la vela flamea. Las ventanas
Abro, ya estrecho en mí. Muda, rompiendo
Las hojas del clavel, como una nube
Que enturbia el cielo, Cuba, viuda, pasa...

1883–1889?/1933

Two Countries

I have two countries: Cuba and the night.
Or are both one? No sooner does the sun
Withdraw its majesty, than Cuba,
With long veils and holding a carnation,
Appears as a sad and silent widow.
I know about the bloodstained carnation
That trembles in her hand! My breast
Is empty, destroyed and empty
Where the heart lay. Now is the time
To commence dying. Night is a good time
To say farewell. Light is a hindrance
As is the human word. The universe
Talks better than man.
          Like a flag
That calls to battle, the candle's
Red flame flutters. I feel a closeness
And open windows. Crushing the carnation's
Petals silently, widowed Cuba passes by
Like a cloud that dims the heavens...

trans. Elinor Randall

João da Cruz e Sousa

BRAZIL
1861–1898

Despite a strong tradition of abolitionist writing, including in literature the reformist impulses of the Romantics and the less idealizing representations of slave life by Naturalist writers, Brazil was the last country in the Southern Hemisphere to abolish slavery (in 1888). João da Cruz e Sousa was born the child of enslaved black parents in 1861. His master's wife taught him to read, and he received some education while still enslaved. After his manumission he benefited from a more formal education and traveled widely throughout Brazil as a member of an itinerant theatrical troupe. That travel, and Cruz e Sousa's later work as a journalist, made him familiar with the desperate conditions of life for other enslaved peoples and set the tone of compassionate indignation that characterizes much of his work: from the humanitarian prose of his first book, *Tropos e fantasias* (*Tropes and Fantasies*, 1885), to his later, more meditative, poems.

When he moved to Rio de Janeiro in 1890, Cruz e Sousa discovered Poe, Baudelaire, and Huysmans. The influence of those writers is evident in the Parnassian polish of his first major work, *Broquéis* (*Shields*, 1893). His lyrics subsequently turned more Symbolist and austere, more dedicated to a cultivated despair of meaning and to a Baudelairean cult of ugliness, Satanism, and cynical laughter. His bitterness about social conditions was exacerbated by a difficult adult life: his four children died, and his wife, a white woman to whom he had dedicated the poem "Antífona" on their wedding day, suffered periodic bouts of mental illness. Cruz e Sousa died of tuberculosis when he was barely thirty-seven years old.

When literary historians call João da Cruz e Sousa the "Black Swan" of Brazilian Symbolism, they mean to indicate his race, his eloquence and eminence, his Modernist imagery, his Platonism, his sonorous elegance and intimate formalism. Often, however, the characterization also carries some implications about Cruz e Sousa's attitude with respect to his negritude. He is sometimes read as a writer who was self-depletingly devoted to European structures of thought (white "codes," to use Manuel Bandeira's terminology), who bitterly resented his blackness and its enforced limitations, who rebelled against Christianity with an Oedipal resentfulness, and who internalized racial injustice in a way that generated masochism and envy. It is true that Cruz e Sousa's lyrics are often organized around pairs of white and black symbols (which figure other dualities: form versus chaos, purity versus suffering, dream versus pain, transcendence versus sensuality), but he tries to subsume the racial overtones of those dualities into philosophical systems, patterns of color symbolism derived from the French Symbolists, and so on. He attempts to make sense of personal differentness by organizing its representation into almost mystical linguistic patterns. By contrast, his last poems, in *Últimos sonetos (Final Sonnets,* 1905 posthum.), represent an effort, influenced by Schopenhauer, to focus his personal anguish on questions of mortality and on the meaning of private suffering in the absence of coherent philosophical systems of belief.

Antífona	*Antiphony*
Ó Formas alvas, brancas, Formas claras de luares, de neves, de neblinas!... Ó Formas vagas, fluidas, cristalinas... Incensos dos turíbulos das aras...	Oh pale, white Forms, clear Forms of moonlight, snow, and mist!... Oh vague, fluid, translucent Forms... Incense burning on altars...
Formas do Amor, constelarmente puras, de Virgens e de Santas vaporosas... Brilhos errantes, mádidas frescuras e dolências de lírios e de rosas...	Forms set with pure, bright lights of the love of Virgins and vaporous Saints... Wandering brilliances, drenched coolnesses and sorrows of lilies and of roses...
Indefiníveis músicas supremas, harmonias da Côr e do Perfume... Horas do Ocaso, trêmulas, extremas, Réquiem do Sol que a Dor da Luz resume...	Indescribable music from heaven, harmonies of Color and of Fragrance... Sunset's hesitant last moments, Requiem for the Sun in Light's Pain...
Visões, salmos e cânticos serenos, surdinas de órgãos flébeis, soluçantes... Dormências de volúpicos venenos sutis e suaves, mórbidos, radiantes...	Visions, psalms and peaceful hymns, muffled sounds of organs, sobbing... Suspension of sensual malices morbid, ecstatic, subtle and soothing...
Infinitos espíritos dispersos, inefáveis, edênicos, aéreos, fecundai o Mistério dêstes versos com a chama ideal de todos os mistérios.	Infinite spirits, scattered, inexpressible, Edenic, ethereal, fertilize the Mystery of these verses with the ideal flame of all mysteries.
Do Sonho as mais azuis diafaneidades que fuljam, que na Estrofe se levantem e as emoções, tôdas as castidades da alma do Verso, pelos versos cantem.	Let the Dream's bluest gauzes be bright let the Stanza be exalted and let the emotions, the chastities of the soul of Verse, sing in these verses.

Que o pólen de ouro dos mais finos astros
fecunde e inflame a rima clara e ardente...
Que brilhe a correção dos alabastros
sonoramente, luminosamente.

Fôrças originais, essência, graça
de carnes de mulher, delicadezas...
Todo êsse eflúvio que por ondas passa
do Éter nas róseas e áureas correntezas...

Cristais diluídos de clarões alacres,
desejos, vibrações, âncias, alentos,
fulvas vitórias, triunfamentos acres,
os mais estranhos estremecimentos...

Flôres negras do tédio e flôres vagas
de amôres vãos, tantálicos, doentios...
Fundas vermelhidões de velhas chagas
em sangue, abertas, escorrendo em rios...

Tudo! vivo e nervoso e quente e forte,
nos turbilhões quiméricos do Sonho,
passe, cantando, ante o perfil medonho
e o tropel cabalístico da Morte...

1893

Let the gold pollen of the finest stars
fill and inflame the rhyme with clear passion...
Let the purification of alabasters glisten
sonorously, luminously.

Primitive forces, essences, grace
in women's bodies, kindnesses...
All those auras that flow from Ether
in waves of rose-scented, gilded currents...

Crystals flawed by eager flashes,
desires, vibrations, longings, gusts
of courage, bitter triumphs, dark conquests,
the most peculiar quiverings...

Dark flowers of boredom and vague flowers
of empty, unwholesome, elusive loves...
Crimson depths of old sores,
open, bleeding in rivers...

Let all! alive, nervous, hot, and strong,
in the Dream's fantastical whirlpool
pass singing before Death's occult
confusion and terrible profile...

trans. Nancy Vieira Couto

Acrobata da dor

Gargalha, ri, num riso de tormenta,
como um palhaço, que desengonçado,
nervoso, ri, num riso absurdo, inflado
de uma ironia e de uma dor violenta.

Da gargalhada atroz, sanguinolenta,
agita os guizos, e convulsionado.
Salta, gavroche, salta *clown*, varado
pelo estertor dessa agonia lenta...

Pedem-te bis e um bis não se despreza!
Vamos! reteza os músculos, reteza
nessas macabras piruêtas d'aço...

E embora caias sôbre o chão, fremente,
afogado em teu sangue estuoso e quente,
ri! Coração, tristíssimo palhaço.

1893

Acrobat of Pain

Chortle, laugh, in a laughter of storm
like a clown who, lanky and nervous,
laughs, in an absurd laughter, inflated
with violent irony and pain.

With that atrocious and bloody guffaw—:
rattle the jester's bells, convulsing.
Jump, puppet: jump, clown, pierced
by the stertor of this slow agony—

You're asked for an encore, and that's not to be sneered at.
Come on! Tighten the muscles up, tighten up
in these macabre steel pirouettes...

And though you fall on the ground, quivering,
drowned in your hot and seething blood,
laugh! Heart, saddest of clowns.

trans. Flavia Vidal

Sexta-feira Santa

Lua absíntica, verde, feiticeira,
pasmada como um vício monstruoso...

Good Friday

Absinthe, green, bewitching moon,
amazed as a monstrous vice...

Um cão estranho fuça na esterqueira,
uivando para o espaço fabuloso.

É esta a negra e santa Sexta-feira!
Cristo está morto, como um vil leproso,
chagado e frio, na feroz cegueira
da Morte, o sangue roxo e tenebroso.

A serpente do mal e do pecado
um sinistro veneno esverdeado
verte do Morto na mudez serena.

Mas da sagrada Redenção do Cristo
em vez do grande Amor, puro, imprevisto,
brotam fosforescências de gangrena!

1905

A strange dog scrabbles in the dunghill,
howling at the fabulous space.

This is the black and holy Friday!
Christ is dead, like a vile leper,
ulcerous and cold, in the ferocious blindness
of Death, his blood purple and shadowy.

The serpent of evil and of sin
a sinister greenish poison
spills from the dead Man in serene muteness.

But from the sacred Redemption of the Christ
instead of the great, pure unforeseen Love,
sprout up phosphorescences of gangrene!

trans. Flavia Vidal

Ódio sagrado

Ó meu ódio, meu ódio majestoso,
meu ódio santo e puro e benfazejo,
unge-me a fronte com teu grande beijo,
torna-me humilde e torna-me orgulhoso.

Humilde, com os humildes generoso,
orgulhoso com os sêres sem Desejo,
sem Bondade, sem Fé e sem lampejo
de sol fecundador e carinhoso.

Ó meu ódio, meu lábaro bendito,
de minh'alma agitado no infinito,
através de outros lábaros sagrados,

ódio são, ódio bom! sê meu escudo
contra os vilões do Amor, que infamam tudo,
das sete tôrres dos mortais Pecados!

1905

Sacred Hatred

Oh, my hatred, my majestic hatred,
my holy and pure and benevolent hatred,
annoint my forehead with your great kiss,
render me humble and render me lofty.

Humble, but generous to the humble:
lofty to those beings without Desire,
without Goodness, without Faith, without the gleam
of the fertilizing, affectionate sun.

Oh, my hatred, my blessed standard-banner
waving in the infinity of my soul,
beyond other sacred banners.

Sound, hatred: good hatred! Be my shield
against the villains of Love, who defame everything,
from the seven towers of the mortal Sins!

trans. Flavia Vidal

Rubén Darío

NICARAGUA
1867–1916

Born in Nicaragua to a mestizo and creole family of the local ascendancy, Rubén Darío lived in Chile, Argentina, and Spain before returning to his native land. During his international travels, as a student and later as a diplomat, Darío read widely in French and Castilian literature. His version of Modernism fused essentially European Symbolist elements (interiority, elegance, formalism, chromatic and musical structures) with Latin American thematics (nationalist sentiments, images derived from a tropical landscape, a sense of the autonomy of Latin American spoken Spanish). "Words should paint the color of a sound, the aroma of a star; they should capture the very soul of things," Darío wrote in 1888. (See the discussion of Darío above, pp. 8–9.)

Darío's book *Azul...* (*Blue...*), published that same year, exemplified the terms of this synthetic Modernism, which in literary practical terms amounts to a Hispano-American version of Continental Symbolism. Although the movement eventually took different forms in different Latin American countries, Darío's position as the "Prince of Modernism" is indisputable. Darío invented forms and a diction to record a new mode of consciousness for Latin American poetics, and even those who opposed the influence of his elegance took his terms and suggestive images—including his famous swan—as the primary referent for their discussion. (See, for instance, the debate about Enrique González Martínez' poem of anti-Rubénist response, "Tuércele el cuello al cisne.") Darío's poems are committed to a beauty that can be intuited but never apprehended. As a result, although Darío's favorite poet was Verlaine, his energetic and nationalistic Modernism has made his reputation as influential as Whitman's is for North American cultural poetics.

Darío's private life was often as troubled as his poems were austerely formal. While lecturing on the peace movement, in New York in 1916, he suffered an embolism. Sensing his imminent death, Darío traveled through Guatemala in order to die in his native Nicaragua.

Primaveral

Mes de rosas. Van mis rimas
en ronda, a la vasta selva,
a recoger miel y aromas
en las flores entreabiertas.
Amada, ven. El gran bosque
es nuestro templo; allí ondea
y flota un santo perfume
de amor. El pájaro vuela
de un árbol a otro y saluda
tu frente rosada y bella
como a un alba; y las encinas
robustas, altas, soberbias,
cuando tú pasas agitan
sus hojas verdes y trémulas,
y enarcan sus ramas como
para que pase una reina.
¡Oh amada mía! Es el dulce
tiempo de la primavera.

Mira en tus ojos los míos,
da al viento la cabellera,
y que bañe el sol ese aro
de la luz salva y espléndida.
Dame que aprieten mis manos
las tuyas de rosa y seda
y ríe, y muestren tus labios
su púrpura húmeda y fresca.
Yo voy a decirte rimas,

Springtime

Month of roses. My poems
wander through the vast forest
to gather honey and fragrance
from the half-opened flowers.
Come, my belovèd. The great
wood is our temple; a blessed
perfume of love is drifting
and wavering there. A bird flies
from tree to tree, and salutes
your brow, which is as rosy
as daybreak; and the live oaks,
tall and staunch and haughty,
rustle their tremulous green
leaves as you approach,
and form an arch with their boughs,
as though a queen were passing.
Oh, my belovèd! It is
the sweet season of spring.

Look: in your eyes, my own;
free your locks to the wind,
so that the sun may burnish
that wild, magnificent gold.
Allow me to clasp your hands,
which are rose petals and silk,
and smile at me with the moist
cool crimson of your lips.
I will recite you verses;

tú vas a escuchar risueña;
si acaso algún ruiseñor
viniese a posarse cerca
y a contar alguna historia
de ninfas, rosas o estrellas,
tú no oirás notas ni trinos,
sino, enamorada y regia,
escucharás mis canciones
fija en mis labios que tiemblan.
¡Oh amada mía! Es el dulce
tiempo de la primavera.

Allá hay una clara fuente
que brota de una caverna,
donde se bañan desnudas
las blancas ninfas que juegan.
Ríen al son de la espuma,
hienden la linfa serena;
entre el polvo cristalino
esponjan sus cabelleras
y saben himnos de amores
en hermosa lengua griega,
que en glorioso tiempo antiguo
Pan inventó en las florestas.
Amada, pondré en mis rimas
la palabra más soberbia
de las frases de los versos
de los himnos de esa lengua;
y te diré esa palabra
empapada en miel hiblea...
¡Oh amada mía! Es el dulce
tiempo de la primavera.
Van en sus grupos vibrantes
revolando las abejas
como un áureo torbellino
que la blanca luz alegra;
y sobre el agua sonora
pasan radiantes, ligeras,
con sus alas cristalinas
las irisadas libélulas.
Oye: Canta la cigarra
porque ama al sol, que en la selva
su polvo de oro tamiza
entre las hojas espesas.
Su aliento nos da en un soplo
fecundo la madre tierra,
con el alma de los cálices
y el aroma de las hierbas.

¿Ves aquel nido? Hay un ave.
Son dos: el macho y la hembra.
Ella tiene el buche blanco,

you will listen with delight,
and if a nightingale
should perch nearby and sing
of nymphs, roses, or stars,
you will not hear his trills:
amorous and enchanted,
you will hear only my songs,
your gaze fixed on my lips.
Oh, my belovèd! It is
the sweet season of spring.

There is a limpid stream
that surges from a cavern,
and beautiful white nymphs
bathe there, playful and naked.
They laugh to the sound of the foam,
they splash the clear water,
moistening their long locks
with crystal drops of dew,
and all know hymns of love
in the splendid Greek tongue
that Pan invented in the woods
in the great days of antiquity.
Belovèd, I will place
in my verses the fairest word
from all the phrases and lines
in the hymns of that language;
and you will speak that word,
which drips the honey of Hybla—
Oh, my belovèd! It is
the sweet season of spring.

A vibrant swarm of bees
is flying in the white sunlight
like a small gold whirlwind,
and the rainbow dragonflies
are darting above the sonorous
waters on crystalline wings.
Listen: the cicada is singing
because it loves the sun,
which filters its golden dust
through the clustering leaves.
Its breath gives us a fecund
sense of our mother earth,
with the very souls of the flowers,
the fragrance of the grasses.

See that nest. See the two
birds, the male and the female.
The female has a white breast,
the male's plumage is black.
A song swells their throats,

él tiene las plumas negras.
En la garganta el gorjeo,
las alas blancas y trémulas;
y los picos que se chocan
como labios que se besan.
El nido es cántico. El ave
incuba el trino, ¡oh poetas!
de la lira universal,
el ave pulsa una cuerda.
Bendito el calor sagrado
que hizo reventar las yemas.
¡Oh amada mía! Es el dulce
tiempo de la primavera.
Mi dulce musa Delicia
me trajo una ánfora griega
cincelada de alabastro,
de vino de Naxos llena;
y una hermosa copa de oro,
la base henchida de perlas,
para que bebiese el vino
que es propicio a los poetas.
En el ánfora está Diana,
real, orgullosa y esbelta,
con su desnudez divina
y en su actitud cinegética.
Y en la copa luminosa
está Venus Citerea
tendida cerca de Adonis
que sus caricias desdeña.
No quiero el vino de Naxos
ni el ánfora de ansas bellas,
ni la copa donde Cipria
al gallardo Adonis ruega.
Quiero beber del amor
sólo en tu boca bermeja.
¡Oh amada mía! Es el dulce
tiempo de la primavera.

1888/1893

their soft wings are trembling,
and their beaks, meeting, are like
two pairs of lips kissing.
The nest is a canticle. Birds
incubate music, oh poets!
Birds vibrate one string
of the universal lyre.
Blessèd be the sacred warmth
that caused the eggs to hatch,
oh, my belovèd, in this
the sweet season of spring.

My sweet muse Delicia
brought me a Greek amphora
carved out of alabaster
and filled with Naxos wine;
and a lovely golden cup,
the base studded with pearls,
so that I might drink the wine
appropriate to poets.
Diana is on the amphora,
regally proud and tall,
with her divine nakedness
and her stance of a huntress
And the Cytherean Venus
is on the luminous cup,
reclining beside Adonis,
who scorns her fond caresses.
But I do not want the wine
of Naxos, nor the fine amphora,
nor the cup where the Cyprian
pleads with that elegant youth.
No, I want to drink love
only from your red mouth,
oh, my belovèd, in this
the sweet season of spring!

trans. Lysander Kemp

Yo persigo una forma...

Yo persigo una forma que no encuentra mi estilo,
botón de pensamiento que busca ser la rosa;
se anuncia con un beso que en mis labios se posa
al abrazo imposible de la Venus de Milo.

Adornan verdes palmas el blanco peristilo;
los astros me han predicho la visión de la Diosa;
y en mi alma reposa la luz, como reposa
el ave de la luna sobre un lago tranquilo.

I Seek a Form...

I seek a form that my style cannot discover,
a bud of thought that wants to be a rose;
it is heralded by a kiss that is placed on my lips
in the impossible embrace of the Venus de Milo.

The white peristyle is decorated with green palms;
the stars have predicted that I will see the goddess;
and the light reposes within my soul like the bird
of the moon reposing on a tranquil lake.

Y no hallo sino la palabra que huye,
la iniciación melódica que de la flauta fluye
y la barca del sueño que en el espacio boga;

y bajo la ventana de mi Bella-Durmiente,
el sollozo continuo del chorro de la fuente
y el cuello del gran cisne blanco que me interroga.

1896

Era un aire suave...

Era un aire suave de pausados giros;
el Hada Harmonía ritmaba sus vuelos;
e iban frases vagas y tenues suspiros,
entre los sollozos de los violoncelos.

Sobre la terraza, junto a los ramajes,
diríase un trémolo de liras eolias,
cuando acariciaban los sedosos trajes
sobre el tallo erguido las altas magnolias.

La marquesa Eulalia, risas y desvíos
daba a un tiempo mismo para dos rivales;
el vizconde ribio de los desafíos
y el abate joven de los madrigales.

Cerca, coronado con hojas de viña,
reía en su máscara Término barbudo,
y como un efebo que fuese una niña,
mostraba una Diana su mármol desnudo.

Y bajo un boscaje, del amor palestra,
sobre el rico zócalo al modo de Jonia,
con un candelabro prendido en la diestra
volaba el Mercurio de Juan de Bolonia.

La orquesta perlaba sus mágicas notas,
un coro de sones alados se oía;
galantes pavanas, fugaces gavotas,
cantaban los dulces violines de Hungría.

Al oír las quejas de sus caballeros
ríe, ríe, ríe la divina Eulalia,
pues son su tesoro las flechas de Eros,
el cinto de Cipria, la rueca de Onfalia.

¡Ay de quien sus mieles y frases recoja!
¡Ay de quien del canto de su amor se fíe!
Con sus ojos lindos y su boca roja,
la divina Eulalia, ríe, ríe, ríe!

And I only find the word that runs away,
the melodious introduction that flows from the flute,
the ship of dreams that rows through all space,

and, under the window of my sleeping beauty,
the endless sigh from the waters of the fountain,
and the neck of the great white swan, that questions me.

trans. Lysander Kemp

It Was a Gentle Air...

It was a gentle air, with turns and pauses;
the sprite Harmony guided all its flights;
and there were whispered words and tenuous sighs
among the sobbings of the violoncellos.

Along the terrace, next to the crowded leaves,
there was a tremolo as of aeolian harps
whenever the silken gowns, in passing, stroked
the white magnolias erect upon their stems.

The Marchioness Eulalia bestowed
her smiles and snubs on two rivals at once;
the blond viscount with his challenges,
the young *abbé* with his madrigals.

Near them, beneath a coronet of grape leaves,
bearded Terminus laughed behind his mask,
and like an ephebe that might have been a girl,
the huntress Diana revealed her naked marble.

The Mercury of Jean de Boulogne was flying
beneath a leafy bower, palestra of love,
on a sumptuous pedestal in the Ionic style;
there was a lighted torch in his right hand.

The orchestra strung its magic notes like pearls;
we heard a chorus of clear and wingèd sounds;
the sweet violins of Hungary sang out
both slow pavannes and volatile gavottes.

On hearing how her two gallants complain,
divine Eulalia laughs and laughs and laughs,
because her treasures are the arrows of Eros,
the Cyprian's girdle, and Omphale's distaff.

Alas for the man who hears her honeyed words!
Alas for the man who believes her songs of love!
With her shining eyes and curving crimson mouth
divine Eulalia laughs and laughs and laughs.

Tiene azules ojos, es maligna y bella;
cuando mira vierte viva luz extraña;
se asoma a sus húmedas pupilas de estrella
el alma del rubio cristal de Champaña.

Es noche de fiesta, y el baile de trajes
ostenta su gloria de triunfos mundanos.
La divine Eulalia, vestida de encajes,
una flor destroza con sus tersas manos.

El teclado armónico de su risa fina
a la alegre música de un pájaro iguala,
con los *staccatti* de una bailarina
y las locas fugas de una colegiala.

¡Amoroso pájaro que trinos exhala
bajo el ala a veces ocultando el pico;
que desdenes rudos lanza bajo el ala,
bajo el ala aleve del leve abanico!

Cuando a media noche sus notas arranque,
y en arpegios áureos gima Filomela,
y el ebúrneo cisne, sobre el quieto estanque,
como blanca góndola imprima su estela,

la marquesa alegre llegaría al boscaje,
boscaje que cubre la amable glorieta
donde han de estrecharla los brazos de un paje,
que siendo su paje será su poeta.

Al compás de un canto de artista de Italia
que en la brisa errante la orquesta deslíe,
junto a los rivales, la divina Eulalia,
la divina Eulalia ríe, ríe, ríe.

¿Fué, acaso, en el tiempo del Rey Luis de Francia,
sol con corte de astros, en campo de azur?
¿Cuando los alcázares llenó de fragancia
la regia y pomposa rosa Pompadour?

¿Fué, cuando la bella su falda cogía,
con dedos de ninfa, bailando el minué,
y de los compases el ritmo seguía
sobre el tacón rojo, lindo y leve el pie?

¿O cuando pastoras de floridos valles
ornaban con cintas sus albos corderos
y oían, divinas Tirsis de Versalles,
las declaraciones de los caballeros?

¿Fué en ese buen tiempo de duques pastores,
de amantes princesas y tiernos galanes,

Her eyes are blue, she is lovely and perverse,
and her glances shed a strange and living light:
the soul of the crystal paleness of champagne
looks out of her pupils, which are moist and starry.

It is a festive night, and the dress ball
shows off the glory of its mundane triumphs.
Divine Eulalia, radiant in her lace,
destroys a flower with her dainty fingers.

[The harmonious keyboard of her soft laughter
seemed like the restless music of a bird:
with the *staccatti* of a ballerina
and a schoolgirl's raging fugues.]

Ah! that amorous bird who breathes pure song
and hides her bill at times beneath her wing;
who trills her insults from beneath her wing,
the soft and guileful wing of her wide fan.

And when, at midnight, Philomel pours out
her timeless grief in arpeggios of golden notes,
and the white swan, like an ivory gondola, prints
its wake upon the tranquility of the pool,

the marchioness will vanish among the leaves,
among the clustering green that hides a bower
in which she will be clasped by the arms of a page
who, being her page, will also be her poet.

But now, divine Eulalia is with her gallants,
and now, to the rhythm of an Italian air
which the musicians loose to the wandering breeze,
divine Eulalia laughs and laughs and laughs.

Was this in the reign of Louis, king of France,
a sun with a court of stars, on an azure field?
When that majestic—that imperial—rose,
Pompadour, filled the castles with perfume?

Was this when the belle plucked up her gorgeous skirt
with a nymph's fingers, to dance the minuet,
her light and lovely feet, in crimson slippers,
following all the measures of the music?

Or was it when shepherdesses, in flowering vales,
adorned their soft white lambs with silken ribbons;
when those divine Thyrses of Versailles listened
to the overtures of the gentlemen who loved them?

Was this in those good days of shepherd dukes,
of loving princesses and tender gallants,

cuando entre sonrisas y perlas y flores
iban las casacas de los chambelanes?

¿Fué, acaso, en el Norte o en el Mediodía?
Yo el tiempo y el día y el país ignoro,
pero sé que Eulalia ríe todavía
¡y es cruel y es eterna su risa de oro!

1896

the days when chamberlains in their livery
moved among shining smiles and pearls and flowers?

Was this in the north, perhaps, or in the south?
I do not know the age, the hour, the country;
but this I know: Eulalia is still laughing,
and her golden laugh is cruel and eternal.

trans. Lysander Kemp

El cisne

A Ch. Del Guffre

Fué en una hora divina para el género humano.
El cisne antes cantaba sólo para morir.
Cuando se oyó el acento del Cisne wagneriano
fué en medio de una aurora, fué para revivir.

Sobre las tempestades del humano oceano
se oye el canto del Cisne; no se cesa de oír,
dominando el martillo del viejo Thor Germano
a las trompas que cantan la espada de Argantir.

¡Oh Cisne! ¡Oh sacro pájaro! Si antes la blanca Helena
del huevo azul de Leda brotó de gracia llena,
siendo de la Hermosura la princesa inmortal,

bajo tus blancas alas la nueva Poesía
concibe en una gloria de luz y de armonía
la Helena eterna y pura que encarna el ideal.

1896

The Swan

To Ch. Del Guffre

It was a divine hour for the human race.
Before, the Swan sang only at its death.
But when the Wagnerian Swan began to sing,
there was a new dawning, and a new life.

The song of the swan is heard above the storms
of the human sea; its aria never ceases;
it dominates the hammering of old Thor,
and the trumpets hailing the sword of Argentir.

O Swan! O sacred bird! If once white Helen,
immortal princess of Beauty's realms, emerged
all grace from Leda's sky-blue egg, so now,

beneath the white of your wings, the new Poetry,
here in a splendor of music and light, conceives
the pure, eternal Helen who is the Ideal.

trans. Lysander Kemp

Sonatina

La princesa está triste... ¿Qué tendrá la princesa?
Los suspiros se escapan de su boca de fresa
que ha perdido la risa, que ha perdido el color.
La princesa está pálida en su silla de oro,
está mudo el teclado de su clave sonoro,
y en un vaso olvidada se desmaya una flor.

El jardín puebla el triunfo de los pavos reales;
parlanchina, la dueña dice cosas banales,
y vestido de rojo piruetea el bufón.
La princesa no ríe, la princesa no siente;
la princesa persigue por el cielo de Oriente
la libélula vaga de una vaga ilusión.

¿Piensa acaso en el príncipe de Golconda o de China,
o en el que ha detenido su carroza argentina

Sonatina

The Princess is sad. What ails the Princess?
Nothing but sighs escape from her lips,
which have lost their smile and their strawberry red.
The Princess is pale in her golden chair,
the keys of her harpsichord gather dust,
and a flower, forgotten, droops in its vase.

The garden is bright with the peacocks' triumph,
the duenna prattles of commonplace things,
the clown pirouettes in his crimson and gold;
but the Princess is silent, her thoughts are far-off:
the Princess traces the dragonfly course
of a vague illusion in the eastern sky.

Are her thoughts of a prince of Golconda or China?
Of a prince who has halted his silver coach

para ver de sus ojos la dulzura de luz?
¿O en el rey de las islas de las rosas fragantes,
o en el que es soberano de los claros diamantes,
o en el dueño orgulloso de las perlas de Ormuz?

¡Ay! la pobre princesa de la boca de rosa
quiere ser golondrina, quiere ser mariposa,
tener alas ligeras, bajo el cielo volar,
ir al sol por la escala luminosa de un rayo,
saludar a los lirios con los versos de Mayo,
o perderse en el viento sobre el trueno del mar.

Ya no quiere el palacio, ni la rueca de plata,
ni el halcón encantado, ni el bufón escarlata,
ni los cisnes unánimes en el lago de azur.
Y están tristes las flores por la flor de la corte;
los jazmines de Oriente, los nelumbos del Norte,
de Occidente las dalias y las rosas del Sur.

¡Pobrecita princesa de los ojos azules!
Está presa en sus oros, está presa en sus tules,
en la jaula de mármol del palacio real;
el palacio soberbio que vigilan los guardas,
que custodian cien negros con sus cien alabardas,
un lebrel que no duerme y un dragón colosal.

¡Oh, quién fuera hipsipila que dejó la crisálida!
(La princesa está triste. La princesa está pálida.)
¡Oh visión adorada de oro, rosa y marfil!
¡Quién volara a la tierra donde un príncipe existe
(La princesa está pálida. La princesa está triste)
más brillante que el alba, más hermoso que Abril!

Calla, calla, princesa —dice el hada madrina—
en caballo con alas hacia acá se encamina,
en el cinto la espada y en la mano el azor,
el feliz caballero que te adora sin verte,
y que llega de lejos, vencedor de la Muerte,
a encenderte los labios con su beso de amor.

1893

Caracol

A Antonio Machado

En la playa he encontrado un caracol de oro
macizo y recamado de las perlas más finas;
Europa le ha tocado con sus manos divinas
cuando cruzó las ondas sobre el celeste toro.

to see the soft light that glows in her eyes?
Of the king of the fragrant isle of roses,
or the lord who commands the clear-shining diamonds,
or the arrogant lord of the pearls of Ormuz?

Alas, the poor Princess, whose mouth is a rose,
would be a swallow or a butterfly;
would skim on light wings, or mount to the sun
on the luminous stair of a golden sunbeam;
would greet the lilies with the verses of May,
or be lost in the wind on the thundering sea.

She is tired of the palace, the silver distaff,
the enchanted falcon, the scarlet buffoon,
the swans reflected on the azure lake.
And the flowers are sad for the flower of the court:
the jasmines of the east, the water lilies of the north,
the dahlias of the west, and the roses of the south.

The poor little Princess with the wide blue eyes
is imprisoned in her gold, imprisoned in her tulle,
in the marble cage of the royal palace,
the lofty palace that is guarded by sentries,
by a hundred Negroes with a hundred halberds,
a sleepless greyhound, and the monstrous dragon.

Oh to be a butterfly leaving its cocoon!
(The Princess is sad. The Princess is pale.)
Oh adorable vision of gold, marble, and rose!
Oh to fly to the land where there is a prince—
(The Princess is pale. The Princess is sad.)—
more brilliant than daybreak, more handsome than April!

"Hush, Princess, hush," says her fairy godmother;
"the joyous knight who adores you unseen
is riding this way on his wingèd horse,
a sword at his waist and a hawk on his wrist,
and comes from far off, having conquered Death,
to kindle your lips with a kiss of true love!"

trans. Lysander Kemp

The Seashell

To Antonio Machado

I found a golden seashell on the beach.
It is massive, and embroidered with the finest pearls.
Europa touched it with her sacred hands
as she rode the waves astride the celestial bull.

He llevado a mis labios el caracol sonoro
y he suscitado el eco de las dianas marinas;
le acerqué a mis oídos, y las azules minas
me han contado en voz baja su secreto tesoro.

Así la sal me llega de los vientos amargos
que en sus hinchadas velas sintió la nave Argos
cuando amaron los astros el sueño de Jasón;

y oigo un rumor de olas, y un incógnito acento,
y un profundo oleaje, y un misterioso viento...
(El caracol la forma tiene de un corazón.)

1904

I raised that sounding seashell to my lips
to rouse the echoes of the ocean's reveilles,
and pressed it to my ear and heard the blue
fathoms whisper the secret of their treasures.

Hence I have tasted the salt of the bitter winds
that swelled the sails of the Argonauts when all
the stars were in love with Jason's golden dream,

and I hear a murmur of waves and an unknown voice
and a vast tide-swell and a mysterious wind—
(The shell I found is in the shape of a heart.)

trans. Lysander Kemp

Lo fatal

A René Pérez

Dichoso el árbol que es apenas sensitivo,
y más la piedra dura, porque ésa ya no siente,
pues no hay dolor más grande que el dolor de ser vivo,
ni mayor pesadumbre que la vida consciente.

Ser, y no saber nada, y ser sin rumbo cierto,
y el temor de haber sido y un futuro terror...
Y el espanto seguro de estar mañana muerto,
y sufrir por la vida y por la sombra y por

lo que no conocemos y apenas sospechamos,
y la carne que tienta con sus frescos racimos,
y la tumba que aguarda con sus fúnebres ramos,
¡y no saber adónde vamos,
ni de dónde venimos!...

1904

Fatality

To René Pérez

The tree is happy because it is scarcely sentient;
the hard rock is happier still, it feels nothing:
there is no pain as great as being alive,
no burden heavier than that of conscious life.

To be, and to know nothing, and to lack a way,
and the dread of having been, and future terrors...
And the sure terror of being dead tomorrow,
and to suffer through all life and through the darkness,

and through what we do not know and hardly suspect...
And the flesh that tempts us with bunches of cool grapes,
and the tomb that awaits us with its funeral sprays,
and not to know where we go,
nor whence we came!...

trans. Lysander Kemp

A Roosevelt

Es con voz de la Biblia, o verso de Walt Whitman,
que habría de llegar hasta ti, Cazador,
primitivo y moderno, sencillo y complicado,
con un algo de Wáshington y cuatro de Nemrod.

Eres los Estados Unidos,
eres el futuro invasor
de la América ingenua que tiene sangre indígena,
que aún reza a Jesucristo y aún habla en español.

Eres soberbio y fuerte ejemplar de tu raza;
eres culto, eres hábil; te opones a Tolstoy.

To Roosevelt

The voice that would reach you, Hunter, must speak
with Biblical tones, or in the poetry of Walt Whitman.
You are primitive and modern, simple and complex;
you are one part George Washington and one part Nimrod.

You are the United States,
future invader of our naive America
with its Indian blood, an America
that still prays to Christ and still speaks Spanish.

You are a strong, proud model of your race;
you are cultured and able; you oppose Tolstoy.

Y domando caballos, o asesinando tigres,
eres un Alejandro-Nabucodonosor.
(Eres un profesor de Energía,
como dicen los locos de hoy.)

Crees que la vida es incendio,
que el progreso es erupción,
que en donde pones la bala
el porvenir pones.
                No.

Los Estados Unidos son potentes y grandes.
Cuando ellos se estremecen hay un hondo temblor
que pasa por las vértebras enormes de los Andes.
Si clamáis, se oye como el rugir del león.
Ya Hugo a Grant lo dijo: Las estrellas son vuestras.
(Apenas brilla, alzándose, el argentino sol
y la estrella chilena se levanta...) Sois ricos.
Juntáis al culto de Hércules el culto de Mammón;
y alumbrando el camino de la fácil conquista,
a Libertad levanta su antorcha en Nueva-York.

Mas la América nuestra, que tenía poetas
desde los viejos tiempos de Netzahualcoyotl,
que ha guardado las huellas de los pies del gran Baco,
que el alfabeto pánico en un tiempo aprendió;
que consultó los astros, que conoció la Atlántida
cuyo nombre nos llega resonando en Platón,
que desde los remotos momentos de su vida
vive de luz, de fuego, de perfume, de amor,
la América del grande Moctezuma, del Inca,
la América fragante de Cristóbal Colón,
la América católica, la América española,
la América en que dijo el noble Guatemoc:
"Yo no estoy en un lecho de rosas"; esa América
que tiembla de huracanes y que vive de amor,
hombres de ojos sajones y alma bárbara, vive.
Y sueña. Y ama, y vibra, y es la hija del Sol.
Tened cuidado. ¡Vive la América española!
Hay mil cachorros sueltos del León Español.
Se necesitaría, Roosevelt, ser, por Dios mismo,
el Riflero terrible y el fuerte Cazador,
para poder tenernos en vuestras férreas garras.

Y, pues contáis con todo, falta una cosa: ¡Dios!

1905

You are an Alexander-Nebuchadnezzar,
breaking horses and murdering tigers.
(You are a professor of Energy,
as the current lunatics say.)

You think that life is a fire,
that progress is an irruption,
that the future is wherever
your bullet strikes.
                No.

The United States is grand and powerful.
Whenever it trembles, a profound shudder
runs down the enormous backbone of the Andes.
If it shouts, the sound is like the roar of a lion.
And Hugo said to Grant: "The stars are yours."
(The dawning sun of the Argentine barely shines;
the star of Chile is rising...) A wealthy country,
joining the cult of Mammon to the cult of Hercules;
while Liberty, lighting the path
to easy conquest, raises her torch in New York.

But our own America, which has had poets
since the ancient times of Nezahualcóyotl;
which preserved the footprints of great Bacchus,
and learned the Panic alphabet once,
and consulted the stars; which also knew Atlantis
(whose name comes ringing down to us in Plato)
and has lived, since the earliest moments of its life,
in light, in fire, in fragrance, and in love—
the America of Moctezuma and Atahualpa,
the aromatic America of Columbus,
Catholic America, Spanish America,
the America where noble Cuauhtémoc said:
"I am not on a bed of roses"—our America,
trembling with hurricanes, trembling with Love:
O men with Saxon eyes and barbarous souls,
our America lives. And dreams. And loves.
And it is the daughter of the Sun. Be careful.
Long live Spanish America!
A thousand cubs of the Spanish lion are roaming free.
Roosevelt, you must become, by God's own will,
the deadly Rifleman and the dreadful Hunter
before you can clutch us in your iron claws.

And though you have everything, you are lacking
    one thing: God!

trans. Lysander Kemp

Tarde del trópico

Es la tarde gris y triste.
Viste el mar de terciopelo,
y el cielo profundo viste
de duelo.

    Del abismo se levanta
la queja amarga y sonora.
La onda, cuando el viento canta,
llora.

    Los violines de la bruma
saludan al sol que muere.
Salmodia la blanca espuma:
¡Miserere!

    La armonía el cielo inunda,
y la brisa va a llevar
la canción triste y profunda
del mar.

    Del clarín del horizonte
brota sinfonía rara,
como si la voz del monte
vibrara.

    Cual si fuese lo invisible...
Cual si fuese el rudo son
que diese al viento un terrible
león.

Tropical Afternoon

The afternoon is sad and gray.
The sea is dressed in velvet
and the sky is swathed in grief.

A bitter, sonorous complaint
arises from the abyss.
The waves, when the wind sings, weep.

The violins of the fog lament
for the dying day. The white foam
intones a *miserere*.

Harmony floods the sky
and the wind carries the deep
and mournful song of the sea.

Strange music bursts from the horizon's
trumpets, as if it were
the reverberating voice of the mountain—

as if it were the Invisible—
as if it were the thunder that a lion
hurls into the wind.

trans. Lysander Kemp

1905

Nocturno

Silencio de la noche, doloroso silencio
nocturno... ¿Por qué el alma tiembla de tal manera?
Oigo el zumbido de mi sangre,
dentro mi cráneo pasa una suave tormenta.
¡Insomnio! No poder dormir, y, sin embargo,
soñar. Ser la auto-pieza
de disección espiritual, ¡el auto-Hamlet!
Dilüir mi tristeza
en un vino de noche,
en el maravilloso cristal de las tinieblas...
Y me digo: ¿a qué hora vendrá el alba?
Se ha cerrado una puerta...
Ha pasado un transeúnte...
Ha dado el reloj trece horas... ¡Si será Ella!...

Nocturne

Silence of the night, a sad, nocturnal
silence—Why does my soul tremble so?
I hear the humming of my blood,
and a soft storm passes through my brain.
Insomnia! Not to be able to sleep, and yet
to dream. I am the autospecimen
of spiritual dissection, the auto-Hamlet!
To dilute my sadness
in the wine of the night
in the marvelous crystal of the dark—
And I ask myself: When will the dawn come?
Someone has closed a door—
Someone has walked past—
The clock has rung three—If only it were She!—

1907

trans. Lysander Kemp

Tríptico de Nicaragua

I. LOS BUFONES

Recuerdo, allá en la casa familiar, dos enanos
como los de Velázquez. El uno, varón, era
llamado "el Capitán". Su vieja compañera
era su madre. Y ambos parecían hermanos.

Tenían de peleles, de espectros, de gusanos;
él cojeaba, era bizco, ponía cara fiera;
fabricaba muñecos y figuras de cera
con sus chicas, horribles y regordetas manos.

También fingía ser obispo y bendecía;
predicaba sermones de endemoniado enredo
y rezaba contrito *páter* y avemaría.

Luego, enano y enana se retiraban quedo;
y en tanto que la gente hacendada reía;
yo, silencioso, en un rincón, tenía miedo.

II. EROS

Es en mi juventud, mi juventud que juega
con versos e ilusiones, espada de oro al cinto;
hay en mi mente un sueño siempre vario y distinto,
y mi espíritu ágil al acaso se entrega...

En cada mujer miro como una ninfa griega;
en poemas sonoros sus frescas gracias pinto;
y esto pasa al amor del puerto de Corinto,
o en la rica en naranjas de almíbar, Chinandega.

¡Tiempo lejano ya! Mas aún veo azahares
en los naranjos verdes, impregnados de aromas;
o las viejas fragatas que llegan de los mares

lejanos; o el hicaco, o tupidos manglares;
o tú, rostro adorado en ese tiempo, asomas
con primeros amores y primeros pesares.

III. TERREMOTO

Madrugada. En silencio reposa la gran villa
donde de niño supe de cuentos y consejas,
o asistí a serenatas de amor junto a las rejas
de alguna novia bella, timorata y sencilla.

El cielo lleno de constelaciones brilla,
y su oriente disputan suaves luces bermejas.

Nicaraguan Triptych

I. THE CLOWNS

I remember two dwarfs, back there in our country home,
two dwarfs like those of Velázquez. One was a man
they called The Captain. The other, his old companion,
was his mother. And they looked as if they were brothers.

They were like straw men, like specters, like caterpillars.
The Captain limped, he was cross-eyed, he made
    wild faces;
he used to fashion dolls and small wax figures
with his short, puffy, horrible little fingers.

At times he played he was a bishop, and blessed us all;
the sermons he preached were devilishly complex;
he said the Pater Noster and the Ave Maria.

Then the two dwarfs would quietly leave the room,
and while the country people were all laughing,
I, silent in a corner, was afraid.

II. EROS

It is the time of my youth, my youth that plays
with rhymes and illusions, a golden sword at its hip;
my mind holds a dream always different and distinct,
and my agile spirit surrenders itself to chance—

I see in every woman a Grecian nymph;
I paint their charm and grace in sonorous poems;
and then this passes to love of the port of Corinth,
or of Chinandega, rich in succulent oranges.

That time is far off now. But I still see blossoms
on the green, aromatic trees in the orange grove;
or the old ships arriving from distant lands;

or the cocoa plum; or the clustered mangrove trees;
or you, the face I adored in that time, looking
out at me with a first love or a first repentance.

III. EARTHQUAKE

Daybreak. The great town reposes in its silence.
As a child, I listened to tales and counsels there,
or attended serenades under the barred window
of some young, simple, God-fearing, lovely sweetheart.

The constellations still glitter in the sky,
but there is a soft pink light on the Eastern horizon—

De pronto, un terremoto mueve las casas viejas
y la gente en los patios y calles se arrodilla

    medio desnuda, y clama: "¡Santo Dios! ¡Santo fuerte!
¡Santo inmortal!" La tierra tiembla a cada momento.
¡Algo de apocalíptico mano invisible vierte!...

    La atmósfera es pesada como plomo. No hay viento.
Y se diría que ha pasado la Muerte
ante la impasibilidad del firmamento.

1912

when suddenly an earthquake shakes the old houses,
and the people kneel to pray in the streets and patios,

half-naked, crying: "Dear God! Immortal God!"
The earth trembles each moment, as if it were shaken
by some invisible and apocalyptic hand—

The air is heavy as lead. There is no wind.
And it could be said that Death has passed this way
under the impassivity of the firmament.

trans. Lysander Kemp

Ricardo Jaimes Freyre

BOLIVIA
1870?–1933

A close friend of Rubén Darío from early on, Ricardo Jaimes Freyre shared Darío's commitment to Modernist thematics, to tones of melancholy and aestheticism, and to the formal musicality of verse. Influenced also by Wagner, and fascinated by Teutonic myths played out in landscapes of operatically exotic ice and snow, Jaimes Freyre attempted, at times, to introduce the resonances of the musical leitmotif as a poetic refrain, to effect a sense of time and repetition in his lyrics. Moreover, Jaimes Freyre's contribution to Darío's theories of Modernism was formally musical. That contribution was made through the Bolivian poet's systematization of the rules of Spanish verse in *Leyes de la versificación castellana* (*Laws of Castilian Versification*, 1919). Rejecting traditional theories that counted syllables as either long or short, Jaimes Freyre insisted instead that Spanish verse is essentially accentual. In his "laws" Jaimes Freyre maintained that instead of counting syllables, the reader parses the Spanish-language poem by attending to "prosodic periods," which may range from one to seven syllables, within the single line. The last syllable of each prosodic period carries the "rhythmic accent" of closure that defines the line's integrity. The musical freedom that Jaimes Freyre's theories made possible helped to shape much of the subsequent free-verse work in Latin America even after the heyday of Latin American Modernism had passed.

Aeternum vale

    Un Dios misterioso y extraño visita la selva.
Es un Dios silencioso que tiene los brazos abiertos.
Cuando la hija de Thor espoleaba su negro caballo,
le vió erguirse, de pronto, a la sombra de un añoso fresno.
        Y sintió que se helaba su sangre
ante el Dios silencioso que tiene los brazos abiertos.

    De la fuente de Imer, en los bordes sagrados, más tarde,
la Noche a los dioses absortos reveló el secreto;
de Águila negra y los Cuervos de Odín escuchaban,
y los cisnes que esperan la hora del canto postrero;

Eternal Farewell

    A strange mysterious God visits the forest,
a silent God Who holds His arms outstretched.
And as Thor's daughter passes, riding her black horse,
suddenly she sees him rise in the shade of an ancient ash;
        she feels her blood run cold
before this silent God Who holds His arms outstretched.

    Later, in the precinct of Imer's sacred spring,
Night told the secret to the astonished gods;
the dark Eagle and the Crows of Odin listened,
and the swans who wait the hour of the final song.

y a los dioses mordía el espanto
de ese Dios silencioso que tiene los brazos abiertos.

En la selva agitada se oían extrañas salmodias;
mecía la encina y el sauce quejumbroso viento;
el bisonte y el alce movían las ramas espesas,
y a través de las ramas espesas huían mugiendo.
En la lengua sagrada de Orga
despertaban del canto divino los divinos versos.

Thor, el rudo, terrible guerrero que blande la maza,
—en sus manos es arma la negra montaña de hierro,—
va a aplastar, en la selva, a la sombra del árbol sagrado,
a ese Dios silencioso que tiene los brazos abiertos.
Y los dioses contemplan la maza rugiente
que gira en los aires y nubla la lumbre del cielo.

Ya en la selva sagrada no se oyen las viejas salmodias,
ni la voz amorosa de Freya cantando a lo lejos;
agonizan los dioses que pueblan la selva sagrada,
y en la lengua de Orga se extinguen los divinos versos.

Solo, erguido a la sombra de un árbol,
hay un Dios silencioso que tiene los brazos abiertos.

1899

El alba

Las auroras pálidas,
Que nacen entre penumbras misteriosas,
Y enredados en las orlas de sus mantos
Llevan girones de sombra,
Iluminan las montañas,
Las crestas de las montañas, rojas;
Bañan las torres erguidas,
Que saludan su aparición silenciosa,
Con la voz de sus campanas
Soñolienta y ronca;
Ríen en las calles
Dormidas de la ciudad populosa,
Y se esparcen en los campos
Donde el invierno respeta las amarillentas hojas.
Tienen perfumes de Oriente
Las auroras;
Los recojieron al paso, de las florestas ocultas
De una extraña Flora.
Tienen ritmos y músicas harmoniosas,
Porque oyeron los gorjeos y los trinos de las aves
Exóticas.

And the gods were filled with dread
of the silent God Who holds His arms outstretched.

Then in the quaking wood, strange noises:
rumbling, a wind made oaks and willows shake;
the bison and the elk crashed through thick branches
and vanished roaring through the heavy brush.
In Orga's consecrated tongue
sacred verses of the sacred song poured out.

Thor, the rough, grim soldier who wields
the mace, black iron mountain, as his weapon,
enters the woods, in the shade of the sacred tree, to fight
the silent God Who holds His arms outstretched.
The gods watch as the mace groans,
spinning through air, and dims the light of heaven.

Now in the sacred wood the ancient songs are silent,
and Freya's amorous voice singing in the distance.
The gods of the sacred wood are dying;
in Orga's sacred tongue the holy songs are dying out.

He stands alone, erect in the shadow of a tree:
the silent God Who holds His arms outstretched.

trans. Victor Tulli

The Dawn

Colorless dawns,
born among mysterious penumbras,
carry shreds of darkness with them
tangled in the fringes of their cloaks;
they illuminate the mountains,
the crests of the mountains, reddish;
they wash across the proud towers,
which salute their silent manifestation
with the sleepy and hoarse
voice of their bells;
they laugh through the drowsy
streets of the crowded city
and disperse across the fields
where winter honors the yellowing leaves.
The dawns contain
perfumes of the Orient,
having gathered them, in passing, from the secret forests
of an unfamiliar Flora.
They bring a rhythmic, harmonious music,
for they have heard the trills and warbles
of exotic birds.

Su luz fría,
Que conserva los girones de la sombra,
Enredóse, vacilante, de los lotos
En las anchas hojas.
Chispeó en las aguas dormidas,
Las aguas del viejo Ganges, dormidas y silenciosas;
Y las tribus de los árabes desiertos,
Saludaron con plegarias a las pálidas auroras.
Los rostros de los errantes bedüinos
Se bañaron con arenas ardorosas,
Y murmuraron las suras del Profeta
Voces roncas.

Tendieron las suaves alas
Sobre los mares de Jonia,
Y vieron surgir a Venus
De las suspirantes olas.

En las cimas,
Donde las nieblas eternas sobre las nieves se posan,
Vieron monstruos espantables
Entre las rocas,
Y las crines de los búfalos que huían
Por la selva tenebrosa.
Reflejaron en la espada
Simbólica,
Que a la sombra de una encina
Yacía, olvidada y polvorosa.

Hay ensueños,
Hay ensueños en las pálidas auroras...
Hay ensueños,
Que se envuelven en sus girones de sombra...
Sorprenden los amorosos
Secretos de las nupciales alcobas,
Y ponen pálidos tintes en los labios
Donde el beso dejó huellas voluptuosas...

Y el Sol eleva su disco fulgurante,
Sobre la tierra, los aires y las suspirantes olas.

1899

Their cold light,
still holding the colored plumes of the darkness,
has saturated through the broad leaves
of the lotus, tenuously;
has sparkled across the sleeping waters,
the water of the ancient Ganges, sleeping and quiet;
and the tribes of the Arabian desert
have greeted the colorless dawns with their prayers;
those nomad-Bedouins
have bathed their faces with the burning sands
and have murmured the words of the Prophet
with droning voices.

They have opened their gentle wings
over Ionian waters
and have watched Venus rise
from the sighing waves.

On the peaks
where the clouds settle forever on the snows,
they have seen astonishing monsters
among the rocks
and the manes of the buffaloes that ran off
through the dark forest.
They have reflected
on the symbolic sword
lying dusty and forgotten
in the shadow of an oak-tree.

There are dreams,
there are dreams in those colorless dawns...
There are dreams
that mingle with their shredded shadows...
They startle the lovers
who had hidden away in amorous corners,
and they spread a pallid color over lips
where kisses had left voluptuous blushes...

And the Sun lifts its brilliant disk
over the earth, and the air, and the sighing waves.

trans. Victor Tulli

Las voces tristes

Por las blancas estepas
Se desliza el trineo;
Los lejanos aullidos de los lobos
Se unen al jadëante resoplar de los perros.

The Sad Voices

Over the white steppes
the sledge slides along;
the distant howling of the wolves
joins with the snorting pants of the dogs.

Nieva.	It snows.
Parece que el espacio se envolviera en un velo,	It seems as if space is covered by a veil,
Tachonado e lirios	adorned with lilies
Por las alas del cierzo.	on the wings of the cold north wind.
El infinito blanco...	The endless whiteness:
Sobre el vasto desierto	over a vast desert
Flota una vaga sensación de angustia,	floats a vague sensation of anguish,
De supremo abandono, de profundo y sombrío	of supreme abandonment, of deep and dark
desaliento.	discouragement.
Un pino solitario	A lone pine
Dibújase a lo lejos,	makes itself evident from far off,
En un fondo de brumas y de nieve	in an underworld of fog and snow,
Como un largo esqueleto.	like a huge skeleton.
Entre los dos sudarios	Between the two shrouds
De la tierra y el cielo,	of the earth and the sky,
Avanza en el Naciente	the sun advances
El helado crepúsculo de invierno...	in the icy twilight of winter.

1899   *trans. Iver Lofving*

Amado Nervo

MEXICO
1870–1919

As a young adult Amado Nervo studied for the priesthood. When he left the seminary, his vestments (in the image offered by the critic Santiago Arguello) metaphorically still clung to him. Although Nervo led an active public life as a diplomat and as a journalist, a fiction writer, and a biographer of Sor Juana Inés de la Cruz, his simple and esteemed poems earned him the sobriquet "The Monk of Poetry."

A contributor to the periodical *Revista Azul* and a cofounder of the influential magazine *Revista Moderna*, early in his career Nervo was an advocate of a plangent, sometimes ornamental Modernism. In 1901 he went to Paris, where he became a close friend of Darío. In 1905 he was appointed secretary to the Mexican diplomatic delegation in Madrid, where he remained until 1918. His poems gradually shed their glamorous experimentalism and found the clear voice of serene religious sincerity that characterizes his mature work. After the death of his beloved Ana Daillez, with whom he had lived for eleven years, he wrote a series of poems offering even his grief to God, because grief was what he had to offer. In later collections, especially *Serenidad* (*Serenity*, 1914) and *Elevación* (*Elevation*, 1917), Nervo's devout images suggest at times a compassionate, almost Buddhistic, instinct toward inclusiveness and mercy. As he liked to point out, even his first name, Amado, means "beloved."

Venganza

Hay quien arroja piedras a mi techo, y después
hurta hipócritamente las manos presurosas
que me dañaron...
                        Yo no tengo piedras, pues
solo hay en mi huerto rosales de olorosas
rosas frescas, y tal mi idiosincrasia es,
que aun escondo la mano tras de tirar las rosas.

1914

El dolor vencido

Dolor, pues no me puedes
quitar a Dios, ¡qué resta a tu eficacia!
"¿Dónde está tu aguijón?"

                        Huyen las horas,
y entre sus alas lleva cada una
cierta porción de tu energía negra.

¡Oh dolor, tú también eres esclavo
del tiempo; tu potencia
se va con los instantes desgranando:
mientras que el Dios que en mi interior anida
más y más agigántase, a medida
que más le voy amando!

1917

El don

¡Oh vida!, ¿me reservas por ventura algún don?
(Atardece. En la torre suena ya la oración.)
¡Oh vida!, ¿me reservas por ventura algún don?

Plañe en las ramas secas el viento lastimero;
se desgrana el crepúsculo en un vivo reguero...
¡Oh vida!, ¿dime cuál será ese don postrero?

¿Será un amor muy grande tu regalo mejor?
(¡Unos ojos azules, unos labios en flor!)
¡Oh, qué dicha, qué dicha si fuese un gran amor!

¿O será una gran paz: ese que necesita
mi pobre alma, tras tanto peregrinar con cuita?
¡Sí, tal vez una paz..., una paz infinita!

...¿O más bien el enigma del que camino en pos,
se aclarará, encendiéndose como una estrella en los
hondos cielos, y entonces, ¡por fin!, hallaré a Dios?

Revenge

Someone throws stones at my roof, then
hypocritically hides the quick hands
that harmed me...
                        I have no stones, only
fragrant fresh roses in my arbor,
and yet—idiosyncratically—
I also hide my hand after throwing roses.

trans. Sue Standing

Sorrow Vanquished

Sorrow, since you cannot make me
quit God, where is your power?
"Where is thy sting?"

                        The hours
fly, carrying away on each wing
a certain portion of your dark energy.

Sorrow, you are also a slave
of time; your potency
diminishes as the moments wear thin,
while God, sheltered inside me,
grows larger and larger, the more
I keep loving Him.

trans. Sue Standing

The Gift

Life, are you keeping something in reserve?
(Late afternoon. Prayer sounds from the tower.)
Life, are you keeping something in reserve?

The sad wind laments in the dry branches;
twilight bleeds away in a bright stream;
life, tell me what will be your last gift?

Will your best present be a great love?
(Some blue eyes, some lips in flower?)
O what luck! What luck if it's a great love!

Or will it be a great peace? which my tired soul
needs after its long, anxious pilgrimage?
Yes, perhaps peace... infinite peace.

...Or, better still, will the riddle of the road
I travel be revealed, flaring like a star
in deep skies, until at last I find God?

¡Oh vida, que devanas aún esta porción
de mis días obscuros! Suena ya la oración;
cae la tarde... ¡Apresúrate a traerme tu don!

1917

Life, who spins out this portion
of my dark days, the prayer sounds;
Evening falls... hurry to bring your gift!

trans. Sue Standing

Éxtasis

Cada rosa gentil ayer nacida,
cada aurora que apunta entre sonrojos,
dejan mi alma en el éxtasis sumida...
¡Nunca se cansan de mirar mis ojos
el perpetuo milagro de la vida!

Años ha que contemplo las estrellas
en las diáfanas noches españolas
y las encuentro cada vez más bellas.
¡Años ha que en el mar, conmigo a solas,
de las olas escucho las querellas,
y aún me pasma el prodigio de las olas!

Cada vez hallo a la Naturaleza
más sobrenatural, más pura y santa.
Para mí, en rededor, todo es belleza;
y con la misma plenitud me encanta
la boca de la madre cuando reza
que la boca del niño cuando canta.

Quiero ser inmortal, con sed intensa,
porque es maravilloso el panorama
con que nos brinda la creación inmensa;
porque cada lucero me reclama,
diciéndome al brillar: "¡Aquí se piensa
también, aquí se lucha, aquí se ama!"

1917

Ecstasy

Each perfect rose that unfolded yesterday,
each sunrise I note between blushes,
fills me with deep pleasure...
I never tire of seeing with my own eyes
the perpetual miracle of life.

Long ago, I looked at the stars
in the transparent nights of Spain,
finding them more exquisite each time.
Long ago, by the sea, alone,
I heard the waves quarrelling,
and still the waves' wonder stuns me.

Each time I find nature
more supernatural, more pure and holy.
For me, here, everything is beautiful
and everything enchants me equally:
the mouth of the mother, praying,
the mouth of the child, singing.

I want passionately to be immortal,
because it is marvelous, the panorama
that invites us to immense creation;
because every star calls to me,
saying with brilliant light, "here, also,
they think, here they struggle, here they love."

trans. Sue Standing

Enrique González Martínez

MEXICO
1871–1952

The career of Enrique González Martínez summarizes much of the paradox of the influence of Modernism in Mexico. Although through the examples of Darío and Lugones other Latin Americans followed the Modernist impulse to value the fertile models of European tradition (including a verbal lushness from Gongorism, a clean formality from Parnassianism, and the allure of abstract beauty from Symbolism), through the example of González Martínez Mexican writers learned, by contrast, those values of landscape, conscience, and verbal austerity that have given the tradition of Mexican poetry a particular and serene gravity. In his most famous poem, a sonnet from 1905 that at times has taken on an iconic quality in Latin American literary studies, González Martínez advises writers to "wring the swan's neck"—that is, to avoid the Parnassian rhetoric, the residue of Romantic sentiment, that had characterized much of the poetics of the nineteenth century and of several generations of Modernists. (Because of a popular misunderstanding of that poem, González Martínez later felt obliged to explain that he had not had in mind either Rubén Darío or his swan, but the poems of many subsequent imitators of Darío. In any case, he would not accuse the author of *Cantos de vida y esperanza* [*Songs of Life and Hope*] of aesthetic frivolity!)

As he pared away those early excesses from his poems, González Martínez opened the way from late Modernism to post-Modernism, toward contemporary aesthetics. He introduced to Mexican poetics a new sensibility and originality—paradoxically, values firmly in keeping with the "Modernist" impulse he is most famous for challenging. "He is not therefore a denier of Modernism," Octavio Paz concludes, "but the only true Modernist poet Mexico has had." Though ironically famous for his image of iconoclastic symbolic violence against the Parnassian "swan," Enrique González Martínez was a kind, reclusive man. In his parallel careers as a poet and as a medical doctor, he exhibited a profound respect for the physical world and an almost mystical respect for the unity of created beings.

Tuércele el cuello al cisne...

Tuércele el cuello al cisne de engañoso plumaje
que da su nota blanca al azul de la fuente;
él pasea su gracia no más, pero no siente
el alma de las cosas ni la voz del paisaje.

Huye de toda forma y de todo lenguaje
que no vayan acordes con el ritmo latente
de la vida profunda... y adora intensamente
la vida, y que la vida comprenda tu homenaje.

Mira al sapiente buho cómo tiende las alas
desde el Olimpo, deja el regazo de Palas
y posa en aquel árbol el vuelo taciturno...

Él no tiene la gracia del cisne, mas su inquieta
pupila, que se clava en la sombra, interpreta
el misterioso libro del silencio nocturno.

1905/1911

Como hermana y hermano

Como hermana y hermano
vamos los dos cogidos de la mano...

En la quietud de la pradera hay una
blanca y radiosa claridad de luna,
y el paisaje nocturno es tan risueño

Wring the Swan's Neck

Wring the swan's neck who with deceiving plumage
inscribes his whiteness on the azure stream;
he merely vaunts his grace and nothing feels
of nature's voice or of the soul of things.

Every form eschew and every language
whose processes with deep life's inner rhythm
are out of harmony... and greatly worship
life, and let life understand your homage.

See the sapient owl who from Olympus
spreads his wings, leaving Athene's lap,
and stays his silent flight on yonder tree.

His grace is not the swan's, but his unquiet
pupil, boring into the gloom, interprets
the secret book of the nocturnal still.

trans. Samuel Beckett

Like Sister and Brother

Like sister and brother
we go holding hands...

In the stillness of the meadow there is
white and radiant moonlight,
and the nocturnal scenery is so cheerful

que con ser realidad parece sueño.
De pronto, en un recodo del camino,
oímos cantar... Parece el trino
de un ave nunca oída,
un canto de otro mundo y de otra vida...
"¿Oyes?" —me dices—. Y a mi rostro juntas
tus pupilas preñadas de preguntas.
La dulce calma de la noche es tanta
que se escuchan latir los corazones.
Yo te digo: "No temas, hay canciones
que no sabremos nunca quién las canta..."

Como hermana y hermano
vamos los dos cogidos de la mano...

Besado por el soplo de la brisa,
el estanque cercano se divisa...
Bañándose en las ondas hay un astro;
un cisne alarga el cuello lentamente
como blanca serpiente
que saliera de un huevo de alabastro.
Mientras miras el agua silenciosa,
como un vuelo fugaz de mariposa
sientes sobre la nuca el cosquilleo,
la pasajera onda de un deseo,
el espasmo sutil, el calosfrío
de un beso ardiente cual si fuera mío...
Alzas a mí tu rostro amedrentado
y trémula murmuras: "¿Me has besado?"
Tu breve mano oprime
mi mano: y yo a tu oído: "¿Sabes? Esos
besos nunca sabrás quién los imprime...
Acaso, ni siquiera si son besos."

Como hermana y hermano
vamos los dos cogidos de la mano...

En un desfalleciente desvarío
tu rostro apoyas en el pecho mío,
y sientes resbalar sobre tu frente
una lágrima ardiente...
Me clavas tus pupilas soñadoras
y tiernamente me preguntas: "¿Lloras?"
"Secos están mis ojos... Hasta el fondo
puedes mirar en ellos... Pero advierte
que hay lágrimas nocturnas —te respondo—
que no sabemos nunca quién las vierte..."

Como hermana y hermano
vamos los dos cogidos de la mano...

1911

that while real, it seems a dream.
Suddenly, in a bend of the road,
we hear singing... It appears to be the trill
of a bird never before heard,
a song from another world and another life...
"Do you hear?"—you say—and you draw your
questioning eyes near my face.
The sweet calm of the night is such
that the beating of our hearts is heard.
I say to you: "Don't be afraid, there are songs
that we'll never know who sings them..."

Like sister and brother
we go holding hands...

The nearby pond is discerned,
kissed by the breeze...
Bathing in the waves there is a star;
A swan slowly stretches its neck
like a white serpent
leaving an alabaster egg...
While you look at the silent water,
you feel a tickling at the nape of your neck,
like a butterfly's fleeting flight,
the passing wave of a desire,
the subtle spasm, the chill
of a burning kiss, as if it were mine...
You raise your frightened face to mine,
and trembling you murmur: "Did you kiss me?"
Your small hand squeezes
my hand: and I, in your ear: "Did you know?
You'll never know who gave those kisses...
You won't even know if they are kisses..."

Like sister and brother
we go holding hands...

On a faint whim,
you lean your face against my chest,
and you feel a burning tear
trickle down your forehead...
You fix your dreamy eyes on me
and tenderly you ask: "Are you crying?"
"My eyes are dry... You can look
clear to the bottom of them... But be warned
that there are nocturnal tears—I respond—
that we'll never know who spills them."

Like sister and brother
we go holding hands...

trans. Nancy Christoph

El néctar de Ápam

La pulquería policromada
con sus óleos murales de arte ingenuo
y sus festones de papel de china,
es como una banderilla de fuego
clavada en el morrillo
del pueblo,
que enardece el domingo
su semana de tedio
y venga en el sonámbulo gendarme de la esquina
casi cuatro centurias de dolor y silencio...

1925

The Nectar of Ápam

Polychromatic beauty—
with your oil-painted murals of primitive art,
your garlands of crepe-paper—:
you are like a fiery banderilla,
a taunt from the throat
of the people,
igniting a Sunday,
your week of tedium,
to avenge, through the sleepwalking policeman in
    the corner,
nearly four centuries of sorrow and silence...

trans. Elizabeth Gordon

La ventana

Ventana mía, ventana
abierta al oriente de par en par,
ventana que al subir la marea
queda a ras del mar...

Tu reja en cruz deja pasar mis sueños
a la hora del milagro lunar
y los miro bañarse desnudos
en la insondable claridad...

Ventana desde donde contemplo
noche a noche un barco que se va,
nave sin rumbo ni destino
sin bandera y sin capitán...

Ventana mía, ventana
abierta al mundo de par en par,
tu barra en cruz deja pasar mi mano
que al viento fía su señal...

1925

The Window

My window, window
open wide, toward the east,
window that descends with the tide
down to the level of the sea...

Your cross-shaped grills pass
through my dreams, through the miracle the moon
and I behold the naked bathers
through an incomprehensible clarity...

Window through which I watch,
night after night, a ship that goes
sailing, with neither direction
nor destiny, no flag, no captain...

My window, window
open wide, toward the world,
your cross-shaped bars pass through my hands,
yielding their signs to the wind.

trans. Elizabeth Gordon

Dolor

Mi abismo se llenó de su mirada,
y se fundió en mi ser, y fue tan mía,
que dudo si este aliento de agonía
es vida aún o muerte alucinada.

Llegó el Arcángel, descargó la espada
sobre el doble laurel que florecía
en el sellado huerto... Y aquel día
volvió la sombra y regresé a mi nada.

Pain

Its gaze filled my abyss, its gaze melted
into my being, became so mine that I
am doubtful if this breath of agony
is life still or hallucinated death.

The archangel came, cast his sword
upon the double laurel flourishing
in the sealed garden... And that day brought back
the shadow and I returned to my nothingness.

Creí que el mundo, ante el humano asombro,
iba a caer envuelto el en escombro
de la ruina total del firmamento...

¡Mas vi la tierra en paz, en paz la altura,
sereno el campo, la corriente pura,
el monte azul y sosegado el viento!

1935

I thought the world, witnessing man's appal,
would crumble, overwhelmed beneath the ruins
of the entire firmament crashing down.

But I saw the earth at peace, at peace the heavens,
the fields serene, limpid the running stream,
blue the mountain and the wind at rest.

trans. Samuel Beckett

Último viaje

Camino del silencio
se ha ido. Va delante
de mí. Lleva su antorcha
a salvo ya de la traición del aire.

Va musitando el verso que no pudo
decir la última tarde.
Se perdió su sonrisa, y en sus ojos
tiembla el hondo pavor del que *ya sabe*.

Lo llamo, lo persigo. Ya no vuelve
el rostro a mí para decirme: "Padre,
ésta es mi juventud, yo te la entrego;
éste es mi corazón, y ésta es mi sangre."

Cuando mis pasos, que la ausencia anima
y le siguen en pos, le den alcance,
juntos los dos ante el cristal que funde
liberadas del tiempo las imágenes,
veré su faz y miraré su frente
en el hombro paterno desmayarse.

Allí sabremos ambos quién ordena
partir un día, y la razón del viaje.

1942

Last Journey

He has gone
the silent road. He goes
before me. He carries his torch
clear already of the traitorous air.

He goes murmuring the verse he could not say
the last evening.
His smile died and in his eyes
the deep dread trembled of what now he knows.

I call him, follow him. He turns no more
his face to me to say, "father,
here is my youth, I give it up to you,
here is my heart, here is my blood."

When my pursuing steps, by absence quickened,
come up with him,
and we are joined before the burning glass
of time-delivered images,
I shall see his face and see his brow
sink on my breast.

There he and I shall know who sets a day
for the departing, and the journey's why.

trans. Samuel Beckett

José María Eguren

PERU
1874–1942

Within the debate about the nature of the Modernist experiment, especially in Peruvian literature, José María Eguren's work represents a position systematically opposed to that of José Santos Chocano. Antideclamatory and anti-Realist from his first publication, *Simbólicas* (*Symbols*, 1911), Eguren wrote poems that flickered with lambent suggestiveness. Articulated in brilliant colors, in a haunting music, figures appear as if in a dream or nightmare, among animals, plants, stars, and objects that seem to exist autonomously, static and mysterious. In Lima, where he was renowned as the premier Symbolist poet of Peru, Eguren sponsored the young Vallejo early in his career. By temperament and conviction Eguren was a poet of sensation in early Vanguardist experimental tones; he was what Rubén Darío called a "raro." Against the Native Americanist commitment of Chocano and his followers, José María Eguren offers an elegant and Europeanized alternative.

Las torres	*The Towers*
Brunas lejanías...	Dark brown, distant...
batallan las torres	the towers battle
presentando	presenting
siluetas enormes.	enormous silhouettes.
Áureas lejanías...	Golden, distant...
las torres monarcas	the royal towers
se confunden	are confused
en sus iras llamas.	in their angry flames.
Rojas lejanías...	Red, distant...
se hierren las torres;	the towers bristle
purpurados	purple;
se oyen sus clamores.	one hears their cries.
Negras lejanías...	Black, distant...
horas cenicientas	grey hours
se oscurecen,	are darkened.
¡ay!, las torres muertas.	Alas!, the dead towers.
1911	*trans. Iver Lofving*

Los muertos	*The Dead*
Los nevados muertos,	The snow-covered dead
bajo triste cielo,	under a sad sky
van por la avenida	pass along the avenue of pain
doliente que nunca termina.	that never ends.
Van con mustias formas	They go with the wandering forms
entre las auras silenciosas:	among the silent auras
y de la muerte dan el frío	and from dead they give the cold
a sauces y lirios.	to the willows and the irises.
Lentos brillan blancos	Slowly they shine white
por el camino desolado;	on the desolate road;
y añoran las fiestas del día	and they long for the daytime parties
y los amores de la vida.	and the loves of their lives.
Al caminar los muertos una	When walking, the dead
esperanza buscan;	search for hope;
y miran sólo la guadaña,	they look only at the scythe,
la triste sombra ensimismada.	their sad shapes absorbed in thought.

En yerma noche de las brumas
y en el penar y la pavura,
van los lejanos caminantes
por la avenida interminable.

1911

In the desolate night of the mists,
and in the prison, in the terror,
the distant walkers pass along
on the unending road.

trans. Iver Lofving

Las niñas de luz

Las niñas de luz
que al sol rodean,
centellean
y sonríen;
como cambiante pedrería,
van por la nube harmonía.
Las niñas del sol,
de albinos cabellos
y purpúrea tez
nadan en ígneos destellos.
Desde un arrebol
su vuelo aseguran,
aterrizar procuran;
y, cual coloridas notas,
mueren en las nublas remotas.
Las niñas de luz
que al sol rodean,
centellean
y sonríen.

1911

The Girls of the Light

The girls of the light
who revolve around the sun
sparkle
and laugh
like changeable stones,
they travel on the harmonious cloud.
The girls of the light;
with albino tresses
and flushed faces,
they swim in the sparkling granite.
From a red cloud
their flight secures
a landing
where colorful notes
die in the remote storm-clouds.
The girls of the light
who revolve around the sun
sparkle
and smile.

trans. Iver Lofving

Peregrín, cazador de figuras

En el mirador de la fantasía,
al brillar del perfume
tembloroso de armonía;
en la noche que llamas consume;
cuando duerme el ánade implume,
los oríficos insectos se abruman
y luciérnagas fuman;
cuando lucen los silfos galones, entorcho,
y vuelan mariposas de corcho
o los rubios vampiros cecean,
o las firmes jorobas campean,
por la noche de los matices,
de ojos muertos y largas narices;
en el mirador distante,
por las llanuras;
Peregrín cazador de figuras,
con ojos de diamante
mira desde las ciegas alturas.

1916

Peregrin, Wandering Hunter of Faces

In the watchtower of fantasy,
in the twinkle of perfume
trembling with harmony:
in the night that flames consume,
when the featherless duck sleeps,
the golden insects annoy,
and fireflies smoulder;
when the striped fairies light up,
when cork butterflies fly
and blonde vampires lisp
or the solid lamp stands out,
in the night of the mothers
with dead eyes and prominent noses;
in the distant watchtower,
by the plains:
the wandering huntsman of faces
watches with diamond eyes
from the sightless heights.

trans. Iver Lofving

Leopoldo Lugones

ARGENTINA
1874–1938

With his erudition, his smooth irony, his fresh images, his "arrogant gallantry" and free-verse liberties, Leopoldo Lugones brought a spirit of Modernist French insouciance into Argentine letters. Widely read in the Parnassian poets and in Hugo, Poe, Laforgue, and Verlaine, Lugones was also a close friend of Rubén Darío. In his early work, *Los crepúsculos del jardín* (*Twilight of the Garden*, 1905), Lugones emerged as an influential Vanguardist and a passionate advocate of free poetic expression. Subsequently, in *Lunario sentimental* (*Sentimental Calendar*, 1909), he seemed to mock some of the excesses of Romantic and Modernist emotion. With stunning mastery of rhythm and rhyme, he later reinvented some traditional forms, often in colloquial diction, to accommodate an increasingly nationalistic pride, especially in *Odas seculares* (*Secular Odes*, 1910) and *Romancero* (*Balladeer*, 1924). As his literary commitments evolved—from Romantic emotion to irony, from free verse to a refurbished formalism—his political commitments evolved as well, from cosmopolitan socialism to a passionate nationalism, even to an advocacy of militaristic authoritarianism.

For much of his life, Lugones served as director of national education in Argentina. Although his early poems can occasionally smack of preciousness, both his technical virtuosity and his cosmopolitan sense of aesthetic models made him a strong influence in Argentine letters, especially on the young Borges. (Borges dedicated his 1960 book *El hacedor* [*Dreamtigers*] to Lugones, as a gesture of "exorcism.")

Delectación morosa

La tarde, con ligera pincelada
que iluminó la paz de nuestro asilo,
apuntó en su matiz crisoberilo
una sutil decoración morada.

Surgió enorme la luna en la enradmada;
los hojas agravaban su sigilo,
y una araña, en la punta de su hilo,
tejía sobre el astro, hipnotizada.

Poblóse de murciélagos el combo
cielo, a manera de chinesco biombo;
tus rodillas exangües sobre el plinto

manifestaban la delicia inerte,
y a nuestros pies un río de jacinto
corría sin rumor hacia la muerte.

1909

Indulgence

The afternoon, with light strokes
that lit the peace of our asylum,
sketched in chrysoberylic shades
a subtle violet decoration.

The moon surged enormous in the thicket;
the leaves increased their secret;
and a spider, on the point of its thread,
was weaving hypnotized above the spheric moon.

Bats filled the crooked arc
of sky, as on a Chinese screen;
your bloodless knees against the plinth

revealed our motionless delight,
at our feet a sapphire river
ran in silence toward its death.

trans. Julie Schumacher

La blanca soledad

Bajo la calma del sueño,
calma lunar de luminosa seda,

White Solitude

In calm of sleep,
lunar calm of luminous silk,

la noche
como si fuera
el blando cuerpo del silencio,
dulcemente en la inmensidad se acuesta...
Y desata
su cabellera,
en prodigioso follaje
de alamedas.

Nada vive sino el ojo
del reloj en la torre tétrica,
profundizando inútilmente el infinito
como un agujero abierto en la arena.
El infinito,
rodado por las ruedas
de los relojes,
como un carro que nunca llega.

La luna cava un blanco abismo
de quietud, en cuya cuenca
las cosas son cadáveres
y las sombras viven como ideas,
y uno se pasma de lo próxima
que está la muerte en la blancura aquella,
de lo bello que es el mundo
poseído por la antigüedad de la luna llena.
Y el ansia tristísima de ser amado,
en el corazón doloroso tiembla.

Hay una ciudad en el aire,
una ciudad casi invisible suspensa,
cuyos vagos perfiles
sobre la clara noche transparentan.
Como las rayas de agua en un pliego,
su cristalización poliédrica.
Una ciudad tan lejana,
que angustia con su absurda presencia.

¿Es una ciudad o un buque
en el que fuésemos abandonando la tierra,
callados y felices,
y con tal pureza,
que sólo nuestras almas
en la blancura plenilunar vivieran?...

Y de pronto cruza un vago
estremecimiento por la luz serena.
Las líneas se desvanecen,
la inmensidad cámbiase en blanca piedra,
y sólo permanece en la noche aciaga
la certidumbre de tu ausencia.

1909

the night, as if it were
the white body of silence,
lies sweet in that great space.
And loosens
its hair,
the lavish foliage
of poplars.

Nothing is alive except the eye
of a clock in a dark tower,
uselessly fathoming infinity
like a needle in the sand.
Infinity,
revolving on the wheels
of clocks
like a car that will never come near.

The moon carves a white abyss
of silence, socket in which
objects are corpses
and shadows alive like ideas.
And one is frightened at how near
death is, within that whiteness,
at how beautiful the world is
in the age of that full moon.
And the sad desire to be loved
trembles in the aching heart.

There's a city in the sky,
suspended and nearly invisible,
whose restless profile
in the clear night shines transparent,
like rays of water on a sheet of paper,
in crystal polyhedral shapes.
A city so distant
its absurd presence is disconcerting.

Is it a city or a ship
we'd leave the earth in,
silent and happy,
so pure
that only our souls
would survive the full whiteness?

Suddenly an errant
tremor cuts the calm light.
The lines are undone,
the great space turns to white stone,
and in the melancholy night
all that remains is the fact of your absence.

trans. Julie Schumacher

Salmo pluvial

Tormenta
Érase una caverna de agua sombría el cielo;
el trueno, a la distancia, rodaba su peñón;
y una remota brisa de conturbado vuelo,
se acidulaba en tenue frescura de limón.

Como caliente polen exhaló el campo seco
un relente de trébol lo que empezó a llover.
Bajo la lenta sombra, colgada en denso fleco,
se vió al cardal con vívidos azules florecer.

Una fulmínea verga rompió el aire al soslayo;
sobre la tierra atónita cruzó un pavor mortal;
y el firmamento entero se derrumbó en un rayo,
como un inmenso techo de hierro y de cristal.

Lluvia
Y un mimbreral vibrante fue el chubasco revuelto
que plantaba sus líquidas varillas al trasluz,
o en pajonales de agua se espesaba revuelto
descerrajando al paso su pródigo arcabuz.

Saltó la alegre lluvia por taludes y cauces;
descolgó del tejado sonoro caracol;
y luego, allá a lo lejos, se desnudó en los sauces,
transparente y dorada bajo un rayo de sol.

Calma
Delicia de los árboles que abrevó el aguacero.
Delicia de los gárrulos raudales en desliz.
Cristalina delicia del trino del jilguero.
Delicia serenísima de la tarde feliz.

Plenitud
El cerro azul estaba fragante de romero,
y en los profundos campos silbaba la perdiz.

1917

Rain Psalm

Tempest
The sky was a somber cave of water;
thunder, in the distance, rolled down a hill;
and a distant breeze in crooked flight
smelled of acid, a subtle lemon chill.

Like warm pollen the dry land exhaled
a clover dew; it began to shower.
Beneath the slow shadow, hung in thick fringe,
thistle fields, in vivid blue, flowered clearly.

Sudden branches tore the air;
the startled earth succumbed to fear,
and the firmament collapsed in thunder
like a great ceiling of crystal and steel.

Rain
And the squall was a vibrant willow
that set its liquid twigs upright in filtered sun,
or, condensing, fell in tangled clots of straw,
suddenly unlocking in rapid downpour, like a gun.

The happy rain jumped screes and riverbeds;
down tile rooves, like snails, it slid away,
and then, undressing in the distant trees,
it glowed transparent, lightly gold in the sun's thin rays.

Calm
Pleasure of the trees that the rain has fed cattle.
Pleasure of the garrulous rapids slipping by.
Crystalline pleasure of the trilling of the linnet.
Pleasure, tranquil pleasure, in the afternoon gone by.

Fullness
The blue hill smelled of rosemary,
and in the deep valley fields a partridge whistled.

trans. Julie Schumacher

Olas grises

Llueve en el mar con un murmullo lento.
La brisa gime tanto, que da pena.
El día es largo y triste. El elemento
duerme el sueño pesado de la arena.

Llueve. La lluvia lánguida trasciende
su olor de flor helada y desabrida.
El día es largo y triste. Uno comprende
que la muerte es así..., que así es la vida.

Gray Waves

It rains above the sea in gentle murmurs.
The wind is moaning so, one feels its grief.
The day is long and sad. The rain
sleeps deeply on the sand.

It rains. The languid drops transcend
their smell of cold, bleak flowers.
The day is long and sad. One understands
that death is like that..., life is like that.

Sigue lloviendo. El día es triste y largo.
En el remoto gris se abisma el ser.
Llueve... Y uno quisiera, sin embargo,
que no acabara nunca de llover.

1917

The rain continues. The day is long and sad.
Within the grayish distance one is lost.
It rains... And nevertheless one wishes
the rain would never stop.

trans. Julie Schumacher

José Santos Chocano

PERU
1875–1934

The "poetic trumpet" of the South American continent, José Santos Chocano celebrates himself, his place, and his race with a daring that recalls Whitman's. Writing as if in opposition to the fascination with French culture and French models (as in works by Darío, Lugones, and others), Chocano blares his prophetic advocacy of local cultural forms. At the same time, he maintains that some Continental models can be useful; he argues for a cultural realignment with Spain, and he reminds Peruvian readers of the glories and heroism of the conquistadores. Conversely, Chocano wrote many of his vigorous declamatory poems, including those in the Whitman-like *Alma América* (*American Spirit*, 1906), while in prison for political activity considered seditious by the Manuel Estrada Cabrera government of Guatemala. Chocano alternately befriended and opposed strong leaders at extremes of the political spectrum. After killing another poet, Chocano spent time in prison, was pardoned, and went into exile in Chile. Eventually his idealistic, sometimes bombastic tone was to influence Darío and others toward an aesthetic of overt political anti-imperialism. Chocano's series *Tres notas de nuestra alma indígena* (*Three Notes of Our Indigenous Spirit*, 1941 posthum.), in which the poem "¡Quién sabe!" ("Who Knows?") appeared, was a touchstone in the *indianismo* movement. The poem was admired at first for its sympathy and light irony, but later was criticized for its apparent idealization of Indian passivity and victimization.

In form, Chocano's poems belong to a Modernist tradition. He imitates Lugones, for instance, in welcoming the liberties that free verse makes possible, but he is suspicious of the licence the form seems to invite. The result is at times a peculiarly moving hybrid, as befits a mestizo who trumpets both his noble Spanish lineage and his Indian heritage. Chocano's radical sonnets aggressively celebrate the spirit of Andean place, including its animals and plants, with a compassionate descriptive splendor. Significantly, they do so in a form derived directly from classical Spanish models.

Blasón

    Soy el cantor de América autóctono y salvaje;
mi lira tiene un alma, mi canto un ideal.
Mi verso no se mece colgado de un ramaje
con un vaivén pausado de hamaca tropical...

    Cuando me siento Inca, le rindo vasallaje
al Sol, que me da el cetro de su poder real;
cuando me siento hispano y evoco el Coloniaje,
parecen mis estrofas trompetas de cristal...

A Manifesto

    I sing America, in its wild and autochthonous state;
my lyre has a soul, and my song has an ideal.
My poem does not hang from a branch,
calmly swinging like a tropical hammock...

    When I feel Incan, I honor that king,
the Sun, who offers me the scepter of his royal power;
when I feel Spanish, I invoke the Empires;
my strophes seem like crystal trumpets...

Mi fantasía viene de un abolengo moro:
los Andes son de plata, pero el León de oro;
y las dos castas fundo con épico fragor.

La sangre es española e incaico es el latido;
¡y de no ser Poeta, quizás yo hubiese sido
un blanco Aventurero o un indio Emperador!

1906

My imagination comes from ancient Moorish blood:
the Andes are of silver, but León is of gold;
I fuse both races with a noise like a thunder.

My blood is Spanish and Incan in its throb;
if I were not a poet, I might have had the job
of a white Adventurer, or Incan emperor!

trans. Andrew Rosing

Los volcanes

Cada volcán levanta su figura,
cual si de pronto, ante la faz del cielo,
suspendiesen el ángulo de un velo
dos dedos invisibles de la altura.

La cresta es blanca y como blanca pura:
la entraña hierve en inflamado anhelo;
y sobre el horno aquel constrasta el hielo,
cual sobre una pasión un alma dura.

Los volcanes son túmulos de piedra,
pero a sus pies los valles que florecen
fingen alfombras de irisada yedra;

y por eso, entre campos de colores,
al destacarse en el azul, parecen
cestas volcadas derramando flores...

1906

The Volcanoes

Each volcano lifts its profile
as if abruptly from the face of the sky
invisible fingers from on high
lifted the corner of a hanging veil.

White, pure white, the crest of the mountain,
while its breast seethes with enflamed desires;
the head's ice strains against the body's fire,
like a pure soul rising past a passion.

Volcanoes are rubbly mounds of rock,
but at their feet the valleys, green
and rainbow-scattered as an Asian rug;

there, among those fields of color,
outlined against the blue, they seem
like tumbled baskets, spilling flowers...

trans. Andrew Rosing

El sueño del caimán

Enorme tronco que arrastró la ola,
yace el caimán varado en la ribera:
espinazo de abrupta cordillera,
fauces de abismo y formidable cola.

El Sol lo envuelve en fúlgida aureola;
y parece lucir cota y cimera,
cual monstruo de metal que reverbera
y que al reverberar se tornasola.

Inmóvil como un ídolo sagrado,
ceñido en mallas de compacto acero,
está ante el agua extático y sombrío,

a manera de un príncipe encantado
que vive eternamente prisionero
en el palacio de cristal de un río...

1906

The Dream of the Caiman

Enormous tree-trunk crawling on the waves,
the alligator wallows up the river's wall:
spine like a sudden mountain-range,
jaws an abyss, and formidable tail.

The sunlight wraps him in an aureole
like shining armor and a plumed cuirass:
glaring in the light, a monster of metal
that echoes the sun's iridescence.

Motionless as a sacred idol,
adrift in the water, ecstatic
and sleepy, wrapped in strong steel mail,

like a prince who lives in an enchantment,
held a prisoner forever
in the crystal palace of a river...

trans. Andrew Rosing

El sueño del cóndor

Al despuntar el estrellado coro,
pósase en una cúspide nevada:
lo envuelve el día en la postrer mirada;
y revienta a sus pies trueno sonoro.

Su blanca gola es imperial decoro;
su ceño varonil, pomo de espada;
sus garfios siempre en actitud airada,
curvos puñales de marfil con oro.

Solitario en la cúspide se siente:
en las pálidas nieblas se confunde;
desvanece el fulgor de su aureola;

y esfumándose, entonces, lentamente,
se hunde en la noche, como el alma se hunde
en la meditación cuando está sola...

1906

The Dream of the Condor

As the choir of stars begins,
he perches on a snowy peak;
the last of daylight envelops him;
at his feet the thunder breaks.

His white throat, like a king's medallion,
beak ferocious as a war-sword's hilt;
eternally sharp for wrath, his talons
curve like daggers of ivory and gold.

Solitary there, he settles on the heights
blending with pallid fogs; his aureole
dwindles, its splendid light

gone shadowy, and slowly he goes
does into the dark, as the soul goes
down in meditation when alone...

trans. Andrew Rosing

Indignación

Levantase a los cielos en raudo torbellino
del polvo de la tierra confuso nubarrón,
y cubre con sus alas el disco diamantino
        del refulgente sol.

Y dícele con burla: —¡Prosigue tu carrera!
Tus rayos de topacio nublados por mí son:
tu orgullo he confundido, monarca de la esfera,
        tu luz amenguo yo.—

1937

Indignation

Blurred in a whirlwind, a mighty cloud of dust
rises obscurely from earth to the heavens.
With its wings it covers the brilliant disc
        of the dazzling sun

and sneers: "On your way. Get out of here.
I dimmed your beams, which were topaz-bright.
I brought down your loftiness, king of the spheres.
        I blotted out your light."

trans. Andrew Rosing

¡Quién sabe!

Indio que asomas a la puerta
de esa tu rústica mansión:
¿para mí no tienes agua?
¿para mi frío, cobertor?
¿parco maíz para mi hambre?
¿para mi sueño, mal rincón?
¿breve quietud para mi andanza?...
        —¡Quién sabe, señor!

Indio que labras con fatiga
tierras que de otros dueños son:
¿ignoras tú que deben tuyas
ser, por tu sangre y tu sudor?

Who Knows?

Oh Indian watching from the doorway
of your rustic home,
for my thirst, have you no water?
for my cold, no clothes?
no corn for my hunger?
no corner, to dream in?
no momentary calm for my fears?
        —"Ah, Milord: who knows?"

Oh Indian, who labors hard
in fields that someone else owns,
don't you understand, by right
of blood and sweat they should be yours?

¿ignoras tú que audaz codicia
siglos atrás, te las quitó?
¿ignoras tú que eres el Amo?
      —¡Quién sabe, señor!

    Indio de frente taciturna
y de pupilas sin fulgor:
¿que pensamiento es el que escondes
en tu enigmática expresión?
¿qué es lo que buscas en tu vida?
¿qué es lo que imploras a tu Dios?
¿qué es lo que sueña tu silencio?
      —¡Quién sabe, señor!

    ¡Oh Raza antigua y misteriosa,
de impenetrable corazón
que sin gozar ves la alegría
y sin sufrir ves el dolor:
eres augusta como el Ande,
el Grande Océano y el Sol!
Ese tu gesto que parece
como de vil resignación
es de una sabia indiferencia
y de un orgullo sin rencor....
    Corre en mis venas sangre tuya,
y, por tal sangre, si mi Dios
me interrogase qué prefiero
—cruz o laurel, espina o flor,
beso que apague mis suspiros
o hiel que colme mi canción—
responderíale dudando:
      —¡Quién sabe, señor!

don't you understand that brazen greed
stole them from you, long ago?
don't you know you are the Master?
      —"Ah, Milord: who knows?"

    Oh Indian, with your taciturn brow
and your eyes with no gleam in them,
what thought is there, hidden
in your secretive expression?
what is it you look for in life?
what is it you pray for, to your God?
what is it your silence dreams?
      —"Ah, Milord: who knows?"

    Oh ancient mysterious race
with your impenetrable heart,
who looks on joy without pleasure
and looks on suffering without grief;
sublime as an Andes mountain,
as the broad ocean, the sun!
This bearing of yours, which seems
a petty resignation,
is actually a wise indifference
and a pride, without rancor....
    Yours is the blood in my veins,
and—by that blood—I swear, if my God
should ask me which I prefer—
the cross or the laurel, thorns or flowers,
the kiss that would quiet my sighs
or a gall that would fill up my song—
trusting my doubt, I would answer:
      —"Ah, My Lord: who knows?"

        1941   *trans. Andrew Rosing*

Julio Herrera y Reissig

URUGUAY
1875–1910

The history of Julio Herrera y Reissig's work presents several paradoxes. Although he took intense somatic sensation as the starting point of many of his poems, he committed his style to the translation of experience into hermetic tropes. Although he was a strong influence on subsequent generations of Latin Americans, intellectually Herrera y Reissig orientated himself toward Europe. Like the French Symbolist poets whom he revered, Herrera y Reissig directed special attention toward nocturnal states of mind: dreams, the eruption of the irrational, the imagistic suggestiveness of the subconscious. Although he often drew on Uruguayan village life for the locating metaphors of his poems, during much of his Modernist period he lived and worked in the attic of his father's house in Montevideo. (Members of his Bohemian coterie jokingly called their group the "Tower of Parnassians" or "Tower of Panoramas," after that attic meetingplace and literary salon.)

Although by the end of his life (in poems written after 1905) Herrera y Reissig had worked beyond the tenets of his early commitment to Modernism and was writing surreal poems that adumbrated Ultraism and Creationism, he is revered as one of the most important Modernist poets of Latin America. Moreover, the example of his exquisite lyricism would make him one of the most influential poets of Latin America, even though most of Herrera y Reissig's poems were published posthumously.

Julio

Frío, frío, frío!
Pieles, nostalgias y dolores mudos.

Flota sobre el esplín de la campaña
una jaqueca sudorosa y fría,
y las ranas celebran en la umbría
una función de ventriloquia extraña.

La Neurastenia gris de la montaña
piensa, por singular telepatía,
con la adusta y claustral monomanía
del convento senil de la Bretaña.

Resolviendo una suma de ilusiones,
como un Jordán de cándidos vellones
la majada eucarística se integra;

y a lo lejos el cuervo pensativo
sueña acaso en un Cosmos abstractivo
como una luna pavorosa y negra.

1902

July

Cold, cold, cold!
Furs, memories, and mute sadnesses.

Above the spleen of the landscape,
calm, and damp, floats a migraine;
and there in the shadows the frogs celebrate,
with a strange ventriloquism.

The mountain's mind—its grey neurasthenia—
with a peculiar telepathy
recalls in its close and gloomy mania
a senile convent in Brittany.

To add up the sum of these illusions,
the eucharistic flock is fused
like a Jordan of fleeces, white as snow;

and far away the pensive crow
is dreaming, maybe, of an abstract Cosmos
like a black and terrifying moon.

trans. Andrew Rosing

La sombra dolorosa

Gemían los rebaños. Los caminos
llenábanse de lúgubres cortejos;
una congoja de holocaustos viejos
ahogaba los silencios campesinos.

Bajo el misterio de los velos finos,
evocabas los símbolos perplejos,
hierática, perdiéndote a lo lejos
con tus húmedos ojos mortecinos.

Mientras unidos por un mal hermano,
me hablaban con suprema confidencia
los mudos apretones de tu mano,

manchó la soñadora transparencia
de la tarde infinita el tren lejano,
aullando de dolor hacia la ausencia.

1909

The Sorrowful Shadow

The flocks went bleating; the roads
were crowded with sorrowful crowds;
an agony of ancient holocausts
smothered-over the silent countryside.

Under mysterious elegant veils
you call forth perplexing symbols,
O Priestess, lost and claimed into the distance
with your moist and deathly gaze.

Even your evil brother joined us, but
meanwhile your hand—with an utmost confidence—
squeezed mine, speaking to me with silent touches,

and the distant rain, wailing that sorrow
that moves toward absence, stained
the lucid dreaminess of the infinite evening.

trans. Andrew Rosing

El regreso

La tierra ofrece el ósculo de un saludo paterno...
Pasta un mulo la hierba mísera del camino
y la montaña luce, al tardo sol del invierno,
como una vieja aldeana, su delantal de lino.

Un cielo bondadoso y un céfiro tierno...
La zagala descansa de codos bajo el pino,
y densos los ganados, con paso paulatino,
acuden a la música sacerdotal del cuerno.

Trayendo sobre el hombro leña para la cena,
el pastor, cuya ausencia no dura más de un día,
camina lentamente rumbo de la alquería.

Al verlo la familia le da la enhorabuena...
Mientras el perro, en ímpetus de lealtad amena,
describe coleando círculos de alegría.

1909

The Return

Earth offers its greeting, with a paternal kiss...
A mule grazes in the meager vegetation,
and in the late winter sun the mountain displays
her snowy apron, like a village matron.

A kindly sky, a gentle zephyr...
A shepherd-girl rests under a pine in the hollow
and in thick rows, with gradual steps, the cattle
come, obeying the priestly music of her horn.

Carrying wood to cook the evening meal,
the shepherd, who has been absent from his home
only all day, walks slowly toward the farm.

His family hurries to see him, and welcome...
even the dog, who wags his lively tail,
inscribing fast circles of joy in the air.

trans. Andrew Rosing

Alba gris

Gris en el cielo y en el alma gris;
rojo en Oriente y en el alma rojo

Todo fue así. Preocupaciones lilas
turbaban la ilusión de la mañana,
y una garza pueril su absurda plana
paloteaba en las ondas intranquilas...

Un estremecimiento de Sibilas
epilepsiaba a ratos la ventana,
cuando de pronto un mito tarambana
rodó en la oscuridad de mis pupilas.

"Adiós, adiós", grité, y hasta los cielos
el gris sarcasmo de su fino guante
ascendió con el rojo de mis celos.

Wagneriaba en el aire una corneja,
y la selva sintió en aquel instante
una infinita colisión compleja.

1909

Grey Dawn

Grey in the sky and grey in my soul;
red in the East and red in my soul.

This is how it was. Lilac preoccupations
disturbed the morning's illusions,
and a childish heron on his inane blank page
stroked backwards on the restless waves.

And a shuddering—like a Sibyl's fit—
rattled at the windows, when all
at once a wind-minded myth
intruded, through my darkened pupils.

"Good-by, good-by," I cried: into the sky
grey sarcasm rose, from her delicate glove,
flying like my own red jealousy.

A crow croaked Wagnerisms into the air, and the woods
felt at the very moment a complete
and cataclysmic crash.

trans. Andrew Rosing

Decoración heráldica

Señora de mis pobres homenajes,
Débote siempre amar aunque me ultrajes.
— GÓNGORA

Heraldic Decoration

O Lady, the object of my abject homage,
I will always love you, though you abuse me.
— GÓNGORA

Soñé que te encontrabas junto al muro glacial donde termina la existencia, paseando tu magnífica opulencia de doloroso terciopelo oscuro.	I dreamed I met you beside the wall that is like a glacier, there where existence ends— you were promenading your opulent greatness, its sad dark velvet.
Tu pie, decoro del marfil más puro, hería, con satánica inclemencia, las pobres almas, llenas de paciencia, que aún brindaban a tu amor perjuro.	Your foot, decorous in purest ivory, with satanic mercilessness scorned the poor souls full of patience who offered themselves to your perjured love, nevertheless.
Mi dulce amor que sigue sin sosiego, igual que un triste corderito ciego, la huella perfumada de tu sombra,	My tender love, which tirelessly as a sad little lamb, follows the track of your shadow's fragrant step
buscó el suplicio de tu regio yugo, y bajo el raso de tu pie verdugo puse mi esclavo corazón de alfombra.	searched for the torment of your noble yoke; under your satin executioner's foot, like a carpet I lay my slave-heart.

1926

trans. Andrew Rosing

Delmira Agustini

URUGUAY
1886–1914

The great poet of Uruguay and an early spokesperson in Latin American letters for the autonomous energy of female consciousness, Delmira Agustini combines in her poems traditional Spanish metrical forms with a vitalistic myth of boundless human desire as a vehicle toward spiritual transcendence. In this combination of carnal and religious elements, her work plays against the metaphors of the great mystic writer of the Spanish American tradition, Sor Juana Inés de la Cruz. Thanks in part to Rubén Darío's energetic advocacy, Agustini was celebrated in literary circles from early in her career. Socially, however, her frankly erotic lyrics alienated her from Uruguayan bourgeois society. In 1913, while working on the two collections of poems for which she is best known, *Los cálices vacíos* (*The Empty Chalices*) and *El rosario de Eros* (*Rosary of Eros*), she married Enrique Job Reyes. After less than a month, Agustini left him and returned to her parents' home. In August 1914, in a hotel room in downtown Montevideo, her estranged husband murdered her and then killed himself.

A powerful consistency unites Agustini's poems, influenced (as Alberta Zum Felde has observed) by both Nietzsche and by Herrera y Reissig. The elegance of her voice and the bravery of her example have made Agustini the "lay saint" of Latin America (as Juana de Ibarbourou called her) and the "older sister" of many later women writers.

Las alas	*The Wings*

Yo tenía...
    ¡dos alas!...
	I once had...
	    two wings!

Dos alas
que del Azur vivían como dos siderales
raíces...
Dos alas,
con todos los milagros de la vida, la muerte
y la ilusión. Dos alas,
fulmíneas
como el velamen de una estrella en fuga;
dos alas,
como dos firmamentos
con tormentas, con calmas y con astros...

    ¿Te acuerdas de la gloria de mis alas?...
El áureo campaneo
del ritmo, el inefable
matiz atesorando
el Iris todo, mas un Iris nuevo
ofuscante y divino,
que adorarán las plenas pupilas del Futuro
(¡las pupilas maduras a toda luz!)... el vuelo...

    El vuelo ardiente, devorante y único,
que largo tiempo atormentó los cielos,
despertó soles, bólidos, tormentas,
abrillantó los rayos y los astros;
y la amplitud: tenían
calor y sombra para todo el Mundo,
y hasta incubar un *más allá* pudieron.

    Un día, raramente
desmayada a la tierra,
yo me adormí en las felpas profundas de este bosque...
¡Soñé divinas cosas!
Una sonrisa tuya me despertó, paréceme...
¡Y no siento mis alas!...
¿Mis alas?...

    Yo las vi deshacerse entre mis brazos...
¡Era como un deshielo!

1910

Two wings
that *did* exist, like two sidereal bases
of the Blue.
Two wings
with all the miracles of life itself, of death,
and of illusion. Two wings
flashing
like flying sails of some bright star in flight;
two wings
like two firmaments
with storms, and calms, and stars.

Do you remember the glory of my wings?
The golden harmony
of their rhythm, their ineffable
bright colors saturated with all the treasures
of the rainbow—but a new rainbow,
and dazzling, and divine—
so that the Future's perfect eyes (eyes that can see all
light!) will worship... the flight.

The fiery, ravenous, singular flight,
that for so long twisted the heavens,
woke up suns and meteors and storms,
shedding brilliance and fullness
onto lightning and the stars: with enough heat
and shade for all the World—
enough, even, to hatch the idea
of the "Beyond."

One day, when I lay strangely
exhausted, on the earth,
I fell asleep in the forest's deep carpet...
I dreamed... divine things!
I thought a smile of yours awakened me...
I did not feel my wings!...
My wings?...

I saw them melt away—between my arms—
exactly as if they were thawing!

trans. Elizabeth Gordon

Otra estirpe

Eros, yo quiero guiarte, Padre Ciego...
Pido a tus manos todopoderosas
¡su cuerpo excelso derramado en fuego
sobre mi cuerpo desmayado en rosas!

La eléctrica corola que hoy despliego
brinda el nectario de un jardín de Esposas;
para sus buitres en mi carne entrego
todo un enjambre de palomas rosas.

Another Race

Eros, let me lead you, Blind Father...
And at your almighty hands I ask
for his prodigal body arrayed in fire
covering mine, pale among petals of damask!

Today the electric corolla I unfurl
offers the attar of a garden of Wives;
for his vultures in my flesh, their feel,
I give up a whole cote of pink doves.

Da a las dos sierpes de su abrazo, crueles,
mi gran tallo febril... Absintio, mieles,
viérteme de sus venas, de su boca...

¡Así tendida soy el surco ardiente
donde puede nutrirse la simiente
de otra Estirpe sublimemente loca!

1913

Give my feverish stem to the twinned cruel serpent
of his embrace... Absinthe and honey spent
in me from his utter veins and from his mouth...

I am one ardent furrow stretched
where the seed of another race will flourish
feeding madness and beauty both!

trans. Karl Kirchwey

Visión

¿Acaso fue en un marco de ilusión,
en el profundo espejo del deseo,
o fue divina y simplemente en vida
que yo te vi velar mi sueño la otra noche?
En mi alcoba agrandada de soledad y miedo,
taciturno a mi lado apareciste
como un hongo gigante, muerto y vivo,
brotado en los rincones de la noche,
húmedos de silencio,
y engrasados de sombra y soledad.

Te inclinabas a mí, supremamente,
como a la copa de cristal de un lago
sobre el mantel de fuego del desierto;
te inclinabas a mí, como un enfermo
da la vida a los opios infalibles
y a las vendas de piedra de la Muerte.

Te inclinabas a mí como el creyente
a la oblea de cielo de la hostia...
—Gota de nieve con sabor de estrellas
que alimenta los lirios de la carne,
chispa de Dios que estrella los espíritus—.
Te inclinabas a mí como el gran sauce
de la Melancolía
a las hondas lagunas del silencio;
te inclinabas a mí como la torre
de mármol del Orgullo,
minada por un monstruo de tristeza,
a la hermana solemne de su sombra...
Te inclinabas a mí como si fuera
mi cuerpo la inicial de tu destino
en la página oscura de mi lecho;
te inclinabas a mí como al milagro
de una ventana abierta al más allá.
¡Y te inclinabas más que todo eso!

Y era mi mirada una culebra
apuntada entre zarzas de pestañas,
al cisne reverente de tu cuerpo.

Vision

Was it perhaps in an imagined frame,
in the bottomless mirror of desire,
or was it divinely and simply in real life
that I saw you watch me sleep the other night?
In my alcove enlarged with loneliness and dread,
quietly, you appeared at my side,
like a gigantic mushroom, dead and alive,
budding in the corners of the night,
damp with silence,
glistening with shadow and with loneliness.

You bent supremely over me, as if
toward the crystal chalice of a lake
on the desert's altar-cloth of fire;
you turned to me as one invalided by life
turns to his infallible opiates
and to the stony bandages of Death.

You leaned toward me in the way the believer
does toward the spotless oblation of the Host...
—Morsel of snow with the savor of stars
that feeds the lilies of mortal flesh,
spark of God to apotheosize the spirit—.
You leaned over me as the great willow
of Melancholy
does over the deep lagoons of silence;
you loomed over me as the marble
tower of Pride,
quarried by a monster of sadness,
does over the solemn sister of its own shadow...
You bent over me as if
my body were the majuscule initial of your fate
written on the dark page of my bed;
you leaned out over me as if toward the miracle
of a window open on the furthest beyond.
And even beyond all these you leaned!

And my glance was a snake
fanged between the brambles of eyelashes,
toward the reverent swan of your body.

Y era mi deseo una culebra
glisando entre los riscos de la sombra
a la estatua de lirios de tu cuerpo.
Tú te inclinabas más y más... y tanto,
y tanto te inclinaste,
que mis flores eróticas son dobles,
Toda tu vida se imprimió en mi vida...

Yo esperaba suspensa el aletazo
del abrazo magnífico; un abrazo
de cuatro brazos que la gloria viste
de fiebre y de milagro; ¡será un vuelo!
Y pueden ser los hechizados brazos
cuatro raíces de una raza nueva.

Yo esperaba suspensa el aletazo
del abrazo magnífico...
        Y cuando
te abrí los ojos como un alma, vi
¡que te hacías atrás y te envolvías
en yo no sé qué pliegue inmenso de la sombra!

1913

And my lust was a snake
slipping between cliffs of shadow
toward the lily statue of your body.
Further you leaned, and further... and so far,
so far you leaned,
that my sexual flowers have doubled their size,
Your entire life is printed on mine...

Apprehensively I waited for the wing-beat
of the magnificent embrace; an embrace
of four arms that beatitude dresses
in fever and miracle; it may be flight!
And it may be that those enchanted arms
are four roots of a new race.

Apprehensively I waited for the wing-beat
of the magnificent embrace...
        And when
I opened my eyes to you like a soul, I saw
you edging backwards, wrapping yourself
in I know not what huge fold of darkness!

trans. Karl Kirchwey

Lo inefable

Yo muero extrañamente... No me mata la Vida,
no me mata la Muerte, no me mata el Amor;
muero de un pensamiento mudo como una herida...
¿No habéis sentido nunca el extraño dolor

de un pensamiento inmenso que se arraiga en la vida,
devorando alma y carne y no alcanza a dar flor?
¿Nunca llevasteis dentro una estrella dormida
que os abrasaba enteros y no daba un fulgor?

¡Cumbre de los Martirios!... ¡Llevar eternamente,
desgarradora y árida, la trágica simiente
clavada en las entrañas como un diente feroz!...

Pero arrancarla un día en una flor que abriera
milagrosa, inviolable... ¡Ah, más grande no fuera
tener entre las manos la cabeza de Dios!

1910

The Ineffable

I am dying strangely... it is not Life
that kills me, not Love; it is not even Death;
I am dying of a thought mute as a wound's mouth...
Have you never felt the extraordinary pain, as if

some huge thought had simply settled down in your life,
devouring flesh and spirit, but stunted, so it never blooms?
Have you never endured a star like a white dwarf
inside you that gives no light but entirely consumes?

Height of Martyrdom!... To carry forever,
tearing and barren, driven into your
body like a feral tooth, this tragic seed!...

But you might root it out one day and find a flower
miraculous, inviolate... Ah, it could be no greater
to hold between your two hands the head of God.

trans. Karl Kirchwey

La barca milagrosa

Preparadme una barca como un gran pensamiento...
La llamarán "La Sombra" unos; otros, "La Estrella."
No ha de estar al capricho de una mano o de un viento;
¡yo la quiero consciente indomable y bella!

The Miraculous Ship

Provision a ship for me like a great idea...
Some will call her The Shadow; others, The Star.
She need not lie at the mercy of hand or cat's paw;
I want her conscious, untameable and fair!

La moverá el gran ritmo de un corazón sangriento
de Vida sobrehumana; he de sentirme en ella
fuerte como en los brazos de Dios. En todo viento,
en todo mar templadme su prora de centella.

La cargaré de toda mi tristeza, y, sin rumbo,
iré como la rota corola de un nelumbio,
por sobre el horizonte líquido de la mar...

Barca, alma hermana: ¿hacia qué tierras nunca vistas,
de hondas revelaciones, de cosas imprevistas
iremos?... Yo ya muero de vivir y soñar...

1913

What will drive her is the rhythm of a bloodstained heart
of superhuman Life; in her I will feel strong
as if in the arms of God. Whatever seas and what-
ever quarter the wind her prow will temper with a
    cinder's sparkling.

I will freight her with all of my sadness, and without a fix
will spin like the lotus flower's broken calyx
across the liquid horizon of the sea...

Ship, sister soul: toward what unseen land,
what deep soundings or things unimagined
will we bear?... Already living and dreaming make me die...

trans. Karl Kirchwey

Manuel Bandeira

BRAZIL
1886–1968

In 1942 Dudley Fitts characterized the early poems of Manuel Carneiro Bandeira de Souza Filho by their subtle method, their "Franciscan gentleness of tone," and their clear speaking voice. That description is an accurate account of the younger Bandeira's poems, especially those he wrote during his friendship with Paul Éluard. However, it is difficult to characterize succinctly the rest of Bandeira's long and varied career. In his poems, in his continuous evolution, in his tireless example to younger poets and his influence on Brazilian letters, Bandeira's changes are a metonymy for the evolution of twentieth-century Brazilian poetry.

    Because of childhood tuberculosis Bandeira was educated at home in his native Recife and in Rio de Janeiro. His early poems, from *A cinza de horas* (*Ash of the Hours*, 1917), with their Penumbrist scrupulousness of diction and Parnassian elegance of form, are saturated with a tone of melancholy that Bandeira later effaced but never entirely abandoned. For the famous Week of Modern Art (1922) Bandeira submitted an "ars poetica" poem from his book *Carnaval* (*Carnival*, 1919). His droll manifesto poems, like "Poética" included here, became touchstones of Brazilian Modernism. (Mário de Andrade would later call Bandeira the "St. John the Baptist of Modernism," because of the power of his example as a precursor to the High Modernist movement in Brazil.) Bandeira's poems after *Libertagem* (*Libertinism*, 1930) helped redefine the landscape of Brazilian writing. Those poems changed the diction and tone of contemporary Brazilian poetry, bringing into it the verve and humor and gentle irony that characterize the idiomatic spoken Portuguese of Brazil. His shift in subject matter toward the mundane, the idiomatic, and the elemental anticipated much subsequent Brazilian work, marking the transition from Modernist to post-Modernist poetics toward Concretism, and beyond.

    Bandeira described these changes in his surprisingly popular memoirs, *Itinerário de Pasárgada* (*The Road to Pasárgada*, 1954). In his capacity as a teacher and man of letters, Bandeira also wrote criticism, edited anthologies of Romantic, Parnassian, and Symbolist poets, and translated Shakespeare, German poets, Dickinson, Eliot, García Lorca, and e. e. cummings. A loyal friend and a generous mentor, Bandeira maintained close relations with many Brazilian poets of several generations. His poem "Retrato" ("Portrait"), for instance, is a tribute to Carlos Drummond de Andrade.

Boda espiritual

Tu não estás comigo em momentos escassos:
No pensamento meu, amor, tu vives nua
—Toda nua, pudica e bela, nos meus braços.

O teu ombro no meu, ávido, se insinua.
Pende a tua cabeça. Eu amacio-a... Afago-a...
Ah, como a minha mão treme... Como ela é tua...

Põe no teu rosto o gozo uma expressão de mágoa.
O teu corpo crispado alucina. De escorço
O vejo estremecer como uma sombra n'água.

Gemes quase a chorar. Suplicas com esforço.
E para amortecer teu ardente desejo
Estendo longamente a mão pelo teu dorso...

Tua boca sem voz implora en um arquejo.
Eu te estreito cada vez mais, e espio absorto
A maravilha astral dessa nudez sem pejo...

E te amo como se ama um passarinho morto.

1917

Spiritual Wedding

You are not with me in fleeting moments
but live, my love, within my mind
—Chaste, beautiful and wholly nude within my arms.

Your shoulder eagerly presses ever closer against mine.
You bow your head. I stroke, caress it.
How my hand trembles... How it has become yours...

Pleasure gives your face an expression of sorrow.
Your tensed body fills me with desire. From this angle
I see it shudder like a shadow on the water.

Your moan is almost a sob. You plead insistently
and to quench your feverish desire
I slowly trail my hand along your back...

Wordless, you implore me in a gasp.
I hold you closer, closer, and spellbound, observe
the starlike marvel of this nudity that knows no shame...

And I love you as one loves a small and lifeless bird.

trans. Candace Slater

Poética

Estou farto do lirismo comedido
Do lirismo bem comportado
Do lirismo functionário público com livro de ponto
        expediente protocolo e manifestações de apreço
    ao sr. diretor.

Estou farto do lirismo que pará e vai averiguar no
        dictionário o cunho vernáculo de um vocábulo

Abaixo os puristas
Todas as palavras sobretudo os barbarismos universais
Todas as construções sobretudo as sintaxes de exceção
Todos os ritmos sobretudo os inumeráveis

Estou farto do lirismo namorador
Político
Raquítico
Sifilítico
De todo lirismo que capitula ao que quer que seja fora de
        si mesmo.

De resto não é lirismo
Será contabilidade tabela de co-senos secretário do amante

Poetics

I'm sick of cautious lyricism
of well-behaved lyricism
of a civil servant lyricism complete with time card
        office hours set procedures and expressions of
    esteem for Mr. Boss, Sir.

I'm sick of the lyricism that has to stop in midstream
        to look up the precise meaning of a word.

Down with purists!
Up with
all words, especially those that everyone gets wrong
all constructions, above all exceptions to the rule
all rhythms, above all those that can't be counted.

I'm sick of philandering lyricism—
political
raquitical
syphilitical
—of all lyricism that gives in to any outside force.

Besides, all this other business isn't lyricism—
It's accounting cosine tables a handbook for the model lover

exemplar com cem modelos de cartas e as diferentes
    maneiras de agradar às mulheres, etc.

Quero antes a lirismo dos loucos
O lirismo dos bêbados
O lirismo difícil e pungente dos bêbados
O lirismo dos clowns de Shakespeare

—Não quero mais saber do lirismo que não é libertação.

1930

Evocação do Recife

Recife
Não a Veneza americana
Não a Mauritsstad dos armadores das Índias Ocidentais

Não o Recife dos Mascates
Nem mesmo o Recife que aprendi a amar depois—
    Recife das revoluções libertárias
Mas o Recife sem história nem literatura
Recife sem mais nada
Recife da minha infância

A Rua da União onde eu brincava de chicote-queimado e
    partia as vidraças da casa de dona Aninha Viegas
Totônio Rodrigues era muito velho e botava o pincenê na
    ponta do nariz
Depois do jantar as famílias tomavam a calçada com
    cadeiras, mexericos, namoros, risadas
A gente brincava no meio da rua
Os meninos gritavam:

    Coelho sai!
    Não sai!

À distância as vozes macias das meninas politonavam:

    Roseira dá-me uma rosa
    Craveiro dá-me um botão

(Dessas rosas muita rosa
Terá morrido em botão...)

De repente
        nos longes da noite
                um sino

Uma pessoa grande dizia:
Fogo em Santo Antônio!

with a hundred form letters and different ways of
    pleasing women, etc.

I prefer the lyricism of madmen
the lyricism of drunks
the difficult and bitter lyricism of the drunk
the lyricism of Shakespeare's clowns

I want nothing more of lyricism that isn't liberation.

trans. Candace Slater

Evocation of Recife

Recife
Not the American Venice,
not the Mauritsstad of the merchants of the Dutch East
    India Company
not the Recife of Portuguese peddlers
not even the Recife I later learned to love—
    the Recife of freedom-seeking revolutions
but a Recife without history or literature
Recife plain and simple
the Recife of my childhood

Union Street where I played crack-the-whip and broke
    Dona Aninha Viegas's windows
Totônio Rodrigues was very old and wore his pince-nez
    on the tip of his nose
After dinner the families took their chairs out on the
    sidewalk,—gossip, flirting, laughter
We children played in the street
The boys shouted:

    Run Rabbit!
    Don't run!

In the distance the little girls' petal-soft voices sung out in
    varied tones:

    Rosebush give me a rose
    Carnation give me a bud

(Of those roses many a rose
must have died in the bud...)

Suddenly
        in the far corners of the night
                a bell

One grown-up said:
"Fire in Saint Anthony!"

Outra contrariava: São José!
Totônio Rodrigues achava sempre que era São José.
Os homens punham o chapéu saíam fumando
E eu tinha raiva de ser menino porque não podia ir ver
       o fogo

Rua da União...
Como eram lindos os nomes das ruas da minha infância
Rua do Sol
(Tenho medo que hoje se chame do Dr. Fulano de Tal)
Atrás de casa ficava a Rua da Saudade...
    ...onde se ia fumar escondido
Do lado de lá era o cais da Rua da Aurora...
      ...onde se ia pescar escondido
Capiberibe
—Capibaribe

Lá longe o sertãozinho de Caxangá
Banheiros de palha
Um dia eu vi uma moça nuinha no banho
Fiquei parado o coração batendo
Ela se riu
       Foi o meu primeiro alumbramento

Cheia! As cheias! Barro boi morto árvores destroços
      redomoinho sumiu
E nos pegões da ponte do trem de ferro os caboclos
      destemidos em jangadas de bananeiras

Novenas
      Cavalhadas
Eu me deitei no colo da menina e ela começou a passar a
      mão nos meus cabelos
Capiberibe
—Capibaribe

Rua da União onde tôdas as tardes passava a preta das
      bananas
          Com o xale vistoso de pano da Costa
E o vendedor de roletes de cana
O de amendoim
    que se chamava midubim e não era torrado era cozido

Me lembro de todos os pregões:
    Ovos frescos e baratos
    Dez ovos por uma pataca
Foi há muito tempo...

A vida não me chegava pelos jornais nem pelos livros
Vinha da boca do povo na língua errada do povo
Língua certa do povo

Another exclaimed, "No, in Saint John!"
Totônio Rodrigues always thought it was Saint John.
The men put on their hats and went out, smoking
and I hated being a boy because I couldn't go with them
      to see the fire

Union Street...
The streets of my childhood had such lovely names!
Sun Street
(I hate to think they may have renamed it after some
      So-and-So)
Behind the house Nostalgia Street...
    ...where we used to sneak a smoke
On the other side the Dawn Street wharf...
      ...where we used to fish in secret.
Capiberibe
—Capibaribe

There way in the distance, the fields of Caxangá
and its straw bathhouses
One day I saw a young girl completely naked in her bath
I froze there, my heart beating wildly
She laughed
       It was my first ecstatic vision

Floods! The floods! Mud dead ox trees debris whirlpools
    —all gone
And between the pillars of the railway bridge daredevil
      country boys in rafts of banana logs

Novenas
      Cavalcades
I lay my head in the girl's lap and she began to run her
      fingers through my hair
Capiberibe
—Capibaribe

Union Street where every afternoon the black woman who
      sold bananas passed by in her bright coarse shawl
and the sugar-cane peddler
and the vendor of peanuts
    we called beenuts and that were boiled instead of
      roasted

I remember all their chants:
    Eggs, fresh and cheap
    Ten eggs for a quarter
That was so long ago...

Life didn't reach me through newspapers or books
but came from the mouths of the people, bad speech of
      the people

Porque ele é que fala gostoso o português do Brasil
    Ao passo que nós
        O que fazemos
        É macaquear
        A sintaxe lusíada
A vida com uma porção de coisas que eu não entendia bem
Terras que não sabia onde ficavam

Recife...
    Rua da União...
        A casa de meu avô...
Nunca pensei que ela acabasse!
Tudo lá parecia impregnado de eternidade

Recife...
    Meu avô morto.
Recife morto, Recife bom, Recife brasileiro como a casa
    de meu avô.

1930

good speech of the people
because it's the people who speak Brazilian Portuguese
    with gusto
   while we
   all we do
   is imitate, monkey see, monkey do
   the language of the classics
Life with a whole slew of things I didn't really understand
Territories for me yet uncharted

Recife...
    Union Street...
        My grandfather's home...
I never thought that house could disappear!
Everything there seemed charged with eternity

Recife...
    My grandfather, dead.
Recife, now dead, bighearted Recife, Recife Brazilian as my
    grandfather's home.

trans. Candace Slater

Mozart no céu

No dia 5 de dezembro de 1791 Wolfgang Amadeus
Mozart entrou no céu, como um artista de circo,
fazendo piruetas extraordinárias sôbre um
mirabolante cavalo branco.

Os anjinhos atônitos diziam: Que foi? Que não foi?
Melodias jamais-ouvidas voavam nas linhas suplementares
    superiores da pauta.
Um momento se suspendeu a contemplação inefável.
A Virgem beijou-o na testa
E desde então Wolfgang Amadeus Mozart foi o mais moço
    dos anjos.

1930

Mozart in Heaven

On the 5th of December 1791 Wolfgang Amadeus
Mozart entered heaven as a circus performer,
turning marvelous pirouettes on a dazzling
white horse.

The small astonished angels said: Who can that be? Who in
    the world can that be?
As never-before-heard melodies began to soar
Line after line above the staff.
For a moment the ineffable contemplation paused.
The Virgin kissed him on the forehead
And from then on Wolfgang Amadeus Mozart was the
    youngest of the angels.

trans. Dudley Poore

Vou-me embora pra Pasárgada

Vou-me embora pra Pasárgada
Lá sou amigo do rei
Lá tenho a mulher que eu quero
Na cama que escolherei
Vou-me embora pra Pasárgada

Vou-me embora pra Pasárgada
Aqui eu não sou feliz

Off to Pasárgada

I'm heading off to Pasárgada
—there I'm a friend of the king,
there I can have any woman
anytime, any bed, anything!
I'm heading off to Pasárgada.

I'm heading off to Pasárgada.
Here I can't get what I need.

Lá a existência é uma aventura
De tal modo inconseqüente
Que Joana a Louca de Espanha
Rainha e falsa demente
Vem a ser contraparente
Da nora que nunca tive

E como farei ginástica
Andarei de bicicleta
Montarei em burro brabo
Subirei no pau-de-sebo
Tomarei banhos de mar!
E quando estiver cansado
Deito na beira do rio
Mando chamar a mãe-d'água
Pra me contar as histórias
Que no tempo de eu menino
Rosa vinha me contar
Vou-me embora pra Pasárgada

Em Pasárgada tem tudo
É outra civilização
Tem um processo seguro
De impedir a concepção
Tem telefone automático
Tem alcalóide à vontade
Tem prostitutas bonitas
Para a gente namorar

E quando eu estiver mais triste
Mas triste de não ter jeito
Quando de noite me der
Vontade de me matar
—Lá sou amigo do rei—
Terei a mulher que eu quero
Na cama que escolherei
Vou-me embora pra Pasárgada

There, you see, life's an adventure
so unpredictably free
that mad Joan of Spain's a relation
of the daughter-in-law never-to-be.

And all the sports that I'll play there…
I'll go bicycling (bicycling, me!),
ride a wild burro,
climb a greased pole,
and swim for miles in the sea.
And then when I'm tired I'll stretch out
beside the river to dream.
To hear those old tales Rosa told once
I'll summon the Mother-of-Streams.
I'm heading off to Pasárgada!

Pasárgada has all you could want.
(Another civilization, I'm told.)
They've got birth control,
they've got dope there,
they've got dial telephones.
They are plenty of good-looking hookers
just waiting for someone to hold.

And when I become even sadder
so sad nothing does any good
when at night all I want
is to die, is to take my own life
—There I'm a friend of the king—
there I can have any woman
anytime, any bed, anything!
I'm heading off to Pasárgada.

trans. Candace Slater

1930

Rondó dos cavalinhos

Os cavalinhos correndo,
E nós, cavalões, comendo…
Tua beleza, Esmeralda,
Acabou me enlouquecendo.

Os cavalinhos correndo,
E nós, cavalões, comendo…
O sol tão claro lá fora,
E em minh'alma—anoitecendo!

Rondeau of the Little Horses

The little horses fleeing
and we, big horses, eating…
Your beauty, Esmeralda,
finally drove me wild.

The little horses fleeing
and we, big horses, eating…
The sun so bright outside,
and in my soul—night coming on!

Os cavalinhos correndo,
E nós, cavalões, comendo...
Alfonso Reyes partindo,
E tanta gente ficando...

Os cavalinhos correndo,
E nós, cavalões, comendo...
A Itália falando grosso,
A Europa se avacalhando...

Os cavalinhos correndo,
E nós cavalões, comendo...
O Brasil politicando,
Nossa! A poesia morrendo...
O sol tão claro lá fora,
O sol tão claro, Esmeralda,
E em minh'alma—anoitecendo!

1936

The little horses fleeing
and we, big horses, eating...
Alfonso Reyes departing
and so many people sitting tight...

The little horses fleeing
and we, big horses, eating...
Italy talking big
and Europe cowering...

The little horses fleeing
and we, big horses, eating...
Brazil talk-talk-talking
—Lord!—while poetry dies on the vine...
The sun so bright outside...
The sun so bright, Esmeralda,
and in my soul—night coming on!

trans. Candace Slater

Retrato

O sorriso escasso,
O riso-sorriso,
A risada nunca.
(Como quem consigo
Traz o sentimento
Do madrasto mundo.)

Com os braços colados
Ao longo do corpo,
Vai pela cidade
Grande e cafajeste,
Com o mesmo ar esquivo
Que escolheu nascendo
Na esquiva Itabira.

Aprendeu com ela
Os olhos metálicos
Com que vê as coisas:
Sem ódio, sem ênfase,
Às vezes com náusea.

Ferro de Itabira,
Em cujos recessos
Um vedor, um dia,
Um vedor—o neto—
Descobriu infante
As fundas nascentes,
O veio, o remanso
De escusa ternura.

1952

Portrait

The rare smile.
The half-laugh more like a smile
and never really laughter.
(Like one who carries with him
the awareness
of a step-mother world.)

Arms glued
to either side,
you move through the city
vulgar and sublime
with the same air of aloofness
you chose by being born
in aloof Itabira.

The metallic eyes
through which you observe the world
learned with Itabira to see
without hatred or expression,
sometimes with revulsion.

Iron of Itabira
in whose recesses
a prospector, one day,
a prospector—the grandson—
discovered early on
the deep springs,
the vein, the calm
of hidden love.

trans. Candace Slater

Entrevista

Vida que morre e que subsiste
Vária, absurda, sórdida, ávida,
Má!

      Se me indagar um qualquer
Repórter:
    "Que há de mais bonito
No ingrato mundo?"
              Não hesito;
Responderei:
           "De mais bonito
Não sei dizer, Mas de mais triste,
—De mais triste é uma mulher
Grávida. Qualquer mulher grávida."

1960

Interview

Life that dies and that subsists
fickle, ludicrous, grasping, vile
defiled!

      If some reporter one day
asks me:
      "What is the most lovely thing you find
in this thankless world?"
            I won't hesitate; I'll
tell him:
        "Most lovely?
I don't know. But saddest by a mile—
the saddest is a woman—
any woman with child."

trans. Candace Slater

Ramón López Velarde

MEXICO
1888–1921

If Darío and González Martínez provided the bridge for Mexican poetry to move from an early cosmopolitan sense of Modernism to a local, second-generation application of Modernist ideals, Ramón López Velarde shows the way from those second-generation ambitions toward contemporary Mexican writing. Energized by the Mexican Revolution and dedicated to aesthetic ambitions of personalism and verbal surprise, López Velarde forges from colloquial Mexican Spanish an idiom of his own, infusing his intensely meditative arguments with abrupt sui generis images and extraordinary word choices. "I long to eject every syllable that is not born of the combustion of my bones," he wrote. Especially after his second book of poems (*Zozobra*) appeared in 1919, some of López Velarde's contemporaries claimed to find his poems tortuous in their pacing, affected in their diction, strained in their imagery, and provincial in their fondness for regional themes and Catholic ritual. By contrast, later readers have often found other qualities in López Velarde's intensely personal voice: authenticity and subjective insight; the sound of one local individual articulating his own tragic relation to universal themes, in a diction that resolutely avoids commonplaces.

Mi prima Agueda

Mi madrina invitaba a mi prima Agueda
a que pasara el día con nosotros,
y mi prima llegaba
con un contradictorio
prestigio de almidón y de temible
luto ceremonioso.

My Cousin Agueda

My godmother invited my cousin
Agueda to spend the day
with us, and my cousin
came with a conflicting
prestige of starch and fearful
ceremonious weeds.

Agueda aparecía, resonante
de almidón, y sus ojos
verdes y sus mejillas rubicundas
me protegían contra el pavoroso
luto...

        Yo era rapaz
y conocía la o por lo redondo,
y Agueda que tejía
mansa y perseverante en el sonoro
corredor, me causaba
calosfríos ignotos...
        (Creo que hasta la debo la costumbre
heróicamente insana de hablar solo).

        A la hora de comer, en la penumbra
quieta del refectorio,
me iba embelesando un quebradizo
sonar intermitente de vajilla
y el timbre carisioso
de la voz de mi prima.

        Agueda era
(luto, pupilas verdes y mejillas
rubicundas) un cesto policromo
de manzanas y uvas
en el ébano de un armario añoso.

                            1916

Agueda appeared, sonorous
with starch, and her green eyes
and ruddy cheeks protected
me against the fearsome
weeds.

        I was a small boy,
knew O was the round one,
and Agueda knitting,
mild and persevering,
in the echoing gallery,
gave me unknown shivers.
(I think I even owe her the heroically
morbid habit of soliloquy.)

At dinner-time in the quiet
shadowy dining-room,
I was spellbound by the brittle
intermittent noise of dishes
and the caressing timbre
of my cousin's voice.

        Agueda was
(weeds, green pupils, ruddy cheeks)
a polychromatic basket of
apples and grapes
in the ebony of an ancient cupboard.

                            trans. Samuel Beckett

Domingos de provincia

En los claros domingos de mi pueblo, es costumbre
que en la Plaza descubran las gentiles cabezas
las mozas, y sus ojos reflejan dulcedumbre
y la banda en el kiosco toca lánguidas piezas.

Y al caer sobre el pueblo la noche ensoñadora,
los amantes se miran con la mejor mirada
y la orquesta en sus flautas y violín atesora
mil sonidos románticos en la noche enfiestada.

Los días de guardar en pueblos provincianos
regalan al viandante gratos amaneceres
en que frescos los rostros, el Lavalle en las manos,

camino de a iglesia van las mozas aprisa;
que en los días festivos, entre aquellas mujeres
no hay una cara hermosa que se quede sin misa.

                            1916

Provincial Sundays

On Sundays when the weather's good, traditionally
in my home town, young ladies show their pretty heads
in the main square, their eyes reflecting sweetness
and the town band playing languid melodies.

And when the dreamy night descends on the town,
the lovers look at one another with fine expressions
in their eyes, the orchestra's flutes and violins
coin a thousand romantic sounds in the festive night.

In provincial towns at dawn, holidays
offer visitors a lovely scene:
with their fresh faces, their missals in their hands,

young ladies on the way to church—
because on a holiday, among them there is not one,
not one beauty, who would miss Mass.

                            trans. Julián Manríquez

El retorno maléfico

a D. Ignacio I. Gastelum

Mejor será no regresar al pueblo,
al éden subvertido que se calla
en la mutilación de la metralla.

Hasta los fresnos mancos,
los dignatarios de cúpula oronda,
han de rodar las quejas de la torre
acribillada en los vientos de fronda.

Y la fusilería grabó en la cal
de todas las paredes
de la aldea espectral,
negros y aciagos mapas,
porque en ellos leyese el hijo pródigo
al volver a su umbral
en un anochecer de maleficio,
a la luz de petróleo de una mecha,
su esperanza deshecha.

Cuando la tosca llave enmohecida
tuerza la chirriante cerradura,
en la añeja clausura
del zaguán, los dos púdicos
medallones de yeso,
entornando los párpados narcóticos,
se mirarán y se dirán: "¿Qué es eso?"

Y yo entraré con pies advenedizos
hasta el patio agorero
en que hay un brocal ensimismado,
con un cubo de cuero
goteando su gota categórica
como un estribillo plañidero.

Si el sol inexorable, alegre y tónico,
hace hervir a las fuentes catecúmenas
en que bañábase mi sueño crónico;
si se afana la hormiga;
si en los techos resuena y se fatiga
de los buches de tórtola el reclamo
que entre las telarañas zumba y zumba;
mi sed de amar será como una argolla
empotrada en la losa de una tumba.

Las golondrinas nuevas, renovando
con sus noveles picos alfareros
los nidos tempraneros;
bajo el ópalo insigne

Baleful Return

To D. Ignacio I. Gastelum

It is better not to go back to the village,
to Eden in ruins, silent now,
among the mutilations of the guns.

Even the crippled ash-trees,
dignitaries with their pompous domes,
must have dropped their foliage in rings,
around that tower, groaning when the winds blow.

Fusileers engraved
their ominous black maps
on the lime of each of the walls
of the ghostly village:
so that the son who returns
as a prodigal to his own beginnings,
while night is falling in an evil spell,
could read his ruined hopes
by the light of an oil lamp.

When the crude rusty key
turns creaking in the lock,
inside the old enclosure
the entryway frames
two modest plaster medallions,
half-open sleepy eyes, looking at each other,
will ask, "what's that?"

And I will enter with a stranger's steps
into the foreboding patio
where an absent-minded well-curb
with its leather bucket stands,
categorically dripping its drop
like something weeping.

If the relentless cheerful bracing sun
heats up the fountains (like catechumens)
where my chronic sleep would be floating;
if the ant is busy,
if up on the roof bird-calls from the bills
of turtle-doves sound till they wear out,
humming and humming among the spider webs,
my thirst for love would be like a ring
embedded in a slab above a tomb.

New arrivals, the swallows renew
their early nests, with beaks
that are still new to masonry;
under the opalescent flag

de los atardeceres monacales,
el lloro de recientes recentales
por la ubérrima ubre prohibida
de la vaca, rumiante y faraónica,
que al párvulo intimida;
campanario de timbre novedoso;
remozados altares;
el amor amoroso
de las parejas pares;
noviazgos de muchachas
frescas y humildes, como humildes coles,
y que la mano dan por el postigo
a la luz de dramáticos faroles;
alguna señorita
que canta en algún piano
alguna vieja aria;
el gendarme que pita...
...Y una íntima tristeza reaccionaria.

1919

of the monastic evening
the crying of the new-born calves
for what was taken, the overflowing udders
of ruminant Pharaonic cows
that frighten a small child;
the bell-tower with its fluctuating tones;
renovated altars;
the affectionate love
of married couples, in pairs;
girls' fiancés
holding their hands between the shutters,
as fresh and humble as a humble cabbage:
by the light of the dramatic lanterns
some young woman
who sings some ancient aria
at some piano;
the constable who tweets his whistle...
...and the intimate responsive sadness.

trans. Victor Tulli

Tierra mojada

Tierra mojada de las tardes líquidas
en que la lluvia cuchichea
y en que se reblandecen las señoritas, bajo
el redoble del agua en la azotea...

Tierra mojada de las tardes olfativas
en que un afán misántropo remonta las lascivas
soledades del éter, y en ellas se desposa
con la ulterior paloma de Noé;
mientras se obstina el tableteo
del rayo, por la nube cenagosa...

Tarde mojada, de hálitos labriegos,
en la cual reconozco estar hecho de barro,
porque en sus llantos veraniegos,
bajo el auspicio de la media luz,
el alma se licúa sobre los clavos
de su cruz...

Tardes en que el teléfono pregunta
por consabidas náyades arteras,
que salen del baño al amor
a volcar en el lecho las fatuas cabelleras
y a balbucir, con alevosía y con ventaja,
húmedos y anhelantes monosílabos,
según que la llovizna acosa las vidrieras...

Tardes como una alcoba submarina
con su lecho y su tina;
tardes en que envejece una doncella

Wet Earth

Wet earth of liquid evenings when the rain
whispers and girls soften
under the redoubled pelting of the drops
on the roof terrace.

Wet earth of odoriferous evenings when
misanthropy toils up to the lascivious
solitudes of air and on them lights
with the last dove of Noah;
while the thunder crackles tirelessly
along the miry clouds.

Wet evenings of steaming earth when I
acknowledge I am made
of clay, for in its summer tears, beneath
the auspice of the light that is half gone,
the soul turns to water on the nails
of its cross.

Evenings when the telephone invites
naiads known for their knowingness,
who leave their bath for love,
to strew their fatuous tresses on the bed
and to lisp, with perfidy and profit,
damp and panting monosyllables
as the fine rain harries the window-panes...

Evenings like an alcove under the sea,
its bed its bath;
evenings when a maiden

ante el brasero exhausto de su casa,
esperando a un galán que le lleve una brasa;
tardes en que descienden
los ángeles, a arar surcos derechos
en edificantes barbechos;
tardes de rogativa y de cirio pascual;
tardes en que el chubasco
me induce a enardecer a cada una
de las doncellas frígidas con la brasa oportuna;
tardes en que, oxidada
la voluntad, me siento
acólito del alcanfor,
un poco pez espada
y un poco San Isidro Labrador...

1919

grows old in front of her extinguished hearth,
waiting for a swain to bring her a live coal;
evenings when on earth
angels descend to plough unerring furrows
on edifying fallows;
evenings of supplication and Pascal candle;
evenings when the squall
incites me to inflame
each frigid maiden with the opportune coal;

evenings when, my soul
oxidized, I feel
an acolyte of camphor,
slightly swordfish, slightly
Saint Isidore Labrador...

trans. Samuel Beckett

Hormigas

A la cálida vida que transcurre canora
con garbo de mujer sin letras ni antifaces,
a la invicta belleza que salva y que enamora,
responde, en la embriaguez de la encantada hora,
un encono de hormigas en mis venas voraces.

Fustigan el desmán del perenne hormigueo
el pozo del silencio y el enjambre del ruido,
la harina rebanada como doble trofeo
en los fértiles bustos, el Infierno en que creo,
el estertor final y el preludio del nido.

Mas luego mis hormigas me negarán su abrazo
y han de huir de mis pobres y trabajados dedos
cual se olvida en la arena un gélido bagazo;
y tu boca, que es cifra de eróticos denuedos,
tu boca, que es mi rúbrica, mi manjar y mi adorno,
tu boca, en que la lengua vibra asomada al mundo
como réproba llama saliéndose de un horno,
en una turbia fecha de cierzo gemebundo
en que ronde la luna porque robarte quiera,
ha de oler a sudario y a hierba machacada,
a droga y a responso, a pábilo y a cera.

Antes de que deserten mis hormigas, Amada,
déjalas caminar camino de tu boca
a que apuren los viáticos del sanguinario fruto
que desde sarracenos oasis me provoca.

Antes de que tus labios mueran, para mi luto,
dámelos en el crítico umbral del cementerio
como perfume y pan y tósigo y cauterio.

1919

Ants

To warm life passing singing with the grace
of a woman without wile or veil,
to unconquered beauty, enamouring, saving,
responds, amid the magic hour's elation,
a rancour of ants in my voracious veins.

The pit of silence and the swarm of sound,
the flour cloven like a double trophy
on fertile busts, the Hell of my belief,
the rattle of death and prelude to the nest,
chastise the ceaseless truant formication.

But soon my ants will deny me their embrace
and from my poor and diligent fingers fly
as a cold bagasse is forgotten on the sand;
and your mouth, cypher of erotic prowess,
your mouth that is my rubric, food, adornment,
your mouth that in its flaunting tongue vibrates
like a reprobate flame escaping from a kiln
into a throng of bitter howling gales
where the moon prowls intent to ravish you,
your mouth will smell of shroud and crushed grass,
of opiate and respond, wick and wax.

Before my ants abandon me, Amada,
let them journey the journey of your mouth
to gorge viatica of the sanguinary fruit
provoking me from Saracen oases.

Before your lips die for my sorrow give
them to me on the graveyard's critical threshold,
their bread and perfume, venom and cautery.

trans. Samuel Beckett

Gabriela Mistral
[Lucila Godoy Alcayaga]

CHILE
1889–1957

Although Gabriela Mistral's early schooling was erratic, she received university training in the field of primary and secondary education, and for the first third of her professional life she taught in the local schools of rural Chile. Later she served as an educational consultant to the governments of Mexico and Chile. Those consultancies led to other diplomatic positions: she served as Chile's consular representative to Madrid, Lisbon, Nice, Los Angeles, and other cities. Mistral moved to Brazil at the time of the Nazi rise to power in Europe, lived in Chile after the war, and spent her last years in the United States as a university professor and as a spokesperson for programs of the United Nations. Although she never married, she adopted a nephew, "Yinyin," to whom she addressed many of her most eloquently maternal poems.

Celebrated as a poet from the publication of her first book, *Sonetos de la muerte* (*Sonnets of Death*, 1914), Mistral in her early poems pursued the creation of an intense Symbolist life-myth, based on the story of a passionate affair, at eighteen, with a young working-class man. According to this poetic legend, the young man was unfaithful; she broke with him reluctantly; shortly afterward, he shot himself. In her mature work, Mistral moved away from the Catholic and Symbolist influences of her early poems and developed a uniquely songlike, limpid style, a voice of almost maternal lullaby that murmurs through simple, traditional forms. This voice continued through her later books, notably in *Desolación* (*Desolation*, 1922), *Ternura* (*Tenderness*, 1924), and *Tala* (*Harvesting*, 1938).

Her later lyrics, which count among the most beloved and influential poems of Latin America, are infused with an affection for experience, a gentleness that expands: toward objects, toward a single infant, toward clusters of children and mothers, toward the small-town community, toward marginalized races, toward the Americas, toward God. Lyric poetry, claimed Mistral, springs from the "wound of love inflicted on us by things." Her poetry's combination of passion and pathos, articulated in an authentic, intimate, even rustic voice, makes it recognizably human and original—and thus universal. In 1945 her beloved nephew Yinyin killed himself, at age fifteen. Mistral received the news of his death shortly before she learned she had won the Nobel Prize in literature (she was the first Latin American writer to win that award). While representing Chile in the United Nations, Mistral spent the last years of her life in Chile and on Long Island, New York, where she lived with her long-time companion, Doris Dana.

Decálogo del artista

i. Amarás la belleza, que es la sombra de Dios sobre el Universo.

ii. No hay arte ateo. Aunque no ames al Creador, lo afirmarás creando a su semejanza.

iii. No darás la belleza como cebo para los sentidos, sino como el natural alimento del alma.

Decalogue of the Artist

i. You shall love beauty, which is the shadow of God over the Universe.

ii. There is no godless art. Although you love not the Creator, you shall bear witness to Him creating His likeness.

iii. You shall create beauty not to excite the senses but to give sustenance to the soul.

iv. No te será pretexto para la lujuria ni para la vanidad, sino ejercicio divino.

v. No la buscarás en las ferias ni llevarás tu obra a ellas, porque la Belleza es virgen, y la que está en las ferias no es Ella.

vi. Subirá de tu corazón a tu canto y te habrá purificado a ti el primero.

vii. Tu belleza se llamará también misericordia, y consolará el corazón de los hombres.

viii. Darás tu obra como se da un hijo: restando sangre de tu corazón.

ix. No te será la belleza opio adormecedor, sino vino generoso que te encienda para la acción, pues si dejas de ser hombre o mujer, dejarás de ser artista.

x. De toda creación saldrás con vergüenza, porque fué inferior a tu sueño, e inferior a ese sueño maravilloso de Dios, que es la Naturaleza.

1922

iv. You shall never use beauty as a pretext for luxury and vanity but as a spiritual devotion.

v. You shall not seek beauty at carnival or fair or offer your work there, for beauty is virginal and is not to be found at carnival or fair.

vi. Beauty shall rise from your heart in song, and you shall be the first to be purified.

vii. The beauty you create shall be known as compassion and shall console the hearts of men.

viii. You shall bring forth your work as a mother brings forth her child: out of the blood of your heart.

ix. Beauty shall not be an opiate that puts you to sleep but a strong wine that fires you to action, for if you fail to be a true man or a true woman, you will fail to be an artist.

x. Each act of creation shall leave you humble, for it is never as great as your dream and always inferior to that most marvelous dream of God which is Nature.

trans. Doris Dana

La casa

La mesa, hijo, está tendida,
en blancura quieta de nata,
y en cuatro muros azulea,
dando relumbres, la cerámica.
Esta es la sal, éste el aceite
y al centro el Pan que casi habla.
Oro más lindo que oro del Pan
no está ni en fruta ni en retama,
y da su olor de espiga y horno
una dicha que nunca sacia.
Lo partimos, hijito, juntos,
con dedos duros y palma blanda,
y tú lo miras asombrado
de tierra negra que da flor blanca.

Baja la mano de comer,
que tu madre también la baja.
Los trigos, hijo, con del aire,
y son del sol y de la azada;
pero este Pan "cara de Dios"

The House

The table, son, is laid
with the quiet whiteness of cream,
and on four walls ceramics
gleam blue, glint light.
Here is the salt, here the oil,
in the center, bread that almost speaks.
Gold more lovely than gold of bread
is not in broom plant or fruit,
and its scent of wheat and oven
gives unfailing joy.
We break bread, little son, together
with our hard fingers, our soft palms,
while you stare in astonishment
that black earth brings forth a white flower.

Lower your hand that reaches for food
as your mother also lowers hers.
Wheat, my son, is of air,
of sunlight and hoe;
but this bread, called "the face of God,"*

*In Chile, the people call bread "The face of God." (G. M.)

no llega a mesas de las casas;
y si otros niños no lo tienen,
mejor, mi hijo, no lo tocaras,
y no tomarlo mejor sería
con mano y mano avergonzadas.

Hijo, el Hambre, cara de mueca,
en remolino gira las parvas,
y se buscan y no se encuentran
el Pan y el Hambre corcovada.
Para que lo halle, si ahora entra,
el Pan dejemos hasta mañana;
el fuego ardiendo marque la puerta,
que el indio quechua nunca cerraba,
¡y miremos comer al Hambre,
para dormir con cuerpo y alma!

1924

is not set on every table.
And if other children do not have it,
better, my son, that you not touch it,
better that you do not take it
with ashamed hands.

My son, Hunger with his grimaced face
in eddies circles the unthrashed wheat.
They search and never find each other,
Bread and hunchbacked Hunger.
So that he find it if he should enter now,
we'll leave the bread until tomorrow.
Let the blazing fire mark the door
that the Quechuan Indian never closed,
and we will watch Hunger eat
to sleep with body and soul.

trans. Doris Dana

Apegado a mí

Velloncito de mi carne,
que en mi entraña yo tejí,
velloncito friolento,
¡duérmete apegado a mí!

La perdiz duerme en el trébol
escuchándole latir:
no te turben mis alientos,
¡duérmete apegado a mí!

Hierbecita temblorosa
asombrada de vivir,
no te sueltes de mi pecho:
¡duérmete apegado a mí!

Yo que todo lo he perdido
ahora tiemblo de dormir.
No resbales de mi brazo:
¡duérmete apegado a mí!

1924

Close to Me

Little fleece of my flesh
that I wove in my womb,
little shivering fleece,
sleep close to me!

The partridge sleeps in the clover
hearing its heart beat.
My breathing will not wake you.
Sleep close to me!

Little trembling blade of grass
astonished to be alive,
don't leave my breast.
Sleep close to me!

I who have lost everything
am now afraid to sleep.
Don't slip away from my arms.
Sleep close to me!

trans. Doris Dana

La flor del aire

Yo la encontré por mi destino,
de pie a mitad de la pradera,
gobernadora del que pase,
del que le hable y que la vea.

The Flower of Air*

I met her, not by chance,
standing in the middle of the meadow,
governing all who passed,
all who addressed her.

*I wanted to call this "The Adventure," my adventure
with Poetry. (G. M.)

Y ella me dijo: "Sube al monte.
Yo nunca dejo la pradera,
y me cortas las flores blancas
como nieves, duras y tiernas."

Me subí a la ácida montaña,
busqué las flores donde albean,
entre las rocas existiendo
medio dormidas y despiertas.

Cuando bajé, con carga mía,
la hallé a mitad de la pradera,
y fuí cubriéndola frenética,
con un torrente de azucenas.

Y sin mirarse la blancura,
ella me dijo: "Tú acarrea
ahora sólo flores rojas.
Yo no puedo pasar la pradera."

Trepé las peñas con el venado,
y busqué flores de demencia,
las que rojean y parecen
que de rojez vivan y mueran.

Cuando bajé se las fuí dando
con un tremblor feliz de ofrenda,
y ella se puso como el agua
que en ciervo herido se ensangrienta.

Pero mirándome, sonámbula,
me dijo: "Sube y acarrea
las amarillas, las amarillas.
Yo nunca dejo la pradera."

Subí derecho a la montaña
y me busqué las flores densas,
color de sol y de azafranes,
recién nacidas y ya eternas.

Al encontrarla, como siempre,
a la mitad de la pradera,
segunda vez yo fuí cubriéndola,
y la dejé como las eras.

Y todavía, loca de oro,
me dijo: "Súbete, mi sierva,
y cortarás las sin color,
ni azafranadas ni bermejas.

"Las que yo amo por recuerdo
de la Leonora y la Ligeia,

She said to me: "Climb the mountain—
I never leave the meadow.
Cut me flowers white
as snow, crisp and tender."

I climbed the mountain
and searched where flowers whiten
among the rocks,
half sleeping, half waking.

When I came down with my burden
I found her in the middle of the meadow.
Like a crazy one, I covered her
with a deluge of lilies.

She never glanced at their whiteness.
She said to me: "Now bring me
red flowers, only the red.
I cannot leave the meadow."

I clambered up crags with deer
and searched for flowers of madness,
those that grow red and appear
to live and die of redness.

When I came down, I offered them
in trembling tribute;
she became red as water bloodied
by the wounded deer.

She gazed at me, half dreaming,
and said: "Go climb again and bring me
the yellow, only the yellow.
I never leave the meadow."

I went straightway to the mountain
and searched for clustered flowers,
color of sun, color of saffron,
newly born, already eternal.

When I returned, I found her still standing
in the middle of the meadow.
I showered her with sun-burst blossoms
till she was golden as the threshing floor.

And once again, crazy with gold,
she said: "Go up, my servant,
and cut flowers that have no color,
not saffron, not burnished red.

"Bring me flowers that I love,
remembering Eleonora and Ligeia,

color del Sueño y de los sueños.
Yo soy Mujer de la pradera."

Me fuí ganando la montaña,
ahora negra como Medea,
sin tajada de resplandores,
como una gruta vaga y cierta.

Ellas no estaban en las ramas,
ellas no abrían en las piedras
y las corté del aire dulce,
tijereteándolo ligera.

Mc las corté como si fuese
la cortadora que está ciega.
Corté de un aire y de otro aire,
tomando el aire por mi selva...

Cuando bajé de la montaña
y fuí buscándome a la reina,
ahora ella caminaba,
ya no era blanca ni violenta;

ella se iba, la sonámbula,
abandonando la pradera,
y yo siguiéndola y siguiéndola
por el pastal y la alameda,

cargada así de tantas flores,
con espaldas y mano aéreas,
siempre cortándolas del aire
y con los aires como siega...

Ella delante va sin cara;
ella delante va sin huella,
y yo la sigo todavía
entre los gajos de la niebla,

con estas flores sin color,
ni blanquecinas ni bermejas,
hasta mi entrega sobre el límite,
cuando mi Tiempo se disuelva...

1938

flowers color of dream, color of dreaming.
I am the woman of the meadow."

I approached the mountain
now black as Medea,
with not a crevice of brightness,
vague and clear as a cavern.

Those flowers did not grow on branches
or open among rocks.
I cut them from the soft air;
I cut them with gentle shears.

I cut as if I the cutter
walked blind.
I cut from one air and another
as if air were my forest.

When I came down from the mountain
and went in search of my queen,
I found her now walking,
no longer white or violent red.

Somnambulant, she was leaving,
abandoning the meadow,
and I followed her, following
through pastures and poplar groves.

Burdened thus with so many flowers,
shoulders, hands, garlanded with air,
from the air ever cutting more flowers,
I went reaping a harvest of air.

She goes before me, faceless,
leaving no footprint,
and I follow her, still follow
through dense clusters of fog,

bearing colorless flowers,
not white or burnished red,
until my release at the farthest limit
when my time dissolves...

trans. Doris Dana

Una palabra

Yo tengo una palabra en la garganta
y no la suelto, y no me libro de ella
aunque me empuje su empellón de sangre.
Si la soltase, quema el pasto vivo,
sangra al cordero, hace caer al pájaro.

One Word

I have in my throat one word
that I cannot speak, will not free
though its thrust of blood pounds me.
If I voiced it, it would scorch the living grass,
bleed the lamb, fell the bird.

Tengo que desprenderla de mi lengua,
hallar un agujero de castores
o sepultarla con cales y cales
porque no guarde como el alma el vuelo.

No quiero dar señales de que vivo
mientras que por mi sangre vaya y venga
y suba y baje por mi loco aliento.
Aunque mi padre Job la dijo, ardiendo,
no quiero darle, no, mi pobre boca
porque no ruede y la hallen las mujeres
que van al río, y se enrede a sus trenzas
o al pobre matorral tuerza y abrase.

Yo quiero echarle violentas semillas
que en una noche la cubran y ahoguen
sin dejar de ella el cisco de una sílaba.
O rompérmela así, como a la víbora
que por mitad se parte con los dientes.

Y volver a mi casa, entrar, dormirme,
cortada de ella, rebanada de ella,
y despertar después de dos mil días
recién nacida de sueño y olvido.

¡Sin saber más que tuve una palabra
de yodo y piedra-alumbre entre los labios
ni saber acordarme de una noche,
de una morada en país extranjero,
de la celada y el rayo a la puerta
y de mi carne marchando sin su alma!

1954

I have to cut it from my tongue,
find a beaver's hole,
or bury it beneath lime and more quicklime
lest, soul-like, it break free.

I wish to give no sign of what I live
as this word courses through my blood, ebbs and flows,
rises, falls with each mad breath.
Though Job, my father, burning, spoke it,
I will not give it utterance
lest it roll vagrant
and be found by river-women,
twist itself in their braids,
or mangle and blaze the poor thicket.

I wish to throw seeds so violent
they burst and smother it in one night
leaving not even a syllable's trace.
Or rip it from myself
with the serpent's severing tooth.

And return to my house, enter and sleep,
torn from it, sliced from it;
wake after two thousand days
newly born out of sleep and oblivion.

Never again to remember the word between my lips,
that word of iodine and alum stone,
or ever again that one night,
the ambush in a foreign land,
the lightning bolt at the door
and my flesh abroad with no soul.

trans. Doris Dana

Una mujer

Donde estaba su casa sigue
como si no hubiera ardido.
Habla sólo la lengua de su alma
con los que cruzan, ninguna.

Cuando dice "pino de Alepo"
no dice árbol que dice un niño
y cuando dice "regato"
y "espejo de oro," dice lo mismo.

Cuando llega la noche cuenta
los tizones de su casa
o enderezada su frente
ve erguido su pino de Alepo.

A Woman

Where her house stood, she goes on living
as if it had never burned.
The only words she speaks
are the words of her soul;
to those who pass by she speaks none.

When she says "pine of Aleppo"
she speaks of no tree, but a child;
and when she says "little stream"
or "mirror of gold" she speaks of the same.

When night falls she counts
the charred beams of her house.
Lifting her forehead she sees
the pine of Aleppo stand tall.

(El día vive por su noche
y la noche por su milagro.)

En cada árbol endereza
al que acostaron en tierra
y en el fuego de su pecho
lo calienta, lo enrolla, lo estrecha.

1954

(The day lives for its night,
the night for its miracle.)

In every tree, she raises the one
they laid upon the earth.
She warms and wraps and holds him close
to the fire of her breast.

trans. Doris Dana

Último árbol

Esta solitaria greca
que me dieron en naciendo:
lo que va de mi costado
a mi costado de fuego;

lo que corre de mi frente
a mis pies calenturientos;
esta Isla de mi sangre,
esta parvedad de reino,

yo lo devuelvo cumplido
y en brazada se lo entrego
al último de mis árboles,
a tamarindo o a cedro.

Por si en la segunda vida
no me dan lo que ya dieron
y me hace falta este cuajo
de frescor y de silencio,

y yo paso por el mundo
en sueño, carrera o vuelo,
en vez de umbrales de casas,
quiero árbol de paradero.

Le dejaré lo que tuve
de ceniza y firmamento,
mi flanco lleno de hablas
y mi flanco de silencio;

soledades que me dí,
soledades que me dieron,
y el diezmo que pagué al rayo
de mi Dios dulce y tremendo;

mi juego de toma y daca
con las nubes y los vientos,
y lo que supe, temblando,
de manantiales secretos.

Final Tree

This solitary fretwork
they gave me at birth
that goes from side
to fiery side,

that runs from my forehead
to my hot feet,
this island of my blood,
this minuteness of kingdom,

I return it fulfilled.
With arms outstretched I give it
to the last of my trees,
to tamarinth or cedar.

In case in the second life
they will not give again what has been given
and I should miss this solace
of freshness and silence,

and if I should pass through the world
in dream, running or flying,
instead of thresholds of houses
I shall want a tree to rest under.

I bequeath it all I had
of ash and firmament,
my flank of speech,
my flank of silence.

Loneliness I gave myself,
loneliness they gave me,
the small tithe I paid the lightning
of my God, sweet and tremendous.

My play of give and take
with clouds and with the winds
and what I knew, trembling,
of secret springs.

¡Ay, arrimo tembloroso
de mi Arcángel verdadero,
adelantado en las rutas
con el ramo y el ungüento!

Tal vez ya nació y me falta
gracia de reconocerlo,
o sea el árbol sin nombre
que cargué como a hijo ciego.

A veces cae a mis hombros
una humedad o un oreo
y veo en contorno mío
el cíngulo de su ruedo.

Pero tal vez su follaje
ya va arropando mi sueño
y estoy, de muerta, cantando
debajo de él, sin saberlo.

Ay! Tremulous shelter
of my true Archangel,
ahead on every road
with branch and balsam.

Perhaps it is already born
and I lack the grace to know it,
or it was that nameless tree
I carried like a blind son.

At times a dampness falls
around my shoulders, a soft breeze,
and I see about me
the girdle of my tree.

Perhaps its foliage
already clothes my dream
and in death I sing beneath it
without knowing.

1954

trans. Doris Dana

Alfonso Reyes

MEXICO
1889–1959

Alfonso Reyes belongs to the tradition of eminent Mexican men of letters. For many years Reyes served as Mexico's ambassador to Spain, where he became known also as an authority on the literature of the Golden Age. After his return to Mexico, Reyes was acknowledged as one of the country's leading essayists, appreciated for his elegant prose style. The author of more than a hundred books of prose, he was, as Valéry Larbaud described him, "a polyglot traveler, a militant critic, and a literary portrait painter" as well as an erudite, witty poet in free verse.

La amenaza de la flor

Flor de las adormideras:
engáñame y no me quieras.

¡Cuánto el aroma exageras,
cuánto extremas tu arrebol,
flor que te pintas ojeras
y exhalas el alma al sol!

Flor de las adormideras.

Una se te parecía
en el rubor con que engañas,
y también porque tenía
como tú negras pestañas.

The Menace of the Flower

Flower of drowsiness,
lull me but love me not.

How you profuse your perfume,
how overdo your rouge,
flower who kohl your lids
and exhale your soul in the sun!

Flower of drowsiness.

There is one resembles you
in your deceiving blush,
and too because she has
black eyelashes like you.

Flor de las adormideras.

Una se te parecía...
(Y tiemblo sólo de ver
tu mano puesta en la mía:
tiemblo no amanezca un día
en que te vuelvas mujer.)

1917

Apenas

A veces, hecho de nada,
sube un efluvio del suelo.
De repente, a la callada,
suspira de aroma el cedro.

Como somos la delgada
disolución de un secreto,
a poco que cede el alma
desborda la fuente un sueño.

¡Mísera cosa la vaga
razón cuando, en el silencio,
una como resolana
me baja, de tu recuerdo!

1927

Yerbas del tarahumara

Han bajado los indios tarahumaras,
que es señal de mal año
y de cosecha pobre en la montaña.

Desnudos y curtidos,
duros en la lustrosa piel manchada,
denegridos de viento y sol, animan
las calles de Chihuahua,
lentos y recelosos,
con todos los resortes del miedo contraídos,
como panteras mansas.

Desnudos y curtidos,
bravos habitadores de la nieve
—como hablan de tú—
contestan siempre así la pregunta obligada:
—"Y tú ¿no tienes frío en la cara?"

Mal año en la montaña,
cuando el grave deshielo de las cumbres

Flower of drowsiness.

There is one resembles you...

(And I tremble alone to see
your hand in mine,
tremble lest you turn
into a woman one day!)

trans. Samuel Beckett

Scarcely...

Sometimes an effluence rises,
made of nothing, from the ground.
Suddenly, hiddenly,
a cedar sighs its scent.

We who are a secret's
tenuous dissolution,
our soul no sooner yields
than dream wells over.

What a poor thing the wandering
reason, when in the still,
sunlight seems to fall
upon me from your memory!

trans. Samuel Beckett

Tarahumara Herbs

The Tarahumara Indians have come down,
sign of a bad year
and a poor harvest in the mountains.

Naked and tanned,
hard in their daubed lustrous skins,
blackened with wind and sun, they enliven
the streets of Chihuahua,
slow and suspicious,
all the springs of fear coiled,
like meek panthers.

Naked and tanned,
wild denizens of the snow,
they—for they thee and thou—
always answer thus the inevitable question:
"And is thy face not cold?"

A bad year in the mountains
when the heavy thaw of the peaks

escurre hasta los pueblos la manada
de animales humanos con el hato a la espalda.

La gente, al verlos, gusta
aquella desazón tan generosa
de otra belleza que la acostumbrada.

Los hicieron católicos
los misioneros de la Nueva España
—esos corderos de corazón de león.
Y, sin pan y sin vino,
ellos celebran la función cristiana
con su cerveza-chicha y su pinole,
que es un polvo de todos los sabores.

Beben tesgüino de maíz y peyote,
yerba de los portentos,
sinfonía lograda
que convierte los ruidos en colores;
y larga borrachera metafísica
los compensa de andar sobre la tierra,
que es, al fin y a la postre,
la dolencia común de las razas de hombres.
Campeones del Maratón del mundo,
nutridos en la carne ácida del venado,
llegarán los primeros con el triunfo
el día que saltemos la muralla
de los cinco sentidos.

A veces, traen oro de sus ocultas minas,
y todo el día rompen los terrones,
sentados en la calle,
entre la envidia culta de los blancos.
Hoy sólo traen yerbas en el hato,
las yerbas de salud que cambian por centavos:
yerbaniz, limoncillo, simonillo,
que alivian las difíciles entrañas,
junto con la orejuela de ratón
para el mal que la gente llama "bilis";
la yerba del venado, el chuchupaste
y la yerba del indio, que restauran la sangre;
el pasto de ocotillo de los golpes contusos,
contrayerba para las fiebres pantanosas,
la yerba de la víbora que cura los resfríos;
collares de semillas de ojo de venado,
tan eficaces para el sortilegio;
y la sangre de grado, que aprieta las encías
y agarra en la raíz los dientes flojos.

(Nuestro Francisco Hernández
—el Plinio Mexicano de los Mil y Quinientos—
logró hasta mil doscientas plantas mágicas

drains down to the villages the drove
of human beasts, their bundles on their backs.

The people, seeing them, experience
that so magnanimous antipathy
for beauty unlike that to which they are used.

Into Catholics
by the New Spain missionaries they were turned
—these lion-hearted lambs.
And, without bread or wine,
they celebrate the Christian ceremony
with their chicha beer and their pinole
which is a powder of universal flavour.

They drink spirits of maize and peyote,
herb of portents,
symphony of positive esthetics
whereby into colours forms are changed;
and ample metaphysical ebriety
consoles them for their having to tread the earth,
which is, all said and done,
the common affliction of all humankind.
The finest Marathon runners in the world,
nourished on the bitter flesh of deer,
they will be first with the triumphant news
the day we leap the wall
of the five senses.

Sometimes they bring gold from their hidden mines
and all the livelong day they break the lumps,
squatting in the street,
exposed to the urbane envy of the whites.
Today they bring only herbs in their bundles,
herbs of healing they trade for a few nickels:
mint and cuscus and birthroot
that relieve unruly innards,
not to mention mouse-ear
for the evil known as "bile";
sumac and chuchupaste and hellebore
that restore the blood;
pinesap for contusions
and the herb that counters marsh fevers,
and viper's grass that is a cure for colds;
canna seeds strung in necklaces,
so efficacious in the case of spells;
and dragon's blood that tightens the gums
and binds fast the roots of loose teeth.

(Our Francisco Hernández
—the Mexican Pliny of the Cinquecento—
acquired no fewer than one thousand two hundred

de la farmacopea de los indios.
Sin ser un gran botánico,
don Felipe Segundo
supo gastar setenta mil ducados,
¡para que luego aquel herbario único
se perdiera en la incuria y en el polvo!
Porque el padre Moxó nos asegura
que no fué culpa del incendio
que en el siglo décimo séptimo
aconteció en el Escorial.)

Con la paciencia muda de la hormiga,
los indios van juntando sobre el suelo
la yerbecita en haces
—perfectos en su ciencia natural.

1934

Sol de Monterrey

No cabe duda: de niño,
a mí me seguía el sol.
Andaba detrás de mí
como perrito faldero;
    despeinado y dulce,
    claro y amarillo:
    ese sol con sueno
    que sigue a los niños.

Saltaba de patio en patio,
se revolcaba en mi alcoba.
Aun creo que algunas veces
lo espantaban con la escoba.
Y a la mañana siguiente,
ya estaba otra vez conmigo,
    despeinado y dulce,
    claro y amarillo:
    ese sol con sueño
    que sigue a los niños.

    (El fuego de mayo
    me armó caballero:
    yo era el Niño Andante,
    y el sol, mi escudero.)

Todo el cielo era de añil;
toda la casa, de oro.
¡Cuánto sol se me metía
por los ojos!
Mar adentro de la frente,
adonde quiera que voy,

magic plants of the Indian pharmacopoeia.
Don Philip the Second,
though not a great botanist,
contrived to spend twenty thousand ducats
in order that this unique herbarium
might disappear beneath neglect and dust!
For we possess the Reverend Father Moxó's
assurance that this was not due to the fire
that in the seventeenth century occurred
in the Palace of the Escorial.)

With the silent patience of the ant
the Indians go gathering their herbs
in heaps upon the ground—
perfect in their natural science.

trans. Samuel Beckett

Monterrey Sun

No doubt: the sun
dogged me when a child.
It followed at my heels
like a Pekinese;
    dishevely and soft,
    luminous and gold:
    the sun that sleepy dogs
    the footsteps of the child.

It frisked from court to court,
in my bedroom weltered.
I even think they sometimes
shooed it with a broom.
And next morning there
it was with me again,
    dishevely and soft,
    luminous and gold,
    the sun that sleepy dogs
    the footsteps of the child.

    (I was dubbed a knight
    by the fire of May:
    I was the Child-Errant
    and the sun my squire.)

Indigo all the sky,
all the house of gold.
How it poured into me,
the sun, through my eyes!
A sea inside my skull,
go where I may,

aunque haya nubes cerradas,
¡oh, cuánto me pesa el sol!
¡oh, cuánto me duele, adentro,
esa cisterna de sol
que viaja conmigo!

Yo no conocí en mi infancia
sombra, sino resolana.—
Cada ventana era sol,
cada cuarto era ventanas.
Los corredores tendían
arcos de luz por la casa.
En los árboles ardían
las ascuas de las naranjas,
y la huerta en lumbre viva
se doraba.

Los pavos reales eran
parientes del sol. La garza
empezaba a llamear
a cada paso que daba.

Y a mí el sol me desvestía
para pegarse conmigo,
   despeinado y dulce,
   claro y amarillo:
   ese sol con sueño
   que sigue a los niños.

Cuando salí de mi casa
con mi bastón y mi hato,
le dije a mi corazón:
—¡Ya llevas sol para rato!
Es tesoro—y no se acaba:
no se me acaba—y lo gasto.
Traigo tanto sol adentro
que ya tanto sol me cansa.—
Yo no conocí en mi infancia
sombra, sino resolana.

1936

and though the clouds be drawn,
oh what weight of sun
upon me, oh what hurt
within me of that cistern
of sun that journeys with me!

No shadow in my childhood
but was red with sun.

Every window was sun,
windows every room.
The corridors bent bows
of sun through the house.
On the trees the coals
of the oranges burned redhot,
and in the burning light
the orchard turned to gold.

The royal peacocks were
kinsmen of the sun.
The heron at every step
it took went aflame.

And me the sun stripped bare
the fiercer to cleave to me,
   dishevely and soft,
   luminous and gold,
   the sun that sleepy dogs
   the footsteps of the child.

When I with my stick
and bundle went from home,
to my heart I said:
Now bear the sun awhile!
It is a hoard—unending,
unending—that I squander.
I bear within me so
much sun that so much sun
already wearies me.

No shadow in my childhood
but was red with sun.

trans. Samuel Beckett

Oswald de Andrade

BRAZIL
1890–1954

The wit and the linguistic play of José Oswald de Souza Andrade's poems and manifesto-poems occasionally threaten to obscure their pointed satire. Andrade's anarchic restlessness accounts for much of the influence his poems—and his example—had on the Brazilian Modernist movement.

Born and educated in São Paulo, in 1912 Andrade traveled to Italy, where he met the Brazilian sculptor Vítor Brécheret and came into contact with Italian Futurist ideals through Filippo Tommaso Marinetti. Andrade responded especially to the Futurists' ambition to dismantle the forms and influence of the past and to forge a cosmopolitan culture from the lyrical scraps of history. After his return to Brazil, Andrade worked as a journalist. In 1920 his essay "O meu poeta futurista" ("My Futurist Poet") rang like a Modernist manifesto in the *Jornal do Comércio*.

In that essay, which introduced a poem by the young Mário de Andrade (no relation) as a model of the art it advocated, Oswald de Andrade called for a modern skepticism, for an iconoclastic liberation of visual and verbal arts, and—in poetry—for a free-verse informality and a new local diction distinguished both from Continental Portuguese and from Symbolist/Parnassian academic vagueness. The ambition of this mode of synthetic Modernism was, as Mário de Andrade would argue later, "to make Brazilians 100% Brazilian, to nationalize a nation that is as yet so lacking in national characteristics." (Despite Oswald's appropriation of the vocabulary of the international avant-garde, these nationalistic and indigenist impulses were part of what distinguished Brazilian Modernism from Italian Futurism.) With Mário de Andrade and other *paulistas*, Oswald organized the famous Semana de Arte Moderna (Week of Modern Art) in São Paulo, February 1922, on the hundredth anniversary of Brazil's independence. The week of the new independence featured a series of concerts (music by Heitor Villa-Lobos and Ernani Braga), exhibitions (paintings by Cubist artists), readings (poems by Manuel Bandeira and Mário de Andrade, fiction by Oswald de Andrade), and manifesto lectures. The critic Graça Aranha announced "the emotional birth of art in Brazil itself." The popular audience reportedly booed at several of these events, but the terms had been set for a radically new configuration of literary values.

In manifestoes for movements which he called "Brazilwood" and "Cannibalism," Oswald laid perceptions across a two-dimensional grid—the page—implicitly arguing for (as Mike Gonzalez and David Treece explain) a historically dialectical essence of Brazilian identity. In his "Brazilwood" manifestoes, taking Brazilwood (then the primary export of Brazil to First World nations) as his defining metaphor, Oswald showed historical Brazilian poetry to be the "product" of a Brazilian subconscious mind, ironically both sophisticated by European standards (viz., those of Blaise Cendrars) and yet an agent of "savage thinking." Through this collage, the Brazilian Modernist impulse could be enacted. In his poems, essays, and, later, dramas Oswald's constant resynthesis of the fundamental elements of Modernism helped the movement to evolve from these first rebellious and iconoclastic manifestations. Oswald made possible the larger conceptual change toward Tropicalism and Cannibalism (see Raul Bopp), toward a less sentimental use of models from the Amazon Indians and other indigenous peoples, and eventually toward Concretism, praxis, and the "process poem." Oswald's political conscience, however, led him to oppose some subsequent developments in Brazilian post-Modernism and to maintain, at times with a combative insistence, the primacy of traditional Modernist values of experimentation and verbal formalism.

In the 1930s Oswald turned to overt social criticism and expressionistic theater. Although in 1945 he officially repudiated his commitment to international Marxism, his influence in the mode of "satiric criticism" is one of his most lasting contributions to Brazilian letters. Underappreciated at the time of his death, Oswald de Andrade's presence has recently been felt more strongly in Brazilian intellectual life because of the influence of the Concretists, neo-Concretists, and semioticians and because of a resurgence of Brazilian theater and film.

falação

O Cabralismo. A civilização dos donatários. A Querência e a Exportação.
O Carnaval. O Sertão e a Favela. Pau-Brasil. Bárbaro e nosso.

A formação étnica rica. A riqueza vegetal. O minério. A cozinha. O vatapá, o ouro e a dança.

Tôda a história de Penetração e a história comercial da América. Pau-Brasil.

Contra a fatalidade do primeiro branco aportado e dominando diplomàticamente as selvas selvagens. Citando Virgílio para os tupiniquins. O bacharel.

País de dores anônimas. De doutôres anônimos. Sociedade de náufragos eruditos.
Donde a nunca exportação de poesia. A poesia emaranhada na cultura. Nos cipós das metrificações.

Século vinte. Um estouro nos aprendimentos. Os homens que sabiam tudo se deformaram como babéis de borracha. Rebentaram de enciclopedismo.

A poesia para os poetas. Alegria da ignorância que descobre. Pedr'Álvares.

Uma sugestão de Blaise Cendrars: —Tendes as locomotivas cheias, ides partir. Um negro gira a manivela do desvio rotativo em que estais. O menor descuido vos fará partir na direção oposta ao vosso destino.

Contra o gabinetismo, a palmilhação dos climas.

A língua sem arcaísmos. Sem erudição. Natural e neológica. A contribuição milionária de todos os erros.

Passara-se do naturalismo à pirogravura doméstica e à kodak excursionista.

Todas as meninas prendadas. Virtuoses de piano de manivela.
As procissões saíram do bôjo das fábricas.
Foi preciso desmanchar. A deformação através do impressionismo e do símbolo. O lirismo em fôlha. A apresentação dos materiais.

A coincidência da primeira construção brasileira no movimento de reconstrução geral. Poesia Pau-Brasil.

Babbling

Cabralism. The civiliation of the donées. The Willing and the Exportation.
The Carnival. The Hinterland and the Slum. Brazilwood. Barbaric and ours.

The rich ethnic formation. The richness of the vegetation. The minerals. The food. The vatapá, the gold and the dance.

All the history of Penetration and the commercial history of America. Brazilwood.

Against the fatality of the first white man who entered the port and diplomatically dominated the savage jungles. Citing Virgil to the Tupíníquím people. The bachelor.

Country of anonymous pains. Of anonymous doctors. Society of erudite shipwrecked people.
From where the never exportation of poetry. The poetry tangled in the culture. In the lianas of the versifications.

Twentieth century. A burst in the learning. The men who knew everything were deformed like rubber babels. They burst free of encyclopaedism.

The poetry for the poets. Happiness of the ignorance that discovers. Pedr'Álvares.

A suggestion from Blaise Cendrars: —You have the locomotives full, you leave. A black man turns the handle of the rotary where you are. The smallest carelessness will make you leave, in a direction opposite to that of your destiny.

Against cabinetism, the tramping of the climates.

The language without archaisms. Without erudition. Natural and neo-logic. The millionaire contribution of all of the mistakes.

From naturalism one had passed to domestic pyrography and to the excursionist kodak.

All the girls talented. Virtuosos of the player piano.
The processions went out of the bulge of the factories.
It was necessary to un-do. Deformation through impressionism and the symbol. The lyricism brand-new. The presentation of the materials.

Contra a argúcia naturalista, a síntese. Contra a cópia, a invenção e a surprêsa.

Uma perspectiva de outra ordem que a visual. O correspondente ao milagre físico em arte. Estrêlas fechadas nos negativos fotográficos.

E a sábia preguiça solar. A reza. A energia silenciosa. A hospitalidade.

Bárbaros, pitorescos e crédulos. Pau-Brasil. A floresta e a escola. A cozinha, o minério e a dança. A vegetação. Pau-Brasil.

1925/1926

The coincidence of the first Brazilian construction in the movement of general reconstruction. Brazilwood poetry.

Against the naturalistic subtlety, the synthesis. Against the copy, the invention and the surprise.

A perspective of an order other than visual. The correspondent to the physical miracle in art. Closed stars in the photographic negatives.

And the wise solar laziness. The prayer. The silent energy. The hospitality.

Barbaric, picturesque and credulous. Brazilwood. The forest and the school. The food, the minerals and the dance. The vegetation. Brazilwood.

trans. Flavia Vidal

erro de português

Quando o português chegou
Debaixo duma bruta chuva
Vestiu o índio
Que pena!
Fosse uma manhã de sol
O índio tinha despido
O português

1926

Portuguese Mistake

When the Portuguese arrived
It was raining like crazy
He dressed the Indian in clothes
What a shame!
If only it had been a sunny day
The Indian would have undressed
The Portuguese.

trans. Flavia Vidal

fronteira

Quero estudar filosofia em Paris
Não pode ser
Só se o compadre Antunes te mandar
Mas a vida mesmo assim é boa
O compadre Antunes faliu
a vida é boa
O compadre Antunes morreu
Velho sino mudo
que paras o teu ritmo no pânico
e aceleras os teus passos
na sedição

A semente frutifica sem aviso
o mascarado encherá de guizos tua mesa farta
Não pode ser
Mesmo assim a vida é boa

Frontier

I want to study philosophy in Paris
That can't happen
Only if your godfather Antunes pays your way
But life is good anyhow
Godfather Antunes went bankrupt
Life is good
Godfather Antunes died
Mute old church-bell,
you slow your rhythm in a panic
and speed up your ringing
in a rebellion

The seed sprouts with no announcement
The man in the mask will fill your table with joys
That's not going to happen
But life is good anyhow

Poeta nasceste compromissado com a liberdade
e inutilmente conheceste a Estrela do Pastor

1945

Poet, you were born destined for liberty;
what a waste to meet the Shepherds' Christmas Star.

trans. Flavia Vidal

o hierofante

Não há possibilidade de viver
com essa gente
nem com nenhuma gente
A desconfiança te cercará como um escudo
Pinta o escaravelho
de vermelho
e tinge os rumos da madrugada
Virão de longe as multidões suspirosas
escutar o bezerro plangente

1945

Hierofant

It's impossible to live
with these people
or with anybody at all
Suspicion surrounds you like an escutcheon
Dye the scarab
red
and paint the dawn's directions
Sighing multitudes will come from far away
to attend the plangent calf

trans. Flavia Vidal

buena-dicha

Há quatrocentos anos
desceste no trópico de Capricórnio
da tábua carbunculosa
das velas
que conduziam pelas negras estrelas
o pálido escaravelho
das marés
Cada degredado era um rei
magro insone incolor
como o barro

Criarás o mundo
dos risos alvares
das colas infecundas
dos risos alvares
Semearás ódios insubmissos lado a lado
de ódios frustrados
Evocarás a humanidade, o orvalho e a rima
Nas lianas constituirás o palácio termita
e da terra cercada de cerros
balida de sinceros cincerros
na lua subirás
como a esperança

O espaço é um cativeiro

1945

Good Luck

Four hundred years ago
you landed in the Tropic of Capricorn
on the carbuncular plank
of ships
steered by dark stars
the pale beetle
of the seas
Every exile was a king
skinny, insomniac, colorless
as clay

You will create a world
from coarse laughter
from sterile glues
from coarse laughter
You will plant insurgent hatreds side by side
frustrated hatreds
You will evoke humanity, mist and frost
Among the lianas you will build a palace of termites
and from a tower circled by hills
bleating with sincere cincerre-bells
you will rise toward the moon
like hope

Space is a prison

trans. Flavia Vidal

<table>
<tr><td>plebiscito</td><td>Election</td></tr>
</table>

plebiscito	*Election*
Venceu o sistema de Babilônia	Who won: the Babylonian system
e o garção de costeleta	and the waiter with the side-burns
1945	*trans. Flavia Vidal*

César Vallejo

PERU/FRANCE
1892?–1938

Born the last of eleven children to a mestizo family, César Abraham Vallejo was raised in the rural highlands of Peru; he published his first book, *Los heraldos negros* (*The Black Heralds*), in 1918. Arrested on specious charges in Lima in 1921, Vallejo spent three months in prison; during that time, he drafted many of the poems of his second book, *Trilce* (1922). The latter book's rebellious shattering of conventional syntax and logic, its neologisms and bold experimentation with themes of temporality, make it one of the major texts of Latin American Vanguardist writing. Vallejo left his homeland at age thirty-one. He never returned, and he never published another book of poems. During his last fourteen years, Vallejo traveled restlessly, motivated by his passion for the ideals of the Russian Revolution and by the fate of the Republic in the Spanish Civil War. Expelled from France as a communist, he traveled to Spain, where he worked with Neruda and others to raise support for the Republican cause. Vallejo spent his last three years in Paris, often impoverished and ill.

After the luminous psychological intensity of his first book and the Surrealist Vanguardism of his second, Vallejo aspired to a more inclusive, passionately sympathetic form. The poems he left in manuscript, including the texts of the *Poemas humanos* (*Human Poems*, 1939 posthum.) and of a book addressed to the partisans of Spain, *España, aparta de mí este cáliz* (*Spain, Take This Cup from Me*, 1940 posthum.), were edited and published by his widow. Those late poems, rich in metaphor and eloquent in their associative meditations, track the evolution of a consciousness so committed to compassionate participation in the agonies of humankind that Vallejo seems to make himself a pure voice of suffering and grace. During his last years Vallejo also concentrated on fiction, following his proletarian protest novel, *Tungsteno* (*Tungsten*, 1931).

Vallejo's is the most eloquently lyrical, personally rich voice in Latin American poetry. His poems are intense in personal emotion, yet articulate about the dynamics of the Latin American mind; unique in form and tone, yet echoing the musical and intellectual sources of his Andean heritage (its songs, history, folklore); aware of the absurdity and incommunicability of modern life, yet devoted to poetry's power to redeem time; deeply solitary, yet hopeful about the possibilities of meaningful collective action in the face of injustice. Vallejo's experiences in Spain, his registry of sensual and ideal love, made him a universal poet. In one of his elegies for his friend, Pablo Neruda emphasized the force of Vallejo's fierce internalization of Spain's suffering. Neruda's metaphors also measure the distance between his own political commitments and Vallejo's: "Spain was chewing at your soul. That soul so whittled away by your own spirit, so stripped, so wounded by your own ascetic need. Spain was the daily drill into your immense virtue." If Neruda is the public conscience of Latin American poetry, the poet of exuberant partisan commitment, Vallejo is its private and soulful conscience, "the greatest universal poet"—writes Thomas Merton—"since Dante."

Los heraldos negros

Hay golpes en la vida, tan fuertes... ¡Yo no sé!
Golpes como del odio de Dios; como si ante ellos,
la resaca de todo lo sufrido
se empozara en el alma... ¡Yo no sé!

Son pocos, pero son... Abren zanjas oscuras
en el rostro más fiero y en el lomo más fuerte.
Serán tal vez los potros de bárbaros atilas;
o los heraldos negros que nos manda la Muerte.

Son las caídas hondas de los Cristos del alma,
de alguna fe adorable que el Destino blasfema.
Esos golpes sangrientos son las crepitaciones
de algún pan que en la puerta del horno se nos quema.

¡Y el hombre... Pobre... pobre! Vuelve los ojos, como
cuando por sobre el hombro nos llama una palmada;
vuelve los ojos locos, y todo lo vivido
se empoza, como un charco de culpa, en la mirada.

Hay golpes en la vida, tan fuertes... ¡Yo no sé!

1918

The Black Messengers

There are some blows in life so hard... I don't know!
Blows that seem to come from God's hatred; as if before
    them,
the backwash of all suffering
were welling into my soul... I don't know!

They are few, but they are... They open dark furrows
in the toughest faces and the strongest backs.
Perhaps they are the colts of barbarous attilas;
or the black messengers sent us by Death.

They are the grave downfall of the soul's Christs,
of some adorable faith that Destiny curses.
Those bloody blows are the crackling
of bread heating for us at the oven door.

And man... Poor... poor man! He turns his head
the way we do when a hand is clapped on our shoulder;
he turns his crazed eyes, and all living
is damned up in that glance, like a puddle of guilt.

There are some blows in life so hard... I don't know!

trans. Rachel Benson

Heces

Esta tarde llueve como nunca; y no
tengo ganas de vivir, corazón.

Esta tarde es dulce. Por qué no ha de ser?
Viste gracia y pena; viste de mujer.

Esta tarde en Lima llueve. Y yo recuerdo
las cavernas crueles de mi ingratitud;
mi bloque de hielo sobre su amapola,
más fuerte que su "No seas así!"

Mis violentas flores negras; y la bárbara
y enorme pedrada; y el trecho glacial.
Y pondrá el silencio de su dignidad
con óleos quemantes el punto final.

Por eso esta tarde, como nunca, voy
con este buho, con este corazón.

Y otras pasan; y viéndome tan triste,
toman un poquito de ti
en la abrupta arruga de mi hondo dolor.

Down to the Dregs

This afternoon it rains as never before; and I
don't feel like staying alive, heart.

The afternoon is pleasant. Why shouldn't it be?
It is wearing grace and pain; it is dressed like a woman.

This afternoon in Lima it is raining. And I remember
the cruel caverns of my ingratitude;
my block of ice laid on her poppy,
stronger than her crying "Don't be this way!"

My violent black flowers; and the barbarous
and staggering blow with a stone; and the glacial pause.
And the silence of her dignity will pour
scalding oils on the end of the sentence.

Therefore, this afternoon, as never before, I walk
with this owl, with this heart.

And other women go past; and seeing me sullen,
they sip a little of you
in the abrupt furrow of my deep grief.

Esta tarde llueve, llueve mucho. Y no
tengo ganas de vivir, corazón!

1918

Ágape

Hoy no ha venido nadie a preguntar;
ni me han pedido en esta tarde nada.

No he visto ni una flor de cementerio
en tan alegre procesión de luces.
Perdóname, Señor: qué poco he muerto!

En esta tarde todos, todos pasan
sin preguntarme ne pedirme nada.

Y no sé qué se olvidan y se queda
mal en mis manos, como cosa ajena.

He salido a la puerta,
y me da ganas de gritar a todos:
Si echan de menos algo, aquí se queda!

Porque en todas las tardes de esta vida,
yo no sé con qué puertas dan a un rostro,
y algo ajeno se toma el alma mía.

Hoy no ha venido nadie;
y hoy he muerto qué poco en esta tarde!

1918

El pan nuestro

(para Alejandro Gamboa)

Se bebe el desayuno... Húmeda tierra
de cimenterio huele a sangre amada.
Ciudad de invierno... La mordaz cruzada
de una carreta que arrastrar parece
una emoción de ayuno encandenada!

Se quisiera tocar todas las puertas,
y preguntar por no sé quién; y luego
ver a los pobres, y, llorando quedos,
dar pedacitos de pan fresco a todos.
Y saquear a los ricos sus viñedos
con las dos manos santas
que a un golpe de luz
volaron desclavadas de la Cruz!

This afternoon it rains, rains endlessly. And I
don't feel like staying alive, heart.

trans. James Wright

Agape

Today no-one has come to inquire;
they haven't this evening asked anything of me.

I haven't seen a single cemetery flower
in such a gay procession of lights.
Forgive me, Lord; how little I have died.

On this evening everyone, everyone goes by
not inquiring or asking anything of me.

And I don't know what they forget and is left
wrong in my hands, like someone else's thing.

I've gone out to the door
and would shout to them all:
If you miss anything, it's here!

Because on all the evenings of this life,
I don't know what doors get slammed in my face,
and something alien seizes my soul.

Today no-one has come by:
and today I have died how little on this evening.

trans. Ed Dorn and Gordon Brotherston

Our Daily Bread

(for Alejandro Gamboa)

Breakfast is drunk down... Damp earth
of the cemetery gives off the fragrance of the precious
    blood.
City of winter... the mordant crusade
of a cart that seems to pull behind it
an emotion of fasting that cannot get free!

I wish I could beat on all the doors,
and ask for somebody; and then
look at the poor, and, while they wept softly,
give bits of fresh bread to them.
And plunder the rich of their vineyards
with those two blessed hands
which blasted the nails with one blow of light,
and flew away from the Cross!

Pestaña matinal, no os levantéis!
¡El pan nuestro de cada día dánoslo,
Señor...!

Todos mis huesos son ajenos;
yo tal vez los robé!
Yo vine a darme lo que acaso estuvo
asignado para otro;
y pienso que, si no hubiera nacido,
otro pobre tomara este café!
Yo soy un mal ladrón... A dónde iré!

Y en esta hora fría, en que la tierra
trasciende a polvo humano y es tan triste,
quisiera yo tocar todas las puertas,
y suplicar a no sé quién, perdón
y hacerle pedacitos de pan fresco
aquí, en el horno de mi corazón...!

                                        1918

Eyelash of morning, you cannot lift yourselves!
Give us our daily bread,
Lord...!

Every bone in me belongs to others;
and maybe I robbed them.
I came to take something for myself that maybe
was meant for some other man;
and I start thinking that, if I had not been born,
another poor man could have drunk this coffee.
I feel like a dirty thief... Where will I end?

And in this frigid hour, when the earth
has the odor of human dust and is so sad,
I wish I could beat on all the doors
and beg pardon from someone,
and make bits of fresh bread for him
here, in the oven of my heart...!

                                        trans. James Wright

A mi hermano Miguel

in memoriam

Hermano, hoy estoy en el poyo de la casa,
donde nos haces una falta sin fondo!
Me acuerdo que jugábamos esta hora, y que mamá
nos acariciaba: "Pero, hijos..."

Ahora yo me escondo,
como antes, todas estas oraciones
vespertinas, y espero que tú no des conmigo.
Por la sala, el zaguán, los corredores.
Después, te ocultas tú, y yo no doy contigo.
Me acuerdo que nos hacíamos llorar,
hermano, en aquel juego.

Miguel, tú te escondiste
una noche de agosto, al alborear;
pero, en ves de ocultarte riendo, estabas triste.
Y tu gemelo corazón de esas tardes
extintas se ha aburrido de no encontrarte. Y ya
cae sombra en el alma.

Oye hermano, no tardes
en salir. Bueno? Puede inquietarse mamá.

                                        1918

To My Brother Miguel

in memoriam

Brother, today I sit on the brick bench outside the house,
where you make a bottomless emptiness.
I remember we used to play at this hour of the day, and
        mama
would calm us: "There now, boys..."

Now I go hide
as before, from all these evening
prayers, and I hope that you will not find me.
In the parlor, the entrance hall, the corridors.
Later, you hide, and I do not find you.
I remember we made each other cry,
brother, in that game.

Miguel, you hid yourself
one night in August, nearly at daybreak,
but instead of laughing when you hid, you were sad.
And your other heart of those dead afternoons
is tired of looking and not finding you. And now
shadows fall on the soul.

Listen, brother, don't be too late
coming out. All right? Mama might worry.

                                        trans. John Knoepfle and James Wright

"Pienso en tu sexo"

Pienso en tu sexo.
Simplificado el corazón, pienso en tu sexo,
ante el hijar maduro del día.
Palpo el botón de dicha, está en sazón.
Y muere un sentimiento antiguo
degenerado en seso.

Pienso en tu sexo, surco más prolífico
y armonioso que el vientre de la Sombra,
aunque la Muerte concibe y pare
de Dios mismo.
Oh Conciencia,
pienso, sí, en el bruto libre
que goza donde quiere, donde puede.

Oh, escándalo de miel de los crepúsculos.
Oh estruendo mudo.

¡Odumodneurtse!

1922

"I'm thinking of your sex"

I'm thinking of your sex.
My heart simplified, I'm thinking of your sex,
faced with the ripe flank of the day.
I stroke your bud of pleasure, it's in season.
And an old awareness dies,
degenerated in brains.

I'm thinking of your sex, furrow more prolific
and harmonious than the womb of Darkness,
though Death conceives and gives birth
from God himself.
Oh Conscience,
I'm thinking, yes, of the free beast
rutting wherever he pleases, wherever he can.

Oh, honeyed scandal of twilights.
Oh mute outcry.

Odumodneurtse!

trans. Sandy McKinney

"Fué Domingo en las claras orejas de mi burro"

Fué Domingo en las claras orejas de mi burro,
de mi burro peruano en el Perú (Perdonen la tristeza)
Mas hoy ya son las once en mi experiencia personal,
experiencia de un solo ojo, clavado en pleno pecho,
de una sola burrada, clavada en pleno pecho,
de una sola hecatombe, clavada en pleno pecho.

Tal de mi tierra veo los cerros retratados,
ricos en burros, hijos de burros, padres hoy de vista,
que tornan ya pintados de creencias,
cerros horizontales de mis penas.

En su estatua, de espalda,
Voltaire cruza su capa y mira el zócalo,
pero en sol me penetra y espanta de mis dientes incisivos
un número crecido de cuerpos inorgánicos.

Y entonces sueño en una piedra
verduzca, diecisiete,
peñasco numeral que he olvidado,
sonido de años en el rumor de aguja de mi brazo,
lluvia y sol en Europa, y ¡cómo toso! ¡cómo vivo!
¡cómo me duele el pelo al columbrar los siglos semanales!
y cómo, por recodo, mi ciclo microbiano,
quiero decir mi trémulo, patriótico peinado.

1923–1937/1939

"It was Sunday in the fair ears of my burro"

It was Sunday in the fair ears of my burro,
my Peruvian burro in Peru (Pardon my sadness)
But already it's eleven o'clock in my personal experience,
experience of a single eye nailed right in the chest,
of a single asininity nailed right in the chest,
of a single hecatomb nailed right in the chest.

So from my country I see the portrayed hills
rich in burros, sons of burros, parents today by sight
altering now painted with beliefs,
hills horizontal to my sorrows.

In his statue, back turned,
Voltaire closes his cape and looks at the socle,
but the sun penetrates me and frightens a grown
number of inorganic bodies from my incisors.

Then I dream on a greenish
seventeen stone,
numeral boulder I've forgotten,
sound of years in the murmur of needle of my arm,
rain and sun in Europe, and how I cough! how I live!
how my hair aches me descrying the weekly centuries!
and how, by its swerve, my microbial cycle,
I mean my tremulous patriotic hairdo.

trans. Clayton Eshleman

"Voy a hablar de la esperanza"

Yo no sufro este dolor como César Vallejo. Yo no me duelo ahora como artista, como hombre ni como simple ser vivo siquiera. Yo no sufro este dolor como católico, como mahometano ni como ateo. Hoy sufro solamente. Si no me llamase César Vallejo, también sufriría este mismo dolor. Si no fuese artista, también lo sufriría. Si no fuese católico, ateo ni mahometano, también lo sufriría. Hoy sufro desde más abajo. Hoy sufro solamente.

Me duelo ahora sin explicaciones. Mi dolor es tan hondo, que no tuvo ya causa ni carece de causa. ¿Qué sería su causa? ¿Dondé está aquello tan importante, que dejase de ser su causa? Nada es su causa; nada ha podido dejar se ser su causa. ¿A qué ha nacido este dolor, por sí mismo? Mi dolor es del viento del norte y del viento del sur, como esos huevos neutros que algunas aves raras ponen del viento. Si hubiera muerto mi novia, mi dolor sería igual. Si me hubieran cortado el cuello de raíz, mi dolor sería igual. Si la vida fuese, en fin, de otro modo, mi dolor sería igual. Hoy sufro desde más arriba. Hoy sufro solamente.

Miro el dolor del hambriento y veo que su hambre anda tan lejos de mi sufrimiento, que de quedarme ayuno hasta morir, saldría siempre de mi tumba una brizna de yerba al menos. ¡Lo mismo el enamorado! ¡Qué sangre la suya más engendrada, para la mía sin fuente ni consumo!

Yo creía hasta ahora que todas las cosas del universo eran, inevitablemente, padres o hijos. Pero he aquí que mi dolor de hoy no es padre ni es hijo. Le falta espalda para anochecer, tanto como le sobra pecho para amanecer y si lo pusiesen en la estancia oscura, no daría luz y si lo pusiesen en una estancia luminosa, no echaría sombra. Hoy sufro suceda lo que suceda. Hoy sufro solamente.

1923–1937/1939

Piedra negra sobre una piedra blanca

Me moriré en París con aguacero,
un día del cual tengo ya el recuerdo.
Me moriré en París—y no me corro—
tal vez un jueves, como es hoy, de otoño.

"I am going to talk about hope"

I do not feel this suffering as César Vallejo. I am not suffering now as a creative person, or as a man, nor even as a simple living being. I don't feel this pain as a Catholic, or as a Mohammedan, or as an atheist. Today I am simply in pain. If my name weren't César Vallejo, I'd still feel it. If I weren't an artist, I'd still feel it. If I weren't a man, or even a living being, I'd still feel it. If I weren't a Catholic, or an atheist, or a Mohammedan, I'd still feel it. Today I am in pain from further down. Today I am simply in pain.

The pain I have has no explanations. My pain is so deep that it never had a cause, and has no need of a cause. What could its cause have been? Where is that thing so important that it stopped being its cause? Its cause is nothing, and nothing could have stopped being its cause. Why has this pain been born all on its own? My pain comes from the north wind and from the south wind, like those hermaphrodite eggs that some rare birds lay conceived of the wind. If my bride were dead, my suffering would still be the same. If they had slashed my throat all the way through, my suffering would still be the same. If life, in other words, were different, my suffering would still be the same. Today I'm in pain from higher up. Today I am simply in pain.

I look at the hungry man's pain, and I see that his hunger walks somewhere so far from my pain that if I fasted until death, one blade of grass at least would always sprout from my grave. And the same with the lover! His blood is too fertile for mine, which has no source and no one to drink it.

I always believed up till now that all things in the world had to be either fathers or sons. But here is my pain that is neither a father nor a son. It hasn't any back to get dark, and it has too bold a front for dawning, and if they put it into some dark room, it wouldn't give light, and if they put it into some brightly lit room, it wouldn't cast a shadow. Today I am in pain, no matter what happens. Today I am simply in pain.

trans. Robert Bly

Black Stone Lying on a White Stone

I will die in Paris, on a rainy day,
on some day I can already remember.
I will die in Paris—and I don't step aside—
perhaps on a Thursday, as today is Thursday, in autumn.

Jueves será, porque hoy, jueves, que proso
estos versos, los húmeros me he puesto
a la mala y, jamás como hoy, me he vuelto,
con todo mi camino, a verme solo.

César Vallejo ha muerto, le pegaban
todos sin que él les haga nada;
le daban duro con un palo y duro

también con una soga; son testigos
los días jueves y los huesos húmeros,
la soledad, la lluvia, los caminos...

1923–1937/1939

It will be a Thursday, because today, Thursday,
    setting down
these lines, I have put my upper arm bones on
wrong, and never so much as today have I found myself
with all the road ahead of me, alone.

César Vallejo is dead. Everyone beat him,
although he never does anything to them;
they beat him hard with a stick and hard also

with a rope. These are the witnesses;
the Thursdays, and the bones of my arms,
the solitude, and the rain, and the roads...

trans. Robert Bly and John Knoepfle

"Hoy me gusta la vida mucho menos"

Hoy me gusta la vida mucho menos,
pero siempre me gusta vivir: ya lo decía.
Casi toqué la parte de mi todo y me contuve
con un tiro en la lengua detrás de mi palabra.

Hoy me palpo el mentón en retirada
y en estos momentáneos pantalones yo me digo:
¡Tánta vida y jamás!
¡Tántos años y siempre mis semanas!...
Mis padres enterrados con su piedra
y su triste estirón que no ha acabado;
de cuerpo entero hermanos, mis hermanos,
y, en fin, mi sér parado y en chaleco.

Me gusta la vida enormemente
pero, desde luego,
con mi muerte querida y mi café
y viendo los castaños frondosos de París
y diciendo:
Es un ojo éste, aquél; una frente ésta, aquella...
    Y repitiendo:
¡Tánta vida y jamás me falla la tonada!
¡Tántos años y siempre, siempre, siempre!

Dije chaleco, dije
todo, parte, ansia, dije casi por no llorar.
Que es verdad que sufrí en aquel hospital que queda al lado
y está bien y está mal haber mirado
de abajo para arriba mi organismo.

Me gustará vivir siempre, así fuese de barriga,
porque, como iba diciendo y lo repito,

"Today I like life much less"

Today I like life much less,
but still I like being alive: I knew it.
I almost touched the part of my whole and checked
myself with a shot in the tongue behind my word.

Today I touch my chin in retreat
and in these momentary trousers I tell myself
So much life and never!
So many years and always my weeks!
My parents buried with their stone
and their sad death-jerk that's not ended;
completely portrayed brothers, my brothers,
in short, my béing erect in a vest.

I like life enormously
but, after all,
with my beloved death and my coffee
and seeing the leafy chestnuts of Paris
and saying:
this is an eye, and that one; this is a forehead,
    and that one... And repeating:
So much life and the tune never fails me!
So many years and always always always!

I said vest, said
whole, part, anxiety, said almost by not weeping.
For it's true I suffered in that hospital next door
and it's good and it's bad to have watched
from below up my organism.

I'd like to live always, even flat on my belly,
because as I was saying and I say it again

¡tánta vida y jamás! ¡Y tantos años,
y siempre, mucho siempre, siempre, siempre!

1923–1937/1939

So much life and never! And so many years,
and always, much always, always always!

trans. Clayton Eshleman

Poema para ser leído y cantado

    Sé que hay una persona
que me busca en su mano, día y noche,
encontrándome, a cada minuto, en su calzado.
¿Ignora que la noche está enterrada
con espuelas detrás de la cocina?

    Sé que hay una persona compuesta de mis partes,
a la que integro cuando va mi talle
cabalgando en su exacta piedrecilla.
¿Ignora que a su cofre
no volverá moneda que salió con su retrato?

    Sé el día,
pero el sol se ma ha escapado;
sé el acto universal que hizo en su cama
con ajeno valor y esa agua tibia, cuya
superficial frecuencia es una mina.
¿Tan pequeña es, acaso, esa persona,
que hasta sus proprios pies así la pisan?

    Un gato es el lindero entre ella y yo,
al lado mismo de su tasa de agua.
La veo en las esquinas, se abre y cierra
su veste, antes palmera interrogante...
¿Qué podrá hacer sino cambiar de llanto?

Pero me busca y busca. ¡Es una historia!

7 septiembre 1937/1939

Poem to Be Read and Sung

    I know there is a person
who looks for me in her hand, day and night,
finding me, every minute, in her shoes.
Doesn't she know that the night is buried
with spurs behind the kitchen?

    I know there is a person made up of my parts,
who I make whole when my waist
goes galloping off on its exact little stone.
Doesn't she know that the coin
imprinted with her effigy will not return to her coffer?

    I know the day,
but the sun has escaped me;
I know the universal act she performed on her bed
with alien courage and that tepid water, whose
superficial frequency is a gold mine.
Is that person, perhaps, so small
that even her own feet step on her?

    A cat is the boundary between her and me,
right at the edge of her measure of water.
I see her on the corners, her clothing
opens and closes, formerly an inquiring palm tree...
What can she do but change crying?

But she looks and looks for me. What a story!

trans. Clayton Eshleman

"La cólera que quiebra al hombre en niños"

    La cólera que quiebra al hombre en niños,
que quiebra al niño, en pájaros iguales,
y al pájaro, después, en huevecillos;
la cólera del pobre
tiene un aceite contra dos vinagres.

    La cólera que al árbol quiebra en hojas,
a la hoja en botones desiguales
y al botón, en ranuras telescópicas;
la cólera del pobre
tiene dos ríos contra muchos mares.

Anger

Anger which breaks a man into children,
Which breaks the child into two equal birds,
And after that the bird into a pair of little eggs:
The poor man's anger
Has one oil against two vinegars.

Anger which breaks a tree into leaves
And the leaf into unequal buds
And the bud into telescopic grooves;
The poor man's anger
Has two rivers against many seas.

La cólera que quiebra al bien en dudas,
a la duda, en tres arcos semejantes
y al arco, luego, en tumbas imprevistas;
la cólera del pobre
tiene un acero contra dos puñales.

La cólera que quiebra el alma en cuerpos,
al cuerpo en órganos desemejantes
y al órgano, en octavos pensamientos;
la cólera del pobre
tiene un fuego central contra dos cráteres.

26 octubre 1937/1939

Anger which breaks good into doubts
And doubt into three similar arcs
And then the arc into unexpected tombs;
The poor man's anger
Has one steel against two daggers.

Anger which breaks the soul into bodies
And the body into dissimilar organs
And the organ into octave thoughts;
The poor man's anger
Has one central fire against two craters.

trans. Thomas Merton

"Un hombre pasa con un pan al hombro"

Un hombre pasa con un pan al hombro.
¿Voy a escribir, después, sobre mi doble?

Otro se sienta, ráscase, extrae un piojo de su axila,
    mátalo.
¿Con qué valor hablar del psicoanálisis?

Otro ha entrado a mi pecho con un palo en la mano.
¿Hablar luego de Sócrates al médico?

Un cojo pasa dando el brazo a un niño.
¿Voy, después, a leer a André Breton?

Otro tiembla de frío, tose, escupe sangre.
¿Cabrá aludir jamás al Yo profundo?

Otro busca en el fango huesos, cáscaras.
¿Cómo escribir, después, del infinito?

Un albañil cae de un techo, muere y ya no almuerza.
¿Innovar, luego, el tropo, la metáfora?

Un comerciante roba un gramo en el peso a un cliente.
¿Hablar, después, de cuarta dimensión?

Un banquero falsea su balance.
¿Con qué cara llorar en el teatro?

Un paria duerme con el pie a la espalda.
¿Hablar, después, a nadie de Picasso?

Alguien va en un entierro sollozando.
¿Cómo luego ingresar a la Academia?

"A man walks by with a loaf of bread on his shoulder"

A man walks by with a loaf of bread on his shoulder.
I'm going to write, after that, about my double?

Another sits, scratches, gets a louse out of his armpit,
cracks it. How dare one speak about psychoanalysis?

Another has entered my chest with a stick in his hand.
After that chat with the doctor about Socrates?

A cripple walks by arm in arm with a child.
After that I'm going to read André Breton?

Another shakes from cold, hacks, spits blood.
Is it possible to even mention the profound I?

Another searches in the mud for bones, rinds.
How write after that about the infinite?

A bricklayer falls from the roof, dies, and no longer
    eats lunch.
After that innovate the trope, the metaphor?

A merchant cheats a customer out of a gram.
After that talk about the fourth dimension?

A banker falsifies his balance.
With what face to cry in the theater?

An outcast sleeps with his foot behind his back.
After that, not talk about Picasso?

Someone goes to a burial sobbing.
How then enter the Academy?

Alguien limpia un fusil en su cocina.
¿Con qué valor hablar del más allá?

Alguien pasa contando con sus dedos.
¿Cómo hablar del no-yó sin dar un grito?

5 noviembre 1937/1939

Someone cleans a rifle in his kitchen.
How dare one speak about the beyond?

Someone walks by counting on his fingers.
How speak of the not-I without crying out?

trans. Clayton Eshleman

España, aparta de mí este cáliz

IX. PEQUEÑO RESPONSO A UN HÉROE DE LA REPÚBLICA

Un libro quedó al borde de su cintura muerta,
un libro retoñaba de su cadáver muerto.
Se llevaron al héroe,
y corpórea y aciaga entró su boca en nuestro aliento;
sudamos todos, el hombligo a cuestas;
caminantes las lunas nos seguían;
también sudaba de tristeza el muerto.

Y un libro, en la batalla de Toledo,
un libro, atrás un libro, arriba un libro, retoñaba del
    cadáver.

Poesía del pómulo morado, entre el decirlo
y el callarlo,
poesía en la carta moral que acompañara
a su corazón.
Quedóse el libro y nada más, que no hay
insectos en la tumba,
y quedó al borde de su manga el aire remojándose
y haciéndose gaseoso, infinito.

Todos sudamos, el hombligo a cuestas,
también sudaba de tristeza el muerto
y un libro, yo lo ví sentidamente,
un libro, atrás un libro, arriba un libro
retoñó del cadáver ex abrupto.

10 septiembre 1937/1939

Spain, Take This Cup from Me

IX. SHORT PRAYER FOR A LOYALIST HERO

A book remained at the edge of his dead waist,
a book was sprouting from his dead corpse.
The hero was carried off,
and corporeal and ominous his mouth entered our breath;
we all sweated, under the load of our navels;
the moons were following us on foot;
the dead man was also sweating from sadness.

And a book, during the battle for Toledo,
a book, a book behind, a book above, was sprouting from
    the corpse.

Poetry of the purple cheekbone, between saying it
and not saying it,
poetry in the moral map that had accompanied
his heart.
The book remained and nothing else, for there are no
insects in his tomb,
and at the edge of his sleeve the air remained soaking
and becoming gaseous, infinite.

We all sweated, under the load of our navels,
the dead man was also sweating from sadness
and a book, I saw it feelingly,
a book, a book behind, a book above
abruptly sprouted from the corpse.

XII. MASA

    Al fin de la batalla,
y muerto el combatiente, vino hacia él un hombre
y le dijo: "¡No mueras; te amo tánto!"
Pero el cadáver ¡ay! siguió muriendo.

    Se le acercaron dos y repitiéronle:
"¡No nos dejes! ¡Valor! ¡Vuelve a la vida!"
Pero el cadáver ¡ay! siguió muriendo.

XII. MASS

    At the end of the battle,
and the combatant dead, a man came toward him
and said: "Don't die; I love you so much!"
But the corpse, alas! kept on dying.

    Two approached him and repeated:
"Don't leave us! Be brave! Return to life!
But the corpse, alas! kept on dying.

Acudieron a él veinte, cien, mil, quinientos mil,
clamando: "Tánto amor, y no poder nada contra la
muerte!"
Pero el cadáver ¡ay! siguió muriendo.

Le rodearon millones de individuos,
con un ruego común: "¡Quédate, hermano!"
Pero el cadáver ¡ay! siguió muriendo.

Entonces, todos los hombres de la tierra
le rodearon; les vió el cadáver triste, emocionado;
incorporóse lentamente,
abrazó al primer hombre; echóse a andar...

10 noviembre 1937/1939

XIV. ESPAÑA, APARTA DE MÍ ESTE CÁLIZ

Niños del mundo,
si cae España—digo, es un decir—
si cae
del cielo abajo su antebrazo que asen,
en cabestro, dos láminas terretres;
niños, ¡que edad la de las sienes cóncavas!
¡qué temprano en el sol lo que os decía!
¡qué pronto en vuestro pecho el ruido anciano!
¡qué viejo vuestro 2 en el cuaderno!

¡Niños del mundo, está
la madre España con su vientre a cuestas;
está nuestra maestra con sus férulas,
está madre y maestra
cruz y madera, porque os dió la altura,
vértigo y división y suma, niños;
está con ella, padres procesales!

Si cae—digo, es un decir—si cae
España, de la tierra para abajo,
niños, ¡cómo vais a cesar de crecer!
¡cómo va a castigar el año al mes!
¡cómo van a quedarse en diez los dientes,
en palote el diptongo, la medalla en llanto!
¡Cómo va el corderillo a continuar
atado por la pata al gran tintero!
¡Cómo vais a bajar las gradas del alfabeto
hasta la letra en que nació la pena!

Niños,
hijos de los guerreros, entre tanto,
bajad la voz, que España está ahora mismo repartiendo
la energía entre el reino animal,

Twenty, a hundred, a thousand, five hundred thousand,
came up to him, crying out:
"So *much* love and no power against death!"
But the corpse, alas! kept on dying.

Millions of persons surrounded him,
with a common plea: "Do not leave us, brother!"
But the corpse, alas! kept on dying.

Then, all the inhabitants of the earth
surrounded him; the corpse looked at them sadly, moved;
he sat up slowly,
embraced the first man; started to walk...

XIV. SPAIN, TAKE THIS CUP FROM ME

Children of the world,
if Spain falls—I mean, it's just a thought—
if she falls
from the sky downward let her forearm be seized,
in a halter, by two terrestrial plates;
children, what age in those concave temples!
how early in the sun what I was telling you!
how soon in your chest the ancient noise!
how old your 2 in your notebook!

Children of the world,
mother Spain is with her belly on her shoulders;
our teacher is with her ferules,
she appears as mother and teacher,
cross and wood, because she gave you the height,
vertigo and division and addition, children;
she is with herself, procedural fathers!

If she falls—I mean, it's just a thought—if Spain
falls, from the earth downward,
children, how you are going to stop growing!
how the year is going to punish the month!
how you're never going to have more than ten teeth,
how the dipthong will remain in downstroke,
    the medal in tears!
How the little lamb is going to continue
bound by its leg to the great inkwell!
How you're going to descend the steps of the alphabet
to the letter in which pain was born!

Children,
sons of warriors, meanwhile,
lower your voice, for Spain is right this moment
    distributing

las florecillas, los cometas y los hombres.
¡Bajad la voz, que está
con su rigor, que es grande, sin saber
qué hacer, y está en su mano
la calavera hablando y habla y habla,
la calavera, aquélla de la trenza,
la calavera, aquélla de la vida!

    ¡Bajad la voz, os digo;
bajad la voz, el canto de las sílabas, el llanto
de la materia y el rumor menor de las pirámides, y aún
el de las sienes que andan con dos piedras!
¡Bajad el aliento, y si
el antebrazo baja,
si las férulas suenan, si es la noche,
si el cielo cabe en dos limbos terrestres,
si hay ruido en el sonido de las puertas,
si tardo,
si no veis a nadie, si os asustan
los lápices sin punta, si la madre
España cae—digo, es un decir—
salid, niños del mundo; id a buscarla!...

                                        1939

energy among the animal kingdom,
little flowers, comets and men.
Lower your voice, for she is
with her rigor, which is great, not knowing
what to do, and she has in her hand
the talking skull and it talks and talks,
the skull, the one with the braid,
the skull, the one with life!

    Lower your voice, I tell you;
lower your voice, the song of syllables, the crying
of matter and the minor rumor of the pyramids, and even
that of your temples which walk with two stones!
Lower your breathing, and if
the forearm comes down,
if the ferules sound, if it is night,
if the sky fits into two terrestrial limbos,
if there is noise in the sound of the doors,
if I am late,
if you don't see anyone, if the blunt pencils
frighten you, if mother
Spain falls—I mean, it's just a thought—
go out, children of the world, go and look for her!...

                                trans. Clayton Eshleman

Alfonsina Storni

ARGENTINA
1892–1938

Born of Italian parents in Switzerland, Alfonsina Storni came to Argentina with her family when she was three years old. Trained and licenced in the field of rural education, she supported herself as a teacher and free-lance journalist from the age of eighteen. At twenty, alone with her son, she moved to Buenos Aires, where she spent the rest of her life. Storni published her first book, *La inquietud del rosal* (*The Restlessness of the Rose*), in 1916. Almost immediately her Modernist-influenced poems of female consciousness and of plangent complaint against sexual injustice became a sensation in the literary world of Buenos Aires. Her poems in *Irremediablemente* (*Irremediably*, 1919) and *Languidez* (*Languor*, 1920) often explore this thematic territory with daring and courage. These poems made her, somewhat ambivalently, the first woman writer to be seriously included in the literary café culture of Buenos Aires. In fiction, essays, and reviews, Storni intensified her formal explorations of gender politics, and this wider formal perspective enabled her to write poems of greater historical perspective, as well. Throughout the 1920s Storni directed the Teatro Infantil, which the city government of Buenos Aires created for her. The professional admiration and financial security of those years, however, did little to assuage her aggrieved sense of gender injustice or her dismay over her sexual dependency on men.

Eventually Storni moved away from the thematics of her early work, calling them "overcharged with romantic honeys." Her later poems, dominated by images of the sea and of release, are concerned less with immediate emotions and more with the general cultural status of women in the twentieth century, as in *El mundo de siete pozos* (*World of Seven Wells*, 1934) and *Mascarilla y trébol* (*Mask and Clover*, 1938). As her poems became angrier and more ironic, Storni also repudiated the formalism of her early work and wrote increasingly in compressed, fourteen-line unrhymed "antisonnets." Depressed and in bad health, she walked into the sea in October 1938.

Peso ancestral

Tú me dijiste: no lloró mi padre;
Tú me dijiste: no lloró mi abuelo;
No han llorado los hombres de mi raza,
Eran de acero.

Así diciendo te brotó una lágrima
Y me cayó en la boca... más veneno.
Yo no he bebido nunca en otro vaso
Así pequeño.

Débil mujer, pobre mujer que entiende,
Dolor de siglos conocí al beberlo:
Oh, el alma mía soportar no puede
Todo su peso.

1919

Ancestral Burden

Once you told me my father never wept;
Once you told me his father never wept;
The men of my line have never wept;
They were made of steel.

As you were saying this you cried a tear
That dropped into my mouth... I have never
drunk more of poison than I did
from that little cup.

Vulnerable woman, poor and comprehending woman,
When I tasted it I knew the pain of centuries.
Oh, my soul cannot endure
All of its burden.

trans. Andrew Rosing

La garra blanca

En esta esplendidez del cielo limpio
Hundo los ojos y al hundirlos lloro.
Cubren el cielo lágrimas de oro,
El cielo limpio.

Ah, me parece que una garra blanca
Ha de bajar de pronto a arrebatarme
Y por el cielo en curva ha de llevarme,
La garra blanca.

1919

The White Claw

In this splendor of white sky
I sink my eyes, and sinking them I weep.
The sky is covered with golden tears:
the clean sky.

And ah, it seems that a white claw
must swoop down and carry me
through the curving sky:
the white claw.

trans. Andrew Rosing

Carta lírica a otra mujer

Vuestro nombre no sé, ni vuestro rostro
Conozco yo, y os imagino blanca,

Débil como los brotes iniciales,
Pequeña, dulce... Ya ni sé... Divina.

En vuestros ojos placidez de lago
Que se abandona al sol y dulcemente

Lyrical Letter to the Other Woman

I do not know your name, I have never seen
your face: I imagine you fair,

delicate as young buds,
small and sweet and... somehow, I don't know... divine.

In your eyes a tranquil lake
lies open to the sun: sweetly its gold

Le absorbe su oro mientras todo calla.
Y vuestras manos, finas, como aqueste

Dolor, el mío, que se alarga, alarga,
Y luego se me muere y se concluye

Así, como lo veis, en algún verso.
Ah, ¿sois así? Decidme si en la boca

Tenéis un rumoroso colmenero,
Si las orejas vuestras son a modo

De pétalos de rosas ahuecados...
Decidme si lloráis, humildemente,

Mirando las estrellas tan lejanas,
Y si en las manos tibias se os aduermen

Palomas blancas y canarios de oro.
Porque todo eso y más, vos sois, sin duda;

Vos, que tenéis el hombre que adoraba
Entre las manos dulces, vos la bella

Que habéis matado, sin saberlo acaso,
Toda esperanza en mí... Vos, su criatura.

Porque él es todo vuestro: cuerpo y alma
Estáis gustando del amor secreto

Que guardé silencioso... Dios lo sabe
Por qué, que yo no alcanzo a penetrarlo.

Os lo confieso que una vez estuvo
Tan cerca de mi brazo, que a extenderlo

Acaso mía aquella dicha vuestra
Me fuera ahora... ¡sí! acaso mía...

Mas ved, estaba el alma tan gastada
Que el brazo mío no alcanzó a extenderse:

La sed divina, contenida entonces,
Me pulió el alma... ¡Y él ha sido vuestro!

¿Comprendéis bien? Ahora, en vuestros brazos
El se adormece y le dices palabras

Pequeñas y menudas que semejan
Pétalos volanderos y muy blancos.

Acaso un niño rubio vendrá luego
A copiar en los ojos inocentes

drinks in the light, and all is quiet.
And your hands, fine, like

my grief that grows, grows,
and will kill me—eventually—, and ends up

like this, as you see, in a poem.
Ah, *are* you like that? Tell me if you have

a murmuring rumor of bees in your voice,
if your ears are like

curled rose-petals...
Tell me if you cry, humbly,

when you look at distant stars,
whether white doves and golden canaries

grow sleepy in your slender hands.
Because you are all of this and more, I'm sure:

You, who hold the man I adored
between your sweet hands, you—the beauty—

who (perhaps you didn't know?) have killed
all hope in me... He's yours, your creature,

completely yours: body and soul.
You enjoy the secret love

that I kept silent... God alone knows why
(I have not penetrated why.)

I confess to you, once he was so near
that all I had to do was to open my arms,

and what you enjoy now
might have been mine.

But you see, my soul was so exhausted
that my arms wouldn't reach any further:

the divine thirst, which I controlled just then,
burnished my soul for me... And now he is yours!

Do you understand? Now he drowses
in your arms and you whisper a myriad

of little words to him, words like
the whitest, fluttering petals.

Maybe a blonde child will come to you, one day,
and his innocent eyes will copy

Los ojos vuestros y los de él
Unidos en un espejo azul y cristalino...

¡Oh, ceñidle la frente! ¡Era tan amplia!
¡Arrancaban tan firmes los cabellos

A grandes ondas, que a tenerla cerca
No hiciera yo otra cosa que ceñirla!

Luego dejad que en vuestras manos vaguen
Los labios suyos; él me dijo un día

Que nada era tan dulce al alma suya
Como besar las femeninas manos...

Y acaso, alguna vez, yo, la que anduve
Vagando por afuera de la vida,

—Como aquellos filósofos mendigos
Que van a las ventanas señoriales

A mirar sin envidia toda fiesta—
Me allegue humildemente a vuestro lado

Y con palabras quedas, susurrantes,
Os pida vuestras manos un momento,

Para besarlas, yo, como él las besa...
Y al recubrirlas, lenta, lentamente,

Vaya pensando: aquí se aposentaron
¿Cuánto tiempo, sus labios, cuánto tiempo

En las divinas manos que son suyas?
¡Oh, qué amargo deleite, este deleite

De buscar huellas suyas y seguirlas
Sobre las manos vuestras tan sedosas,

Tan finas, con sus venas tan azules!
Oh, que nada podría, ni ser suya,

Ni dominarle el alma, ni tenerlo
Rendido aquí a mis pies, recompensarme

Este horrible deleite de hacer mío
Un inefable, apasionado rastro.

Y allí en vos misma, sí, pues sois barrera,
Barrera ardiente, viva, que al tocarla

Ya me remueve este cansancio amargo.
Este silencio de alma en que me escudo,

your eyes, and his too,
united on a clear blue mirror.

Oh, wreath his brow with honor! (It is wide enough
for that.) The strong waves of his hair

broke across that brow. And yet, if I were near it
I could do nothing else but wreath it around.

Let his lips wander
over your hands; one day he told me

that nothing was as sweet to his soul
as kissing a woman's hands...

And maybe, someday, I, who wander
outside of life,—

like those mendicant philosophers
who look in through mansion windows

and watch each feast without envy—
I will humbly come up beside you

and quietly, whispering,
ask to hold your hands for just a moment,

so that I can kiss them, I, as he kisses them...
and when I return them, slow, slowly back,

I will be thinking: his lips,
how long were they fixed there, how long

in your divine hands?
Oh, what a bitter delight, this pleasure

of watching for his traces, following them
over your hands that are so

delicate, with their veins that are so blue.
Oh, nothing—not

even to be his, not to dominate his soul, not to have it
surrendered at my feet—nothing could compensate me

for this awful delight, to have what is left
to me passionate and—ineffable.

And there in your own self: yes, you are the obstacle,
flaming, alive: when I touch it, already

this bitter heaviness eases from me.
This silence of the soul in which I sink myself—

Este dolor mortal en que me abismo,
Esta inmovilidad del sentimiento

¡Que sólo salta, bruscamente, cuando
Nada es posible!

this mortal grief in which I destroy myself—
this paralysis of feeling

that only leaps to life
when nothing is possible!—

1920

trans. Dana Stangel

Dolor

Quisiera esta tarde divina de Octubre
Pasear por la orilla lejana del mar;

Que la arena de oro y las aguas verdes
Y los cielos puros me vieran pasar.

Ser alta, soberbia, perfecta, quisiera,
Como una romana, para concordar

Con las grandes olas, y las rocas muertas
Y las anchas playas que ciñen el mar.

Con el paso lento y los ojos fríos
Y la boca muda dejarme llevar:

Ver cómo se rompen las olas azules
Contra los granitos y no parpadear;

Ver cómo las aves rapaces se comen
Los peces pequeños y no suspirar;

Pensar que pudieran las frágilas barcas
Hundirse en las aguas y no despertar;

Ver que se adelanta, la garganta libre,
El hombre más bello: no desear amar...

Perder la mirada, distraídamente,
Perderla y que nunca la vuelva a encontrar;

Y, figura erguida entre cielo y playa,
Sentirme el olvido perenne del mar.

1925

Sorrow

This divine October morning
I would like to walk along the shore

And to let the gold sand and green waters
And pure sky witness my passing there...

I would like to be tall, proud, perfect,
Like a Roman matron, in harmony

With the giant waves and the flat rocks
And the huge beaches beside the water.

I would let myself be carried along
With slow steps and cold eyes and mute mouth,

To see how the blue waves break
Against the sand, and not stir;

To see how the birds of prey devour
The little fish, and not even a whisper;

To think that the delicate little boats
Might falter in the water, and not care;

To see the handsomest man approach, a giant
On the loose, and not want love, no desire...

To lose the sense of sight, abstractedly—
Lose, and not recover;

And standing upright between the sky and sand,
To feel the sea's oblivion forever.

trans. Andrew Rosing

Yo en el fondo del mar

En el fondo del mar
hay una casa
de cristal.

Me at the Bottom of the Sea

At the bottom of the sea
is a crystal
house.

A una avenida
de madréporas,
da.

Un gran pez de oro,
a las cinco,
me viene a saludar.

Me trae
un rojo ramo
de flores de coral.

Duermo en una cama
un poco más azul
que el mar.

Un pulpo
me hace guiños
a través del cristal.

En el bosque verde
que me circunda
—din don... din dan—
se balancean y cantan
las sirenas
de nácar verdemar.

Y sobre mi cabeza
arden, en el crepúsculo,
las erizadas puntas del mar.

1934

It looks out
onto a soft-stone
avenue.

At five o'clock
a great gold fish
comes to visit.

He brings me
a red spray
of coral flowers.

I sleep in a bed
a little bluer
than the sea.

An octopus
winks at me
through the glass.

In the green woods
around me,
ding dong... ding dong...
sirens of sea-green
mother-of-pearl
flutter and sing.

And over my head
the bristling points of the sea
flare in the dusk.

trans. Andrew Rosing

Voy a dormir

Dientes de flores, cofia de rocío,
manos de hierbas, tú, nodriza fina,
ténme prestas las sábanas terrosas
y el edredón de musgos escardados.

Voy a dormir, nodriza mía, acuéstame.
Ponme una lámpara a la cabecera;
una constelación; la que te guste;
todas son buenas; bájala un poquito.

Déjame sola: oyes romper los brotes...
te acuna un pie celeste desde arriba
y un pájaro te traza unos compases

para que olvides... Gracias. ¡Ah, un encargo!
Si él llama nuevamente por teléfono,
le dices que no insista, que he salido.

1938

I'm Going to Sleep

Teeth of flowers, hair of dew,
hands of the grasses: my fine nurse,
make the sheets of the earth ready for me,
and the quilt of smooth mosses.

Nurse, I'm going to sleep now; come tuck me in;
put a light beside my bed;
a constellation, whatever you choose—
they are all lovely—only turn it down a little.

Now leave me. Listen to the plants begin to sprout...
High above, a celestial foot rocks your cradle,
a bird sings some lullaby notes

so you can forget... Thank you. Oh, and please:
if he calls again, tell him
not to ask for me; tell him I have gone...

trans. Andrew Rosing

Mário de Andrade

Mário Raul de Morais de Andrade called his book *Macunaíma* (1929) at first a "story," later a "novel," and finally a "rhapsody." Arguably the most famous Brazilian book ever written, *Macunaíma* presents "a hero without character" (as Andrade describes him) who is made to seem an embodiment of the Brazilian national character. Restless, witty, sensual, adaptive, and sentimental, the character Macunaíma, an ethnic Indian of the tropics, "becomes" a white man in order to pursue an ideal of stolen treasure in the city. Through Macunaíma's allegorical adventures, Andrade invents primarily a style—rich with colloquial Brazilian idioms, folklore, neologisms, and proverbs—to articulate his persistent vision of the uniqueness of Brazilian life and the autonomy of the Portuguese language in Brazil. These same ideals, and much of that style, pervade Andrade's poems, from the early pre-Modernist Futurist poems of *Paulicéia desvairada* (*Hallucinated City*, 1922) through his enthusiastic contributions to the nationalist wave of the Modernist movement in Brazil. The values this style carries continue through Andrade's long subsequent career as an influential poet, novelist, dramatist, critic, civic leader, ethnographer, educator, and journalist.

Born in São Paulo and educated there as a pianist, Andrade worked at first as a professor in the Conservatory. In an essay entitled "O meu poeta futurista" ("My Futurist Poet"), anticipating the Week of Modern Art in 1922, Oswald de Andrade "presented" a poem from Mário de Andrade's then-unpublished manuscript *Pauficéia desvairada* as a model of the anti-Parnassian new work Oswald was then advocating: "Did you discern the change in rhythm, the new form, the daring sentence? . . . We also have our own remodelers renewing pathways of expression and ecstasy!" Mário himself soon dissociated himself from the pure Futurist model, but his career was launched. Through the power of his literary manifestoes and journalism throughout the 1920s, he came to be known as the "Pope of Modernism."

After 1935 Mário de Andrade assumed the leadership of the Department of Culture of the city of São Paulo. His achievements there were diverse, from designing playgrounds to establishing the Society for Ethnography and Folklore. (He was responsible for inviting the French anthropologist Claude Lévi-Strauss to become a visiting professor at the new University of São Paulo.) Mário spent much of the latter part of his life in Rio de Janeiro, returning finally to his beloved São Paulo, although his poems increasingly reverted to the tropical interior for their imagery, their idioms, and their verve. His nonfiction prose works, published late in life, include voluminous correspondence, the comprehensive *Aspectos da literatura brasileira* (*Aspects of Brazilian Literature*, 1943), and—because of his staggeringly cosmopolitan knowledge—much of the first *Brazilian National Encyclopedia*.

Inspiração	*Inspiration*
Onde até na fôrça do verão havia tempestades de ventos e frios de crudelíssimo inverno.	Where even at the height of summer there were storms of wind and cold like unto the harshest winter.
FR. LUIS DE SOUSA	FRA LUIS DE SOUSA

São Paulo! comoção de minha vida...
Os meus amores são flores feitas de original...

São Paulo! tumult of my life...
My loves are flowers made from the original...

Arlequinal!... Traje dc losangos... Cinza e ouro...
Luz e bruma... Forno e inverno morno...
Elegâncias sutis sem escândalos, sem ciúmes...
Perfumes de Paris... Arys!
Bofetadas líricas no Trianon... Algodoal!...

São Paulo! comoção de minha vida...
Galicismo a berrar nos desertos da América!

1922

Harlequinate!... Diamond tights... Gray and gold...
Light and mist... Oven and warm winter...
Subtle refinements without scandals, without jealousy...
Perfumes from Paris... Arys!
Lyrical slaps in the Trianon... Cotton field!...

São Paulo! tumult of my life...
Gallicism crying in the wilderness of America!

trans. Jack E. Tomlins

Os cortejos

Monotonias das minhas retinas...
Serpentinas de entes frementes a se desenrolar...
Todos os sempres das minhas visões! "Bon giorno, caro."

Horríveis as cidades!
Vaidades e mais vaidades...
Nada de asas! Nada de poesia! Nada de alegria!
Oh! os tumultuários das ausências!
Paulicea—a grande boca de mil dentes;
e os jôrros dentre a lingua trissulca
de pús e de mais pús de distinção...
Giram homens fracos, baixos, magros...
Serpentinas de entes frementes a se desenrolar...

Estes homens de São Paulo,
todos iguais e desiguais,
quando vivem dentro dos meus olhos tão ricos,
parecem-me uns macacos, uns macacos.

1922

The Processions

Monotonies of my retinas...
Serpentines of quivering beings unrolling...
All the forevers of my visions! "Bon giorno, caro."

Horrid cities!
Vanities and more vanities...
No wings whatsoever! No poetry whatsoever!
    No joy whatsoever!
Oh! the agitatings of absences!
São Paulo—the great mouth with a thousand teeth;
and amidst the trifid tongue the torrents
of pus and more pus of distinction...
Men whirl past feeble, short, skinny...
Serpentines of quivering beings unrolling...

These men of São Paulo,
all equal and unequal,
when they live within my eyes so rich,
seem to me just so many monkeys, just so many monkeys.

trans. Jack E. Tomlins

Domingo

Missas de chegar tarde, em rendas,
e dos olhares acrobáticos...
Tantos telégrafos sem fio!
Santa Cecília regorgita de corpos lavados
e de sacrilégios picturais...
Mas Jesus Cristo nos desertos,
mas o sacerdote no "Confiteor"... Contrastar!
—Futilidade, civilização...

Hoje quem joga?... O Paulistano
Para o Jardim América das rosas e dos ponta-pés!
Friedenreich fez goal! Corner! Que juiz!
Gostar de Bianco? Adoro. Qual Bartô...
E o meu xará maravilhoso!...
—Futilidade, civilização...

Sunday

Late arrivals at Mass, in lace,
exchanging acrobatic glances....
So much wireless telegraphy!
St. Cecilia exudes from washed bodies
and pictorial sacrileges...
But Jesus Christ in the wilderness,
but the priest at the Confiteor... Contrast!
"Futility, civilization..."

Who's playing today?... The Paulistano Team.
Off to America Garden of the roses and kick-offs!
Friedenreich made a goal! Corner! What a referee!
Do I like Bianco? Crazy about him. Better than Barto...
And my wonderful fellow-Mario!...
"Futility, civilization..."

Mornamente em gazolinas... Trinta e cinco contos!
Tens dez milreis? vamos ao corso...
E filar cigarros a quinzena inteira...
Ir ao corso é lei. Viste Marília?
E Filis? Que vestido: pele só!
Automóveis fechados... Figuras imóveis...
O bocejo do luxo... Entêrro.
E tambem as famílias dominicais por atacado,
entre os convenientes perenemente...
—Futilidade, civilização.

Central. Drama de adultério.
A Bertini arranca os cabellos e morre.
Fugas... Tiros... Tom Mix!
Amanhã fita alemã... de beiços...
As meninas mordem os beiços pensando em fita alemã...
As romas de Petronio...
E o leito virginal... Tudo azul e branco!
Descansar... Os anjos... Imaculado!
As meninas sonham masculinidades...
—Futilidade, civilização.

1922

Warmly in gasolines... Thirty-five thousand!
Do you have ten bucks? let's go make the main drag...
And mooch cigarettes for two weeks on end...
You've got to go down to the main drag. Did you see
    Marilia?
And Phyllis! What a dress: practically naked!
Closed automobiles... Motionless figures...
The yawn of luxury... Burial.
And also the wholesale Sunday families,
among the perenially proper...
"Futility, civilization..."

Main jail. A drama of adultery.
Bertini tears her hair and dies.
Getaways... Hold-ups... Tom Mix!
Tomorrow a German film... For free!
The young girls are disturbed from thinking about
    German films...
The romes of Petronius...
And the virgin's bed... All blue and white!
Rest... The angels... Immaculate!
The young girls dream masculinities...
"Futility, civilization..."

trans. Jack E. Tomlins

Nocturno

Luzes do Cambucí pelas noites de crime...
Calor!... E as nuvens baixas muito grossas,
feitas de corpos de mariposas,
rumorejando na epiderme das árvores...

Gingam os bondes como um fôgo de artifício,
sapateando nos trilhos,
cuspindo um orifício na treva cor de cal...

Num perfume de heliotrópios e de pôças
gira uma flor-do-mal... Veio do Turquestan;
e traz olheiras que escurecem almas...
Fundiu esterlinas entre as unhas roxas
nos oscilantes de Ribeirão Preto...

—Batat'assat'ô furnn!...

Luzes do Cambucí pelas noites de crime!...
Calor... E as nuvens baixas muito grossas,
feitas de corpos de mariposas,
rumorejando na epiderme das árvores...

Nocturne

Lights from the Cambucí district on nights of crime...
Hot weather!... And the lowering thick clouds,
made from the bodies of moths,
rustling on the epidermis of the trees...

The trolleys swish like a skyrocket,
clicking their heels on the tracks,
spitting out an orifice into the whitewashed gloom...

In a perfume of heliotropes and puddles
whirls a flower-of-evil... She came from Turkestan;
and she has circles under her eyes that obscure souls...
She has smelted English pounds between her purple
    fingernails
in the bordellos of Ribeirão Preto...

    Get-a you roast-a yams!...

Lights from Cambucí on nights of crime...
Hot weather!... And the lowering thick clouds,
made from the bodies of moths,
rustling on the epidermis of the trees...

Um mulato cor de oiro,
com uma cabeleira feita de alianças polidas...
Violão! "Quando eu morrer..." Um cheiro pesado de
    baunilhas
oscila, tomba e rola no chão...
Ondula no ar a nostalgia das Baías...

E os bondes passam como um fôgo de artifício,
sapateando nos trilhos,
ferindo um orifício na treva cor de cal...

—Batat'assat'ô furnn!...

Calor!... Os diabos andam no ar
corpos de nuas carregando...
As lassitudes dos sempres imprevistos!
e as almas acordando às mãos dos enlaçados!
Idílios sob os plátanos!...
E o ciume universal às fanfarras gloriosas
de saias cor de rosa e gravatas cor de rosa!...

Balcões na cautela latejante, onde florem Iracemas
para os encontros dos guerreiros brancos... Brancos?
E que os cães latam nos jardins!
Ninguem, ninguem, ninguem se importa!
Todos embarcam na Alameda dos Beijos da Aventura!
Mas eu... Estas minhas grades em girândolas de jasmins,
enquanto as travessas do Cambucí nos livres
da liberdade dos lábios entreabertos!...

Arlequinal! Arlequinal!
As nuvens baixas muito grossas,
feitas de corpos de mariposas,
rumorejando na epiderme das árvores...
Mas sôbre estas minhas grades em girândolas de jasmins,
o estelário delira em carnagens de luz,
e meu céu é todo um rojão de lágrimas!...

E os bondes riscam como um fôgo de artifício,
sapateando nos trilhos,
jorrando um orifício na treva cor de cal...

—Batat'assat'ô furnn!...

1922

A golden mulatto
with hair like lustrous wedding rings...
Guitar! "When I die..." A heady scent of vanilla
pivots, falls, and rolls on the ground...
In the air undulates the nostalgia of the Bahias.

And the trolleys pass by like a skyrocket,
clicking their heels on the tracks,
wounding an orifice in the whitewashed gloom...

    Get-a you roast-a yams!...

Hot weather!... Devils in the air
bodies of naked girls carrying...
The lassitudes of the unforeseen forevers!
and souls awakening to the hands of embracing lovers!
Idyls under the plantain trees!...
And the universal jealousy with magnificent fanfares
in pink skirts and pink necktics!...

Balconies in the pulsating caution, where Iracemas
    blossom
for rendezvous with white warriors... White?
So let the dogs bark in the gardens!
No one, no one, no one cares!
They all embark on the Promenade of the Kisses of
    Adventure!
But I... Behind these garden fences of mine with
    pinwheels of jazmine,
remain while the alley ways of Cambucí in the free
of the freedom of parted lips!...

Harlequinate! Harlequinate!
The lowering thick clouds,
made from the bodies of moths,
rustling on the epidermis of the trees...
But on these my garden fences with pinwheels of jazmine,
the stars grow delirious in carnages of light,
and my sky is all a skyrocket of tears!...

And the trolleys trace like fireworks,
clicking their heels on the tracks,
jetting an orifice into the whitewashed gloom...

    Get-a you roast-a yams!...

trans. Jack E. Tomlins

Alfonso Cortés

NICARAGUA
1893–1969

Alfonso Cortés occupies an almost mythical place in Latin American letters. The legend of Cortés involves both the deep interiority of his poetic gift and the onset of his periodic madness (reputedly exactly at midnight on February 18, 1927). He is renowned as much for his status as the exemplary and mystical *poeta loco* of Nicaragua as for his devoutly spiritual, richly connotative poems. Cortés spent his last forty years in the house in León where Rubén Darío had spent his childhood; Ernesto Cardenal claims to recall walking to school as a child and seeing Cortés chained to a wall, writing. In lucid periods Cortés translated Baudelaire, Verlaine, Mallarmé, and Edgar Allan Poe.

In his best poems Cortés presents an enigmatic, visionary, metaphysical, and self-enclosed universe that shimmers with prophetic apparitions of space, being, form, and the deity. These apparitions take form in a language that is virtually without history, Cortés maintained, a language written "in the origin of things which is not anterior to them, but permanent." Accordingly, his poetic style underwent little evolution throughout his long life.

La canción del espacio

La distancia que hay de aquí a
una estrella que nunca ha existido
porque Dios no ha alcanzado a
pellizcar tan lejos la piel de la
noche! Y pensar que todavía creamos
que es más grande o más
útil la paz mundial que la paz
de un solo salvaje...

Este afán de relatividad de
nuestra vida contemporánea—es—
lo que da al espacio una importancia
que sólo está en nosotros,—
y quién sabe hasta cuándo aprenderemos
a vivir como los astros—
libres en medio de lo que es sin fin
y sin que nadie nos alimente.

La tierra no conoce los caminos
por donde a diario anda—y
más bien esos caminos son la
conciencia de la tierra... —Pero si
no es así, permítaseme hacer una
pregunta: —Tiempo, dónde estamos
tú y yo, yo que vivo en tí y
tú que no existes?

1928

Space Song

The distance that lies from here
To some star that never existed
Because God has not yet managed
To pull the skin of night that far!

And to think we still believe greater
More useful world peace
Than the peace of one lone savage...

This relativity craze
In our contemporary life: There's
What gives space an importance
Found only in ourselves!

Who knows how long we'll take to learn
To live as stars—
Free in the midst of what is without end
And needing no one to feed us.

Earth knows nothing of the paths it daily travels—
Yet those paths are the conscience of earth.... But if
This is not so, allow me just
One question: —Time, you and I
Where are we,
I who live in you
And you who do not exist?

trans. Thomas Merton

La gran plegaria

El tiempo es hambre y el espacio es frío
orad, orad, que sólo la plegaria
puede saciar las ansias del vacío.

El sueño es una roca solitaria
en donde el águila del alma anida:
soñad, soñad, entre la vida diaria.

1927?

Great Prayer

Time is hunger, space is cold
Pray, pray, for prayer alone can quiet
The anxieties of void.

Dream is a solitary rock
Where the soul's hawk nests:
Dream, dream, during
Ordinary life.

trans. Thomas Merton

Vicente Huidobro

CHILE
1893–1948

Vicente Huidobro lived much of his life in Paris and Madrid, where in the years before World War I he came into contact with many of the experimental writers of the early Continental Vanguardist movements, including Apollinaire and Gertrude Stein. His poems from this period, some written in French, track his responses to a series of aesthetic ideologies, from Symbolism forward through Cubism, Futurism, and Ultraism. In 1917, in Buenos Aires, he proclaimed his theory of "Creationism," in manifestoes that insisted on the artificial and verbal nature of the poetic artifact, which derives its power from the writer's intelligent exercise of will. Huidobro described the new poem as "neither anecdote nor description": "emotion gives birth to the only creative virtue." Mounting images in a collage without punctuation, using intransitive verbs as transitive, distributing the text in nonlinear forms across the page, the Creationist poem as Huidobro actually wrote it behaved much like a Cubist painting—fracturing and reorganizing perception, leaving the work of connection and interpretation to the reader.

The freedom of imaginative association that this super-Realist aesthetic permits often shapes a vision of a desolate world of deeply private, even solipsistic subjectivity. Although many of his Creationist poems were written in French, Huidobro's long poem *Altazor* (1931), in Spanish, enacts many of these theories. The central narrative character of that poem, Altazor himself, summarizes the emotional and epistemological drama of the modern will. *Altazor* is a vision of the human creature as a "metaphysical animal freighted with anxieties," whose salvation from the absurdity and incoherence of the world might lie in the willful assertion of his powerful imagination. "The poet creates the world that ought to exist outside of the one that does exist," Huidobro writes. "The poet is concerned with expressing only the inexpressible."

Arte poética

Que el verso sea como una llave
Que abra mil puertas.
Una hoja cae; algo pasa volando;
Cuanto miren los ojos creado sea,
Y el alma del oyente quede temblando.

Ars Poetica

Let poetry be like a key
Opening a thousand doors.
A leaf falls; something flies by;
Let all the eye sees be created
And the soul of the listener tremble.

Inventa mundos nuevos y cuida tu palabra;
El adjetivo, cuando no da vida, mata.

Estamos en el ciclo de los nervios.
El músculo cuelga,
Como recuerdo, en los museos;
Mas no por eso tenemos menos fuerza:
El vigor verdadero
Reside en la cabeza.

Por qué cantáis la rosa, ¡oh Poetas!
Hacedla florecer en el poema;

Sólo para nosotros
Viven todas las cosas bajo el Sol.

El poeta es un pequeño Dios.

1916

Invent new worlds and watch your word;
The adjective, when it doesn't give life, kills it.

We are in the age of nerves.
The muscle hangs,
Like a memory, in museums;
But we are not the weaker for it:
True vigor
Resides in the head.

Oh Poets, why sing of roses!
Let them flower in your poems;

For us alone
Do all things live beneath the Sun.

The poet is a little God.

trans. David M. Guss

Marino

Aquel pájaro que vuela por primera vez
Se aleja del nido mirando hacia atrás

Con el dedo en los labios
                    os he llamado

Yo inventé juegos de agua
En la cima de los árboles

Te hice la más bella de las mujeres
Tan bella que enrojecías en las tardes

                La luna se aleja de nosotros
                Y arroja una corona sobre el polo

Hice correr ríos
            que nunca han existido

De un grito eleve una montaña
Y en torno bailamos una nueva danza

                Corté todas las rosas
                De las nubes del este

Y enseñé a cantar un pájaro de nieve

Marchemos sobre los meses desatados

Soy el viejo marino
                que cose los horizontes cortados

1918

Sailor

That bird flying for the first time
Leaves its nest looking back

With a finger to my lips
                    I called to you

I invented waterfalls
In the tops of trees

I made you the most beautiful woman
So beautiful that you blushed in the evenings

                The moon drifts off
                And plants a wreath around the pole

I made rivers run
            where none had been before

With a shout I made a mountain rise
And now we do a new dance around it

                I cut all the roses
                From the clouds of the East

And I taught a snowbird how to sing

Let's depart upon the floating months

I'm the old sailor
                who mends torn horizons

trans. David M. Guss

Altazor [Selecciones]

Así eres molino de viento
Molino de asiento
Molino de asiento del viento
Que teje las noches y las mañanas
Que hila las nieblas de ultratumba
Molino de aspavientos y del viento en aspas
El paisaje se llena de tus locuras

Y el trigo viene y va
De la tierra al cielo
Del cielo al mar
Los trigos de las olas amarillas
Donde el viento se revuelca
Buscando la cosquilla de las espigas

Escucha
Pasa el palpador en eléctricas corrientes
El viento norte despeina tus cabellos
Hurra molino moledor
Molino volador
Molino charlador
Molino cantador
Cuando el cielo trae de la mano una tempestad
Hurra molino girando en la memoria
Molino que hipnotiza las palomas viajeras

Habla habla molino de cuento
Cuando el viento narra tu leyenda etérea
Sangra sangra molino del descendimiento
Con tu gran recuerdo pegado a los ocasos del mundo
Y los brazos de tu cruz fatigados por el huracán

Así reímos y cantamos en esta hora
Porque el molino ha creado el imperio de su luz escogida
Y es necesario que lo sepa
Es necesario que alguien se lo diga

Sol tú que naciste en mi ojo derecho
Y moriste en mi ojo izquierdo
No creas en los vaticinios del zodíaco
Ni en los ladridos de las tumbas
Las tumbas tienen maleficios de luna
Y no saben lo que hablan

Yo te lo digo porque mi sombrero está cansado de
    recorrer el mundo
Y tengo una experiencia de mariposa milenaria

Profetiza profetiza
Molino de las constelaciones
Mientras bailamos sobre el azar de la risa

Altazor [Selections]

So you're a windmill
A millstone
A windmillstone that
Weaves together nights and mornings
Spins the fog beyond the grave
Mill blown through and overblown
The landscape overflows with your follies

And the wheat comes and goes
From earth to heaven
From heaven to sea
The yellow waves of wheat
Where the wind wallows
Inviting a tickling from the ears

Listen
The pulsar passes in electric currents
The north wind musses your hair
Hurray grinding mill
Flying mill
Chatter mill
Singing mill
When the sky brings a storm by hand
Hurray mill whirling in memory
Hypnotizing the carrier pigeons

Speak speak mill of story
When the wind recites your ethereal legend
Bleed bleed mill of descent
With your grand memento stuck to the sunsets of the
    world
And the arms of your cross tired out by the hurricane

So this is the hour we laugh and sing
Because the mill created its empire of chosen light
And it must be known
Someone must say it

Sun you who were born in my right eye
And died in my left eye
Don't believe in predictions from the zodiac
Or in barks from the tombs
The tombs are full of moon spells
And don't know what they're saying

I tell you because my hat is tired of roaming the world
And I'm having a millennial butterfly experience

Prophesy prophesy
Mill of the constellations
While we dance upon the laugh's accident

Ahora que la grúa que nos trae el día
Volcó la noche fuera de la tierra

Empiece ya
La farandolina en la lejantaña de la montanía
El horimento bajo el firmazonte
Se embarca en la luna
Para dar la vuelta al mundo
Empiece ya
La faranmandó mandó liná
Con su musiquí con su musicá

[. . .]

Y he aquí que ahora me diluyo en múltiples cosas
Soy luciérnaga y voy iluminando las ramas de la selva
Sin embargo cuando vuelo guardo mi modo de andar
Y no sólo soy luciérnaga
Sino también el aire en que vuela
La luna me atraviesa de parte a parte
Dos pájaros se pierden en mi pecho
Sin poderlo remediar
Y luego soy árbol
Y en cuanto a árbol conservo mis modos de luciérnaga
Y mis modos de cielo
Y mi andar de hombre mi triste andar
Ahora soy rosal y hablo con lenguaje de rosal
Y digo
Sal rosa rorosalía
Sal rosa al día
Salía al sol rosa sario
Fueguisa mía sonrodería rososoro oro
Ando pequeño volcán del día
Y tengo miedo del volcán
Mas el volcán responde
Prófugo rueda al fondo donde ronco
Soy rosa de trueno y sueno mis carrasperas
Estoy preso y arrastro mis propios grillos
Los astros que trago crujen en mis entrañas
Proa a la borrasca en procesión procreadora
Proclamo mis proezas bramadoras
Y mis bronquios respiran en la tierra profunda
Bajo los mares y las montañas
Y luego soy pájaro
Y me disputo el día en gorjeos
El día que me cruza la garganta
Ahora solamente digo
Callaos que voy a cantar
Soy el único cantor de este siglo
Mío mío es todo el infinito
Mis mentiras huelen a cielo
Y nada más

Now that the crane that scoops us the day
Tossed the night right out of the earth

Begin now
The farandolina in the distain of the mountance
The horiment under the firmazon
Sails away on the moon
To turn the world around
Begin now
The faranmandó mandó liná
With its musiquí with its musicá

[. . .]

Here and now I have to dilute myself into many things
I am firefly and I go lighting the boughs of the forest
However when I fly I watch the way I move
And I'm not only firefly
But also the air it flies on
The moon passes over me from one side to the other
Two birds are lost in my breast
And they can't help it
And soon I'm a tree
And while a tree I keep my firefly ways
And my sky ways
And my human movement my sad walking
Now I'm rosebush and speak in rosebush language
And I say
Rise rose rorosarose
Rise rose to the day
Rose ary arose to the sun
My fireling smilerounding rosesore ore
I move into the day's volcano
And I'm afraid of volcanos
But the volcano replies
Fugitive roller at the depths where I snore
I'm rose of thunder sounding my hoarse voice
I'm a prisoner dragging my own irons
The stars I swallow sizzle my guts
Prow to the storm in procreative procession
I proclaim my roaring prowess
And my bronchials breathe in the deep earth
Under the seas and the mountains
And then I'm bird
And I argue all day in chirps
The day my throat comes across me
I alone will say
Be quiet I'm going to sing
I am this age's only singer
Mine mine is all the infinite
My lies smell of heaven
And nothing else

Y ahora soy mar
Pero guardo algo de mis modos de volcán
De mis modos de árbol de mis modos de luciérnaga
De mis modos de pájaro de hombre y de rosal
Y hablo como mar y digo
De la firmeza hasta el horicielo
Soy todo montalas en la azulaya
Bailo en las volaguas con espurinas
Una corriela tras de la otra
Ondola en olañas mi rugazuleo
Las verdondilas bajo la luna del selviflujo
Van en montonda hasta el infidondo
Y cuando bramuran los hurafones
Y la ondaja lanza a las playas sus laziolas
Hay un naufundo que grita pidiendo auxilio
Yo me hago el sordo
Miro las butraceas lentas sobre mis tornadelas
La subaterna con sus brajidos
Las escalolas de la montasca
Las escalolas de la desonda
Que no descansan hasta que roen el borde de los altielos
Hasta que llegan al abifunda
En tanto el pirata canta
Y yo lo escucho vestido de verdiul

La luna en el mar riela
En la luna gime el viento
Y alza en blanco crujimiento
Alas de olas en mi azul

El mar se abrirá para dejar salir los primeros náufragos
Que cumplieron su castigo
Después de tantos siglos y más siglos
Andarán por la tierra con miradas de vidrio
Escalarán los montes de sus frases proféticas
Y se convertirán en constelaciones
Entonces aparecerá un volcán en medio de las olas
Y dirá yo soy el rey
Traedme el armonio de las nebulosas
Y sabed que las islas son las coronas de mi cabeza
Y las olas mi único tesoro
Yo soy el rey

[. . .]

Yo soy el rey
Los ahogados florecen cuando yo lo mando
Atad el arco iris al pirata
Atad el viento a los cabellos de la bruja
Yo soy el rey
Y trazaré tu horóscopo como un plan de batalla

And now I'm sea
But I keep some of my volcano ways
Of my tree ways of my firefly ways
Of my bird ways of man and of rosebush
And I speak like sea and I say
From the firmahcad to the horisky
I'm all mountwings on the blueach
I dance on the soarwaters with swalloams
One glimmerun after the other
Swellave on wavetain my blueripplish
The greenfinches under the moon of the flowood
Rise in mountwave toward the infiround
And when the huraphoons haulroar
And the lowave throws its lassowaves at the coast
There's a shipdeep cries pleading for help
I become deaf
I look at the slow traptraces over my backtracks
The sublighthouse with its bellowmoos
The stairwaves of the stormount
The stairwaves of the swellow
That won't rest until they eat away the border of higheaven
Until they reach the opundity
Meanwhile the pirate sings
And I listen dressed in veridue

The sail in the sea shimmers
On the moon the wind moans
And heaves in white creaking
Wings of waves in my blue

The sea will open to free the first of the shipwrecked
Who fulfilled their punishment
After so many ages and more ages
They will walk on the land with glances of glass
They will scale the mountains of their prophetic phrases
And be transformed into constellations
Then will appear a volcano in the midst of the waves
And it will say I am king
Bring me the harmonium of the misties
And know that the islands are the crowns on my head
And the waves my only treasure
I am king

[. . .]

I am king
The drowned flower when I command it
Tie the rainbow to the pirate
Tie the wind to the witch's hair
I am king
And I will trace your horoscope like a battle plan

Oyendo esto el arco iris se alejaba	Hearing this the rainbow edged away
¿A dónde vas arco iris	Where are you going rainbow
No sabes que hay asesinos en todos los caminos?	Don't you know murderers lurk on every road?
El iris encadenado en la columna montante	The rainbow chained in the upright column
Columna de mercurio en fiesta para nosotros	Column of mercury on holiday for us
Tres mil doscientos metros de infrarojo	Three thousand two hundred meters of infrared
Un extremo se apoya en mi pie y el otro en la llaga	One end leans on my foot and the other on the wound
de Cristo	of Christ
Los domingos del arco iris para el arcángel	The rainbow's Sundays for the archangel
¿En dónde está el arquero de los meteoros?	Where is the archer of the meteors?
El arquero arcaico	The archaic archer
Bajo la arcada eterna el arquero del arcano con su violín	Under the eternal arcade the archer of the arcanum with
violeta con su violín violáceo con su violín violado	his violet violin with his violaceous violin with his
	violin violated
Arco iris arco de las cejas en mi cielo arqueológico	Rainbow arch of eyebrows in my archeological sky
Bajo el área del arco se esconde el arca de tesoros	Under the area of the arch is hidden the ark of precious
preciosos	treasure
Y la flor montada como un reloj	And the flower mounted as a clock
Con el engranaje perfecto de sus pétalos	With the perfect gears of its petals
Ahora que un caballo empieza a subir galopando por el	Just now a horse begins to gallop up the rainbow
arco iris	Now the glance unloads the swollen eyes
Ahora la mirada descarga los ojos demasiado llenos	At the moment when the sunsets flee across the plains
En el instante en que huyen los ocasos a través de las	The sky is looking for an aeroplane
llanuras	And I hear the laughter of the dead beneath the earth
El cielo está esperando un aeroplano	
Y yo oigo la risa de los muertos debajo de la tierra	

trans. Stephen Fredman

1917–1931/1931

Rincones sordos

El mundo se detiene a medio camino
Con su cielo prendido en las montañas
Y el alba en ciertas flores que yo conozco

Esconde en tus cabellos los secretos de la noche
Esconde las mentiras en tu alma de alegres sombras
Esconde tus alas bajo tus besos
Esconde el collar de suspiros en torno a tus senos
Esconde la barca de tu lengua en las fuentes de la sed
En el puerto de la boca amarrada
Esconde la luz a la sombra
Las lágrimas al abrigo del viento que va a soplar
Porque tiene derecho a la vida
Como yo lo tengo a la más alta cumbre
Y al abismo que ha caído tan bajo

Esconde las caídas del sueño
Esconde los colores al fondo de los ojos
Esconde el mar detrás del cielo
Y vuelve a subir a la superficie
Para ser tú mismo al sol de los destinos
A flor de mano como el ciego olvidado

Quiet Spaces

The world stops in the middle of its course
Its sky caught on mountains
And the sunrise on certain flowers I recognize

It hides the secrets of the night in your hair
It hides lies in your soul of bright shadows
It hides your wings beneath your kisses
It hides the necklace of sighs around your breasts
It hides the barge of your tongue in its fountains of thirst
In the harbor of the fastened mouth
It hides the light from the darkness
The tears in the shelter of the wind soon to burst
Because it has a right to life
Just as I have it from the highest peak
To the abyss which has fallen so low

It hides dreams' failures
It hides colors at the bottom of eyes
It hides the sea behind the sky
And comes back up to the surface
To be yourself beneath the sun of destiny
Like the soft touch of the forgotten blind man

Esconde los suspiros en su estuche
Esconde las palabras en su fruto
Y llora tu vida en el hastío de las cosas

1941

It hides sighs in its case
It hides words in its fruit
And your life weeps for the boredom of it all

trans. Stephen Fredman

La poesía es un atentado celeste

Yo estoy ausente pero en el fondo de esta ausencia
Hay la espera de mí mismo
Y esta espera es otro modo de presencia
La espera de mi retorno
Yo estoy en otros objetos
Ando en viaje dando un poco de mi vida
A ciertos árboles y a ciertas piedras
Que me han esperado muchos años

Se cansaron de esperarme y se sentaron

Yo no estoy y estoy
Estoy ausente y estoy presente en estado de espera
Ellos querrían mi lenguaje para expresarse
Y yo querría el de ellos para expresarlos
He aquí el equívoco el atroz equívoco

Angustioso lamentable
Me voy adentrando en estas plantas
Voy dejando mis ropas
Se me van cayendo las carnes
Y mi esqueleto se va revistiendo de cortezas

Me estoy haciendo árbol Cuántas veces me he ido
    convirtiendo en otras cosas...
Es doloroso y lleno de ternura

Podría dar un grito pero se espantaría la
    transubstanciación
Hay que guardar silencio Esperar en silencio

1948

Poetry Is a Heavenly Crime

I am absent but deep in this absence
There is the waiting for myself
And this waiting is another form of presence
The waiting for my return
I am in other objects
I am away travelling giving a little of my life
To some trees and some stones
That have been waiting for me many years

They got tired of waiting for me and sat down

I'm not here and I'm here
I'm absent and I'm present in a state of waiting
They wanted my language so they could express themselves
And I wanted theirs to express them
This is the ambiguity, the horrible ambiguity

Tormented wretched
I'm moving inward on these soles
I'm leaving my clothes behind
My flesh is falling away on all sides
And my skeleton's putting on bark

I'm turning into a tree How often I've turned into other
    things...
It's painful and full of tenderness

I could cry out but it would scare away the
    transubstantiation
Must keep silence Wait in silence

trans. W. S. Merwin

Juana de Ibarbourou
[Juanita Fernández Morales]

URUGUAY
1895–1979

Juana de Ibarbourou's early poems, especially those in *Las lenguas de diamante* (*Diamond Tongues*, 1919), celebrate the flesh, the sacramental power of affection, and the renewal of life through physical love. In subsequent poems, as in *Perdida* (*Lost*, 1950), she explored the terrors of aging, the corruption of the flesh, and the continuity of identity through time. Ibarbourou's tight, passionate poems made her celebrated, early in her career, as a representative poet of female energy, "Juana of America." Her influence has been ambiguous, offering to other writers, especially women poets, an example of strong emotion and bold declaration—and yet also influencing many sentimental imitators. An immensely popular figure at the height of her career, Ibarbourou spent her last years in Montevideo in solitude, neglect, and ill health.

La hora

Tómame ahora que aún es temprano
Y que llevo dalias nuevas en la mano.

Tómame ahora que aún es sombría
Esta taciturna cabellera mía.

Ahora, que tengo la carne olorosa.
Y los ojos limpios y la piel de rosa.

Ahora, que calza mi planta ligera.
La sandalia viva de la primavera.

Ahora, que en mis labios repica la risa
Como una campana sacudida a prisa.

Después... ¡ah, yo sé
Que ya nada de eso más tarde tendré!

Que entonces inútil será tu deseo
Como ofrenda puesta sobre un mausoleo.

¡Tómame ahora que aún es temprano
Y que tengo rica de nardos la mano!

Hoy, y no más tarde. Antes que anochezca
Y se vuelva mustia la corola fresca.

Hoy, y no mañana. Oh amante, ¿no ves
Que la enredadera crecerá ciprés?

1919

The Hour

Take me now while it's still early
And new dahlias fill my hands.

Take me now while it's still dark,
This silent long hair of mine.

Now, while my flesh is fragrant
And my eyes are clear, my skin pink.

Now while my light foot traces
The bright sandal of springtime.

Now while on my lips laughter rings
Like a bell shaken quickly.

Afterwards... I know
That later I'll have nothing of this.

And then your desire will be as useless
As a gift left in a tomb.

Take me now while it's still early
And my hands are rich with tuberoses.

Today, not later. Before it grows dark
And the fresh corolla fades.

Today, not tomorrow. Love, don't you see
The climbing plant grows into cypress.

trans. Sophie Cabot Black

El fuerte lazo

Crecí
Para ti.
Tálame. Mi acacia
Implora a tus manos su golpe de gracia.

The Strong Bond

I grew
For you.
Devastate me. My acacia
Begs from your hands the final coup de grace.

Florí
Para ti.
Córtame. Mi lirio
Al nacer dudaba ser flor a ser cirio.

Fluí
Para ti.
Bébeme. El cristal
Envidia lo claro de mi manantial.

Alas di
Por ti.
Cázame. Falena,
Rodeo tu llama de impaciencia llena.

Por ti sufriré.
¡Bendito sea el daño que tu amor me dé!
¡Bendita sea el hacha, bendita la red,
Y loadas sean tijera y sed!

Sangre del costado
Manaré, mi amado.
¿Qué broche más bello, qué joya más grata,
Que por ti una llaga color escarlata?

En vez de abalorios para mis cabellos,
Siete espinas largas hundiré entre ellos,
Y en vez de zarcillos pondré en mis orejas
Como dos rubíes dos ascuas bermejas.

Me verás reír
Viéndome sufrir.

Y tú llorarás
Y entonces... ¡más mío que nunca serás!

1919

I bloomed
For you.
Cut me. My lily
When it was born didn't know if it was flower or wax.

I flowed
For you.
Drink me. Even crystal
Envies the clarity of my spring.

I grew wings
For you.
Hunt me. Like a moth
filled with impatience, I circle your flame.

I will suffer for you.
Blessed be the damage your love gives me.
Blessed be the axe, blessed the net
And praised be the shears and the thirst.

Blood from my side:
I will bleed, my love.
What brooch is more beautiful, what jewel finer
Than this wound going crimson, for you?

Instead of ornaments for my hair,
I will sink in seven long thorns,
instead of tendrils I will put in my ears
Two rubies, two vermillion embers.

You'll watch me laugh.
See me suffer.

You will cry
And then... you'll be mine more than ever.

trans. Sophie Cabot Black and Maria Negroni

Vida-garfio

Amante: no me lleves, si muero, al camposanto.
A flor de tierra abre mi fosa, junto al riente
Alboroto divino de alguna pajarera
O junto a la encantada charla de alguna fuente.

A flor de tierra, amante. Casi sobre la tierra
Donde el sol me caliente los huesos, y mis ojos,
Alargados en tallos, suban a ver de nuevo
La lámpara salvaje de los ocasos rojos.

Life-Hook

Love: if I die don't take me to the cemetery.
Dig my grave just at ground level, near the laughing
Divine disturbance of a birdhouse.
Or by a fountain's haunting talk.

Just at ground level, my love. And almost above earth
Where the sun can heat the bones, and my eyes,
Extended, as if into stalks, rise to see again
The savage lamp of the setting sun.

A flor de tierra, amante. Que el tránsito así sea
      Más breve. Yo presiento
La lucha de mi carne por volver hacia arriba,
Por sentir en sus átomos la frescura del viento.

      Yo sé que acaso nunca allá abajo mis manos
      Podrán estarse quietas.
Que siempre como topos arañarán la tierra.
En medio de las sombras estrujadas y prietas.

      Arrójame semillas. Yo quiero que se enraicen
En la greda amarilla de mis huesos menguados.
¡Por la parda escalera de las raíces vivas
Yo subiré a mirarte en los lirios morados!

                                             1919

Just at ground level, my love. So the passage
      Will be even shorter. I sense
Already my flesh fighting, trying to return
To feel the atoms of a freshening wind.

      I know my hands
      May never stay still down there.
That like moles they will scrape the earth
In the middle of dark, compacted shadows.

      Cover me with seeds. I want them to root
In the yellow chalk of my diminishing bones.
Up the gray staircase of living roots
I will rise to watch you. I'll be the purple lilies.

                trans. Sophie Cabot Black and Maria Negroni

Noche de lluvia

Llueve..., espera, no te duermas,
Quédate atento a lo que dice el viento
Yo a lo que dice el agua que golpea
Con sus dedos menudos en los vidrios.

Todo mi corazón se vuelve oídos
Para escuchar a la hechizada hermana,
Que ha dormido en el cielo,
Que ha visto el sol de cerca,
Y baja ahora, elástica y alegre,
De la mano del viento,
Igual que una viajera
Que torna de un país de maravilla.

¡Cómo estará de alegre el trigo ondeante!
¡Con qué avidez se esponjará la hierba!
¡Cuántos diamantes colgarán ahora
Del ramaje profundo de los pinos!

Espera, no te duermas. Escuchemos
El ritmo de la lluvia.
Apoya entre mis senos
Tu frente taciturna.
Yo sentiré el latir de tus dos sienes,
Palpitantes y tibias,
Tal cual si fueran dos martillos vivos
Que golpearan mi carne.

Espera, no te duermas. Esta noche
Somos los dos un mundo,
Aislado por el viento y por la lluvia
Entre las cuencas tibias de una alcoba.

Rainy Night

It's raining... don't sleep yet,
Listen to what the wind says
And to the water striking
With small fingers against glass.

All my heart turns, intent
On hearing the enchanted sister
Who sleeps in the sky,
Who has seen the sun up close,
And who now comes down, resilient and blithe,
Her hand in the wind's,
Like the traveller
Who returns from a marvelous land.

And how happy the waving wheat will be,
The grass eagerly takes in and grows.
How many diamonds will now hang
From branches of the deep pines!

Wait, don't sleep. Listen
To the rhythm of the rain.
Rest your silent forehead
Between my breasts.
I'll feel the beating of your temples
Pulsing and warm,
As if they were two living hammers
Striking on my flesh.

Wait, don't sleep. Tonight
The two of us are a world,
Isolated by wind and rain
Between the warm hollows of a bedroom.

Espera, no te duermas. Esta noche
Somos acaso la raíz suprema
De donde debe germinar mañana
El tronco bello de una raza nueva.

1922

Wait, don't sleep. Tonight,
Perhaps, we are an ultimate root,
From where a beautiful stalk must begin,
Tomorrow, a new race.

trans. Sophie Cabot Black

Raíz salvaje

Me ha quedado clavada en los ojos
La visión de ese carro de trigo,
Que cruzó rechinante y pesado,
Sembrando de espigas el recto camino.

¡No pretendas, ahora, que ría!
¡Tú no sabes en qué hondos recuerdos
            Estoy abstraída!

Desde el fondo del alma me sube
Un sabor de pitanga a los labios.
Tiene aún mi epidermis morena
No sé qué fragancias de trigo emparvado.
¡Ay, quisiera llevarte conmigo
A dormir una noche en el campo
Y en tus brazos pasar hasta el día
Bajo el techo alocado de un árbol!

Soy la misma muchacha salvaje
Que hace años trajiste a tu lado.

1922

Wild Root

It has stayed stuck in my eyes:
The vision of that cart of wheat,
As it crosses, creaking and sluggish,
Scattering stalks all over the clear road.

Don't claim that now, I laugh.
You don't know in what deep memories
            I wander.

From the bottom of the soul a taste
Of cherry climbs to the lips.
Still held in my browned skin,
I-don't-know-what fragrances of baled hay.
I want to take you with me
Into the country to spend one night
In your arms till day,
Under the maddened root of a tree.

I'm the same wild girl
You brought to your side years ago.

trans. Sophie Cabot Black and Maria Negroni

Mujer

Si yo fuera hombre, ¡qué hartazgo de luna,
de sombra y silencio me había de dar!
¡Cómo, noche a noche, solo ambularía
por los campos quietos y por frente al mar!

Si yo fuera hombre, ¡qué extraño, qué loco,
tenaz vagabundo que había de ser!
¡Amigo de todos los largos caminos
que invitan a ir lejos para no volver!

Cuando así me acosan ansias andariegas,
¡qué pena tan honda me da ser mujer!

1922

Woman

If I were a man, I'd have all the moonlight—
and shadow—and silence—I wanted!
How I'd walk, night after night
through the quiet fields, and watch the ocean!

If I were a man, what a strange, odd,
purposeful vagabond I'd become!
Friend of all the open roads
that beckon, on and on and on!

When restless travel pesters me, tempting,
how deeply I resent I am a woman!

trans. Sophie Cabot Black

Jorge de Lima

BRAZIL
1895–1953

Trained as a physician in his home state of Alagôas in the Northeast of Brazil, Jorge Mateus de Lima practiced medicine for much of his adult life, while also pursuing careers as a writer, a professor of literature, a sculptor, a photographer, and a politician. (After the restoration of democracy in Brazil in 1945, he served a term as president of the city council of Rio de Janeiro.) Like Fernando Pessoa, the Portuguese poet he most admired, Jorge de Lima seems almost to be several poets: at times a folklorist who registers the rhythms of Afro-Brazilian experience, at times a mystic devoted to Mariology, at times a muralistic regionalist, a cerebral Surrealist, a Proustian memoirist. Near the end of his life, in poems from the 1940s leading toward *Invenção de Orfeo* (*Invention of Orpheus*, 1952), Lima's remarkable integrity asserted itself in lyrical meditations based on his Christian millennialism. In his last poems, Lima forged a style of neo-Baroque collage that helped him synthesize many of his emotional and intellectual interests.

Essa negra Fulô

Ora, se deu que chegou
(isso já faz muito tempo)
no bangüê dum meu avô
uma negra bonitinha
chamada negra Fulô.

    Essa negra Fulô!
    Essa negra Fulô!

Ó Fulô! Ó Fulô!
(Era a fala da Sinhá)
—Vai forrar a minha cama
pentear os meus cabelos
vem ajudar a tirar
a minha roupa, Fulô!

    Essa negra Fulô!

Essa negrinha Fulô!
ficou logo pra mucama
para vigiar a Sinhá
pra engomar pro Sinhó!

    Essa negra Fulô!
    Essa negra Fulô!

Ó Fulô! Ó Fulô!
(Era a fala da Sinhá)
vem me ajudar, ó Fulô,
vem abanar o meu corpo

That Black Girl Fulô

Now it so happened she came
(a long long time ago)
on grandfather's wagon,
a pretty little black girl
by the name of Fulô

    That black girl Fulô!
    That black girl Fulô!

Oh Fulô! Come, Fulô!
(the voice of the Mistress)
—come make up my bed
come brush my hair
come help me lay out
my wardrobe, oh Fulô!

    That black girl Fulô!

That little Fulô
became the companion
to look after Mistress
to iron for the Master

    That black girl Fulô!
    That black girl Fulô!

Oh Fulô! Come, Fulô!
(the voice of the Mistress)
come help me now, Fulô
come fan my body,

que eu estou suada, Fulô!
vem coçar minha coceira,
vem me catar cafuné,
vem balançar minha rêde,
vem me contar uma história,
que eu estou com sono, Fulô!

    Essa negra Fulô!

"Era um dia uma princesa
que vivia num castelo
que possuía um vestido
com os peixinhos do mar.
Entrou na perna dum pato
saiu na perna dum pinto
o Rei-Senhô me mandou
que vos contasse mais cinco."

    Essa negra Fulô!
    Essa negra Fulô!

Ó Fulô? Ó Fulô?
Vai botar para dormir
esses meninos, Fulô!
"Minha mãe me penteou
minha madrasta me enterrou
pelos figos da figueira
que o Sabiá beliscou".

    Essa negra Fulô!
    Essa negra Fulô!

Fulô? Ó Fulô?
(Era a fala da Sinhá
chamando a negra Fulô.)
Cadê meu frasco de cheiro
que teu Sinhô me mandou?

—Ah! Foi você que roubou!
Ah! Foi você que roubou!

O Sinhô foi ver a negra
levar couro do feitor.
A negra tirou a roupa.
O Sinhô disse: Fulô!
(A vista se escureceu
que nem a negra Fulô)

    Essa negra Fulô!
    Essa negra Fulô!

I sweat so in this heat, Fulô!
come scratch an itch,
come stroke my hair,
come swing my net,
come tell me a story,
I'm sleepy now, Fulô!

    That black girl Fulô!

" 'Once there was a princess
who lived in a castle
and once had a dress
with the fish of sea on it.
Up one side the leg of a duck,
down the other the leg of a chicken...'
Now the King-Master he say
I got to tell you five more."

    That black girl Fulô!
    That black girl Fulô!

Oh Fulô! Come, Fulô!
Now put the children
to bed, my Fulô!
"My mother she comb me,
my stepmother bury me
by the figs from the figtree
the songbird swiped."

    That black girl Fulô!
    That black girl Fulô!

Oh Fulô! Where are you, Fulô?
(the voice of the Mistress
calling the black girl Fulô)
Where is the bottle of cologne
the Master sent to me?

—Oh, It was you who stole it!
Oh, it was you who stole it!

The Master goes to see
the black girl whipped.
The black girl stripped.
The Master said: Fulô!
(His vision had turned
as dark as Fulô.)

    That black girl Fulô!
    That black girl Fulô!

Ó Fulô? Ó Fulô?
Cadê meu lenço de rendas,
cadê meu cinto, meu broche,
cadê meu têrco de ouro
que teu Sinhô me mandou?
Ah! foi você que roubou.
Ah! foi você que roubou.

    Essa negra Fulô!
    Essa negra Fulô!

O Sinhô foi açoitar
sozinho a negra Fulô.
A negra tirou a saia
e tirou o cabeção,
de dentro dele pulou
nuinha a negra Fulô.

    Essa negra Fulô!
    Essa negra Fulô!

Ó Fulô? Ó Fulô?
Cadê, cadê teu Sinhô
que nosso Senhor me mandou?
Ah! Foi você que roubou,
foi você, negra Fulô!

    Essa negra Fulô!

                    1928

Oh Fulô! Where are you, Fulô?
Where are my lace kerchief,
where are my belt, my brooch,
the golden rosary
the Master sent to me?
—Oh, it was you who stole them!
Oh, it was you who stole them!

    That black girl Fulô!
    That black girl Fulô!

The Master alone
took hold of the whip.
She took off her skirt
and then her shift too.
She jumped out of her shift:
naked Fulô, the black girl.

    That black girl Fulô!
    That black girl Fulô!

Oh, Fulô! Where are you, Fulô?
Where?—and oh where is your
    Master,
the man Our Lord gave to me?
—Oh, it was you who stole him,
    you, black Fulô!

    That black girl Fulô!

trans. Elizabeth Gordon

As trombetas

Ouço o baque dos anjos precipitados
cavando vales na terra.
Vejo do ventre primeiro, da Eva, da Madre,
os cordões umbilicais enleando os sêres até hoje.
E ouço o clamor das trombetas
acompanhando a queda das asas.
E em cada cordão que se rompe,
ressoa no choro nascente
a memória das trombetas.
E ouço outras trombetas e outras quedas e outros baques,
e sempre o sangue jorrando
e sempre o som legendário
reboando pelos vales.
Mal se extingue no ar a trombeta do anjo das guerras
nos vales coagulados de sangue;
nos antípodas dos vales, —novas trombetas anunciam
o choro dos que vão nascer para batalhar,
dos que vão nascer para se acabar.

The Trumpets

I hear the trumpets of flying angels
scooping valleys out of the earth.
From the First Womb, the womb of Eve, of the Mother,
    I see
umbilical cords dangling between beings, even now.
And I hear the clangor of trumpets
with the drift of wings.
And in each severed cord
the new cry's echoes are
the memory of those trumpets.
And I hear other trumpets and other falls and other
    declines,
and always the blood pounding
and always the legendary sound
echoing down the valleys.
The trumpet of the angel of war is hardly silenced in the air
in valleys clotted with blood,
in the depths of the valleys, when new trumpets announce

Ouço as trombetas finais reunindo
os meus membros esfacelados na morte.
Serei leve.
Sereis leves, —corpos ensangüentados que subireis do Vale
ao clangor majestoso das trombetas finais.

1938

Estrangeiro, estrangeiro

para José Osório de Oliveira

E quando os assírios acabaram de brigar com os caldeus
    enterraram os mortos;
e outros povos começaram a brigar pela posse da terra;
mas antes do dia findar, filisteus, hebreus, persas, gregos,
    árias, romanos, africanos, russos, espanhóis, chineses,
    japoneses,
brigaram, brigaram, brigaram.
E houve paz para enterrar os mortos.
E nem o Sinédrio, nem os Conselhos, nem a Liga das
    Nações,
nada fizeram, nada resolveram, nada adiantaram.
E houve paz para enterrar as ligas.
E rebentaram na carcaça velha do mundo cinqüenta
    revoluções simultâneas
para salvar o homem e garantir a paz.
E deram inúmeros prêmios nóbeis a vários chanceleres, e,
    cantaram hinos a várias democracias,
a vários grandes condutores;
e as polícias continuaram a espancar os sonhadores;
e os generais ganharam grandes soldos para defender as
    pátrias,
e houve bombas em várias partes do globo;
e ainda ontem, num morro do mundo,
a Tísica devorou várias môças,
e os germes continuam a se alimentar de crianças órfãs;
ricos, pobres, moços, e velhos se enforcaram nas árvores.
A massa tem fome, o uivo da humanidade é mais doloroso
    de noite.
A superfície da terra continua do tamanho de uma cova.
Estrangeiro que passais,
sois tão novo e sois tão velho quanto eu sou.
A mesma inquietação e a mesma decepção nos arrazam os
    olhos.
Estrangeiro que passais, quantas vêzes o chão que pisamos
    já mudou?
O senhor comissário já nos deu licença
de olhar as nuvens e aspirar a brisa de Deus?

the cries of those born during the battle,
who are born to disappear.
I hear the final trumpets bringing
my severed members together in death.
I will be light:
You will be light: —bloody bodies that will rise from the
    valley
in the majestic blare of the final trumpets.

trans. Luiz Fernández García

Stranger, Stranger

For José Osório de Oliveira

And when the Assyrians stopped waging war against the
    Chaldeans, they buried the dead;
and others began to fight for possession of the earth;
but before the day was over the Philistines, Hebrews,
    Persians, Greeks, Aryans, Romans, Africans,
    Russians, Spaniards, Chinese, Japanese
fought and fought and fought.
And there was peace to bury the dead.
And neither the Sanhedrin nor the Councils nor the
    Leagues of Nations
did anything, resolved anything, made progress with
    anything.
And there was peace to bury the leagues.
And across the old body of the earth fifty revolutions to
    save humankind and to guarantee peace raged all at
    once.
And they awarded innumerable Nobel Prizes to various
    Foreign Ministers, and they sang hymns to various
    democracies,
to various great leaders;
the police continued to bash the dreamers;
the generals earned huge salaries defending their
    fatherlands,
and bombs exploded in various parts of the globe;
and only yesterday, on a hillock of the earth,
tuberculosis consumed a number of girls
and worms kept feeding on young orphans;
the rich, the poor, the young and old hang themselves
    from trees.
Most are hungry; the wail of humanity is sadder at night.
The surface of the earth is still the size of a grave.
You, stranger passing by,
you are as young and as old as I.
The same anxieties and the same old lies bring tears to
    our eyes.
You, stranger passing by, how many times has the ground
    we walk on changed?

E para olhar o próximo eclipse arranjaremos bilhetes com
    o chefe?
Estrangeiro amigo, escrevamos para os nossos bisnetos
    fictícios
a história eterna do homem decaído e do mundo sem jeito.
Estrangeiro, vós me estendeis vossos braços e somos como
    velhos amigos passeando nos cais,
e olhando no mar—a vela, a asa, a onda e as coisas fugitivas.
Estrangeiro, estrangeiro, as nossas nações, apesar de nossa
    amizade,
continuam isoladas e inimigas como em Mesopotâmia:
e ainda há entre elas raças irreconciliáveis.
Estrangeiro, estrangeiro, eu sou dos vossos.
E se quereis ser dos meus, aceitai
que só a Igreja de Cristo—mais forte que a lei de gravidade,
continua a enterrar os mortos neste planêta errado.

1938

Has the commissioner given us permission
to watch the clouds and to breathe God's breezes?
And to view the next eclipse shall we order tickets from
    the boss?
Stranger, my friend, let us write for our imaginary great-
    grandchildren
the eternal story of fallen man and of the awkward world.
Stranger, you offer me your hand and we are like old
    friends, promenading on the levee
and looking out to sea—the sail, the wing, the wave, the
    transitory things.
Stranger, stranger, despite our friendship our countries still
are alienated from each other, are enemies, as in
    Mesopotamia:
and there still are unreconcilable races among them.
Stranger, stranger, I belong to your kind.
And if you long to belong to mine, believe
that only the Church of Christ—stronger than the law of
    gravity—
continues to bury the dead on this wayward planet.

trans. Luiz Fernández García

As palavras de despedida

E ouvirás em cada século que passa
um ruido que se perde no tempo;
e o último cometa que apenas passou ontem;
e os oceanos renovarem suas águas muitas vezes.
Verás várias constelações te enviarem seus raios e se
    extinguirem depois.
Confrontarás tua infância com as dos filhos do Sol.
Reconhecerás as estrelas que te jogaram pedras
quando eras um simples homem nos caminhos da vida.
Recensearás como Abraão os astros que puderes contar.
Contemplarás a morte prematura das luas
e a vida misteriosa das estrelas.
Reconstituirás o jogo da criação e o trono da primeira
    mulher.
Avistarás centenas de milhões de eclipses se produzirem
    simultâneamente.
E centenas de milhões de labaredas em espiral subirem até
    o trono do Mestre.
E te lembrarás que eras um pobre esquimó entre o gelo da
    terra e a última noite que te libertou do mundo.

1950

Words of Departure

And you will hear in every passing century
a sound lost in time;
and the last comet that passed by only yesterday;
and the oceans renewing their waters over and over.
You will see some constellations sending you their rays
    and then dying.
You will compare your childhood with that of the children
    of the Sun.
You will recognize stars that threw their rocks at you
when you were an ordinary man on life's paths.
You will count as Abraham did the celestial bodies, so that
    you can count.
You will contemplate the premature death of moons
and the mysterious life of the stars.
You will piece together the game of creation and the
    throne of the first woman.
You will watch hundreds of millions of eclipses happening
    all at once.
And hundreds of millions of flames in a spiral rising to the
    throne of the Master.
And you will remember you were a poor Eskimo caught
    between the ice of the earth and the final night that
    freed you from the world.

trans. Luiz Fernández García

Raul Bopp

Raised in the south of Brazil, trained as a lawyer in Recife and Rio, and seasoned as a diplomat in Japan and the United States, Raul Bopp found his true subject in Manaus, where he discovered what he insisted was the authentic Brazil. Bopp brought to the early Modernist movement in Brazil a fascination with the folklore, Indian languages, and culture of the vast hinterland of the Amazon basin. As a contributor to the magazine *Revista de Antropofagia* (*Anthropophagical Review*) in the 1920s and 1930s, Bopp defined the concerns of what he called the "Cannibalist school" of poetry. "Anthropophagical" in their appropriative and assimilative relation to European experimental writing, the theories of Bopp and Oswald de Andrade further associated them with the tenets of the cosmopolitan/indigenist "Verde e Amarelo" writers, who took their name ("The Green and Yellow") from the colors of the Brazilian flag.

His long poem *Cobra Norato* (*The Snake Norato* or, as translated by Renato Rezende, *Black Snake*) was written in 1928 and published in its first version in 1931. In it Bopp embodies his primitivist, mystical sense of the life of Brazil's interior, whose energy he and the other "Cannibalists" proposed as an alternative to the compromising forces of modern urban life. Skeptical, impressionistic, rhythmically complex, and erotically playful, the poem moves at times like a dream or a fairy tale. Its politics, however, are humanitarian and ecologically alert to the dangers of exploiting the rain forest and its indigenous cultures. In later editions, Bopp softened the bluntness and difficulty of the poem's diction, making the tone less austerely visionary and more tender. In his later poems, in his criticism, and in his several volumes of memoirs, Bopp continued his Modernist advocacy of Amazonian and Afro-Brazilian folklore as sources of energy and psychic survival.

Cobra Norato	*Black Snake*
II	II
Começa agora a floresta cifrada.	Begins here, the ciphered forest.
A sombra escondeu as árvores. Sapos beiçudos espiam no escuro.	The shade is hiding the trees. Blubber-lipped frogs spy in the dark.
Aqui um pedaço de mato está de castigo. Árvorezinhas acocoram-se no charco. Um fio de água atrasada lambe a lama.	Here a piece of the forest is being punished. Little trees squat in the pond. A hurried stream licks the mud.
—Eu quero é ver a filha da rainha Luzía.	—I want to see Queen Luzía's daughter!
Agora são os rios afogados bebendo o caminho. A água vai chorando afundando afundando.	Now drowned rivers drink the road. The water goes crying, sinking and sinking.
Lá adiante a areia guardou os rastos da filha da rainha Luzía!	Far ahead the sand held the tracks of Queen Luzía's daughter.

—Agora sim
vou ver a filha da rainha Luzía.

Mas antes tem que passar por sete portas
Ver sete mulheres brancas de ventres despovoados
guardadas por um jacaré.

—Eu só quero a filha da rainha Luzía.

Tem que entregar a sombra para o Bicho do Fundo.
Tem que fazer mironga na lua nova.
Tem que beber três gotas de sangue.

—Ah só se fôr da filha da rainha Luzía!

A selva imensa está com insônia.

Bocejam árvores sonolentas.
Ai que a noite secou. A água do rio se quebrou
Tenho que ir-me embora.

Me sumo sem rumo no fundo do mato
onde as velhas árvores grávidas cochilam.

De todos os lados me chamam:
—Onde vais, Cobra Norato?
Tenho aqui três àrvorezinhas jovens à tua espera.

—Não posso.
Eu hoje vou dormir com a filha da rainha Luzía.

IV

Esta é a floresta de hálito podre,
parindo cobras.

Rios magros obrigados a trabalhar.

A correnteza se arrepia nos remoinhos
descascando as margens gosmentas.

Raízes desdentadas mastigam lodo

Num estirão alagado
o charco engole a água do igarapê.

Fede.
O vento mudou de lugar

Um assobio assusta as árvores.
Silencio se machucou

—Yes, now
I will see Queen Luzía's daughter!

But first you must pass through seven doors.
See seven white women with empty wombs, watched
over by a crocodile.

—I just want to see Queen Luzía's daughter.

First you must give your shadow to the Bottomless Being.
Accomplish extraordinary deeds under the rising moon.
Drink three drops of blood.

—Only if it's the blood
of Queen Luzía's daughter!

The immense forest suffers insomnia.

Sleepy trees are now yawning.
The night is all dried up. The river waters are broken.
I have to go.

I vanish into the ancient forest
where pregnant trees are napping.

From everywhere they call me:
—Where are you going, Cobra Norato?
Here we have three young saplings, awaiting you.

—I can't.
Tonight I will sleep with Queen Luzía's daughter.

IV

This is the rotten-breathed forest
giving birth to cobras.

Meager rivers are forced to work.

The running water shivers in the sworls
husking the slimy banks.

Toothless roots masticate mud.

In a swampy stretch of road
the pond swallows the igarapé's water.

Stinks.
The wind has moved out.

A hiss frightens the trees.
The silence was hurt.

Cai lá adiante um pedaço de pau sêco:
pum.

Um berro avulso atravessa a floresta
Chegam vozes.

O rio se engasgou num barranco

Espia-me um sapo sapo sapo
Por aqui há cheiro de gente
—Quem é você?

—Sou a Cobra Norato
Vou me amaziar a filha da rainha Luzía.

VI

Passo nas beiras de um encharcadiço
lambido pelas enxurradas.
Um plasma visguento se descostura
e alaga as margens rasas debruadas de lama.

Vou furando paredões moles.
Caio num fundo escuro de floresta
inchada alarmada mal-assombrada.

Ouvem-se apitos, um bate-que-bate
Estão soldando serrando serrando
Parece que fabricam terra...
Ué! Estão mesmo fabricando terra.

Chiam longos tanques de lôdo-pacoema
Os velhos andaimes podres se derretem
Lameiros se emendam
Mato amontoado derrama-se no chão.

Correm vozes em desordem.
Berram: *Não pode!*
—Será comigo?

Passo por baixo de arcadas folhudas
que respiram um ar úmido.

A floresta trabalha
Espalha planta pelos estirões de terra fresca

Arbustos incognitos perguntam:
—Já será dia?
Manchas de luz abrem buracos nas copas altas

Àrvores-comadres
passaram a noite tecendo fôlhas em segredo.

Far ahead a dry branch falls:
poom.

A detached howl crosses the forest
Voices arrive.

The river choked itself in a ditch

Frogs spy on me
There is a human scent around here.
—Who are you?

I'm Cobra Norato
Today I will enjoy Queen Luzía's daughter.

VI

I pass the swamp borders
being licked by the torrents.
A viscous plasma rips open,
overflowing the shallow waters with mud.

I thread my way through soft walls.
I fall into a dark bottom of the forest—
it's swollen it's alarmed it's haunted.

Whistles sound, a beat sounds
Something drills and saws and saws
Sounds like a mud factory.
Oh! It really is a mud factory.

Long wide pacoema-slime ponds squeak
The old rotten scaffold melts.
Marshes meet and melt together
Branches and leaves scatter on the ground.

Voices in confusion running
Howling: "*It can't be!*"
—Are they talking to me?

I pass under a tufted arch
that exhales a wet breath.

The forest is working
spreading vegetation over new earth.

Unknown bushes are asking:
—Is it day already?
The light opens holes in the high tree-tops.

Comrade-trees
spent the night secretly weaving leaves.

Vento-ventinho assoprou de fazer cocegas nos ramos
Desmanchou escrituras indecifradas.

XI

Acordo.

A lua nasceu com olheiras.
O silêncio dói dentro do mato.

Abriram-se as estrêlas.
As águas grandes encolheram-se com sono.

A noite cansada parou

Ai compadre!
Tenho vontade de ouvir uma música mole
que se estire por dentro do sangue:
música com gôsto de lua
e do corpo da filha da rainha Luzía;

que me faça ouvir de nôvo
a conversa dos rios
que trazem as queixas do caminho
e vozes que vem de longe
surradas de ai ai ai

Atravessei o Treme-treme

Passei na casa do Minhocão.
Deixei minha sombra para o Bicho-do-Fundo
só por causa da filha da rainha Luzía

Levei puçanga de cheiro
e casca de tinhorão
fanfan com fôlhas de trevo
e raiz de mucura-cáa.

Mas nada deu certo...

Ando com uma jurumenha
que faz um dòizinho na gente
e morde o sangue devagarinho.

Ai compadre.
Não faça barulho
que a filha da
rainha Luzía
talvez ainda esteja dormindo.

Ai onde andará
que eu quero sòmente

A wind—a little wind—blew, tickling the branches
Undid undeciphered writings.

XI

I wake up.

The moon rose with bags under its eyes.
The silence hurts within the forest.

The stars are clean.
The great waters shrank while sleeping.

The tired night has stopped.

Oh, my friend!
I feel like listening to soft music—
that stretches itself within my blood:
a music that tastes like the moon
and like Queen Luzia's daughter's body;

and that makes me hear again
the conversations of the rivers—
which bring the lamentations of the journey
and voices that came from far away
swollen with sobbings

I crossed the Shaken-lands

I stopped at the Big Worm's house.
I left my shadow with the Bottomless Being
only for Queen Luzia's daughter

I brought scented potions
and tinhorão-tree bark
a bunch of clover-leaves
and mucura-cá roots.

But nothing worked out...

I go with such a sadness—
that slowly hurts a little
and bites the blood tenderly.

Oh, my friend.
Do not make noise
because maybe
the daughter of Queen Luzia
is still sleeping.

Oh, where would she be
for I only want to see

ver os seus olhos molhados de verde	*her eyes wet with green*
seu corpo alongado de canarana.	*her body—slim—like sugar-cane.*
Talvez ande longe...	*Maybe she is far away...*
E eu virei vira-mundo	*And I became a vagabond,*
para ter um querzinho	*a world-traveller, wishing*
de apertar o corpo de pele de flor	*to squeeze the body made of skin of flower*
da filha da	*of the daughter*
rainha Luzía	*of Queen Luzia.*
Ai não faça barulho...	*Oh, do not make noise...*

XV

Céu muito azul.	Sky very blue.
Garcinha branca voou voou...	White little heron flew and flew...
Pensou que o lago era lá em cima.	It thought the lake was way above.
Pesa um mormaço. Dói a luz nos olhos.	Heavy dampness. Light hurting the eyes.
Sol parece um espelhinho.	The sun seems like a little mirror.
Vozes se dissolvem:	Dissolving voices:
Passarão sòzinho risca a paisagem bojuda.	A lone enormous bird crosses the pregnant horizon.

1928/1931   *trans. Renato Rezende*

Ricardo Molinari

ARGENTINA
1898–

Ricardo Molinari, who maintained that the formal roots of his poems lay in the Spanish classical tradition, lived for many years in Spain, where he was befriended by García Lorca and where he wrote early poems of hermetic intensity. When Molinari returned to Argentina he worked to integrate the austere, image-rich lyricism of his classical training with the rhythms of free verse, to articulate the physical and psychic landscape of his homeland.

If Borges is the poet of Buenos Aires, an urbane and sly and mystical poet, Molinari is the earnest poet of Argentine solitude, of the landscape of the pampas, of the mortal and transitory elements of experience. "My poetry is my world," he once explained. "I sing what I cannot keep, what becomes absence." Thus, in this thematic of absence and verbal repetition, Molinari's poems ally themselves with the mystical themes of time and its verbal echoes in Borges. Molinari's ablest critic, Julio Arístedes, characterized this central thematic as "the agony of being in time." This combination of solitude and elegance, evident in Molinari's "odes" and in the collection *Un día, el tiempo, y las nubes* (*A Day, Time, and the Clouds*, 1964), largely explains his enduring influence on younger Argentine poets.

Poema de la Niña Velázqueña

Ah, si el pueblo fuera tan pequeño
que todas sus calles pasaran por mi puerta.

Yo deseo tener una ventana
que sea el centro del mundo,
y una pena
como la de la flor de la magnolia,
que si la tocan se obscurece.

Por qué no tendrá el pueblo una cintura
amurallada
hasta el día de su muerte,
o un río turbulento que lo rodee
para guardar a la niña velazqueña.

Ah, sus pasos son como los de la paloma,
remansados;
para la amistad yo siempre la pinto sin pareja;
en una de sus manos lleva un globo
de agua,
en el que se ve lo frágil del destino
y lo continuado del vivir.
Su voz
es tan suave, que en su atmósfera convalece
la pena desgraciada,
y como en las coplas:
de su cabellera
nace la noche
y de sus manos el alba.
En qué piedad o dulzura se irán aclimatando
las cosas que ella mira
o le son familiares,
como el incienso,
la goma de límon
y la tardanza
con que siempre la miro.

Por qué no tendrá el pueblo allá
en su fondo,
un acueducto,
para que el paisaje que ven sus ojos
esté húmedo,
y nunca se fatigue de mirarlo.

Yo sé que su bondad
tiene más horas que el día,
y que todos sus pensamientos van entre el alba
y el atardecer
conmoviéndola.
Los días que se van la agrandan.

Poem of the Girl from Velázquez

Ah, if only the village were so small
that all the streets passed by my door.

I wish I had a window
that would be the center of the world,
and a sorrow
like that of the magnolia-flower,
which darkens when you touch it.

Why does the village not have a wall
surrounding it
until the day of her death,
or a turbulent river encircling it
to guard the girl from Velazquez.

Ah, her steps are like the dove's,
tranquil;
for friendship's sake I always imagine her alone,
holding in one of her hands a balloon
full of water
in which the fragility of destiny can be seen
and the continuity of life.
Her voice
is so gentle that in its atmosphere
sad grief heals,
as also in poems:
from her hair
the night is born,
and the dawn from her hands.
What piety, or sweetness, will they be used to,
the things she looks at
or things familiar to her,
like the incense,
the lemon-jellies,
the longing
with which I look at her.

Why doesn't the village have
an aqueduct
there, behind it,
so that the landscape her eyes see
is watered,
and she never grows tired of looking at it.

I know her goodness
has more hours than the day,
and that all her thoughts pass between dawn
and dusk,
touching her.
The days that pass make her grow.

Qué horizonte estará más cercano
de su corazón,
para encaminar todos mis pasos
hacia él,
aunque se quede descalza la esperanza.

Quién la rescatará de la castidad,
mientras yo sólo anhelo
que en su voz,
algún día, llegue a oírme....

1927

Oda a una larga tristeza

Quisiera cantar una larga tristeza que no olvido,
una dura lengua. Cuántas veces.

En mi país el Otoño nace de una flor seca,
de algunos pájaros; a veces creo que de mi nuca
    abandonada
o del vaho penetrante de ciertos ríos de la llanura
cansados de sol, de la gente que a sus orillas
goza una vida sin majestad.

Cuando se llega para vivir entre unos sacos de carbón y se
    siente que la piel
se enseñorea de hastío,
de repugnante soledad; que el ser es una isla sin un clavel,
se desea el Otoño, el viento que coge a las hojas
igual que a las almas; el viento
que inclina sin pesadez las embriagadas hierbas,
para envolverlas en el consuelo de la muerte.

No; no quisiera volver jamás a la tierra;
me duele toda la carne, y donde ha habido un beso se me
    pudre el aire.
En el Verano florido he visto un caballo azulado y un toro
    transparente
beber en el pecho de los ríos, inocentes, su sangre;
los árboles de las venas, llenos, perdidos en los laberintos
    tibios del cuerpo,
en la ansiosa carne oprimida. En el Verano...
Mis días bajaban por la sombra de mi cara
y me cubrían el vientre, la piel pura, rumorosa,
envueltos en la claridad
más dulce.
Como un demente, ensordecido, inagotable,
quebrada la rosa el junco, el agitado seno deslumbrante,
sin velos, en el vacío descansa indiferente un día sin
    pensamiento,

What horizon will be closest
to her heart,
so that I can take each of my steps
toward it,
although hope stays barefoot.

Who will rescue her from chastity,
while I hope only
that in her voice,
some day, she comes to hear me....

trans. Inés Probert

Ode to a Long Sorrow

I would like to tell about an enduring sorrow I have
    not forgotten,
a difficult story. So many times.

In my country autumn is born from a dry flower,
from certain birds; sometimes I believe it is born from my
    forsaken throat
or from a penetrant odor of certain rivers on the plain,
tired of the sun, from people on the river-banks
who live an unmajestic life.

When you arrive there, to live among the bags of coal,
    and feel the skin
seize the ennui,
the repugnant solitude, that one's being is an island with
    no carnations,
one longs for the autumn, the wind that grasps at leaves
as if at souls; the wind
without oppressiveness bending the drunken weeds,
to wrap them in the consolation of death.

No, I don't want ever to return to the earth;
all my flesh aches, and where a kiss has been my breath
    festers.
In blossoming summer I have seen a blue horse and a
    transparent bull
drink from the breast of the rivers—innocent, their blood;
the tree of the veins, full, lost in the lukewarm labyrinths
    of the body,
in the anxious worried flesh. In summer...
my days went down along the shadow of my face
and they covered my womb, the pure skin, whispering,
wrapped in the sweetest
clarity.
Like a madman, deafened, inexhaustible,
the bullrush broke the rose, the agitated bewildered
    bosom,

sin hombre, con un anochecer que llega con una espada.

Un sucio resplandor me quema las flores del cielo,
las grandes llanuras majestuosas.
Quisiera cantar esta larga tristeza desterrada,
pero, ay, siento llegar el mar hasta mi boca.

1940

without veils, in the emptiness resting indifferent, a day
    with no consciousness,
without humans, with an evening that arrives with the
    sword.

A dirty glare burns the flowers of heavens,
the great majestic plains.
I would like to tell about this long and exiled sorrow,
but, oh, I feel the sea arriving in my mouth!

trans. Inés Probert

Pequeña oda a la melancolía

Encima de las anchas y duras hojas frías del tiempo llegas
    manchada
por el huyente sol de las estaciones húmedas en las
    planicies.
Tibia de color y tiritante vienes, y mi corazón siente la
    dicha, la guarda, de una palabra
callada, y el susurrante paso en las hierbas cubre el hastío,
    la lumbre,
de una retenida esencia ahogada y remota.

Derecha y unida, la veste recoges replegada, deshecha
    junto al hueso.
¡Cuánto y hondo del alma quieres para entrar en ti,
    rozarte! Sí, igual que el aire
dentro de la boca abrumada y llameante.
Pasas con las mareas del océano y el brillo empapado de
    los cielos lentos, últimos, que acuden
velados por el sur, donde vuela y anida la avutarda
    colorada, y la noche
se vuelve y llama angustiosa debajo de las floridas
    obscuridades,
nostálgica y esparcida.

1966

Little Ode to Melancholy

Over the wide cold leaves of time you arrive, stained
by the fleeting sun of the rainy seasons on the plains.
You come lukewarm in color and shivering, and my heart
    feels the bliss, holds it, from a word
unspoken, and the murmuring steps on the grass cover
    the ennui, the glow,
of an essence withheld, drowned and remote.
You gather a robe around you—proper, singular—,
    folding it around you
around you, curved to fit the bone.
How much of the soul, what depths of the soul you want
    to enter you, to touch you lightly in passing! Yes:
    even as air
enters the mouth, claustral and flaring.
You go with the ocean tides and the watery brilliance of
    the slow, final skies, which go
veiled toward the south where the great red bustard flies
    and nests, and the night
turns back and calls full of anguish under the flowering
    darknesses,
nostalgic and scattered.

trans. Inés Probert

Luis Palés Matos

P U E R T O   R I C O
1898–1959

The most famous poet of Puerto Rico and one of the foremost representatives of Caribbean poetry after the Négritude movement, Luis Palés Matos combines a thematic commitment to the African presence in the New World with a formalist, sometimes surreal and sometimes playful, austerity. "Dreaming is the natural condition," he claimed. Within the freedom this formulation offered him, Palés Matos wrote poems and essays that established him as the artistic conscience of the Antilles. His subject matter includes descriptions of villages and village life, scenes of mythological and social survivals of African customs in Caribbean culture, and angry satires of racial relations in Puerto Rico and Haiti. His style, which borrows from local spoken discourse as well as from Spanish literary models, affords him great tonal range. Luis Palés Matos' poetic world exists, as Federico de Onís describes it, "between the Baroque and the prosaic, between emotion and irony, the spiritual and physical, the dreamed and the real, the exotic and the local: everything is equal and is one and the same."

Pueblo

¡Piedad, Señor, piedad para mi pobre pueblo
donde mi pobre gente se morirá de nada!
Aquel viejo notario que se pasa los días
en su mínima y lenta preocupación de rata;
este alcalde adiposo de grande abdomen vacuo
chapoteando en su vida tal como en una salsa;
aquel comercio lento, igual, de hace diez siglos;
estas cabras que triscan el resol de la plaza;
algún mendigo, algún caballo que atraviesa
tiñoso, gris y flaco, por estas calles anchas;
la fría y atrofiante modorra del domingo
jugando en los casinos con billar y barajas;
todo, todo el rebaño tedioso de estas vidas
en este pueblo viejo donde no ocurre nada,
todo esto se muere, se cae, se desmorona,
a fuerza de ser cómodo y de estar a sus anchas.

¡Piedad, Señor, piedad para mi pobre pueblo!
Sobre estas almas simples, desata algún canalla
que contra el agua muerta de sus vidas arroje
la piedra redentora de una insólita hazaña...
Algún ladrón que asalte ese Banco en la noche,
algún Don Juan que viole esa doncella casta,
algún tahur de oficio que se meta en el pueblo
y revuelva estas gentes honorables y mansas.

¡Piedad, Señor, piedad para mi pobre pueblo
donde mi pobre gente se morirá de nada!

1925

Pueblo

Pity, Lord, pity on my poor town,
where my poor people will die of nothing!

That old notary who spends days
in his minimal and slow, ratlike job;
this adipose mayor with a big, empty belly
wallowing in his life, as though in a sauce;
that slow business the same as ten centuries ago;
these goats that frolic in the sun glare of the square;
some beggar; some horse that crosses,
sordid, gray, and skinny, these wide streets;
the cold atrophying Sunday drowsiness,
playing billiards and cards in the casino;
everything, the whole tedious flock of these lives
in the old town where nothing happens,
all this is dying, falling, crumbling
by dint of being comfortable and unrestricted.
Unleash some villain on these poor souls
to cast the redeeming stone of an extraordinary deed
against the dead water of their lives...;
some thief to assault that bank at night;
some Don Juan to ravage that chaste damsel;
some professional gambler to get into the town
and stir up these honorable docile people...

Pity, Lord, pity on my poor town;
where my poor people will die of nothing!

trans. Barry Luby

Elegía del Duque de la Mermelada

¡Oh mi fino, mi melado Duque de la Mermelada!
¿Dónde están tus caimanes en el lejano aduar del Pongo,
y la sombra azul y redonda de tus baobabs africanos,
y tus quince mujeres olorosas a selva y a fango?

Ya no comerás el suculento asado de niño,
ni el mono familiar, a la siesta, te matará los piojos,

Elegy for the Duke of Marmalade

Oh, my fine, my honey-colored Duke of Marmalade!
Where are your alligators in the distant Pongo village,
and the round blue shadows of your African baobabs,
and your fifteen wives that smell of mud and jungle?

No longer will you eat the succulent roast of child,
nor will your familiar monkey kill your lice at siesta time,

ni tu ojo dulce rasteará el paso de la jirafa afeminada
a través del silencio plano y caliente de las sabanas.

Se acabaron tus noches con su suelta cabellera de fogatas
y su gotear soñoliento y perenne de tamboriles,
en cuyo fondo te ibas hundiendo como en un lodo tibio
hasta llegar a las márgenes últimas de tu gran bisabuelo.

Ahora, en el molde vistoso de tu casaca francesa,
pasas azucarado de saludos como un cortesano cualquiera,
a despecho de tus pies que desde sus botas ducales
te gritan:—Babilongo, súbete por las cornisas del
          palacio—.

¡Qué gentil va mi Duque con la Madama de Cafolé,
todo afelpado y pulcro en la onda azul de los violines,
conteniendo las manos que desde sus guantes de aristócrata
le gritan:—Babilongo, derríbala sobre ese canapé de rosa!—

Desde las márgenes últimas de tu gran bisabuelo,
a través del silencio plano y caliente de las sabanas,
¿por qué lloran tus caimanes en el lejano aduar del Pongo,
¡oh mi fino, mi melado Duque de la Mermelada!?

nor your soft eyes track the step of the effeminate giraffe
across the flat, hot silence of the grasslands.

Ended are your nights with their streaming hair of bonfires
and their sleepy perpetual trickle of timbrels,
in which depth you sank as into a warm mud
until you reached the final limits of your great grandfather.

Now in the flaring mold of your French coat,
you pass sugared with greetings like any other courtier,
in spite of your feet which shriek to you from their
ducal boots: "Babilongo, climb up the cornices of the
          palace!"

How refined goes my Duke with Madame Cafolé,
all velvety and trim on the blue wave of violins,
restraining his hands which from his gentlemanly gloves
shriek at him: "Babilongo, make her on that pink lounge!"

From the final limits of your great grandfather,
across that flat, hot silence of the grasslands,
why do your alligators weep in the distant Pongo village,
oh my fine, my honey-colored Duke of Marmalade?

                                        1937

                              trans. Ellen G. Matilla and Diego de la Texera

---

Jorge Luis Borges

ARGENTINA
1899–1986

Although he was educated in Switzerland and England, Jorge Luis Borges returned to his native Argentina (in 1921) a more passionate advocate of its potential than he had been when he left it. In the prologue to his first book of poems, *Fervor de Buenos Aires* (*Passion for B.A.*, 1923), Borges defined the tenets of the *ultraísta* movement, of which he was the most influential theorist and practitioner. The literary qualities he advocated there were defined largely in contradistinction to the ornate and musical art of Darío and his followers. Instead of the decorative rhetoric of *rubéndarismo*, Borges insisted on the power of the Image ("our universal password and sign"). Instead of the purely auditory or musical phrase, the young Borges admired the forward momentum of free verse. Instead of the early Modernist vision of contemporary life as mechanical and urban and dominated by an elegantly melancholic "nostalgia for Europe," Borges proposed a more immediately local, profound, and mythic reality as the focus of poetic energies.

Borges learned these lessons early, adapting to the idiom of Buenos Aires concepts derived from Lugones, from German Expressionism, from José Hernández' epic *El gaucho Martín Fierro* (1812), and from his own mythic conceptions of Argentine history and identity. By his thirties Borges had come to consider some of the Vanguardist elements of his early poems too sensationalistic, striving too stylishly after effect. Although Borges would later become more interested in questions of narrative truth, metaphysics, memory, and the labyrinths of intertextuality, some of those early

Vanguardist ideals—the primacy of the Symbol, for instance—continued to influence Borges through his long career as a poet, fiction writer, essayist, critic, and author of detective fiction. As he went blind, during his later years, Borges became an iconic figure of world literature, the creator and interpreter of an oneiric literary world. Tightened by his early work in poetry, his allusive prose style—like the glancing brilliant play of sunlight on ice—shapes a glacially ironic imaginative locus: both text and its own interpretation, both source and parody, word and echo, voice and void. In the late pieces of short prose for which he is best known in North America, Borges' "metaphysical restlessness" takes the form of complex ironic parables of the mysteries of time and human consciousness. For many years Borges served as an official of the state library system in Buenos Aires. Although Juan Perón dismissively had him reassigned for a time as an inspector of meat products, Borges later served as director of the National Library of Argentina.

Un patio

Con la tarde
se cansaron los dos o tres colores del patio.
La gran franqueza de la luna llena
ya no entusiasma su habitual firmamento.
Patio, cielo encauzado.
El patio es el declive
por el cual se derrama el cielo en la casa.
Serena,
la eternidad espera en la encrucijada de estrellas.
Grato es vivir en la amistad oscura
de un zaguán, de una parra y de un aljibe.

1923

Patio

With evening
the two or three colors of the patio grew weary.
The huge candor of the full moon
no longer enchants its usual firmament.
Patio: heaven's watercourse.
The patio is the slope
down which the sky flows into the house.
Serenely
eternity waits at the crossway of the stars.
It is lovely to live in the dark friendliness
of covered entrance way, arbor, and wellhead.

trans. Robert Fitzgerald

Casas como ángeles

Donde San Juan y Chacabuco se cruzan
vi las casas azules,
vi las casas que tienen colores de aventura.
Eran como banderas
y hondas como el naciente que suelta las afueras.
Las hay color de aurora y las hay color de alba;
su resplandor es una pasión ante la ochava
de la esquina cualquiera, turbia y desanimada.
Yo pienso en las mujeres
que buscarán el cielo de sus patios fervientes.
Pienso en los claros brazos que ilustrarán la tarde
y en el negror de trenzas: pienso en la dicha grave
de mirarse en sus ojos hondos, como parrales.
Empujaré la puerta cancel que es hierro y patio
y habrá una clara niña, ya mi novia, en la sala,
y los dos callaremos, trémulos como llamas,
y la dicha presente se aquietará en pasada.

1925

Houses like Angels

Where San Juan and Chacabuco intersect
I saw the blue houses,
the houses that wear colors of adventure.
They were like banners
and deep as the dawn that frees the outlying quarters.
Some are daybreak color and some dawn color;
their cool radiance is a passion before the oblique
face of any drab, discouraged corner.
I think of the women
who will be looking skyward from their burning dooryards.
I think of the pale arms that make evening glimmer
and of the blackness of braids: I think of the grave delight
of being mirrored in their deep eyes, like arbors of night.
I will push the gate of iron entering the dooryard
and there will be a fair girl, already mine, in the room.
And the two of us will hush, trembling like flames,
and the present joy will grow quiet in that passed.

trans. Robert Fitzgerald

Fundación mítica de Buenos Aires

¿Y fue por este río de sueñera y de barro
que las proas vinieron a fundarme la patria?
Irían a los tumbos los barquitos pintados
entre los camalotes de la corriente zaina.

Pensando bien la cosa, supondremos que el río
era azulejo entonces como oriundo del cielo
con su estrellita roja para marcar el sitio
en que ayunó Juan Díaz y los indios comieron.

Lo cierto es que mil hombres y otros mil arribaron
por un mar que tenía cinco lunas de anchura
y aun estaba poblado de sirenas y endriagos
y de piedras imanes que enloquecen la brújula.

Prendieron unos ranchos trémulos en la costa,
durmieron extrañados. Dicen que en el Riachuelo,
pero son embelecos fraguados en la Boca.
Fue una manzana entera y en mi barrio: en Palermo.

Una manzana entera pero en mitá del campo
presenciada de auroras y lluvias y suestadas.
La manzana pareja que persiste en mi barrio:
Guatemala, Serrano, Paraguay, Gurruchaga.

Un almacén rosado como revés de naipe
brilló y en la trastienda conversaron un truco;
el almacén rosado floreció en un compadre,
ya patrón de la esquina, ya resentido y duro.

El primer organito salvaba el horizonte
con su achacoso porte, su habanera y su gringo.
El corralón seguro ya opinaba YRIGOYEN,
algún piano mandaba tangos de Saborido.

Una cigarrería sahumó como una rosa
el desierto. La tarde se había ahondado en ayeres,
los hombres compartieron un pasado ilusorio.
Sólo faltó una cosa: la vereda de enfrente.

A mí se me hace cuento que empezó Buenos Aires:
La juzgo tan eterna como el agua y el aire.

1929

The Mythical Founding of Buenos Aires

And was it along this torpid muddy river
that the prows came to found my native city?
The little painted boats must have suffered the steep surf
among the root-clumps of the horse-brown current.

Pondering well, let us suppose that the river
was blue then like an extension of the sky,
with a small red star inset to mark the spot
where Juan Díaz fasted and the Indians dined.

But for sure a thousand men and other thousands
arrived across a sea that was five moons wide,
still infested with mermaids and sea serpents
and magnetic boulders which sent the compass wild.

On the coast they put up a few ramshackle huts
and slept uneasily. This, they claim, in the Riachuelo,
but that is a story dreamed up in the Boca.
It was really a city block in my district—Palermo.

A whole square block, but set down in open country,
attended by dawns and rains and hard southeasters,
identical to that block which still stands in my
    neighborhood:
Guatemala—Serrano—Paraguay—Gurruchaga.

A general store pink as the back of a playing card
shone bright; in the back there was poker talk.
The corner bar flowered into life as a local bully,
already cock of his walk, resentful, tough.

The first barrel organ teetered over the horizon
with its clumsy progress, its habaneras, its wop.
The cart-shed wall was unanimous for YRIGOYEN.
Some piano was banging out tangos by Saborido.

A cigar store perfumed the desert like a rose.
The afternoon had established its yesterdays,
and men took on together an illusory past.
Only one thing was missing—the street had no other side.

Hard to believe Buenos Aires had any beginning.
I feel it to be as eternal as air and water.

trans. Alastair Reid

Poema conjetural

El doctor Francisco Laprida, asesinado
el día 22 de setiembre de 1829 por los
montoneros de Aldao, piensa antes de morir:

Zumban las balas en la tarde última.
Hay viento y hay cenizas en el viento,
se dispersan el día y la batalla
deforme, y la victoria es de los otros.
Vencen los bárbaros, los gauchos vencen.
Yo, que estudié las leyes y los cánones,
yo, Francisco Narciso de Laprida,
cuya voz declaró la independencia
de estas crueles provincias, derrotado,
de sangre y de sudor manchado el rostro,
sin esperanza ni temor, perdido,
huyo hacia el Sur por arrabales últimos.

Como aquel capitán del Purgatorio
que, huyendo a pie y ensangrentando el llano,
fue cegado y tumbado por la muerte
donde un oscuro río pierde el nombre,
así habré de caer. Hoy es el término.
La noche lateral de los pantanos
me acecha y me demora. Oigo los cascos
de mi caliente muerte que me busca
con jinetes, con belfos y con lanzas.

Yo que anhelé ser otro, ser un hombre
de sentencias, de libros, de dictámenes,
a cielo abierto yaceré entre ciénagas;
pero me endiosa el pecho inexplicable
un júbilo secreto. Al fin me encuentro
con mi destino sudamericano.
A esta ruinosa tarde me llevaba
el laberinto múltiple de pasos
que mis días tejieron desde un día
de la niñez. Al fin he descubierto
la recóndita clave de mis años,
la suerte de Francisco de Laprida,
la letra que faltaba, la perfecta
forma que supo Dios desde el principio.
En el espejo de esta noche alcanzo
mi insospechado rostro eterno. El círculo
se va a cerrar. Yo aguardo que así sea.

Pisan mis pies la sombra de las lanzas
que me buscan. Las befas de mi muerte,
los jinetes, las crines, los caballos,
se ciernen sobre mí... Ya el primer golpe,
ya el duro hierro que me raja el pecho,
el íntimo cuchillo en la garganta.

1943

Conjectural Poem

Doctor Francisco Laprida, set upon and killed the
22nd of September 1829 by a band of gaucho militia
serving under Aldao, reflects before he dies:

Bullets whip the air this last afternoon.
A wind is up, blowing full of cinders
as the day and this chaotic battle
straggle to a close. The gauchos have won:
victory is theirs, the barbarians'.
I, Francisco Narciso Laprida,
who studied both canon law and civil
and whose voice declared the independence
of this entire untamed territory,
in defeat, my face marked by blood and sweat,
holding neither hope nor fear, the way lost,
strike out for the South through the back country.

Like that captain in Purgatorio
who fleeing on foot left blood on the plain
and was blinded and then trampled by death
where an obscure river loses its name,
so I too will fall. Today is the end.
The night and to right and left the marshes—
in ambush, clogging my steps. I hear the
hooves of my own hot death riding me down
with horsemen, frothing muzzles, and lances.

I who longed to be someone else, to weigh
judgments, to read books, to hand down the law,
will lie in the open out in these swamps;
but a secret joy somehow swells my breast.
I see at last that I am face to face
with my South American destiny.
I was carried to this ruinous hour
by the intricate labyrinth of steps
woven by my days from a day that goes
back to my birth. At last I've discovered
the mysterious key to all my years,
the fate of Francisco de Laprida,
the missing letter, the perfect pattern
that was known to God from the beginning.
In this night's mirror I can comprehend
my unsuspected true face. The circle's
about to close. I wait to let it come.

My feet tread the shadows of the lances
that spar for the kill. The taunts of my death,
the horses, the horsemen, the horses' manes,
tighten the ring around me... Now the first
blow, the lance's hard steel ripping my chest,
and across my throat the intimate knife.

trans. Norman Thomas di Giovanni

Poema de los dones

A María Esther Vázquez

Nadie rebaje a lágrima o reproche
Esta declaración de la maestría
De Dios, que con magnífica ironía
Me dio a la vez los libros y la noche.

De esta ciudad de libros hizo dueños
A unos ojos sin luz, que sólo pueden
Leer en las bibliotecas de los sueños
Los insensatos párrafos que ceden

Las albas a su afán. En vano el día
Les prodiga sus libros infinitos,
Arduos como los arduos manuscritos
Que perecieron en Alejandría.

De hambre y de sed (narra una historia griega)
Muere un rey entre fuentes y jardines;
Yo fatigo sin rumbo los confines
De esta alta y honda biblioteca ciega.

Enciclopedias, atlas, el Oriente
Y el Occidente, siglos, dinastías,
Símbolos, cosmos y cosmogonías
Brindan los muros, pero inútilmente.

Lento en mi sombra, la penumbra hueca
Exploro con el báculo indeciso,
Yo, que me figuraba el Paraíso
Bajo la especie de una biblioteca.

Algo, que ciertamente no se nombra
Con la palabra *azar*, rige estas cosas;
Otro ya recibió en otras borrosas
Tardes los muchos libros y la sombra.

Al errar por las lentas galerías
Suelo sentir con vago horror sagrado
Que soy el otro, el muerto, que habrá dado
Los mismos pasos en los mismos días.

¿Cuál de los dos escribe este poema
De un yo plural y de una sola sombra?
¿Qué importa la palabra que me nombra
Si es indiviso y uno el anatema?

Groussac o Borges, miro este querido
Mundo que se deforma y que se apaga

Poem of the Gifts

To María Esther Vázquez

Let no one impute to self-pity or censure
The power of the thing I affirm: that God
With magnificent irony has dealt me the gift
Of these books and the dark, with one stroke.

He has lifted these eyes, now made lightless,
To be lords of this city of books, though all that they read
In my dream of a library are insensible paragraphs
Disclosed to their longing

Each passing day. Vainly dawn multiplies book
After book to infinity, each one
Inaccessible, each lost to me now, like the manuscripts
Alexandria fed to the flame.

Greek anecdote tells of a king who lived among
Gardens and fountains, and died of thirst and starvation;
I toil in the breadth and the depth and the blindness
Of libraries, without strength or direction.

Encyclopedias, atlases, Orient,
Occident, dynasties, ages,
Symbols and cosmos, cosmogonies
Call to me from the walls—ineffectual images!

Painfully probing the dark, I grope toward
The void of the twilight with the point of my faltering
Cane—I for whom Paradise was always a metaphor,
An image of libraries.

Something—no need to prattle of chance
Or contingency—presides over these matters;
Long before me, some other man took these books and
    the dark
In a fading of dusk for his lot.

Astray in meandering galleries,
It comes to me now with a holy, impalpable
Dread, that I am that other, the dead man, and walk
With identical steps and identical days to the end.

Which of us two is writing this poem
In the I of the first person plural, in identical darkness?
What good is the word that speaks for me now in my
    name,
If the curse of the dark is implacably one and the same?

En una pálida ceniza vaga
Que se parece al sueño y al olvido.

1960

Groussac or Borges, I watch the delectable
World first disfigure then extinguish itself
In a pallor of ashes, until all that is gone
Seems at one with sleep and at one with oblivion.

trans. Ben Belitt

El otro tigre

> And the craft that createth a semblance
> MORRIS: *Sigurd the Volsung* (1876)

Pienso en un tigre. La penumbra exalta
La vasta Biblioteca laboriosa
Y parece alejar los anaqueles;
Fuerte, inocente, ensangrentado y nuevo,
El irá por su selva y su mañana
Y marcará su rastro en la limosa
Margen de un río cuyo nombre ignora
(En su mundo no hay nombres ni pasado
Ni porvenir, sólo un instante cierto)
Y salvará las bárbaras distancias
Y husmeará en el trenzado laberinto
De los olores el olor del alba
Y el olor deleitable del venado;
Entre las rayas del bambú descifro
Sus rayas y presiento la osatura
Bajo la piel espléndida que vibra.
En vano se interponen los convexos
Mares y los desiertos del planeta;
Desde esta casa de un remoto puerto
De América del Sur, te sigo y sueño,
Oh tigre de las márgenes del Ganges.

Cunde la tarde en mi alma y reflexiono
Que el tigre vocativo de mi verso
Es un tigre de símbolos y sombras,
Una serie de tropos literarios
Y de memorias de la enciclopedia
Y no el tigre fatal, la aciaga joya
Que, bajo el sol o la diversa luna,
Va cumpliendo en Sumatra o en Bengala
Su rutina de amor, de ocio y de muerte.
Al tigre de los símbolos he opuesto
El verdadero, el de caliente sangre,
El que diezma la tribu de los búfalos
Y hoy, 3 de agosto del 59,
Alarga en la pradera una pausada
Sombra, pero ya el hecho de nombrarlo
Y de conjeturar su circunstancia
Lo hace ficción del arte y no criatura
Viviente de las que andan por la tierra.

The Other Tiger

> And the craft that createth a semblance
> MORRIS: *Sigurd the Volsung* (1876)

A tiger comes to mind. The twilight here
Exalts the vast and busy Library
And seems to set the bookshelves back in gloom;
Innocent, ruthless, bloodstained, sleek,
It wanders through its forest and its day
Printing a track along the muddy banks
Of sluggish streams whose names it does not know
(In its world there are no names or past
Or time to come, only the vivid now)
And makes its way across wild distances
Sniffing the braided labyrinth of smells
And in the wind picking the smell of dawn
And tantalizing scent of grazing deer;
Among the bamboo's slanting stripes I glimpse
The tiger's stripes and sense the bony frame
Under the splendid, quivering cover of skin.
Curving oceans and the planet's wastes keep us
Apart in vain; from here in a house far off
In South America I dream of you,
Track you, O tiger of the Ganges' banks.

It strikes me now as evening fills my soul
That the tiger addressed in my poem
Is a shadowy beast, a tiger of symbols
And scraps picked up at random out of books,
A string of labored tropes that have no life,
And not the fated tiger, the deadly jewel
That under sun or stars or changing moon
Goes on in Bengal or Sumatra fulfilling
Its rounds of love and indolence and death.
To the tiger of symbols I hold opposed
The one that's real, the one whose blood runs hot
As it cuts down a herd of buffaloes,
And that today, this August third, nineteen
Fifty-nine, throws its shadow on the grass;
But by the act of giving it a name,
By trying to fix the limits of its world,
It becomes a fiction, not a living beast,
Not a tiger out roaming the wilds of earth.

Un tercer tigre buscaremos. Este
Será como los otros una forma
De mi sueño, un sistema de palabras
Humanas y no el tigre vertebrado
Que, más allá de las mitologías,
Pisa la tierra. Bien lo sé, pero algo
Me impone esta aventura indefinida,
Insensata y antigua, y persevero
En buscar por el tiempo de la tarde
El otro tigre, el que no está en el verso.

We'll hunt for a third tiger now, but like
The others this one too will be a form
Of what I dream, a structure of words, and not
the flesh and bone tiger that beyond all myths
Paces the earth. I know these things quite well,
Yet nonetheless some force keeps driving me
In this vague, unreasonable, and ancient quest.
And I go on pursuing through the hours
Another tiger, the beast not found in verse.

trans. Norman Thomas di Giovanni

1960

Arte poética

Mirar el río hecho de tiempo y agua
Y recordar que el tiempo es otro río,
Saber que nos perdemos como el río
Y que los rostros pasan como el agua.

Sentir que la vigilia es otro sueño
Que sueña no soñar y que la muerte
Que teme nuestra carne es esa muerte
De cada noche, que se llama sueño.

Ver en el día o en el año un símbolo
De los días del hombre y de sus años,
Convertir el ultraje de los años
En una música, un rumor y un símbolo,

Ver en el muerte el sueño, en el ocaso
Un triste oro, tal es la poesía
Que es inmortal y pobre. La poesía
Vuelve como la aurora y el ocaso.

A veces en las tardes una cara
Nos mira desde el fondo de un espejo;
El arte debe ser como ese espejo
Que nos revela nuestra propia cara.

Cuentan que Ulises, harto de prodigios,
Lloró de amor al divisar su Itaca
Verde y humilde. El arte es esa Itaca
De verde eternidad, no de prodigios.

También es como el río interminable
Que pasa y queda y es cristal de un mismo
Heráclito inconstante, que es el mismo
Y es otro, como el río interminable.

Ars Poetica

To look at the river made of time and water
And remember that time is another river,
To know that we are lost like the river
And that faces dissolve like water.

To be aware that waking dreams it is not asleep
While it is another dream, and that the death
That our flesh goes in fear of is that death
Which comes every night and is called sleep.

To see in the day or in the year a symbol
Of the days of man and of his years,
To transmute the outrage of the years
Into a music, a murmur of voices, and a symbol,

To see in death sleep, and in the sunset
A sad gold—such is poetry,
Which is immortal and poor. Poetry
Returns like the dawn and the sunset.

At times in the evenings a face
Looks at us out of the depths of a mirror;
Art should be like that mirror
Which reveals to us our own face.

They say that Ulysses, sated with marvels,
Wept tears of love at the sight of his Ithaca,
Green and humble. Art is that Ithaca
Of green eternity, not of marvels.

It is also like the river with no end
That flows and remains and is the mirror of one same
Inconstant Heraclitus, who is the same
And is another, like the river with no end.

1960

trans. W. S. Merwin

Límites

Hay una línea de Verlaine que no volveré a recordar,
Hay una calle próxima que está vedada a mis pasos,
Hay un espejo que me ha visto por última vez,
Hay una puerta que he cerrado hasta el fin del mundo.
Entre los libros de mi biblioteca (estoy viéndolos)
Hay alguno que ya nunca abriré.
Este verano cumpliré cincuenta años:
La muerte me desgasta, incesante.

De Inscripciones *(Montevideo, 1923)*
de Julio Platero Haedo.

1960

Limits (or Good-byes)

There's a line of Verlaine's that I'm not going to
          remember again.
There's a nearby street that's forbidden to my footsteps.
There's a mirror that has seen me for the last time.
There's a door I've closed until the end of the world.
Among the books in my library (I'm looking at them)
There are some I'll never open again.
This summer I'll be fifty years old:
Death invades me, constantly.

From Inscripciones *by Julio Platero Haedo*
(Montevideo, 1923)

trans. Alan Dugan

Everness

Sólo una cosa no hay. Es el olvido.
Dios, que salva el metal, salva la escoria
Y cifra en Su profética memoria
Las lunas que serán y las que han sido.
Ya todo está. Los miles de reflejos
Que entre los dos crepúsculos del día
Tu rostro fue dejando en los espejos
Y los que irá dejando todavía.
Y todo es una parte del diverso
Cristal de esa memoria, el universo;
No tienen fin sus arduos corredores
Y las puertas se cierran a tu paso;
Sólo del otro lado del ocaso
Verás los Arquetipos y Esplendores.

1964

Everness

One thing does not exist: Oblivion.
God saves the metal and he saves the dross,
And his prophetic memory guards from loss
The moons to come, and those of evenings gone.
Everything *is:* the shadows in the glass
Which, in between the day's two twilights, you
Have scattered by the thousands, or shall strew
Henceforward in the mirrors that you pass.
And everything is part of that diverse
Crystalline memory, the universe;
Whoever through its endless mazes wanders
Hears door on door click shut behind his stride,
And only from the sunset's farther side
Shall view at last the Archetypes and the Splendors.

trans. Richard Wilbur

Spinoza

Las traslúcidas manos del judío
Labran en la penumbra los cristales
Y la tarde que muere es miedo y frío.
(Las tardes a las tardes son iguales.)
Las manos y el espacio de jacinto
Que palidece en el confín del Ghetto
Casi no existen para el hombre quieto
Que está soñando un claro laberinto.
No lo turba la fama, ese reflejo
De sueños en el sueño de otro espejo,
Ni el temeroso amor de las doncellas.
Libre de la metáfora y del mito

Spinoza

The Jew's hands, translucent in the dusk,
Polish the lenses time and again.
The dying afternoon is fear, is
Cold, and all afternoons are the same.
The hands and the hyacinth-blue air
That whitens at the Ghetto edges
Do not quite exist for this silent
Man who conjures up a clear labyrinth—
Undisturbed by fame, that reflection
Of dreams in the dream of another
Mirror, nor by maidens' timid love.
Free of metaphor and myth, he grinds

Labra un arduo cristal: el infinito
Mapa de Aquél que es todas Sus estrellas.

1964

A stubborn crystal: the infinite
Map of the One who is all His stars.

trans. Richard Howard and César Rennert

El mar

Antes que el sueño (o el terror) tejiera
Mitologías y cosmogonías,
Antes que el tiempo se acuñara en días.
El mar, el siempre mar, ya estaba y era.
¿Quién es el mar? ¿Quién es aquel violento
Y antiguo ser que roe los pilares
De la tierra y es uno y muchos mares
Y abismo y resplandor y azar y viento?
Quien lo mira lo ve por vez primera,
Siempre. Con el asombro que las cosas
Elementales dejan, las hermosas
Tardes, la luna, el fuego de una hoguera.
¿Quién es el mar, quién soy? Lo sabré el día
Ulterior que sucede a la agonía.

1967

The Sea

Before our human dream (or terror) wove
Mythologies, cosmogonies, and love,
Before time coined its substance into days,
The sea, the always sea, existed: was.
Who is the sea? Who is that violent being,
Violent and ancient, who gnaws the foundations
Of earth? He is both one and many oceans;
He is abyss and splendor, chance and wind.
Who looks on the sea, sees it the first time,
Every time, with the wonder distilled
From elementary things—from beautiful
Evenings, the moon, the leap of a bonfire.
Who is the sea, and who am I? The day
That follows my last agony shall say.

trans. John Updike

Claudia Lars
[Carmen Brannon Beers]

EL SALVADOR
1899–1974

Claudia Lars was one of the first Latin American writers to bring issues of female consciousness, physical experience, and emotion into a lyrical structure. Her work, as the critic Hugo Emilio Pedemonte describes it, "notices the sharp brightness of things: she is a woman of a very fine lyrical intuition, who seems to say less than she knows, and of an idiomatic elegance that continually affirms her complex culture." Throughout a long career spanning from *Estrellas en el pozo* (*Stars in the Ditch*, 1934) through the poems published in her *Póstuma* (*Posthumous Poems*, 1975), Lars was a writer of integrity and continuity whose example and generosity toward younger writers, especially young women poets, made her a beloved—and even symbolically maternal—figure in Latin American poetry.

Dibujo de la mujer que llega

En el lodo empinada.
No como el tallo de la flor
y el ansia de la mariposa...
Sin raíces ni juegos:
más recta, más segura
y más libre.

Sketch of the Frontier Woman

Standing erect in the mire.
Unlike the flower's stalk
and the butterfly's eagerness...
Without roots or fluttering:
more upright, more sure,
and more free.

Conocedora de la sombra y de la espina.
Con el milagro levantado
en los brazos triunfantes.
Con la barrera y el abismo
debajo de su salto.

Dueña absoluta de su carne
para volverla centro del espíritu:
vaso de lo celeste,
domus áurea,
gleba donde se yerguen, en un brote,
la mazorca y el nardo.

Olvidada la sonrisa de Gioconda.
Roto el embrujo de los siglos.
Vencedora de miedos.
Clara y desnuda bajo el día limpio.

Amante inigualable
en ejercicio de un amor tan alto
que hoy ninguno adivina.
Dulce,
con filtrada dulzura
que no daña ni embriaga a quien la prueba.

Maternal todavía,
sin la caricia que detiene el vuelo,
ni ternuras que cercan,
ni mezquinas daciones que se cobran.

Pionera de las nubes.
Guía del laberinto.
Tejedora de vendas y de cantos.
Sin más adorno que su sencillez.

Se levanta del polvo...
No como el tallo de la flor
que es apenas belleza.

1937

Familiar with the shadow and the thorn.
With the miracle uplifted
in her triumphant arms.
With the barrier and the abyss
beneath her leap.

Absolute mistress of her flesh
to make it the core of her spirit:
vessel of the heavenly,
domus aurea,
a lump of earth from which rise, budding,
the corn and the tuberose.

Forgotten the Gioconda smile.
Broken the spell of centuries.
Vanquisher of fears.
Clear and naked in the limpid day.

Lover without equal
in a love so lofty
that today no one divines it.
Sweet,
with a filtered sweetness
that neither harms nor intoxicates him who tastes it.

Maternal always,
without the caress that hinders flight,
or the tenderness that confines,
or the petty yieldings that must be redeemed.

Pioneer of the clouds.
Guide to the labyrinth.
Weaver of tissues and songs.
Her only adornment, simplicity.

She rises from the dust...
Unlike the flower's stalk
which is less than beauty.

trans. Donald D. Walsh

Evocación de Gabriela Mistral

(En su casa de Santa Barbara, California)

Tu retiro apenas recogía
rumores de la ciudad mecanizada:
isla para viajeros locos,
llena de ciruelas y libros.

    No olvido nuestras lecturas
    bajo una lámpara,
    ni las visitas del escritor noruego

Recollection of Gabriela Mistral

(At her home in Santa Barbara, California)

Your retreat hardly prompted
murmurs from the mechanized city:
an island full of plums and books
awaiting crazy travellers.

    I'll not forget our readings
    by lamplight
    nor the visits from the Norwegian writer

que hablaba de la cuarta dimensión
como si hablara de Oslo.
Fácilmente regreso a los álamos azules
y a ciertos afanes mañaneros
entre remolachas y coles.

Mariposas sin rumbo
querían descansar en tu cabeza
y el perro destructor de escarabajos
se transformaba al oír nuestras voces
en cordero de Felpa.

   Un Buda de marfil tenía asiento
   cerca del libro más cristiano entre todos
   y el Cristo medioeval en su cruz de viernes
   agonizaba encima de la consola.

Tu profunda mirada
iba del Tranquilo Compasivo al Amoroso Sufriente
afirmando que los dos podían alumbrar la tierra entera
desde un mismo candelabro.

   Casa tan quieta y limpia
   me obligaba a caminar de puntillas
   y era dulce recibir, sin pedirlo,
   el oro de tu palabra.

Gocé un verano inmerecido
y rompí noches del corazón
queriendo descubrir abismos.
Por eso al fin dijiste con voz resignada:
"Amiga curiosísima:
llegas hasta mis huesos para observarme
y ya ves: me han matado mis muertos"...

   Entonces comprendí las líneas
   de un rostro severo
   y ahora padezco el largo fuego
   de todos tus versos.

                                        1973

who spoke of the fourth dimension
as if he were speaking of Oslo.
Effortlessly I return to the blue poplars
and to certain early morning tasks
between beets and cabbages.

Wandering butterflies
would want to rest on your head
and the beetle-destroying dog
would become a cuddly lamb
upon hearing our voices.

   An ivory Buddha was placed
   near the most Christian book of them all
   and the medieval Christ on his crucifix
   agonized above the console.

Your profound gaze
would move from the Peaceful, Compassionate One
   to the Loving, Suffering One
confirming that the two could light up the whole world
from the same candelabra.

   The house, so still and clean,
   compelled me to tiptoe about
   and it was sweet to receive, without asking,
   the gold of your word.

I enjoyed an undeserved summer
and I interrupted peaceful nights
wanting to discover abysses.
Because of this, in the end you said with resignation in
   your voice:
"My dear, curious friend:
you've penetrated me to the bone in order to observe me
and now you see: my own dead have killed me."

   Then I understood the lines
   in a harsh face
   and now I suffer the prolonged fire
   of all of your verses.

                                        trans. Nancy Christoph

Carlos Pellicer

M E X I C O
1899–1977

Carlos Pellicer was friendly with many of the writers associated with the influential journal *Contemporáneos* (1928–1931), including Gorostiza, Torres Bodet, and Villaurrutia. In his attention to the chromatic light, the sculptural forms, and the dynamic energy of the tropical American landscape, however, from the start of his writing career Pellicer distinguished essential elements of his aesthetic from those of the *Contemporáneos* group and the Creationists: from their verbalism, from their musical and subjective intensity, and from their interest in the seductiveness of death as an informing poetic myth.

After having been imprisoned for political reasons, during the 1930s, Pellicer traveled, both as an individual and as a cultural attaché, for much of his adult life. In compensation, though, his poems often register the rhythms and visual intensity of his native Tabasco. "I am from the tropics," he wrote, "and in the land where I was born . . . the Mayan culture flourished. Therefore, the ancient cultures of Mexico have had a level of meaning for me which I could call a passion. All this has inclined me more toward nature and to heroes than anything else. Simón Bolívar and Cuauhtémoc have been the personalities whom I have studied most and who have most embellished my modest poetic works." His early poems, as in *Colores en el mar* (*Colors in the Sea*, 1921) and *Piedra de sacrificios* (*Stone of Sacrifice*, 1924), were often joyous pictorial evocations of tropical landscapes, charged with a sense of the mutability of natural forces (the sea, the moon, the flight of birds). In later works Pellicer tamed that exuberance slightly, to include more historical and spiritual meditations in his profoundly visual style.

Deseos

a Salvador Novo

Trópico, para qué me diste
las manos llenas de color.
Todo lo que yo toque
se llenará de sol.
En las tardes sutiles de otras tierras
pasaré con mis ruidos de vidrio tornasol.
Déjame un solo instante
dejar de ser grito y color.
Déjame un solo instante
cambiar de clima el corazón,
beber la penumbra de una cosa desierta,
inclinarme en silencio sobre un remoto balcón,
ahondarme en el manto de pliegues finos,
dispersarme en la orilla de una suave devoción,
acariciar dulcemente las cabelleras lacias
y escribir con un lápiz muy fino mi meditación.
¡Oh, dejar de ser un solo instante
el Ayudante de Campo del sol!
¡Trópico, para qué me diste
las manos llenas de color!

1924

Wishes

to Salvador Novo

Tropics, why did you give me
these hands so full of color?
Whatever I touch
fills up with sunlight.
I move through the delicate evening hours of other lands
like a great noisy sunflower made of glass.
Let me for one moment
stop being all cry and color.
Let me for one moment
change the climate of my heart,
drink in the twilight of some lonely place,
lean on a distant balcony in silence,
sink deep into a finely tailored cloak,
be broken on the shores of some quiet passion,
softly caress the long straight locks of women
and set my reflections down with a nice little pencil.
Oh, for one moment not to be
Aide-de-Camp to the sun!
Tropics, why did you give me
these hands so full of color!

trans. Donald Justice

Estudios

I

Relojes descompuestos,
    voluntarios caminos

Studies

I

Clocks out of order,
    wayward roads

sobre la música del tiempo.
    Hora y veinte.
Gracias a vuestro
paso
lento,
llego a las citas mucho después
y así me doy todo a las máquinas
gigantescas y translúcidas del silencio.

II

Diez kilómetros sobre la vía
de un tren retrasado.
El paisaje crece
dividido de telegramas.
Las noticias van a tener tiempo
de cambiar de camisa.
La juventud se prolonga diez minutos,
el ojo caza tres sonrisas.
Kilo de panoramas
pagado con el tiempo
que se gana perdiendo.

III

Las horas se adelgazan;
de una salen diez.
Es el trópico,
prodigioso y funesto.
Nadie sabe qué hora es.

1927

A la poesía

Sabor de octubre en tus hombros,
de abril tu mano da olor.
Reflejo de cien espejos
    tu cuerpo.
Noche en las flautas mi voz.

Tus pasos fueron caminos
de música. La danzó
la espiral envuelta en hojas
    de horas.
Desnuda liberación.

La cifra de tu estatura,
la de la ola que alzó
tu peso de tiempo intacto.
    Mi brazo
sutilmente la ciñó.

---

across the music of time.
    Twenty after.
Thanks to your
slow
pace,
I keep appointments much later
and thus am entirely given over
to the gigantic and translucent machines of silence.

II

Ten kilometers down the line
of a train behind schedule.
The countryside stretches out,
marked off by telegrams.
The news is going to have time
to change its shirt.
Youth lasts ten minutes longer,
one's eye surprises three smiles.
A kilo of panoramas
paid for with the time
won by losing.

III

The hours thin down;
out of one come ten.
These are the tropics,
prodigious and sad.
Nobody knows what time it is.

trans. Donald Justice

To Poetry

The taste of October on your shoulders.
Your hands give off a scent of April.
Like a hundred mirrors, I reflect
    your body.
Night-time in the flutes of my voice.

Your footsteps were paths
of music. It danced
tangled up in leaves: the helix
    of hours.
Naked liberation.

The measure of your height,
of the wave that raised
your weight of time, untouched.
    My arm
softly circled it.

En medio de las espigas
y a tu mirada estival,
afilé la hoz que alía
    al día
la cosecha sideral.

Trigo esbelto a fondo azul
cae al brillo de la hoz.
Grano de oro a fondo negro
    aviento
con un cósmico temblor.

Sembrar en el campo aéreo,
crecer alto a flor sutil.
Sudó la tierra y el paso
    a ocaso
del rojo cedía al gris.

Niveló su ancha caricia
la mano sobre el trigal.
Todas e idénticas: ¡una!
    Desnuda
la voz libre dio a cantar.

Sabor de octubre en tus hombros,
de abril tu mano da olor.
Espejo de cien espejos
    mi cuerpo,
anochecerá en tu voz.

Siracusa 1928/1929

Among the aftergrowths
and your summery gaze
I sharpened the sickle that conjoined
    the day
with the heavenly harvest.

From the blue depths the willowy wheat
falls to the brilliance of the sickle.
From the black depths a grain of gold
    a pitchfork
with a cosmic shiver.

To plant in the breezy countryside—
to grow, swellingly, a delicate flower:
the earth sweated, and the path
    toward the red
sunset yields to grey.

He lifted his narrow stroke,
his hand above the wheat-field.
All the grains identical: One!
    Naked.
The free voice begins to sing.

The taste of October on your shoulders.
Your hands give off a scent of April.
A mirror of a hundred mirrors,
    my body
will sleep darkly in your voice.

trans. Alexandra Migoya

Grupos de palomas

A la señora Lupe Medina de Ortega

1

Los grupos de palomas,
notas, claves, silencios, alteraciones,
modifican el ritmo de la loma.
La que se sabe tornasol afina
las ruedas luminosas de su cuello
con mirar hacia atrás a su vecina.
Le da al sol la mirada
y escurre en una sola pincelada
plan de vuelos a nubes campesinas.

2

La gris es una joven extranjera
cuyas ropas de viaje
dan aire de sorpresas al paisaje
sin compradoras y sin primaveras.

Flocks of Doves

For Sra. Lupe Medina de Ortega

1

The flocks of doves—
notes, musical keys, silences, changes—
modify the rhythm of the hill.
The one who knows how to shine, purifies
the bright rings of her neck
by looking back at her neighbor.
She gives the sun a look
and quietly glides on with a single touch,
the form of flights into country clouds.

2

The grey one is a young tourist
whose travelling clothes
lend an air of surprise to the countryside—
without commerce, without springtime.

3

Hay una casi negra
que bebe astillas de agua en una piedra.
Después se pule el pico,
mira sus uñas, ve las de las otras,
abre un ala y la cierra, tira un brinco
y se para debajo de las rosas.
El fotógrafo dice:
para el jueves, señora.
Un palomo amontona sus *erres* cabeceadas,
y ella busca alfileres
en el suelo que brilla por nada.
Los grupos de palomas
—notas, claves, silencios, alteraciones—,
modifican lugares de la loma.

4

La inevitablemente blanca,
sabe su perfección. Bebe en la fuente
y se bebe a sí misma y se adelgaza
cual un poco de brisa en una lente
que recoge el paisaje.
Es una simpleza
cerca del agua. Inclina la cabeza
con tal dulzura,
que la escritura desfallece
en una serie de sílabas maduras.

5

Corre un automóvil y las palomas vuelan.
En la aritmética del vuelo,
los *ochos* árabes desdóblanse
y la suma es impar. Se mueve el cielo
y la casa se vuelve redonda.
Un viraje profundo.
Regresan las palomas.
Notas. Claves. Silencios. Alteraciones.
El lápiz se descubre, se inclinan las lomas,
y por 20 centavos se cantan las canciones.

México 1925/1941

3

There's an almost-black one,
who drinks twigs of water in a stone.
After he polishes his beak,
he checks his claws and observes the others,
he opens a wing and closes it, gives a hop
and stops beneath the rose.
The photographer speaks:
by Thursday, Ma'am.
One dove rolls the Rs in her tight throat.
She watches for pins
on the ground, which shines for no reason.
The flocks of doves—
notes, musical keys, silences, changes—
modify the spaces of the hill.

4

One, inevitably white:
she knows her perfection. Drinks from the fountain
and drinks herself in, and thins out
like a light breeze in front of a lens
that captures the countryside.
It is a simplicity
close to water. She tilts her head
with such sweetness
that writing weakens
into a series of over-ripe syllables.

5

When cars drive past, the doves fly off.
In the arithmetic of their flight
an *eight* in Arab script unfolds,
and the addition is uneven. The sky moves,
the house becomes round.
A sharp turn.
The doves return—
notes, musical keys, silences, changes—:
the pencil declares and the hill tilts,
and for 20 cents -–small change—they sing themselves
  the songs.

trans. Alexandra Migoya

José Gorostiza

MEXICO

1901–1973

José Gorostiza was one of the founding members of the *Contemporáneos* group in Mexico during the 1920s. Those poets, including also Villaurrutia and Torres Bodet, challenged the strenuous national-ism of postrevolutionary Mexican art and advocated a countervailing aestheticism. Gorostiza's poems present this aesthetic commitment with remarkable scrupulousness and careful emotion. "Poetry, for me," Gorostiza wrote, "is an investigation of certain essences—love, life, death, God—that happen with such force that they break language open—in such a way as, speaking with the greatest transparency, to allow language to cross over into those essences."

The poem sequence from which several of the following poems come, *Muerte sin fin* (*Death without End*, 1939), is Gorostiza's masterwork, the rendering of his essentialist ambitions in a flexible form and a "luminous, exact, and palpitating" diction. The sequence threads through a long dialectic in which the metaphorical terms alternate: between life and death, between water and the vessel that holds it, between phantom and material, between nothingness and presence—and between emotion and its verbal form. According to Octavio Paz, Gorostiza's sequence signaled the end of a poetic era as well as the effective end of Gorostiza's writing career. The poem, Paz claims, "is the monument that form has erected to its own death." Gorostiza's account of the poem's thematics is more direct: "It simply occurred to me (and this was nothing new) that life and death constitute a single, unitary process and that each one, life and death, could be admired in its full splendor from the opposite shore."

¿Quién me compra una naranja?

A Carlos Pellicer

¿Quién me compra una naranja
para mi consolación?
Una naranja madura
en forma de corazón.

La sal del mar en los labios
¡Ay de mí!
la sal del mar en las venas
y en los labios recogí.

Nadie me diera los suyos
para besar.
La blanda espiga de un beso
yo no la puedo segar.

Nadie pidiera mi sangre
para beber.
Yo mismo no sé si corre
o si deja de correr.

Como se pierden las barcas
¡Ay de mí!
como se pierden las nubes
y las barcas, me perdí.

Y pues nadie me lo pide,
ya no tengo corazón.
¿Quién me compra una naranja
para mi consolación?

1925

Who Will Buy Me an Orange?

To Carlos Pellicer

Who will buy me an orange
to console me now?
A ripe perfect orange
shaped like a heart.

The sea salt on my lips,
alas for me!
On my lips and in my veins
I gathered the salt of the sea.

No one will offer
her lips to me.
I cannot harvest the tender
wheat ear of a kiss.

No one will ask to drink
my blood.
I myself cannot tell
whether or not it still flows.

As ships are wrecked,
alas for me!
I was lost as clouds are lost
and ships are lost at sea!

And since no one asks me for it,
I no longer have a heart.
Who will buy me an orange
to console me now?

trans. Rachel Benson

Elegía

A Ramón López Velarde

Solo, con ruda soledad marina,
se fue por un sendero de la luna,
mi dorada madrina,
apagando sus luces como una
pestaña de lucero en la neblina.

El dolor me sangraba el pensamiento,
y en los labios tenía,
como una rosa negra, mi lamento.

Las azules canéforas de la melancolía
derramaron sus frágiles cestillos,
y el sueño se dolía
con la luna de lánguidos lebreles amarillos.

Se pusieron de púrpura las liras;
las mujeres, en hilos de lágrimas suspensas,
cortaron las espiras
blandamente aromadas de sus trenzas.

Y al romper mis quietudes vesperales
lo gris de estas congojas,
las oí resbalar como a las hojas
en los rubios jardines otoñales.

Apaguemos las lámparas, hermanos.
De los dulces laúdes
no muevan el cordaje nuestras manos.
Se nos murieron las siete virtudes,
al asomar
los finos labios del amanecer.
¡Ponga Dios una lenta lágrima de mujer
en los ojos del mar!

1925

Luciérnagas

A Enrique González Rojo

I

Una delgada niebla
florecía las copas de durazno.
Primaveral delicia se difunde en el aire
rosa de la madrugada
y entre las olas niñas
de pie ligero como pluma de pájaro.

¿Qué buscará de noche la luciérnaga
con su farol opaco?

Elegy

To Ramón López Velarde

Alone, with harsh marine aloneness,
he went down a pathway of the moon,
my gilded protectress,
snuffing out her lamps
like a star's eyelash in the mist.

Sorrow was bleeding my thoughts,
and I held my lament between my lips
like a black rose.

The blue caryatids of melancholy
spilled their fragile little baskets,
and dream grieved
with the moon of languid yellow greyhounds.

The lyres were adorned with murex;
women suspended on threads of tears
cut the faintly scented
coils of their hair.

And the grey of these sorrows
broke my evening quietude;
I heard them slither like leaves
into tawny autumn gardens.

Let us put out the lanterns, brothers.
Let our hands not stir
the sweet lutes' rigging.
The seven virtues died for us
as the delicate lips of dawn
appeared.
May God put a slow woman's tear
in the eyes of the sea.

trans. Rachel Benson

Fireflies

To Enrique González Rojo

I

A thin mist
has flowered the tips of peach tree branches
Spring delight is diffused in the air—
rose of the dawn—
and among the waves—girls
with feet light as a bird's feather.

What will the firefly seek by night
with its opaque lantern?

II

Sonrojada de brisa te pareces
a Lady Yang Kuei-Fei
en la fiesta imperial de la peonía,
porque, también así, jugaba entonces
a ser la luna de colores lenta
y el rocío traslúcido de la tarde.

¡Qué lejanías
tienes para jugar a las ausencias!
Como el hueledenoche embelesado,
sólo das un perfume
que se pierde distante a la sordina.

¿Qué buscarás tan lejos, en la luna,
si no luciérnagas?

III

Pobre de mí, borracho.
Li Po desandará conmigo
las acuarelas malvas del crepúsculo,
y desde las colinas taciturnas
haremos de luciérnagas perdidas,
con los faroles de papel al hombro.

1925

II

Flushed with breeze you are
like Lady Yang Kuei Fei
at the imperial peony festival,
for then she too played
at being the slow colored moon
and the pellucid dew of evening.

What distances
you keep to play at absences!
Like some ravishing night-blooming flower,
you emit only a perfume
that is lost far away and secretly.

What will you seek in the moon so far off,
if not fireflies?

III

Alas for me, drunken.
Li Po will retrace with me
the mild watercolors of dusk
and leaving the taciturn hills
we shall become lost fireflies
with paper lanterns on our shoulders.

trans. Rachel Benson

Muerte sin fin [Selección]

Lleno de mí, sitiado en mi epidermis
por un dios inasible que me ahoga,
mentido acaso
por su radiante atmósfera de luces
que oculta mi conciencia derramada,
mis alas rotas en esquirlas de aire,
mi torpe andar a tientas por el lodo;
lleno de mí—ahíto—me descubro
en la imagen atónita del agua,
que tan sólo es un tumbo inmarcesible,
un desplome de ángeles caídos
a la delicia intacta de su peso,
que nada tiene
sino la cara en blanco
hundidas a medias, ya, como una risa agónica
en las tenues holandas de la nube
y en los funestos cánticos del mar
—más resabio de sal o albor de cúmulo
que sola prisa de acosada espuma.
No obstante—oh paradoja—constreñida
por el rigor del vaso que la aclara,
el agua toma forma.
En él se asienta, ahonda y edifica,

Death without End [Selection]

Filled with myself, walled up in my skin
by an inapprehensible god that is stifling me,
deceived perhaps
by his radiant atmosphere of light
that hides my drained conscience,
my wings broken into splinters of air,
my listless groping through the mire;
filled with myself—gorged—I discover my essence
in the astonished image of water,
that is only an unwithering cascade,
a tumbling of angels fallen
of their own accord in pure delight,
that has nothing
but a whitened face
half sunken, already, like an agonized laugh
in the thin sheets of the cloud
and the mournful canticles of the sea—
more aftertaste of salt or cumulus whiteness
than lonely haste of foam pursued.
Nevertheless—oh paradox—constrained
by the rigor of the glass that clarifies it,
the water takes shape.
In the glass it sits, sinks deep and builds,

cumple una edad amarga de silencios	attains a bitter age of silences
y un reposo gentil de muerte niña,	and the grateful repose of a child smiling
sonriente, que desflora	in death, that deflowers
un más allá de pájaros	a beyond of disbanded
en desbandada.	birds.
En la red de cristal que la estrangula,	In the crystal snare that strangles it,
allí, como en el agua de un espejo,	there, as in the water of a mirror,
se reconoce;	it recognizes itself;
atada allí, gota con gota,	bound there, drop with drop,
marchito el tropo de espuma en la garganta	the trope of foam withered in its throat.
¡qué desnudez de agua tan intensa,	What intense nakedness of water,
qué agua tan agua,	what water so strongly water,
está en su orbe tornasol soñando,	is dreaming in its iridescent sphere,
cantando ya una sed de hielo justo!	already singing a thirst for rigid ice!
¡Mas qué vaso—también—mas providente	But what a provident glass—also—
éste que así se hinche	that swells
como una estrella en grano,	like a star ripe with grain,
que así, en heroica promisión, se enciende	that flames in heroic promise
como un seno habitado por la dicha,	like a heart inhabited by happiness,
y rinde así, puntual,	and that punctually yields up
una rotunda flor	to the water
de transparencia al agua,	a round transparent flower,
un ojo proyectil que cobra alturas	a missile eye that attains heights
y una ventana a gritos luminosos	and a window to luminous cries
sobre esa libertad enardecida	over that smoldering liberty
que se agobia de cándidas prisiones!	oppressed by white fetters!

1939

trans. Rachel Benson

Cecília Meireles

B R A Z I L

1901–1964

Cecília Meireles is the most important female poet to have written in modern Brazilian Portuguese. Orphaned at age three and raised by her maternal grandmother, Meireles concluded her formal education at the Normal School in Rio in 1917 and devoted her professional life to journalism, teaching, library work, and educational reform. In part because of her other careers, as a poet Meireles defined herself as working somewhat outside the Brazilian literary mainstream. Her early poems, in *Espectros* (*Ghosts*, 1919), were influenced by Parnassianism and Brazilian Modernism, but Meireles resisted the pull toward nationalism that influenced other Modernist poets in Brazil. In the middle of her literary career, the disciplined formalism of Meireles' poems attracted the criticism of more avant-garde Modernists in Brazil. From the dawn of what she considered her mature work, starting with *Viagem* (*Voyage*, 1939), Meireles worked toward a synthesis of European Symbolism and Asian mysticism. She became an expert also on Brazilian folklore and, in particular, on Afro-Brazilian culture. In her later years Meireles traveled widely as a Brazilian cultural attaché, wrote travel chronicles, and edited anthologies of Asian writing.

Perhaps in response to the early loss of her parents—and the suicide of her husband in 1935—Meireles turned the visionary exoticism of earlier Brazilian poets toward more internal themes of time, change, and mortality. Though full of tactile metaphors and verbal sensuality, her poems increasingly address a state of vivid internal "exile," an ideal transcendental solitude, described in figures of a timeless, elemental physical universe.

Retrato

Eu não tinha êste rosto de hoje,
assim calmo, assim triste, assim magro,
nem êstes olhos tão vazios,
nem o lábio amargo.

Eu não tinha estas mãos sem fôrça,
tão paradas e frias e mortas;
eu não tinha êste coração
que nem se mostra.

Eu não dei por esta mudança,
tão simples, tão certa, tão fácil:
—Em que espelho ficou perdida
a minha face?

1938

Portrait

I didn't have this face then,
so calm, and sad, and thin,
nor these eyes that are so empty,
nor these bitter lips.

I didn't have these weak hands then,
so still and cool and dead;
I didn't have this heart then
that I hate to bare, today.

I was never aware of changing—
so simple, so certain, so easy.
—Into what mirror then
was my face lost?

trans. Luiz Fernández García

Desenho

Fui morena e magrinha como qualquer polinésia,
e comia mamão, e mirava a flor de goiaba.
E as lagartixas me espiavam, entre os tijolos e as
    trepadeiras,
e as teias de aranha mas minhas árvores se entrelaçavam.

Isso era num lugar de sol e nuvens brancas,
onde as rôlas, à tarde, soluçavam mui saudosas...
O eco, burlão, de pedra em pedra ia saltando,
entre vastas mangueiras que choviam ruivas horas.

Os pavões caminhavam tão naturais pos meu caminho,
e os pombos tão felizes se alimentavam pelas escadas,
que era desnecessário crescer, pensar, escrever poemas,
pois a vida completa e bela e terna ali já estava.

Como a chuva caía das grossas nuvens, perfumosas!
E o papagaio como ficava sonolento!
O relógio era festa de ouro; e os gatos enigmáticos
fechavam os olhos, quando queriam caçar o tempo.

Vinham morcegos, à noite, picar os sapotis maduros,
e os grandes cães ladravam como nas noites do Império.
Mariposas, jasmins, tinhorões, vaga-lumes
moravam nos jardins sussurrantes e eternos.

Sketch

I was as dark and slim as a Polynesian girl.
I ate papayas and gazed at guava-flowers.
And the lizards peeked at me between the bricks and vines,
and the spider-webs were tangled in my trees.

That was all in a place of sun and white clouds,
where doves moaned a sweet sadness, all afternoon...
An echo, a jester, danced from rock to rock
among huge mango-trees, that rained reddish hours.

The peacocks walked naturally along my path,
and the pigeons, contented, fed among the steps:
there was no need to expand, to think, to write poems,
because life—whole and lovely and tender—was already
    there.

How the rain fell, fragrant, from the heavy clouds!
And the parrot, how he snoozed!
The clock was a golden festival, and the enigmatic cats
shut their eyes when they wanted to hunt for time.

Bats came at night to peck the ripe sapoti,
and big dogs barked in the nights of the Empire.
Butterflies, jasmines, caladiums, lightning-bugs
lived in the humming, eternal gardens.

E minha avó cantava e cosia. Cantava
canções de mar e de arvoredo, em língua antiga.
E eu sempre acreditei que havia música em seus dedos
e palavras de amor en minha roupa escritas.

Minha vida começa num vergel colorido,
por onde as noites eram só de luar e estrêlas.
Levai-me aonde quiserdes!—aprendi com as primaveras
a deixar-me cortar e a voltar sempre inteira.

1945

And my grandmother sang and sewed, sang
songs of the sea and the forest, in an ancient tongue.
And I always believed there was music in her fingers
and words of love written into my clothes.

My life began in a garden of color,
where nights were all moonlight and stars.
Take me wherever you want!—I learned with the Spring
how to be cut apart and always come back whole.

trans. Luiz Fernández García

Vigília

Como o companheiro é morto,
todos juntos morreremos
um pouco.

O calor de nossas lágrimas
sôbre quem perdeu a vida,
Não é nada.

Amá-lo, nesta tristeza,
é suspiro numa selva
imensa.

Por fidelidade reta
ao companheiro perdido,
que nos resta?

Deixar-nos morrer um pouco
por aquêle que hoje vemos
todo morto.

1949

Vigil

As the companion is dead,
so we must all together die
somewhat.

Shed for him who lost his life,
our tears are worth
nothing.

Love for him, within this grief,
is a faint sigh lost in a vast
forest.

Faith in him, the lost
companion—what but that
is left?

To die ourselves somewhat
through him we see today
quite dead.

trans. James Merrill

Balada das dez bailarinas do cassino

Dez bailarinas deslizam
por um chão de espelho.
Têm corpos egípcios com placas douradas,
pálpebras azuis e dedos vermelhos.
Levantam véus brancos, de ingênuos aromas,
e dobram amarelos joelhos.

Andam as dez bailarinas
sem voz, em redor das mesas.
Há mãos sôbre facas, dentes sôbre flôres
e os charutos toldam as luzes acesas.
Entre a música e a dança escorre
uma sedosa escada de vileza.

Ballad of the Ten Casino Dancers

Ten dancers glide
across a mirror floor.
They have thin gilt plaques on Egyptian bodies,
fingertips reddened, blue lids painted,
lift white veils naively scented,
bend yellow knees.

The ten dancers go
voiceless among customers,
hands above knives, teeth above roses,
little lamps befuddled by cigars.
Between the music and the movement flows
depravity, a flight of silken stairs.

As dez bailarinas avançam
como gafanhotos perdidos.
Avançam, recuam, na sala compacta,
empurrando olhares e arranhando o ruído.
Tão nuas se sentem que já vão cobertas
de imaginários, chorosos vestidos.

As dez bailarinas escondem
nos cílios verdes as pupilas.
Em seus quadris fosforescentes,
passa uma faixa de morte tranqüila.
Como quem leva para a terra um filho morto,
levam seu próprio corpo, que baila e cintila.

Os homens gordos olham com um tédio enorme
as dez bailarinas tão frias.
Pobres serpentes sem luxúria,
que são crianças, durante o dia.
Dez anjos anêmicos, de axilas profundas,
embalsamados de melancolia.

Vão perpassando como dez múmias,
as bailarinas fatigadas.
Ramo de nardos inclinando flôres
azuis, brancas, verdes, douradas.
Dez mães chorariam, se vissem
as bailarinas de mãos dadas.

                                        1949

The dancers now advance
like ten lost grasshoppers,
advance, recoil, avoiding glances
in the close room, and plucking at the din.
They are so naked, you imagine
them clothed in the stuff of tears.

The ten dancers screen
their pupils under great green lashes.
Death passes tranquil as a belt around
their phosphorescent waists.
As who should bear a dead child to the ground
each bears her flesh that moves and scintillates.

Fat men watch in massive tedium
those cold, cold dancers,
pitiful serpents without appetite
who are children by daylight.
Ten anemic angels made of hollows,
melancholy embalms them.

Ten mummies in a band,
back and forth go the tired dancers.
Branch whose fragrant blossoms bend
blue, green, gold, white.
Ten mothers would weep at the sight
of those dancers hand in hand.

                                        trans. James Merrill

O cavalo morto

Vi a névoa da madrugada
deslizar seus gestos de prata,
mover densidade de opala
naquele pórtico de sono.

Na fronteira havia um cavalo morto.

Grãos de cristal rolavam pelo
Seu flanco nítido: e algum vento
torcia-lhe as crinas, pequeno,
leve arabesco, triste adôrno.

—e movia a cauda ao cavalo morto.

As estrêlas ainda viviam
e ainda não eram nascidas
ai! as flôres daquele dia...
—mas era um canteiro o seu corpo:

um jardim de lírios, o cavalo morto.

The Dead Horse

I saw the early morning mist
make silver passes, shift
densities of opal
within sleep's portico.

On the frontier, a dead horse.

Crystal grains were rolling down
his lustrous flank, and the breeze
twisted his mane in a littlest,
lightest arabesque, sorry adornment

—and his tail stirred, the dead horse.

Still the stars were shining
and that day's flowers, sad to say,
had not yet come to light
—but his body was a plot,

garden of lilies, the dead horse.

Muitos viajantes contemplaram	Many a traveler took note
a fluida música, a orvalhada	of fluid music, the dewfall
das grandes môscas de esmeralda	of big emerald flies
chegando em rumoroso jôrro.	arriving in a noisy gush.
Adernava triste, o cavalo morto.	He was listing sorely, the dead horse.
E viam-se uns cavalos vivos,	And some live horses could be seen
altos como esbeltos navios,	slender and tall as ships,
galopando nos ares finos,	galloping through the keen air
com felizes perfis de sonho.	in profile, joyously dreaming.
Branco e verde via-se o cavalo morto,	White and green the dead horse
no campo enorme e sem recurso	in the enormous field without recourse
—e devagar girava o mundo	—and slowly the world between
entre as suas pestanas, turvo	his eyelashes revolved, all blurred
como em luas de espelho roxo.	as in red mirror moons.
Dava o sol nos dentes do cavalo morto.	Sun shone on the teeth of the dead horse.
Mas todos tinham muita pressa,	But everybody was in a frantic rush
e não sentiram como a terra	and could not feel how earth
procurava, de légua em légua,	kept searching league upon league
o ágil, o imenso, o etéreo sôpro	for the nimble, the immense, the ethereal breath
que faltava àquele arcabouço.	which had escaped that skeleton.
Tão pesado, o peito do cavalo morto!	O heavy breast of the dead horse!

1949

trans. James Merrill

Carlos Drummond de Andrade BRAZIL
1902–1987

In the later years of his long life, younger Brazilian poets called Carlos Drummond de Andrade "The Master." In some senses, though, he occupied this position of respect from early in his career. When Oswald de Andrade published Drummond's "No meio de caminho" ("In the Middle of the Road") in the *Revista de Antropofagia* (1928), many readers saw that poem as embodying some of the best characteristics of Brazilian Modernism, both in its nationalism and in its aestheticism. By late 1934, however, in *Brejo das almas* (*Fen of Souls*), Drummond was already skeptical about a nationalistic Brazilian poetry, and with that questioning came a skepticism about the literary project of defining a Brazilian national identity. Drummond's poems had begun their crucial inward turn, by which public issues are found implied in subjective experience. This poetic attitude would persist throughout the rest of Drummond's career.

That "turn" suggests also why the French existentialist writers were important to Drummond de Andrade. A poet of realism concerning the individual's solitary place in the universe, he found stability in the self-knowledge shaped by a clear poetic voice (despite his declarations of shyness and social awkwardness). Drummond resisted identification with any single "school" of poetics or literary politics. His early longing for community remained, however, and his search for community led him down many paths: regional identity, in *Confissões de Minas* (*Confessions from Minas*, 1944); solidarity with the international struggle against fascism, in *A rosa de povo* (*The People's Rose*, 1944); familial reconciliation and domestic continuity, in *Claro enigma* (*Clear Enigma*, 1951) and in other books; even poetry itself as a way to formulate identity and yet also a "secret death," in *A vida passada a limpo* (*Life in a New Copy*, 1959).

The threads that connect these thematic evolutions are Drummond de Andrade's style of calm urbanity in the service of political ideals, his emotional authenticity, his deeply personal internalization of idiomatic Brazilian speech, and his tone of serene acceptance of life's disillusionments. Because of his friendship with Elizabeth Bishop, his first English-language translator, Drummond de Andrade is known in North America as a poet of equanimity. In Brazil, his reputation is somewhat more political, perhaps because of the anti-U.S. and anti-Modernist attitudes of some of his late poems directed against the materialism and mechanization of Brazilian daily life.

Poema de sete faces

Quando nasci, um anjo torto
desses que vivem na sombra
disse: Vai, Carlos! ser *gauche* na vida.

As casas espiam os homens
que correm atrás de mulheres.
A tarde talvez fosse azul,
não houvesse tantos desejos.

O bonde passa cheio de pernas:
pernas brancas pretas amarelas.
Para que tanta perna, meu Deus, pergunta meu coração.
Porém meus olhos
não perguntam nada.

O homem atrás do bigode
é sério, simple e forte.
Quase não conversa.
Tem poucos, raros amigos
o homem atrás dos óculos e do bigode.

Meu Deus, por que me abandonaste
se sabias que eu não era Deus
se sabias que eu era fraco.

Mundo mundo vasto mundo,
se eu se chamasse Raimundo,
seria uma rima, não seria uma solução.
Mundo mundo vasto mundo,
mais vasto é meu coração.

Seven-sided Poem

When I was born, one of the crooked
angels who live in shadow, said:
Carlos, go on! Be *gauche* in life.

The houses watch the men,
men who run after women.
If the afternoon had been blue,
there might have been less desire.

The trolley goes by full of legs:
white legs, black legs, yellow legs.
My God, why all the legs?
my heart asks. But my eyes
ask nothing at all.

The man behind the moustache
is serious, simple, and strong.
He hardly ever speaks.
He has a few, choice friends,
the man behind the spectacles and the moustache.

My God, why hast Thou forsaken me
if Thou knew'st I was not God,
if Thou knew'st that I was weak?

Universe, vast universe,
if I had been named Eugene
that would not be what I mean
but it would go into verse
faster.

Eu não devia te dizer,
mas essa lua
mas esse conhaque
botam a gente comovido como o diabo.

1930

Universe, vast universe,
my heart is vaster.

I oughtn't to tell you,
but this moon
and this brandy
play the devil with one's emotions.

trans. Elizabeth Bishop

Infância

A Abgar Renault

Meu pai montava a cavalo, ia para o campo.
Minha mãe ficava sentada cosendo.
Meu irmão pequeno dormia.
Eu sozinho menino entre mangueiras
lia a história de Robinson Crusoé,
comprida história que não acaba mais.

No meio-dia branco de luz uma voz que aprendeu
a ninar nos longes da senzala—e nunca se esqueceu
chamava para o café.
Café preto que nem a preta velha
café gostoso
café bom.

Minha mãe ficava sentada cosendo
olhando para mim:
—Psiu... Não acorde o menino.
Para o berço onde pousou um mosquito.
E dava um suspiro... que fundo!

Lá longe meu pai campeava
no mato sem fim da fazenda.

E eu não sabia que minha história
era mais bonita que a de Robinson Crusoé.

1930

Infancy

To Abgar Renault

My father got on his horse and went to the field.
My mother stayed sitting and sewing.
My little brother slept.
A small boy alone under the mango trees,
I read the story of Robinson Crusoe,
the long story that never comes to an end.

At noon, white with light, a voice that had learned
lullabies long ago in the slave-quarters—and never
    forgot—
called us for coffee.
Coffee blacker than the black old woman
delicious coffee
good coffee.

My mother stayed sitting and sewing
watching me:
Shh—don't wake the boy.
She stopped the cradle when a mosquito had lit
and gave a sigh... how deep!
Away off there my father went riding
through the farm's endless wastes.

And I didn't know that my story
was prettier than that of Robinson Crusoe.

trans. Elizabeth Bishop

No meio do caminho

No meio do caminho tinha uma pedra
tinha uma pedra no meio do caminho
tinha uma pedra
no meio do caminho tinha uma pedra.

Nunca me esquecerei dêsse acontecimento
na vida de minhas retinas tão fatigadas.
Nunca me esquecerei que no meio do caminho

In the Middle of the Road

In the middle of the road was a stone
was a stone in the middle of the road
was a stone
in the middle of the road was a stone.

I shall never forget that event
in the life of my so tired eyes.
I shall never forget that in the middle of the road

tinha uma pedra
tinha uma pedra no meio do caminho
no meio do caminho tinha uma pedra.

1930

was a stone
was a stone in the middle of the road
in the middle of the road was a stone.

trans. John Nist

Não se mate

Carlos, sossegue, o amor
é isso que você está vendo:
hoje beija, amanhã não beija,
depois de amanhã é domingo
e segunda-feira ninguém sabe
o que será.

Inútil você resistir
ou mesmo suicidar-se.
Não se mate, oh não se mate,
reserve-se todo para
as bodas que ninguém sabe
quando virão,
se é que virão.

O amor, Carlos, você telúrico,
a noite passou em você,
e os recalques se sublimando,
lá dentro um barulho inefável,
rezas,
vitrolas,
santos que se persignam,
anúncios do melhor sabão,
barulho que ninguém sabe
de quê, praquê.

Entretanto você caminha
melancólico e vertical.
Você é a palmeira, você é o grito
que ninguém ouviu no teatro
e as luzes todas se apagam.
O amor no escuro, não, no claro,
é sempre triste, meu filho, Carlos,
mas não diga nada a ninguém,
ninguém sabe nem saberá.

1934

Don't Kill Yourself

Carlos, keep calm, love
is what you're seeing now:
today a kiss, tomorrow no kiss,
day after tomorrow's Sunday
and nobody knows what will happen
Monday.

It's useless to resist
or to commit suicide.
Don't kill yourself. Don't kill yourself!
Keep all of yourself for the nuptials
coming nobody knows when,
that is, if they ever come.

Love, Carlos, tellurian,
spent the night with you,
and now your insides are raising
an ineffable racket,
prayers,
victrolas,
saints crossing themselves,
ads for a better soap,
a racket of which nobody
knows the why or wherefore.

In the meantime you go on your way
vertical, melancholy.
You're the palm tree, you're the cry
nobody heard in the theatre
and all the lights went out.
Love in the dark, no, love
in the daylight, is always sad,
sad, Carlos, my boy,
but tell it to nobody,
nobody knows nor shall know.

trans. Elizabeth Bishop

Viagem na família

A Rodrigo M. F. de Andrade

No deserto de Itabira
a sombra de meu pai

Traveling as a Family

for Rodrigo M. F. de Andrade

In the desert of Itabira
the shade of my father

tomou-me pela mão.
Tanto tempo perdido.
Porém nada dizia.
Não era dia nem noite.
Suspiro? Vôo de pássaro?
Porém nada dizia.

Longamente caminhamos.
Aqui havia uma casa.
A montanha era maior.
Tantos mortos amontoados,
o tempo roendo os mortos.
E nas casas em ruína,
desprezo frio, umidade.
Porém nada dizia.

A rua que atravessava
a cavalo, de galope.
Seu relógio. Sua roupa.
Seus papéis de circunstância.
Suas histórias de amor.
Há um abrir de baús
e de lembranças violentas.
Porém nada dizia.

No deserto de Itabira
as coisas voltam a existir,
irrespiráveis e súbitas.
O mercado de desejos
expõe seus tristes tesouros;
meu anseio de fugir;
mulheres nuas; remorso.
Porém nada dizia.

Pisando livros e cartas,
viajamos na família.
Casamentos; hipotecas;
os primos tuberculosos;
a tia louca; minha avó
traída com as escravas,
rangendo sedas na alcova.
Porém nada dizia.

Que cruel, obscuro instinto
movia sua mão pálida
sùtilmente nos empurrando
pelo tempo e pelos lugares
defendidos?

Olhei-o nos olhos brancos.
Gritei-lhe: Fala! Minha voz
vibrou no ar um momento,
bateu nas pedras. A sombra

took me by the hand.
So much lost time.
However he didn't speak.
It was neither day nor night.
Sigh? bird's flight?
However he didn't speak.

We walked a long way.
Here, there'd been a house.
The mountains were bigger, then.
So many deaths piled up
and time gnawing the dead.
And in the ruined homes,
cold disdain, and damp.
However he didn't speak.

The street he used to cross
on horseback, at a gallop.
His watch. His suit.
His many title-deeds.
His anecdotes on sex.
Here's his foot-locker full
of rash souvenirs.
However he didn't speak.

In the deserts of Itabira
things start coming back
in an unbreathable rush.
The marketplace of desires
displays its sorry trash:
my anxiety to leave,
naked women, remorse.
However he didn't speak.

Stamping letters and books
we travel as a clan.
Weddings, mortgages,
the tuberculous branch,
the crazy aunt; the granny
betrayed among her slave girls,
tearing silks on her bed.
However he didn't speak.

What cruel dark instinct
made his pale hand twitch
subtly pushing us
through time, through places
with barricades?

I looked in his white eyes.
I shouted: Talk! My voice
made the air shake a bit, it
rattled stones. The shade

prosseguia devagar
aquela viagem patética
através do reino perdido.
Porém nada dizia.

Vi mágoa, incompreensão
e mais de uma velha revolta
a dividir-nos no escuro.
A mão que eu não quis beijar,
o prato que me negaram,
recusa em pedir perdão.
Orgulho. Terror noturno.
Porém nada dizia.

Fala fala fala fala.
Puxava pelo casaco
que se desfazia em barro.
Pelas mãos, pelas botinas
prendia a sombra severa
e a sombra se desprendia
sem fuga nem reação.
Porém ficava calada.

E eram distintos silêncios
que se entranhavam no seu.
Era meu avô já surdo
querendo escutar as aves
pintadas no céu da igreja;
a minha falta de amigos;
a sua falta de beijos;
eram nossas difíceis vidas
e uma grande separação
na pequena área do quarto.

A pequena área da vida
me aperta contra o seu vulto,
e nesse abraço diáfano
é como se eu me queimasse
todo, de pugente amor.
Só hoje nos conhecermos!
Óculos, memórias, retratos
fluem no rio do sangue.
As águas já não permitem
distinguir seu rosto longe,
para lá de setenta anos...

Senti que me perdoava
porém nada dizia.

As águas cobrem o bigode,
a família, Itabira, tudo.

kept his slow, picking pace,
that pathetic trip
through a lost kingdom.
However he didn't speak.

I saw hurt. Misunderstanding.
More than one old tiff
splitting us in the dark:
the hand I wouldn't kiss,
the dish he wouldn't share,
the refusal to admit a wrong.
Pride. Terror at night.
However he didn't speak.

Talk Talk Talk Talk Talk.
I pulled him by his coat
which fell apart like clay.
By his hands. By the boots
I caught the angry shade
who veered, and got away.
Without sweat. Without a scene.
However it didn't speak.

There were specific silences
that burgeoned from his.
There was a deaf grandfather
who drooled to hear the birds
painted on the church ceiling;
my own lack of friends;
his own too-chary kisses.
There were our two grim lives
and the vast division
wrought in a small bedroom.

The small bedroom of life
squeezes me to his side,
and this diaphanous embrace
is like an all-over burn
from rank, pungent love.
Only now do we meet!
Glasses, memories, portraits,
run in the river of blood.
The waves never permit
the distinguishing of a face
on the far side of seventy...

I felt he pardoned me.
However he didn't speak.

The waters reach his mustache,
the family, Itabira, the rest.

1942

trans. Virginia de Araújo

Resíduo

De tudo ficou um pouco.
Do meu medo. Do teu asco.
Dos gritos gagos. Da rosa
ficou um pouco.

Ficou um pouco de luz
captada no chapéu.
Nos olhos do rufião
de ternura ficou um pouco
(muito pouco).

Pouco ficou deste pó
de que teu branco sapato
se cobriu. Ficaram poucas
roupas, poucos véus rotos
pouco, pouco, muito pouco.

Mas de tudo fica um pouco.
Da ponte bombardeada,
de duas folhas de grama,
do maço
—vazio—de cigarros, ficou um pouco.

Pois de tudo fica um pouco.
Fica um pouco de teu queixo
no queixo de tua filha.
De teu áspero silêncio
um pouco ficou, um pouco
nos muros zangados,
nas folhas, mudas, que sobem.

Ficou um pouco de tudo
no pires de porcelana,
dragão partido, flor branca,
ficou um pouco
de ruga na vossa testa,
retrato.

Se de tudo fica um pouco,
mas por que não ficaria
um pouco de mim? no trem
que leva ao norte, no barco,
nos anúncios de jornal,
um pouco de mim em Londres,
um pouco de mim algures?
na consoante?
no poço?

Um pouco fica oscilando
na embocadura dos rios
e os peixes não o evitam,

Residue

Of everything, a little stayed.
Of my fear. Of your temper.
Of stammered screams. Of the rose,
a little.

A little of the light stayed
pooled in the hat.
In the bully's eyes
a trace stayed, of gentleness
(only one).

A little of the dust
with which your white shoe
was covered. Random
clothes, some mass-veils, rotted,
a little, a little, a touch.

But of everything, a little stays.
Of the blasted bridge,
of two stalks of grass,
of the empty
box of cigarettes, a little stayed.

For of everything, a little stays.
The line of your chin stayed
in your daughter's.
Of your dry silence,
a little stayed, a little
in the angry walls,
in non-vocal leaves which spin.

A little of everything stayed
in the china saucer,
cracked dragon, pale flower;
the lines on your brow,
I mirror.

If a little stays of everything,
why shouldn't something mine stay,
too? in the train
running north, on a ship,
in newspaper ads;
a little of me in London,
some farther off?
in the consonant?
in the well?

A little buoys in the drift
at the river's mouth
and fish don't mind it,
a little, it's not in books.

um pouco: não está nos livros.
De tudo fica um pouco.
Não muito: de uma torneira
pinga esta gota absurda,
meio sal e meio álcool,
salta esta perna de rã,
este vidro de relógio
partido em mil esperanças,
este pescoço de cisne,
este segredo infantil...
De tudo ficou um pouco:
de mim; de ti; de Abelardo.
Cabelo na minha manga,
de tudo ficou um pouco;
vento nas orelhas minhas,
simplório arroto, gemido
de víscera inconformada,
e minúsculos artefatos:
campânula, alvéolo, cápsula
de revólver... de aspirina.
De tudo ficou um pouco.

E de tudo fica um pouco.
Oh abre os vidros de loção
e abafa
o insuportável mau cheiro da memória.

Mas de tudo, terrível, fica um pouco,
e sob as ondas ritmadas
e sob as nuvens e os ventos
e sob as pontes e sob os túneis
e sob as labaredas e sob o sarcasmo
e sob a gosma e sob o vômito
e sob o soluço, o cárcere, o esquecido
e sob os espetáculos e sob a morte de escarlete
e sob as bibliotecas, os asilos, as igrejas triunfantes
e sob tu mesmo e sob teus pés já duros
e sob os gonzos da família e da classe,
fica sempre um pouco de tudo.
Às vezes um botão. Às vezes um rato.

1945

Of everything a little stays.
Not much: from the faucet drips
this ludicrous drop
half alcohol, half salt,
this frog-leg that leaps,
this wrist watch lens
split in a thousand hopes,
this swan neck,
this secret, infantile...
Of everything, a little stays:
of me, of you; of Abelard.
Hair on my sleeve,
of everything a little stays,
wind in these ears,
buffoon burp, groan
from the abused entrails,
and tiny artifacts:
glass bell, honeycomb, shell
of revolver... aspirin.
Of everything, a little stays.
Oh, open the lotion bottles
and smother
the intolerable stench of memory.

But of everything terrible, a little stays,
and under the beating waves
and under the clouds and the winds
and under the bridges and the tunnels
and under the flames and under the sarcasm
and under the drool and under the vomit
and under the sob within the cell, the forgotten prisoner
and under the performances and the scarlet death
and under the libraries, the asylums, the triumphant
    churches
and under you yourself and under your feet, half stiff
    already,
and under the gross canopy of family and class,
a little something always stays.
A button, sometimes. Sometimes a rat.

trans. Virginia de Araújo

Retrato de família

Este retrato de família
está um tanto empoeirado.
Já não se vê no rosto do pai
quanto dinheiro ele ganhou.

Nas mãos dos tios não se percebem
as viagens que ambos fizeram.

Portrait of a Family

This family portrait
is rather dusty.
You can't see Papa's face
or the big stack he made.

In the uncles' hands
the foreign travel doesn't show.

A avó ficou lisa, amarela,
sem memórias da monarquia.

Os meninos, como estão mudados.
O rosto de Pedro é tranqüilo,
usou os melhores sonhos.
E João não é mais mentiroso.

O jardim tornou-se fantástico.
As flores, são placas cinzentas.
E a areia, sob pés extintos,
é um oceano de névoa.

No semicírculo das cadeiras
Nota-se certo movimento.
As crianças trocam de lugar,
mas sem barulho: é um retrato.

Vinte anos é um grande tempo.
Modela qualquer imagem.
Se uma figura vai murchando,
outra, sorrindo, se propõe.

Esses estranhos assentados,
meus parentes? Não acredito.
São visitas se divertindo
numa sala que se abre pouco.

Ficaram traços da família
perdidos no jeito dos corpos.
Bastante para sugerir
que um corpo é cheio de surpresas.

A moldura deste retrato
em vão prende suas personagens.
Estão ali voluntariamente,
saberiam—se preciso—voar.

Poderiam sutilizar-se
no claro-escuro do salão,
ir morar no fundo dos móveis
ou no bolso de velhos coletes.

A casa tem muitas gavetas
e papéis, escadas compridas.
Quem sabe a malícia das coisas,
quando a matéria se aborrece?

O retrato não me responde,
ele me fita e se contempla
nos meus olhos empoeirados.
E no cristal se multiplicam

Granny's smooth now, yellow,
finished with the monarchy.

The boys are quite changed.
Pedro's face is placid,
His dreams are improved.
And João's stopped telling tales.

The garden's strange:
flowers like lead disks;
sand, under the dead feet,
an ocean of mist.

One notes a certain rush
of kids in the formal group:
they play musical chairs
—no music, no bodies.

Twenty years is a lot.
Anyone would seem odd.
But if one shape gives up,
another comes and smiles.

These queer seated people
my relatives? Who said!
They're visitors who wandered in
to a rarely opened room.

Family features stay on
in the blind tumble of flesh.
Just enough to suggest
the grab-bag a body is.

The picture frame isn't what
holds the pictured in:
free-will keeps them there;
they'd flee, if they wished.

They could blend subtly
in the parlor chiaroscuro,
silt to the bottoms of seats
and into winter clothes.

The house is full of drawers
and papers, deep stairwells.
Who knows how mean things get
once matter is disturbed?

The picture keeps its place.
It watches me, it contemplates
itself in my dusty eyes.
In my lenses, there multiply

os parentes mortos e vivos.
Já não distingo os que se foram
dos que restaram. Percebo apenas
a estranha idéia de família

viajando através da carne.

1945

relatives dead and alive.
I can't tell which is which.
I do know what a strange
notion of family does trace

the long road of the flesh.

trans. Virginia de Araújo

Canto esponjoso

Bela
esta manhã sem carência de mito,
e mel sorvido sem blasfêmia.

Bela
esta manhã ou outra possível,
esta vida ou outra invenção
sem, na sombra, fantasmas.

Umidade de areia adere ao pé.
Engulo o mar, que me engole.
Valvas, curvos pensamentos, matizes da luz
azul
      completa
cobro formas constituídas.

Bela
a passagem do corpo, sua fusão
no corpo geral do mundo.

Vontade de cantar. Mas tão absoluta
que me calo, repleto.

1947

Diminutive

Beautiful
this morning, no myth felt lacking,
and honey in the mouth without sin.

Beautiful
this morning or another possible,
this life or some other invention,
lived in the clear.

Dampness of sand clings to the feet.
I swallow the wave that swallows me in.
Valves, thoughts curving, light shimmer
blue
      complete
          over forms that keep.

Beautiful
the body's passage, its fusion
into the even body of the world.

A wish to sing. But so total,
I control it, replete.

trans. Virginia de Araújo

Um boi vê os homens

Tão delicados (mais que um arbusto) e correm
e correm de um para outro lado, sempre esquecidos
de alguma coisa. Certamente, falha-lhes
não sei que atributo essencial, posto se apresentem nobres
e graves, por vezes. Ah, espantosamente graves,
até sinistros. Coitados, dir-se-ia não escutam
nem o canto do ar nem os segredos de feno,
como também parecem não enxergar o que é visível
e comum a cada um de nós, no espaço. E ficam tristes
e no rasto da tristeza chegam à crueldade.
Toda a expressão deles mora nos olhos—e perde-se
a um simples baixar de cílios, a uma sombra.
Nada nos pêlos, nos extremos de inconcebível fragilidade,

An Ox Looks at Man

They are more delicate even than shrubs and they run
and run from one side to the other, always forgetting
something. Surely they lack I don't know what
basic ingredient, though they present themselves
as noble or serious, at times. Oh, terribly serious,
even tragic. Poor things, one would say that they hear
neither the song of air nor the secrets of hay;
likewise they seem not to see what is visible
and common to each of us, in space. And they are sad,
and in the wake of sadness they come to cruelty.
All their expression lives in their eyes—and loses itself
to a simple lowering of lids, to a shadow.
And since there is little of the mountain about them—

e como neles há pouca montanha,
e que secura e que reentrâncias e que
impossibilidade de se organizarem em formas calmas,
permanentes e necessárias. Têm, talvez,
certa graça melancólica (um minuto) e com isto se fazem
perdoar a agitação incômoda e o translúcido
vazio interior que os torna tão pobres e carecidos
de emitir sons absurdos e agônicos: desejo, amor, ciúme
(que sabemos nós?), sons que se despedaçam e tombam
    no campo
como pedras aflitas e queimam a erva e a água,
e difícil, depois disto, é ruminarmos nossa verdade.

1951

nothing in the hair or in the terribly fragile limbs
but coldness and secrecy—it is impossible for them
to settle themselves into forms that are calm, lasting,
and necessary. They have, perhaps, a kind
of melancholy grace (one minute) and with this they allow
themselves to forget the problems and translucent
inner emptiness that make them so poor and so lacking
when it comes to uttering silly and painful sounds:
    desire, love, jealousy
(what do we know?)—sounds that scatter and fall in
    the field
like troubled stones and burn the herbs and the water,
and after this it is hard to keep chewing away at our truth.

trans. Mark Strand

Elegia

Ganhei (perdi) meu dia.
E baixa a coisa fria
também chamada noite, e o frio ao frio
em bruma se entrelaça, num suspiro.

E me pergunto e me respiro
na fuga deste dia que era mil
para mim que esperava
os grandes sóis violentos, me sentia
tão rico deste dia
e lá se foi secreto, ao serro frio.

Perdi minha alma à flor do dia ou já perdera
bem antes sua vaga pedraria?
Mas quando me perdi, se estou perdido
antes de haver nascido
e me nasci votado à perda
de frutos que não tenho nem colhia?

Gastei meu dia. Nele me perdi.
De tantas perdas uma clara via
por certo se abriria
de mim a mim, estela fria.
As árvores lá fora se meditam.
O inverno é quente em mim, que o estou berçando,
e em mim vai derretendo
este torrão de sal que está chorando.

Ah, chega de lamento e versos ditos
ao ouvido de alguém sem rosto e sem justiça,
ao ouvido do muro,
ao liso ouvido gotejante
de uma piscina que não sabe o tempo, e fia
seu tapete de água, distraída.

Elegy

I've won (lost) my day.
And the cold thing lowers
called night, as well, and cold into cold
in haze merges, with a sigh.

And I question myself and breathe myself
in the flight of this day which was a thousand
days for me, who awaited
the violence of great suns, who felt
so rich for it,
and there it goes in secret past the cold peaks.

Did I lose my soul at noon? or was that treasure
taken since or before? Does timing matter
if I am lost
since birth (before?) if I was
born bonded to a loss of what
I hadn't, and could never hope to gain?

I spent my day. I lost myself in it.
Among such losses, a single path
surely will emerge
from me to me, blank monolith, to compensate.
The trees here are lost in meditation.
Winter is still hot in me who cradled winter
tight, and, inside, this uninscribed column
of salt begins to thaw in tears.

Enough pity. Enough verse
said in the ear of the faceless and unjust
said in the ear of a wall
said in the smooth dripping ear
of a pool which knows no hours, but spills away
its water carpet in indifference.

E vou me recolher
ao cofre de fantasmas, que a notícia
de perdidos lá não chegue nem açule
os olhos policiais do amor-vigia.
Não me procurem que me perdi eu mesmo
como os homens se matam, e as enguias
à loca se recolhem, na água fria.

Dia,
espelho de projeto não vivido,
e contudo viver era tão flamas
na promessa dos deuses; e é tão ríspido
em meio aos oratórios já vazios
em que a alma barroca tenta confortar-se
mas só vislumbra o frio noutro frio.

Meu Deus, essência estranha
ao vaso que me sinto, ou forma vã,
pois que, eu essência, não habito
vossa arquitetura imerecida;
meu Deus e meu conflito,
nem vos dou conta de mim nem desafio
as garras inefáveis: eis que assisto
a meu desmonte palmo a palmo e não me aflijo
de me tornar planície em que já pisam
servos e bois e militares em serviço
da sombra, e uma criança
que o tempo novo me anuncia e nega.

Terra a que me inclino sob o frio
de minha testa que se alonga,
e sinto mais presente quanto aspiro
em ti o fumo antigo dos parentes,
minha terra, me tens; e teu cativo
passeias brandamente
como ao que vai morrer se estende a vista
de espaços luminosos, intocáveis:
em mim o que resiste são teus poros.
Corto o frio da folha. Sou teu frio.

E sou meu próprio frio que me fecho
longe do amor desabitado e líquido,
amor em que me amaram, me feriram
sete vezes por dia, em sete dias
de sete vidas de ouro,
amor, fonte de eterno frio,
minha pena deserta, ao fim de março,
amor, quem contaria?
E já não sei se é jogo, ou se poesia.

1954

And I withdraw
to the safe of ghosts, for rumor
of loss cannot reach me there, and the sharp eye
of the watchman, Love, counts nothing lost.
Don't follow—I lose myself
as men do who rush to death, as eels
do that withdraw in mud on shelves under cataracts.

Day,
mirror of a project never lived:
but to live was flames! so the gods
proclaimed. But to live was harsh
where vacant chapels clutter the scene
and the baroque soul strains to be comforted
only to feel fresh chill, from another face.

My God, essence stranger
to this vessel I-myself, to this manic
form I-am; this essence-I is not fit
for such architecture as yours.
My Lord and my conflict:
I neither meet your demands nor challenge them,
I know your claws ineffable, I observe
my slow decomposition and am not disturbed
to be a parade-ground upon which roam
serfs, cattle, military gentlemen in death's
employ, and a child
time promised, and then stole.

Earth I bow to, below the chill
on my tall forehead which grows taller still,
earth I sense most present when I inhale
the dry scent and dust of my family dead,
Earth, have me for your hostage,
I walk with a light step,
a man with counted days who sees the landscape stretch
into space luminous and intangible.
What keeps me yet? In my skin, the pores of Earth.
I break the cold of the leaf. I am coldness.

I'm chill with the cold of closing breath.
I'm lost to any unlived and liquid love
such as they loved me with when they hurt
seven times a day in sets of seven days for seven
golden lives. Love, frozen,
love, source of eternal cold,
drop my pen by March's end.
Love, who'll care? if I'm unsure myself
whether it's poetry still, or a mere game.

trans. Virginia de Araújo

Nicolás Guillén

In 1936 Nicolás Guillén was jailed in Cuba for publishing "subversive materials." Released, he moved to Spain in 1937 to join the International Congress for the Defense of Culture, and he remained in Spain through the civil war. Guillén's early poems, written in the idiom and rhythms of impoverished Afro-Caribbean peoples, had been strongly influenced by the *poesía negra* movement of the Antilles (including the poems of Luis Palés Matos in Puerto Rico). Guillén's experiences in Spain moved him to a more international perspective.

Although Guillén began as a Modernist, the form of his poems followed his political commitments. He abandoned his early Modernist diction in favor of an "Afro-Cuban" formalism, finding in residually African speech forms and in song forms of an Afro-Cuban tradition analogies for his experiments in the Cuban *son* (sweet sound). Guillén's adaptation of that musical form—like the African-based experimentation by writers of the Harlem Renaissance and of the international Négritude movement—drew on cultural and formal memories of African songs and of the planting songs of enslaved peoples (in Guillén's case, peoples of the Caribbean). Although he remained an avowed communist, Guillén, a mestizo by birth, writes in a vernacular that nevertheless resists the exoticism of other Afro-Cuban theorists, such as the novelist Alejo Carpentier. Guillén's connective is voice (and not, for instance, Naturalist narrative representations of specific injustices), and as a result his poems are more psychological, more theoretically generalized, than those of the overtly political writers with whom he is frequently compared.

Without compromising his commitment to the speech rhythms and physical realities of Afro-Cuban life, Guillén increasingly addressed his poems to issues of cross-cultural Marxist dialectic. Exiled by the Fulgencio Batista regime in the early 1950s, Guillén lived in Buenos Aires until 1960; after Fidel Castro's coup, Guillén returned to Cuba. From 1961 until his death, Nicolás Guillén served as president of the Writers' and Artists' Union in Havana.

Pequeña oda a un negro boxeador cubano	*Small Ode to a Black Cuban Boxer*
Tus guantes puestos en la punta de tu cuerpo de ardilla, y el *punch* de tu sonrisa.	Your gloves cocked before a squirrel-quick body and the punch in your smile!
El Norte es fiero y rudo, boxeador. Ese mismo Broadway, que en actitud de vena se desangra para chillar junto a los *rings* en que tú saltas como un moderno mono elástico, sin el resorte de las sogas, ni los almohadones del *clinch;* ese mismo Broadway, que unta de asombro su boca de melón ante tus puños explosivos y tus actuales zapatos de charol; ese mismo Broadway,	Boxer, the North is hard and cruel. The very Broadway that like a vein bleeds out to scream beside the ring wherein you bound, a brand new rubber monkey, without resorting to the ropes or the cushions of a clinch... the very Broadway that oils its melon-mouth with fear before your fists of dynamite and stylish patent leather shoes... is the same Broadway

es el que estira su hocico con una enorme lengua húmeda,
para lamer glotonamente
toda la sangre de nuestro cañaveral.

De seguro que tú
no vivirás al tanto de ciertas cosas nuestras,
ni de ciertas cosas de allá,
porque el *training* es duro y el músculo traidor,
y hay que estar hecho un toro,
como dices alegremente, para que el golpe duela más.

Tu inglés,
un poco más precario que tu endeble español,
sólo te ha de servir para entender sobre la lona
cuanto en su verde slang
mascan las mandíbulas de los que tú derrumbas
jab a *jab*.

En realidad acaso no necesites otra cosa,
porque como seguramente pensarás.
ya tienes tu lugar.

Es bueno, al fin y al cabo,
hallar un *punching bag*,
eliminar la grasa bajo el sol.
saltar,
sudar,
nadar,
y de la suiza al *shadow boxing*,
de la ducha al comedor,
salir pulido, fino, fuerte
como un baston recién labrado
con agresividades de *black jack*.

Y ahora que Europa se desnuda
para tostar su carne al sol
y busca en Harlem y en La Habana
jazz y son
lucirse negro mientras aplaude el bulevar,
y frente a la envidia de los blancos
hablar en negro de verdad.

1931

---

that stretches out its snout, its moist enormous tongue,
to lick and glut upon
our canefields' vital blood!

It's clear
you're not aware of certain things down here,
nor of certain things up there;
for training is tough, muscle a traitor,
and one must gain—you say with joy
—a bull-like strength, to make the punch hurt more.

Your English,
only a bit more shaky than your feeble Spanish,
is good enough inside the ring
for you to understand that filthy slang
spit from the jaws of those you waste
jab by jab.

In truth, perhaps that's all you need.
And, as you certainly will think,
you've got it made.

For after all, it's great
to find a punching bag,
work off some fat beneath the sun—
to leap,
to sweat,
to swim—
and from shadow-boxing to a fight,
from the shower to the table,
come out polished, fine, and strong,
like a newly-crafted cane
with the aggressiveness of a black jack.

So now that Europe strips itself
to brown its hide beneath the sun
and seeks in Harlem and Havana
jazz and *son:*
the Negro reigns while boulevards applaud!
Let the envy of the whites
know proud, authentic black!

trans. Robert Márquez and David Arthur McMurray

El apellido

Elegía familiar

I

Desde la escuela
y aún antes... Desde el alba, cuando apenas

My Last Name

A family elegy

I

Ever since school
and even before... Since the dawn, when I was

era una brizna yo de sueño y llanto,
desde entonces,
me dijeron mi nombre. Un santo y seña
para poder hablar con las estrellas.
Tú te llamas, te llamarás...
Y luego me entregaron
esto que veis escrito en mi tarjeta,
esto que pongo al pie de mis poemas:
las trece letras
que llevo a cuestas por la calle,
que siempre van conmigo a todas partes.
¿Es mi nombre, estáis ciertos?
¿Tenéis todas mis señas?
¿Ya conocéis mi sangre navegable,
mi geografía llena de oscuros montes,
de hondos y amargos valles
que no están en los mapas?
¿Acaso visitásteis mis abismos,
mis galerías subterráneas
con grandes piedras húmedas,
islas sobresaliendo en negras charcas
y donde un puro chorro
siento de antiguas aguas
caer desde mi alto corazón
con fresco y hondo estrépito
en un lugar lleno de ardientes árboles,
monos equilibristas,
loros legisladores y culebras?
¿Toda mi piel (debí decir)
toda mi piel viene de aquella estatua
de mármol español? ¿También mi voz de espanto,
el duro grito de mi garganta? ¿Vienen de allá
todos mis huesos? ¿Mis raíces y las raíces
de mis raíces y además
estas ramas oscuras movidas por los sueños
y estas flores abiertas en mi frente
y esta savia que amarga mi corteza?
¿Estáis seguros?
¿No hay nada más que eso que habéis escrito,
que eso que habéis sellado
con un sello de cólera?
(¡Oh, debí haber preguntado!).

Y bien, ahora os pregunto:
¿no veis estos tambores en mis ojos?
¿No veis estos tambores tensos y golpeados
con dos lágrimas secas?
¿No tengo acaso
un abuelo nocturno
con una gran marca negra
(más negra todavía que la piel)

barely a patch of sleep and wailing,
since then
I have been told my name. A password
that I might speak with stars.
Your name is, you shall be called...
And then they handed me
this you see here written on my card,
this I put at the foot of all poems:
thirteen letters
that I carry on my shoulders through the street,
that are with me always, no matter where I go.
Are you sure it is my name?
Have you got all my particulars?
Do you already know my navigable blood,
my geography full of dark mountains,
of deep and bitter valleys
that are not on the maps?
Perhaps you have visited my chasms,
my subterranean galleries
with great moist rocks,
islands jutting out of black puddles,
where I feel the pure rush
of ancient waters
falling from my proud heart
with a sound that's fresh and deep
to a place of flaming trees,
acrobatic monkeys,
legislative parrots and snakes?
Does all my skin (I should have said),
Does all my skin come from that Spanish marble?
My frightening voice too,
the harsh cry in my throat?
Are all my bones from there?
My roots and the roots
of my roots and also
these dark branches swayed by dreams
and these flowers blooming on my forehead
and this sap embittering my bark?
Are you certain?
Is there nothing more than this that you have written,
than this which you have stamped
with the seal of anger?
(Oh, I should have asked!)

Well then, I ask you now:
Don't you see these drums in my eyes?
Don't you see these drums, tightened and
beaten with two dried-up tears?
Don't I have, perhaps,
a nocturnal grandfather
with a great black scar
(darker still than his skin)

una gran marca hecha de un latigazo?
¿No tengo pues
un abuelo mandinga, congo, dahomeyano?
¿Cómo se llama? ¡Oh, sí decídmelo!
¿Andrés? ¿Francisco? ¿Amable?
¿Cómo decís Andrés en congo?
¿Cómo habéis dicho siempre
Francisco en dahomeyano?
En mandinga ¿cómo se dice Amable?
¿O no? ¿Eran, pues, otros nombres?
¡El apellido, entonces!
¿Sabéis mi otro apellido, el que me viene
de aquella tierra enorme, el apellido
sangriento y capturado, que pasó sobre el mar
entre cadenas, que pasó entre cadenas sobre el mar?

¡Ah, no podéis recordarlo!
Lo habéis disuelto en tinta inmemorial.
Lo habéis robado a un pobre negro indefenso.
Los escondisteis, creyendo
que iba a bajar los ojos yo de la vergüenza.
¡Gracias!
¡Os lo agradezco!
¡Gentiles gentes, thank you!
Merci!
Merci bien!
Merci beaucoup!
Pero no... ¿Podéis creerlo? No.
Yo estoy limpio.
Brilla mi voz como un metal recién pulido
Mirad mi escudo: tiene un baobab,
tiene un rhoceronte y una lanza.
Yo soy también el nieto,
biznieto,
tataranieto de un esclavo.
(Que se avergüence el amo).
¿Seré Yelofe?
¿Nicolás Yelofe, acaso?
¿O Nicolás Bakongo?
¿Tal vez Guillén Banguila?
¿O Kumbá?
¿Quizá Guillén Kumbá?
¿O Kongué?
¿Pudiera ser Guillén Kongué?
¡Oh, quién lo sabe!
¡Qué enigma entre las aguas!

II

Siento la noche inmensa gravitar
sobre profundas bestias,
sobre inocentes almas castigadas;

---

a great scar made by a whip?
Have I not, then,
a grandfather who's Mandingo, Dahoman, Congolese?
What is his name? Oh, yes, give me his name!
Andrés? Francisco? Amable?
How do you say Andrés in Congolese?
How have you always said
Francisco in Dahoman?
In Mandingo, how do you say Amable?
No? Were they, then, other names?
The last name then!
Do you know my other last name, the one that comes
to me from that enormous land, the captured,
bloody last name, that came across the sea
in chains, which came in chains across the sea.

Ah, you can't remember it!
You have dissolved it in immemorial ink.
You stole it from a poor, defenseless Black.
You hid it, thinking that I would
lower my eyes in shame.
Thank you!
I am grateful to you!
Noble people, thanks!
Merci!
Merci bien!
Merci beaucoup!
But no... Can you believe it? No.
I am clean.
My voice sparkles like newly polished metal.
Look at my shield: it has a baobab,
it has a rhinoceros and a spear.
I am also the grandson,
great grandson,
great great grandson of a slave.
(Let the master be ashamed.)
Am I Yelofe?
Nicolás Yelofe, perhaps?
Or Nicolás Bakongo?
Maybe Guillén Banguila?
Or Kumbá?
Perhaps Guillén Kumbá?
Or Kongué?
Could I be Guillén Kongué?
Oh, who knows!
What a riddle in the waters!

II

I feel immense night fall
on profound beasts,
on innocent castigated souls;

pero también sobre voces en punta,
que despojan al cielo de sus soles,
los más duros,
para condecorar la sangre combatiente.
De algún país ardiente, perforado
por la gran flecha ecuatorial,
sé que vendrán lejanos primos,
remota angustia mía disparada en el viento;
sé que vendrán pedazos de mis venas,
sangre remota mía,
con duro pie aplastando las hierbas asustadas;
sé que vendrán hombres de vidas verdes,
remota selva mía,
con su dolor abierto en cruz y el pecho rojo en llamas.
Sin conocernos nos reconoceremos en el hambre,
en la tuberculosis y en la sífilis,
en el sudor comprado en bolsa negra,
en los fragmentos de cadenas
adheridos todavía a la piel;
sin conocernos nos reconoceremos
en los ojos cargados de sueños
y hasta en los insultos como piedras
que nos escupen cada día
los cuadrumanos de la tinta y el papel.
¿Qué ha de importar entonces
(¡que ha de importar ahora!)
¡ay! mi pequeño nombre
de trece letras blancas?
¿Ni el mandinga, bantú,
yoruba, dahomeyano
nombre del triste abuelo ahogado
en tinta de notario?
¿Qué importa, amigos puros?
¡Oh sí, puros amigos,
venid a ver mi nombre!
Mi nombre interminable,
hecho de interminables nombres;
el nombre mío, ajeno,
libre y mío, ajeno y vuestro,
ajeno y libre como el aire.

1958

but also on ready voices,
which steal suns from the sky,
the brightest suns,
to decorate combatant blood.
From some flaming land pierced through
by the great equatorial arrow,
I know there will come distant cousins,
my ancestral anguish cast upon the winds;
I know there will come portions of my veins,
my ancestral blood,
with calloused feet bending frightened grasses;
I know there will come men whose lives are green,
my ancestral jungle,
with their pain open like a cross and their breasts red
      with flames.
Having never met, we will know each other by the hunger,
by the tuberculosis and the syphilis,
by the sweat bought in a black market,
by the fragments of chain
still clinging to the skin;
Having never met we will know each other
by the dream-full eyes
and even by the rock-hard insults
the quadrumanes of ink and paper
spit at us each day.
What can it matter, then.
(What does it matter now!)
ah, my little name
of thirteen letters?
Or the Mandingo, Bantu,
Yoruba, Dahoman name
of the sad grandfather drowned
in notary's ink.
Good friends, what does it matter?
Oh, yes, good friends
come look at my name!
My name without end,
made up of endless names;
My name, foreign,
free and mine, foreign and yours,
foreign and free as the air.

trans. Robert Márquez and David Arthur McMurray

Bares

Amo los bares y tabernas
junto al mar,
donde la gente charla y bebe
sólo por beber y charlar.
Donde Juan Nadie llega y pide

Bars

I love the bars and taverns
next to the sea,
where people talk and drink
just to drink and talk.
Where Joe Nobody walks in and asks

su trago elemental,
y están Juan Bronco y Juan Navaja
y Juan Narices y hasta Juan Simple,
el sólo, el simplemente Juan.

Allí la blanca ola
bate de la amistad;
una amistad de pueblo, sin retórica,
una ola de ¡hola! ¿cómo estás?
Allí huele a pescado,
a mangle, a ron, a sal
y a camisa sudada puesta a secar al sol.

Búscame, hermano, y me hallarás
(en La Habana, en Oporto,
en Jacmel, en Shanghai)
con la sencilla gente
que sólo por beber y charlar
puebla los bares y tabernas
junto al mar.

1958

for his drink straight
and there are Joe Fisticuffs and Joe Blade too
and Joe Blow and even Joe Simple,
alone, and just-plain Joe.

There white waves
break into a friendliness:
a friendliness of a small town, without rhetoric,
a wave "hi!" and "how're you doing?"
It smells like fish there,
of mangrove, of rum, of salt
and a sweaty shirt hung out in the sun to dry.

Look for me, brother, and you'll find me
(in Havana, in Oporto,
in Jacmel, in Shanghai)
with ordinary folks
who—just to drink and talk—
people the bars and the taverns
next to the sea.

trans. Eric Orozco

Jaime Torres Bodet

MEXICO
1902–1974

The poems of Jaime Torres Bodet suggest a different model for the integration of lyricism and public responsibility than the more overtly political assertions of Neruda, Cardenal, or the Brazilian avant-garde. The poet, he writes, is the "subtle educator" of democracy. Torres Bodet's commitments to poetry, to mass education, and to human rights infused both of his careers, as writer and as public servant. With the publication of his first book, *Fervor* (1918), Torres Bodet joined the circle of poets around Enrique González Martínez, who praised Torres Bodet's early poems as "limpid and serene verse . . . purified in his own heart." As his public career developed—he worked as a professor of French literature, as director of the Mexican government's "each one, teach one" literacy program in the 1940s, and as director general of UNESCO in the late 1950s—Torres Bodet wrote increasingly "public" poems that register a compassion for the suffering of others. At the same time, Torres Bodet's technique evolved gradually from the traditional formalism of his early poems, with their emphasis on the music of the line, toward a surreal and serenely meditative free verse. In later works—including *Sonetos* (*Sonnets*, 1949) and his autobiography, *Tiempo de arena* (*Time on Stage*, 1955)—Torres Bodet insists on forms of freedom that bridge political rights and emotional liberation. His late poems, in effect, enact that integrity of poetry and spiritual wholeness that Torres Bodet lived, faithful to "the forgiveness that life offers to all our mistakes."

Vivir

Sentimientos vulgares
en las caras vulgares
de las gentes vulgares.

Las mismas calles viejas
con sus tristezas viejas...
¡Las mismas almas viejas!

Todo lo conocido:
el dolor conocido,
el placer conocido.

¡Y tener que vivir
sabiendo que vivir
ya no es más que vivir!

1923

Living

Common feelings
in common faces
of common people.

The same old streets
with their old sadness...
The same old souls!

All that is known:
the sorrow known,
the pleasure known.

And to have to live
knowing that life
is no more than living!

trans. Sonja Karsen

Dédalo

Enterrado vivo
en un infinito
dédalo de espejos,
me oigo, me sigo,
me busco en el liso
muro del silencio.

Pero no me encuentro.

Palpo, escucho, miro.
Por todos los ecos
de este laberinto,
un acento mío
está pretendiendo
llegar a mi oído...

Pero no lo advierto.

Alguien está preso
aquí, en este frío
lúcido recinto,
dédalo de espejos...
Alguien, al que imito.
Si se va, me alejo.
Si regresa, vuelvo.
Si se duerme, sueño.
—"¿Eres tú?" me digo...

Pero no contesto.

Labyrinth

Buried alive
in an infinite
labyrinth of mirrors
I hear myself, follow myself,
look for myself
in this smooth wall of silence.

But I do not find myself.

I grope, listen, look.
Through all the echoes
of this labyrinth
my voice
is trying
to reach my ear...

But I do not hear it.

Someone here is a prisoner
in this cold
brilliant enclosure,
labyrinth of mirrors:
someone whom I imitate.
If he goes, I go away.
If he returns, I return.
If he sleeps, I dream,
"Is it you?"

But I do not answer.

Perseguido, herido
por el mismo acento
—que no sé si es mío—
contra el eco mismo
del mismo recuerdo,
en este infinito
dédalo de espejos
enterrado vivo.

1937

Pursued, wounded
by this same voice
—which I do not know
is mine or not—
against the same echo
of the same memory,
in this infinite
labyrinth of mirrors
buried alive.

trans. Sonja Karsen

Patria

Esta piedad profunda es tierra mía.
Aquí, si avanzo, lo que toco es patria:
presencia donde siento a cada instante
el acuerdo del cuerpo con el alma.

Esta es mi voz. Pero la escucho
en bocas diferentes. Y aunque nada
de cuanto dice pueda sorprenderme,
oírla me cautiva porque canta
en ella un corazón siempre distinto
que nos lo explica todo sin palabras.

Aquí, si avanzo, el mundo se detiene.
Todo es verdad primera y espontánea:
¡día, hasta fallecer, hecho de aurora!
¡vida, hasta concluir, hecha de infancia!

1957

My Country

This profound piety is my own country.
Here, if I advance, what I touch is my country:
a presence where I feel with each instant
the harmony of body and soul.

This is my voice. But I hear it
in different mouths. And although nothing
of what it says can surprise me,
to listen to it charms me because in it
sings a heart always different
which explains it all without words.

Here, if I advance, the world is stayed.
All is primal and spontaneous truth:
day, until death, made of dawn!
life, until the end, made of childhood!

trans. Sonja Karsen

Éxodo

Venían del terror y del tumulto,
huyendo de provincias bombardeadas
en donde solamente
siguen doblando a muerto esas campanas
que nadie ha visto y que ninguno atiende.
Venían de los límites de un mundo
perdido para siempre... ¡y perdido por nada!

Traían a caballo, a pie, en carrozas
de pompas funerarias,
o sobre antiguos coches de bomberos,
todo lo que se salva
—en el minuto ciego de la angustia—
de lo que fue un hogar, una costumbre,
un paisaje, una época del alma:
el retrato de un niño vestido de almirante,

Exodus

They came from the terror and tumult
fleeing the bombarded provinces
where only
those bells keep tolling death
that nobody has seen and nobody heeds.
They came from the confines of a world
lost forever... and lost for nothing!

They brought on horseback, on foot, in hearses
or on old fire-engines
all that one saves
—in the blind moment of anguish—
of what was a home, a custom,
a landscape, a period of the soul:
a picture of a child dressed as an admiral,
the projector of a magic lantern,

el proyector de una linterna mágica,
un reloj descompuesto, un calendario,
la funda de un paraguas,
el pasaporte oculto donde sangran las visas
y, junto al corazón, no una medalla,
ni una carta de amor, sino un paquete
de billetes de banco—porque todos,
hasta los más modestos, esperaban
comprarse un porvenir dichoso y libre
al llegar a la aduana deseada.

Venían sin rencor, sin pensamiento,
formando un gran ciempiés de sombras cautas,
sorprendidos de ser tan numerosos
y de no descubrir en tantas caras
ni una sonrisa amable, ni unos ojos
donde verse, al pasar, sin desconfianza.

Iban hacia el destierro con el mismo
premioso paso, anónimo y oscuro,
que los llevó—en la paz abandonada—
al taller, a la escuela, a la oficina,
pidiéndose perdón unos a otros
cuando la multitud los agolpaba
en un recodo estrecho
de la ruta polvosa, ardiente y larga.

A veces una cólera surgía.
Era una llama rápida,
la luz de un grito que lograba apenas
probar hasta qué punto les mentían
el cielo, el sol, el viento, las distancias.

Pero pronto volvía a integrarse el silencio.
Porque nada hay tan mudo como una
      tribu en marcha
desde el amanecer hasta el exilio,
a pie, a caballo, en coche,
en carros de combate, en ambulancias,
ejército que avanza preguntándose
a cada instante si la blanca torre
adivinada al pie de la colina
anuncia ya la etapa:
el pajar donde pueden los vencidos
hallar al fin un sueño sin fronteras
sobre un suelo que ayer era una patria...

1957

a broken clock, a calendar,
the cover of an umbrella,
the hidden passport where visas bleed,
and, close to the heart, not a medal,
or a love letter, but a bundle
of banknotes—because all,
even the poorest, hoped
to buy a happy and free future
upon their arrival at the desired border.

They came without rancor, without thinking,
forming a large centipede of careful shadows,
surprised at being so numerous
at not discovering in so many faces
a kind smile, a pair of eyes
to look into, on passing, without mistrust.

They went into exile with the same
rigid step, anonymous and obscure,
which took them—during the abandoned peace—
to the workshop, to school, to the office,
asking forgiveness of each other
when the multitude crowded them
on a narrow bend
of the dusty, burning and long road.

At times a fury raged.
It was a rapid flame,
a sudden outcry which could hardly
prove up to what point lied to them
heaven, sun, wind, distances.

But soon silence returned.
Because there is nothing more silent
      than a people on the march
from dawn to exile,
on foot, on horseback, by car,
in combat cars, in ambulances
an army which advances asking itself
at each instant if the white tower
discovered at the foot of the hill
already announces the end:
the barn where the vanquished
can finally find a dream without borders
on a soil that yesterday was a country.

trans. Sonja Karsen

Resumen

Vivimos de no ser... De ser morimos.
Somos proyecto en todo mientras somos.

Summary

We live by not being... By being we die.
We are a project in everything while we live.

Proyecto de esperanza en el deseo;   Project of hope in desire;

Proyecto de esperanza en el deseo;	Project of hope in desire;
y, cuando poseemos lo esperado,	and, when we possess the desired end,
proyecto de evasión, sed de abandono.	project of evasion, thirst of abandon.
En el joven trigal, lo verde es siempre	In the young wheatfield, green is always
ansiedad de la espiga. Acaba en oro.	anxiety of the stem. It ends in gold.
Pero ¿dónde comienza cuanto acaba?	But, where begins all that ends?
Vivimos de inventar lo que no somos.	We live by inventing what we are not.
En cambio, este magnífico absoluto	In contrast, the magnificent absolute
de lo que ya no sufre deterioros,	of what no longer suffers change
de lo que ya no pueden	of what no longer
modificar ni el tiempo ni el olvido,	either time or oblivion can change,
este sólido trozo	this solid piece
de vida inalterable que es la muerte	of unalterable life which is death,
¡cómo nos garantiza y nos define	how it guarantees, defines,
y nos revela y nos demuestra en todo!	reveals and shows us up in everything.
Vivimos sólo de creer que fuimos.	We live only believing that we existed.
Seremos siempre póstumos.	We will always be posthumous.

1957   *trans. Sonja Karsen*

Jorge Carrera Andrade

ECUADOR
1903–1978

William Carlos Williams wrote of Jorge Carrera Andrade's *Registro del mundo* (translated as *Selected Poems*, 1940): "I don't know when I have had so clear a picture, so unaffected by the torments of the mind which are our daily bread." Likening this painterly precision to the worldview of animist cultures, Williams concludes, "It is a sad picture, but a great one." Carrera Andrade, Ecuador's greatest poet, arrived early at this tonic clarity of spirit, which he associated with an anti-Modernist, or indigenist, resistance to literary complexity. In his poems Carrera Andrade often incorporated subtly surreal metaphors, thus opening the way for a more overt influence of Surrealism in Latin American poetics. His literary antecedents were the prose poems of the French writer Francis Jammes, the poems of Anglo-American Imagists, and the Japanese haiku he studied while serving as a diplomat in Asia.

Carrera Andrade himself was hardly a simple man. A poet, a politician, and an influential essayist, Carrera Andrade was an energetically public figure. He was active in the Republic of Spain in the 1930s; he traveled widely and represented Ecuador in the foreign service; he vigorously defended indigenous peoples' rights in South America. Carrera Andrade's commitment to the terse, visual form of his poems came to represent a complex spiritual discipline. "True poetry," he wrote, "is only that which has fallen from combat with the angel."

La vida perfecta	*The Perfect Life*
Conejo: hermano tímido, mi maestro y filósofo!	Rabbit: timid brother! My teacher and philosopher!
Tu vida me ha enseñado la lección del silencio.	Your life has taught me the lesson of silence.

Como en la soledad hallas tu mina de oro
no te importa la eterna marcha del universo.

Pequeño buscador de la sabiduría,
hojeas como un libro la col humilde y buena,
y observas las maniobras que hacen las golondrinas,
como San Simeón, desde tu oscura cueva.

Pídele a tu buen Dios una huerta en el cielo,
una huerta con coles de cristal en la gloria,
un salto de agua dulce para tu hocico tierno
y sobre tu cabeza un vuelo de palomas.

Tú vives en olor de santidad perfecta.
Te tocará el cordón del padre San Francisco
el día de tu merte. ¡Con tus largas orejas
jugarán en el cielo las almas de los niños!

1928/1930

For since in solitude you find your mine of gold,
the world's eternal onward march means nothing to you.

Tiny seeker after wisdom,
you leaf, as through a book, the good and humble cabbage;
and like Saint Simeon, from your dark hole
you watch the evolutions of the swallows.

Ask your good God for a garden in Heaven,
a garden with crystal cabbages in glory,
a spring of fresh water for your tender nose,
and a flight of doves above your head.

You live in the odour of perfect sanctity.
The cincture of Father Saint Francis will touch you
on the day of your death. And in Heaven
the souls of children will play with your long ears!

trans. Dudley Fitts

El reloj

Reloj:
picapedrero del tiempo.

Golpea en la muralla más dura de la noche,
pica tenaz, el péndulo.

La despierta vainilla
compone partituras de olor en los roperos.

Vigilando el trabajo del reloj
anda con sus pantuflas calladas el silencio.

1928/1930

The Clock

Clock:
time's stone-mason.

It chips at the night's hardest wall:
persistent hammer: pendulum.

Still awake, the heliotrope
composes scores of scent, in the clothes-closet.

Watching over the clock's work,
silence walks in its muffled slippers.

trans. Michael Surman

Domingo

Iglesia frutera
sentada en una esquina de la vida:
naranjas de cristal de las ventanas.
Organo de cañas de azúcar.

Ángeles: polluelos
de la Madre María.

La campanilla de ojos azules
sale con los pies descalzos
a corretear por el campo.

Reloj de Sol;
burro angelical con su sexo inocente;

Sunday

Fruit-vender church,
seated at a corner of life:
crystal oranges of windows.
Organ of sugarcane stalks.

Angels: chicks
of Mother Mary.

The little blue-eyed bell
runs out barefoot
to scamper over the countryside.

Clock of the sun;
angelical donkey with its innocent sex:

viento buen mozo del domingo
que trae noticias del cerro;
indias con su carga de legumbres
abrazada a la frente.

El cielo pone los ojos en blanco
cuando sale corriendo de la iglesia
la campanilla de los pies descalzos.

1929/1930

Segunda vida de mi madre

Oigo en torno de mí tu conocido paso,
tu andar de nube o lento río,
tu presencia imponiendo, tu humilde majestad
visitándome, súbdito de tu eterno dominio.

Sobre un pálido tiempo inolvidable,
sobre verdes familias, de bruces en la tierra,
sobre trajes vacíos y baúles de llanto,
sobre un país de lluvia, calladamente reinas.

Caminas en insectos y en hongos, y tus leyes
por mi mano se cumplen cada día
y tu voz, por mi boca, furtiva se resbala
ablandando mi voz de metal y ceniza.

Brújula de mi larga travesía terrestre.
Origen de mi sangre, fuente de mi destino.
Cuando el polvo sin faz te escondió en su guarida,
me desperté asombrado de encontrarme aún vivo.

Y quise echar abajo las invisibles puertas
y dí vueltas en vano, prisionero.
Con cuerda de sollozos me ahorqué sin ventura
y atravesé. llamándote, los pantanos del sueño.

Mas te encuentras viviendo en torno mío.
Te siento mansamente respirando
en esas dulces cosas que me miran
en un orden celeste dispuestas por tu mano.

Ocupas en su anchura el sol de la mañana
y con tu acostumbrada solicitud me arropas
en su manta sin peso, de alta lumbre,
aún fría de gallos y de sombras.

Mides el silbo líquido de insectos y de pájaros
la dulzura entregándome del mundo
y tus tiernas señales van guiándome,
mi soledad llenando con tu lenguaje oculto.

handsome Sunday wind
bringing news from the hill;
Indian women with their vegetable loads
bound to their foreheads.

The sky rolls up its eyes
when the little barefoot bell
comes scampering out of church.

trans. Muna Lee de Muñoz Marín

Second Life of My Mother

I hear your familiar footsteps all about me,
your pace like a cloud's or a slow river's,
your presence making itself felt: your humble majesty
visiting me, subject of your eternal dominion.

Over a pale unforgettable time,
over green families prostrate on the ground,
over empty dresses and trunkfuls of weeping,
over a land of rain, you rule silently.

You walk in insects and in toadstools, your laws
are executed by my hand every day,
and your voice slips furtively through my mouth
softening the metal and ash of my voice.

Compass of my long earthly voyage.
Origin of my blood, source of my destiny.
When the featureless dust hid you in its lair
I woke astonished to find myself still alive.

And I tried to tear down the invisible doors,
and vainly, a prisoner, I prowled about them.
I hanged myself haplessly with a rope of sobs,
and calling on you, traversed the marshes of dreams.

But you are here, living, all about me.
I am aware of you breathing gently
through those sweet things that gaze upon me
in heavenly order, ranged by your hand.

You inhabit the breadth of the morning sunlight
and with your accustomed care enfold me
in its weightless mantle of lofty light
still chilly with cocks and shadows.

You measure the liquid chirrup of insects and birds
making me a gift of the sweetness of earth,
and your tender signals keep guiding me,
my solitude filled with your hidden speech.

Te encuentras en mis actos, habitas mis silencios.
Por encima de mi hombro tu mandato me dictas
cuando la noche sorbe los colores
y llena el hueco espacio tu presencia infinita.

Oigo dentro de mí tus palabras proféticas
y la vigilia entera me acompañas
sucesos avisándome, claves incompresibles,
nacimientos de estrellas, edades de las plantas.

Moradora del cielo, vive, vive sin años.
Mi sangre original, mi luz primera.
Que tu vida inmortal alentando en las cosas
en vasto coro simple me rodee y sostenga.

1939/1940

You are in all I do, you inhabit my silence.
Yours is the mandate that stands at my shoulder
when night drinks up the colours
and your infinite presence fills hollow space.

I hear within me your prophetic words,
and throughout the vigil you companion me,
warning of things to come, incomprehensible keys,
births of stars, ages of the plants.

Dweller in the skies, live, live without years.
My original blood, my earliest light.
May your immortal life, breathing through all things
in vast simple chorus, surround and sustain me!

trans. Muna Lee de Muñoz Marín

Transfiguración de la lluvia

La lluvia de cabellos dorados por el sol
llega hasta mis manos con sus alas mojadas.
Me cubre con su gran beso de niña difunta.
Lluvia que resbalas con tu cuerpo transparente,
deja caer tus sucesivas túnicas
y tiéndete en el suelo como una virgen de cristal.
Haz correr tus lágrimas en las ventanas.
Sueña cantando, ¡oh reina sombría!
entre las columnas y los juncos de tu reino.
Mueve los títeres terrestres con tus cordeles líquidos.
Sembradora venida del cielo,
arroja tus semillas y flores que se deshacen.
Encierra al hombre en tu inmensa jaula de vidrio,
tu océano vertical que sepulta las cosas.
En memoria de tu paso,
refúgiate en el hongo fugaz de una burbuja
durante miles de años
hasta ser un eterno ojo de piedra.

1966

Transfiguration of the Rain

The rain with its hair gilded by the sun
touches my hands with its moist wings.
It covers me with its great kiss, that of a lifeless girl.
Rain that slides in its transparent body:
let your series of veils drop
and stretch out on the ground like a crystalline virgin.
Let your tears fall across the windows,
ringing your song, o dark queen!,
through the columns and rushes of your kingdom.
Move the earth's puppets with your liquid strings.
Sower come down from the sky,
scatter your seeds and vanishing flowers.
Wrap the human in your glass cage,
your vertical ocean that buries everything.
Remembering your passing,
take refuge in the quick mushroom of a bubble
for thousands of years,
till you become an eternal eye of stone.

trans. Michael Surman

Eugenio Florit

CUBA

1903–

The child of a Spanish father and a Cuban mother, Eugenio Florit was born in Spain but lived from 1915 through 1940 in Havana, where he was trained as a lawyer. Since 1940 Florit has lived in New York City, where he worked first as a member of the Cuban embassy and for many years as a professor of hispanic literature at Columbia University. In 1936 Florit met the Spanish poet José Ramón Jiménez, from whom Florit learned the Modern Spanish values of neo-Symbolist formality, suggestiveness, and *poesía pura*. In his introduction to Florit's 1937 volume *Doble acento* (*Double Stress*), Jiménez praised Florit's "honest and slow lyricism that can bring itself to completion with a delightful intellectual steadiness." The restrained elegance of Florit's poems, such as his elegy for his father ("Elegía para tu ausencia"), indicate also the influence of British Romantic poets, especially Keats and Shelley. Florit collected most of his mature work in the 1970 volume *Antología penúltima* (*Penultimate Anthology*).

Elegía para tu ausencia

"Peace, peace, he is not dead, he doth not sleep.
He hath awakened from the dream of life."

SHELLEY

Te fuiste aquel minuto para toda la muerte
a navegar en hondos océanos de silencio
con un largo camino de pupilas dormidas
y un bando de palomas prendido a tus ensueños.

Ya estarás por ausentes claridades de luna,
más tuyo que en las flechas de tu reloj de oro,
donde contabas tanto minuto sin orillas
para la sed de alas que quemaba tus hombros.

Y habrás saltado mares que la inquietud miraba,
abismos en la tímida soledad de tu ausencia;
y en la noche habrás sido tenue brisa caliente
junto a aquel pedacito de tu amorosa tierra.

Largo abrazo de alientos sobre las amapolas
y una risa, y un canto sin palabras ni música;
y un aquí estoy gozoso de pasados insomnios,
y un para siempre cálido en la fría llanura.

Como partiste en brazos del silencio apretado,
resonará más viva la luz de tus palabras;
y en cada estrofa de aire se enredará un acento,
y en cada mariposa te nacerán más alas.

Gozo de estar ya vivo para el eterno día,
de saberte en el agua, y en el sol, y en la hierba.
Harás entre las nubes Nacimientos de plata
y encontrarás tu nido en un árbol de estrellas.

1937

Elegy for Your Absence

"Peace, peace, he is not dead, he doth not sleep.
He hath awakened from the dream of life."

SHELLEY

In that moment you sailed for all of death
Into profound oceans of silence
With long hours of sleeping pupils,
And a flock of doves caught in your dreams.

Now you are already in distant moonlight,
More yourself than in the arrows of your golden clock
Where you reckoned such a shoreless moment
For the thirst of wings that was burning on your shoulders.

You shall have vaulted seas stared at by inquietude,
Abysses in the timid solitude of your absence;
And in the night you shall have been delicate warm breeze
Close to that crumb of your amorous earth.

Long embrace of breath over the poppies
And a laugh and a song without words or music;
With a "Here I am," glad of past wakefulness,
And a "forever" warm in the cool plain.

As you leave pressed in the arms of silence
The light of your words shall echo more clearly
And in each stanza of air an accent shall be entangled
And in each butterfly more wings shall be born to you.

Gladness of being alive for that eternal day,
Knowing yourself in the water, in the sun, and in the grass.
Among the clouds you shall make nativities of silver
And you shall discover your nest in a tree of stars.

trans. H. R. Hays

Martirio de San Sebastián

A Ricardo, mi hermano

Sí, venid a mis brazos, palomitas de hierro;
palomitas de hierro, a mi vientre desnudo.

The Martyrdom of Saint Sebastian

To Ricardo, my brother

Yes, come to my arms, little doves of iron,
little doves of iron, to my naked belly!

Qué dolor de caricias agudas.
Sí, venid a morderme la sangre,
a este pecho, a estas piernas, a la ardiente mejilla.
Venid, que ya os recibe el alma entre los labios.
Sí, para que tengáis nido de carne,
y semillas de huesos ateridos.
Para que hundáis el pico rojo
en el haz de mis músculos.
Venid a mis ojos, que puedan ver la luz,
a mis manos, que toquen forma imperecedera,
a mis oídos, que se abran a las aéreas músicas,
a mi boca, que guste las mieles infinitas,
a mi nariz, para el perfume de las eternas rosas.
Venid, sí, duros ángeles de fuego,
pequeños querubines de alas tensas.
Sí, venid, a soltarme las amarras
para lanzarme al viaje sin orillas.
¡Ay!, qué acero feliz, qué piadoso martirio.
¡Ay!, punta de coral, águila, lirio
de estremecidos pétalos. Sí. Tengo
para vosotras, flechas, el corazón ardiente,
pulso de anhelo, sienes indefensas.
Venid, que está mi frente
ya limpia de metal para vuestra caricia.
Ya, qué río de tibias agujas celestiales!...
Qué nieves me deslumbran el espíritu!...
Venid! Una tan sólo do vosotras, palomas,
para que anide dentro de mi pecho
y me atraviese el alma con sus alas!...
Señor, ya voy, por cauce de saetas!...
Sólo una más y quedaré dormido.
Este largo morir despedazado
cómo me ausenta del dolor. Ya apenas
el pico de estos buitres me lo siento...
Qué poco falta ya, Señor, para mirarte!...
y miraré con ojos que vencieron las flechas,
y escucharé tu voz con oídos eternos,
y al olor de tus rosas me estaré como en éxtasis,
y tocaré con manos que nutrieron estas fieras palomas,
y gustaré tus mieles con los labios del alma!...
Ya voy, Señor. ¡Ay!, qué sueño de soles,
qué camino de estrellas en mi sueño...
Ya sé que llega mi última paloma...
¡Ay! Ya está bien, Señor, que te la llevo
hundida en un rincón de las entrañas!

1937

What pain, the stab of your caress—
Yes, come to bite my blood,
this breast, these legs, come to my burning cheek.
Come, for my soul admits you: enter by way of the lips.
Yes, I have a nest of flesh for you,
for you, the seeds of my frozen bones—
Sink your red beaks
into my sheaf of muscles.
Come to my eyes, that they may see the light,
to my hands, that they may touch the imperishable,
to my ears, that they open to ethereal music,
to my mouth, that it taste the honey of infinitude,
to my nostrils, for the perfume of eternal roses.
Come, yes, hard angels of fire,
tiny cherubim on stiff wings.
Yes, come unbind me, cast me loose,
launch me on my boundless voyage.
What an ecstasy of steel—what merciful release!!
Oh coral point! Eagle, lily
with trembling petals! Yes. For you, arrows,
this yearning, this hot heart pulsing, my undefended
    temples.
Come, that the place between my eyes be opened
and unarmored, cleansed by your caress.
Now the warm stream of celestial needles!...
Now the sudden snow dazzling my spirit!
Come! One alone from among you, doves,
to nestle in my breast
and with your wings to penetrate my soul!...
Lord, I come, along the river-way of arrow!...
Only one more and I shall fall asleep.
This dying long, by pieces
how it frees me from the pain! Now I barely feel
the vultures picking me apart...
So little time, Lord, before I see you!...
and I shall see with eyes that never die,
and the odor of your roses shall be my ecstasy,
and I will touch the hands that fed those fierce doves,
and taste the honey with my soul's own lips!...
I come, Lord, ah, dreaming in the sunlight,
what a course of stars streaming in my sleep...
I know that now my last dove comes...
Here, Lord, ah! I bring it to you
lodged within the contents of my heart.

trans. Peter Fortunato

Tarde presente

Entre el ocaso y yo, toda la vida.
Como si detenido

The Present Evening

Between me and the sunset, the whole of life.
As if time, arrested,

el tiempo se cayera
a florecer en una gota de agua.
Como si Dios en su alto pensamiento
secara el llanto de sus hijos;
y Ella, la sin color, durmiera al borde florecido
de sus innumerables tumbas.
Como si ayer llegara con su recuerdo escrito
y mañana estuviera ya en su cárcel de letras;
como si hoy fuera una enorme rosa
de millones de pétalos unidos
en una sola esquina del mundo revelado.
O aún mejor: como si todo beso
de amante hubiera roto su semilla
y se alzaran al viento del crepúsculo
sus alas libres.
                        Como el vuelo
apretado de ejércitos de ángeles
en su más alto círculo.
Como ascensión de un pensamiento libre
hasta el principio
donde nació la luz y se formaron
entraña de dolor, gérmen de grito
y lágrima primera bajo el cielo.
Como si todo junto de repente
se pusiera entre el hombre y su destino.
Como si ante el ocaso rojo abriera
un girasol sus rayos amarillos.
Como si aquella mano
de ayer regara azules lirios
y fuera el mar bajo la mano
un palomar de pétalos heridos.
Y como si los barcos emergieran
de su muerte de hierros, de su sueño
de peces, de su olvido,
para tender sus velas inmortales
a los vientos y al sol.
                        Como si fríos
los huesos de la tierra,
por fuego inmaterial enrojecidos
hasta el blanco del alma
volvieran a pesar, a estremecerse,
a reír y a llorar, en risa y llanto
de verdad, en latidos
de pecho verdadero, en ojos limpios,
en bocas sin pecado, en tibia
caricia de sus carnes.
                        Así dicho
frente al ocaso, desde tierra al mar,
con la ternura junto a mí.
                        Se alegra
el corazón de manso gris vestido.

1940

Were falling
To blossom in a drop of water.
As if God in his lofty meditation
Were drying the tears of his sons;
And She, the colorless one, were sleeping on the
            flowering border
Of her innumerable tombs.
As if yesterday were to come with its written memory
And tomorrow were already in its prison of letters;
As if today were an enormous rose
Of millions of petals, united
In a single corner of the revealed world.
Or better still; as if all lovers' kisses
Had burst from their seedbed
And were raising in the twilight wind
Their liberated wings.
                        Like the compact flight
Of armies of angels
In their highest sphere.
Like the ascension of a thought at liberty
Toward the source
Where light is born and the core of sorrow,
The germ of a cry and a first tear
Have taken form under the sky.
As if all of this together suddenly
Intervened between man and his destiny.
As if a sunflower were opening its yellow petals
In front of the red west.
As if the hand of yesterday
Were sprinkling blue lilies
And the sea beneath the hand
Were a dovecote of wounded petals.
And as if the ships were emerging
From their dead iron, from their dream of fishes,
From their oblivion
To stretch their immortal sails
In the winds and the sun.
                        As if the cold
Bones of the earth,
Reddened by immaterial fire,
Were returning to the white heat of the soul
To ponder, to tremble,
To laugh, and to weep, with laughter and tears
Of truth, in the beating
Of an actual breast, in clean eyes,
In sinless mouths, in the warm
Caress of its flesh.
                        These words,
Facing the west, from sea to sky,
With tenderness close to me.
                        The heart,
Dressed in gray humility, rejoices.

trans. H. R. Hays

Henriqueta Lisboa

"I would say that the poetry of Henriqueta is characterized by a constant perfection, like that of Cecília Meireles," wrote Manuel Bandeira in 1983. "But this perfection is not the fruit of a facile virtuosity: it is the perfection of a natural aesceticism, acquired by the force of a difficult spiritual discipline, of a rigorously economic vocabulary." In her early poems, Lisboa addressed traditional lyrical themes with clarity and precision. That combination made her famous, as Sérgio Milliet described her, as one of the "purest" poets of Brazil. In later works, especially those addressing the history of her native Minas Gerais, with a deeply internalized Christian spirituality Lisboa meditates almost obsessively on death and change. Throughout her work Lisboa maintained her uniqueness of diction and her pure aesthetic commitment. Modernism and feminism seem to have influenced her less than a vision of an intense, stately, lyrical integrity.

Idílio

Senhor, perdoa que eu não te procure
em teus dias de abundância e púrpura.
Perdoa que eu não esteja presente
a teus rituais de luz e incenso.
Perdoa que não me associe à turba
quando és aclamado nas praças públicas.
E que nunca tenha sido
porta-estandarte de tuas insígnias.

Não é que me envergonhe de Ti, Senhor.
Foste tu mesmo que me deste esse pudor
pelas coisas que se oferecem à claridade.
Não sei cantar em altas vozes.
Não sei expandir-me em gestos largos e notórios.
Não sei utilizar-me das cores fulgurantes.

Amo em silêncio, como as monjas.
Da penumbra, como os que amam sem esperança.
Com extrema delicadeza,
como se o meu amor estivesse para morrer...

Na tristeza e na obscuridade,
quandos os homens se distraírem de Ti
e se forem para a faina ou para o ócio
deixando os teus templos vazios,
então, Senhor,
minha hora será chegada.
Entrarei devagarinho no teu santuário,
acenderei de mãos trêmulas tua lâmpada de óleo
e sentar-me-ei no chão, junto ao teu tabernáculo,
imersa em pensamentos inefáveis.

Idyll

Lord, forgive me if I do not look for you
in your days of opulence and of purple.
Forgive me for not being present
during your rituals of light and incense.
Forgive me for not mingling with the mob
when you are hailed in public squares.
And for the fact that I have never been
a color-bearer for your banners.

It is not that I am ashamed of You, my Lord.
It was you yourself who gave me this bashfulness
for the things that propose themselves to brightness.
I do not know how to sing aloud.
I do not know how to extend myself in broad and garish
    actions.
I do not know how to make use of the gaudy colors.

I love quietly, like the nuns.
From the dusk, like those who love hopelessly.
With the utmost refinement,
as if my Beloved were about to die...

In grief and in dimness,
when the men put You aside
and go away to their work or their spare time
leaving the temples empty,
then, oh Lord,
my time will have come.
I shall slowly enter your shrine,
with trembling hands I shall light your oil lamp
and I'll sit on the ground, close to your tabernacle
absorbed in unutterable thoughts.

Não rezarei, talvez, Senhor.
Meus lábios não sabem pronunciar em vão
aquelas fórmulas
que o tempo desfigurou em minha imaginação.
Meus lábios ficarão imóveis.
Mas haverá em todo meu ser
tanto abandono,
tanta afinidade da minha atitude com teu ambiente
que sentirás meu coração bater
dentro de tuas mãos.

Serei então feliz, feliz docemente
como uma enamorada tímida
a quem se adivinha.

1935

Maybe, I shall not pray, oh Lord.
My lips cannot articulate in vain
those expressions
that time has defaced from my imagery.
My lips will remain motionless.
But in my whole being there will be
so much surrender,
so much rapport between my posture and your
    environment
that you will feel my heart beat
inside your hands.

Then I shall be happy, sweetly blissful
like a shy *enamorada*
whom one foresees.

trans. *Hélcio Veiga Costa*

Eco

Papagaio verde
deu um grito agudo.
Rocha numa raiva
brusca, respondeu.

Ganhou a floresta
um grande escarcéu.
Papagaios mil
o grita gritaram
rocha repetiu.

De um e de outro lado
metralhando o espaço
os gritos choveram
e choveram, de aço.

Gritos agudíssimos!

Mas ninguém morreu.

1941

Echo

Green parrot
let out a shrill scream.
Rock in sudden
anger, replied.

A great uproar
invaded the forest.
Thousands of parrots
screamed together
and rock echoed.

From all sides
strafing space
steely screams rained
and rained down.

Very piercing screams!

But no one died.

trans. *Hélcio Veiga Costa*

Elegia

A princípio os mortos
eram dois ou três.
Não mortos, sombras:
um velho, uma criança,
mais alguém talvez.

Elegy

At first the dead
were two or three.
Not dead, shadows:
an old man, a child,
someone else perhaps.

Tranqüilos corpos
sob umas lápides.
Em cima e em torno
flores e pássaros.

Os mortos pertenciam à morte
como as pedras e as plantas
a seus reinos.

Com isso aos poucos
foi crescendo o número.
De várias pessoas
quedavam lacunas.

E também para os lazeres
vinham vestidos de luto,
confidências, soluços,
delicados bocejos.

Nesse tempo a morte
pertencia ao quotidiano.

Foi então que o raio
caiu sobre o cedro.
Seiva de minha seiva
corria dentro do cedro.
Carne de cera fria
com minhas mãos toquei.
Olhos neutros de vidro
com meus próprios olhos vi.

Que noite, que tempestade,
que impetuosos aquilões,
ai! que torrente dos vales,
que babel com seus dilúvios,
que bando de salteadores,
com que espadas, com que foices,
com que brutais extorsões,
que abutres ávidos ávidos
e com que garras aduncas,
que nuvem de gafanhotos
e com que bocas hediondas
se haviam juntado acaso
nesse campo devastado?...

Náusea, horror, despojamento,
primeiro corpo sem brio!

De então a vida
pertence à morte.

Still bodies
under tombstones.
Above and around
flowers and birds.

The dead belonged to death
like the stones and the plants
to their own kingdoms.

And thus, little by little,
the number was increasing.
There were gaps
of several people.

And for leisure, too,
they came dressed in mourning,
confidences, sobs,
gentle yawns.

At that time death
belonged to daily life.

It was then that the lightning
fell upon the cedar.
Sap of my sap
ran inside the cedar.
With my hands I touched
flesh of cold wax.
With my own eyes I saw
lifeless, glassy eyes:

What a night, what a tempest,
what impetuous north winds,
alas! what torrents from the valleys,
what a babel with its floods
what a gang of brigands,
with what swords, and scythes,
with what brutal extortions,
what rapacious rapacious vultures
and with what hooked claws,
what throngs of locusts
and with what hideous mouths
had they perchance been gathered together
in that devastated battlefield?...

Loathing, horror, despoilment,
the first body without self respect!

Since then life
belongs to death.

De então na lua
se acendem verdes
círios diluentes
sobre marfim.

De então nas curvas
das cordilheiras
surpreendo os mortos
nos seus espasmos.

De então na mesa
tenho-os presentes:
cada conviva
com seu silêncio.

De então nas ruas
caminham soltos.
E tocam flautas
uns pelos outros.

Esse de esquina
de amplas espáduas
vede: está morto.
Porém não sabe.

Mas já na sombra
secretos dedos
preparam certo
ramo de goivos.

1945

Since then in the moon
green, guttering, large candles
are lit
on ivory.

Since then on the curves
of mountain ridges
I take the dead unawares
in their spasms.

Since then at the table
they are present for me:
each commensal
lost in his silence.

Since then along the streets
they walk freely.
And they play the flute
for one another.

That one at the corner,
broad shouldered,
look: he is dead.
But he does not know it.

But in the shadow
hidden fingers already
arrange a certain
nosegay of gillyflowers.

trans. Hélcio Veiga Costa

Camélia

Vinde ver a camélia
pela madrugada nascida,
antes que o sol lhe tisne
a epiderme.

Tão plácida na sua intimidade. É o círculo
em que se encontram os corações. É o elo
do entendimento recíproco. São as asas
do anjo cerradas pela paz. É a pomba
que em palma oferecida pousa. A lua
que se esqueceu das nuvens e queda
em singelo convívio. O nó
macio e branco da amizade. O ninho
que se fecha sobre si mesmo—completo.

1959

Camellia

Come to see the camellia,
born at daybreak,
before the sun tans
its skin.

So mild in its privacy. It is the circle
where hearts meet. The bond
of mutual understanding. The wings
of the angel clenched by peace. The dove
which perches upon the offered palm. The moon
that has forgotten the clouds and is still
in an unadorned intimacy. The soft
and white knot of friendship. The nest
that closes upon itself—perfect.

trans. Hélcio Veiga Costa

Além da Imagem

Além da Imagem: trama do inefável
para mudar contorno definido.
Ou não bem definido. Além da Imagem
treme de ser lembrança o que era olvido.

1967

Beyond the Image

Beyond the Image: plot of what is unutterable
to change a defined configuration.
Or something not so explicit. Beyond the Image
a remembrance that was forgetfulness trembles into being.

trans. Hélcio Veiga Costa

Xavier Villaurrutia

MEXICO
1903–1950

The founder of the first experimental theater group in Mexico City, Xavier Villaurrutia is well known in his home country as a dramatist, especially as the author of the play *Invitación a la muerte* (*Invitation to Death*, 1943). Internationally he is better known as a poet of Rilkean complexity, solitude, and "nocturnal" Romanticism. The disjunction in his reputation, however, reflects an artificial distinction. In fact, Villaurrutia's dramatic interests influenced his poems, which often imply dramatic tensions and scenarios through dispassionate, submerged narratives. With the poet José Gorostiza, Villaurrutia was one of the founding members of the review *Ulises* (1927–1928), which promoted many of the ideals of the *Contemporáneos* group. Resisting the nationalist fervor of postrevolutionary Mexico, writers of the *Contemporáneos* group advocated instead a poetry of emotional intensity, transcendence, and verbalism and a passionate embrace of the shadow side of life. A man of great intellect, wit, and personal loyalty, Villaurrutia never married but lived with his mother and sister. Late in life, Villaurrutia also taught at the national university in Mexico City and served as director of the Bellas Artes theater program.

Recent critical readings of Villaurrutia's poems have valued his nocturnal and deathly serene poems less than his poems of homoerotic energy and love. Eliot Weinstein characterizes Villaurrutia's process in terms that associate both those patterns of his poems: "Technically, he took the prosody and many of the themes of *modernismo* . . . and stripped its high-flown rhetoric to the natural, condensed, and playful speech of the Spanish *vanguardia*. . . . But most of all, he was one of the great poets of desire: one whose beloved, finally, is not another man but Death itself, Death himself."

Poesía

Eres la compañía con quien hablo
de pronto, a solas.
Te forman las palabras
que salen del silencio
y del tanque de sueño en que me ahogo
libre hasta despertar.

Tu mano metálica
endurece la prisa de mi mano
y conduce la pluma
que traza en el papel su litoral.

Poetry

You are the companion I talk with
suddenly, alone.
You are formed by words
that emerge from silence
and from the reservoir of dreams where I drown,
at large, till waking.

Your metallic hand
toughens my quick hand
and leads the pen
that traces your shoreline onto paper.

Tu voz, hoz de eco,
es el rebote de mi voz en el muro,
y en tu piel de espejo
me estoy mirando mirarme por mil Argos,
por mil largos segundos.

    Pero el menor ruido te ahuyenta
y te veo salir
por la puerta del libro
o por el atlas del techo,
por el tablero del piso,
o la página del espejo,
y me dejas
sin más pulso ni voz y sin más cara,
sin máscara como un hombre desnudo
en medio de una calle de miradas.

                1926

Your voice, a narrow echo,
is the return of my voice against the wall,
and on your mirroring skin
I am looking at myself look at myself through a thousand
       Argus-eyes,
through a thousand long seconds.

    But the slightest noise drives you away,—
I see you leave
through the door of the book,
the atlas of the ceiling,
the tablet of pavement,
the page of the mirror,
and you leave me
without another pulse or voice, without another face,
with no mask, like a naked man
in the middle of a street of stares.

            trans. Dana Stangel

Nocturno de Los Ángeles

            a Agustín J. Fink

Se diría que las calles fluyen dulcemente en la noche.
Las luces no son tan vivas que logren desvelar el secreto,
el secreto que los hombres que van y vienen conocen,
porque todos están en el secreto
y nada se ganaría con partirlo en mil pedazos
si, por el contrario, es tan dulce guardarlo
y compartirlo sólo con la persona elegida.

Si cada uno dijera en un momento dado,
en sólo una palabra, lo que piensa,
las cinco letras del DESEO formarían una enorme cicatriz
    luminosa,
una constelación más antigua, más viva aún que las otras.
Y esa constelación sería como un ardiente sexo
en el profundo cuerpo de la noche,
o, mejor, como los Gemelos que por vez primera en
    la vida
se miraran de frente, a los ojos, y se abrazaran ya
    para siempre.

De pronto el río de la calle se puebla de sedientos seres,
Caminan, se detienen, prosiguen.
Cambian miradas, atreven sonrisas,
Forman imprevistas parejas...

Hay recodos y bancos de sombra,
orillas de indefinibles formas profundas
y súbitos huecos de luz que ciega
y puertas que ceden a la presión más leve.

Los Angeles Nocturne

            to Agustín J. Fink

You could say that the streets flow softly in the night.
The lamps are not bright enough to reveal the secret,
the secret known to the men who come and go,
because they are all in the secret
and nothing would be gained by dividing it into a
    thousand pieces
when, on the other hand, it is so delightful to keep it
and only share it with the person one chooses.

If, at a given moment, each man were to say
what he is thinking about in one word only,
the six letters of DESIRE would form a huge, luminous scar,
a constellation more ancient, but more vibrant than
    the others.
And that constellation would be like an ardent sex
in the deep body of the night,
or, better, like the Gemini when for the first time in
    their lives
they look each other in the face, in the eyes, and finally
    embrace forever.

Suddenly the river of the street is peopled with
    thirsty beings.
They walk, pause, go on walking.
They exchange glances, venture smiles,
form into unexpected couples...

There are corners and benches in shadow,
sidewalk shores of dense indefinable shapes

El río de la calle queda desierto un instante.
Luego parece remontar de sí mismo
deseoso de volver a empezar.
Queda un momento paralizado, mudo anhelante
como el corazón entre dos espasmos.

Pero una nueva pulsación, un nuevo latido
arroja al río de la calle nuevos sedientos seres.
Se cruzan, se entrecruzan y suben.
Vuelan a ras de tierra.

Nadan de pie, tan milagrosamente
que nadie se atrevería a decir que no caminan.
Son los Ángeles
Han bajado a la tierra
por invisibles escalas.
Vienen del mar, que es el espejo del cielo,
en barcos de humo y sombra,
a fundirse y confundirse con los mortales,
a rendir sus frentes en los muslos de las mujeres,
a dejar que otras manos palpen sus cuerpos febrilmente,
y que otros cuerpos busquen los suyos hasta encontrarlos
como se encuentran al cerrarse los labios de una
    misma boca,
a fatigar su boca tanto tiempo inactiva,
a poner en libertad sus lenguas de fuego,
a decir las canciones, los juramentos, las malas palabras
en que los hombres concentran el antiguo misterio
de la carne, la sangre y el deseo.

Tienen nombres supuestos, divinamente sencillos.
Se llaman Dick o John, o Marvin o Louis.
En nada sino en la belleza se distinguen de los mortales.

Caminan, se detienen, prosiguen.
Cambian miradas, atreven sonrisas.
Forman imprevistas parejas.

Sonríen maliciosamente al subir en los ascensores de
    los hoteles
donde aún se practica el vuelo lento y vertical.
En sus cuerpos desnudos hay huellas celestiales;
signos, estrellas y letras azules.
Se dejan caer en las camas, se hunden en las almohadas
que los hacen pensar todavía un momento en las nubes.
Pero cierran los ojos para entregarse mejor a los goces de
    su encarnación misteriosa,
y cuando duermen sueñan no con los ángeles sino con
    los mortales.

Los Angeles, California 1936/1939

and sudden gaps of blinding light
and doors that yield to the slightest pressure.

The river of the street remains deserted for an instant.
Then it seems to rise up from itself,
wanting to begin again.
It stays paralyzed for a moment, mute, breathless
as a heart between two beats.

But a new pulsation, a new throbbing
vomits new thirsty beings into the river of the street.
They cross, intersect and take off.
They fly flush with the earth.

They swim on foot, so miraculously
that no one would dare to say that they are not walking.
They are the Angels.
They have descended to earth
by invisible stepladders.
They come from the sea, heaven's mirror,
in boats of smoke and shadow
to fuse and confuse themselves with mortals,
to surrender their faces in women's thighs,
to let other hands feel their bodies feverishly,
and other bodies seek theirs until they find them
the way two lips of the same mouth find each other
    upon closing,
to exhaust their mouths so long inactive,
to free their fiery tongues,
to utter the songs, curses, dirty words
in which men concentrate the ancient mystery
of flesh, blood, and desire.

They have assumed names, divinely simple.
They are called Dick or John or Marvin or Louis.
Only by their beauty can they be distinguished
    from mortals.
They walk, pause, go on walking.
They exchange glances, venture smiles,
form into unexpected couples.

They smile maliciously going up in hotel elevators
where slow vertical flight is still practiced.
On their naked bodies are celestial markings:
signs, stars and blue letters.
They fall into beds, they sink into pillows
which for a minute still make them think of clouds.
But they close their eyes the better to abandon themselves
    to the delights of their mysterious incarnation,
and when they sleep they dream, not of angels, but
    of mortals.

trans. Rachel Benson

Nocturno

Todo lo que la noche
dibuja con la mano
de sombra:
el placer que revela,
el vicio que desnuda.

Todo lo que la sombra
hace oír con el duro
golpe de su silencio:
las voces imprevistas
que a intervalos enciende,
el grito de la sangre,
el rumor de unos pasos
perdidos.

Todo lo que el silencio
hace huir de las cosas:
el vaho del deseo,
el sudor de la tierra,
la fragancia sin nombre
de la piel.

Todo lo que el deseo
unta en mis labios:
la dulzura soñada
de un contacto,
el sabido sabor
de la saliva.

Y todo lo que el sueño
hace palpable:
la boca de una herida,
la forma de una entraña
la fiebre de una mano
que se atreve.

¡Todo!
circula en cada rama
del árbol de mis venas,
acaricia mis muslos,
inunda mis oídos,
vive en mis ojos muertos,
muere en mis labios duros.

1939

Nocturne

All that the night
sketches with its hand
of shadow:
the pleasure it reveals,
the vice it uncovers.

All that the shadow
lets hear with its
blow of silence:
the voices unforeseen
it burns between spaces,
the cry of the blood,
the murmur of some strayed
steps.

All that the silence
makes flee from things:
the steam of desire,
the sweat of the earth,
the nameless fragrance
of the skin.

All that desire
anoints on my lips:
the dreamed sweetness
of a contact,
the tasted taste
of saliva.

And all that the dream
turns palpable:
the mouth of a wound,
the shape of an entrail,
the fever in a hand
that dares.

Everything!
Flows in each branch
of the veins of my tree,
fondles my thighs,
floods my ears,
lives in my dead eyes,
dies on my hard lips.

trans. Xavier Leroux

Nocturno de la estatua

a Agustín Lazo

Soñar, soñar la noche, la calle, la escalera
y el grito de la estatua desdoblando la esquina.

Correr hacia la estatua y encontrar sólo el grito,
querer tocar el grito y sólo hallar el eco,
querer asir el eco y encontrar sólo el muro
y correr hacia el muro y tocar un espejo.

Hallar en el espejo la estatua asesinada,
sacarla de la sangre de su sombra,
vestirla en un cerrar de ojos,
acariciarla como a una hermana imprevista
y jugar con las fichas de sus dedos
y contar a su oreja cien veces cien cien veces
hasta oírla decir: "estoy muerta de sueño."

1939

Nuestro amor

Si nuestro amor no fuera,
al tiempo que un secreto,
un tormento, una duda,
una interrogación;

si no fuera una larga
espera interminable,
un vacío en el pecho
donde el corazón llama
como un puño cerrado
a una puerta impasible;

si nuestro amor no fuera
el sueño doloroso
en que vives sin mí,
dentro de mí, una vida
que me llena de espanto;

si no fuera un desvelo,
un grito iluminado
en la noche profunda;

si nuestro amor no fuera
como un hilo tendido
en que vamos los dos
sin red sobre el vacío;

Nocturne of the Statue

To Agustín Lazo

Dreaming, dreaming the night, the street, the stairway,
and the statue's cry spreading the corner open.

Running toward the statue and finding only the cry,
wanting to feel the cry and finding only the echo,
wanting to seize the echo and finding only the wall,
and running to the wall and finding a mirror.

Finding the murdered statue in the mirror,
removing it from the shadow's blood,
dressing it with closing eyes,
caressing it like an unexpected sister,
playing with the cards of its fingers
and whispering into its ear a hundred times a hundred
　　　　hundred times
till hearing it say, "I am sick to death of dreaming."

trans. Dana Stangel

Our Love

If our love were not
simultaneously a secret,
a torment, a doubt,
a questioning;

if it were not a long
interminable waiting,
an emptiness in the chest
where the heart pounds
like a closed fist
on some immovable door;

if our love were not
the sad dream
in which you live without me,
inside me, a life
that fills me with dread;

if it were not insomnia,
a lighted cry
in the deep night;

if our love were not
like a tightrope
where the two of us walk
without a net, across the void;

si tus palabras fueran	if your words were
sólo palabras para	only words for
nombrar con ellas cosas	naming things
tuyas, no más, y mías;	of yours, no more, and of mine;
si no resucitaran,	if they did not come to life again,
si no evocaran trágicas	if they did not evoke tragic
distancias y rencores	distances and angers,
traspuestos y olvidados;	displaced and forgotten;
si tu mirada fuera	if your glance were
siempre la que un instante	always the one that for a moment
—¡pero qué instante eterno!—	—but what an eternal moment!—
es tu más honda entrega;	is your deepest surrender;
si tus besos no fueran	if your kisses were not
sino para mis labios	trembling and submissing
trémulos y sumisos;	for any lips but mine;
si tu lenta saliva	if the lingering moistness of your mouth
no fundiera en mi boca	did not blend its infinite flavor
su sabor infinito;	in my mouth;
si juntos nuestros labios	if together our lips
desnudos como cuerpos,	naked as bodies
y nuestros cuerpos juntos	and our bodies together
como labios desnudos	naked as lips
no formaran un cuerpo	did not form one body
y una respiración,	and one breath,
¡no fuera amor el nuestro,	O ours would not be love,
no fuera nuestro amor!	our love would not be!

1948   *trans. Michael Surman*

Pablo Neruda
[Neftalí Ricardo Reyes Basoalto]

C H I L E

1904–1973

The child who was to become the most popular, best-known, and arguably the most influential poet of Latin America, "Pablo Neruda" was born Neftalí Reyes Basoalto in the seaside village of Parral, in south-central Chile, during the summer rainy season. His mother died within a month of his birth. (Several biographers have associated this early loss of maternal affection with Neruda's sometimes obsessive poetic images of rain, sea, femininity, and emotional integrity.) He was raised at home and educated in the public schools of Temuco, where Gabriela Mistral, then in her early twenties, was teaching elementary school. He began to write poems at an early age, even though his family—especially his father, a railroad worker—forbade him. By late adolescence, Neftalí Reyes Basoalto was writing emotionally capacious poems of surrealist intensity. Apparently in part to avoid his father's disapproval, he restyled himself "Pablo Neruda," choosing a working-class first name and a surname that recalled the nationalistic Czech historical novelist Jan Neruda (1834–1891).

After *Crepusculario* (*Twilight Book*, 1923), Neruda's first major publication was *Veinte poemas de amor y una canción desesperada* (*Twenty Love Poems and a Song of Despair*, 1924 in Santiago), which introduced a meditative young poet of Romantic intensity and confident lyricism. When he joined the diplomatic corps and was stationed in Burma in 1927, Neruda's lyrical inclination responded to the solitude of his life there and to the humid exotic reality that in its fecundity seemed to border on the surreal. The poems of his *Residencia en la tierra, 1925–1931* (*Residence on the Earth*, 1st ed. 1933) immersed the lyrical perceiver in a welter of images suggesting the turbulence of this physical world, with which the mediating consciousness must contend. Neruda counters the richness of that external world with a correspondingly inventive verbal lushness, in "dynamic forms" that enact the poems' emotions of disintegration, despair, claustral ennui, and sexual tumult. The poems of the *Residencias* (1933, 1935, 1947), claims Julio Cortázar, effected a "radical mutation of our deepest speech." Although the theories behind the form of those poems owe something to Vicente Huidobro's "creationism," the difference lodges in the world's external truths that inform Neruda's dynamic syntax. Still, it is a world of "primordial dough," as Octavio Paz characterizes the timeless and placeless spatiality of the poems of *Residencia:* "It is a mythical geography . . . a planet that is fermenting, rotting, germinating."

Transferred to Barcelona in 1934 and later located in Madrid, Neruda came into contact with pre–civil war politics and with some of the most important poets of the Spanish "Generation of '27," including Federico García Lorca, Rafael Alberti, and Miguel Hernández. Under the influence of those writers, and responding to the tumultuous politics of Spain on the verge of the civil war, once again Neruda transformed his aesthetic. He enlarged the field of his poems' concerns to include political and social arguments, and there he found a wealth of possibilities within the tones of sympathy and difficult joy that were to characterize much of his best work for the rest of his life. (Some readers, like John Felstiner, have demonstrated how the formal concomitants of these changes, such as Neruda's ability to sustain an argument by counterpointing systematic metaphors derived from an essentially private mythology, in fact preceded the political application of those formal possibilities.) Critics have called this apparent shift an evolution, even a conversion; certainly the change involved a double transformation, both a turning *from* the subjectivity of his early poems and a turning *toward* the collective struggle. "The world has changed, and my poetry has changed," Neruda explained, claiming that his earlier poems, beginning with *Residencia*, had been "saturated with pessimism." Neruda's new tones of sympathy differed from the more personal tenderness of César Vallejo (although Vallejo later suggested that only he and Neruda wrote in a mode Vallejo called *verdadismo*, "truthism"). In *España en el corazón* (*Spain in My Heart*, 1937), a tribute both to the Spanish Republic and to his friend Vallejo, Neruda's poems were more prophetic and more rhetorically directive, like the poems of Blake and Whitman that he loved and translated. In fact, Roberto González Echevarría has suggested that Neruda later chose the title of his *Canto general* (*General Song*, 1950) to distinguish his new tones of outwardness and collectivity from those of Whitman's "Song of Myself"—and implicitly from Whitman's democratic naivete—while still paying indirect homage to Whitman's generalizing energies.

Returning to the Americas on the eve of World War II, Neruda served as ambassador to Mexico and—on his way back to Chile in 1943—visited Macchu Picchu, the "lost" city of the Incas, in Peru. That trip occasioned the most important and resonant single poem of Latin America, Neruda's *Alturas de Macchu Picchu* (*The Heights of Macchu Picchu*). That majestic meditation on the nature of American reality—with its Whitmanian sympathies, its moving imaginative addresses to the vanished human realities that survive in the ruins among the rock and plants of the Andes, its realization of the survival of human work in the stones of the ruined city—marks Neruda's emergence as a major poet of Latin American essences, a poet who inscribed Latin American experience into the world's conscience. Written on Isla Negra in 1945, *Macchu Picchu* was published as a section of the longer sequence *Canto general*, which located those essences in the context of other historical meditations and personal addresses to the vistas, flora, and human customs of the continent (including the Araucanian Indian traditions of southern Chile). This new "impure poetry," Neruda insisted, should open itself to the landscape and drama and conditions of the New World. Paradoxically, Neruda's experiences in Spain both confirmed him as a poet in the language of Spain and reoriented him toward Latin America.

By the late 1940s Neruda had declared himself a communist. Although his incessant preoccupation with immediate realities flavored his political allegiances, his overt political commitment helped Neruda to contextualize several of his obsessive concerns: the material conditions of the Americas, registered in the *Odas elementales* (*Elemental Odes*, 1954, 1955, 1957, 1963, 1964); the ironically Whitman-like resistance to North American imperialist attitudes vis-à-vis Latin America; an endearingly limpid attention to the local and the particular, in *Memorial de Isla Negra* (*Remembrance of Isla Negra*, 1964). Throughout this period, Neruda enacts his identification with the democratic individual in surprisingly accessible poems carried by a personal mythology and by repetitive, personally encoded symbols. Neruda wrote several poems in praise of Stalin, traveled to the Soviet Union, and accepted the Stalin Prize for poetry in 1953. He later tried to repudiate some of the excesses of the Stalinist regime. Charles Tomlinson, among other critics, has pointed out not only the political compromises this admiration for the Soviet system after World War II required, but also how many of Neruda's later poems rely on a tone of almost "coercive" smugness, a "sinisterly autistic" oversimplification of political realities. According to Tomlinson, the attitude sometimes takes the form of direct invective and at other times the form of a startling intimacy with his readers, whom the poem conceives, sentimentally but coercively, as both "you" and "the masses."

Neruda's later love poems, addressed to his third wife Matilde Urrutia, surprised his readers by their passion, their clarity, and their submergence of public themes into private and domestic affections (*Los versos del capitán* [*The Captain's Verses*, 1953] and *Cien sonetos de amor* [*One Hundred Love Sonnets*, 1959]). In an important sense, these late poems come full circle, returning Neruda to the image-rich affection of his *Veinte poemas de amor*.

In 1970 Neruda declared himself a candidate for the presidency of Chile. After ascertaining the depth of the support for the Socialist candidate, Salvador Allende Gossens, he withdrew from the race, as planned, and threw his support to Allende's Popular Front. Neruda won the Nobel Prize in 1971 while he was living in Paris, serving as the Chilean ambassador to France. Already suffering from cancer, he died of a heart attack two weeks after the CIA-backed coup in 1973 that toppled Allende's democratically elected government.

Veinte poemas de amor y una canción desesperada

I. CUERPO DE MUJER

Cuerpo de mujer, blancas colinas, muslos blancos,
te pareces al mundo en tu actitud de entrega.
Mi cuerpo de labriego salvaje te socava
y hace saltar el hijo del fondo de la tierra.

Fui solo como un túnel. De mí huían los pájaros,
y en mí la noche entraba su invasión poderosa.
Para sobrevivírme te forjé como un arma,
como una flecha en mi arco, como una piedra en mi honda.

Pero cae la hora de la venganza, y te amo.
Cuerpo de piel, de musgo, de leche ávida y firme.
Ah los vasos del pecho! Ah los ojos de ausencia!
Ah las rosas del pubis! Ah tu voz lenta y triste!

Cuerpo de mujer mía, persistiré en tu gracia.
Mi sed, mi ansia sin límite, mi camino indeciso!
Oscuros cauces donde la sed eterna sigue,
y la fatiga sigue, y el dolor infinito.

VII. INCLINADO EN LAS TARDES...

Inclinado en las tardes tiro mis tristes redes
a tus ojos oceánicos.

Allí se estira y arde en la más alta hoguera
mi soledad que da vueltas los brazos como un náufrago.

Hago rojas señales sobre tus ojos ausentes
que olean como el mar a la orilla de un faro.

Sólo guardas tinieblas, hembra distante y mía,
de tu mirada emerge a veces la costa del espanto.

Inclinado en las tardes echo mis tristes redes
a ese mar que sacude tus ojos oceánicos.

Los pájaros nocturnos picotean las primeras estrellas
que centellean como mi alma cuando te amo.

Galopa la noche en su yegua sombría
desparramando espigas azules sobre el campo.

Twenty Love Poems and a Song of Despair

I. BODY OF A WOMAN

Body of a woman, white hills, white thighs,
you look like a world, lying in surrender.
My rough peasant's body digs in you
and makes the son leap from the depth of the earth.

I was alone like a tunnel. The birds fled from me,
and night swamped me with its crushing invasion.
To survive myself I forged you like a weapon,
like an arrow in my bow, a stone in my sling.

But the hour of vengeance falls, and I love you.
Body of skin, of moss, of eager and firm milk.
Oh the goblets of the breast! Oh the eyes of absence!
Oh the roses of the pubis! Oh your voice, slow and sad!

Body of my woman, I will persist in your grace.
My thirst, my boundless desire, my shifting road!
Dark river-beds where the eternal thirst flows
and weariness follows, and the infinite ache.

VII. LEANING INTO THE AFTERNOONS...

Leaning into the afternoons I cast my sad nets
towards your oceanic eyes.

There in the highest blaze my solitude lengthens and
    flames,
its arms turning like a drowning man's.

I send out red signals across your absent eyes
that wave like the sea or the beach by a lighthouse.

You keep only darkness, my distant female,
from your regard sometimes the coast of dread emerges.

Leaning into the afternoons I fling my sad nets
to that sea that is thrashed by your oceanic eyes.

The birds of night peck at the first stars
that flash like my soul when I love you.

The night gallops on its shadowy mare
shedding blue tassels over the land.

beds where the eternal thirst flows
and weariness follows, and the infinite ache.

XX. PUEDO ESCRIBIR LOS VERSOS...

Puedo escribir los versos más tristes esta noche.

Escribir, por ejemplo: "La noche está estrellada,
y tiritan, azules, los astros, a lo lejos."

El viento de la noche gira en el cielo y canta.

Puedo escribir los versos más tristes esta noche.
Yo la quise, y a veces ella también me quiso.

En las noches como ésta la tuve entre mis brazos.
La besé tantas veces bajo el cielo infinito.

Ella me quiso, a veces yo también la quería.
Cómo no haber amado sus grandes ojos fijos.

Puedo escribir los versos más tristes esta noche.
Pensar que no la tengo. Sentir que la he perdido.

Oír la noche inmensa, más inmensa sin ella.
Y el verso cae al alma como al pasto el rocío.

Qué importa que mi amor no pudiera guardarla.
La noche está estrellada y ella no está conmigo.

Eso es todo. A lo lejos alguien canta. A lo lejos.
Mi alma no se contenta con haberla perdido.

Como para acercarla mi mirada la busca.
Mi corazón la busca, y ella no está conmigo.

La misma noche que hace blanquear los mismos árboles.
Nosotros, los de entonces, ya no somos los mismos.

Ya no la quiero, es cierto, pero cuánto la quise.
Mi voz buscaba el viento para tocar su oído.

De otro. Será de otro. Como antes de mis besos.
Su voz, su cuerpo claro. Sus ojos infinitos.

Ya no la quiero, es cierto, pero tal vez la quiero.
Es tan corto el amor, y es tan largo el olvido.

Porque en noches como ésta la tuve entre mis brazos,
mi alma no se contenta con haberla perdido.

Aunque éste sea el último dolor que ella me causa,
y éstos sean los últimos versos que yo le escribo.

1924

XX. TONIGHT I CAN WRITE...

Tonight I can write the saddest lines.

Write, for example, "The night is shattered
and the blue stars shiver in the distance."

The night wind revolves in the sky and sings.

Tonight I can write the saddest lines.
I loved her, and sometimes she loved me too.

Through nights like this one I held her in my arms.
I kissed her again and again under the endless sky.

She loved me, sometimes I loved her too.
How could one not have loved her great still eyes.

Tonight I can write the saddest lines.
To think that I do not have her. To feel that I have lost her.

To hear the immense night, still more immense without her.
And the verse falls to the soul like dew to the pasture.

What does it matter that my love could not keep her.
The night is shattered and she is not with me.

This is all. In the distance someone is singing. In the
    distance.
My soul is not satisfied that it has lost her.

My sight searches for her as though to go to her.
My heart looks for her, and she is not with me.

The same night whitening the same trees.
We, of that time, are no longer the same.

I no longer love her, that's certain, but how I loved her.
My voice tried to find the wind to touch her hearing.

Another's. She will be another's. Like my kisses before.
Her voice. Her bright body. Her infinite eyes.

I no longer love her, that's certain, but maybe I love her.
Love is so short, forgetting is so long.

Because through nights like this one I held her in my arms
my soul is not satisfied that it has lost her.

Though this be the last pain that she makes me suffer
and these the last verses that I write for her.

trans. W. S. Merwin

Galope muerto

Como cenizas, como mares poblándose,
en la sumergida lentitud, en lo informe,
o como se oyen desde el alto de los caminos
cruzar las campanadas en cruz,
teniendo ese sonido ya aparte del metal,
confuso, pesando, haciéndose polvo
en el mismo molino de las formas demasiado lejos,
o recordadas o no vistas,
y el perfume de las ciruelas que rodando a tierra
se pudren en el tiempo, infinitamente verdes.

Aquello todo tan rápido, tan viviente,
inmóvil sin embargo, como la polea loca en sí misma,
esas ruedas de los motores, en fin.
Existiendo como las puntadas secas en las costuras
      del árbol,
callado, por alrededor, de tal modo,
mazclando todos los limbos sus colas.
Es que de dónde, por dónde, en qué orilla?
El rodeo constante, incierto, tan mudo,
como las lilas alrededor del convento,
o la llegada de la muerte a la lengua del buey
que cae a tumbos, guardabajo, y cuyos cuernos
      quieren sonar.

Por eso, en lo inmóvil, deteniéndose, percibir,
entonces, como aleteo inmenso, encima,
como abejas muertas o números,
ay, lo que mi corazón pálido no puede abarcar,
en multitudes, en lágrimas saliendo apenas,
y esfuerzos humanos, tormentas,
acciones negras descubiertas de repente
como hielos, desorden vasto,
oceánico, para mí que entro cantando,
como con una espada entre indefensos.

Ahora bien, de qué está hecho ese surgir de palomas
que hay entre la noche y el tiempo, como una
      barranca húmeda?
Ese sonido ya tan largo
que cae listando de piedras los caminos,
más bien, cuando sólo una hora
crece de improviso, extendiéndose sin tregua.

Adentro del anillo del verano
una vez los grandes zapallos escuchan,
estirando sus plantas conmovedoras,
de eso, de lo que solicitándose mucho,
de lo lleno, oscuros de pesadas gotas.

Dead Gallop

Like ashes, like oceans swarming,
in the sunken slowness, in what's unformed,
or like high on the road hearing
bellstrokes cross by crosswise,
holding that sound just free of the metal,
blurred, bearing down, reducing to dust
in the selfsame mill of forms far out of reach,
whether remembered or never seen,
and the aroma of plums rolling to earth
that rot in time, endlessly green.

All of it so quick, so livening,
immobile though, like a pulley idling on itself,
those wheels that motors have, in short.
Existing like dry stitches in the seams of trees,
silenced, encircling, in such a way,
all the planets splicing their tails.
Then from where, which way, on what shore?
The ceaseless whirl, uncertain, so still,
like lilacs around the convent,
or death as it gets to the tongue of an ox
who stumbles down unguarded, and whose horns want
      to sound.

That's why, in what's immobile, holding still, to perceive
then, like great wingbeats, overhead,
like dead bees or numbers,
oh all that my spent heart can't embrace,
in crowds, in half-shed tears,
and human toiling, turbulence,
black actions suddenly disclosed
like ice, immense disorder,
oceanwide, for me who goes in singing,
as with a sword among defenseless men.

Well that what is it made of—that spurt of doves
between night and time, like a damp ravine?
That sound so drawn out now
that drops down lining the roads with stones,
or better, when just one hour
buds up suddenly, extending endlessly.

Within the ring of summer,
once, the enormous calabashes listen,
stretching their poignant stems—
of that, of that which urging forth,
of what's full, dark with heavy drops.

trans. John Felstiner

1925

Walking around

Sucede que me canso de ser hombre.
Sucede que entro en las sastrerías y en los cines
marchito, impenetrable, como un cisne de fieltro
navegando en un agua de origen y ceniza.

El olor de las peluquerías me hace llorar a gritos.
Sólo quiero un descanso de piedras o de lana,
sólo quiero no ver establecimientos ni jardines,
ni mercaderías, ni anteojos, ni ascensores.

Sucede que me canso de mis pies y mis uñas
y mi pelo y mi sombra.
Sucede que me canso de ser hombre.

Sin embargo sería delicioso
asustar a un notario con un lirio cortado
o dar muerte a una monja con un golpe de oreja.
Sería bello
ir por las calles con un cuchillo verde
y dando gritos hasta morir de frío.

No quiero seguir siendo raíz en las tinieblas,
vacilante, extendido, tiritando de sueño,
hacia abajo, en las tripas mojadas de la tierra,
absorbiendo y pensando, comiendo cada día.

No quiero para mí tantas desgracias.
No quiero continuar de raíz y de tumba,
de subterráneo solo, de bodega con muertos,
aterido, muriéndome de pena.

Por eso el día lunes arde como el petróleo
cuando me ve llegar con mi cara de cárcel,
y aúlla en su transcurso como una rueda herida,
y da pasos de sangre caliente hacia la noche.

Y me empuja a ciertos rincones, a ciertas casas
        húmedas,
a hospitales donde los huesos salen por la ventana,
a ciertas zapaterías con olor a vinagre,
a calles espantosas como grietas.

Hay pájaros de color de azufre y horribles intestinos
colgando de las puertas de las casas que odio,
hay dentaduras olvidadas en una cafetera,
hay espejos
que debieran haber llorado de vergüenza y espanto,
hay paraguas en todas partes, y venenos, y ombligos.

Walking Around

It so happens I'm tired of just being a man.
I go to a movie, drop in at the tailor's—it so happens—
feeling wizened and numbed, like a big, wooly swan,
awash on an ocean of clinkers and causes.

A whiff from a barbershop does it: I yell bloody murder.
All I ask is a little vacation from things: from boulders
        and woolens,
from gardens, institutional projects, merchandise,
eyeglasses, elevators—I'd rather not look at them.

It so happens I'm fed up—with my feet and my fingernails
and my hair and my shadow.
Being a man leaves me cold: that's how it is.

Still—it would be lovely
to wave a cut lily and panic a notary,
or finish a nun with a left to the ear.
It would be nice
just to walk down the street with a green switchblade
        handy,
whooping it up till I die of the shivers.

I won't live like this—like a root in a shadow,
wide-open and wondering, teeth chattering sleepily,
going down to the dripping entrails of the universe
absorbing things, taking things in, eating three squares
        a day.

I've had all I'll take from catastrophe.
I won't have it this way, muddling through like a root or
        a grave,
all alone underground, in a morgue of cadavers,
cold as a stiff, dying of misery.

That's why Monday flares up like an oil-slick,
when it sees me up close, with the face of a jailbird,
or squeaks like a broken-down wheel as it goes,
stepping hot-blooded into the night.

Something shoves me toward certain damp houses, into
        certain dark corners,
into hospitals, with bones flying out of the windows;
into shoe stores and shoemakers smelling of vinegar,
streets frightful as fissures laid open.

There, trussed to the doors of the houses I loathe
are the sulphurous birds, in a horror of tripes,
dental plates lost in a coffeepot,
mirrors

Yo paseo con calma, con ojos, con zapatos,
con furia, con olvido,
paso, cruzo oficinas y tiendas de ortopedia,
y patios donde hay ropas colgadas de un alambre:
calzoncillos, toallas y camisas que lloran
lentas lágrimas sucias.

1935

that must surely have wept with the nightmare and shame
of it all;
and everywhere, poisons, umbrellas, and belly buttons.

I stroll unabashed, in my eyes and my shoes
and my rage and oblivion.
I go on, crossing offices, retail orthopedics,
courtyards with laundry hung out on a wire;
the blouses and towels and the drawers newly washed,
slowly dribbling a slovenly tear.

trans. Ben Belitt

Explico algunas cosas

Preguntaréis: Y dónde están las lilas?
Y la metafísica cubierta de amapolas?
Y la lluvia que a menudo golpeaba
sus palabras llenándolas
de agujeros y pájaros?

Os voy a contar todo lo que me pasa.

Yo vivía en un barrio
de Madrid, con campanas,
con relojes, con árboles.

Desde allí se veía
el rostro seco de Castilla
como un océano de cuero.
                    Mi casa era llamada
la casa de las flores, porque por todas partes
estallaban geranios: era
una bella casa
con perros y chiquillos.
                    Raúl, te acuerdas?
Te acuerdas, Rafael?
                    Federico, te acuerdas
debajo de la tierra,
te acuerdas de mi casa con balcones en donde
la luz de Junio ahogaba flores en tu boca?
                    Hermano, hermano!

Todo
eran grandes voces, sal de mercaderías,
aglomeraciones de pan palpitante,
mercados de mi barrio de Argüelles con su estatua
como un tintero pálido entre las merluzas:
el aceite llegaba a las cucharas,
un profundo latido
de pies y manos llenaba las calles,
metros, litros, esencia

I'm Explaining a Few Things

You are going to ask: and where are the lilacs?
and the poppy-petalled metaphysics?
and the rain repeatedly spattering
its words and drilling them full
of apertures and birds?

I'll tell you all the news.

I lived in a suburb,
a suburb of Madrid, with bells,
and clocks, and trees.

From there you could look out
over Castille's dry face:
a leather ocean.
                    My house was called
the house of flowers, because in every cranny
geraniums burst: it was
a good-looking house
with its dogs and children.
                    Remember, Raúl?
Eh, Rafael?
                    Federico, do you remember
from under the ground
where the light of June drowned flowers
    in your mouth?
                    Brother, my brother!

Everything
loud with big voices, the salt of merchandises,
pile-ups of palpitating bread,
the stalls of my suburb of Argüelles with its statue
like a drained inkwell in a swirl of hake:
oil flowed into spoons,
a deep baying
of feet and hands swelled in the streets,
metres, litres, the sharp

aguda de la vida,
                    pescados hacinados,
contextura de techos con sol frío en el cual
la flecha se fatiga,
delirante marfil fino de las patatas,
tomates repetidos hasta el mar.

Y una mañana todo estaba ardiendo
Y una mañana las hogueras
salían de la tierra
devorando seres,
y desde entonces fuego,
pólvora desde entonces,
y desde entonces sangre.
Bandidos con aviones y con moros,
bandidos con sortijas y duquesas,
bandidos con frailes negros bendiciendo
venían por el cielo a matar niños,
y por las calles la sangre de los niños
corría simplemente, como sangre de niños.

Chacales que el chacal rechazaría,
piedras que el cardo seco mordería escupiendo,
víboras que las víboras odiaran!

Frente a vosotros he visto la sangre
de España levantarse
para ahogaros en una sola ola
de orgullo y de cuchillos!

Generales
traidores:
mirad mi casa muerta,
mirad España rota:
pero de cada casa muerta sale metal ardiendo
en vez de flores,
pero de cada hueco de España
sale España,
pero de cada niño muerto sale un fusil con ojos,
pero de cada crimen nacen balas
que os hallarán un día el sitio
del corazón.

Preguntaréis por qué su poesía
no nos habla del sueño, de las hojas,
de los grandes volcanes de su país natal?

Venid a ver la sangre por las calles.
venid a ver
la sangre por las calles,
venid a ver la sangre
por las calles!

1947

measure of life,
                    stacked-up fish,
the texture of roofs with a cold sun in which
the weather vane falters,
the fine, frenzied ivory of potatoes,
wave on wave of tomatoes rolling down to the sea.

And one morning all that was burning,
one morning the bonfires
leapt out of the earth
devouring human beings—
and from then on fire,
gunpowder from then on,
and from then on blood.
Bandits with planes and Moors,
bandits with finger-rings and duchesses,
bandits with black friars spattering blessings
came through the sky to kill children
and the blood of children ran through the streets
without fuss, like children's blood.

Jackals that the jackals would despise,
stones that the dry thistle would bite on and spit out,
vipers that the vipers would abominate!

Face to face with you I have seen the blood
of Spain tower like a tide
to drown you in one wave
of pride and knives!

Treacherous
generals:
see my dead house,
look at broken Spain:
from every house burning metal flows
instead of flowers,
from every socket of Spain
Spain emerges
and from every dead child a rifle with eyes,
and from every crime bullets are born
which will one day find
the bull's eye of your hearts.

And you will ask: why doesn't his poetry
speak of dreams and leaves
and the great volcanoes of his native land?

Come and see the blood in the streets.
Come and see
the blood in the streets.
Come and see the blood
in the streets!

trans. Nathaniel Tarn

Algunas bestias

Era el crepúsculo de la iguana.
Desde la arcoirisada crestería
su lengua como un dardo
se hundía en la verdura,
el hormiguero monacal pisaba
con melodioso pie la selva,
el guanaco fino como el oxígeno
en las anchas alturas pardas
iba calzando botas de oro,
mientras la llama abría cándidos
ojos en la delicadeza
del mundo lleno de rocío.
Los monos trenzaban un hilo
interminablemente erótico
en las riberas de la aurora,
derribando muros de polen
y espantando el vuelo violeta
de las mariposas de Muzo.
Era la noche de los caimanes,
la noche pura y pululante
de hocicos saliendo del légamo,
y de las ciénagas soñolientas
un ruido opaco de armaduras
volvía al origen terrestre.

El jaguar tocaba las hojas
con su ausencia fosforescente,
el puma corre en el ramaje
como el fuego devorador
mientras arden en él los ojos
alcohólicos de la selva.
Los tejones rascan los pies
del río, husmean el nido
cuya delicia palpitante
atacarán con dientes rojos.

Y en el fondo del agua magna,
como el círculo de la tierra,
está la gigante anaconda
cubierta de barros rituales,
devoradora y religiosa.

1950

Some Beasts

It was the twilight of the iguana.
From the rainbow-arch of the battlements,
his long tongue like a lance
sank down in the green leaves,
and a swarm of ants, monks with feet chanting,
crawled off into the jungle,
the guanaco, thin as oxygen
in the wide peaks of cloud,
went along, wearing his shoes of gold,
while the llama opened his honest eyes
on the breakable neatness
of a world full of dew.
The monkeys braided a sexual
thread that went on and on
along the shores of the dawn,
demolishing walls of pollen
and startling the butterflies of Muzo
into flying violets.
It was the night of the alligators,
the pure night, crawling
with snouts emerging from ooze,
and out of the sleepy marshes
the confused noise of scaly plates
returned to the ground where they began.

The jaguar brushed the leaves
with a luminous absence,
the puma runs through the branches
like a forest fire,
while the jungle's drunken eyes
burn from inside him.
The badgers scratch the river's
feet, scenting the nest
whose throbbing delicacy
they attack with red teeth.

And deep in the huge waters
the enormous anaconda lies
like the circle around the earth,
covered with ceremonies of mud,
devouring, religious.

trans. James Wright

Alturas de Macchu Picchu

VI

Entonces en la escala de la tierra he subido
entre la atroz maraña de las selvas perdidas
hasta ti, Macchu Picchu.

The Heights of Macchu Picchu

VI

Then up the ladder of the earth I climbed
through the barbed jungle's thickets
until I reached you Macchu Picchu.

Alta ciudad de piedras escalares,
por fin morada del que lo terrestre
no escondió en las dormidas vestiduras.
En ti, como dos líneas paralelas,
la cuna del relámpago y del hombre
se mecían en un viento de espinas.

Madre de piedra, espuma de los cóndores.

Alto arrecife de la aurora humana.

Pala perdida en la primera arena.

Esta fué la morada, éste es el sitio:
aquí los anchos granos del maíz ascendieron
y bajaron de nuevo como granizo rojo.

Aquí la hebra dorada salió de la vicuña
a vestir los amores, los túmulos, las madres,
el rey, las oraciones, los guerreros.

Aquí los pies del hombre descansaron de noche
junto a los pies del águila, en las altas guaridas
carniceras, y en la aurora
pisaron con los pies del trueno la niebla enrarecida,
y tocaron las tierras y las piedras
hasta reconocerlas en la noche o la muerte.

Miro las vestiduras y las manos,
el vestigio del agua en la oquedad sonora,
la pared suavizada por el tacto de un rostro
que miró con mis ojos las lámparas terrestres,
que aceitó con mis manos las desaparecidas
maderas: porque todo, ropaje, piel, vasijas,
palabras, vino, panes,
se fué, cayó a la tierra.

Y el aire entró con dedos
de azahar sobre todos los dormidos:
mil años de aire, meses, semanas de aire,
de viento azul, de cordillera férrea,
que fueron como suaves huracanes de pasos
lustrando el solitario recinto de la piedra.

X

Piedra en la piedra, el hombre, dónde estuvo?
Aire en el aire, el hombre, dónde estuvo?
Tiempo en el tiempo, el hombre, dónde estuvo?
Fuiste también el pedacito roto

Tall city of stepped stone,
home at long last of whatever earth
had never hidden in her sleeping clothes.
In you two lineages that had run parallel
met where the cradle both of man and light
rocked in a wind of thorns.

Mother of stone and sperm of condors.

High reef of the human dawn.

Spade buried in primordial sand.

This was the habitation, this is the site:
here the fat grains of maize grew high
to fall again like red hail.

The fleece of the vicuña was carded here
to clothe men's loves in gold, their tombs and mothers,
the king, the prayers, the warriors.

Up here men's feet found rest at night
near eagles' talons in the high
meat-stuffed eyries. And in the dawn
with thunder steps they trod the thinning mists,
touching the earth and stones that they might recognize
that touch come night, come death.

I gaze at clothes and hands,
traces of water in the booming cistern,
a wall burnished by the touch of a face
that witnessed with my eyes the earth's carpet of tapers,
oiled with my hands the vanished wood:
for everything, apparel, skin, pots, words,
wine, loaves, has disappeared,
fallen to earth.

And the air came in with lemon blossom fingers
to touch those sleeping faces:
a thousand years of air, months, weeks of air,
blue wind and iron cordilleras—
these came with gentle footstep hurricanes
cleansing the lonely precinct of the stone.

trans. Nathaniel Tarn

X

Stone upon stone, and man, where was he?
Air upon air, and man, where was he?
Time upon time, and man, where was he?
Were you too then the broken bit

de hombre inconcluso, de águila vacía
que por las calles de hoy, que por las huellas,
que por las hojas del otoño muerto
va machacando el alma hasta la tumba?
La pobre mano, el pie, la pobre vida...
Los días de la luz deshilachada
en ti, como la lluvia
sobre las banderillas de la fiesta,
dieron pétalo a pétalo de su alimento oscuro
en la boca vacía?
               Hambre, coral del hombre,
hambre, planta secreta, raíz de los leñadores,
hambre, subió tu raya de arrecife
hasta estas altas torres desprendidas?

Yo te interrogo, sal de los caminos,
muéstrame la cuchara, déjame, arquitectura,
roer con un palito los estambres de piedra,
subir todos los escalones del aire hasta el vacío,
rascar la entraña hasta tocar el hombre.

Macchu Picchu, pusiste
piedra en la piedra, y en la base, harapo?
Carbón sobre carbón, y en el fondo la lágrima?
Fuego en el oro, y en él, temblando el rojo
goterón de la sangre?
Devuélveme el esclavo que enterraste!
Sacude de las tierras el pan duro
del miserable, muéstrame los vestidos
del siervo y su ventana.
Dime cómo durmió cuando vivía.
Dime si fue su sueño
ronco, entreabierto, como un hoyo negro
hecho por la fatiga sobre el muro.
El muro, el muro! Si sobre su sueño
gravitó cada piso de piedra, y si cayó bajo ella
como bajo una luna, con el sueño!

Antigua América, novia sumergida,
también tus dedos,
al salir de la selva hacia el alto vacío de los dioses,
bajo los estandartes nupciales de la luz y el decoro,
mezclándose al trueno de los tambores y de las lanzas,
también, también tus dedos,
los que la rosa abstracta y la línea del frío, los
que el pecho sangriento del nuevo cereal trasladaron
hasta la tela de materia radiante, hasta las duras cavidades,
también, también, América enterrada, guardaste en lo
    más bajo,
en el amargo intestino, como un águila, el hambre?

of half-spent humankind, an empty eagle, that
through the streets today, through footsteps,
through the dead autumn's leaves,
keeps crushing its soul until the grave?
The meager hand, the foot, the meager life...
Did the days of unraveled light
in you, like rain
on pennants at a festival,
give off their dark food petal by petal
into your empty mouth?
               Hunger, coral of humankind,
hunger, hidden plant, root of the woodcutter,
hunger, did your reef-edge climb
to these high and ruinous towers?

I question you, salt of the roads,
show me the trowel; architecture, let me
grind stone stamens with a stick,
climb every step of air up to the void,
scrape in the womb till I touch man.

Macchu Picchu, did you set
stone upon stone on a base of rags?
Coal over coal and at bottom, tears?
Fire on the gold and within it, trembling, the red
splash of blood?
Give me back the slave you buried!
Shake from the earth the hard bread
of the poor, show me the servant's
clothes and his window.
Tell me how he slept while he lived.
Tell me if his sleep
was snoring, gaping like a black hole
that weariness dug in the wall.
The wall, the wall! If every course of stone
weighed down his sleep, and if he fell underneath
as under a moon, with his sleep!

Ancient America, sunken bride,
your fingers too,
leaving the jungle for the empty height of the gods,
under bridal banners of light and reverence,
blending with thunder from the drums and lances,
yours, your fingers too,
those that the abstract rose and the rim of cold, the
bloodstained body of the new grain bore up
to a web of radiant matter, to the hardened hollows,
you too, buried America, did you keep in the deepest part
of your bitter gut, like an eagle, hunger?

trans. John Felstiner

XII

Sube a nacer conmigo, hermano.

Dame la mano desde la profunda
zona de tu dolor diseminado.
No volverás del fondo de las rocas.
No volverás del tiempo subterráneo.
No volverá tu voz endurecida.
No volverán tus ojos taladrados.

Mírame desde el fondo de la tierra,
labrador, tejedor, pastor callado:
domador de guanacos tutelares:
albañil del andamio desafiado:
aguador de las lágrimas andinas:
joyero de los dedos machacados:
agricultor temblando en la semilla:
alfarero en tu greda derramado:
traed a la copa de esta nueva vida
vuestros viejos dolores enterrados.
Mostradme vuestra sangre y vuestro surco,
decidme: aquí fuí castigado,
porque la joya no brilló o la tierra
no entregó a tiempo la piedra o el grano:
señaladme la piedra en que caísteis
y la madera en que os crucificaron,
encendedme los viejos pedernales,
las viejas lámparas, los látigos pegados
a través de los siglos en las llagas
y las hachas de brillo ensangrentado.

Yo vengo a hablar por vuestra boca muerta.

A través de la tierra juntad todos
los silenciosos labios derramados
y desde el fondo habladme toda esta larga noche,
como si yo estuviera con vosotros anclado.

Contadme todo, cadena a cadena,
eslabón a eslabón, y paso a paso,
afilad los cuchillos que guardasteis,
ponedlos en mi pecho y en mi mano,
como un río de rayos amarillos,
como un río de tigres enterrados,
y dejadme llorar, horas, días, años,
edades ciegas, siglos estelares.

Dadme el silencio, el agua, la esperanza.

Dadme la lucha, el hierro, los volcanes.

Apegadme los cuerpos como imanes.

Acudid a mis venas y a mi boca.

Hablad por mi palabras y mi sangre.

1945/1950

XII

Rise up, brother, be born with me.

Give me your hand from the deep
territory seeded with your griefs.
You won't come back from the depths of the rock.
You won't come back from underground time.
No coming back for your roughened voice.
No coming back for your drilled eyes.
Look at me from the depths of the earth,
farmer, weaver, quiet shepherd;
trainer of sacred llamas;
mason on a risky scaffold:
water-bearer of Andean tears:
jeweller with bruised fingers:
farmer trembling among seedlings:
potter among spilled clay:
bring to the cup of this new life
your ancient buried sorrows.
Show me your blood and your furrows,
say to me: Here I was whipped
because a jewel didn't shine or the earth
hadn't yielded its grain or stone on time.
Pick out the stone on which you stumbled
and the wood on which they crucified you,
kindle the old flints for me,
the old lamps, the whips
that stuck to the wounds through the centuries,
and the bright axes stained with blood.
I come to speak for your dead mouth.
You silent scattered lips,
come join throughout the earth
and speak to me from the depths of this long night
as if we were anchored here together,
tell me everything, chain by chain,
link by link and step by step,
sharpen the knives you hid,
put them in my chest and into my hand,
like a river of yellow lightning,
like a river of buried jaguars,
and let me cry, hours, days, years,
blind ages, stellar centuries.

Give me silence, water, hope.

Give me struggle, iron, volcanoes.

Fasten your bodies to mine like magnets.

Come into my veins and into my mouth.

Speak through my words and my blood.

trans. David Young

La United Fruit Co.

Cuando sonó la trompeta, estuvo
todo preparado en la tierra,
y Jehová repartió el mundo
a Coca-Cola Inc., Anaconda,
Ford Motors, y otras entidades:
la Compañía Frutera Inc.
se reservó lo más jugoso,
la costa central de mi tierra,
la dulce cintura de América.
Bautizó de nuevo sus tierras
como "Repúblicas Bananas,"
y sobre los muertos dormidos,
sobre los héroes inquietos
que conquistaron la grandeza,
la libertad y las banderas,
estableció la ópera bufa:
enajenó los albedríos
regaló coronas de César,
desenvainó la envidia, atrajo
la dictadura de las moscas,
moscas Trujillos, moscas Tachos,
moscas Carías, moscas Martínez,
moscas Ubico, moscas húmedas
de sangre humilde y mermelada,
moscas borrachas que zumban
sobre las tumbas populares,
moscas de circo, sabias moscas
entendidas en tiranía.
Entre las moscas sanguinarias
la Frutera desembarca,
arrasando el café y las frutas,
en sus barcos que deslizaron
como bandejas el tesoro
de nuestras tierras sumergidas.

Mientras tanto, por los abismos
azucarados de los puertos,
caían indios sepultados
en el vapor de la mañana:
un cuerpo rueda, una cosa
sin nombre, un número caído,
un racimo de fruta muerta
derramada en el pudridero.

1950

United Fruit Co.

When the trumpet blared everything
on earth was prepared
and Jehovah distributed the world
to Coca-Cola Inc., Anaconda,
Ford Motors and other entities:
United Fruit Inc.
reserved for itself the juiciest,
the central seaboard of my land,
America's sweet waist.
It rebaptized its lands
the "Banana Republics,"
and upon the slumbering corpses,
upon the restless heroes
who conquered renown,
freedom and flags,
it established the comic opera:
it alienated self-destiny,
regaled Caesar's crowns,
unsheathed envy, drew
the dictatorship of flies:
Trujillo flies, Tacho flies,
Carías flies, Martínez flies,
Ubico flies, flies soaked
in humble blood and jam,
drunk flies that drone
over the common graves,
circus flies, clever flies
versed in tyranny.

Among the bloodthirsty flies
the Fruit Co. disembarks,
ravaging coffee and fruits
for its ships that spirit away
our submerged lands' treasures
like serving trays.

Meanwhile, in the seaports'
sugary abysses,
Indians collapsed, buried
in the morning mist:
a body rolls down, a nameless
thing, a fallen number,
a bunch of lifeless fruit
dumped in the rubbish heap.

trans. Jack Schmitt

América, no invoco tu nombre en vano

América, no invoco tu nombre en vano.
Cuando sujeto al corazón la espada,

America, I Do Not Call Your Name without Hope

America, I do not call your name without hope.
When I hold the sword against the heart,

cuando aguanto en el alma la gotera,
cuando por las ventanas
un nuevo día tuyo me penetra,
soy y estoy en la luz que me produce,
vivo en la sombra que me determina,
duermo y despierto en tu esencial aurora:
dulce como las uvas, y terrible,
conductor del azúcar y el castigo,
empapado en esperma de tu especie,
amamantado en sangre de tu herencia.

1950

when I live with the faulty roof in the soul,
when one of your new days
pierces me coming through the windows,
I am and I stand in the light that produces me,
I live in the darkness which makes me what I am,
I sleep and awake in your fundamental sunrise:
as mild as the grapes, and as terrible,
carrier of sugar and the whip,
soaked in the sperm of your species,
nursed on the blood of your inheritance.

trans. Robert Bly

Oda a los calcetines

Me trajo Maru Mori
un par
de calcetines
que tejió con sus manos
de pastora,
dos calcetines suaves
como liebres.
En ellos
metí los pies
como en
dos
estuches
tejidos
con hebras del
crepúsculo
y pellejo de ovejas.
Violentos calcetines,
mis pies fueron
dos pescados
de lana,
dos largos tiburones
de azul ultramarino
atravesados
por una trenza de oro,
dos gigantescos mirlos,
dos cañones:
mis pies
fueron honrados
de este modo
por
estos
celestiales
calcetines.
Eran
tan hermosos
que por primera vez
mis pies me parecieron

Ode to My Socks

Maru Mori brought me
a pair
of socks
which she knitted herself
with her sheepherder's hands,
two socks as soft
as rabbits.
I slipped my feet
into them
as though into
two
cases
knitted
with threads of
twilight
and goatskin.
Violent socks,
my feet were
two fish made
of wool,
two long sharks
sea-blue, shot
through
by one golden thread,
two immense blackbirds,
two cannons:
my feet
were honored
in this way
by
these
heavenly
socks.
They were
so handsome
for the first time
my feet seemed to me

inaceptables
como dos decrépitos
bomberos, bomberos,
indignos
de aquel fuego
bordado,
de aquellos luminosos
calcetines.

Sin embargo
resistí
la tentación aguda
de guardarlos
como los colegiales
preservan
las luciérnagas,
como los eruditos
coleccionan
documentos sagrados,
resistí
el impulso furioso
de ponerlos
en una jaula
de oro
y darles cada día
alpiste
y pulpa de melón rosado.
Como descubridores
que en la selva
entregan el rarísimo
venado verde
al asador
y se lo comen
con remordimiento,
estiré
los pies
y me enfundé
los
bellos
calcetines
y
luego los zapatos.

Y es ésta
la moral de mi oda:
dos veces es belleza
la belleza
y lo que es bueno es doblemente
bueno
cuando se trata de dos calcetines
de lana
en el invierno.

unacceptable
like two decrepit
firemen, firemen
unworthy
of that woven
fire,
of those glowing
socks.

Nevertheless
I resisted
the sharp temptation
to save them somewhere
as schoolboys
keep
fireflies,
as learned men
collect
sacred texts,
I resisted
the mad impulse
to put them
into a golden
cage
and each day give them
birdseed
and pieces of pink melon.
Like explorers
in the jungle who hand
over the very rare
green deer
to the spit
and eat it
with remorse,
I stretched out
my feet
and pulled on
the magnificent
socks
and then my shoes.

The moral
of my ode is this:
beauty is twice
beauty
and what is good is doubly
good
when it is a matter of two socks
made of wool
in winter.

trans. Robert Bly

1954

Oda a César Vallejo

A la piedra en tu rostro,
Vallejo,
a las arrugas
de las áridas sierras
yo recuerdo en mi canto,
tu frente
gigantesca
sobre tu cuerpo frágil,
el crepúsculo negro
en tus ojos
recién desenterrados,
días aquellos,
bruscos,
desiguales,
cada hora tenía
ácidos diferentes
o ternuras
remotas,
las llaves
de la vida
temblaban
en la luz polvienta
de la calle,
tú volvías
de un viaje
lento, bajo la tierra,
y en la altura
de las cicatrizadas cordilleras
yo golpeaba las puertas,
que se abrieran
los muros,
que se desenrollaran
los caminos,
recién llegado de Valparaíso
me embarcaba en Marsella,
la tierra
se cortaba
como un limón fragante
en frescos hemisferios amarillos,
tú
te quedabas
allí, sujeto
a nada,
con tu vida
y tu muerte,
con tu arena
cayendo,
midiéndote
y vaciándote,
en el aire,

Ode to César Vallejo

The stone in your face,
Vallejo,
the creases
of the dry sierras:
I recollect them in my song:
your enormous
forehead
above your delicate body,
the black twilight
in your eyes,
freshly unearthed,
those harsh
unstable
days,
each hour held
different acids
or distant
gentlenesses,
the keys
of life
trembled
in the powdery light
of the street,
you returned
from a slow
journey, from under the earth,
and in the heights
of the scarred mountain-ranges
I pounded on the doors,
to make the walls
open,
to make the roads
unroll,
just arrived from Valparaiso
I disembarked at Marseille,
the earth
broke open
like a fragrant lemon
in fresh yellow hemispheres,
you
stayed
there, subject
to nothing,
with your life
and your death,
with your sand
dropping,
measuring you
and draining you,
in the air,

en el humo,
en las callejas rotas
del invierno.
Era en París, vivías
en los descalabrados
hoteles de los pobres.
España
se desangraba.
Acudíamos.
Y luego
te quedaste
otra vez en el humo
y así cuando
ya no fuiste, de pronto,
no fue la tierra
de las cicatrices,
no fue
la piedra andina
la que tuvo tus huesos,
sino el humo,
la escarcha
de París en invierno.

Dos veces desterrado,
hermano mío,
de la tierra y el aire,
de la vida y la muerte,
desterrado
del Perú, de tus ríos,
ausente
de tu arcilla.
No me faltaste en vida,
sino en muerte.
Te busco
gota a gota,
polvo a polvo,
en tu tierra,
amarillo
es tu rostro,
escarpado
es tu rostro,
estás lleno
de viejas pedrerías,
de vasijas
quebradas,
subo
las antiguas
escalinatas,
tal vez
estés perdido,
enredado
entre los hilos de oro,

in the smoke,
in the defeated alleys
of the winter.
You were in Paris, living
in the wounded
hostels of the poor.
Spain
was bleeding.
We left.
And again
that time
you remained, in the smoke,
so that when
suddenly you just *weren't* any longer,
it was not the earth
with its scars,
it was not
the stone of the Andes
that held your bones
but the smoke,
the frost,
of Paris in winter.

Exiled twice,
my brother:
from the earth and the air
from life and death,
exiled
from Peru, from your rivers,
absent
from your clay soil.
I never missed you in life,
only in death.
I search for you
drop by drop,
dust by dust,
in the earth,
your face is
yellow,
your face is
craggy,
you are full
of old jewels,
of broken
pots,
I climb
the ancient
terraces,
maybe you have
gotten lost,
caught netted
in threads of gold,

cubierto
de turquesas,
silencioso,
o tal vez
en tu pueblo,
en tu raza,
grano
de maíz extendido,
semilla
de bandera.
Tal vez, tal vez ahora
transmigres
y regreses,
vienes
al fin
de viaje,
de manera
que un día
te verás en el centro
de tu patria,
insurrecto,
viviente,
cristal de tu cristal, fuego en tu fuego,
rayo de piedra púrpura.

1954

covered
with turquoise,
silent,
or maybe
in your village,
in your race,
a grain
of corn spread wide,
seed
of a flag.
Maybe, maybe now
you are transmigrating,
and you are returning,
you are coming
to the end
of the journey,
so that
one day
you will find yourself in the middle
of your homeland,
insurgent,
alive,
crystal of your crystal, flame in your flame,
beam of purple stone.

trans. Stephen Tapscott

Oda a la pereza

Ayer sentí que la oda
no subía del suelo.
Era hora, debía
por lo menos
mostrar una hoja verde.
Rasqué la tierra: "Sube,
hermana oda
—le dije—
te tengo prometida,
no me tengas miedo,
no voy a triturarte,
oda de cuatro hojas,
oda de cuatro manos,
tomarás té conmigo.
Sube,
te voy a coronar entre las odas,
saldremos juntos, por la orilla
del mar, en bicicleta."
Fue inútil.

Entonces,
en lo alto de los pinos,

Ode to Laziness

Yesterday I felt this ode
would not get off the floor.
It was time, I ought
at least
show a green leaf.
I scratch the earth: "Arise,
sister ode
—said to her—
I have promised you,
do not be afraid of me,
I am not going to crush you,
four-leaf ode,
four-hand ode,
you shall have tea with me.
Arise,
I am going to crown you among the odes,
we shall go out together along the shores
of the sea, on a bicycle."
It was no use.

Then,
on the pine peaks,

la pereza
apareció desnuda,
me llevó deslumbrado
y soñoliento,
me descubrió en la arena
pequeños trozos rotos
de sustancias oceánicas,
maderas, algas, piedras,
plumas de aves marinas.
Busqué sin encontrar
ágatas amarillas.
El mar
llenaba los espacios
desmoronando torres,
invadiendo
las costas de mi patria,
avanzando
sucesivas catástrofes de espuma.
Sola en la arena
abría un rayo
una corola.
Vi cruzar los petreles plateados
y como cruces negras
los cormoranes
clavados en las rocas.
Liberté una abeja
que agonizaba en un velo de araña,
metí una piedrecita
en un bolsillo,
era suave, suavísima
como un pecho de pájaro,
mientras tanto en la costa,
toda la tarde,
lucharon sol y niebla.
A veces
la niebla se impregnaba
de luz
como un topacio,
otras veces caía
un rayo de sol húmedo
dejando caer gotas amarillas.

En la noche,
pensando en los deberes de mi oda
fugitiva,
me saqué los zapatos
junto al fuego,
resbaló arena de ellos
y pronto fui quedándome
dormido.

laziness
appeared in the nude,
she led me dazzled
and sleepy,
she showed me upon the sand
small broken bits
of ocean substance,
wood, algae, pebbles,
feathers of sea birds.
I looked for but did not find
yellow agates.
The sea
filled all spaces
crumbling towers,
invading
the shores of my country,
advancing
successive catastrophes of the foam.
Alone on the sand
spread wide
its corolla.
I saw the silvery petrels crossing
and like black creases
the cormorants
nailed to the rocks.
I released a bee
that was agonizing in a spider's net.
I put a little pebble
in my pocket,
it was smooth, very smooth
as the breast of a bird,
meanwhile on the shore,
all afternoon
sun struggled with mist.
At times
the mist was steeped
in thought,
topaz-like,
at others fell
a ray from the moist sun
distilling yellow drops.

At night,
thinking of the duties of my
fugitive ode,
I pulled off my shoes
near the fire;
sand slid out of them
and soon I began to fall
asleep.

1954   *trans. William Carlos Williams*

Oda a la sal

Esta sal
del salero
yo la ví en los salares.
Sé que
no
van a creerme,
pero
canta,
canta la sal, la piel
de los salares
canta
con una boca ahogada
por la tierra.
Me estremecí en aquellas
soledades
cuando escuché
la voz
de
la sal
en el desierto.
Cerca de Antofagasta
toda
la pampa salitrosa
suena:
es una
voz
quebrada,
un lastimero
canto.

Luego en sus cavidades
la sal gema, montaña
de una luz enterrada,
catedral transparente,
cristal del mar, olvido
de las olas.

Y luego en cada mesa
de este mundo,
sal,
tu substancia
ágil
espolvoreando
la luz vital
sobre
los alimentos.
Preservadora
de las antiguas
bodegas del navío,
descubridora

Ode to Salt

This salt
in the saltcellar
I once saw in the salt mines.
I know
you won't
believe me,
but
it sings,
salt sings, the skin
of the salt mines,
sings
with a mouth smothered
by the earth.
I shivered in those
solitudes
when I heard
the voice
of
the salt
in the desert.
Near Antofagasta
the nitrous
pampa
resounds:
a
broken
voice,
a mournful
song.

In its caves
the salt moans, mountain
of buried light,
translucent cathedral,
crystal of the sea, oblivion
of the waves.

And then on every table
in the world,
salt,
we see your piquant
powder
sprinkling
vital light
upon
our food. **Preserver**
of the ancient
holds of ships,
discoverer

fuiste
en el océano,
materia
adelantada
en los desconocidos, entreabiertos
senderos de la espuma.
Polvo del mar, la lengua
de ti recibe un beso
de la noche marina:
el gusto funde en cada
sazonado manjar tu oceanía
y así la mínima,
la minúscula
ola del salero
nos enseña
no sólo su doméstica blancura,
sino el sabor central del infinito.

on
the high seas,
earliest
sailor
of the unknown, shifting
byways of the foam.
Dust of the sea, in you
the tongue receives a kiss
from ocean night:
taste imparts to every seasoned
dish your ocean essence;
the smallest,
miniature
wave from the saltcellar
reveals to us
more than domestic whiteness;
in it, we taste infinitude.

1957

trans. Margaret Sayers Peden

Cien sonetos de amor

V

No te toque la noche ni el aire ni la aurora,
sólo la tierra, la virtud de los racimos,
las manzanas que crecen oyendo el agua pura,
el barro y las resinas de tu país fragante.

Desde Quinchamalí donde hicieron tus ojos
hasta tus pies creados para mí en la Frontera
eres la greda oscura que conozco:
en tus caderas toco de nuevo todo el trigo.

Tal vez tú no sabías, araucana,
que cuando antes de amarte me olvidé de tus besos
mi corazón quedó recordando tu boca

y fui como un herido por las calles
hasta que comprendí que había encontrado,
amor, mi territorio de besos y volcanes.

XVI

Amo el trozo de tierra que tú eres,
porque de las praderas planetarias
otra estrella no tengo. Tú repites
la multiplicación del universo.

Tus anchos ojos son la luz que tengo
de las constelaciones derrotadas,

One Hundred Love Sonnets

V

I did not touch your night, or your air, or dawn:
only the earth, the truth of the fruit in clusters,
the apples that swell as they drink the sweet water,
the clay and the resins of your sweet-smelling land.

From Quinchamalí where your eyes began,
to the Frontera where your feet were made for me,
you are my dark familiar clay: touching your hips,
I touch the wheat in its fields again.

Woman from Arauco, maybe you didn't know
how before I loved you I forgot your kisses.
But my heart went on, remembering your mouth—and
    I went on

and on through the streets like a man wounded,
until I understood, Love: I had found
my place, a land of kisses and volcanoes.

XVI

I love the handful of the earth you are.
Because of its meadows, vast as a planet,
I have no other star. You are my model
of the multiplying universe.

Your wide eyes are the only light I know
from extinguished constellations;

tu piel palpita como los caminos
que recorre en la lluvia el meteoro.

De tanta luna fueron para mí tus caderas,
de todo el sol tu boca profunda y su delicia,
de tanta luz ardiente como miel en la sombra

tu corazón quemado por largos rayos rojos,
y así recorro el fuego de tu forma besándote,
pequeña y planetaria, paloma y geografía.

XCII

Amor mío, si muero y tú no mueres,
amor mío, si mueres y no muero,
no demos al dolor más territorio:
no hay extensión como la que vivimos.

Polvo en el trigo, arena en las arenas,
el tiempo, el agua errante, el viento vago
nos llevó como grano navegante.
Pudimos no encontrarnos en el tiempo.

Esta pradera en que nos encontramos,
oh pequeño infinito! devolvemos.
Pero este amor, amor, no ha terminado,

y así como no tuvo nacimiento
no tiene muerte, es como un largo río,
sólo cambia de tierras y de labios.

1959

your skin throbs like the streak
of a meteor through rain.

Your hips were that much of the moon for me,
your deep mouth and its delights, that much sun;
your heart, fiery with its long red rays,

was that much ardent light, like honey in the shade.
And so I pass across your burning form, kissing
you—compact and planetary, my dove, my globe.

XCII

My love, if I die and you don't—,
My love, if you die and I don't—,
let's not give grief an even greater field.
No expanse is greater than where we live.

Dust in the wheat, sand in the deserts,
time, wandering water, the vagrant wind
swept us like a sailing seed.
We might not have found one another in time.

This meadow where we find ourselves,
O little infinity!: we give it back.
But, Love, this love has not ended:

just as it never had a birth,
it has no death: it is like a long river,
only changing lands, and changing lips.

trans. Stephen Tapscott

Sara de Ibáñez

URUGUAY
1910–1971

In his introduction to Sara de Ibáñez' first book of poems, *Canto* (*Song*, 1940), Pablo Neruda wrote: "This woman retrieves from Sor Juana de la Cruz a treasure we had lost till now: one of mystical transport subdued into rigor, one of containment transformed to an eternal spray of sea-foam." Ibáñez' ability to ring crystalline changes on poetic forms derived from the poets of the Spanish Golden Age (including Sor Juana, Garcilaso, Fray Luis de León, Góngora, and San Juan de la Cruz), in poems of surprisingly personal and mysterious images, made her one of the most enduring and admired Latin American poets. In the rich Uruguayan tradition that includes not only Juana de Ibarbourou and Alfonsina Storni but also such poets as Clara Silva, Susana Soca, Ida Vitale, Amanda Berenguer, and Ester de Cáceres, Ibáñez' voice is still distinctive: pure, musical, erotic, elegant. Her poetry is delicate in its emotional accuracy and austere in its images, at the same time avoiding preciousness and hermeticism.

Isla en la tierra

Al norte el frío y su jazmín quebrado.
Al este un ruiseñor lleno de espinas.
Al sur la rosa en sus aéreas minas,
y al oeste un camino ensimismado.

Al norte un ángel yace amordazado.
Al este el llanto ordena sus neblinas.
Al sur mi tierno haz de palmas finas,
y al oeste mi puerta y mi cuidado.

Pudo un vuelo de nube o de suspiro
trazar esta finísima frontera
que defiende sin mengua mi retiro.

Un lejano castigo de ola estalla
y muerde tus olvidos de extranjera,
mi isla seca en mitad de la batalla.

1940

Island in the Earth

To the north, the cold and its broken jasmine.
To the east, a nightingale full of thorns.
To the south, the rose in its subtle abundance,
to the west a pensive road.

To the north, an angel lies silenced.
To the east, weeping arranges its mists.
To the south, my tender packet of fine palms,
to the west, my door and caution.

Maybe the flight of a cloud, or a sigh,
might trace this frontier that defends
my retreat bravely.

A distant wave of punishment explodes
and gnaws at your strange forgetfulness,
my dry island in the midst of the battle.

trans. Inés Probert

Isla en la luz

Se abrasó la paloma en su blancura.
Murió la corza entre la hierba fría.
Murió la flor sin nombre todavía
y el fino lobo de inocencia oscura.

Murió el ojo del pez en la onda dura.
Murió el agua acosada por el día.
Murió la perla en su lujosa umbría.
Cayó el olivo y la manzana pura.

De azúcares de ala y blancas piedras
suben los arrecifes cegadorcs
en invasión de lujuriosas hiedras.

Cementerio de angélicos desiertos:
guarda entre tus dormidos pobladores
sitio también para mis ojos muertos.

1943

Island in the Light

The dove burned in its whiteness.
The doe died in the cold grass.
Dead, the flower—still unnamed—
and the shrewd wolf of dark innocence.

The eye of the fish died in the rugged wave.
The water died, driven by the day.
The pearl in its luxurious darkness died.
Oblivion and the pure apple fell.

The blinding cliffs rise
up from flying sugars and white rocks,
like an invasion of wild ivies.

Graveyard of angelic deserts:
among your sleeping inhabitants, keep
also a place for my lifeless eyes.

trans. Inés Probert

Tú, por mi pensamiento

¿Que se estiró la tierra
hasta el gemido?
¿Que fue el cielo sonando sus campanas azules
desde el pálido sueño a la sangre que sufre?

You, for My Meditation

Did the earth stretch out
until it cried?
Did the sky deepen its blue fields
from the pale dream to the blood that suffers?

¿Que se ha cruzado un río,
llanto y llanto?
¿Que se han cruzado veinte galopes de cristales,
con sus veinte misterios llenos de claridades?

¿Que se alzó la montaña
poderosa?
¿Que alargó el alto hielo su selva inmaculada?
¿Que las rocas crecieron para tapar tu cara?

¿Que el viento se hizo espeso
como piedra,
como una inmensa rueda de vidrio turbulento
girando entre tus sienes y el rumor de mis besos?

¿Que el espacio se burla
de mis ojos?
¡Ah, no! Yo sé el camino para poder hallarte.
La muerte me ha mirado caminar por sus valles.

1943

Did the river travel,
crying and crying?
Did twenty crystal gallopings ride across the field,
with their twenty mysteries full of brightnesses?

Did the heavy mountain
lift itself?
Did the frost extend its immaculate forest?
Did the cliff grow huger, blurring its face?

Did the wind thicken
like a stone,
like a great and stormy wheel of glass,
spinning between your temples and the hint of my kisses?

Did this huge distance
deceive my sight?
Oh, no: I know the path I need to find you.
Death has shown me how to walk its valleys.

trans. Andrew Rosing

La página vacía

A Stéphane Mallarmé

Cómo atrever esta impura
cerrazón de sangre y fuego,
esta urgencia de astro ciego
contra tu feroz blancura.
Ausencia de la criatura
que su nacimiento espera,
de tu nieve prisionera
y de mis venas deudora,
en el revés de la aurora
y el no de la primavera.

1967

The Empty Page

For Stéphane Mallarmé

How to make this impure
storminess of blood and fire,
urgency of the blind planet,
oppose your terrible whiteness.
The absence of the creature
who waits to be born,
held captive by your snows
and by my mortgaged veins,
in the disillusionment of dawn
and in spring's no.

trans. Andrew Rosing

No puedo

No puedo cerrar mis puertas
ni clausurar mis ventanas:
he de salir al camino
donde el mundo gira y clama,
he de salir al camino
a ver la muerte que pasa.

He de salir a mirar
cómo crece y se derrama
sobre el planeta encogido
la desatinada raza
que quiebra su fuente y luego
llora la ausencia del agua.

I Cannot

I cannot close my doors
nor fasten my windows
—which look out on the road
where the world spins and clamors
—which look out on the road
to see death passing by.

—Which look out and see
how the restless species,
flourishing and spreading
over the shrunken planet,
destroys its origins and then
laments the absence of water.

He de salir a esperar
el turbión de las palabras
que sobre la tierra cruza
y en flor los cantos arrasa,
he de salir a escuchar
el fuego entre nieve y zarza.

No puedo cerrar las puertas
ni clausurar las ventanas,
el laúd en las rodillas
y de esfinges rodeada,
puliendo azules respuestas
a sus preguntas en llamas.

Mucha sangre está corriendo
de las heridas cerradas,
mucha sangre está corriendo
por el ayer y la mañana,
y un gran ruido de torrente
viene a golpear en el alba.

Salgo al camino y escucho,
salgo a ver la luz turbada;
un cruel resuello de ahogado
sobre las bocas estalla,
y contra el cielo impasible
se pierde en nubes de escarcha.

Ni en el fondo de la noche
se detiene la ola amarga,
llena de niños que suben
con la sonrisa cortada,
ni en el fondo de la noche
queda una paloma en calma.

No puedo cerrar mis puertas
ni clausurar mis ventanas.
A mi diestra mano el sueño
mueve una iracunda espada
y echa rodando a mis pies
una rosa mutilada.

Tengo los brazos caídos
convicta de sombra y nada;
un olvidado perfume
muerde mis manos extrañas,
pero no puedo cerrar
las puertas y las ventanas,
y he de salir al camino
a ver la muerte que pasa.

—which look out to wait for
the wildness of the words
that cross the earth and, blossoming,
crack the stones apart.
—which look out to attend
the fire between snow and brambles.

I cannot close the doors
nor fasten the windows,
the lute on the knees
and the sphinx, enclosed,
polishing blue responses
to its questions, in tears.

Much blood is flowing
from the closed wounds;
much blood is flowing
for yesterday and tomorrow,
and a great flooding noise
comes to crash against the dawn.

I go out to the road and I listen,
I go out to watch the troubling light;
a fierce breath of anguish
explodes in front of the mouths
and is lost in clouds of frost
against the impenetrable sky.

It never stops, not even in the depths
of the night, the bitter wave
filled with children rising
with half-smiles,
not even in the depths of the night
does the dove rest calmly.

I cannot close my doors
nor fasten my windows.
At my right hand the dream
flourishes an angry sword
and throws a mutilated rose,
rolling, to my feet.

My arms fall, convicted
of shadow and nothingness,
a forgotten scent
destroys my strange hands,
but I cannot close
the doors or the windows
—which look out on the road
to see death passing by.

1967   *trans. Andrew Rosing*

José Lezama Lima

In the English-speaking world José Lezama Lima is best known for his epic novel *Paradiso*, published in Cuba in 1966. That book won him almost instant international acclaim, ironically as a writer of prose. It is clear, though, that the novel's complex re-creation of the braided flow of consciousness, narrative events, and affection through several generations owes much to Lezama Lima's long commitment to poetry. He has been called the "Góngora of the tropics" because of his belief in poetry as the "absolute form of liberty," embodied in an allusive, cerebral, elegantly disciplined style. The Catholic poet Cintio Vitier characterizes the central element of Lezama Lima's sorcery as a "barbarous naturalism" which articulates the mystical connection of consciousness with objects, within a larger pursuit of the "verbal imitation of the unfathomable appearances" of things. The desire for transcendence in his work sometimes wars against an acknowledgment of hermeneutic limitations. The results of this conflict—a struggle toward completeness but against the systemization of experience—are his "metonymical poetry and metaphorical prose." Julio Ortega calls Lezama Lima's poetry, collected in the posthumous *Poesías completas* (*Complete Poems*, 1970), "the summa theologica" of Latin American poetry in the latter half of the century, both because of Lezama Lima's address to the "problematics" of poetry and because of his importance to younger writers.

For many years an employee of the National Cultural Council in Castro's Cuba, Lezama Lima fell into disfavor with the regime when he published *Paradiso*. The official skepticism toward that book centered on its bildungsroman accounts of homosexuality in Cuba and on the fiction's refusal to take fixed positions about the political questions it raised. Official censors harassed Lezama Lima because of his book's representations of sexuality. Social Realists suspected him because of the complexity of his neo-Baroque style, which reflects influences ranging from Dante through Rilke and Proust. Because of his international stature as a writer and critic, however, Lezama Lima proved immune to serious governmental persecution. From his relatively secure position, he was able to help and protect many younger Cuban intellectuals and writers.

Ah, *que tú escapes*

Ah, que tú escapes en el instante
en el que ya habías alcanzado tu definición mejor.
Ah, mi amiga, que tú no quieras creer
las preguntas de esa estrella recién cortada,
que va mojando sus puntas en otra estrella enemiga.
Ah, si pudiera ser cierto que a la hora del baño,
cuando en una misma agua discursiva
se bañan el inmóvil paisaje y los animales más finos:
antílopes, serpientes de pasos breves, de pasos evaporados,
parecen entre sueños, sin ansias levantar
los más extensos cabellos y el agua más recordada.
Ah, mi amiga, si en el puro mármol de los adioses
hubieras dejado la estatua que nos podía acompañar,

Ah, *That You Escape*

Ah, that you escape in the flash
when you had come upon your best definition.
Ah, my love, that you don't want to be taken in by
the questions of that newly cut star
that keeps drenching its tips in another enemy star.
Ah, if I could be sure that during the hour of bathing
a still landscape and the most delicate animals
bathed in one discursive water:
antelope, snakes with short and evaporated gait
appear in dreams to raise quite comfortably
the fullest hair and most remembered water.
Ah, my love, if in the pure marble of goodbyes
you had left the statue that could go with us,

pues el viento, el viento gracioso,
se extiende como un gato para dejarse definir.

1941

since wind, the gracious wind,
stretches out like a cat to let itself be defined.

trans. Willis Barnstone

Una oscura pradera me convida

Una oscura pradera me convida,
sus manteles estables y ceñidos,
giran en mí, en mi balcón se aduermen.
Dominan su extensión, su indefinida
cúpula de alabastro se recrea.
Sobre las aguas del espejo,
breve la voz en mitad de cien caminos,
mi memoria prepara su sorpresa:
gamo en el cielo, rocío llamarada.
Sin sentir que me llaman
penetro en la pradera despacioso,
ufano en nuevo laberinto derretido.
Allí se ven, ilustres restos,
cien cabezas, cornetas, mil funciones
abren su cielo, su girasol callando.
Extraña la sorpresa en este cielo,
donde sin querer vuelven pisadas
y suenan las voces en su centro henchido.
Una oscura pradera va pasando.
Entre los dos, viento o fino papel,
el viento, herido viento de esta muerte
mágica, una y despedida.
Un pájaro y otro ya no tiemblan.

1945

A Dark Meadow Invites Me

A dark meadow invites me,
its firm and tight tablecloths
spin in me, doze off on my balcony.
They dominate its extension, its indefinite
alabaster cupola is recreated.
Over the waters of the mirror
a quick voice in the middle of a hundred roads,
my memory readies its surprise:
a fallow deer in the sky, dew, sudden blaze.
Oblivious to their calling me,
I slowly penetrate the meadow,
arrogant in the new melted labyrinth.
There one sees illustrious remains,
a hundred heads, bugles, a thousand operations
open their sky, silencing their sunflower.
Surprise is strange in their sky
where footsteps involuntarily fly back
and voices echo in their swollen center.
A dark meadow goes by.
Between the two, wind or fine paper,
the wind, wounded wind with this magic
death, unanimous and chased away.
One bird and another no longer shiver.

trans. Willis Barnstone

Llamado del deseoso

Deseoso es aquel que huye de su madre.
Despedirse es cultivar un rocío para unirlo con la
        secularidad de la saliva.
La hondura del deseo no va por el secuestro del fruto.
Deseoso es dejar de ver a su madre.
Es la ausencia del sucedido de un día que se prolonga
y es a la noche que esa ausencia se va ahondando como
        un cuchillo.
En esa ausencia se abre una torre, en esa torre baila un
        fuego hueco.
Y así se ensancha y la ausencia de la madre es un mar
        en calma.
Pero el huidizo no ve el cuchillo que le pregunta,
es de la madre, de los postigos asegurados, de quien
        se huye.
Lo descendido en vieja sangre suena vacío.

Call of the Desirous

Desirous is one who gets away from his mother.
To say farewell is to cultivate dew so as to join it to
        saliva's secularity.
The depth of desire does not go with the abduction of
        the fruit.
Desirous is to quit seeing your mother.
It is the absence of a day's event that lingers
and it is into night that that absence deepens like a knife.
In that absence a tower opens, in that tower a hollow
        flame dances.
So it grows immense and the mother's absence is a
        calm sea.
But the one who gets away doesn't spot the knife
        asking him,
it is the mother, the safe posterns he is fleeing.
What has descended in old blood sounds empty.

La sangre es fría cuando desciende y cuando se esparce
    circulizada.
La madre es fría y está cumplida.
Si es por la muerte, su peso es doble y ya no nos suelta.
No es por las puertas donde se asoma nuestro abandono.
Es por un claro donde la madre sigue marchando, pero
    ya no nos sigue.
Es por un claro, allí se ciega y bien nos deja.
Ay del que no marcha esa marcha donde la madre ya no
    le sigue, ay.

No es desconocerse, el conocerse sigue furioso como en
    sus días,
pero el seguirlo sería quemarse dos en un árbol,
y ella apetece mirar el árbol como una piedra,
como una piedra con la inscripción de ancianos juegos.
Nuestro deseo no es alcanzar o incorporar un fruto ácido.
El deseoso es el huidizo
y de los cabezazos con nuestras madres cae el planeta
    centro de mesa
y ¿de donde huimos, si no es de nuestras madres de
    quien huimos
que nunca quieren recomenzar el mismo naipe, la misma
    noche de igual ijada descomunal?

                                            1945

The blood is cold when it descends and when it spreads
    in circles.
The mother is cold and is fulfilled.
If it's for death, her weight is double and won't let us loose.
Our abandonment doesn't come through doors.
The mother is marching along a clearing, but no longer
    trails us.
It's along a clearing, there she is blinded and really
    leaves us.
Ay the one who doesn't tread that step where the mother
    no longer trails him, ay.

It's not being blind to oneself, the self-knower is mad
    as before,
but the pursuit would be to burn them both in a tree,
and she longs to see the tree as a stone,
as a stone inscribed with ancient games.
Our desire is not to attain or incorporate an acid fruit.
The desirous is one who gets away
and the planet at the center of the table falls from
    bumping heads against our mothers
and where are we fleeing if not from our mothers
who never want to rebegin the same card, the same night
    with its same monstrous flank?

                                    trans. Willis Barnstone

Rapsodia para el mulo

Con qué seguro paso el mulo en el abismo.

Lento es el mulo. Su misión no siente.
Su destino frente a la piedra, piedra que sangra
creando la abierta risa en las granadas.
Su piel rajada, pequeñísimo triunfo ya en lo oscuro,
pequeñísimo fango de alas ciegas.
La ceguera, el vidrio y el agua de tus ojos
tienen la fuerza de un tendón oculto
y así los inmutables ojos recorriendo
lo oscuro progresivo y fugitivo.
El espacio de agua comprendido
entre sus ojos y el abierto túnel,
fija su centro que la faja
como la carga de plomo necesaria
que viene a caer como el sonido
del mulo cayendo en el abismo.

Las salvadas alas en el mulo inexistentes,
más apuntala su cuerpo en el abismo
la faja que le impide la dispersión

Rhapsody for the Mule

How certain the mule's step in the abyss.

Slow is the mule. He does not sense his mission.
His fate facing the stone, stone that bleeds
creating the open laughter of pomegranates.
His cracked skin, tiniest triumph now in the dark,
tiniest blind-winged clod.
The blindness, the glassiness, the water of your eyes
have the strength of a hidden tendon:
just so his motionless eyes scanning
the increasing fugitive dark.
The space of water between
his eyes and the open tunnel
fixes the centre that cinches him
like the necessary load of lead
to fall like the sound of the mule
falling in the abyss.

No saving wings existing for the mule,
his body is more sustained in the abyss
by the swath belting-in the dispersion

de la carga de plomo que en la entraña
del mulo pesa cayendo en la tierra húmeda
de piedras pisadas con un nombre.
Seguro, fajado por Dios,
entra el poderoso mulo en el abismo.

Las sucesivas coronas del desfiladero
—van creciendo corona tras corona—
y allí en lo alto la carroña
de las ancianas aves que en el cuello
muestran corona tras corona.
Seguir con su paso en al abismo.
Él no puede, no crea ni persigue,
ni brincan sus ojos
ni sus ojos buscan el secuestrado asilo
al borde preñado de la tierra.
No crea, eso es tal vez decir:
¿No siente, no ama ni pregunta?
El amor traído a la traición de alas sonrosadas,
infantil en su oscura caracola.
Su amor a los cuatro signos
del desfiladero, a las sucesivas coronas
en que asciende vidrioso, cegato,
como un oscuro cuerpo hinchado
por el agua de los orígenes,
no la de la redención y los perfumes.
Paso es el paso del mulo en el abismo.

Su don ya no es estéril: su creación
la segura marcha en el abismo.
Amigo del desfiladero, la profunda
hinchazón del plomo dilata sus carrillos.
Sus ojos soportan cajas de agua
y el jugo de sus ojos
—sus sucias lágrimas—
son en la redención ofrenda altiva.
Entontado el ojo del mulo en el abismo
y sigue en lo oscuro con sus cuatro signos.
Peldaños de agua soportan sus ojos,
pero ya frente al mar
la ola retrocede como el cuerpo volteado
en el instante de la muerte súbita.
Hinchado está el mulo, valerosa hinchazón
que le lleva a caer hinchado en el abismo.
Sentado en el ojo del mulo,
vidrioso, cegato, el abismo
lentamente repasa su invisible.
En el sentado abismo,
paso a paso, sólo se oyen
las preguntas que el mulo
va dejando caer sobre la piedra al fuego.

of the leaden charge heavy in the bowels
of the mule as he falls to the moist earth
of stones trampled with a name.
Steadily, cinched by God,
the strong mule enters the abyss.

The successive crests of the ravine—
crest crescent beyond crest—
and there on high the carrion
of ancient birds, their necks
displaying crest upon crest.
The step onward in the abyss.
He has no power of creation or pursuit,
his eyes neither leap
nor seek the sanctuary sequestered
at earth's teeming border.
No creation: and is that perhaps
no feeling, no loving, no questioning?
Love brought by betrayal of rosy wings,
childlike in the dark conch.
His love for the four hoof-signs
in the ravine, the successive crests
of his glassy blind ascent,
the dark body swollen
by the water of origins,
not the water of redemption and perfume.
Each step is a step of the mule in the abyss.

His gift is no longer sterile: his creation
the steady march in the abyss.
Familiar of the ravine, the deep
lead swelling puffs out his cheeks.
His eyes hold boxes of water,
and the juice of his eyes—
his grimy tears—
are proud oblation for redemption.
Bewildered the eye of the mule in the abyss,
and he marches on in the dark with his four hoof-signs.
Steps of water are shored up in his eyes,
but now confronting the sea
the wave retreats like a wrestler thrown
at the moment of sudden death.
Swollen is the mule, a mighty swelling
that bears him swollen to fall into the abyss.
Settled in the mule's eye,
glassy, myopic, the abyss
slowly reviews its invisible.
In the settled abyss,
step by step, are heard only
the questions which the mule
treads into the burning stone.

Son ya los cuatro signos
conque se asienta su fajado cuerpo
sobre el serpentín de calcinadas piedras.
Cuando se adentra más en el abismo
la piel le tiembla cual si fuesen clavos
las rápidas preguntas que rebotan.
En el abismo sólo el paso del mulo.
Sus cuatro ojos de húmeda yesca
sobre la piedra envuelven rápidas miradas.
Los cuatro pies, los cuatro signos
maniatados revierten en las piedras.
El remolino de chispas sólo impide
seguir la misma aventura en la costumbre.
Ya se acostumbra, colcha del mulo,
a estar clavado en lo oscuro sucesivo;
a caer sobre la tierra hinchado
de aguas nocturnas y pacientes lunas.
En los ojos del mulo, cajas de agua.
Aprieta Dios la faja del mulo
y lo hincha de plomo como premio.
Cuando el gamo bailarín pellizca el fuego
en el desfiladero prosigue el mulo
avanzando como las aguas impulsadas
por los ojos de los maniatados.
Paso es el paso del mulo en el abismo.

El sudor manando sobre el casco
ablanda la piedra entresacada
del fuego no en las vasijas educado,
sino al centro del tragaluz, oscuro miente.
Su paso en la piedra nueva carne
formada de un despertar brillante
en la cerrada sierra que oscurece.
Ya despertado, mágica soga
cierra el desfiladero comenzado
por hundir sus rodillas vaporosas.
Ese seguro paso del mulo en el abismo
suele confundirse con los pintados guantes de lo estéril.
Suele confundirse con los comienzos
de la oscura cabeza negadora.
Por ti suele confundirse, descastado vidrioso.
Por ti, cadera con lazos charolados
que parece decirnos yo no soy y yo no soy,
pero que penetra también en las casonas
donde la araña hogareña ya no alumbra
y la portátil lámpara traslada
de un horror a otro horror.
Por ti suele confundirse, tú, vidrio descastado,
que paso es el paso del mulo en el abismo.

La faja de Dios sigue sirviendo.
Así cuando sólo no es chispas la caída

Now there are four hoof-signs,
and so his cinched body settles
upon the serpentine calcined stones.
Entering deeper into the abyss
his skin trembles as if the swift
bouncing questions were nails.
In the abyss only the mule's step.
His four eyes of humid tinder
weave quick glances on the rock.
The four feet; the four manacled
signs, overflow on the stones.
Only the flurry of sparks impedes
the repetition of the familiar story.
Now the mule is used to his quilt:
to being nailed to successive darkness;
to falling, swollen with nocturnal
waters and suffering moons, upon the earth.
In the mule's eyes, boxes of water.
God tightens the mule's cinch
and swells him with lead for a prize.
When the dancing buck plucks at the fire
in the ravine, the mule continues
advancing like waters raised
by the stares of manacled men.
Each step is a step of the mule in the abyss.

Sweat oozing over the hoof
softens stones sifted
from fire formed not in vessels,
but in the skylight-centre, giving the lie to darkness.
His step on the stone new flesh
fashioned of a bright awakening
in the dense darkening mountains.
Alert now, the ravine completes
the magic cord begun
with the bending of its vapoury knees.
That steady step of the mule in the abyss
is often confused with sterility's painted gloves,
confused often with the first probings
of the dark denying head.
Confused through you, glossy outcast:
through you, haunch with glassy looping braids
that seem to tell us *I am not* and *I am not*,
but pierce also those mansions
no longer lit by ancestral candelabra,
where the lamp is carried
from one horror to another horror.
Through you confused, you, outcast glass,
for each step is a step of the mule in the abyss.

The buckle of God still serves.
Thus when the fall is not merely sparks,

sino una piedra que volteando
arroja el sentido como pelado fuego
que en la piedra deja sus mordidas intocables.
Así contraída la faja, Dios lo quiere,—
la entraña no revierte sobre el cuerpo,
aprieta el gesto posterior a toda muerte.
Cuerpo pesado, tu plomada entraña,
inencontrada ha sido en el abismo,
ya que cayendo, terrible vertical
trenzada de luminosos puntos ciegos,
aspa volteando incesante oscuro,
has puesto en cruz los dos abismos.
Tu final no siempre es la vertical de dos abismos.
Los ojos del mulo parecen entregar
a la entraña del abismo, húmedo árbol.
Árbol que no se extiende en acanalados verdes
sino cerrado como la única voz de los comienzos.
Entontado, Dios lo quiere,
el mulo sigue transportando en sus ojos
árboles visibles y en sus músculos
los árboles que la música han rehusado.
Árbol de sombra y árbol de figura
han llegado también a la última corona desfilada.
La soga hinchada transporta la marea
y en el cuello del mulo nadan voces
necesarias al pasar del vacío al haz del abismo.

Paso es el paso, cajas de agua, fajado por Dios
el poderoso mulo duerme temblando.
Con sus ojos sentados y acuosos,
al fin el mulo árboles encaja en todo abismo.

1949

but a bounding stone
hurling the sense like a blazing fire
that leaves its intangible bite upon the stone.
The buckle thus tightened (God wills it),
the bowels do not burst out in bodily rupture;
the look that follows every death grows strong.
Heavy body, your lead-like bowels
were unencountered in the abyss,
for in falling, a horrible vertical braided
with shining blind points,
wheel spinning incessant dark,
of two abysses you have formed a cross.
Your terminus is not always the vertical of two abysses.
The mule's eyes seem to yield
a humid tree to the heart of the abyss.
A tree that does not spread out in channelled greens,
but thick like the single voice of the beginnings.
Bewildered, God wills it,
the mule carries in his eyes
trees visible, and in his muscles
the trees that have rejected music.
Tree of shade and tree of shape,
they too have won the last crest of the ravine.
The swollen rope carries the tides over
and in the mule's neck voices are swimming
as he passes from the void to the face of the deep.

Each step is a box, boxes of water, God-cinched,
trembling sleeps the powerful mule.
With his set and watery eyes
in each abyss the mule plants trees at last.

trans. José Rodríguez Feo, Dudley Fitts, and Donald D. Walsh

Los fragmentos de la noche

Cómo aislar los fragmentos de la noche
para apretar algo con las manos,
como la liebre penetra en su oscuridad
separando dos estrellas
apoyadas en el brillo de la yerba húmeda.
La noche respira en una intocable humedad,
no en el centro de la esfera que vuela,
y todo lo va uniendo, esquinas o fragmentos,
hasta formar el irrompible tejido de la noche,
sutil y completo como los dedos unidos
que apenas dejan pasar el agua,
como un cestillo mágico
que nada vacío dentro del río.
Yo quería separar mis manos de la noche,
pero se oía una gran sonoridad que no se oía,
como si todo mi cuerpo cayera sobre una serafina

The Fragments of the Night

How to isolate the fragments of the night
to grab something in one's hands
as a hare slips into darkness
separating two stars
held up in the shine of damp grass.
The night breathes an intangible dampness,
not in the center of the flying sphere,
and it ties up everything, corners or fragments,
till it forms an unbreakable web of night,
subtle and whole like fingers joined together
that scarcely let any water drip through
like a magic basket
swimming empty inside the river.
I wanted to separate my hands from the night,
but a great resonance that was not heard was heard
as if my whole body fell upon a silent

silenciosa en la esquina del templo.
La noche era un reloj, no para el tiempo
sino para la luz,
era un pulpo que era una piedra,
era una tela como una pizarra llena de ojos.
Yo quería rescatar la noche
aislando sus fragmentos,
que nada sabían de un cuerpo,
de una tuba de órgano
sino la sustancia que vuela
deconociendo los pestañeos de la luz.
Quería rescatar la respiración
y se alzaba en su soledad y esplendor
hasta formar el neuma universal
anterior a la aparición del hombre.
La suma respirante
que forma los grandes continentes
de la aurora que sonríe
con zancos infantiles.
Yo quería rescatar los fragmentos de la noche
y formaba una sustancia universal,
comencé entonces a sumergir
los dedos y los ojos en la noche,
le soltaba todas las amarras a la barcaza.
Era un combate sin término,
entre lo que yo le quería quitar a la noche
y lo que la noche me regalaba.
El sueño, con contornos de diamante,
detenía a la liebre
con orejas de trébol.
Momentáneamente tuve que abandonar la casa
para darle paso a la noche.
Qué brusquedad rompió esa continuidad,
entre la noche trazando el techo,
sosteniéndolo como entre dos nubes
que flotaban en la oscuridad sumergida.
En el comienzo que no anota los nombres,
la llegada de lo diferenciado con campanillas
de acero, con ojos
para la profundidad de las aguas
donde la noche reposaba.
Como en un incendio,
yo quería sacar los recuerdos de la noche,
el tintineo hacia dentro del golpe mate,
como cuando con la palma de la mano
golpeamos la masa de pan.
El sueño volvió a detener a la liebre
que arañaba mis brazos
con palillos de aguarrás.
Riéndose, repartía por mi rostro grandes cicatrices.

1960

seraphin in the temple corner.
Night was a watch, not for time
but for light,
it was an octopus that was a stone,
it was a web like a blackboard full of eyes.
I wanted to rescue the night,
isolating its fragments
that knew nothing of a body,
of an organ pipe,
but only that substance that might fly about
not recognizing the blinking light.
I wanted to rescue the breathing
and it rose in its loneliness and splendor
to form a universal pneuma
before man's first appearance.
The breathing summation
forming the great continents
of dawn that smiles
with childlike stilts.
I wanted to rescue the fragments of the night
and I formed a universal substance.
Then I started to dip
my fingers and eyes into the night,
I cut loose all the barge cables.
It was unending combat
between what I wanted to take from the night
and what the night was giving me.
A sleep, with diamond contours,
stopped the hare
with clover ears.
Momentarily I had to abandon my house
to let the night come through.
What roughness broke that continuity
amid the night tracing the roof,
holding it up as between two clouds
drifting in buried darkness.
In the beginning that ignores the names,
the arrival of distinctness by means of tiny steel
bells and eyes
for the depth of the waters
where night was resting.
Like a fire
I wanted to rescue the recollections of night,
the chiming within the checkmate
as when we pound bread dough
with the palm of our hand.
Sleep again stopped the hare
scratching my arms
with sticks of turpentine.
Laughing, it distributed great scars on my face.

trans. Willis Barnstone

Retrato de José Cemí [de la novela Paradiso]

No libró ningún combate, pues jadear
fue la costumbre establecida entre su hálito
y la brisa o la tempestad.
Su nombre es también Thelema Semí,
su voluntad puede buscar un cuerpo
en la sombra, la sombra de un árbol
y el árbol que está a la entrada del Infierno.
Fue fiel a Orfeo y a Proserpina.
Reverenció a sus amigos, a la melodía,
ya la que se oculta, o la que hace temblar
en el estío a las hojas.
El arte lo acompañó todos los días,
la naturaleza le regaló su calma y su fiebre.
Calmoso como la noche,
la fiebre le hizo agotar la sed
en ríos sumergidos,
pues él buscaba un río y no un camino.
Tiempo le fue dado para alcanzar la dicha,
pudo oirle a Pascal:
los ríos son caminos que andan.
Así todo lo que creyó en la fiebre,
lo comprendió después calmosamente.
Es en lo que cree, está donde conoce,
entre una columna de aire y la piedra del sacrificio.

1966

Portrait of José Cemí [from the novel Paradiso]

No combat did he unleash, as panting
was the custom set between his breath
and the breeze or tempest.
His name was also Thelema Semí,
his will can seek a body
in the shade, the shadow of a tree
and the tree that is at the gates of hell.
He was faithful to Orpheus and Proserpina.
He revered his friends, the melody,
both the one that is hidden and the one that shakes
the summer leaves.
Art went with him every day,
nature bestows her calm, her fever.
Calming as the night,
the fever made him quench his thirst
in sunken rivers,
for he sought a river, not a path.
Time to come to happiness was given him,
he could hear Pascal:
rivers are walking paths.
So that everything he believed in fever
he later understood in calm.
Within what he believes, he is where he knows,
between a column of air and the sacrificial stone.

trans. Gregory Rabassa

Enrique Molina

ARGENTINA
1910–

A poet as strongly influenced by Continental models (including Rilke, Breton, and Rimbaud, whom he translated) as by contemporary Latin American writers, Enrique Molina is the great Argentine poet of interiority. His poems explore an emotional terrain of desire and loss and compensation, celebrating the diversity of the physical world as it informs the diversity of the self.

Mientras corren los grandes días

Arde en las cosas un terror antiguo, un profundo y
    secreto soplo,
un ácido orgulloso y sombrío que llena las piedras de
    grandes agujeros,
y torna crueles las húmedas manzanas, los árboles que el
    sol consagró;
las lluvias entretejidas a los largos cabellos con salvajes
    perfumes y su blanda y ondeante música;

As the Great Days Flow

An ancient terror burns in things, a deep and secret sigh,
a proud, somber acid that fills the stones with giant holes
and drives the damp apples to cruelty, and the trees the
    sun made sacred;
the rains interwoven in the long hair with wild fragrances
    and their soft, undulating music;
the dress-up and vain objects, the tender, aching wood in
    the tense violins

los ropajes y los vanos objetos; la tierna madera dolorosa
    en los tensos violines
y honrada y sumisa en la paciente mesa, en el
    infausto ataúd,
a cuyo alrededor los ángeles impasibles y justos se reúnen
    a recoger su parte de muerte;
las frutas de yeso y la íntima lámpara donde el atardecer
    se condensa,
y los vestidos caen como un seco follaje a los pies de la
    mujer desnudándose,
abriéndose en quietos círculos en torno a sus tobillos
    como un espeso estanque
sobre el que la noche flamea y se ahonda, recogiendo ese
    cuerpo melodioso,
arrastrando las sombras tras los cristales y los sueños tras
    los semblantes dormidos;
en tanto, junto a la tibia habitación, el desolado viento
    plañe bajo las hojas de la hiedra.
¡Oh, Tiempo! ¡Oh, enredadera pálida! ¡Oh, sagrada fatiga
    de vivir...!
¡Oh, estéril lumbre que en mi carne luchas! Tus puras
    hebras trepan por mis huesos,
envolviendo mis vértebras tu espuma de suave ondular.
Y así, a través de los rostros apacibles, del invariable giro
    del Verano,
a través de los muebles inmóviles y mansos, de las
    canciones de alegre esplendor,
todo habla al absorto e indefenso testigo, a las postreras
    sombras trepadoras,
de su incierta partida, de las manos transformándose en la
    gramilla estival.
Entonces mi corazón lleno de idolatría se despierta
    temblando,
como el que sueña que la sombra entra en él y su adorable
    carne se licua
a un son lento y dulzón, poblado de flotantes animales y
    neblinas,
y pasa la yema de sus dedos por sus cejas, comprueba de
    nuevo sus labios y mira una vez más sus desiertas
    rodillas,
acariciando en torno sus riquezas, sin penetrar su secreto,
mientras corren los grandes días sobre la tierra inmutable.

1941

and chaste and docile on the patient table, in the
    hapless coffin,
with just, impassive angels circling round to gather in
    their share of death;
the plaster fruits and the intimate lamp where dusk
    condenses
and the garments drop like dead leaves around the feet of
    the woman undressing,
opening out in quiet circles about her ankles like a
    dense pool
with the night upon it flaming out and diving deep,
    drawing that melodious body to itself,
pulling the shadows along past the windowpanes and the
    dreams behind the sleeping faces,
while, close by the tepid room, the desolate wind laments
    beneath the ivy leaves.
Oh, Time! Oh, pallid vine! Oh, sacred weariness of
    living...!
Oh, sterile fire, how you struggle in my flesh! Your pure
    tendrils twine along my bones,
your gently undulating foam enclosing my spine.
And so, through the peaceful faces, the changeless turning
    of the Summer
through the still, meek furniture, the songs of joyful
    splendor,
everything speaks to the rapt, helpless witness, to the last
    creeping shadows,
of its unsure departure, of the hands turning into summer
    graze grass.
Then my heart, filled with idolatry, wakes up trembling,
as one who dreams that the shadow gets inside him and
    his adorable flesh melts down
to a slow, sweet song, crowded with floating animals
    and mists,
and runs his fingertips over his eyebrows, makes sure
    again of his lips and checks once more his deserted
    knees,
caressing his riches all around, not penetrating
    their secret,
as the great days flow across the changeless land.

trans. Naomi Lindstrom

Como debe de ser

Aquí está mi alma, con su extraña
insatisfacción, como los dientes del lobo:
la narradora de naturaleza cruel e insumisa
que nunca encuentra la palabra;

The Way It Must Be

Here is my soul, with its strange
dissatisfaction, like the teeth of the wolf:
the taleteller, cruel and unruly by nature,
who never finds the word;

y por allá se aleja un viejo tren, momentáneo y perdido,
como una luz en la lluvia, pero vuelve
a repetir su jadeo férreo y a llevarnos de nuevo
en el verde aire de los amores errantes.
Pues un tren no sólo moviliza sus hierros
sino sangre soñadora deslumbrada por el viaje,
rostros arena, rostros relámpagos, rostros que
    hacen música,
y puede crujir burlonamente también
cuando los demonios, en el salón comedor,
al cruzar por una pequeña estación de provincia
con un cerco de tunas y el mendigo predilecto de la Virgen,
sacaban la lengua y aplastaban su trasero desnudo contra
    el vidrio de la ventanilla.
Y nunca más vuelvas a despedirte de mí,
en medio de esta tierra cabeza abajo que se eriza en
    el aire frío.

1941

and over there an old train pulls out of sight, there a
    moment, gone,
like a light in the rain, but starts back
up with its iron panting and takes us once more
through the green air of errant loves.
For a train throws into motion not just its works
but the dreamy blood bedazzled by the journey,
sandfaces, flashfaces, faces that make music,
and also it can creak with mockery
when the demons, in the dining room,
passing through a little backwoods station
with a prickly pear hedge and the beggar most beloved
    of the Virgin,
stuck out their tongues and plastered their naked rumps
    against the windowpane.
And never tell me goodbye again,
amid this upside down land that pricks up in the cold air.

trans. Naomi Lindstrom

Pablo Antonio Cuadra

NICARAGUA
1912–

Pablo Antonio Cuadra is a poet of intense intimacy and verbal implication. His early poems of childhood, place, and familiarity with his landscape made him one of the leaders of the *vanguardia* renewal of Nicaraguan poetry after Rubén Darío. Cuadra carries his native place into his lyrics in ways that Darío adumbrated but did not often achieve. In this poetry of incarnate verbal place, Cuadra walks a delicate balance. Although thematically he represents a firm commitment to nationalism, he recognizes the dangers of a superficial national folklore; although he advocates a strong mistrust of international political and cultural imperialism, he has resisted overt identification with particular political parties in contemporary Nicaragua. His commitments are different from the iconoclastic political radicalism of Neruda and from the psychological experimentation of Vallejo, although Cuadra is sometimes compared with those writers. Cuadra's aesthetic derives from a deeply felt Christian humanism, which meditates on the suffering Christ as a common and democratizing image of Latin American reality.

El nacimiento del sol

He inventado mundos nuevos. He soñado
noches construidas con sustancias inefables.
He fabricado astros radiantes, estrellas sutiles
en la proximidad de unos ojos entrecerrados.
    Nunca, sin embargo,
repetiré aquel primer día cuando nuestros padres
salieron con sus tribus de la húmeda selva
y miraron al oriente. Escucharon el rugido

The Birth of the Sun

I have invented new worlds. I have dreamed
Nights built out of ineffable substances.
I have made burning stars, subtle lights
Next to half-closed eyes.

            Yet never
Can I recover that first day when our fathers
Emerged, with their tribes, from the humid jungle

del jaguar. El canto de los pájaros. Y vieron
levantarse un hombre cuya faz ardía.
Un mancebo de faz resplandeciente,
cuyas miradas luminosas secaban los pantanos.
Un joven alto y encendido cuyo rostro ardía.
Cuya faz iluminaba el mundo.

1959

And looked to the East. They listened to the roar
Of the jaguar, the song of birds; and they saw
Rise up a man with a burning face,
A youth with a resplendent face,
Whose looks, full of light, dried up the marshes,
A tall, burning youth whose face was aflame:
Whose face lit up the whole world!

trans. Thomas Merton

Caballos en el lago

Los caballos bajan al amanecer.

Entran al lago de oro y avanzan
—ola contra ola
el enarcado cuello y crines—
a la cegadora claridad.
Muchachos desnudos
bañan sus ancas
    y ellos yerguen
        ebrios de luz
su estampa antigua.
Escuchan
—la oreja atenta—
el sutil clarín de la mañana
y miran
el vasto campo de batalla.
Entonces sueñan—
    bullo
        la remota osadía—
se remontan
a los días heroicos
cuando el hierro
devolvía al sol sus lanzas
potros blancos
escuadrones de plata
y el grito
lejanísimo de los pájaros
y el viento.

Pero vuelven

    (Látigo
    es el tiempo)

Al golpe
enfilan hacia tierra
—bajan la frente—
y uncido
    al carro
        el sueño

Horses in the Lake

The horses go down at dawn.

They enter the golden lake and move on—
wave against wave
of arched necks and manes—
into the dazzling light.
Naked boys
bathe their haunches
    and they raise
        their antique figures,
drunk with light.
They listen,
ears attentive,
to the delicate bugle of morning,
and see
the vast battlefield.
Then they dream—
    a remote boldness
        breaks through—
soaring back
to the heroic days
when swords
returned the sun's thrusts,
white stallions
squadrons of silver
and distant cries
of birds
and wind.

But they return

    (Time
    is the whip)

With the lash
they file toward land,
heads bowed,
and yoked
    to the wagon
        the dream

queda
    atrás
        dormido
            el viento.

1977

remains
    behind;
        the wind's
           asleep.

trans. Grace Schulman and Ann McCarthy de Zavala

Manuscrito en una botella

Yo había mirado los cocoteros y los tamarindos
y los mangos
las velas blancas secándose al sol
el humo del desayuno sobre el cielo
del amanecer
y los peces saltando en la atarraya
y una muchacha vestida de rojo
que bajaba a la playa y subía con el cántaro
y pasaba detrás de la arboleda
y aparecía y desaparecía
y durante mucho tiempo
yo no podía navegar sin esa imagen
de la muchacha vestida de rojo
y los cocoteros y los tamarindos y los mangos
me parecía que sólo existían
porque ella existía
y las velas blancas sólo eran blancas
cuando ella se reclinaba
con su vestido rojo y el humo era celeste
y felices los peces y los reflejos de los peces
y durante mucho tiempo quise escribir un poema
sobre esa muchacha vestida de rojo
y no encontraba el modo de describir
aquella extraña cosa que me fascinaba
y cuando se lo contaba a mis amigos se reían
pero cuando navegaba y volvía
siempre pasaba por la isla de la muchacha de vestido rojo
hasta que un día entré en la bahía de su isla
y eché el ancla y salté a tierra
y ahora escribo estas líneas y las lanzo a las olas en
    una botella
porque ésta es mi historia
porque estoy mirando los cocoteros y los tamarindos
y los mangos
las velas blancas secándose al sol
y el humo del desayuno sobre el cielo
y pasa el tiempo
y esperamos y esperamos
y gruñimos
y no llega con las mazorcas
la muchacha vestida de rojo.

1977

Manuscript in a Bottle

I had seen coconut trees and tamarinds
and mangos
the white sails drying in the sun
the smoke of breakfast across the sky
at dawn
and fish jumping in the net
and a girl in red
who would go down to the shore and come up with a jug
and pass behind a grove
and appear and disappear
and for a long time
I could not sail without that image
of the girl in red
and the coconut trees and tamarinds and mangos
that seemed to live only
because she lived
and the white sails were white only
when she lay down
in her red dress and the smoke was blue
and the fish and the reflection of the fish
were happy
and for a long time I wanted to write a poem
about that girl in red
and couldn't find the way to describe
the strange thing that fascinated me
and when I told my friends they laughed
but when I sailed away and returned
I always passed the island of the girl in red
until one day I entered the bay of her island
and cast anchor and leaped to land
and now I write these lines and throw them into the
    waves in a bottle
because this is my story
because I am gazing at coconut trees and tamarinds
and mangos
the white sails drying in the sun
and the smoke of breakfast across the sky
and time passes
and we wait and wait
and we grunt
and she does not come with ears of corn
the girl in red.

trans. Grace Schulman and Ann McCarthy de Zavala

La estrella vespertina

Vimos las llamas levantar la noche
y ensangrentar las aguas como un sol ahogado.
—¡Es la isla de Inés!—gritaron los marinos
y tiré la red y puse mano al remo
hundiéndolo en las aguas rojas.
Gritos se alzaban de ribera a ribera
y aves despertadas de sus nidos
giraban como cenizas.
¡Ya era tarde! Como una Y griega
escarlata escrita sobre mi sueño
la vi desnuda correr
y hundirse entre las olas.

    Hablo de Inés.
Siempre hablo de Inés
cuando la triste y vesperal estrella
baja a las ondas
y su desnudo ardor baña en las aguas.

1977

The Evening Star

We saw the flames raise the night
and stain the waters with blood like a drowned sun.
—It's the island of Inés!—shouted the sailors
and I threw down the net and put my hands to the oars
plunging them into the red waters.
Cries rose up from shore to shore
and birds awakened from their nests,
circling like ashes.
It was too late! Like a scarlet Y
written on my dream
I saw her run
naked
and sink in the waves.

    I am speaking of Inés.
I always speak of Inés
when the sad evening star
goes down to the waves
and bathes its naked ardor in the waters.

trans. Grace Schulman and Ann McCarthy de Zavala

Julio Cortázar

ARGENTINA
1914 1984

Born in Brussels of Argentine parents, Julio Cortázar spent much of his childhood in Argentina. In the 1950s, under pressure from the Peronist regime, he moved permanently to Paris, where he maintained French citizenship and where he worked for many years as a translator for UNESCO. A committed Marxist, Cortázar took seriously the public responsibilities of an engaged intellectual; he was an outspoken cultural critic and a prominent member of international groups dedicated to social activism. Best known as a fiction writer and essayist, Cortázar worked extensively in the mode of "magic realism," in which a tonal structure of calm factuality encloses events of illogical causality, fairy-tale-like transformations, and psychological revelation.

Beside Gabriel García Márquez' *Cien años de soledad* (*One Hundred Years of Solitude*, 1967), Cortázar's novel *Rayuela* (*Hopscotch*, 1963) most famously exemplifies storytelling in the "magic realist" mode. Organized like a circular labyrinth, *Rayuela* dismantles and reassembles the linear structure of the traditional novel. Encompassing several sets of dualities (including doubled characters, two "Muse" figures, two loci of action, even two types of readers and reading encounters, lit by the flicker of textual presence and absence), the vertiginous "plot" of *Rayuela* comes to seem wholly congruent with its formal method. With such rangy cleverness, in his narratives and poems and prose poems Cortázar works this combination of dry tone, fabulous image, and formal experiment toward astute critiques of bourgeois life and of the metaphysic of traditional cause and effect that underpins it.

The following selections, from Cortázar's *Historias de cronopios y de famas* (*Stories of Cronopios and Famas*, 1962), continue a rich line of Latin American experimentation with hybrid forms, such as the prose poem, that can sustain the intensity and clarity of verse while borrowing momentum from the narrative. Following Cortázar's lead, other writers have worked this equation in other directions, infusing narratives with moments of lyrical intensity and even—like José Lezama Lima in his *Paradiso*—embedding poems within linear narratives.

Conducta de los espejos en la isla de Pascua

Cuando se pone un espejo al oeste de la isla de Pascua, atrasa. Cuando se pone un espejo al este de la isla de Pascua, adelanta. Con delicadas mediciones puede encontrarse el punto en que ese espejo estará en hora, pero el punto que sirve para ese espejo no es garantía de que sirva para otro, pues los espejos adolecen de distintos materiales y reaccionan según les da la real gana. Así Salomón Lemos, el antropólogo becado por la Fundación Guggenheim, se vio a sí mismo muerto de tifus al mirar su espejo de afeitarse, todo ello al este de la isla. Y al mismo tiempo un espejito que había olvidado al oeste de la isla de Pascua, reflejaba para nadie (estaba tirado entre las piedras) a Salomón Lemos de pantalón corto yendo a la escuela, después a Salomón Lemos desnudo en una bañadera, jabonado entusiastamente por su papá y su mamá, después a Salomón Lemos diciendo ajó para emoción de su tía Remeditos en una estancia del partido de Trenque Lauquen.

1962

Historia verídica

A un señor se le caen al suelo los anteojos, que hacen un ruido terrible al chocar con las baldosas. El señor se agacha afligidísimo porque los cristales de anteojos cuestan muy caro, pero descubre con asombro que por milagro no se le han roto.

Ahora este señor se siente profundamente agradecido, y comprende que lo ocurrido vale por una advertencia amistosa, de modo que se encamina a una casa de óptica y adquiere en seguida un estuche de cuero almohadillado doble protección, a fin de curarse en salud. Una hora más tarde se le cae el estuche, y al agacharse sin mayor inquietud descubre que los anteojos se han hecho polvo. A este señor le lleva un rato

The Behavior of Mirrors on Easter Island

When you set up a mirror on the western side of Easter Island, it runs backwards. When you set one up on the eastern side of the island, it runs forward. Delicate surveys may discover the point at which that mirror will run on time, but finding the point at which that mirror works correctly is no guarantee that that point will serve for any other, since mirrors are subject to the defects of the individual substances of which they are made and react the way they really and truly want to. So that Solomon Lemos, an anthropologist on fellowship from the Guggenheim Foundation, looking into the mirror to shave, saw himself dead of typhus—this was on the eastern side of the island. And at the same time a tiny mirror which he'd forgotten on the western side of Easter Island (it'd been dropped between some stones) reflected for no one Solomon Lemos in short pants on his way to school, then Solomon Lemos naked in a bathtub being enthusiastically soaped by his mummy and daddy, then Solomon Lemos going da-da-da, to the thrilled delight of his Aunt Remeditos on a cattle ranch in Trenque Lanquen county.

trans. Paul Blackburn

A Very Real Story

It happened that a gentleman dropped his glasses on the floor, which, when they hit the tiles, made a terrible noise. The gentleman stoops down to pick them up, very dejected, as the lenses are very expensive, but he discovers with astonishment that by some miracle he hasn't broken them.

Now this gentleman feels profoundly thankful and understands that what has happened amounts to a friendly warning, in such a way that he walks down to an optician's shop and immediately acquires a leather glasses case, padded and double-protected, an ounce of prevention is worth a pound of, etc. An hour later the

comprender que los designios de la Providencia son inescrutables, y que en realidad el milagro ha ocurrido ahora.

1962

case falls, and stooping down to recover it without any great anxiety, he discovers that the glasses are in smithereens. It takes this gentleman a while to understand that the designs of Providence are inscrutable, and that in reality the miracle has just now occurred.

trans. Paul Blackburn

Las líneas de la mano

De una carta tirada sobre la mesa sale una línea que corre por la plancha de pino y baja por una pata. Basta mirar bien para descubrir que la línea continúa por el piso de parqué, remonta el muro, entra en una lámina que reproduce un cuadro de Boucher, dibuja la espalda de una mujer reclinada en un diván, y por fin escapa de la habitación por el techo y desciende en la cadena del pararrayos hasta la calle. Ahí es difícil seguirla a causa del tránsito pero con atención se la verá subir por la rueda del autobús estacionado en la esquina y que lleva al puerto. Allí baja por la media de nilón cristal de la pasajera más rubia, entra en el territorio hostil de las aduanas, rampa y repta y zigzaguea hasta el muelle mayor, y allí (pero es difícil verla, sólo las ratas la siguen para trepar a bordo) sube al barco de turbinas sonoras, corre por las planchas de la cubierta de primera clase, salva con dificultad la escotilla mayor, y en una cabina donde un hombre triste bebe coñac y escucha la sirena de partida, remonta por la costura del pantalón, por el chaleco de punto, se desliza hasta el codo, y con un último esfuerzo se guarece en la palma de la mano derecha, que en ese instante empieza a cerrarse sobre la culata de una pistola.

1962

The Lines of the Hand

From a letter thrown on the table a line comes which runs across the pine plank and descends by one of the legs. Just watch, you see that the line continues across the parquet floor, climbs the wall and enters a reproduction of a Boucher painting, sketches the shoulder of a woman reclining on a divan, and finally gets out of the room via the roof and climbs down the chain of lightning rods to the street. Here it is difficult to follow it because of the transit system, but by close attention you can catch it climbing the wheel of a bus parked at the corner, which carries it as far as the docks. It gets off there down the seam on the shiny nylon stocking of the blondest passenger, enters the hostile territory of the customs sheds, leaps and squirms and zigzags its way to the largest dock, and there (but it's difficult to see, only the rats follow it to clamber aboard) it climbs onto the ship with the engines rumbling, crosses the planks of the first-class deck, clears the major hatch with difficulty, and in a cabin where an unhappy man is drinking cognac and hears the parting whistle, it climbs the trouser seam, across the knitted vest, slips back to the elbow, and with a final push finds shelter in the palm of the right hand, which is just beginning to close around the butt of a revolver.

trans. Paul Blackburn

Costumbres de los famas

Sucedió que un fama bailaba tregua y bailaba catala delante de un almacén lleno de cronopios y esperanzas. Las más irritadas eran las esperanzas porque buscan siempre que los famas no bailen tregua ni catala sino espera, que es el baile que conocen los cronopios y las esperanzas.

Los famas se sitúan a propósito delante de los almacenes, y esta vez el fama bailaba tregua y bailaba catala para molestar a las esperanzas. Una de las esperanzas dejó en el suelo su pez de flauta—pues las esperanzas, como el Rey del Mar, están siempre asistidas de peces de flauta—y salió a imprecar al fama, diciéndole así:

Normal Behavior of the Famas

It happened that a fama was dancing respite and dancing catalan in front of a shop filled with cronopios and esperanzas. The esperanzas were the most irritated. They are always trying to see to it that the famas dance hopeful, not respite or catalan, since hopeful is the dance the cronopios and esperanzas know best.

The famas deliberately, always, locate directly in front of the shops, and at this time the fama was dancing respite and dancing catalan just to annoy the esperanzas. One of the esperanzas laid his flute fish on the floor—esperanzas, like the King of the Sea, are always accompanied by flute

—Fama, no bailes tregua ni catala delante de este almacén.

El fama seguía bailando y se reía.

La esperanza llamó a otras esperanzas, y los cronopios formaron corro para ver lo que pasaría.

—Fama —dijeron las esperanzas—. No bailes tregua ni catala delante de este almacén.

Pero el fama bailaba y se reía, para menoscabar a las esperanzas.

Entonces las esperanzas se arrojaron sobre el fama y lo lastimaron. Lo dejaron caído al lado de un palenque, y el fama se quejaba, envuelto en su sangre y su tristeza.

Los cronopios vinieron furtivamente, esos objetos verdes y húmedos. Rodeaban al fama y lo compadecían, diciéndole así:

—Cronopio cronopio cronopio.

Y el fama comprendía, y su soledad era menos amarga.

1962

fishes—and went outside to curse at the fama, speaking to him like this:

—Fama, don't dance respite or catalan in front of this store.

The fama kept on dancing, and laughed.

The esperanza called out the other esperanzas, and the cronopios formed a circle around to see what would happen.

—Fama—said the esperanzas—don't dance respite or catalan either in front of this store.

But the fama kept on dancing and laughing to undermine the esperanzas.

Then the esperanzas hurled themselves upon the fama and wounded him. They left him lying beside a palisade, and the fama was lying there, lapped in his blood and gloom.

The cronopios, those wet green objects, came forward furtively and commiserated with him, speaking like this:

—Cronopio cronopio cronopio.

And the fama understood, and his solitude was less embittered.

trans. Paul Blackburn

Viajes

Cuando los famas salen de viaje, sus costumbres al pernoctar en una ciudad son las siguientes: Un fama va al hotel y averigua cautelosamente los precios, la calidad de las sábanas y el color de las alfombras. El segundo se traslada a la comisaría y labra un acta declarando los muebles e inmuebles de los tres, así como el inventario del contenido de sus valijas. El tercer fama va al hospital y copia las listas de los médicos de guardia y sus especialidades.

Terminadas estas diligencias, los viajeros se reúnen en la plaza mayor de la ciudad, se comunican sus observaciones, y entran en el café a beber un aperitivo. Pero antes se toman de las manos y danzan en ronda. Esta danza recibe el nombre de "Alegría de los famas".

Travel

When famas go on a trip, when they pass the night in a city, their procedure is the following: one fama goes to the hotel and prudently checks the prices, the quality of the sheets, and the color of the carpets. The second repairs to the commissariat of police and there fills out a record of the real and transferable property of all three of them, as well as an inventory of the contents of their valises. The third fama goes to the hospital and copies the lists of the doctors on emergency and their specialties.

After attending to these affairs diligently, the travelers join each other in the central plaza of the city, exchange observations, and go to a café to take an *apéritif.* But before they drink, they join hands and do a dance in a circle. This dance is known as "The Gayety of the Famas."

Cuando los cronopios van de viaje, encuentran los hoteles llenos, los trenes ya se han marchado, llueve a gritos, y los taxis no quieren llevarlos o les cobran precios altísimos. Los cronopios no se desaniman porque creen firmemente que estas cosas les ocurren a todos, y a la hora de dormir se dicen unos a otros: "La hermosa ciudad, la hermosísima ciudad". Y sueñan toda la noche que en la ciudad hay grandes fiestas y que ellos están invitados. Al otro día se levantan contentísimos, y así es como viajan los cronopios.

Las esperanzas, sedentarias, se dejan viajar por las cosas y los hombres, y son como las estatuas que hay que ir a ver porque ellas no se molestan.

1962

When cronopios go on a trip, they find that all the hotels are filled up, the trains have already left, it is raining buckets and taxis don't want to pick them up, either that or they charge them exorbitant prices. The cronopios are not disheartened because they believe firmly that these things happen to everyone. When they manage, finally, to find a bed and are ready to go to sleep, they say to one another, "What a beautiful city, what a very beautiful city!" And all night long they dream that huge parties are being given in the city and that they are invited. The next day they arise very contented, and that's how cronopios travel.

Esperanzas are sedentary. They let things and people slide by them. They're like statues one has to go visit. They never take the trouble.

trans. Paul Blackburn

Efraín Huerta

MEXICO
1914–1982

Efraín Huerta gave up a promising career as a lawyer, but his early legal training clearly influenced the logic and diction of his poems. Urbane, social, socioerotic, Huerta's poems bring a loose-jointed exuberance into Mexican poetry. Although he strips the Whitmanian line of its idealist philosophical underpinnings and insists on an antirhetorical lyricism, Huerta retains much of Whitman's rebellious nonconformity and vitality. Besides writing poems, for almost fifty years Huerta worked as a professional journalist and film critic.

Declaración de odio

Estar simplemente como delgada carne ya sin piel,
como huesos y aire cabalgando en el alba,
como un pequeño mustio tiempo
duradero entre penas y esperanzas perfectas.
Estar vilmente atado por absurdas cadenas
y escuchar con el viento los penetrantes gritos
que brotan del océano:
agonizantes pájaros cayendo en la cubierta
de los barcos oscuros y eternamente bellos,
o sobre largas playas ensordecidas, ciegas
de tanta fina espuma como miles de orquídeas.

Porque, ¡que alto mar, sucio y maravilloso!
Hay olas como árboles difuntos,

Declaration of Hate

To be simply like thin flesh without skin,
like bones and air mounting in the dawn,
like a small, withered time
lasting between perfect griefs and hopes.
To be vilely tied by absurd chains
and listen with the wind to the penetrating shouts
that gush from the ocean:
dying birds falling on the decks
of dark and eternally beautiful ships,
or onto long deafened beaches, blind
from such delicate foam like thousands of orchids.

Because, what a tall sea, dirty and marvelous!
There are waves like dead trees,

hay una rara calma y una fresca dulzura,
hay horas grises, blancas y amarillas.
Y es el cielo del mar, alto cielo con vida,
que nos entra en la sangre, dando luz y sustento
a lo que hubiera muerto en las traidoras calles,
en las habitaciones turbias de esta negra ciudad.
Esta ciudad de ceniza y tezontle cada día menos puro,
de acero, sangre y apagado sudor.

Amplia y dolorosa ciudad donde caben los perros,
la miseria y los homosexuales,
las prostitutas y la famosa melancolía de los poetas,
los rezos y las oraciones de los cristianos.
Sarcástica ciudad donde la cobardía y el cinismo son
      alimento diario
de los jovencitos alcahuetes de talles ondulantes,
de las mujeres asnas, de los hombres vacíos.

Ciudad negra o colérica o mansa o cruel,
o fastidiosa nada más: sencillamente tibia.
Pero valiente y vigorosa porque en sus calles viven
      los días rojos y azules
de cuando el pueblo se organiza en columnas,
los días y las noches de los militantes comunistas,
los días y las noches de las huelgas victoriosas,
los crudos días en que los desocupados adiestran su rencor
agazapados en los jardines o en los quicios dolientes.

¡Los días en la ciudad! Los días pesadísimos
como una cabeza cercenada con los ojos abiertos.
Estos días como frutas podridas.
Días enturbiados por salvajes mentiras.
Días incendiarios en que padecen las curiosas estatuas
y los monumentos son más estériles que nunca.

Larga, larga ciudad con sus albas como vírgenes hipócritas,
con sus minutos como niños desnudos,
con sus bochornosos actos de vieja díscola y aparatosa,
con sus callejuelas donde mueren extenuados, al fin,
los roncos emboscados y los asesinos de la alegría.

Ciudad tan complicada, hervidero de envidias,
criadero de virtudes deshechas al cabo de una hora,
páramo sofocante, nido blando en que somos
como palabra ardiente desoída,
superficie en que vamos como un tránsito oscuro,
desierto en que latimos y respiramos vicios,
ancho bosque regado por dolorosas y punzantes lágrimas,
lágrimas de desprecio, lágrimas insultantes.

there is a rare calm and a fresh sweetness,
there are grey hours, white and yellow.
And it is the sea sky, tall sky with life,
that enters in our blood, giving light and sustenance
to that which might have died in treacherous streets,
in the turbid rooms of this black city.
The city of ash and porous stone, each day less pure,
of steel, blood, and extinguished sweat.

Ample and sorrowful city with room for dogs,
misery and homosexuals,
prostitutes and the famous melancholy of poets
prayers and orations of Christians.
Sarcastic city where cowardice and cynicism are the
      daily bread
of young pimps with undulating waists,
of donkey women, of superficial men.

Black city or furious or mild or cruel,
of nothing more than vexing: simply lukewarm.
But valiant and vigorous because in its streets live red
      and blue days
when the people organize in columns,
the days and nights of the militant communists,
the days and nights of the victorious strikes,
the crude days in which the unemployed train their anger
crouched in the gardens or in the aching joints.

Days in the city! Laborious days
like an amputated head with open eyes.
These days like rotten fruits.
Days muddied by savage lies.
Inflammatory days in which the curious statues suffer
and the monuments are more sterile than ever.

Large, large city with its dawns like hypocritical virgins,
with its minutes like naked children,
with its shameful acts of an unruly and ostentatious
      old woman,
with its alleys where, in the end, stretched out,
the hoarse ambushers and the assassins of happiness die.

City so complicated, bubbling spring of envies,
breeding-ground of virtues undone in an hour's time,
suffocating wasteland, soft nest in which we are
like a burning word unheard,
surface we go over like a dark passage,
desert where we beat and breathe vices,
broad wood watered by painful and biting tears,
tears of disdain, insulting tears.

Te declaramos nuestro odio, magnífica ciudad.
A ti, a tus tristes y vulgarísimos burgueses,
a tus chicas de aire, caramelos y films americanos,
a tus juventudes ice cream rellenas de basura,
a tus desenfrenados maricones que devastan
las escuelas, la plaza Garibaldi,
la viva y venenosa calle de San Juan de Letrán.

Te declaramos nuestro odio perfeccionado a fuerza de
    sentirte cada día más inmensa,
cada hora más blanda, cada línea más brusca.
Y si te odiamos, linda, primorosa ciudad sin esqueleto,
no lo hacemos por chiste refinado, nunca por neurastenia,
sino por tu candor de virgen desvestida,
por tu mes de diciembre y tus pupilas secas,
por tu pequeña burguesía, por tus poetas publicistas,
¡por tus poetas, grandísima ciudad por ellos y su enfadosa
    categoría de descastados,
por sus flojas virtudes de ocho sonetos diarios,
por sus lamentos al crepúsculo y a la soledad interminable,
por sus retorcimientos histéricos de prometeos sin sexo
o estatuas del sollozo, por su ritmo de asnos en busca
    de una flauta.

Pero no es todo, soberana ciudad de lenta vida.
Hay por ahí escondidos, asustados, acaso masturbándose,
varias docenas de cobardes, niños de la teoría,
de la envidia y el caos, jóvenes del "sentido práctico de
    la vida",
ruines abandonados a sus propios orgasmos,
viles niños sin forma mascullando su tedio,
especulando en libros ajenos a lo nuestro.
¡A lo nuestro, ciudad lo que nos pertenece,
lo que vierte alegría y hace florecer júbilos,
risas, risas de gozo de unas bocas hambrientas,
hambrientas de trabajo,
de trabajo orgullo de ser al fin varones
en un mundo distinto.

Así hemos visto limpias decisiones que saltan
paralizando el ruido mediocre de las calles,
pudiendo caracteres, dando voces de alerta,
de esperanza y progreso.
Son rosas o geranios, claveles o palomas,
saludos de victoria y puños retadores.
Son las voces, los brazos y los pies decisivos,
y los rostros perfectos, y los ojos de fuego,
y la táctica en vilo de quienes hoy te odian
para amarte mañana cuando el alba sea alba
y no chorro de insultos, y no río de fatigas,
y no una puerta falsa para huir de rodillas.

1944

We declare to you our hate, magnificent city.
To you, to your sad and vulgar bourgeoisie,
to your girls of air, caramels, and American films,
to your ice cream black pudding youths of garbage,
to your licentious queers who devastate
the schools, the Garibaldi Plaza,
the living and venomous street of Saint John of Letrán,

We declare to you our hate perfected by force of feeling it
    each day more immense,
each hour softer, each line more brusque.
And if we hate you, beautiful, exquisite city without
    skeleton,
we do not do it for a refined joke, never for neurasthenia,
but rather for your candor of a disrobed virgin,
for your month of December and your dry pupils,
for your little bourgeoisie, for your publicist poets,
for your poets, grandest city! for them and for their
    annoying category of untouchables,
for their slack virtues of eight sonnets a day,
for their laments to the dawn and to interminable solitude,
for their hysterical twistings of sexless prometheuses
or statues of the sob, for their rhythm of asses in search
    of a flute.

But that is not all, sovereign city of slow life.
There are hidden over there, surprised, perhaps
    masturbating,
a few dozen cowards, children of theory,
of envy and chaos, youth of the "practical sense of life,"
ruins abandoned to their own orgasms,
vile children without form mumbling their tedium,
speculating about books foreign to our own.
To our own, city that which belongs to us!
What pours happiness and makes jubilations flower,
laughs, laughs of enjoyment from some hungry mouths,
hungry from work,
from proud work of being at last men
in a different world.

So we have seen clean decisions that leap,
paralyzing the mediocre noise of the streets,
upsetting characters, giving voices of alert,
of hope and progress.
They are roses or geraniums, carnations or doves,
greetings of victory and defiant fists.
They are the voices, the decisive arms and feet,
and the perfect faces, and the eyes of fire,
and the suspended tactics of those who today hate you
to love you tomorrow when the dawn may be dawn
and not a stream of insults, and not a river of fatigues,
and not a false door for kneeling flight.

trans. Todd Dampier

Los hombres del alba

Y después, aquí, en el oscuro seno del río más oscuro,
en lo más hondo y verde de la vieja ciudad,
estos hombres tatuados: ojos como diamantes,
bruscas bocas de odio más insomnio,
algunas rosas o azucenas en las manos
y una desesperante ráfaga de sudor.

Son los que tienen en vez de corazón
un perro enloquecido,
a una simple manzana luminosa,
o un frasco con saliva y alcohol,
o el murmullo de la una de la mañana,
o un corazón como cualquiera otro.

Son los hombres del alba.
Los bandidos con la barba crecida
y el bendito cinismo endurecido,
los asesinos cautelosos
con la ferocidad sobre los hombros,
los maricas con fiebre en las orejas
y en los blandos riñones,
los violadores,
los profesionales del desprecio,
los del aguardiente en las arterias,
los que gritan, aúllan, como lobos
con las patas heladas.
Los hombres más abandonados,
más locos, más valientes:
los más puros.

Ellos están caídos de sueño y esperanzas,
con los ojos en alto, la piel gris
y un eterno sollozo en la garganta.
Pero hablan. Al fin, la noche es una misma
siempre, y siempre fugitiva:
es un dulce tormento, un consuelo sencillo,
una negra sonrisa de alegría,
un modo diferente de conspirar,
una corriente tibia temerosa
de conocer la vida un poco envenenada.
Ellos hablan del día. Del día,
que no les pertenece, en que no se pertenecen,
en que son más esclavos: del día,
en que no hay más caminos
que un prolongado silencio
o una definitiva rebelión.

Pero yo sé que tienen miedo del alba.
Sé que aman la noche y sus lecciones escalofriantes.
Sé de la lluvia nocturna cayendo

The Men of Dawn

And afterwards, here, in the dark bosom of the
    darkest river,
in the deepest and greenest part of the old city,
these tattooed men: eyes like diamonds,
brusque mouths of hate plus insomnia,
some roses or white lilies in the hands
of an infuriating burst of sweat.

They are the ones that have in place of a heart
a maddened dog,
or a simple luminous apple,
or a flask with saliva and alcohol,
or the murmur of one in the morning,
or a heart like any other.

They are the men of the dawn,
The bandits with the grown-out beard
and the blessed hardened cynicism,
the crafty assassins
with ferocity over their shoulders,
the sissies with fever in their ears
and in their soft kidneys,
the rapists,
the professionals of disdain,
those with the brandy in their arteries,
those that shout, howl, like wolves
with frozen feet.
The most abandoned men,
the most insane, the most valiant:
the most pure.

They are fallen from dreams and hopes,
with their eyes high up, grey skin,
and an eternal sob in their throat.
But they talk. At last, the night is the same
always, and always fugitive:
it is a sweet torment, a simple consolation,
a black smile of happiness,
a different manner of conspiring,
a timid lukewarm current
of knowing life to be a little poisoned.
They talk about the day. About the day,
which doesn't belong to them, in which they don't belong,
in which they are more slaves: about the day,
in which there are no other paths
except a long prolonged silence
or a definitive rebellion.

But I know that they fear the dawn.
I know they love the night and its chilling lessons.

como sobre cadáveres.
Sé que ellos construyen con sus huesos
un sereno monumento a la angustia.
Ellos y yo sabemos estas cosas:
que la gemidora metralla nocturna,
después de alborotar brazos y muertes,
después de oficiar apasionadamente
como madre del miedo,
se resuelve en rumor,
en penetrante ruido,
en cosa helada y acariciante,
en poderoso árbol con espinas plateadas,
en reseca alambrada:
en alba. En alba
con eficacia de pecho desafiante.

Entonces un dolor desnudo y terso
aparece en el mundo.
Y los hombres son pedazos de alba,
son tigres en guardia,
son pájaros entre hebras de plata,
son escombros de voces.
Y el alba negrera se mete en todas partes:
en las raíces torturadas,
en las botellas estallantes de rabia,
en las orejas amoratadas,
en el húmedo desconsuelo de los asesinos,
en la boca de los niños dormidos.
Pero los hombres del alba se repiten
en forma clamorosa,
y ríen y mueren como guitarras pisoteadas,
con la cabeza limpia
y el corazón blindado.

1944

I know of the night rain falling
as if over cadavers.
I know they construct with their bones
a serene monument to anguish.
They and I know these things:
that the moaning nocturnal shrapnel,
after agitating arms and deaths,
after passionately officiating
like the mother of fear,
resolves into a murmur,
into a penetrating noise,
into a frozen and caressing thing,
into a powerful tree with silver thorns,
into a parched barbed-wire fence:
into dawn. Into dawn
with the effectiveness of a defiant breast.

Then a naked and terse pain
appears in the world.
And the men are pieces of dawn,
are tigers on guard,
are birds between threads of silver,
are rubble of voices.
And dawn, the slave trader, gets into everything:
into the tortured roots,
into the bottle bursting with anger,
into the purple ears,
into the humid distress of the assassins,
into the mouths of sleeping children.
But the men of the dawn recur
in clamorous form,
and laugh and die like trampled guitars,
with clean head
and armored heart.

trans. Todd Dampier

Este es un amor

Este es un amor que tuvo su origen
y en un principio no era sino un poco de miedo
y una ternura que no quería nacer y hacerse fruto.

Un amor bien nacido de ese amar de sus ojos,
un amor que tiene a su voz como ángel y bandera,
un amor que huele a aire y a nardos y a cuerpo húmedo,
un amor que ya no tenía remedio porque siempre hay
un amor que no tiene remedio, ni salvación,
ni vida ni muerte ni siquiera una pequeña agonía.

Este es un amor rodeado de jardines y de luces
y de la nieve de una mañana de febrero

This Is a Love

This is a love that began
and in a beginning was nothing but a little bit of fear
and a tenderness that didn't want to be born and bear fruit.

A love well born from that loving of her eyes,
a love that has her voice as angel and flag,
a love that smells of air and of nard and of moist body,
a love that has no remedy because it always is,
a love that has no remedy, nor salvation,
nor life nor death nor even a small agony.

This is a love encircled by gardens and by lights
and by the snow of a February morning

y del ansia que uno respira bajo el crepúsculo de San Ángel
y de todo lo que no se sabe, porque nunca se sabe
por qué llega el amor y luego las manos
—esas terribles manos delgadas como el pensamiento—
se entrelazan y un suave sudor de—otra vez—, miedo,
brilla como las perlas abandonadas
y sigue brillando aún cuando el beso, los besos,
los miles y millones de besos se parecen al fuego
y se parecen a la derrota y al triunfo
y a todo lo que parece poesía—y es poesía.
Esta es la historia de un amor con oscuros y tiernos
        orígenes:
vino como unas alas de paloma y la paloma no tenía ojos
y nosotros nos veíamos a lo largo de los ríos
y a lo ancho de los países
y las distancias eran como inmensos océanos
y tan breves como una sonrisa sin luz
y sin embargo ella me tendía la mano y yo tocaba su piel
        llena de gracia
y me sumergía en sus ojos en llamas
y me moría a su lado y respiraba como un árbol
        despedazado
y entonces me olvidaba de mi nombre
y del maldito nombre de las cosas y de las flores
y quería gritar y gritarle al oído que la amaba
y que yo ya no tenía corazón para amarla
sino tan sólo una inquietud del tamaño del cielo
y tan pequeña como la tierra que cabe en la palma de
        la mano.

Y yo veía que todo estaba en sus ojos—otra vez ese mar—,
ese mal, ese peligrosa bondad,
ese crimen, ese profundo espíritu que todo lo sabe
y que ya ha adivinado que estoy con el amor hasta los
        hombros,
hasta el alma y hasta los mustios labios.
Ya lo saben sus ojos y ya lo sabe el espléndido metal de sus
        muslos,
ya lo saben las fotografías y las calles
y ya lo saben las palabras—y las palabras y las calles y las
        fotografías
ya saben que lo saben y que ella y yo lo sabemos
y que hemos de morirnos toda la vida para no rompernos
        el alma
y no llorar de amor.

1956

and by the anxiousness that one breathes beneath the
        dawn of Saint Angel
and by everything that is not known, because it is never
        known
why love arrives and later the hands
—those terrible hands slim like thought—
intertwine and a soft perspiration of—again—, fear,
shines like abandoned pearls
and continues shining even when the kiss, the kisses,
the thousands and millions of kisses resemble fire
and resemble the downfall and the triumph
and everything that seems to be poetry—and it is poetry.
This is the story of a love with dark and tender origins:
wine like wings of a dove and the dove had no eyes
and we saw each other at the length of rivers
and at the breadth of countries
and the distances were like immense oceans
and so brief like a smile without light
and still she stretched out her hand to me and I touched
        her skin full of grace
and submerged myself in her eyes in flames
and died at her side and breathed like a shredded tree
and then I forgot my name
and forgot the cursed name of things and of flowers
and I wanted to shout and shout in her ear that I loved her
and that already I had no heart to love her
but just only a disquiet the size of the sky
and as small as the land that fits in the palm of the hand.

And I saw that everything was in her eyes—again that
        sea—,
that evil, that dangerous goodness,
that crime, that profound spirit that knows everything
and that had already divined that I am in love up to the
        shoulders,
up to the soul and up to the soft lips.
Her eyes already know it and the splendid metal of her
        muscles already knows it, the photographs and the
        streets already know it
and the words already know it—the words and the streets
        and the photographs
already know that they know it and that she and I know it
and that we have to die all our life so as not to break our
        soul
and not to cry of love.

trans. Todd Dampier

Nicanor Parra

Nicanor Parra's most influential contribution to Latin American poetics has been the theory of "antipoetry." Combining the critical materialism of Brecht with a resolutely colloquial diction, the absurdist fever of Kafka with ironic insights derived from contemporary psychology, Parra's "antipoems" speak personally but stringently, without the intervention of a "sincere" lyrical narrator. For all their critical antecedents, Parra's poems begin from his assumption that "the function of the artist consists in the rigorous expression of his experiences, without commentary of any kind."

Nicanor Parra was trained as a mathematician and physicist at Brown University and at Oxford, where he came to embrace principles of relativity in a physical mode, principles that carry over into the epistemological concerns of his poems. Later he was a professor of physics at the University of Santiago. In an important sense, his poems resemble mathematical theorems of physics: "economy of language, no metaphors, no literary figures." Parra's theories have sometimes been used to counter the dominance of the image-based personalism of Neruda. (Neruda, in fact, was instrumental in finding a publisher for Parra's *Poemas y antipoemas* [*Poems and Antipoems*, 1954]; in his *Extravagario* [1958], Neruda himself seems to imitate some of Parra's strategies.) Even more generally, however, Parra's example has served as an astringent against the florid rhetoric of several generations of Latin American and Spanish lyric poems. Parra's work represents a revolutionary mode of poetic authenticity. Austere, discursive, droll, mercurial, fragmentary, accessible, and conspicuously lacking in sentiment, Parra's "antipoems" have had a strong and liberating effect on poetics in Latin America and elsewhere. In his later years, Parra moved to a form of neo-Symbolism. Partly in response to the oppressive Pinochet regime, Parra devised a satirical character, the Christ of Elqui, whose skewed folk wisdom spoke obliquely but clearly against human rights abuses and against violations of ecological common sense.

Solo de piano

Ya que la vida del hombre no es sino una acción a
   distancia,
Un poco de espuma que brilla en el interior de un vaso;
Ya que los árboles no son sino muebles que se agitan:
No son sino sillas y mesas en movimiento perpetuo;
Ya que nosotros mismos no somos más que seres
(Como el dios mismo no es otra cosa que dios)
Ya que no hablamos para ser escuchados
Sino para que los demás hablen
Y el eco es anterior a las voces que lo producen;
Ya que ni siquiera tenemos el consuelo de un caos
En el jardín que bosteza y que se llena de aire,
Un rompecabezas que es preciso resolver antes de morir
Para poder resucitar después tranquilamente
Cuando se ha usado en exceso de la mujer;
Ya que también existe un cielo en el infierno,
Dejad que yo también haga algunas cosas:

Piano Solo

Since man's life is nothing but a bit of action at a distance,
A bit of foam shining inside a glass;
Since trees are nothing but moving trees;
Nothing but chairs and tables in perpetual motion;
Since we ourselves are nothing but beings
(As the godhead itself is nothing but God);
Now that we do not speak solely to be heard
But so that others may speak
And the echo precede the voice that produces it;
Since we do not even have the consolation of a chaos
In the garden that yawns and fills with air,
A puzzle that we must solve before our death
So that we may nonchalantly resuscitate later on
When we have led woman to excess;
Since there is also a heaven in hell,
Permit me to propose a few things:

Yo quiero hacer un ruido con los pies
Y quiero que mi alma encuentre su cuerpo.

1954

El Túnel

Pasé una época de mi juventud en casa de unas tías
A raíz de la muerte de un señor íntimamente ligado a ellas
Cuyo fantasma las molestaba sin piedad
Haciéndoles imposible la vida.

En el principio yo me mantuve sordo a sus telegramas
A sus epístolas concebidas en un lenguaje de otra época
Llenas de alusiones mitológicas
Y de nombres propios desconocidos para mí
Varios de ellos pertenecientes a sabios de la antigüedad
A filósofos medievales de menor cuantía
A simples vecinos de la localidad que ellas habitaban.

Abandonar de buenas a primeras la universidad
Romper con los encantos de la vida galante
Interrumpirlo todo
Con el objeto de satisfacer los caprichos de tres
      ancianas histéricas
Llenas de toda clase de problemas personales
Resultaba, para una persona de mi carácter,
Un porvenir poco halagador
Una idea descabellada.

Cuatro años viví en El Túnel, sin embargo,
En comunidad con aquellas temibles damas
Cuatro años de martirio constante
De la mañana a la noche.
Las horas de regocijo que pasé debajo de los árboles
Tornáronse pronto en semanas de hastío
En meses de angustia que yo trataba de disimular
      al máximo
Con el objeto de no despertar curiosidad en torno
      a mi persona,
Tornáronse en años de ruina y de miseria
¡En siglos de prisión vividos por mi alma
En el interior de una botella de mesa!

Mi concepción espiritualista del mundo
Me situó ante los hechos en un plano de franca
      inferioridad:
Yo lo veía todo a través de un prisma
En el fondo del cual las imágenes de mis tías se
      entrelazaban como hilos vivientes
Formando una especie de malla impenetrable
Que hería mi vista haciéndola cada vez más ineficaz.

I wish to make a noise with my feet
I want my soul to find its proper body.

trans. William Carlos Williams

The Tunnel

In my youth I lived for a time in the house of some aunts
Following the death of a gentleman with whom they had
      been intimately connected
Whose ghost tormented them without pity
Making life intolerable for them.

At the beginning I ignored their telegrams
And their letters composed in the language of another day,
Full of mythological allusions
And proper names that meant nothing to me
Some referring to sages of antiquity
Or minor medieval philosophers
Or merely to neighbors.

To give up the university just like that
And break off the joys of a life of pleasure,
To put a stop to it all
In order to placate the caprices of three hysterical
      old women
Riddled with every kind of personal difficulty,
This, to a person of my character, seemed
An uninspiring prospect,
A brainless idea.

Four years, just the same, I lived in The Tunnel
In the company of those frightening old ladies,
Four years of uninterrupted torture
Morning, noon, and night.
The delightful hours that I had spent under the trees
Were duly replaced by weeks of revulsion,
Months of anguish, which I did my best to disguise
For fear of attracting their curiosity.
They stretched into years of ruin and misery.
For centuries my soul was imprisoned
In a bottle of drinking water!

My spiritualist conception of the world
Made me feel utterly inferior when facing the facts:
I saw everything through a prism
In the depths of which the images of my aunts intertwined
      like living threads
Forming a sort of impenetrable chain mail
Which hurt my eyes, making them more and more
      useless.

Un joven de escasos recursos no se da cuenta de las cosas.
El vive en una campana de vidrio que se llama Arte
Que se llama Lujuria, que se llama Ciencia
Tratando de establecer contacto con un mundo de
     relaciones
Que sólo existen para él y para un pequeño grupo
     de amigos.

Bajo los efectos de una especie de vapor de agua
Que se filtraba por el piso de la habitación
Inundando la atmósfera hasta hacerlo todo invisible
Yo pasaba las noches ante mi mesa de trabajo
Absorbido en la práctica de la escritura automática.

Pero para qué profundizar en estas materias desagradables
Aquellas matronas se burlaron miserablemente de mí
Con sus falsas promesas, con sus extrañas fantasías
Con sus dolores sabiamente simulados
Lograron retenerme entre sus redes durante años
Obligándome tácitamente a trabajar para ellas
En faenas de agricultura
En compraventa de animales
Hasta que una noche, mirando por la cerradura
Me impuse que una de ellas
¡Mi tía paralítica!
Caminaba perfectamente sobre la punta de sus piernas
Y volví a la realidad con un sentimiento de los demonios.

                    1954

La víbora

Durante largos años estuve condenado a adorar a una
     mujer despreciable
Sacrificarme por ella, sufrir humillaciones y burlas
     sin cuento,
Trabajar día y noche para alimentarla y vestirla,
Llevar a cabo algunos delitos, cometer algunas faltas,
A la luz de la luna realizar pequeños robos,
Falsificaciones de documentos comprometedores,
So pena de caer en descrédito ante sus ojos fascinantes.
En horas de comprensión solíamos concurrir a los parques
Y retratarnos juntos manejando una lancha a motor,
O nos íbamos a un café danzante
Donde nos entregábamos a un baile desenfrenado
Que se prolongaba hasta altas horas de la madrugada.

Largos años viví prisionero del encanto de aquella mujer
Que solía presentarse a mi oficina completamente desnuda
Ejecutando las contorsiones más difíciles de imaginar
Con el propósito de incorporar mi pobre alma a su órbita
Y, sobre todo, para extorsionarme hasta el último centavo.

A young man of scanty means doesn't know what's
     going on
He lives in a bell jar called Art
Or Lust or Science
Trying to make contact with a world of relationships
That only exist for him and a small group of friends.

Under the influence of a sort of water vapor
That found its way through the floor of the room
Flooding the atmosphere till it blotted out everything
I spent the nights at my work table
Absorbed in practicing automatic writing.

But why rake deeper into this wretched affair?
Those old women made a complete fool of me
With their false promises, with their weird fantasies,
With their cleverly performed sufferings.
They managed to keep me enmeshed for years
Making me feel obliged to work for them:
Agricultural labors,
Purchase and sale of cattle,
Until one night, looking through the keyhole
I noticed that one of my aunts—
The cripple!—
Was getting about beautifully on the tips of her toes,
And I came to, knowing I'd been bewitched.

                    trans. W. S. Merwin

The Viper

For years I was doomed to worship a contemptible woman
Sacrifice myself for her, endure endless humiliations
     and sneers,
Work night and day to feed her and clothe her,
Perform several crimes, commit several misdemeanors,
Practice petty burglary by moonlight,
Forge compromising documents,
For fear of a scornful glance from her bewitching eyes.
During brief phases of understanding we used to meet
     in parks
And have ourselves photographed together driving
     a motorboat,
Or we would go to a nightclub
And fling ourselves into an orgy of dancing
That went on until well after dawn.

For years I was under the spell of that woman.
She used to appear in my office completely naked
And perform contortions that defy the imagination,
Simply to draw my poor soul into her orbit

Me prohibía estrictamente que me relacionase con
    mi familia.
Mis amigos eran separados de mí mediante libelos
    infamantes
Que la víbora hacía publicar en un diario de su propiedad.
Apasionada hasta el delirio no me daba un instante
    de tregua,
Exigiéndome perentoriamente que besara su boca
Y que contestase sin dilación sus necias preguntas
Varias de ellas referentes a la eternidad y a la vida futura
Temas que producían en mí un lamentable estado
    de ánimo,
Zumbidos de oídos, entrecortadas náuseas,
    desvanecimientos prematuros
Que ella sabía aprovechar con ese espíritu práctico que
    la caracterizaba
Para vestirse rápidamente sin pérdida de tiempo
Y abandonar mi departamento dejándome con un palmo
    de narices.

Esta situación se prolongó por más de cinco años.
Por temporadas vivíamos juntos en una pieza redonda
Que pagábamos a medias en un barrio de lujo cerca del
    cementerio.
(Algunas noches hubimos de interrumpir nuestra luna
    de miel
Para hacer frente a las ratas que se colaban por la ventana).
Llevaba la víbora un minucioso libro de cuentas
En el que anotaba hasta el más mínimo centavo que yo le
    pedía en préstamo;
No me permitía usar el cepillo de dientes que yo mismo le
    había regalado
Y me acusaba de haber arruinado su juventud:
Lanzando llamas por los ojos me emplazaba a comparecer
    ante el juez
Y pagarle dentro de un plazo prudente parte de la deuda
Pues ella necesitaba ese dinero para continuar sus estudios
Entonces hube de salir a la calle y vivir de la caridad
    pública,
Dormir en los bancos de las plazas,
Donde fuí encontrado muchas veces moribundo por
    la policía
Entre las primeras hojas del otoño.
Felizmente aquel estado de cosas no pasó más adelante,
Porque cierta vez en que yo me encontraba en una plaza
    también
Posando frente a una cámara fotográfica
Unas deliciosas manos femeninas me vendaron de pronto
    la vista
Mientras una voz amada para mí me preguntaba quién
    soy yo.

And above all to wring from me my last penny.
She absolutely forbade me to have anything to do with
    my family.
To get rid of my friends this viper made free with defama-
    tory libels
Which she published in a newspaper she owned.
Passionate to the point of delirium, she never let up for
    an instant,
Commanding me to kiss her on the mouth
And to reply at once to her silly questions
Concerning, among other things, eternity and the afterlife,
Subjects which upset me terribly,
Producing buzzing in my ears, recurrent nausea, sudden
    fainting spells
Which she turned to account with that practical turn of
    mind that distinguished her,
Putting her clothes on without wasting a moment
And clearing out of my apartment, leaving me flat.

This situation dragged on for five years and more.
There were periods when we lived together in a
    round room
In a plush district near the cemetery, sharing the rent.
(Some nights we had to interrupt our honeymoon
To cope with the rats that streamed in through the
    window.)
The viper kept a meticulous account book
In which she noted every penny I borrowed from her,
She would not let me use the toothbrush I had given
    her myself,
And she accused me of having ruined her youth:
With her eyes flashing fire she threatened to take me
    to court
And make me pay part of the debt within a reasonable
    period
Since she needed the money to go on with her studies.
Then I had to take to the street and live on public charity,
Sleeping on park benches
Where the police found me time and again, dying,
Among the first leaves of autumn.
Fortunately that state of affairs went no further,
For one time—and again I was in a park,
Posing for a photographer—
A pair of delicious feminine hands suddenly covered
    my eyes
While a voice that I loved asked me: Who am I.
You are my love, I answered serenely.
My angel! she said nervously.
Let me sit on your knees once again!
It was then that I was able to ponder the fact that she was
    now wearing brief tights.

Tú eres mi amor, respondí con serenidad.
¡Ángel mío, dijo ella nerviosamente,
Permite que me siente en tus rodillas una vez más!
Entonces pude percatarme de que ella se presentaba ahora
    provista de un pequeño taparrabos.
Fué un encuentro memorable, aunque lleno de notas
    discordantes:
Me he comprado una parcela, no lejos del matadero,
    exclamó,
Allí pienso construir una especie de pirámide
En la que podamos pasar los últimos días de nuestra vida.
Ya he terminado mis estudios, me he recibido de abogado,
Dispongo de un buen capital;
Dediquémonos a un negocio productivo, los dos, amor
    mío, agregó,
Lejos del mundo construyamos nuestro nido.
Basta de sandeces, repliqué, tus planes me inspiran
    desconfianza,
Piensa que de un momento a otro mi verdadera mujer
Puede dejarnos a todos en la miseria más espantosa.
Mis hijos han crecido ya, el tiempo ha transcurrido,
Me siento profundamente agotado, déjame reposar un
    instante,
Tráeme un poco de agua, mujer,
Consígueme algo de comer en alguna parte,
Estoy muerto de hambre,
No puedo trabajar más para ti,
Todo ha terminado entre nosotros

1954

It was a memorable meeting, though full of discordant
    notes.
I have bought a plot of land not far from the
    slaughterhouse, she exclaimed.
I plan to build a sort of pyramid there
Where we can spend the rest of our days.
I have finished my studies, I have been admitted to the bar,
I have a tidy bit of capital at my disposal;
Let's go into some lucrative business, we two, my love,
    she added,
Let's build our nest far from the world.
Enough of your foolishness, I answered, I have no
    confidence in your plans.
Bear in mind that my real wife
Can at any moment leave both of us in the most
    frightful poverty.
My children are grown up, time has elapsed,
I feel utterly exhausted, let me have a minute's rest,
Get me a little water, woman,
Get me something to eat from somewhere,
I'm starving,
I can't work for you any more,
It's all over between us.

trans. W. S. Merwin

Pido que se levante la sesión

Señoras y señores:
Yo voy a hacer una sola pregunta:
¿Somos hijos del sol o de la tierra?
Porque si somos tierra solamente
No veo para qué
continuamos filmando la película:
Pido que se levante la sesión.

1962

I Move the Meeting Be Adjourned

Ladies and gentlemen
I have only one question:
Are we children of the Sun or of the Earth?
Because if we are only Earth
I see no reason
To continue shooting this picture!
I move the meeting be adjourned.

trans. Allen Ginsberg

Momias

Una momia camina por la nieve
Otra momia camina por el hielo
Otra momia camina por la arena.

Una momia camina por el prado
Una segunda momia la acompaña.

Mummies

One mummy walks on snow
Another mummy walks on ice
Another mummy walks on sand.

A mummy walks through the meadow
A second mummy goes with her.

Una momia conversa por teléfono	One mummy talks on the phone
Otra momia se mira en un espejo.	Another mummy views herself in the mirror.
Una momia dispara su revólver.	One mummy fires her revolver.
Todas las momias cambian de lugar	All the mummies change places
Casi todas las momias se retiran.	Almost all the mummies withdraw.
Varias momias se sientan a la mesa	A few mummies sit down at the table
Unas momias ofrecen cigarrillos	Some mummies offer cigarettes
Una momia parece que bailara.	One mummy seems to be dancing.
Una momia más vieja que las otras	One mummy older than the others
Da de mamar a su niño de pecho.	Puts her baby to her breast.

1962   *trans. Thomas Merton*

La montaña rusa

Durante medio siglo
La poesía fue
El paraíso del tonto solemne.
Hasta que vine yo
Y me instalé con mí montaña rusa.

Suban, si les parece.
Claro que yo no respondo si bajan
Echando sangre por boca y narices.

Roller Coaster

For half a century
Poetry was the paradise
Of the solemn fool.
Until I came
And built my roller coaster.

Go up, if you feel like it.
I'm not responsible if you come down
Bleeding from your mouth and nose.

1962   *trans. Miller Williams*

El pequeño burgués

El que quiera llegar al paraíso
Del pequeño burgués tiene que andar
El camino del arte por el arte
Y tragar cantidades de saliva:
El noviciado es casi interminable.

Lista de lo que tiene que saber.

Anudarse con arte la corbata
Deslizar la tarjeta de visita
Sacudirse por lujo los zapatos
Consultar el espejo veneciano
Estudiarse de frente y de perfil
Ingerir una dosis de cognac
Distinguir una viola de un violín
Recibir en pijama a las visitas
Impedir la caída del cabello
Y tragar cantidades de saliva.

Litany of the Little Bourgeois

If you want to get to the heaven
Of the little bourgeois, you must go
By the road of Art for Art's sake
And swallow a lot of saliva:
The apprenticeship is almost interminable.

A list of what you must learn how to do:

Tie your necktie artistically
Slip your card to the right people
Polish shoes that are already shined
Consult the Venetian mirror
(Head-on and in profile)
Toss down a shot of brandy
Tell a viola from a violin
Receive guests in your pajamas
Keep your hair from falling
And swallow a lot of saliva.

Todo tiene que estar en sus archivos.	Best to have everything in your kit.
Si su mujer se entusiasma con otro	If the wife falls for somebody else
Le recomiendo los siguientes trucos:	We recommend the following:
Afeitarse con hojas de afeitar	Shave with razor blades
Admirar las bellezas naturales	Admire the Beauties of Nature
Hacer crujir un trozo de papel	Crumple a sheet of paper
Sostener una charla por teléfono	Have a long talk on the phone
Disparar con un rifle de salón	Shoot darts with a popgun
Arreglarse las uñas con los dientes	Clean your nails with your teeth
Y tragar cantidades de saliva.	And swallow a lot of saliva.
Si desea brillar en los salones	If he wants to shine at social gatherings
El pequeño burgués	The little bourgeois
Debe saber andar en cuatro pies	Must know how to walk on all fours
Estornudar y sonreír a un tiempo	How to smile and sneeze at the same time
Bailar un vals al borde del abismo	Waltz on the edge of the abyss
Endiosar a los órganos sexuales	Deify the organs of sex
Desnudarse delante del espejo	Undress in front of a mirror
Deshojar una rosa con un lápiz	Rape a rose with a pencil
Y tragar toneladas de saliva.	And swallow tons of saliva.
A todo esto cabe preguntarse	And after all that we might well ask:
¿Fue Jesucristo un pequeño burgués?	Was Jesus Christ a little bourgeois?
Como se ve, para poder llegar	As we have seen, if you want to reach
Al paraíso del pequeño burgués	The heaven of the little bourgeois,
Hay que ser un acróbata completo:	You must be an accomplished acrobat:
Para poder llegar al paraíso	To be able to get to heaven,
Hay que ser un acróbata completo:	You must be a wonderful acrobat.
¡Con razón el artista verdadero	And how right the authentic artist is
Se entretiene matando matapiojos!	To amuse himself killing bedbugs!
Para salir del círculo vicioso	To escape from the vicious circle
Recomiendan el acto gratuito:	We suggest the *acte gratuite:*
Aparecer y desaparecer	Appear and disappear
Caminar en estado cataléptico	Walk in a cataleptic trance
Bailar un vals en un montón de escombros	Waltz on a pile of debris
Acunar un anciano entre los brazos	Rock an old man in your arms
Sin despegar la vista de su vista	With your eyes fixed on his
Preguntarle la hora al moribundo	Ask a dying man what time it is
Escupir en el hueco de la mano	Spit in the palm of your hand
Presentarse de frac en los incendios	Go to fires in a morning coat
Arremeter con el cortejo fúnebre	Break into a funeral procession
Ir más allá del sexo femenino	Go beyond the female sex
Levantar esa losa funeraria	Lift the top from that tomb to see
Ver si cultivan árboles adentro	If they're growing trees in there
Y atravesar de una vereda a otra	And cross from one sidewalk to the other
Sin referencias ni al porqué ni al cuándo	Without regard for when or why
Por la sola virtud de la palabra	...For the sake of the word alone...
Con su bigote de galán de cine	...With his movie-star mustache...
A la velocidad del pensamiento.	...With the speed of thought...

1962   *trans. James Laughlin*

Octavio Paz

MEXICO

1914–

Essayist, poet, diplomat, and cultural historian, Octavio Paz is Mexico's foremost man of letters of the twentieth century. His most famous prose work, *El laberinto de la soledad* (*The Labyrinth of Solitude*, 1961), explored the complexities of the Mexican psyche. In its unique combination of Indian and European sensibilities, Paz contended, the Mexican consciousness resists both the linguistic hegemony of the Spanish language and the cultural "otherness" of the United States. At the same time, Paz' other essays and poems have explored more universal and international issues of contemporary life, especially questions of psychic alienation and integration.

Paz himself has rejected the dreamy lyricism of his earliest work, as in *Luna silvestre* (*Sylvan Moon*, 1933). Although his early poems were heavily influenced by Surrealism and by Asian philosophy, the history of Paz' poems is a track of restless formalism, ranging from tight imagistic perceptual moments, as in *A la orilla del mundo* (*On the Edge of the World*, 1942) and *La estación violenta* (*The Violent Season*, 1958), to the broader inclusiveness of poems based on Aztec models, to even more humanly universal techniques and themes, as in *Blanco* (*White*, 1967). In politics, Paz describes himself as a "disillusioned leftist." In the 1930s he fought on the side of the Spanish Republic. As a diplomat in the 1950s, he represented Mexico in several countries, including France, where he became friends with the Surrealists, especially Breton. Paz served also as ambassador to India, although he resigned that position in protest against the "Tlatelolco Massacre" (in which students were killed by government security forces, shortly before the opening of the 1968 Olympic Games in Mexico City). Since 1971 Paz has edited the influential magazine *Vuelta*.

The common thread that unites these various literary and social identities is Paz' enduring commitment to the complex communicability of metaphorical language. "Poetry makes things more transparent and clearer and teaches us to respect men and nature," Paz insists. A writer of interpenetrations—of solitude and solitarity, of clarity and allusiveness, of Mexican specificity and international applicability—Paz won the 1990 Nobel Prize in literature.

Misterio	*Mystery*
Relumbra el aire, relumbra,	Glittering of air, it glitters,
el mediodía relumbra,	noon glitters here
pero no veo al sol.	but I see no sun
Y de presencia en presencia	And from seeming to seeming
todo se me transparenta,	all is transparent,
pero no veo al sol.	but I see no sun.
Perdido en las transparencias	Lost in transparencies
voy de reflejo a fulgor,	I move from reflection to blaze
pero no veo al sol.	but I see no sun.
Y él en la luz se desnuda	The sun also is naked in the light
y a cada esplendor pregunta,	asking questions of every splendor,
pero no ve al sol.	but he sees no sun.

1944

trans. Muriel Rukeyser

Lago

Tout pour L'œil,
rien pour les oreilles!

CHARLES BAUDELAIRE

Entre montañas áridas
las aguas prisioneras
reposan, centellean,
como un cielo caído.

Un mitad violeta,
otra de plata, escama,
resplandor indolente,
soñoliento entre nácares.

Nada sino los montes
y la luz entre brumas;
agua y cielo reposan,
pecho a pecho, infinitos.

Como el dedo que roza
unos senos, un vientre,
estremece las aguas,
delgado, un soplo frío.

Vibra el silencio, vaho
de presentida música,
invisible al oído,
sólo para los ojos.

Sólo para los ojos
esta luz y estas aguas,
esta perla dormida
que apenas resplandece.

¡Todo para los ojos!
Y en los ojos un ritmo,
un color fugitivo,
la sombra de una forma,
un repentino viento
y un naufragio infinito.

1944

Himno entre ruinas

donde espumoso el mar siciliano...

GÓNGORA

Coronado de sí el día extiende sus plumas.
¡Alto grito amarillo,

Lake

All for the Eye,
nothing for the ears!

CHARLES BAUDELAIRE

Between arid mountains
the imprisoned waters
rest, sparkle,
like a fallen sky.

One half violet,
the other silver, a fish-scale,
a lazy glittering,
drowsing in mother-of-pearl.

Nothing but mountains
and the light in the mist;
water and sky rest,
breast to breast, infinite.

Like a finger brushing against
breasts, a belly,
a thin, cold breath
shivers the waters.

The silence vibrates, vapor
of presaged music,
invisible to the hearing,
only for the eyes.

Only for the eyes
this light and these waters,
this sleeping pearl
that barely gleams.

All for the eyes!
And in the eyes a rhythm,
a fugitive color,
the shadow of a form,
a sudden wind
and an infinite shipwreck.

trans. Rachel Benson

Hymn among the Ruins

Where foams the Sicilian Sea...

GÓNGORA

Self crowned the day displays its plumage.
A shout tall and yellow,

caliente surtidor en el centro de un cielo
imparcial y benéfico!
Las apariencias son hermosas en esta su verdad
    momentánea.
El mar trepa la costa,
se afianza entre las peñas, araña deslumbrante;
la herida cárdena del monte resplandece;
un puñado de cabras es un rebaño de piedras;
el sol pone su huevo de oro y se derrama sobre el mar.
Todo es dios.
¡Estatua rota,
columnas comidas por la luz,
ruinas vivas en un mundo de muertos en vida!

Cae la noche sobre Teotihuacán.
En lo alto de la pirámide los muchachos fuman marihuana,
suenan guitarras roncas.
¿Qué yerba, qué agua de vida ha de darnos la vida,
dónde desenterrar la palabra,
la proporción que rige al himno y al discurso,
al baile, a la ciudad y a la balanza?
El canto mexicano estalla en un carajo,
estrella de colores que se apaga,
piedra que nos cierra las puertas del contacto.
Sabe la tierra a tierra envejecida.

Los ojos ven, las manos tocan.
Bastan aquí unas cuantas cosas:
tuna, espinoso planeta coral,
higos encapuchados,
uvas con gusto a resurrección,
almejas, virginidades ariscas,
sal, queso, vino, pan solar.
Desde lo alto de su morenía una isleña me mira,
esbelta catedral vestida de luz.
Torres de sal, contra los pinos verdes de la orilla
surgen las velas blancas de las barcas.
La luz crea templos en el mar.

Nueva York, Londres, Moscú.
La sombra cubre al llano con su yedra fantasma,
con su vacilante vegetación de escalofrío,
su vello ralo, su tropel de ratas.
A trechos tirita un sol anémico.
Acodado en montes que ayer fueron ciudades, Polifemo bosteza.
Abajo, entre los hoyos, se arrastra un rebaño de hombres.
(Bípedos domésticos, su carne
—a pesar de recientes interdicciones religiosas—
es muy gustada por las clases ricas.
Hasta hace poco el vulgo los consideraba animales impuros.)

impartial and beneficent,
a hot geyser into the middle sky!
Appearances are beautiful in this their momentary truth.
The sea mounts the coast,
clings between the rocks, a dazzling spider;
the livid wound on the mountain glistens;
a handful of goats becomes a flock of stones;
the sun lays its gold egg upon the sea.
All is god.
A broken statue,
columns gnawed by the light,
ruins alive in a world of death in life!

Night falls on Teotihuacán.
On top of the pyramid the boys are smoking marijuana,
harsh guitars sound.
What weed, what living waters will give life to us,
where shall we unearth the word,
the relations that govern hymn and speech,
the dance, the city and the measuring scales?
The song of Mexico explodes in a curse,
a colored star that is extinguished
a stone that blocks our doors of contact.
Earth tastes of rotten earth.

Eyes see, hands touch.
Here a few things suffice:
prickly pear, coral and thorny planet,
the hooded figs,
grapes that taste of the resurrection,
clams, stubborn maidenheads,
salt, cheese, wine, the sun's bread.
An island girl looks on me from the height of her
    duskiness,
a slim cathedral clothed in light.
A tower of salt, against the green pines of the shore,
the white sails of the boats arise.
Light builds temples on the sea.

New York, London, Moscow.
Shadow covers the plain with its phantom ivy,
with its swaying and feverish vegetation,
its mousy fur, its rats swarm.
Now and then an anemic sun shivers.
Propping himself on mounts that yesterday were cities,
*   Polyphemus yawns.*
Below, among the pits, a herd of men dragging along.
(Domestic bipeds, their flesh—
despite recent religious prohibitions—
is much-loved by the wealthy classes.
Until lately people considered them unclean animals.)

Ver, tocar formas hermosas, diarias.
Zumba la luz, dardos y alas.
Huele a sangre la mancha de vino en el mantel.
Como el coral sus ramas en el agua
extiendo mis sentidos en la hora viva:
el instante se cumple en una concordancia amarilla,
¡oh mediodía, espiga henchida de minutos,
copa de eternidad!

Mis pensamientos se bifurcan, serpean, se enredan,
recomienzan,
y al fin se inmovilizan, ríos que no desembocan,
delta de sangre bajo un sol sin crepúsculo.
¿Y todo ha de parar en este chapoteo de aguas muertas?

¡Día, redondo día,
luminosa naranja de veinticuatro gajos,
todos atravesados por una misma y amarilla dulzura!
La inteligencia al fin encarna,
se reconcilian las dos mitades enemigas
y la conciencia-espejo se licúa,
vuelve a ser fuente, manantial de fábulas:
Hombre, árbol de imágenes,
palabras que son flores que son frutos que son actos.

Nápoles 1948

To see, to touch each day's lovely forms.
The light throbs, all darties and wings.
The wine-stain on the tablecloth smells of blood.
As the coral thrusts branches into the water
I stretch my senses to this living hour:
the moment fulfills itself in a yellow harmony.
Midday, ear of wheat heavy with minutes,
eternity's brimming cup.

My thoughts are split, meander, grow entangled,
start again,
and finally lose headway, endless rivers,
delta of blood beneath an unwinking sun.
And must everything end in this spatter of stagnant water?

Day, round day,
shining orange with four-and-twenty bars,
all one single yellow sweetness!
Mind embodies in forms,
the two hostile become one,
the conscience-mirror liquifies,
once more a fountain of legends:
man, tree of images,
words which are flowers become fruits which are deeds.

trans. William Carlos Williams

Piedra nativa

La luz devasta las alturas
Manadas de imperios en derrota
El ojo retrocede cercado de reflejos

Países vastos como el insomnio
Pedregales de hueso

Otoño sin confines
Alza la sed sus invisibles surtidores
Un último pirú predica en el desierto

Cierra los ojos y oye cantar la luz:
El mediodía anida en tu tímpano

Cierra los ojos y ábrelos:
No hay nadie ni siquiera tú mismo
Lo que no es piedra es luz

1955

Native Stone

Light is laying waste the heavens
Droves of dominions in stampede
The eye retreats surrounded by mirrors

Landscapes enormous as insomnia
Stony ground of bone

Limitless autumn
Thirst lifts its invisible fountains
One last peppertree preaches in the desert

Close your eyes and hear the song of the light:
Noon takes shelter in your inner ear

Close your eyes and open them:
There is nobody not even yourself
Whatever is not stone is light

trans. Muriel Rukeyser

Aquí

Mis pasos en esta calle
Resuenan
        En otra calle
Donde
        Oigo mis pasos
Pasar en esta calle
Donde

Sólo es real la niebla

1961

Here

My steps along this street
resound
        in another street
in which
        I hear my steps
passing along this street
in which

Only the mist is real

trans. Charles Tomlinson

Certeza

Si es real la luz blanca
De esta lámpara, real
La mano que escribe, ¿son reales
Los ojos que miran lo escrito?

De una palabra a la otra
Lo que digo se desvanece.
Yo sé que estoy vivo
Entre dos paréntesis.

1961

Certainty

If it is real the white
light from this lamp, real
the writing hand, are they
real, the eyes looking at what I write?

From one word to the other
what I say vanishes.
I know that I am alive
between two parentheses.

trans. Charles Tomlinson

Pueblo

Las piedras son tiempo
        El viento
Siglos de viento
        Los árboles son tiempo
Las gentes son piedra
        El viento
Vuelve sobre si mismo y se entierra
En el día de piedra

No hay agua pero brillan los ojos

1968

Village

The stones are time
        The wind
Centuries of wind
        The trees are time
The people are stone
        The wind
Turns upon itself and sinks
Into the stone day

There is no water here for all the lustre of its eyes

trans. Charles Tomlinson

La arboleda

A Père Gimferrer

Enorme y sólida
        pero oscilante,
golpeada por el viento
        pero encadenada,

The Grove

For Père Gimferrer

Enormous and solid
        but swaying,
beaten by the winds
        but chained

rumor de un millón de hojas
contra mi ventana.
                    Motín de árboles,
oleaje de sonidos verdinegros.
                         La arboleda,
quieta de pronto,
                    es un tejido de ramas y frondas.
Hay claros llameantes.
                    Caída en esas redes
se revuelve,
               respira
una materia violenta y resplandeciente,
un animal iracundo y rápido,
cuerpo de lumbre entre las hojas:
                         el día.

A la izquierda del macizo,
                    más idea que color,
poco cielo y muchas nubes,
                    el azuleo de una cuenca
rodeada de peñones en demolición,
                    arena precipitada
en el embudo de la arboleda.
                    En la región central
gruesas gotas de tinta
                    esparcidas
sobre un papel que el poniente inflama,
negro casi enteramente allá,
                    en el extremo sudeste,
donde se derrumba el horizonte.
                    La enramada,
vuelta cobre, relumbra.
                    Tres mirlos
atraviesan la hoguera y reaparecen,
                         ilesos,
en una zona vacía: ni luz ni sombra.
                    Nubes
en marcha hacia su disolución.

Encienden luces en las casas.
El cielo se acumula en la ventana.
                    El patio,
encerrado en sus cuatro muros,
                    se aísla más y más.
Así perfecciona su realidad.
                    El bote de basura,
la maceta sin planta,
               ya no son,
sobre el opaco cemento,
                    sino sacos de sombras.

to the soil,
                    murmur of millions of leaves
against the window:
                    the inextricable
mass
          woven dark green branches
and dazzling spaces.
                    Fallen
into these nets
                    there's a material
violent, resplendent,
                    an animal
wrathful and swift,
                    now immobile,
light that lights itself
                    to extinguish itself.
To the left, above the wall,
                    more idea than color,
the blue blue of a basin
                    edged round by large rocks,
crumbling,
          sand silently precipitated
into the funnel of the grove.
                    In the central
part
     thick drops of ink
                    spattered
on a sheet of paper inflamed by the west,
                    black
there, almost entirely,
                    in the far southeast,
where the horizon breaks down.
                    The grove
turns copper, shines.
               Three blackbirds
pass through the blaze and reappear,
                    unharmed,
in an emptiness: neither light nor shade.
                    Vegetation
on fire for its dissolution.
                    In the houses
lights are lit.
               In the window
the sky gathers.
               In its walls of tile
the patio
          grows more and more
secluded:
          it perfects
its reality.
          And now

Sobre sí mismo
                    el espacio
se cierra.
            Poco a poco se petrifican los nombres.

                    Cambridge, England, 28 julio 1970

on the opaque cement
                    nothing but
sackfuls of shadow
                    the trash-can,
the empty flower-pot.
                    Space closes
over itself:
            inhuman.
Little by little, the names petrify.

                    trans. Elizabeth Bishop with Octavio Paz

Viento, agua, piedra

                    A Roger Caillois

El agua horada la piedra,
el viento dispersa el agua,
la piedra detiene al viento.
Agua, viento, piedra.

El viento esculpe la piedra,
la piedra es copa del agua,
el agua escapa y es viento.
Piedra, viento, agua.

El viento en sus giros canta,
el agua al andar murmura,
la piedra inmóvil se calla.
Viento, agua, piedra.

Uno es otro y es ninguno:
entre sus nombres vacíos
pasan y se desvanecen
agua, piedra, viento.

                    1980

Wind and Water and Stone

                    for Roger Caillois

The water hollowed the stone,
the wind dispersed the water,
the stone stopped the wind.
Water and wind and stone.

The wind sculpted the stone,
the stone is a cup of water,
the water runs off and is wind.
Stone and wind and water.

The wind sings in its turnings,
the water murmurs as it goes,
the motionless stone is quiet.
Wind and water and stone.

One is the other, and is neither:
among their empty names
they pass and disappear,
water and stone and wind.

                    trans. Mark Strand

Entre lo que veo y digo...

                    A Roman Jakobson

I
Entre lo que veo y digo,
entre lo que digo y callo,
entre lo que callo y sueño,
entre lo que sueño y olvido,
la poesía.
            Se desliza
entre el sí y el no:
                    dice

Between What I See and What I Say...

                    for Roman Jakobson

I
Between what I see and what I say,
between what I say and what I keep silent,
between what I keep silent and what I dream,
between what I dream and what I forget:
poetry.
            It slips
between yes and no,
                    says

lo que callo,
   calla
lo que digo,
   sueña
lo que olvido.
    No es un decir:
es un hacer.
   Es un hacer
que es un decir.
    La poesía
se dice y se oye:
    es real.
Y apenas digo
   es real,
se disipa.
   ¿Así es más real?

2
Idea palpable,
   palabra
impalpable:
   la poesía
va y viene
   entre lo que es
y lo que no es.
   Teje reflejos
y los desteje.
   La poesía
siembra ojos en la página,
siembra palabras en los ojos.
Los ojos hablan,
   las palabras miran,
las miradas piensan.
   Oír
los pensamientos,
   ver
lo que decimos,
   tocar
el cuerpo de la idea.
   Los ojos
se cierran,
   las palabras se abren.

1980

what I keep silent,
   keeps silent
what I say,
   dreams
what I forget.
   It is not speech:
it is an act.
   It is an act
of speech.
   Poetry
speaks and listens:
   it is real.
And as soon as I say
   it is real,
it vanishes.
   Is it then more real?

2
Tangible idea,
   intangible
word:
   poetry
comes and goes
   between what is
and what is not.
   It weaves
and unweaves reflections.
   Poetry
scatters eyes on a page,
scatters words on our eyes.
Eyes speak,
   words look,
looks think.
   To hear
thoughts,
   see
what we say,
   touch
the body of an idea.
   Eyes close,
the words open.

trans. Eliot Weinberger

Entre irse y quedarse

Entre irse y quedarse duda el día,
enamorado de su transparencia.

La tarde circular es ya bahía:
en su quieto vaivén se mece el mundo.

Between Going and Staying

Between going and staying the day wavers,
in love with its own transparency.

The circular afternoon is now a bay
where the world in stillness rocks.

Todo es visible y todo es elusivo,
todo está cerca y todo es intocable.

Los papeles, el libro, el vaso, el lápiz
reposan a la sombra de sus nombres.

Latir del tiempo que en mi sien repite
la misma terca sílaba de sangre.

La luz hace del muro indiferente
un espectral teatro de reflejos.

En el centro de un ojo me descubro;
no me mira, me miro en su mirada.

Se disipa el instante. Sin moverme,
yo me quedo y me voy: soy una pausa.

                                        1980

All is visible and all elusive,
all is near and can't be touched.

Paper, book, pencil, glass,
rest in the shade of their names.

Time throbbing in my temples repeats
the same unchanging syllable of blood.

The light turns the indifferent wall
into a ghostly theater of reflections.

I find myself in the middle of an eye,
watching myself in its blank stare.

The moment scatters. Motionless,
I stay and go: I am a pause.

                                        trans. Eliot Weinberger

Árbol adentro

Creció en mi frente un árbol,
Creció hacia dentro.
Sus raíces son venas,
nervios sus ramas,
sus confusos follajes pensamientos.
Tus miradas lo encienden
y sus frutos de sombra
son naranjas de sangre,
son granadas de lumbre.
                    Amanece
en la noche del cuerpo.
Allá adentro, en mi frente,
el árbol habla.
                Acércate, ¿lo oyes?

                                        1987

A Tree Within

A tree grew inside my head.
A tree grew in.
Its roots are veins,
its branches nerves,
thoughts its tangled foliage.
Your glance sets it on fire,
and its fruits of shade
are blood oranges
and pomegranates of flame.
                    Day breaks
in the body's night.
There, within, inside my head,
the tree speaks.
                Come closer—can you hear it?

                                        trans. Eliot Weinberger

Julia de Burgos

PUERTO RICO
1917–1953

The eldest of seven children, Julia de Burgos was raised in rural Puerto Rico. She married early and, after a difficult divorce, left Puerto Rico to pursue a doctorate in Cuba. In her poems, however, she retained an affection for the landscape of her native Carolina region, the valley of the Loíza River southeast of San Juan, as a locus of innocence and relief, a pastoral alternative to social injustice, urban poverty, and the personal turmoil of her adult life. She died in New York City in 1953 and was buried in a pauper's anonymous grave; several years later her body was returned, with honors, to

Puerto Rico. In an appreciation of Burgos, Luis Lloréns Torres wrote: "No other poet of the Americas . . . can sustain that lyrical ecstasy, that emotional vibration, which ignite her poems. . . . Julia de Burgos is unique, because [at the same time] no other poet in the Americas can imitate the heights of her ideological flights." At the time of her death Burgos had published two major books of poems, *Poemas en veinte surcos* (*Poems in Twenty Furrows*, 1940) and *Canción de la verdad sencilla* (*Song of the Simple Truth*, 1940). Her sister Consuelo edited and published her posthumous collection *El mar y tú* (*The Sea and You*) in 1954.

A Julia de Burgos

Ya las gentes murmuran que yo soy tu enemiga
    porque dicen que en verso doy al mundo tu yo.

    Mienten, Julia de Burgos. Mienten, Julia de Burgos.
La que se alza en mis versos no es tu voz: es mi voz;
porque tú eres ropaje y la esencia soy yo;
y el más profundo abismo se tiende entre las dos.

    Tú eres fría muñeca de mentira social,
y yo, viril destello de la humana verdad.

    Tú, miel de cortesanas hipocresías; yo no;
que en todos mis poemas desnudo el corazón.

    Tú eres como tu mundo, egoísta; yo no;
que todo me lo juego a ser lo que soy yo.

    Tú eres sólo la grave señora señorona;
yo no; yo soy la vida, la fuerza, la mujer.

    Tú eres de tu marido, de tu amo; yo no;
yo de nadie, o de todos, porque a todos, a todos,
en mi limpio sentir y en mi pensar me doy.

    Tú te rizas el pelo y te pintas; yo no;
a mí me riza el viento; a mí me pinta el sol.

    Tú eres dama casera, resignada, sumisa,
atada a los prejuicios de los hombres; yo no;
que yo soy Rocinante corriendo desbocado
olfateando horizontes de justicia de Dios.

1938

To Julia de Burgos

The people are saying that I am your enemy,
    That in poetry I give you to the world.

    They lie, Julia de Burgos. They lie, Julia de Burgos.
The voice that rises in my verses is not your voice: it is
    my voice;
For you are the clothing and I am the essence;
Between us lies the deepest abyss.

    You are the bloodless doll of social lies
And I the virile spark of human truth;

    You are the honey of courtly hypocrisy; not I—
I bare my heart in all my poems.

    You, like your world, are selfish; not I—
I gamble everything to be what I am.

    You are only the serious lady, Señora. Doña Julia.
Not I. I am life. I am strength. I am woman.

    You belong to your husband, your master. Not I:
I belong to nobody or to all, for to all, to all
I give myself in my pure feelings and thoughts.

    You curl your hair and paint your face. Not I:
I am curled by the wind, painted by the sun.

You are the lady of the house, resigned, submissive,
Tied to the bigotry of men. Not I:
I am Rocinante, bolting free, wildly
Snuffling the horizons of the justice of God.

trans. Grace Schulman

Poema para mi muerte

    Ante un anhelo

Morir conmigo misma, abandonada y sola,
en la más densa roca de una isla desierta.

Poem to My Death

    Confronting a longing

To die with my very self, abandoned and alone,
On the densest rock of a deserted island.

En el instante un ansia suprema de claveles,	At that moment, a final yearning for carnations,
y en el paisaje un trágico horizonte de piedra.	On the landscape, a tragic horizon of stone.
Mis ojos todos llenos de sepulcros de astro,	My eyes filled with graves of stars,
y mi pasión, tendida, agotada, dispersa.	My passion spread out, exhausted, dispersed,
Mis dedos como niños, viendo perder la nube	My fingers like children watching a cloud fade,
y mi razón poblada de sábanas inmensas.	My reason mobbed with enormous sheets.
Mis pálidos afectos retornando al silencio	My pale affections returning to silence
—¡hasta el amor, hermano derretido en mi senda!—	—Even love, consumed brother in my path!—
Mi nombre destorciéndose, amarillo en las ramas,	My name untangling, yellow in the branches,
y mis manos, crispándose para darme a las yerbas.	And my hands, twitching to give me to the grass.
Incorporarme el último, el integral minuto,	To rise to the final, the whole minute,
y ofrecerme a los campos con limpieza de estrella,	And to offer myself to the fields,
doblar luego la hoja de mi carne sencilla,	Then to bend the leaf of my ordinary flesh
y bajar sin sonrisa, ni testigo a la inercia.	And fall unsmiling, without witness to inertia.
Que nadie me profane la muerte con sollozos,	Let nobody dishonor my death with sobs
ni me arropen por siempre con inocente tierra;	Or wrap me forever in plain earth
que en el libre momento me dejen libremente	For in a moment of freedom I may freely
disponer de la única libertad del planeta.	Demand the one liberty of this planet.
¡Con qué fiera alegría comenzarán mis huesos	With what mad joy will my bones begin
a buscar ventanitas por la carne morena	To seek airholes in my brown flesh
y yo, dándome, dándome feroz y libremente	And I, giving myself, giving myself fiercely and boldly
a la intemperie y sola rompiéndome cadenas!	To the elements: in solitude breaking my chains!
¿Quién podrá detenerme con ensueños inútiles	Who will detain me with useless dreams
cuando mi alma comience a cumplir su tarea,	When my soul begins to fulfill its task
haciendo de mis sueños un amasijo fértil	Making of my sleep a rich dough
para el frágil gusano que tocará a mi puerta?	For the frail worm that knocks at my door?
Cada vez más pequeña mi pequeñez rendida,	Smaller and smaller my worn-out humility
cada instante más grande y más simple la entrega;	At every instant greater and easier the surrender
mi pecho quizá ruede a iniciar un capullo,	Perhaps my chest will turn to begin a flower bud
acaso irán mis labios a nutrir azucenas.	Maybe my lips will feed lilies.
¿Cómo habré de llamarme cuando sólo me quede	What shall I be called when all that remains
recordarme, en la roca de una isla desierta?	Is my memory of myself on the rock of the deserted island?
Un clavel interpuesto entre el viento y mi sombra,	A carnation wedged between my shadow and the wind,
hijo mío y de la muerte, me llamarán poeta.	Death's child and mine: My name will be poet.

1961   *trans. Grace Schulman*

Violeta Parra

CHILE

1917–1967

Shortly after Violeta Parra's suicide, Pablo Neruda heard a recording by her on his car radio. In traffic, on the road to Santiago from his Isla Negra home, he wrote an elegy for her. That poem begins with the image of an "earthly violet" that ascends to the heavens—not alone, but accompanied by "la luz de torojil, / de oro ensortijado / de la cebolla frita" ("the light of the lemon-balm, / of braided gold, / of fried onions") while birds chirp and the Chillán volcanoes rumble. The force and range of Neruda's images, from filtered light to fried onions, suggests something about Parra's diverse and forceful, sometimes difficult, character: her elegance, her anger, her austerity, and yet her solidarity with ordinary people and the dynamics of working-class lives. Like Víctor Jara, Violeta Parra was a guiding force of the New Song movement in Chile. A collector and performer of Latin American folk music, Parra recognized the political power of such democratic forms. That music, with its symbolic power of resistance, has represented several popular movements against authoritarian regimes in Chile and other Latin American countries.

Sister of the poet Nicanor Parra and mother of the musicians Ángel and Isabel Parra, Violeta was a woman of complex talents as a musician, as a poet (in her posthumous 1967 collection *Décimas*), and as a sculptor and ceramicist. She is the only Latin American artist to have had a one-person exhibition at the Louvre. The breadth of Parra's influence and talent was largely recognized only after her death. In the following selection Joan Baez, who made the song famous to North American audiences, provides her (edited) performance version of Parra's trademark poem/song.

Gracias a la vida

Gracias a la vida que me ha dado tanto.
Me dió dos luceros, que cuando los abro
perfecto distingo lo negro del blanco,
y en el alto cielo su fondo estrellado
y en las multitudes al hombre que yo amo.

Gracias a la vida que me ha dado tanto.
Me ha dado el oído, que en todo su ancho
graba noche y día grillos y canarios;
martillos, turbinas, ladridos, chubascos,
y la voz tan tierna de mi bienamado.

Gracias a la vida que me ha dado tanto.
Me ha dado el sonido y el abecedario,
con él las palabras que pienso y declaro,
madre, amigo, hermano y luz alumbrando
la ruta del alma del que estoy amando.

Gracias a la vida que me ha dado tanto.
Me ha dado la marcha de mis pies cansados,
con ellos anduve ciudades y charcos,
playas y desiertos, montañas y llanos
y la casa tuya, tu calle y tu patio.

Gracias a la vida que me ha dado tanto.
Me dio el corazón que agita su marco
cuando miro el fruto del cerebro humano,
cuando miro al bueno tan lejos del malo,
cuando miro el fondo de tus ojos claros.

Here's to Life

Thanks to life that has given me so much
It has given me two eyes, when I open them
I can tell black and white clearly apart
The star-covered depths of the lofty sky
The man I love among all the crowd.

Thanks to life that has given me so much
It has given me sound and the alphabet
And with it the words I think and speak
Mother, friend, brother, and light that brightens
the way of the soul of the one I love.

Thanks to life that has given me so much
It has given me hearing that in all its breadth
Night and day records crickets and canaries
Hammers, turbines, barking, squalls
And the soft voice of my beloved.

Thanks to life that has given me so much
It has given me the step of my tired feet
With them I walked around cities and puddles
Beaches and deserts, mountains and plains
And your house, your street, and your courtyard.

Thanks to life that has given me so much
It has given me laughter and it has given me tears
So I can tell happiness from grief
The two things my song is made of
And the song of you all that is my own song.

Gracias a la vida que me ha dado tanto.
Me ha dado la risa y me ha dado el llanto,
así yo distingo dicha de quebranto,
los dos materiales que forman mi canto,
y el canto de ustedes que es el mismo canto
y el canto de todos que es me propio canto.

Thanks to life that has given me so much!

trans. Joan Baez and John Upton

1967

Gonzalo Rojas

CHILE

1917–

After an early affiliation with the Chilean Surrealist group Mandrágora, by the time of his first book, *La miseria del hombre* (*Human Poverty*, 1948), Rojas had located the concerns that have occupied him for much of the rest of his career. In a style of luminous tension that questions the grounds of poetic knowledge itself, Rojas explores the chief currents in his work: erotic love, the nature of time, the powers and limits of language.

Cama con espejos

Ese mandarín hizo de todo en esta cama con espejos,
    con dos espejos:
hizo el amor, tuvo la arrogancia
de creerse inmortal, y tendido aquí miró su rostro por
    los pies,
y el espejo de abajo le devolvió el rostro de lo visible;
así desarrolló una tesis entre dos luces: el de arriba
contra el de abajo, y acostado casi en el aire
llegó a la construcción de su gran vuelo de madera.

La estridencia de los días y el polvo seco del funcionario
no pudieron nada contra el encanto portentoso:
ideogramas carnales, mariposas de alambre distinto,
    fueron muchas y muchas
las hijas del cielo consumidas entre las llamas
de aquestos dos epejos lascivos y sonámbulos
dispuestos en lo íntimo de dos metros, cerrados el uno
    contra el otro:
el uno para que el otro le diga al otro que el Uno es
    el Principio.
Ni el yinn ni el yang, ni la alternancia del esperma y de la
    respiración
lo sacaron de esta liturgia, las escenas eran veloces
en la inmovilidad del paroxismo: negro el navío navegaba
lúcidamente en sus aceites y el velamen de sus barnices,
y una corriente de aire de ángeles iba de lo Alto a
    lo Hondo

Bed with Mirrors

That mandarin did it all on this bed with mirrors,
    two mirrors:
he made love, he had the arrogance
to believe himself immortal, and lying here he watched
    his face between his feet
and the bottom mirror gave him back the face of
    the visible;
thus he developed a thesis between two half-lights:
    the upper
against the lower, and reclining almost in the air
he came to build his great wooden flight.

The shrillness of the days and the dry dust of
    the functionary
were no match for the portentous spell:
ideograms of flesh, butterflies of different wires,
    many and many
were the daughters of heaven consumed in the flames
of these two lewd sleepwalking mirrors
disposed in the intimacy of two meters, closed one upon
    the other:
the one so that the other might tell the other that the One
    is the Beginning.
Neither the yin nor the yang nor sperm alternating
    with breath
took him from this liturgy, swift were the scenes
in the stillness of the paroxysm: shining the black
    ship sailed

sin reparar en que lo Hondo era lo Alto para el seso
del mandarín. Ni el yinn ni el yang, y esto se pierde en
  el Origen.

1977

in its oils and the canvas of its varnishes,
and a current of the air of angels went from the Height
    to the Depths
without noticing that the Depths were the Height for
    the brain
of the mandarin. Neither the yin nor the yang, and this
    gets lost in the Origin.

trans. Christopher Maurer

Versículos

A esto vino al mundo el hombre, a combatir
la serpiente que avanza en el silbido
de las cosas, entre el fulgor
y el frenesí, como un polvo centelleante, a besar
por dentro el hueso de la locura, a poner
amor y más amor en la sábana
del huracán, a escribir en la cópula
el relámpago de seguir siendo, a jugar
este juego de respirar en el peligro.

A esto vino al mundo el hombre, a esto la mujer
de su costilla: a usar este traje con usura,
esta piel de lujuria, a comer este fulgor de fragancia
cortos días que caben adentro de unas décadas
en la nebulosa de los milenios, a ponerse
a cada instante la máscara, a inscribirse en el número de
    los justos
de acuerdo con las leyes de la historia o del arca
de la salvación: a este vino el hombre.

Hasta que es cortado y arrojado a esto vino, hasta que lo
    desovan
como a un pescado con el cuchillo, hasta
que el desnacido sin estallar regresa a su átomo
con la humildad de la piedra,
                              cae entonces,
sigue cayendo nueve meses, sube
ahora de golpe, pasa desde la oruga
de la vejez a otra mariposa
distinta.

1977

Chapter and Verse

It was for this that man came into the world, to fight
the serpent that advances in the whistle
of things, in the glow
and the frenzy, like a glittering dust, to kiss
the bone of madness from within, to put
more and more love on the sheet
of the hurricane, to write on his love act
the lightning of continued being, to play
this game of breathing in danger.

It was for this that man came into the world, for this
    the woman
from his rib; to pay the interest on this suit,
this skin of lust, to eat this glowing perfume
for short days that fit inside a few decades
in the nebula of the millennia, to put on
the mask again and again, to inscribe himself among
    the just
in keeping with the laws of history or the ark
of salvation: for this, man came.

Till he is cut and thrown away, he came for this, till they
    clean him
with the knife like a fish, till
he is un-born and without bursting returns to his atom
humble as stone,
                        then he falls,
keeps falling for nine months, rises
suddenly, passing from the worm
of old age into another butterfly,
a different one.

trans. Christopher Maurer

Y nacer es aquí una fiesta innombrable

A José Lezama Lima (1910–1976)

Respiras por palabras diez mil veces al día,
juras por el amor y la hermosura

And to Be Born Is Here an Unnameable Feast

To José Lezama Lima (1910–1976)

You breathe by words ten thousand times a day,
you swear by love and loveliness

y diez mil veces purificas tus pulmones	and purify your lungs ten thousand times
mordiendo el soplo de la ráfaga extranjera,	biting the gust of the foreign wind,
pero todo es en vano, la muerte, el paladar,	but it is all in vain: death, the palate,
el pájaro verbal que vuela de tu lengua.	the verbal bird that flies from your tongue.

1979   *trans. Christopher Maurer*

Mario Benedetti

URUGUAY

1920–

Mario Benedetti is the most famous and perhaps the most representative writer of Uruguay in the twentieth century. He has worked in virtually every literary genre, including the novella, the novel, the essay, the poem, and the drama. Benedetti's early work embodied an elegant, and implicitly elitist, aesthetic. Until well into his forties Benedetti worked as an accountant in an office; the deliberately bureaucratic, banal, and jargonistic idiom of his famous *Poemas de la oficina* (*Office Poems*, 1956) reflect much of that experience, in works that treat the quotidian experience of middle-class professionals with irony and compassion.

With the publication of his short stories in *Montevideanos* (*Montevideans*, 1959), arguably his best work, Benedetti emerged as a strong voice of social conscience, analyzing the alienated but complacent soul of his contemporary bourgeois society. Benedetti's later poems, collected in *Inventario* (*Inventory*, 1970), are often meditations in the stately lyrical voice of a wise and self-aware individual speaker. In their proselike idioms, however, they address broad social realities. Benedetti has been active in international literary politics, serving often on the boards of literary prizes offered by the Casa de las Américas in Havana, for example. He has also been a bravely outspoken critic of military regimes in Uruguay and Argentina.

Con permiso

Está prohibido escribir sobre cierta violencia
así que voy a hablar de la violencia permitida

el violento autorizado asiste comprensivo y curioso
     a tus cartas de amor acaricia contigo los muslos
     de tu novia escucha tus murmullos tus
     desfallecimientos
duro e infeliz se introduce doméstico en tu casa
pobre gendarme de repente promovido al horror
manoseador de secretos y mayólicas
a veces ladroncito sin vocación ni melancolía
recién llegado al crimen nuevo rico del miedo

el violento autorizado ve con preocupación el camello
     que pasa por el ojo de la aguja
y ordena un silencio sin fisuras para poder vociferarte
     en el oído su higiénico entusiasmo por
     la libertad

With Your Permission

It is forbidden to write about a certain class of violence
so I will speak only of that violence which is permissible

authorized violence is present comprehensive and curious
     in your love letters caresses with you the thighs of
     your sweetheart listens to your whispers your
     expirations
crude and wretched he insinuates himself tamely into
     your house
poor gendarme promoted suddenly to horror
handler of secrets and majolica
at times a minor thief without vocation or melancholy
a parvenu to crime and nouveau riche with fear

authorized violence watches with deep concern the camel
     passing through the eye of a needle
and ordains an imperforate silence so he can vociferate
     in your ear his hygienic enthusiasm
     for liberty

deja el corazón en el hogar junto a los nenes o en
    el apartamento de su hembrita tercera a fin de
    no comprometerlo cuando ultima a los heridos
    de ojos abiertos

el violento autorizado poro a poro te odia pero sobre
    todo se aborrece a sí mismo y como todavía no
    puede reconocerlo sabe que en el espejo ha de
    encontrar puntual su arcada indivisible su
    minifundio de vergüenza

tortura así con la boca seca malbaratando de ese
    modo sus insomnios sus poblados y resecos
    insomnios y sabiendo muy en el fondo que todo
    es una gran postergación inútil porque la
    historia no es impaciente pero mantiene sus ficheros
    al día

el violento autorizado tiene una descomunal tijera
    para cortar las orejas de la verdad pero despúes
    no sabe que hacer con ellas
no entiende de símbolos y lo bien que hace porque
    todo las calles las ventanas los ojos las paredes
    el cielo los puños los dientes son mercados de
    símbolos son ferias donde el futuro se ofrece
    como pichincha inesperada

el violento autorizado se mete en sus metales en sus
    fortalezas semovientes en su noche expugnable
    pero como deja un huequito para respirar por
    ahí se cuela no la bala perdida sino el guijarro
tiene miedo y lo bien que hace

el violento autorizado posee una formidable computadora
    electrónica capaz de informarle qué
    violencia es buena y qué violencia es mala y por
    eso prohibe nombrar la violencia execrable

la computadora por ejemplo advirtió que este poema
    trataba de la violencia buena.

1967

he leaves his heart at home with the kids or in the
    apartment of his third mistress so it will not be
    compromised when he goes out to finish off his
    wide-eyed victims

authorized violence hates your every pore but above all
    loathes himself and as he still cannot confess this
    knows that in the mirror he will find punctilious his
    chronic retching his minifundio of shame
so he torments with his mouth parched squandering
    insomnias desiccated well-populated insomnias
    knowing deep inside it is all a great futile
    postponement because history is not impatient but
    does keep its files up to date

authorized violence owns an extraordinary pair of
    scissors for cutting off the ears of truth but after he
    has no idea what to do with them
he cannot understand symbols and good for him because
    everything the streets windows eyes walls sky fists
    teeth are marketplaces of symbols fairs where the
    future is offered like an unexpected bargain

authorized violence plunges deep into his self-moving
    laminated strongholds expugnable nights but leaves a
    little chink for breathing through which not a stray
    bullet but a small boulder can pass
he is afraid and good for him

authorized violence has a formidable electronic computer
    to inform him which violence is good and which
    violence is bad so that way he can prohibit
    the mentioning of execrable violence

the computer reported for example that this poem
    was about good violence.

trans. David Arthur McMurray

Todos conspiramos

A Raúl Sendic

Estarás como siempre en alguna frontera
jugándote en tu sueño lindo y desvencijado
recordando los charcos y el confort todo junto
tan desconfiado pero nunca incrédulo
nunca más que inocente nunca menos
esa estéril frontera con aduanas
y pelmas y galones y también esta otra
que separa pretérito y futuro

We All Conspire

For Raúl Sendic

You will always be at some border
taking risks in your lovely ragged dream
remembering still waters and comfort at the same time
so mistrustful but never incredulous
never more than innocent never less
that sterile border with its customs
and sluggards and gold braiding and also this other one
that separates past from future

qué bueno que respires que conspires
dicen que madrugaste demasiado
que en plena siesta cívica gritaste
pero tal vez nuestra verdad sea otra
por ejemplo que todos dormimos hasta tarde
hasta golpe hasta crisis hasta hambre
hasta mugre hasta sed hasta vergüenza
por ejemplo que estás sólo o con pocos
que estás contigo mismo y es bastante
porque contigo están los pocos muchos
que siempre fueron pueblo y no lo saben
qué bueno que respires que conspires
en esta noche de podrida calma
bajo esta luna de molicie y asco
quizá en el fondo todos conspiramos
sencillamente das la señal de fervor
la bandera decente con el asta de caña
pero en el fondo todos conspiramos
y no sólo los viejos que no tienen
con qué pintar murales de protesta
conspiran el cesante y el mendigo
y el deudor y los pobres adulones
cuyo incienso no rinde como hace cinco años
la verdad es que todos conspiramos
pero no sólo los que te imaginas
conspiran claro está que sin saberlo
los jerarcas los ciegos poderosos
los dueños de tu tierra y de sus uñas
conspiran qué relajo los peores
a tu favor que es el favor del tiempo
aunque crean que su ira es la única
o que han descubierto su filón y su pólvora
conspiran las pitucas los ministros
los generales bien encuadernados
los venales los flojos los inermes
los crápulas los nenes de mamá
y las mamás que adquieren su morfina
a un abusivo precio inflacionario
todos—quiéranlo o no—van conspirando
incluso el viento que te da en la nuca
y sopla en el sentido de la historia
para que esto se rompa se termine
de romper lo que está resquebrajado
todos conspiran para que al fin logres
y esto es lo bueno que quería decirte
dejar atrás la cándida frontera
y te instales por fin en tus visiones
nunca más que inocente nunca menos
en tu futuro—ahora en ese sueño—
desvencijado y lindo como pocos.

1967

how great that you breathe that you conspire
they say that you rose too early
that you shouted in the middle of the public siesta
but maybe our truth is another one
for instance that we all sleep until too late
until blow until crisis until hunger
until filth until thirst until shame
for instance that you are alone or with a few
that you are with yourself and that is enough
because with you are the many few
that have always been *pueblo* and don't know it
how great that you breathe that you conspire
in this night of putrid calm
under this moon of languidity and loathing
maybe in the end we all conspire
you simply give the signal of fervor
the decent flag with its pole of cane
but in the end we all conspire
not just the old men who have nothing
with which to write graffiti
the dismissed and the beggar
and the indebted and the poor sycophants
whose incense doesn't yield as it did five years ago
the truth is that we all conspire
but not only those you imagine
the old guard the blindly powerful
of course without knowing it
the owners of your lands and their claws
how sick even the worst
for your own good which is the good of time
even though they believe that their anger is unique
or have discovered their motherlode and their own
    explosives
the swanky women the ministers of state
the well-bound generals
the mercenaries the timid the defenseless
the debauched the mama's-boys
and the mommies who buy their morphine
at the exploitive and inflated price
all—wanting to or not—conspiring
including the wind that hits at the back of the neck
and blows in the direction of history
so that this breaks this ends up
breaking what is cracked
all conspire so that in the end you attain
and this is the great thing I wanted to tell you
leave behind the simple border
and finally settle in your visions
never more than innocent never less
in your future—now in that dream—
ragged and lovely as few dreams are.

trans. Sophie Cabot Black and Maria Negroni

João Cabral de Melo Neto

BRAZIL
1920–

João Cabral de Melo Neto accepts only reluctantly the description of himself as a "poet." Skeptical of the lyric celebration of the autobiographical self, dedicated instead to a rationally constructed and antilyrical discursive aesthetic, Cabral de Melo Neto has brought Contructionist attentions into Brazilian lyric poetry, like a South American Valéry. Cabral de Melo Neto was born in Pernambuco and educated at home; ill health prevented him from attending university. He read widely at home and published his Surrealist first book, *Pedra do sono* (*Stone and Sleep*, 1942), shortly before he entered the foreign service. His overseas experience, including many years of residence in Spain, profoundly influenced Cabral de Melo Neto's sense of the poem's discursive and cerebral essence as a verbal artifact. While living abroad he translated works by many of the international Modernists, including Amy Lowell, William Carlos Williams, Marianne Moore, Pablo Neruda (the *Elemental Odes*), and Francis Ponge.

On his permanent return to Brazil, however, Cabral de Melo Neto began to saturate his poems with the landscape of his native Pernambuco. He is well known in Brazil especially through the lyrical-narrative settings of his poems to samba music by Chico Buarque. Although he seems to share little with his contemporaries of the "Generation of '45," Cabral de Melo Neto has increasingly dedicated his poems to formal questions of linguistic communicability and self-conscious verbalism that have much in common with those poets' concerns. Cabral de Melo Neto, however, characteristically works with a commitment to the labor of poems, their connections to the stubbornness of physical reality, their self-sufficiency (like that of a stone), and their nature as achieved human constructs.

A Carlos Drummond de Andrade	*To Carlos Drummond de Andrade*
Não há guarda-chuva	There is no umbrella
contra o poema	against the poem
subindo de regiões onde tudo é surprêsa	rising from regions where everything is a surprise,
como uma flor mesmo num canteiro.	like a flower from a garden.
Não há guarda-chuva	There is no umbrella
contra o amor	against the love
que mastiga e cospe como qualquer bôca,	that chews up and spits out—like a mouth:
que tritura como um desastre.	that grinds like a disaster.
Não há guarda-chuva	There is no umbrella
contra o tédio:	against the tedium,
o tédio das quatro paredes, das quatro	the tedium of four walls, four
estações, dos quatro pontos cardeais.	seasons, four points of the compass.
Não há guarda-chuva	There is no umbrella
contra o mundo	against the world
cada dia devorado nos jornais	the newspapers ruin each day
sob as espécies de papel e tinta.	with this kind of paper, this ink.
Não há guarda-chuva	There is no umbrella
contra o tempo,	against time:

rio fluindo sob a casa, correnteza
carregando os dias, os cabelos.

river flowing under the house, its current
carrying off the days, one's hair.

1945

trans. Guy Pacitti

Cemitério pernambucano

(Nossa Senhora da Luz)

Cemetery in Pernambuco

(Our Lady of Light)

Nesta terra ninguém jaz,
pois também não jaz um rio
noutro rio, nem o mar
é cemitério de rios.

Nobody lies in this earth
because no river is at rest
in any other river, nor is the sea
a potter's field of rivers.

Nenhum dos mortos daqui
vem vestido de caixão.
Portanto, êles não se enterram,
são derramados no chão.

None of these dead men here
comes dressed in a coffin.
Therefore they are not buried
but spilled out on the ground.

Vêm em rêdes de varandas
abertas ao sol e à chuva.
Trazem suas próprias môscas.
O chão lhes vai como luva.

Wrapped in the hammocks they slept in,
naked to sun and rain,
they come bringing their own flies.
The ground fits them like a glove.

Mortos ao ar-livre, que eram,
hoje à terra-livre estão.
São tão da terra que a terra
nem sente sua intrusão.

Dead, they lived in the open air.
Today they are part of open earth,
so much the earth's that the earth
does not feel their intrusion.

1955

trans. Jane Cooper

Uma faca só lâmina [Seleçãoes]

The Knife That Is All Blade [Selections]

Assim como uma bala
enterrada no corpo,
fazendo mais espêsso
um dos lados do morto;

Like a bullet
buried in the body,
making the sides
of a dead man thicker;

assim como uma bala
do chumbo mais pesado,
no músculo de um homem
pesando-o mais de um lado;

like a bullet
of an even heavier lead
in a man's muscle,
making him weigh more on one side;

qual bala que tivesse
um vivo mecanismo,
bala que possuísse
um coração ativo

like a bullet that may have contained
some live mechanism,
a bullet that may have had
an active heart—

igual ao de un relógio
submerso em algum corpo,
ao de um relógio vivo
e também revoltoso,

like that of a clock
submerged in a body
or a clock that's alive
and rebellious,

relógio que tivesse
o gume de uma faca
e tôda a impiedade
de lâmina azulada;

assim como uma faca
que sem bôlso ou bainha
se transformasse em parte
de vossa anatomia;

qual uma faca íntima
ou faca de uso interno,
habitando num corpo
como o próprio esqueleto

de um homem que o tivesse,
e sempre, doloroso,
de homem que se ferisse
contra seus próprios ossos.

A

Seja bala, relógio,
ou a lâmina colérica,
é contudo uma ausência
o que êsse homem leva.

Mas o que não está
nêle está como bala:
tem o ferro do chumbo,
mesma fibra compacta.

Isso que não está
nêle é como um relógio
pulsando em sua gaiola,
sem fadiga, sem ócios.

Isso que não está
nêle está como a ciosa
presença de uma faca,
de qualquer faca nova.

Por isso é que o melhor
dos símbolos usados
é a lâmina cruel
(melhor se de Pasmado):

porque nenhum indica
essa ausência tão ávida
como a imagem da faca
que só tivesse lâmina,

nenhum melhor indica
aquela ausência sôfrega

a clock that might have
a knife's edge
and all the arrogance
of a blue blade;

like a knife
with no pocket or sheath,
changing itself to a part
of your anatomy:

like an intimate knife
or a knife for internal use,
living in a body
like the skeleton itself

of a man who might have had it,
and always, unfortunately,
of a man who might hurt himself
with his own bones.

A

Whether it's bullet, a clock,
or a mean knife-blade,
nevertheless what that man carries
is an absence.

What is not in him
takes the place of a bullet:
the metallic nature of lead,
the same compact texture.

What is not in him
is like a clock
ticking in its cage,
without weariness, without leisure.

What is not in him
is here like the jealous
presence of a knife,
of some fresh knife.

That is why the best
of the symbols used here
is the mean knife-blade
(better still if it was made in Pasmado):

because none of the others suggests
such an eager absence
as the image of the knife does,
a knife that is all blade,

none indicates better
that ravenous absence

que a imagem de uma faca
reduzida à sua bôca,

que a imagem de uma faca
entregue inteiramente
à fome pelas coisas
que nas facas se sente.

1955

as the image of a knife
shrunk to a mouth,

the image of a knife
completely given over to the hunger
for whatever
is felt on knives.

trans. Elizabeth Gordon

Duas das festas da morte

Recepções de cerimônia que dá a morte:
o morto, vestido para um ato inaugural;
e ambìguamente: com a roupa do orador
e a da estátua que se vai inaugurar.
No caixão, meio caixão meio pedestal,
o morto mais se inaugura do que morre;
e duplamente: ora sua própria estátua
ora seu próprio vivo, em dia de posse.

Piqueniques infantis que dá a morte:
os enterros de criança no Nordeste:
reservados a menores de treze anos,
impróprios a adultos (nem o seguem).
Festa meio excursão meio piquenique,
ao ar livre, boa para dia sem classe;
nela, as crianças brincam de boneca,
e aliás, com uma boneca de verdade.

1966

Two of the Festivals of Death

Solemn receptions given by death:
death, dressed for an unveiling;
and ambiguously: dressed like an orator
and like the statue that's to be unveiled.
In the coffin, half coffin half pedestal,
death unveils himself more than he dies;
and in duplicate: now he's his own statue,
now he's himself, alive, for the occasion.

Children's picnics given by death:
children's funerals in the northeast:
no one over thirteen admitted,
no adults allowed, even walking behind.
Party half outing, half picnic,
in the open air, nice for a day when school's out;
the children who go play dolls
or else that's what they really are.

trans. W. S. Merwin

A educacão pela pedra

Uma educação pela pedra: por lições;
para aprender da pedra, freqüentá-la;
captar sua voz inenfática, impessoal
(pela de dicção ela começa as aulas).
A lição de moral, sua resistência fria
ao que flui e a fluir, a ser maleada;
a de poética, sua carnadura concreta;
a de economia, seu adensar-se compacta:
lições da pedra (de fora para dentro,
cartilha muda), para quem soletrá-la.

Outra educação pela pedra: no Sertão
(de dentro para fora, e pré-didática).
No Sertão a pedra não sabe lecionar,
e se lecionasse, não ensinaria nada;
lá não se aprende a pedra: lá a pedra,
uma pedra de nascença, entranha a alma.

1966

Education by Stone

An education by stone: through lessons,
to learn from the stone: to go to it often,
to catch its level, impersonal voice
(by its choice of words it begins its classes).
The lesson in morals, the stone's cold resistance
to flow, to flowing, to being hammered:
the lesson in poetics, its concrete flesh:
in economics, how to grow dense compactly:
lessons from the stone, (from without to within,
dumb primer), for the routine speller of spells.

Another education by stone: in the backlands
(from within to without and pre-didactic place).
In the backlands stone does not know how to lecture,
and, even if it did would teach nothing:
you don't learn the stone, there: there, the stone,
born stone, penetrates the soul.

trans. James Wright

O canavial e o mar

O que o mar sim ensina ao canavial:
o avançar em linha rasteira da onda;
o espraiar-se minucioso, de líquido,
alagando cova a cova onde se alonga.
O que o canavial sim ensina ao mar:
a elocução horizontal de seu verso;
a geórgica de cordel, ininterrupta,
narrada em voz e silêncio paralelos.

2.

O que o mar não ensina ao canavial:
a veemência passional da preamar;
a mão-de-pilão das ondas na areia,
moída e miúda, pilada do que pilar.
O que o canavial não ensina ao mar:
o desmedido do derramar-se da cana;
o comedimento do latifúndio do mar,
que menos lastradamente se derrama.

1966

The Canefield and the Sea

The sea Yes teaches the canefield:
to advance in a creeping line,
to spread itself out
hole by hole up to the tideline.
The canefield Yes teaches the sea
the horizontal eloquence of its verse,
georgics of the news-stand, uninterrupted,
spoken aloud and parallel in silence.

2.

The sea does not teach the canefield:
to rise in a passionate tide;
a pestle pounding the beach,
crushing the sand, making it finer.
The canefield does not teach the sea:
how the sugarcane is always flowing;
that the sea is held, and flows
less heavily, for it is held.

trans. Louis Simpson

O mar e o canavial

O que o mar sim aprende do canavial:
a elocução horizontal de seu verso;
a geórgica de cordel, ininterrupta
narrada em voz e silêncio paralelos.
O que o mar não aprende do canavial;
a veemência passional da preamar;
a mão-de-pilão das ondas na areia,
moída e miúda, pilada do que pilar.

O que o canavial sim aprende do mar:
o avançar em linha rasteira da onda;
o espraiar-se minucioso, de líquido,
alagando cova a cova onde se alonga.
O que o canavial não aprende do mar:
o desmedido do derrarmar-se da cana;
o comedimento do latifúndio do mar,
que menos lastradamente se derrama.

1966

The Sea and the Canefield

The sea Yes learns from the canefield
the horizontal eloquence of its verse,
georgics of the news-stand, uninterrupted,
spoken aloud and parallel in silence.
The sea does not learn from the canefield
to rise in a passionate tide,
a pestle pounding the beach,
crushing the sand, making it finer.

The canefield Yes learns from the sea
to advance in a creeping line,
to spread itself out
hole by hole up to the tideline.
The canefield does not learn from the sea
how the sugarcane is always flowing;
that the sea is held, and flows
less heavily, for it is held.

trans. Louis Simpson

Tecendo a manhã

Um galo sòzinho não tece uma manhã:
êle precisará sempre de outros galos.
De um que apanhe êsse grito que êle

Weaving the Morning

One rooster does not weave a morning,
he will always need the other roosters,
one to pick up the shout that he

e o lance a outro; de um outro galo
que apanhe o grito que um galo antes
e o lance a outro; e de outros galos
que com muitos outros galos se cruzem
os fios de sol de seus gritos de galo,
para que a manhã, desde uma teia tênue,
se vá tecendo, entre todos os galos.

2.

E se encorpando em tela, entre todos,
se erguendo tenda, onde entrem todos,
se entretendendo para todos, no tôldo
(a manhã) que plana livre de armação.
A manhã, tôldo de um tecido tão aéreo
que, tecido, se eleva por si: luz balão.

1966

and toss it to another, another rooster
to pick up the shout that a rooster before him
and toss it to another, and other roosters
with many other roosters to criss-cross
the sun-threads of their rooster-shouts
so that the morning, starting from a frail cobweb,
may go on being woven, among all the roosters.

2.

And growing larger, becoming cloth,
pitching itself a tent where they all may enter,
inter-unfurling itself for them all, in the tent
(the morning) which soars free of ties and ropes—
the morning, tent of a weave so light
that, woven, it lifts itself through itself: balloon light.

trans. Galway Kinnell

Os vazios do homem

Os vazios do homem não sentem ao nada
do vazio qualquer: do do casaco vazio,
do da saca vazia (que não ficam de pé
quando vazios, ou o homem com vazios);
os vazios do homem sentem a um cheio
de uma coisa que inchasse já inchada;
ou ao que deve sentir, quando cheia,
uma saca: todavia não, qualquer saca.
Os vazios do homem, êsse vazio cheio,
não sentem ao que uma saca de tijolos,
uma saca de rebites; nem têm o pulso
que bate numa de sementes, de ovos.

2.

Os vazios do homem, ainda que sintam
a uma plenitude (gôra mas presença)
contêm nadas, contêm apenas vazios:
o que a esponja, vazia quando plena;
incham do que a esponja, de ar vazio,
e dela copiam certamente a estrutura:
tôda em grutas ou em gotas de vazio,
postas em cachos de bôlha, de não-uva.
Êsse cheio vazio sente ao que uma saca
mas cheia de esponjas cheias de vazio;
os vazios do homem ou o vazio inchado:
ou o vazio que inchou por estar vazio.

1966

The Emptiness of Man

The emptiness of man is not like
any other: not like an empty coat
or empty sack (things which do not stand up
when empty, such as an empty man),
the emptiness of man is more like fullness
in swollen things which keep on swelling,
the way a sack must feel
that is being filled, or any sack at all.
The emptiness of man, this full emptiness,
is not like a sack of bricks' emptiness
or a sack of rivets', it does not have the pulse
that beats in a seed bag or bag of eggs.

2.

The emptiness of man, though it resembles
fullness, and seems all of a piece, actually
is made of nothings, bits of emptiness,
like the sponge, empty when filled,
swollen like the sponge, with air, with empty air;
it has copied its very structure from the sponge,
it is made up in clusters, of bubbles, of non-grapes.
Man's empty fullness is like a sack
filled with sponges, is filled with emptiness:
man's emptiness, or swollen emptiness,
or the emptiness that swells by being empty.

trans. Galway Kinnell

Olga Orozco

A poet of complex sensibilities, Olga Orozco writes poems that resist easy classification. Strongly influenced by French avant-garde writing, she has been responsible for bringing many of the works of French Surrealist writers, including Artaud, Éluard, and Breton, to a Latin American readership. Not surprisingly, considering these antecedents, her work contains a mysteriousness and an imperious nostalgia, embodied in exuberant language. Viewed from another angle, her combination of mystery and precise diction may be seen as a defense of radical subjectivity in the face of the periodic repressiveness of Argentine politics from the 1950s through the 1980s. Her first major book, *Las muertes* (*The Deaths*, 1951), is a series of poems about the deaths of various historical and imaginary figures (the final poem of the book is "Olga Orozco"). In that book and in later collections, Orozco's poems become declared acts of an abstracting imagination, yet so closely tied to the physical world that the surreal and the hyperphysical are seamlessly linked. Orozco's book *Museo salvaje* (1974) collects meditations on various parts of the body, as elements in a "Savage Museum" haunted by consciousness. Alejandra Pizarnik characterized Orozco's work as a poetry "not only of the cerebellum and the spirit, but also of the veins, the stomach, the heart and the sex, the poetry of an inspiration through which . . . all that it is to be human, throbs."

Miss Havisham

Aquí yace Miss Havisham,
lujosa vanidad del desencanto.
Un día se visitó para la dicha con su traje de muerte,
sin saberlo.
Era la hora exacta en que alcanzaba la música de un sueño
cuando alguien cortó con duro golpe las cuerdas
    mentirosas del amor,
y quedó desasida, cayendo hacia lo oscuro como una
    nube rota.
Todo fue clausurado.
No invadir el recinto donde una novia recogió para
    el odio los escarchados trozos de su corazón.
Quien entró fue elegido para expiar ciegamente todo
    el llanto.
No levantar los sellos.
Las manos de la luz habrían despersado los flotantes
    ropajes,
los manteles roído por tenaces dinastías de insectos,
las aguas del espejo enturbiadas aún después de la caída
    de la última imagen,
los lugares desiertos donde los comensales serían calmos
    deudos
alrededor de una desenterrada,
de una novia marchita fosforeciendo aún en venganza
    y desprecio.
Ahora ya está muerta.
Pasad.

Miss Havisham

Here lies Miss Havisham,
the opulent vanity of disappointment.
One day she dressed for happiness in her gown of death,
unaware.
It was the right time to reach toward the music of
    a dream—
when in one rough swoop someone slashed the lying
    strings of love
and she fell apart, falling toward darkness like a
    quashed cloud.
Everything was locked away.
No admittance to the place where a hollow bride, in the
    name of hatred, gathered the frozen remains of
    her heart.
Whoever entered had been chosen, for the blind
    reparation of all that weeping.
It was forbidden to break the seals.
The hands of light would have scattered the floating
    garments,
the table-lace gnawed by determined dynasties of insects,
the mirror's waters still undisturbed after the last image
    had dropped,
the deserted places where the dinner-guests would be
    indifferent relatives
around the body of the disinterred,
around the wilted bride, still phosphorescent with
    vengeance and scorn.

Ésa es la escena que los años guardaron en orgulloso
    polvo de paciencia,
es la suntuosa urdimbre donde cayó como una colgadura
    envuelta por las llamas de su muerte.
Fue una espléndida hoguera.
Sí. Nada hace mejor fuego que la vana aridez,
que ese lóbrego infierno en que está ardiendo por una
    eternidad,
hasta que llegue Pip y escriba debajo de su nombre:
        "la perdono".

1951

Olga Orozco

Yo, Olga Orozco, desde tu corazón digo a todos
    que muero.
Amé la soledad, la heroica peduración de toda fe,
el ocio donde crecen animales extraños y plantas fabulosas,
la sombra de un gran tiempo que pasó entre misterios y
    entre alucinaciones
y también el pequeño temblor de las bujías en el anochecer.
Mi historia está en mis manos y en las manos con que
    otros las tatuaron.
De mi estadía quedan las magias y los ritos,
unas fechas gastadas por el soplo de un despiadado amor,
la humarada distante de la casa donde nunca estuvimos,
y unos gestos dispersos entre los gestos de otros que no
    me conocieron.
Lo demás aún se cumple en el olvido,
aún labra la desdicha en el rostro de aquélla que se buscaba
    en mí igual que en un espejo de sonrientes praderas,
y a la que tú verás extrañamente ajena:
mi propia aparecida condenada a mi forma de este mundo.
Ella hubiera querido guardarme en el desdén o en
    el orgullo,
en el último instante fulmíneo como el rayo,
no en el túmulo incierto donde alzo todavía la voz ronca
    y llorada
entre los remolinos de tu corazón.
No. Esta muerte no tiene descanso ni grandeza.
No puedo estar mirándola por primera vez durante
    tanto tiempo.
Pero debo seguir muriendo hasta tu muerte
porque soy tu testigo ante una ley más honda y más oscura
    que los cambiantes sueños,
allá, donde escribimos la sentencia:
"Ellos han muerto ya.
Se habían elegido por castigo y perdón, por cielo y
    por infierno.

Now she is dead.
Come in.
This is the scene the years have guarded in a proud dust
    of patience,
the sumptuous knotting where she dropped like a tapestry,
    wrapped in the flames of her death.
It was a splendid blaze.
Yes. Nothing's better for a fire than vain desiccation,
than this shadowy hell where she will burn eternally,
till Pip arrives and writes beneath her name:
        "she is forgiven."

trans. Stephen Tapscott

Olga Orozco

I, Olga Orozco, tell everyone, from your heart, that I am
    dying.
I loved: solitude, the heroic lastingness of all faith,
relaxing where strange animals and fabulous plants live,
the shadow of a great era that moved through mysteries
    and exotic visions,
also the candles' little trembling at evening.
My history lies in my hands and the hands of those who
    tattooed them.
The magic and the rites remain from my sojourn,
some dates worn away by gusts of merciless love,
distant smoke from the house where we never were,
some gestures scattered among the gestures of people
    who never knew me.
The rest is still winding itself up, in oblivion,
still carving grief on the face of the one who looked for
    herself in me as in a mirror of smiling fields,
the one you will see as strangely alien:
my ghost, condemned to my form in this world.
She would have liked to regard me with scorn or
    with pride
in the last moment like a bolt of lightning:
not in the confused uproar where I still raise my hoarse
    voice, crying out
among the whirlpools of your heart.
No. For this death, no serenity or grandeur:
I can't look at it for long, the first time.
But I have to keep on dying till your death
because I am your witness, before a law deeper and darker
    than transmogrifying dreams,
there where we pronounce the sentence:
"Now they are dead.
They were chosen for penalty, for pardon, for heaven and
    for hell.

Son ahora una mancha de humedad en las paredes del
  primer aposento."

1951

Now they're a stain of damp on the walls of the first
  room."

trans. Stephen Tapscott

Para hacer un talismán

Se necesita sólo tu corazón
hecho a la viva imagen de tu demonio o de tu dios.
Un corazón apenas, como un crisol de brasas para
  la idolatría.
Nada más que un indefenso corazón enamorado.
Déjalo a la intemperie,
donde la hierba aúlle sus endechas de nodriza loca
y no pueda dormir,
donde el viento y la lluvia dejen caer su látigo en un golpe
  de azul escalofrío
sin convertirlo en mármol y sin partirlo en dos,
donde la oscuridad abra sus madrigueras a todas las jaurías
y no logre olvidar.
Arrójalo después desde lo alto de su amor al hervidero de
  la bruma.
Ponlo luego a secar en el sordo regazo de la piedra,
y escarba, escarba en él con una aguja fría hasta arrancar el
  último grano de esperanza.
Deja que lo sofoquen las fiebres y la ortiga,
que lo sacuda el trote ritual de la alimaña,
que lo envuelva la injuria hecha con los jirones de sus
  antiguas glorias.
Y cuando un día un año aprisione con la garra de un siglo,
antes que sea tarde,
antes que se convierta en momia deslumbrante,
abre de par en par y una por una todas sus heridas:
que las exhiba al sol de la piedad, lo mismo que el mendigo,
que plaña su delirio en el desierto,
hasta que sólo el eco de un nombre crezca en él con la
  furia del hambre:
un incesante golpe de cuchara contra el plato vacío.

Si sobrevive aún,
si ha llegado hasta aquí hecho a la viva imagen de tu
  demonio o de tu dios,
he aquí un talismán más inflexible que la ley,
más fuerte que las armas y el mal del enemigo.
Guárdalo en la vigilia de tu pecho igual que a un centinela.
Pero vela con él.
Puede crecer en ti como la mordedura de la lepra;
puede ser tu verdugo.
¡El inocente monstruo, el insaciable comensal de
  tu muerte!

1962

To Make a Talisman

Your heart is all you need,
fashioned in the living image of your daemon or your god.
Only a heart, like a crucible of coals before an idol.
Nothing but a defenseless, affectionate heart.
Leave it out in the elements,
where the grasses like a crazed nurse will wail their dirges
and it cannot fall asleep,
where the wind and the rain whisper their whips in blue
  cold blasts
without turning it to marble or splitting it in two,
where darkness opens warrens to all the wild animals
and it cannot forget.
Throw it from the summit of its love into the seething
  mist.
Then spread it out to dry in the stone's deaf lap
and scrape, scrape it with a cold nail till the last grain of
  hope has been gouged away.
So that fevers and nettles can suffocate it,
so that predatory beasts can jolt it with their ritual trot,
so that it can be swaddled in insult made from the rags
  of its ancient glories.
And when one day per year imprisons it with the talons
  of a century,
before it's too late,
before it becomes a luminous mummy,
open its wounds wide open, exhibit them one by one,
like a beggar, display them to the piteous sun;
let it wail its delirium in the desert
till only the echo of a name grows inside it, like a raging
  hunger:
the ceaseless pounding of a spoon against an empty plate.

If it still survives,
it has come this far as the living image of your daemon
  or your god;
here is a talisman more inflexible than the law,
stronger than the weapons and the malice of the enemy.
Guard it in the vigil of your chest like a sentry.
But keep watch over it.
It can grow inside you like the gnawing of leprosy;
it can be your executioner.
The innocent monster, insatiable dinner-guest at
  your death!

trans. Stephen Tapscott

La realidad y el deseo

A Luis Cernuda

La realidad, sí, la realidad,
ese relámpago de lo invisible
que revela en nosotros la soledad de Dios.

Es este cielo que huye.
Es este territorio engalanado por las burbujas de la muerte.
Es esta larga mesa a la deriva
donde los comensales persisten ataviados por el prestigio
    de no estar.
A cada cual su copa
para medir el vino que se acaba donde empieza la sed.
Y cada cual su plato
para encerrar el hambre que se extingue sin saciarse jamás.
Y cada dos la división del pan:
el milagro al revés, la comunión tan sólo en lo imposible.
Y en medio del amor,
entre uno y otro cuerpo la caída,
algo que se asemeja al latido sombrío de unas alas que
    vuelven desde la eternidad,
al pulso del adiós debajo de la tierra.

La realidad, sí, la realidad:
un sello de clausura sobre todas las puertas del deseo.

1974

Reality and Desire

For Luis Cernuda

Reality, yes, reality,
is the lightning-bolt of the invisible
that reveals in us the solitude of God.

This is the sky that escapes.
This is the territory adorned with the bubbles of death.
This is the big floating table
where the dinner-guests stay seated, wearing the prestige
    of not-being-there.
Each one has his goblet
to weigh the wine that ends where thirst begins.
Each one has his plate
that holds the hunger that ends but is never satisfied.
And for each pair their share of bread:
the miracle in reverse, solitary communion with the
    impossible.
And in the middle of love,
between one body and another, the fall,
something that seems like the shadowy throb of wings
    flying toward eternity,
to a pulse of farewell in the earth.

Reality, yes, reality:
the seal of cloister on all the gates of desire.

trans. Stephen Tapscott

Eunice Odio

COSTA RICA/MEXICO
1922–1974

Eunice Odio was born in Costa Rica and lived in Guatemala, Cuba, Nicaragua, the United States and, finally, in Mexico, where she wrote most of her best work. The restlessness of her peregrinations is reflected in her poems, which are magisterial, lyrical, difficult diffractions of the single self in almost ecstatically shifting encounters with concepts. The form of those meditations reflects both the heterogeneity of her imagination and her ability to assemble a cultural vision from disparate lyrical shards. Famously beautiful, self-destructive, and loyal, in temperament Odio was essentially a mystic. Her correspondence, published posthumously, is a collection of meditations about poetry as the source of spiritual power, about her personal relations with the archangel Michael, and about her outspoken attitudes toward the literary communities in which she lived. Resistant to group action in politics or in literature, she was nevertheless a friend of poets in the Poema Largo and *Contemporáneos* groups, including Homero Aridjis and Carlos Pellicer. Prolific as a writer but reluctant to publish, she was assembling a comprehensive collection of her poems, *Territorio del alba* (*Territory of the*

Dawn), at the time of her death. Eunice Odio died in Mexico City, alone and under odd circumstances, in 1974.

The text "Prólogo," given here as a separate poem, serves also as the introductory piece to Odio's long sequence *El tránsito del fuego* (*The Fire's Journey*, 1957).

Recuerdo de mi infancia privada

> *Por esas puertas que se*
> *cierran, se abren...*

Son puertas que a lo largo del alma me golpean.

No me hables de esas puertas, amigo, no me hables;

porque yo les conozco sus goznes coronados de ira,
sus barrotes limados por el cielo,

su tácito desvelo en las noches más altas,
por donde algunas veces transcurrió nuestro amado
como a través del grito duele hasta el hueso el alma,
con temblor de pesado miembro oscuro y prohibido.

Yo he pasado a toda hora
por esas puertas húmedas que se cierran, se abren,

y he reído hasta el hombro
de sentir sus profundos maderos alterados,
porque pasaba un niño coral entre pañales
como ríos de cisne sin contorno.

Pero también recuerdo, debajo de mi infancia,
en un secreto abril con habitantes,
con océanos,
con árboles,
una puerta de azul carpintería
por donde algunas veces comenzaba mi madre,
empezaban sus labios,
sus brazos que partían de las olas,
su voz en que cabía la tarde
y apenas mis dos piernas que corrían
desordenando el aire.

Ahora la recuerdo
con mis beligerancias infantiles,
puerta de piedras jóvenes,

mi madre
con sus pasos a ternera boreal, traspasándola,
se incorporaba a la semana

Memory of My Private Childhood

> *Through those doors that*
> *close, are opened...*

Those doors through my soul knock about.

Don't speak to me of those doors, my friend, don't speak;

because I know their hinges crowned with anger,
their braces filed down by the sky,

their tacit vigilance on the highest of nights,
through which our beloved sometimes passed
and the soul cried out, pained to its very bones,
with the trembling of a heavy, dark, forbidden member.

I have passed at all hours
through those damp doors that close, that open,

and I have laughed my head off
from feeling their deep altered wood,
because a coral-colored child passed amid diapers
like rivers of a formless swan.

But I also remember, beneath my childhood,
in a secret April with inhabitants,
with oceans,
with trees,
a door made of blue woodwork
where sometimes my mother began,
her lips began,
her arms which came out of the waves,
her voice which contained the afternoon
and barely my two legs that run
upsetting the air.

Now I remember her
with my childhood belligerence,
door of young stones,

my mother
with her boreal calf's footsteps, passing through her,
becoming the week

ciñéndose el perfil,
la trenza,
la memoria,

la cintura en escombro de paloma,

y me buscaba
entre los habitantes de ese abril
con océanos,

con árboles,

y yo corría,

corría,

con mis piernas de niña
para ser hallada

con la voz

en la tarde.

girding her profile,
the braid,
the memory

her waist in dove debris,

and she sought me
among the inhabitants of that April
with oceans,

with trees,

and I ran,

ran,

with my little girl's legs
to be found

with my voice

in the afternoon.

1946/1974

trans. Suzanne Jill Levine

Creación

Proposiciones de Prometeo

*Y la tierra estaba desordenada y vacía,
y las tinieblas estaban sobre la haz
del abismo, y el espíritu de Dios empollaba
sobre la haz de las aguas.*

EL GÉNESIS, 1–2

Creation

Promethean Propositions

*And the earth was without form, and
void; and darkness was upon the face
of the deep. And the Spirit of God moved
upon the face of the waters.*

GENESIS 1:2

I

Altas proposiciones de lo estéril
por cuyo rastro voy sangrando a media altura
y buscándome,
palpándome,
por detrás de la rosa edificada,
sobre lo que no tiene orilla ni regreso
y es, como lo descubierto recobrado
que acaba él que me siga y me revele.

Me apoyo en ti,
clima desenterrado de lo estéril
para fundar el aire de la gracia y el asombro;
y el metaloide aciago y desmentido,
primero en rama llega,
y luego en flor el metaloide oscuro,

I

High propositions of barrenness
by whose sign I am bleeding at half height,
seeking myself,
touching myself,
from behind the constructed rose,
over what has no return or border
but is, like what is exposed and restored
to finish whoever would follow and reveal me.

As I lean on you,
climate unearthed from barrenness
to establish the air of grace and amazement,
the fated, refuted metalloid
arrives, first as branch;
then the dark one, as flower

y en fruto de sabor martirizado,
baja junto a la lengua enajenada,
pasa de mano en mano hasta la altura.

Porque no es lo posible lo seguro
sino lo que inseguro se doblega,
lo que hay que abrir y sojuzgar por dentro,
y es como polvo en cantidad de sombra.

Porque el fruto no es puerto
sin rumbo entre las aguas,
sino estación secreta de la carne;
íntima paz de cotidiana guerra
donde reposa el vientre silvestre y revestido
de accidentes geológicos y espesos.

Y la alegría purísima,
la honda gracia presente y madurada,
que rebota hasta el fondo de la sangre,
que hace correr y madrugar en pájaros,
y equivocarse de pecho y ponerse,
como ciertas flores,
un corazón de pana en la mañana.

La alegría de caer en inocencia de sí mismo
y disfrutarse junto a otras criaturas
en el descubrimiento de su nombre,
madrugando de pecho para arriba
donde los alimentos perseveran
hallados para el cielo.

II

Y será como el árbol plantado
junto a arroyos de aguas,
que da su fruto en su tiempo,
y su hoja no cae; y todo lo que
hace, prosperará.

SALMO 1–3

Al borde estoy de herirme y escucharme
ahora que le propongo al polvo una ecuación
para el deslizamiento de la garganta,

Ahora que inauguro mi regreso
junto a mi pequeñez iluminada,

Ahora que me busco revelada
y transida en otros nombres,

Cuando por mí descienden y se agrupan
anchas temperaturas matinales,

Y han gran fiesta cerval en los caminos.

and fruit with a tortured taste,
descends beside the estranged tongue
and passes from hand to hand to the height.

Because the possible can't be certain
unless the uncertain yields:
it must be opened and conquered inside,
and its shadow is thick as dust.

Because the fruit is not a port
without a course through the waters
but a hidden condition of flesh:
inner peace from daily war
where the wild belly rests, dressed
in dense geological accidents,

and the purest joy,
the deep grace, present and ripened,
rebounding to the depths of the blood,
making it run and arise like birds
and make a wrong turn in the breast
and put on, like certain flowers,
a plush heart in the morning.

The joy of falling, innocent of itself,
enjoying itself beside other creatures
in the discovery of its name,
awakening from the breast upwards
where sustenance is found,
persevering, for the sky.

II

And he shall be like a tree planted
by the rivers of waters, that bringeth
forth his fruit in his season; and
whatsoever he doeth shall prosper.

PSALM 1:3

On the verge of wounding myself and hearing myself,
I now propose to the dust an equation
for sliding down the throat.

I inaugurate my return,
with my smallness lit beside me,

I seek myself revealed
and overcome with other names,

while comfortable morning temperatures
descend on me and gather together

and make a great festival, like deer, in the streets.

III

Pasa mi corazón
con su pastosa identidad doliente.

Mi aliento transitivo que enarbolo
y el niño cuyos pasos me prolongan.

Pero la sangre está ya en marcha,
repercute,
hacia un país recóndito y anclado,
entre pesados hierros con nombre de muchacho,
y extensos materiales fuera del pulso mío.

La sangre está ya en marcha
hacia una parte mía donde llego de pronto,
y me conoce el pecho en que tropiezo,
y mis extensas, pálidas, boreales coronarias.

El cuerpo es ya contagio de azucena,
estación de la rama y su eficacia;
palacio solitario en cuya orilla
crece el suelo y afluye entre rebaños
y entre sueños secretos y pacíficos.

IV

Puede pasar mi pecho errante,
mi instantáneo cabello
y mi atroz rapidez que no me alcanza,

Pero se ha vuelto inaugural
mi peso de habitante recobrado.
Y aires de nacimiento me convocan,

¡Ah, feliz muchedumbre de huesos en reposo!

Refluyen a mi forma y se congregan
los elementos suaves y terrestres
y la pulpa negada y transcurrida.

Los pájaros me cambian
a traslados mayores del sonido,

Y la tierra a empujones de llanura.

Al borde estoy de herirme y escucharme
ahora que me lleno de retoños y párpados tranquilos,

Cuando tengo costumbre de nacer
donde bajan los huesos temporales,

III

My heart goes on
with its soft grieving density,

my transitive breath which I raise
and the child whose steps extend me.

But the blood is already marching—
it reverberates—
toward a hidden and anchored country,
among heavy metals named for a boy
and vast materials outside my pulse.

The blood is already marching
toward a part of me where I will come soon:
the breast where I stumble knows me,
and my vast pale northern crowns.

The body is already a contagion of lilies,
a condition of the branch and its effects;
a solitary palace on whose border
the soil grows and flows among flocks,
among secret, peaceful dreams.

IV

My wandering breast can go on,
my instant hair
and my inhuman speed which cannot catch me,

but my weight has become inaugural,
its residence restored,
and airs of origin call me,

ah happy crowd of resting bones!

The smooth earthly elements
and the dull elapsed pulp
flow back to my form and gather.

The birds change me
and major shifts of sound,

and the earth by thrusts of its plains.

On the verge of wounding myself and hearing myself,
now that I'm full of sprouts and quiet eyelids,

when I have my time of birth
in which the temporal bones descend,

Cuando me llamo para mí, callada,
y alguien que no soy yo ya me recuerda,

Sollozante y sangrando a media altura,
sobre lo detenido
descubierto
y recobrado.

1948/1974

Prólogo del tiempo que no está en sí

I
Nada estaba previsto.
Todo era inminente.

II
Un día después de un tiempo inmemorial,
mientras el cielo se movía de pie,
de un ojo a otro;

y se pensaba de un corazón a otro
en las ciudades,

el orden del vacío preparaba
una palabra que no sabía su nombre.

(La palabra, aquella, del tamaño del aire.)

III
También, potencia descansada, el viento,
alzado tumbador de estrellas,
desde el trueno que escucho sin memoria
esclarecer para contar sus ángeles,
rasgaba los templos ardorosos.

IV
También un toro, sí, también un toro pálido
tenía la cara terrenal
y con su grande uña cardial golpeaba el mundo.

V
Los ríos conjugándose, ordenándose en sílabas de agua,
trasoían su límite de peces y de fuego.

VI
Apenas se escribían los frutos y los niños,
con el palote antiguo que reunía los verbos

antes en libertad, acéfalos, sin vías
en la ruta de una mañana eterna.

when I name myself for myself, silent,
and someone I'm not already remembers me,

weeping and bleeding at half height
over what is stopped
exposed
and then restored.

trans. Martha Collins

Prologue to a Time That Is Not Itself

I
Nothing was foreseen.
Everything was imminent.

II
One day after a time immemorial,
while the sky walked
from eye to eye,

thinking itself from heart to heart
in the cities,

the arrangement of empty space prepared
a word that did not know its name.

(That word: it was the size of air.)

III
Also: strength renewed, the wind,
raised up to assault stars—
from the thunder to which I listen
for light to count its angels, the wind
tore down the burning temples.

IV
Also a bull, yes a pale bull
with an earthly face
pounded the world with its large heart-like hoof.

V
The rivers converging, arranging themselves in syllables
    of water,
would misunderstand the limits of fish and of fire.

VI
New fruit and young children barely wrote each other
using the old-fashioned stroke that joined verbs

that once were free, headless, without roads
on the path of an eternal morning.

VII

La noche se soñaba su figura de mayo.
¿Cómo sería su verde partiendo de las hojas?
¿Cómo sería su verde y cercano
a tan claro designio de laureles
y razonado en pétalo profundo?

Quería una palabra para escuchar su color en la noche.

VIII

Los ángeles buscaban un cuerpo para el llanto,
con el sexo menor posado en una lámpara,
y su peinado, apenas pronombre de las olas.

IX

Las islas navegaban rumbo un pueblo de cobre,
madurando en peceras su sol de porcelana,
mas noche y día las encontró la arena,
con el oído al pie de la colmena,
y con sus musgos dando su lámpara ordenada.

X

Más allá de su arrullo, a un año de sus vísceras amadas,
el arpa desataba su sonrisa, sus tálamos nacientes.

Era ya necesario organizarle la cuerda
y la estatura que crecían a la altura del álamo;
pronto entraría

en sus obligaciones de armonía.

XI

Allá en su edad,
—seca, sin fin memoria de la nieve—
el frío creaba su niñez.
Nadie sabía si era un quelonio mortal,
o el corazón sin fecha de un anillo perenne.

Todos lo amaban y lo confundían
con su asonancia de oro sembrado en el desierto.

Ya lo anunciaba la ciudad llena de cosas jóvenes.
Un día vendría el relámpago a soplarle los hombros,
un huracán liviano lo llevaría consigo;

desde entonces el frío resonaría
con los que lo olvidaron hace siglos,
hace nueve sollozos de abejas insepultas.

XII

El océano sólo era una larga presencia de caballo
alrededor del mundo,

VII

Night dreamed its own image of May.
What would its green be like, removed from the leaves?
What would its green be like, next
to such a clear pattern of laurels,
rendered petal by deep petal?

It would wish for a word to listen to night's color.

VIII

The angels looked for a body for tears,
the smaller sex posed in the light,
its hair just barely the pronoun of waves.

IX

The islands charted a course through a copper country,
ripening porcelain sunlight in fishbowls,
but night and day the sand found them,
its ear held to the base of the beehive,
its mosses giving orderly light.

X

Beyond its lullaby, after a year of its beloved insides,
the harp unfastened its smile, its marriage beds.

It needed to organize string
and stature, now grown to the height of a poplar:
soon it would enter into

its harmonic obligations.

XI

There in its age—
dry, with endless memory of snow—
the cold invented its childhood.
No one knew whether it was a mortal turtle
or the undated heart of an unchanging ring.

Everyone loved it, confusing it
with its gold counterpart sown in the desert.

The city full of new things already foresaw it:
one day lightning would come to blow on its shoulders,
a frivolous hurricane would carry it off;

from then on the cold would resound
for those who forgot it centuries before,
before nine sobs of unburied grandmothers.

XII

The ocean alone was a long presence of horse
around the world,

y el caballo era, apenas, un labio descifrado
y perdido de súbito,

sal,

víspera del agua,
ingrávida y solemne.

XIII

Los cristales designaban unánimes costumbres y
    gestiones:
el humilde epídoto trepaba por el cuarzo
con gecónida pata;

y el cristal de roca en su perímetro oscilante,
rehuía los contactos con el hierro,
y al pasar por coléricos destellos,

se afirmaba sin mancha.

XIV

Corderillos adentro, mariposas adentro,
dándole honor al polvo,
colmándolo de azules convenciones y seres imprevistos,
se fundaba la gracia carnal de las ciudades.

XV

La abeja resumía en su seno de virgen prematura,
la abreviada dulzura de un padre inagotable.

XVI

Era la paz primera que nadie repetía.

Andaba ya un gran hueso buscándose al oído,
de la mañana al bronce, de la noche a los ciervos.

XVII

Era en la infancia de Dios,
cuando hablaba con una sola sílaba,

y seguía

creciendo en secreto.

1957

Carta a Carlos Pellicer

Señor muy precioso, niño sapientísimo:

    Hoy, que es *La Hora de Junio*, voy a regalarle varias
cosas que me pertenecen: una gota del Sol; un azul que

---

and the horse was, barely, a tongue deciphered
and suddenly lost,

salt,

on the eve of water,
weightless and solemn.

XIII

The crystals appointed unanimous customs and measures:

the humble epidote drilled through the quartz
with its lizard foot,

the rock crystal with shifting perimeter
avoided contacts with iron,
and when it passed through furious flashes,

declared itself without blemish.

XIV

Lambskins inside, butterflies inside,
honoring the dust,
showering it with blue conventions and unexpected beings,
the carnal grace of the cities established itself.

XV

The bee sums up, in its premature virgin's breast,
the brief sweetness of an inexhaustible father.

XVI

It was the first peace that no one repeated.

Soon a great bone went looking for hearing:
the bronze of morning, the deer of night.

XVII

It was the infancy of God,
when he spoke with a single syllable

and kept on

growing in secret.

trans. Martha Collins

Letter to Carlos Pellicer

Most charming sir, most learned young master,

Today, which is the Midsummer Hour, I'm offering you
some things that belong to me: a drop of sun; a blue I

encontré en la calle, la segunda parte de una golondrina; el manto de un insecto del color del mundo; varios sueños diamantinos y multitudinarios. ¿Le gustan estos objetos celestes? ¿Los acepta? ¿Verdad que sí porque los sintió en los ojos desde antes que en su infancia apareciera la primera Luna redonda de marzo?

Y le doy más: un espejo en que se mira el cielo, una pátina de césped, un desplazamiento de mariposa, una cucharada de golondrinas de Chichén Itzá; un gran río que corre al compás de los marinos y los pescadores; un sonido tintineante de Raimundo Lulio; el corazón mío en el momento en que se alegró, porque lo miraban; una mirada verde que fue al aire y regresó al infinito; el son del cielo y el del sonido. Le regalo el fondo de una perla dinosauria que es donde vamos a vivir y morir usted y yo, dentro de tres árboles de años. Le doy una florecita de árbol potente y dulce. Le doy la vida que ya no tienen sus abuelos y sus padres. Le regalo la sonrisa de una bisabuela suya que usted no conoció porque era ángela y árbola y se fue a la eternidad en un segundo, junto con sus trenzas de río y su perfil de escamas resplandecientes. Le regalo una espuma que vi un día que ya he perdido, pero que podemos recobrar a la vuelta de cualquier año bisiesto y poderoso. Le doy mi amor, fugitivo en los bosques; le cedo la mitad de una criatura que no puede morir y que anda en la Tierra, dirigida por el aire; le doy un caballo que se soñó; un rocío que se alejó del tiempo y del espacio para ser inmemorial; mi cabeza desatada por el viento; mi alma vestida de cereza y con un gran afán de aventura; le regalo una calle de abril; un santo que se deshizo en el viento, un niño que se construyó, ojo por ojo y diente por diente, una vez que lo nacieron; un duende que venía cuando iba, porque no le temía al milagro; le regalo un vaso lleno de mariposas que no duermen jamás y que siempre andan en manojos de árboles; una mujer que se perdió de súbito porque el aire la quería y la miraban los cedros masculinos; y también le regalo una mujer hallada en el fuego, a quien nadie pudo entender. Le doy el suelo donde se juntan muchas flores irisadas y desnudas, tal como Dios las trajo al mundo; una mano tendida en medio del mar y usted.

Reciba, Maestro, mis dádivas sin fin. Lo ama profundamente,

Eunice Odio

P.D.—Se me había olvidado regalarle todo el horizonte y sus consecuencias.

29 de junio de 1971, México.

1971/1974

found on the street, half of a swallow; the mantle of an earth-colored insect; some glittering multi-faceted dreams. Do you like these delightful objects? Do you accept them? Is that because you felt them in your eyes even before the first round moon of March appeared in your infancy?

I give you more: a mirror in which the sky looks at itself, a patina of lawn, a butterfly journey, a spoonful of swallows from Chichén Itzá; a great river that runs in time with sailors and fishermen; the ringing sound of Raimundo Lulio; my heart when it rejoices because it is looked at; a green look that went into the air and returned to infinity; the music of sky and of sound. I offer you the depth of the dinosaur pearl where you and I will live and die in the years of three trees. I give you a little tree-flower, strong and sweet. I give you a life which neither your parents nor grandparents have. I offer you the smile of a great-grandmother you never knew because she was an angel and a tree and she went off to eternity in a flash, with her rivery hair and her shining scales. I offer you some foam I found on a day I've already lost, but which we can retrieve in any leap-year. I give you my love, fleeing in the forest; I hand over half of a creature that cannot die and that walks on earth, guided by air. I give you a horse that dreamed itself; a dew that recedes from time and space to become eternal; my head, undone by the wind; my soul, dressed in cherry-red, with its great desire for adventure. I offer you an April street; a saint who came apart in the wind, a child who made himself up, eye by eye and tooth by tooth, as they appeared; a goblin that came when it went, because it was not afraid of a miracle. I offer you a glass full of butterflies, never sleeping, always moving through clusters of trees; a woman who suddenly disappeared because the air desired her and the masculine cedars looked at her; and I offer you also a woman found in the fire, whom no one can understand. I give you the ground where many flowers are gathered, iridescent and un-adorned, just as God brought them into the world; a hand stretched out in the midst of the sea and you.

Receive, master, my endless gifts. I love you profoundly,

Eunice Odio

P.S.: I forgot to offer you the horizon and all its effects.

June 29, 1971, Mexico City

trans. Martha Collins

Álvaro Mutis

Born in Bogotá, Álvaro Mutis spent much of his childhood in Belgium, where he was educated. Since 1956 he has lived much of the time in Mexico, where he has worked for Columbia Pictures TV. In their meditative fullness, Mutis' poems explore the strangeness and the virtually mythological intensity of ordinary objects. Like his countryman Gabriel García Márquez, Mutis articulates his passion for the physical world through a verbal attachment to the numbers, figurations, symbols, and objects of mundane experience, which his poems present in their resonant suggestiveness. Besides three books of poems, Mutis has also published several volumes of fiction, including the three novellas collected in *Maqroll* (1973).

Amén

Que te acoja la muerte
con todos tus sueños intactos.
Al retorno de una furiosa adolescencia,
al comienzo de las vacaciones que nunca te dieron,
te distinguirá la muerte con su primer aviso.
Te abrirá los ojos a sus grandes aguas,
te iniciará en su constante brisa de otro mundo.
La muerte se confundirá con tus sueños
y en ellos reconocerá los signos
que antaño fuera dejando,
como un cazador que a su regreso
reconoce sus marcas en la brecha.

1965

Amen

That death receives you
with all your dreams intact.
At the return of a raging youth,
at the beginning of vacations never given,
death will distinguish you with its first call.
Your eyes will be opened to its big waters, you will be
initiated into its constant wind of another world.
Death will melt with your dreams
and there recognize the signs
left so long ago,
as a hunter coming back
recognizes his own prints along the gap.

trans. Sophie Cabot Black and Maria Negroni

Canción del este

A la vuelta de la esquina
un ángel invisible espera;
una vaga niebla, un espectro desvaído
te dirá algunas palabras del pasado.
Como agua de acequia, el tiempo
cava en ti su manso trabajo
de días y semanas,
de años sin nombre ni recuerdo.
A la vuelta de la esquina
te seguirá esperando vanamente
ese que no fuiste, ese que murió
de tanto ser tú mismo lo que eres.
Ni la más leve sospecha,
ni la más leve sombra
te indica lo que pudiera haber sido

East Song

At any turn
an invisible angel waits;
a vague fog, a faded vision
will tell you words of the past.
Like water in a ditch, time
carves in you a gentle labor
of days and weeks,
of years without name or souvenir.
At any turn
the one you never were, the one that died
of you so much being what you are,
will continue waiting, uselessly, for you.
Not even a hint,
not even the slightest shadow
tells you what that encounter

ese encuentro. Y, sin embargo,
allí estaba la clave
de tu breve dicha sobre la tierra.

1965

could have been. There, however,
there was the key
to your brief happiness on earth.

trans. Sophie Cabot Black and Maria Negroni

Una palabra

Cuando de repente en mitad de la vida llega una palabra
    jamás antes pronunciada,
una densa marea nos recoge en sus brazos y comienza el
    largo viaje entre la magia recién iniciada,
que se levanta como un grito en un inmenso hangar
    abandonado donde el musgo cobija las paredes,
entre el óxido de olvidadas criaturas que habitan un
    mundo en ruinas una palabra basta,
una palabra y se inicia la danza pausada que nos lleva por
    entre un espeso polvo de ciudades,
hasta los vitrales de una oscura casa de salud, a patios
    donde florece el hollín y anidan densas sombras,
húmedas sombras, que dan vida a cansadas mujeres.
Ninguna verdad reside en estos rincones y, sin embargo,
    allí sorprende el mudo pavor
que llena la vida con su aliento de vinagre—rancio vinagre
    que corre por la mojada despensa de una humilde
    casa de placer.
Y tampoco es esto todo.
Hay también las conquistas de calurosas regiones, donde
    los insectos vigilan la copulación de los guardianes del
    sembrado
que pierden la voz entre los cañaduzales sin límite
    surcados por rápidas acequias
y opacos reptiles de blanca y rica piel.
¡Oh el desvelo de los vigilantes que golpean sin descanso
    sonoras latas de petróleo
para espantar los acuciosos insectos que envía la noche
    como una promesa de vigilia!
Camino del mar pronto se olvidan estas cosas.
Y si una mujer espera con sus blancos y espesos muslos
    abiertos como las ramas de un florido písamo
    centenario,
entonces el poema llega a su fin, no tiene ya sentido su
    monótono treno
de fuente turbia y siempre renovada por el cansado cuerpo
    de viciosos gimnastas.

Sólo una palabra.
Una palabra y se inicia la danza
de una fértil miseria.

1965

A Word

When suddenly in the middle of a life arrives a word
    never before pronounced,
A dense tide gathers us in its arms and the long voyage
    starts amidst magic recently begun,
elevating as a scream in a vast abandoned hangar where
    moss shelters the walls,
amidst the rust of forgotten creatures who inhabit a world
    in ruins, a word is enough,
a word and thus starts the serene dance leading us
    through a thick dust of cities,
toward the stained glass of a dark health house, toward
    patios where soot blossoms and dense shadows nest,
humid shadows, which give life to tired women.
No truth resides in these corners and yet there is the
    surprise of a mute dread
which fills up life with its vinegared breath—rancid
    vinegar spilling through the wet cabinet of a humble
    house of pleasure.
And that's not it either.
There are also conquests of hot regions, where insects
    survey the copulating guardians of a sown land
who lose their voices among acres of boundless sugarcane
    furrowed by quick ditches
and opaque reptiles of white and rich skin.
Oh the wakefulness of keepers who restlessly beat loud
    drums of oil
to drive off the eager insects sent by night like a promise
    of vigil!
On the way to the sea you soon forget these things.
And if a woman waits with her white and dense thighs
    open like branches of the hundred year pisamo tree,
then the poem comes to its end, no longer a sense to its
    monotonous dirge
that comes from a cloudy source always renovated by the
    tired bodies of vicious gymnasts.

Only one word.
One word and the dance starts
of a fertile misery.

trans. Sophie Cabot Black and Maria Negroni

Sonata

¿Sabes qué te esperaba tras esos pasos del arpa llamándote
     de otro tiempo, de otros días?
¿Sabes por qué un rostro, un gesto, visto desde el tren que
     se detiene al final del viaje,
antes de perderte en la ciudad que resbala entre la niebla y
     la lluvia,
vuelven un día a visitarte, a decirte con unos labios sin
     voz, la palabra que tal vez iba a salvarte?
¡A dónde has ido a plantar tus tiendas! ¿Por qué esa ancla
     que revuelve las profundidades ciegamente y tú nada
     sabes?
Una gran extensión de agua suavemente se mece en vastas
     regiones ofrecidas al sol de la tarde;
aguas del gran río que luchan contra un mar en extremo
     cruel y helado, que levanta sus olas contra el
     cielo y va a perderlas tristemente en la lodosa
     sabana del delta.

Tal vez eso pueda ser.
Tal vez allí te digan algo.
O callen fieramente y nada sepas.
¿Recuerdas cuando bajó al comedor para desayunar y la
     viste de pronto, más niña, más lejana, más bella que
     nunca?
También allí esperaba algo emboscado.
Lo supiste por cierto sordo dolor que cierra el pecho.
Pero alguien habló.
Un sirviente dejó caer un plato.
Una risa en la mesa vecina,
algo rompió la cuerda que te sacaba del profundo pozo
     como a José los mercaderes.
Hablaste entonces y sólo te quedó esa tristeza que ya sabes
y el dulceamargo encanto por su asombro ante el mundo,
alzado al aire de cada día como un estandarte que señalara
     tu presencia y el sitio de tus batallas.
¿Quién eres, entonces? ¿De dónde salen de pronto esos
     asuntos en un puerto y ese tema que teje la viola
tratando de llevarte a cierta plaza, a un silencioso y viejo
     parque
con su estanque en donde navegan gozosos los veleros
     del verano?
No se puede saber todo.
No todo es tuyo.
No esta vez, por lo menos. Pero ya vas aprendiendo a
     resignarte y a dejar que
otro poco tuyo se vaya al fondo definitivamente
y quedes más solo aun y más extraño,

Sonata

Do you know what was waiting beyond those steps of the
     harp calling you from another time, other days?
Do you know why a face, a gesture, seen from the train
     that stops at voyage's end,
before losing you in the city that slips between fog and
     rain,
comes back one day to visit, to say with voiceless lips, the
     word that could maybe save you?
Where have you gone to set up your tents—why that
     anchor that blindly stirs the depths and you know
     nothing?
A great extension of water gently sways in huge regions
     offered to evening sun;
waters of the big river fighting an extremely cruel and icy
     sea, a sea that lifts its waves against the sky and loses
     them sadly in the muddy savanna of the delta.

Maybe that could be.
Maybe there they will tell you.
Or be furiously silent and you know nothing.
Do you remember when she came down for breakfast and
     you saw her suddenly, more childish, more distant,
     more beautiful than ever?
There too something was waiting in ambush.
You knew because of a dull pain against the chest.
But someone spoke.
A servant let a plate drop.
A laugh at the next table,
something broke the rope that pulled you out of the deep
     well like the merchants did to José.
You talked then, you kept only that already familiar sadness
and the bittersweet charm, her awe, in the face of
     the world,
lifted to the air of each day like a flag that could point to
     your presence, the site of your battles.
Who are you then? Where do these affairs of harbors
     suddenly come from, this theme that knits the viola
trying to take you to a certain square, to a silent old park
with its pond where boats of summer joyously sail?
You cannot know everything.
Not everything is yours.
Not this time at least. But already you are learning to
     resign, to let
yet another part of you hit absolute bottom,
yourself to remain even more alone, more strange.
like a steward screamed at in the morning disorder of
     hotels,

como un camarero al que gritan en el desorden matinal de
    los hoteles,
órdenes, insultos y vagas promesas, en todas las lenguas de
    la tierra.

orders, insults, and vague promises, in all the languages of
    the earth.

trans. Sophie Cabot Black and Maria Negroni

1965

Claribel Alegría

EL SALVADOR
1924–

Born in Nicaragua, Claribel Alegría grew up in El Salvador and studied philosophy at George Washington University in the United States. She has published ten books of poems and (in collaboration with her husband, Darwin Flakoll) a novel, studies of Latin American history, and several anthologies of Hispanic poetry. In 1978 her book of poems *Sobrevivo* (*I Survive*) won Cuba's Casa de las Américas Prize. Although she lives now in Mallorca and in Managua, Alegría conceives of her poems as acts of solidarity—most immediately with the peasants who suffer in political wars and with the women writers of El Salvador and Nicaragua. In this sense, the issues of her later poems recall the dramas of political conscience that characterize the poems of many of her contemporaries, including Gioconda Belli, Ana Ilce, and Rosario Murillo. Austere, vivid, stringent in its avoidance of sentimentality, Alegría's is a poetry of testimony.

Hacia la edad jurásica

Alguien los trajo a Palma
tenían el tamaño de una iguana
y comían insectos
y ratones.
El clima fue propicio
y empezaron a crecer
abandonaron las ratas
por los pollos
y seguían creciendo
se comían los perros
a más de un burro solitario
a los niños que andaban sueltos
pos las calles.
Todas las cloacas
se atascaron
y huyeron al campo
se comieron las vacas
los corderos
y seguían creciendo
derrumbaron murallas
masticaban olivos
se rascaban el lomo

Toward the Jurassic Age

Someone brought them to Palma
the size of an iguana
they ate insects and rats
the climate was favorable
they started to grow
they left rats for chickens and dogs
they ate more than one lonely donkey
children turned loose on the streets
the gutters were clogged as they
fled to the fields
they ate cows, sheep and kept growing
they tore down walls
they chewed up olive trees
they scratched their backs
on jutting rocks until
landslides blocked the roads
they leapt over the landslides
and now they are in Valldemossa
they killed the village doctor
and, frightened, the people hid
there are herbivores

contra rocas salientes
y hube derrumbes que bloquearon el camino
pero saltaron sobre los derrumbes
y están ahora en Valldemossa
y mataron al médico
del pueblo
y todos los vecinos
se asustaron
y corrieron despavoridos a esconderse.
Hay herbívoros
y carnívoros se conocen
por la gorra castrense
que corona su cresta
pero ambos son dañinos
engullen plantaciones
y tienen pulgas del tamaño
de un gran plato
se rascan contra las paredes
y las casas se caen.
Están ahora en Valldemossa
y sólo pueden abatirse
por cohetes proyectados
desde aviones
pero nadie aguanta el hedor
cuando uno muere
y la gente protesta
y no hay manera
de enterrarlos.

and carnivores among them
the carnivores know one another
by the military caps that crown
their crests
but both are harmful
they devour plantations
and carry fleas the size of supper plates
they scratch against walls
until houses tumble
they are now in Valldemossa
and can only be killed
by rockets dropped from planes
but no one can stand the stench
when one of them dies
the people protest that it is
impossible to bury them

trans. Carolyn Forché

1982

Éramos tres

A Paco, a Rodolfo

Era invierno con nieve
era de noche
hoy es día de verdes
de pájaros
de sol
día de cenizas
y lamentos
me empuja el viento
me lleva por el puente
por la tierra agrietada
por el arroyo seco
rebosante de plásticos y latas
la muerte cobra vida
aquí en Deyá
los arroyos
los puentes

We Were Three

To Paco and Rodolfo

It was winter,
there was snow,
it was night,
this is a green day
of doves and sun
of ashes and cries.
The wind pushes me
across the bridge
over the cracked earth
through a dry streambed
strewn with cans.
Death comes to life
here in Deya,
the torrents
the stone bridge.

mis muertos acechando
en cada esquina
las rejas inocentes
de un balcón
el reflejo borroso
de mis muertos
me sonríen de lejos
se despiden
salen del cemeterio
forman muro
se me vuelve translúcida
la piel
me tocan a la puerta
gesticulan
era de piedra el puente
era de noche
los brazos enlazados
por el vaivén de un canto
como pequeñas nubes congeladas
nos salía el aliento
de las bocas
era invierno con nieve
eramos tres
hoy la tierra está seca
reverbera
se me caen los brazos
estoy sola
montan guardia mis muertos
me hacen señas
me asaltan por la radio
en el periódico
el muro de mis muertos
se levanta
se extiende de Aconcagua
hasta el Izalco
continúan su lucha
marcan rumbos
era de piedra el puente
era de noche
nadie sabe decir
cómo murieron
sus voces perseguidas
se confunden
murieron en la cárcel
torturados
se levantan mis muertos
tienen rabia
las calles están solas
me hacen guiños
soy cementerio apátrida
no caben.

My dead wait
at every corner,
the innocent grillwork of balconies
the filmed mirror of my dead.
They smile from the distance
and wave to me,
they leave the cemetery,
a wall of the dead.
My flesh emits light
and they come to my door
waving their arms.
The bridge was stone,
it was night,
our arms circled each other,
we swayed to our songs,
our breath rose from our mouths
in small, crystalline clouds,
it was winter,
there was snow,
we were three.
Today the earth is dry
and resounds like a drum,
my arms fall to my sides,
I am alone.
My dead stand watch
and send signals to me,
they assail me
in the radio and paper.
The wall of my dead
rises and reaches from Aconcagua to Izalco.
The bridge was stone,
it was night,
no one can say
how they died.
Their persecuted voices are one voice
dying by torture in prison.
My dead arise, they rage.
The streets are empty
but my dead wink at me.
I am a cemetery,
I have no country
and they are too many to bury.

trans. Carolyn Forché

1982

Ernesto Cardenal

Ernesto Cardenal's poems bear testimony about his commitment both to the politics of Marxist revolution and to the power of liberation theology. At their integral best, the poems make these two commitments seem movingly reciprocal. Although from the late 1940s Cardenal had been involved in Vanguardist poetry and in political work against the Somoza regime, his overtly religious commitment began in 1954, when he entered a Catholic seminary to train for the priesthood. His theological education took place at the Trappist monastery of Gethsemane, where he worked with Thomas Merton. Later Cardenal studied in Cuernavaca, Mexico, and in Colombia. (He describes those experiences in the 1961 autobiographical work *Gethsemane, Kentucky*.) Ordained in 1965, Cardenal returned to Nicaragua and established a religious community on the island of Solentiname in Lake Nicaragua. Somozan soldiers destroyed the monastery there in 1977, and Cardenal fled the country. After his return from exile in Costa Rica and in Cuba, he served as minister of culture for the Sandinista government.

Grounded in a double commitment to historical liberation and spiritual redemption, Cardenal's poems declare a longing for mystical union with God while they explore the distance the human soul feels from that transcendent communion. Cardenal meditates on the struggles of human experience within this spiritual gap, declares his solidarity with oppressed minorities, and opens his poems to analysis of the dynamics of radical social change. In *Salmos* (*Psalms*, 1969), for instance, Cardenal reaches toward an affirmation of God's benevolence toward sinful and suffering humanity, at the same time detailing guerrilla efforts during the revolutionary period of 1954–1956. His later poems detail these themes in more declamatory and narrative forms. In his movement through doubt toward a positive faith, Cardenal reveals also the influence that North American poets –especially Dickinson, Whitman, and Pound––have had on his poems.

León

Yo vivía en una casa grande junto a la iglesia de San
    Francisco
que tenía una leyenda en el zaguán que decía
             AVE MARIA
y rojos corredores de ladrillos de barro,
viejas tejas rojas,
            y ventanas de rejas ensarradas,
y un gran patio angustioso en las tardes sin aire
con un alcaraván triste que cantaba las horas,
y una tía blanca en el patio rezando el rosario.
En las tardes se oía aquel toque del Angelus
        (*"El Ángel del Señor anunció a María..."*)
la mano de una niña lejana tocando una nota de piano,
        y el clarín de un cuartel.
De noche una enorme luna roja subía del Calvario.
Me contaban cuentos de ánimas en pena y aparecidos.
        A media noche
la sombra del general Arechabala cabalgaba por las calles.

León

I used to live in a big house by the Church of St. Francis
which had an inscription in the entrance hall saying
             AVE MARIA
and red corridors of brick,
an old red-tiled roof,
          and windows with rusty iron grilles,
and a large courtyard just unbearable on stuffy afternoons
with a sad clock bird singing out the hours,
and someone's pale aunt in the courtyard reciting the
    rosary.
In the evenings I'd hear that angelus bell
        (*"The Angel of the Lord declared unto Mary..."*)
the hand of a distant little girl playing a note on the piano,
        and the bugle from some barracks.
At night a huge red moon rose above Calvary
They told me stories of souls in purgatory and ghosts.
        At midnight
the shade of General Arechabala rode a horse through the
    streets.

Y el ruido de una puerta que se cierra... Un coche negro...
Una carreta vacía corriendo, traqueteando, por la Calle
    Real.
Y después todos los gallos del vecindario cantando,
y el canto del alcaraván,
y mi tía que salía cada día a su misa de 4
con las compañas repicando en San Francisco,
               repicando
en el Calvario
               y en el Hospicio de San Juan
y las pichingas de los lecheros chocando en el empedrado
y un panadero golpeando en un zaguán
y gritando
          EL PAN
              EL PAN

                  1954

And the noise of a door closing... A black coach...
An empty cart rattling as it rolled through the Calle Real.
And then all the roosters in the neighborhood crowing,
and the song of the clock bird,
and my aunt who'd leave each morning for mass at 4
with the bells ringing in St. Francis,
               ringing
in Calvary
               and in St. John's Hospital
and the jars of the milkmen clattering on the stone
    pavement
and a bread vendor knocking on a front door
and crying
          BREAD
              BREAD

          trans. Jonathan Cohen

Como latas de cerveza vacías

Como latas de cerveza vacías y colillas
de cigarrillos apagados, han sido mis días.
Como figuras que pasan por una pantalla de televisión
y desaparecen, así ha pasado mi vida.
Como los automóviles que pasaban rápidos por
    las carreteras
con risas de muchachas y música de radios...
Y la belleza pasó rápida, como el modelo de los autos
y las canciones de los radios que pasaron de moda.
Y no ha quedado nada de aquellos días, nada,
más que latas vacías y colillas apagadas,
risas en fotos marchitas, boletos rotos,
y el aserrín con que al amanecer barrieron los bares.

                  1960

Like Empty Beer Cans

Like empty beer cans, like empty
    cigarette butts;
my days have been like that.
Like figures passing on a
    T.V. screen.
And disappearing, so my
    life has gone.
Like cars going by fast
    on the roads
with girls laughing and radios
    playing...
Beauty got obsolete as fast
    as car models
and forgotten radio hits.
Nothing is left of those
    days, nothing,
but empty beer cans,
    cigarette butts,
smiles on faded photos, torn
    tickets
and the sawdust with which,
    in the mornings,
they swept out the bars.

           trans. Thomas Merton

Salmo 5

Escucha mis palabras oh Señor
          Oye mis gemidos

Psalm 5

Give ear to my words, O Lord,
          Harken unto my moaning

Escucha mi protesta
Porque no eres tú un Dios amigo de los dictadores
ni partidario de su política
ni te influencia la propaganda
ni estás en sociedad con el gángster

No existe sinceridad en sus discursos
ni en sus declaraciones de prensa

Hablan de paz en sus discursos
mientras aumentan su producción de guerra
Hablan de paz en las Conferencias de Paz
y en secreto se preparan para la guerra
    Sus radios mentirosos rugen toda la noche
Sus escritorios están llenos de planes criminales y
    expedientes siniestros
Pero tú me salvarás de sus planes
Hablan con la boca de las ametralladoras
Sus lenguas relucientes
    son las bayonetas...

Castígalos oh Dios
    malogra su política
confunde sus memorandums
    impide sus programas
A la hora de la Sirena de Alarma
tú estarás conmigo
tú serás mi refugio el día de la Bomba
Al que no cree en la mentira de sus anuncios comerciales
ni en sus campañas publicitarias ni en sus campañas
    politicas
    tú lo bendices
Lo rodeas con tu amor
    como con tanques blindados

1964

Pay heed to my protest
For you are not a God friendly to dictators
neither are you a partisan of their politics
nor are you influenced by their propaganda
neither are you in league with the gangster

There is no sincerity in their speeches
nor in their press releases

They speak of peace in their speeches
while they increase their war production
They speak of peace at Peace Conferences
and secretly prepare for war
    Their lying radios roar into the night
Their desks are strewn with criminal intentions and
    sinister reports
But you will deliver me from their plans
They speak through the mouth of the submachine-gun
Their flashing tongues are bayonets...

Punish them, O Lord,
    thwart them in their policies
confuse their memorandums
    obstruct their programs
At the hour of Alarm
you shall be with me
you shall be my refuge on the day of the Bomb
To him who believes not in the lies of their commercial
    messages
nor in their publicity campaigns nor in their political
    campaigns
    you will give your blessing
With love do you compass him
    as with armor-plated tanks

trans. Robert Márquez

Oración por Marilyn Monroe

Señor
recibe a esta muchacha conocida en toda la tierra con el
    nombre de Marilyn Monroe
aunque ese no era su verdadero nombre
(pero Tú conoces su verdadero nombre, el de la
    huerfanita violada a los 9 años
y la empleadita de tienda que a los 16 se había querido
    matar)
y que ahora se presenta ante Ti sin ningún maquillaje
sin su Agente de Prensa
sin fotógrafos y sin firmar autógrafos
sola como un astronauta frente a la noche espacial.

Prayer for Marilyn Monroe

Lord
accept this girl called Marilyn Monroe throughout the
    world
though that was not her name
(but You know her real name, that of the orphan raped
    at nine,
the shopgirl who tried to kill herself aged just sixteen)
who now goes into Your presence without make-up
without her Press Agent
without her photographs or signing autographs
lonely as an astronaut facing the darkness of outer space.

Ella soñó cuando niña que estaba desnuda en una iglesia
      (según cuenta el *Time*)
ante una multitud postrada, con las cabezas en el suelo
y tenía que caminar en puntillas para no pisar las cabezas.
Tú conoces nuestros sueños mejor que los psiquiatras.
Iglesia, casa, cueva, son la seguridad del seno materno
pero también algo más que eso...
Las cabezas son los admiradores, es claro
(la masa de cabezas en la oscuridad bajo el chorro de luz).
Pero el templo no son los estudios de la 20th Century-Fox.
El templo—de mármol y oro—es el templo de su cuerpo
en el que está el Hijo del Hombre con un látigo en la mano
expulsando a los mercaderes de la 20th Century-Fox
que hicieron de Tu casa de oración una cueva de ladrones.

Señor
en este mundo contaminado de pecados y radiactividad
Tú no culparás tan sólo a una empleadita de tienda
que como toda empleadita de tienda soñó ser estrella
    de cine.
Y su sueño fue realidad (pero como la realidad
    del technicolor).
Ella no hizo sino actuar según el script que le dimos
—el de nuestras propias vidas—y era un script absurdo.
Perdónala Señor y perdónanos a nosotros
por nuestra 20th Century
por esta Colosal Super-Producción en la que todos hemos
    trabajado.

Ella tenía hambre de amor y le ofrecimos tranquilizantes
para la tristeza de no ser santos
        se le recomendó el Psicoanálisis.
Recuerda Señor su creciente pavor a la cámara
y el odio al maquillaje—insistiendo en maquillarse en
    cada escena—
y cómo se fue haciendo mayor el horror
y mayor la impuntualidad a los estudios.

Como toda empleadita de tienda
soñó ser estrella de cine.
Y su vida fue irreal como un sueño que un psiquiatra
    interpreta y archiva.

Sus romances fueron un beso con los ojos cerrados
que cuando se abren los ojos
se descubre que fue bajo los reflectores
    y apagan los reflectores!
y desmontan las dos paredes del aposento (era un set
    cinematográfico)
mientras el Director se aleja con su libreta
    porque la escena ya fue tomada.
O como un viaje en yate, un beso en Singapur, un baile
    en Río

When she was a girl, she dreamed she was naked in a
    church (according to *Time*)
standing in front of a prostrate multitude, heads to the
    ground,
and had to walk on tiptoe to avoid the heads.
You know our dreams better than the psychiatrists.
Church, house, or cave all represent the safety of the womb
but also something more....
The heads are admirers, so much is clear (that
mass of heads in the darkness below the beam to the
    screen).
But the temple isn't the studios of 20th Century-Fox.
The temple, of gold and marble, is the temple of her body
in which the Son of Man stands whip in hand
driving out the money-changers of 20th Century-Fox
who made Your house of prayer a den of thieves.

Lord,
in this world defiled by radioactivity and sin,
surely You will not blame a shopgirl
who (like any other shopgirl) dreamed of being a star.
And her dream became "reality" (Technicolor reality).
All she did was follow the script we gave her,
that of our own lives, but it was meaningless.
Forgive her Lord and forgive all of us
for this our 20th Century
and the Mammoth Super-Production in whose making
    we all shared.

She was hungry for love and we offered her tranquilizers.
For the sadness of our not being saints
        they recommended Psychoanalysis.
Remember Lord her increasing terror of the camera
and hatred of make-up (yet her insistence on fresh
    make-up
for each scene) and how the terror grew
and how her unpunctuality at the studios grew.

Like any other shopgirl
she dreamed of being a star.
And her life was as unreal as a dream an analyst reads
    and files.

Her romances were kisses with closed eyes
which when the eyes are opened
are seen to have been played out beneath the spotlights
    and the spotlights are switched off
and the two walls of the room (it was a set) are
    taken down
while the Director moves away notebook in hand,
    the scene being safely canned.
Or like a cruise on a yacht, a kiss in Singapore, a dance
    in Rio,

la recepción en la mansión del Duque y la Duquesa
    de Windsor
vistos en la salita del apartamento miserable.

La película terminó sin el beso final.
La hallaron muerta en su cama con la mano en el teléfono.
Y los detectives no supieron a quién iba a llamar.
Fue
como alguien que ha marcado el número de la única voz
    amiga
y oye tan sólo la voz de un disco que le dice: WRONG
    NUMBER
O como alguien que herido por los gángsters
alarga la mano a un teléfono desconectado.

Señor
quienquiera que haya sido el que ella iba a llamar
y no llamó (y tal vez no era nadie
o era Alguien cuyo número no está en el Directorio de
    Los Angeles)
        contesta Tú el teléfono!

                                    1965

Luces

    Aquel vuelo clandestino de noche.
Con peligro de ser derribados. La noche serena.
El cielo lleno, llenísimo de estrellas. La Vía Láctea
clarísima tras el grueso vidrio de la ventanilla,
    masa blancuzca y rutilante en la noche negra
con sus millones de procesos de evoluciones y revoluciones.
Íbamos sobre el mar para evitar la aviación somocista,
    pero cerca de la costa.
El pequeño avión volando bajo, y volando lento.
Primero las luces de Rivas, tomada y retomada por los
    Sandinistas, ahora a medias en poder de los
    Sandinistas.
Después otras luces: Granada, en poder de la guardia
    (sería atacada esa noche).
Masaya, totalmente liberada. Tantos cayeron allí.
Más allá un resplandor: Managua. Lugar de tantos
    combates.
(El Bunker—todavía el bastión de la guardia).
Diriamba, liberada. Jinotepe, con combates. Tanto
    heroísmo
relumbra en esas luces. Montelimar—nos señalaba el
    piloto—:
la hacienda del tirano junto al mar. Al lado, Puerto Somoza.
La Vía Láctea arriba, y las luces de la revolución de
    Nicaragua.
Me parece mirar más lejos, en el norte, la fogata de

a reception in the mansion of the Duke and Duchess of
    Windsor viewed in the sad tawdriness of a cheap
    apartment.

The film ended without the final kiss.
They found her dead in bed, hand on the phone.
And the detectives never learned who she was going to call.
It was as
though someone had dialed the only friendly voice
and heard a prerecorded tape just saying "WRONG NUMBER";
or like someone wounded by gangsters, who
reaches out toward a disconnected phone.

Lord, whoever
it may have been that she was going to call
but did not (and perhaps it was no one at all
or Someone not in the Los Angeles telephone book),
        Lord, You pick up that phone.

                        trans. Robert Pring-Mill

Lights

    That clandestine night flight.
Running the risk of being shot down. The night serene.
The heavens filled, so filled with stars. The Milky Way
so clear beyond the thick glass of the window,
    a whitish and shimmering mass in the black night
with its millions of processes of evolutions and revolutions.
We were flying over the sea to evade the Somoza airforce,
    but near the coast.
The little plane flying low, and flying slow.
First the lights of Rivas, taken and retaken by the
    Sandinistas, now halfway in the Sandinistas' hands.
Then other lights: Granada, in the hands of the guard
    (it would be attacked that night).
Masaya, completely liberated. So many fell there.
Further on, a glitter: Managua. The site of so many battles.
(The Bunker—still the bastion of the guard.)
Diriamba: liberated. Jinotepe, still fighting. So much
    heroism
shines in those lights. Montelimar—the pilot points
    it out—:
the tyrant's seaside estate. Beside it Puerto Somoza.
The Milky Way above, and the lights of Nicaragua's
    revolution.
I seem to see further off, in the north, Sandino's campfire
    ("That light is Sandino").
The stars above us, and the smallness of this earth

Sandino ("Aquella luz es Sandino").
Las estrellas sobre nosotros, y la pequeñez de esta tierra
pero también la importancia de ella, de estas
pequeñitas luces de los hombres. Pienso: todo es luz.
El planeta viene del sol. Es luz hecha sólida.
La electricidad de este avión es luz. El metal es luz. El calor
    de la vida viene del sol.
        "Hágase la luz".
También están las tinieblas.
Hay extraños reflejos—no sé de donde vienen—en
    la superficie transparente de la ventanilla.
Una luminosidad roja: las luces de la cola del avión.
Y reflejos en el mar tranquilo: serán las estrellas.
Miro la lucecita de mi cigarillo—también viene del sol,
    de una estrella.
Y la silueta de un barco grande. ¿El portavión de los
    EE.UU.
enviado a patrullar la costa del Pacífico?
Una gran luz a la derecha nos sobresalta. ¿Un jet contra
    nosotros?
No. La luna que sale, media luna, serenísima, iluminada
    por el sol.
    El peligro de ir volando en una noche tan clara.
Y el radio de pronto. Palabras confusas llenando el
    pequeño avión.
¿La guardia? El piloto dice: "son los nuestros".
    Esas ondas son de nosotros.
Ya estamos cerca de León, el territorio liberado.
Una intensa luz rojo-anaranjada, como la brasa de un
    puro: Corinto:
la potente iluminación de los muelles rielando en el mar.
Y ahora ya la playa de Poneloya, y el avión entrando
    a tierra,
el cordón de espuma de la costa radiante bajo la luna.
    El avión bajando. Un olor a insecticida.
    Y me dice Sergio: "¡El olor de Nicaragua!"
    Es el momento de mayor peligro, la aviación enemiga
        puede estar esperándonos sobre este aeropuerto.
    Y ya las luces del aeropuerto.
Estamos en tierra. Salen de la oscuridad los compas verde-
    olivo a abrazarnos.
Sentimos sus cuerpos calientes, que también vienen del
    sol, que también son luz.
    Es contra las tinieblas esta revolución.
Era la madrugada del 18 de julio. Y el comienzo
    de todo lo que estaba por venir.

but the importance of it as well, of these
tiny little human lights. I think: everything is light.
The planet comes from the sun. It is light made solid.
This plane's electricity is light. The metal is light. Life's
    warmth comes from the sun.
        "Let there be light."
There is darkness too.
There are strange reflections—I don't know where they
    come from—
        on the clear surface of the windows.
A red luminosity: the plane's taillights.
And reflections on the calm sea: they must be the stars.
I look at my cigarette's glow—it too comes from the sun,
    from a star.
And the silhouette of a big ship. The U.S. aircraft carrier
sent to patrol the Pacific coast?
A big light on the right startles us. A jet against us?
No. The moon coming up, a halfmoon, so serene, lit by
    the sun.
    The danger of flying on such a clear night.
And suddenly the radio. Confused words filling the little
    plane.
The guard? The pilot says: "they're ours."
    Those waves are ours.
Now we're near León, liberated territory.
An intense reddish-orange light, like the red-hot glow of a
    cigar: Corinto:
the powerful dock lights shimmering on the sea.
And now the Poneloya beach, and the plane coming in to
    land,
the coast a line of foam radiating light beneath the moon.
    The plane descending. A smell of insecticide.
And Sergio says to me: "The smell of Nicaragua!"
This is the most dangerous part, the enemy airforce
    could be waiting for us over this airport.
And finally the airport lights.
We've landed, Comrades clad in olive-green come out of
    the dark to embrace us.
We feel their warm bodies, which also come from the sun,
which are also light.
    It's against the darkness, this revolution.
It was the dawn of July 18. And the beginning
    of everything that was to come.

trans. Jonathan Cohen

1979

Rosario Castellanos

MEXICO
1925–1974

Born in Mexico City, Rosario Castellanos spent much of her childhood in Comitán, in Mayan southern Mexico. After traveling to Europe and to the United States for advanced study in aesthetics, she returned to the province of Chiapas to work with Indian theater groups and the Indigenous Institute of San Cristóbal. Much of her work, even throughout her involvement with the literary group "The Generation of the '50s," tried to traverse the distance between the pre-Columbian and the European cultural traditions of Mexico. This social division was complicated, for Castellanos, by her awareness of the alienated and disempowered situation of women in both traditions. Castellanos' friend Elena Poniatowska characterized this complex position in personal terms: "Rosario was always alone. Her childhood was lonely, her adolescence desperately so, and as an adult she lived under the sign not just of loneliness but of singleness. Solitude becomes the thread that sews the pages of her books, linking poetry and prose and running from her novel *Balún Canán* [1957] . . . to the poems collected in *Poesía no eres tú* [*You Are Not Poetry*, 1972]." José Emilio Pacheco describes the effect of this alienation on her work: "At that time, no one in this country was so clearly aware of her double status, as a woman and as a Mexican, nor did anyone else make of this awareness the very material of her writing, the central thread of her work."

The evolution of Rosario Castellanos' poems tracks a long sequence of excision, clarification, and self-denial. In the effort to tell an undisguised truth, Castellanos moves from an early poetic style rich in imagery and dislocations toward a style of direct statement, simple diction, and occasionally mordant humor. According to Castellanos, her poetic vision was determined in large part by the Mexican Indian's mystical understanding of the interconnectedness of all life; further, the influence of Gabriela Mistral is sometimes clear in her later poems. Castellanos also wrote formative literary essays, fiction, and a ground-breaking feminist play, the giddy farce *El eterno femenino* (*The Eternal Feminine*, 1975). Her sharp wit is evident even in the title of her most famous poem, "Poesía no eres tú," apparently a response to the nineteenth-century sentimentalization of a woman in one of Gustavo Adolfo Bécquer's Romantic *Rimas*. "¿Qué es poesía?" (What is poetry?), the woman in the Bécquer poem asks; the man responds, "Poesía eres tú" (You are poetry). While serving as Mexican ambassador to Israel, Castellanos died in a freak household accident in Tel Aviv. In an irony she might have enjoyed, she was buried in the Rotunda of Illustrious Men, in Mexico City.

Una palmera

Señora de los vientos,
garza de la llanura,
cuando te meces canta
tu cintura.

Gesto de la oración
o preludio del vuelo,
en tu copa se vierten uno a uno
los cielos.

A Palm Tree

Lady of the winds,
heron of the plains,
when you sway
your being sings.

Gesture of prayer
or prelude to flight,
through your branches
the heavens flow.

Desde el país oscuro de los hombres
he venido, a mirarte, de rodillas.
Alta, desnuda, única.
Poesía.

From the dark land of men
I have come, on my knees, to behold you.
Tall, naked, singular.
Poetry.

1952

trans. Myralyn F. Allgood

El otro

¿Por qué decir nombres de dioses, astros,
espumas de un océano invisible,
polen de los jardines más remotos?
Si nos duele la vida, si cada día llega
desgarrando la entraña, si cada noche cae
convulsa, asesinada.
Si nos duele el dolor en alguien, en un hombre
al que no conocemos, pero está
presente a todas horas y es la víctima
y el enemigo y el amor y todo
lo que nos falta para ser enteros.
Nunca digas que es tuya la tiniebla,
no te bebas de un sorbo la alegría.
Mira a tu alrededor: hay otro, siempre hay otro.
Lo que él respira es lo que a ti te asfixia,
lo que come es tu hambre.
Muere con la mitad más pura de tu muerte.

The Other

Why utter the names of gods or stars,
foam of an invisible ocean,
pollen of the most remote gardens?
If life hurts, if each day breaks
clawing at our gut, if each night falls
convulsed, murdered.
If the hurt in someone else hurts us, in a man
we don't know, who is
present always and is the victim
and the enemy and love and all
we need to be whole.
Never say darkness is yours,
don't gulp down joy.
Look around you: there is the other, always the other.
He breathes what chokes you.
He eats your hunger.
He dies with the purest half of your death.

1959

trans. Maureen Ahern

Poesía no eres tú

Porque si tú existieras
tendría que existir yo también. Y eso es mentira.

Nada hay más que nosotros: la pareja,
los sexos conciliados en un hijo,
las dos cabezas juntas, pero no contemplándose
(para no convertir a nadie en un espejo)
sino mirando frente a sí, hacia el otro.

El otro: mediador, juez, equilibrio
entre opuestos, testigo,
nudo en el que se anuda lo que se había roto.

El otro, la mudez que pide voz
al que tiene la voz
y reclama el oído del que escucha.

El otro. Con el otro
la humanidad, el diálogo, la poesía, comienzan.

You Are Not Poetry

Because if you existed
I too must exist. And that is a lie.

There is nothing more than us: the couple,
sexes conciliated in a child,
two heads together, but not looking at each other
(so that no one is turned into a mirror),
rather staring straight ahead, toward the other.

The other: mediator, judge, balance
between opposites, witness,
knot that binds up all that had broken.

The other, muteness begging a voice
from the speaker,
claiming an ear
from the listener.

The other. With the other
humanity, dialogue, poetry begin.

1972

trans. Maureen Ahern

El retorno

Piso la tierra del Anáhuac que es
la tierra de mis muertos.

Pues bien: como su nombre lo indica—y otros signos—
están muertos. No hablan.

Algunos, los recientes, con el mentón atado
todavía al último pañuelo.
Otros con la mandíbula intacta, calcio vuelto
a su existencia mineral que es muda.

Así pues, no me piden
que yo viva por ellos,
que mire el mundo que no ven, que lleve
adelante un destino que no alcanzó a cumplirse.

Si necesito justificaciones
para estar, para hacer
y, sobre todo, para no borrarme
(que sería lo lógico siguiendo las premisas)
habrá que conseguirlas de otro modo.

¿Con los vivientes, que me dan la espalda,
que no me ven pero que si me vieran
sería con el rechazo del que sabe
que, por ley natural, a menos cuerpos
mayor espacio y aire y esperanza?

¿Con los que llegan ya con la granada lista
para hacerla explotar, entre sus manos?
¿Con los que ven en mí el estorbo, la ruina,
el esperpento
que hay que destruir para construir de nuevo?

No. La respuesta no han
de darla únicamente los humanos.

Quizá hacer una obra...
¿Obra? ¿Cambiar la faz de la naturaleza?
¿Añadir algún libro a las listas bibliográficas?
¿Hacer variar el rumbo de la historia?

Pero si éste es asunto—otra vez—de hombres
y del tiempo medido al modo de los hombres
y según los criterios
con los que ellos aceptan o rechazan.

¿Entonces, qué? ¿Dios? ¿Su mandato?
Es demasiado tarde para inventar ahora
o para regresar a la infancia dorada.

The Return

I walk the land of Anahuac which is
the land of my dead.

Yes: as their names suggest—and other signs—
they are dead. They do not speak.

Some, the most recent, have their chins tied
with the final kerchief.
Others with their jaw intact, calcium reverted
to its mute mineral state.

So, then, do not ask me
to live for them.
To see the world they do not see, to body
forth a destiny left incomplete.

If I need justification
for existing, for doing
and, above all, for not erasing myself
(which would be logical based on the evidence)
I will have to obtain it some other way.

From the living, who turn their backs on me,
who do not see me but who if they did
would reject me like those who know
that, by a law of nature, fewer bodies mean
more space and air and hope?

From those who arrive with the grenade already poised
to explode between their hands?
From those who see in me an obstacle, a ruin,
a hideous sight
that must be destroyed in order to construct the new?

No. The answer will not
come from humans alone.

Perhaps to undertake some great work...
Work? Change nature's face?
Add some book to the bibliographies?
Change the course of history?

But that's a man's job—again—
cut to time measured to fit men
following the criteria
they use to accept or reject.

Then what? God? His reign?
It is too late now to invent
or return to golden childhood.

Acepta nada más los hechos: has venido
y es igual que tu hubieras quedado o que si nunca
tu hubieras ido. Igual. Para ti. Para todos.

Superflua aquí. Superflua allá. Superflua
exactamente igual a cada uno
de los que ves y de los que no ves.

Ninguno es necesario
ni aun para ti, que por definición
eres menesterosa.

Just accept the facts: you are here
and it's all the same as if you had stayed or never
left. The same. For you. For everyone.

Superfluous here. Superfluous there. Superfluous
exactly like each and every one
you see and do not see.

No one is necessary
not even for you, who by definition
are so needy.

1972

trans. Magda Bogin

Roberto Juarróz

ARGENTINA

1925–

In his most famous series, *Poesía vertical* (*Vertical Poetry*), Roberto Juarróz explores poetic space as a sequence of logical relations among numbers, objects, and human beings. The sparkle of paradox, irony, dramatic intelligence, and deductive reason applied to internal events gives his poems the cool inevitability of mathematical theorems. Educated in France, Juarróz heads the Department of Bibliotechnology and Informational Science at the University of Buenos Aires.

Hay puntos de silencio rodeando al corazón...

Hay puntos de silencio rodeando al corazón.
Son él mismo, pero enfrente.
recostado en sus múltiples fechas,
no deshecho en su muerte, pero en tratos con ella.

No es una escritura de silencio en busca de ojo,
ni un Dios asegurado afuera de sí mismo,
ni una lluvia cobarde,
ni un perro perseguido por su propio ladrido.

El corazón es una mano silenciosa
cuyos dedos están enfrente suyo.
Él los imita a latidos,
pero ellos no se dejan seducir

There Are Points of Silence Circling the Heart...

There are points of silence circling the heart.
They are itself, but facing it,
reclining on its multiple days,
not undone at its death, but on terms with her.

It is not a writing of silence looking for an eye,
nor a God safe outside himself,
nor a cowardly rain,
nor a dog tormented by his own barking.

The heart is a silent hand
with its fingers facing it.
It imitates their pulsing
but they won't be tempted.

1978

trans. W. S. Merwin

Véase primero el aire y su elemento negro que no cesa...

Véase primero el aire y su elemento negro que no cesa,
véase el lomo demasiado suave de las cosas que ha rozado
la muerte,

Look First at the Air and Its Black Element Which Never Stops...

Look first at the air and its black element which
never stops,
look at the too-smooth backs of the things which death
has been scraping,

véase cómo crece la mirada torcida, la mirada del hombre,
mientras la recta mirada de las cosas yace tirada en
    cualquier parte,
véase cómo hay orillas que pasan de ríos que no pasan
y violentas imitaciones del corazón rompiendo astas,
véase el trueno de vejez y gestos sin acabar que muerde
    al mundo,
véase el gastado carillón de la muerte,
su dentellada que por morder se muerde hasta a sí misma,
su lunático hipo de tumbas y borrones,
véase las narices que inventan fragancias sin vacíos
y el lecho que llegará cuando no estemos
y el ronquido que sella los amores.

Y tan sólo después
fírmese y cúmplase.

1978

La vida dibuja un árbol...

La vida dibuja un árbol
y la muerte dibuja otro.
La vida dibuja un nido
y la muerte lo copia.
La vida dibuja un pájaro
para que habite el nido
y la muerte de inmediato
dibuja otro pájaro.

Una mano que no dibuja nada
se pasea entre todos los dibujos
y cada tanto cambia uno de sitio.
Por ejemplo:
el pájaro de la vida
ocupa el nido de la muerte
sobre el árbol dibujado por la vida.

Otras veces
la mano que no dibuja nada
borra un dibujo de la serie.
Por ejemplo:
el árbol de la muerte
sostiene el nido de la muerte,
pero no lo ocupa ningún pájaro.

Y otras veces
la mano que no dibuja nada
se convierte a sí misma
en imagen sobrante,
con figura de pájaro,
con figura de árbol,

look how the crooked view is growing, man's view,
while the straight view is lying somewhere, thrown aside,
look how there are shores that are taken for rivers that are
    standing still
and there are violent imitations of the heart breaking
    spears,
look at the thunder of age and faces without end, which
    bites the world,
look at the worn-out carillon of death
with its gnashing that bites itself to have something to bite,
and its lunatic frenzy of tombs and blots,
look at the nostrils that invent fragrances without hollows
and at the bed that will arrive when we are not here
and at the snoring that is the seal of love.

Then and only then
sign and go through with it.

trans. W. S. Merwin

Life Draws a Tree...

Life draws a tree
and death draws another one.
Life draws a nest
and death copies it.
Life draws a bird
to live in the nest
and right away death
draws another bird.

A hand that draws nothing
wanders among the drawings
and at times moves one of them.
For example:
a bird of life
occupies the death's nest
on the tree that life drew.

Other times
the hand that draws nothing
blots out one drawing of the series.
For example:
the tree of death
holds the nest of death,
but there's no bird in it.

And other times
the hand that draws nothing
itself changes
into an extra image
in the shape of a bird,
in the shape of a tree,

con figura de nido.
Y entonces, sólo entonces,
no falta ni sobra nada.
Por ejemplo:
dos pájaros
ocupan el nido de la vida
sobre el árbol de la muerte.

O el árbol de la vida
sostiene dos nidos
en los que habita un solo pájaro.

O un pájaro único
habita un sólo nido
sobre el árbol de la vida
y el árbol de la muerte.

1978

in the shape of a nest.
And then, only then,
nothing's missing and nothing's left over.
For example:
two birds
occupy life's nest
in death's tree.

Or life's tree
holds two nests
with only one bird in them.

Or a single bird
lives in the one nest
on the tree of life
and the tree of death.

trans. W. S. Merwin

En alguna parte hay un hombre...

En alguna parte hay un hombre
que transpira pensamiento.
Sobre su piel se dibujan
los contornos húmedos de una piel más fina,
la estela de una navegación sin nave.

Cuando ese hombre piensa luz, ilumina,
cuando piensa muerte, se alisa,
cuando recuerda a alguien, adquiere sus rasgos,
cuando cae en sí mismo, se oscurece como un pozo.

En él se ve el color de los pensamientos nocturnos
y se aprende que ningún pensamiento carece
de su noche y su día.
Y también que hay colores y pensamientos
que no nacen de día ni de noche,
sino tan sólo cuando crece un poco más el olvido.

Ese hombre tiene la porosidad de una tierra más viva
y a veces, cuando sueña, toma aspecto de fuego,
salpicaduras de una llama que se alimenta con llama,
retorcimientos de bosque calcinado.

A ese hombre se le puede ver el amor,
pero eso tan sólo quien lo encuentre y lo ame.
Y también se podría ver en su carne a dios,
pero sólo después de dejar de ver todo el resto.

(A Octavio Paz)

1978

Somewhere There's a Man...

Somewhere there's a man
who sweats thought.
On his skin are drawn
the moist contours of a finer skin,
the wake of a navigation without a vessel.

When that man thinks light, he shines,
when he thinks death, he becomes polished,
when he remembers somebody, he acquires their features,
when he falls into himself he becomes dark like a well.

In him the color of night thoughts is visible,
and it's obvious that no thought is without
its night and day.
And also that there are colors and thoughts
that are not born of day nor of night
but only when oblivion grows a little bigger.

That man is porous, like an earth with more life in it,
and at times when he dreams, he looks like a fire:
splashes of a flame that feeds itself with flame,
writhings of calcined woods.

In that man love can be seen,
but only by someone who meets him and loves him.
And also in his flesh one could see god,
but only when one had stopped seeing all the rest.

(To Octavio Paz)

trans. W. S. Merwin

Jaime Sabines

MEXICO
1925–

In a daring contemporary idiom, the poems of Jaime Sabines consider the sense and nonsense of existence. Their silky musicality plays against the abruptness of their perceptions. Like the poets of the "impure" poetry he admires, Sabines is a skillful and intellectual writer who seems to enjoy violating taboos. Like the confessional poets, Sabines is also a writer of rapt emotional clarity. That combination of intellectual skepticism and clear emotion has made Sabines one of the most important poets of his generation.

Yo no lo sé de cierto...	*I Do Not Know It for Sure...*

Yo no lo sé de cierto, pero lo supongo
que una mujer y un hombre
algún día se quieren,
se van quedando solos poco a poco,
algo en su corazón les dice que están solos,
solos sobre la tierra se penetran,
se van matando el uno al otro.

Todo se hace en silencio. Como
se hace la luz dentro del ojo.
El amor une cuerpos.
En silencio se van llenando el uno al otro.

Cualquier día despiertan, sobre brazos;
piensan entonces que lo saben todo.
Se ven desnudos y lo saben todo.

(Yo no lo sé de cierto. Lo supongo.)

1950

I do not know it for sure, but I suppose
that a man and a woman
some day love each other,
they are left alone little by little
something in their heart tells them they are alone,
alone over the earth they penetrate each other
they go on killing each other.

Everything is done in silence, as
light is made inside the eye.
Love unites the bodies.
In silence they go on filling each other.

Any day they wake up, over arms;
they think then they know everything.
They see themselves naked and they know everything.

(I do not know it for sure, but I suppose it.)

trans. Isabel Bize

Los amorosos

Los amorosos callan.
El amor es el silencio más fino,
el más tembloroso, el más insoportable.
Los amorosos buscan,
los amorosos son los que abandonan,
son los que cambian, los que olvidan.
Su corazón les dice que nunca han de encontrar,
no encuentran, buscan.

Los amorosos andan como locos
porque están solos, solos, solos,
entregándose, dándose a cada rato,
llorando porque no salvan al amor.

The Lovers

Lovers become quiet.
Love is the most precious silence,
the most shaky, the most intolerable.
Lovers search,
lovers are those who abandon,
are those who change, those who forget.
Their heart tells them that they never have to meet,
they do not meet, they search.

Lovers go about like crazy people
because they are alone, alone, alone,
subjecting themselves, giving themselves over to
    every moment,

Les preocupa el amor. Los amorosos
viven al día, no pueden hacer más, no saben.
Siempre se están yendo,
siempre, hacia alguna parte.
Esperan,
no esperan nada, pero esperan.
Saben que nunca han de encontrar.
El amor es la prórroga perpetua,
siempre el paso siguiente, el otro, el otro.
Los amorosos son los insaciables,
los que siempre—¡qué bueno!—han de estar solos.

Los amorosos son la hidra del cuento.
Tienen serpientes en lugar de brazos.
Las venas del cuello se les hinchan
también como serpientes para asfixiarlos.
Los amorosos no pueden dormir
porque si se duermen se los comen los gusanos.

En la obscuridad abren los ojos
y les cae en ellos el espanto.

Encuentran alacranes bajo la sábana
y su cama flota como sobre un lago.

Los amorosos son locos, sólo locos,
sin Dios y sin diablo.

Los amorosos salen de sus cuevas
temblorosos, hambrientos,
a cazar fantasmas.
Se ríen de las gentes que lo saben todo,
de las que aman a perpetuidad, verídicamente,
de las que creen en el amor como en una lámpara
    de inagotable aceite.

Los amorosos juegan a coger el agua,
a tatuar el humo, a no irse.
Juegan el largo, el triste juego del amor.
Nadie ha de resignarse.
Dicen que nadie ha de resignarse.
Los amorosos se avergüenzan de toda conformación.

Vacíos, pero vacíos de una a otra costilla,
la muerte les fermenta detrás de los ojos,
y ellos caminan, lloran hasta la madrugada
en que trenes y gallos se despiden dolorosamente.

Les llega a veces un olor a tierra recién nacida,
a mujeres que duermen con la mano en el sexo,
    complacidas,

crying because they do not save love.
Love worries them. Lovers
live during the day, they cannot do anything more, they
    do not know.
They are always going,
always, toward somewhere.
They wait,
they do not wait for anything, but they wait.
They know that they never have to meet.
Love is the perpetual continuation,
always the next step, the other, the other.
Lovers are insatiable,
those who always—"how good!"—have to be alone.

Lovers are the hydra in the old story.
They have snakes instead of arms.
The veins in the neck swell
like snakes, also, to suffocate them. Lovers cannot sleep
because if they sleep worms will eat them.

In the darkness they open their eyes
and fear falls into them.

They find scorpions under the sheet
and their bed floats as on a lake.

Lovers are crazy people, only crazy people,
without God and without devil.

Lovers leave their caves
trembling, starving,
to hunt ghosts.
They laugh at people who know everything,
at those who love perpetually, sincerely,
at those who believe in love as in a lamp of
    inexhaustible oil.

Lovers play at collecting water,
at tattooing smoke not to go away.
They play the large, sad game of love.
Nobody has to resign himself.
They tell that no one has to resign himself.
Lovers are ashamed of all conformity.

Empty, but empty from one rib to the other,
death ferments them behind the eyes,
and they walk, they cry until dawn,
when trains and roosters are sent off, painfully.
Sometimes a scent of new-born earth reaches them,
women who sleep with a hand on their sex, satisfied,
to streams of flexible water and to kitchens.

a arroyos de agua tierna y a cocinas.
Los amorosos se ponen a cantar entre labios
una canción no aprendida.
Y se van llorando, llorando
la hermosa vida.

1950

Entresuelo

Un ropero, un espejo, una silla,
ninguna estrella, mi cuarto, una ventana,
la noche como siempre, y yo sin hambre,
con un chicle y un sueño, una esperanza.
Hay muchos hombres fuera, en todas partes,
y más allá la niebla, la mañana.
Hay árboles helados, tierra seca,
peces fijos idénticos al agua,
nidos durmiendo bajo tibias palomas.
Aquí, no hay una mujer. Me falta.
Mi corazón desde hace días quiere hincarse
bajo alguna caricia, una palabra.
Es áspera la noche. Contra muros, la sombra
lenta como los muertos, se arrastra.
Esa mujer y yo estuvimos pegados con agua.
Su piel sobre mis huesos
y mis ojos dentro de su mirada.
Nos hemos muerto muchas veces
al pie del alba.
Recuerdo que recuerdo su nombre,
sus labios, su transparente falda.
Tiene los pechos dulces, y de un lugar
a otro de su cuerpo hay una gran distancia:
de pezón a pezón cien labios y una hora,
de pupila a pupila un corazón, dos lágrimas.
Yo la quiero hasta el fondo de todos los abismos,
hasta el último vuelo de la última ala,
cuando la carne toda no sea carne, ni el alma
sea alma.
Es preciso querer. Yo ya lo sé. La quiero.
¡Es tan dura, tan tibia, tan clara!

Esta noche me falta.
Sube un violín desde la calle hasta mi cama.
Ayer miré dos niños que ante un escaparate
de manequíes desnudos se peinaban.
El silbato del tren me preocupó tres años,
hoy sé que es una máquina.
Ningún adiós mejor que el de todos los días
a cada cosa, en cada instante, alta
la sangre iluminada.

Lovers prepare to sing, through their lips,
a song not understood.
And they go on crying, crying
the beautiful life.

trans. Claudine-Marie D'Angelo

Entresol

A wardrobe, a mirror, a chair,
not one star, my room, a window,
the nights as always, and me without hunger,
with a piece of gum and a dream, a hope.
There are many men outside, all over,
and, further, the fog, the morning.
There are frozen trees, dry earth,
permanent fish, identical to the water,
nests sleeping under lukewarm doves.
Here there is no woman. I lack.
For fifty days my heart has wanted to swell
under some caress, one word.
The night is rough. Against the walls, shadow
slow like the dead, it drags itself.
This woman and I were hit by water.
Her skin over my bones
and my eyes inside her glance.
We had died many times
at the foot of the sunrise.
I remember that I remember her name,
her lips, her transparent skirt.
She has sweet breasts, and from one part
to another of her body there is a great distance:
from nipple to nipple one hundred lips and one hour,
from pupil to pupil one heart, two tears.
I love her to the depth of all the abysses,
till the last flight of the last wing,
when the flesh of all is no longer flesh, and the soul
no longer soul.
It is essential to love. I know that now. I love her.
She is so hard, so lukewarm, so clear!

Tonight I miss her.
A violin rises from the street to my bed.
Yesterday I watched two children who in front of a display
of naked mannequins combed their hair.
The whistle of the train worried me for three years;
now I know that it is a machine.
No goodbye better than that of everyday
to everything, in every instant, high
illuminated blood.

Desamparada sangre, noche blanda,
tabaco del insomnio, triste cama.

Yo me voy a otra parte.
Y me llevo mi mano, que tanto escribe y habla.

1950

Caprichos

Uno
La niña toca el piano
mientras un gato la mira.
En la pared hay un cuadro
con una flor amarilla.
La niña morena y flaca
le pega al piano y lo mira
mientras un duende le jala
las trenzas y la risa.
La niña y el piano siguen
en la casa vacía.

Dos
El cielo estaba en las nubes
y las nubes en los pájaros,
los pájaros en al aire
y el aire sobre sus manos.

La yerba le acariciaba
ásperamente los labios
y sus ojos le contaban
una tristeza de algo:
como ropa de mujer
tendida, limpia, en el campo.

Tres
Llenas de tierra las manos
y los ojos llenos de agua,
voy a decirte un secreto:
no tengo casa.
No, no tengo casa.

Desabróchame la piel
de la espalda
y úntame yodo y arena
para borrar esa marca.
Tengo una marca.

No me dejes en el cuello
la garganta
callándose tanto tiempo

Defenseless blood, mild night,
tobacco of insomnia, sad bed.

I go away to somewhere else.
I take away my hand, which writes and speaks much.

trans. Claudine-Marie D'Angelo

Capriccios

One
The girl plays the piano
while the cat watches her.
On the wall there is a picture
with a yellow flower.
The girl, brown and thin,
strikes the piano and watches it
while a ghost pulls
her braids and laughs at her.
The girl and the piano continue
in the empty house.

Two
The sky was in the clouds
and the clouds in the birds
and birds in the air
and the air above their hands.

The grass caressed
her lips roughly
and her eyes told of
a sadness of something:
like women's clothing
hung out, clean, in the country.

Three
Hands full of earth
and eyes full of water,
I am going to tell you a secret:
I do not have a home.
No, I do not have a home.

Unfasten for me the skin
of my back
and anoint me with iodine and sand
to erase this mark.
I have a mark.

Do not abandon me
mute
all this time

lo de mi casa.
Que me duele, de veras,
no tener casa.

1951

in the neck the throat
of my home.
...because it hurts me, truly,
not to have a home.

trans. Claudine-Marie D'Angelo

Si alguien te dice que no es cierto

Si alguien te dice que no es cierto,
dile que venga,
que ponga sus manos sobre su estómago y jure,
que atestigüe la verdad de todo.
Que mire la luz en el petróleo de la calle,
los automóviles inmóviles,
las gentes pasando y pasando,
las cuatro puertas que dan al este,
las bicicletas sin nadie,
los ladrillos, la cal amorosa,
las estanterías a tu espalda cayéndose,
las canas en la cabeza de tu padre,
el hijo que no tiene tu mujer,
y el dinero que entra con la boca llena de mierda.
Díle que jure, en el nombre de Dios invicto
en el torneo de las democracias,
haber visto y oído.
Porque ha de oír también el crimen de los gatos
y un enorme reloj al que dan cuerda pegado a tu oreja

1956

If Someone Tells You It's Not for Sure

If someone tells you it's not for sure,
tell him to come here,
to put his hands over his stomach and swear,
to bear witness to the whole truth.
To see the light in the oily street,
the stopped cars,
the people passing and passing,
the four doors which face the East,
the empty bicycles,
the bricks, the affectionate quicklime,
the bookshelves tumbling behind you,
the gray hairs on your father's head,
the son your wife never had,
and the money that walks in with its mouth full of shit.
In the name of the undefeated God
in the contest of the democracies,
tell him to swear he's seen and heard.
Because he's also got to hear the crime of the cats
and keep his ears glued to the big clock they keep winding.

trans. Philip Levine

Carlos Germán Belli

PERU

1927–

Carlos Germán Belli is the most important and original Peruvian poet of the generation following César Vallejo. International in outlook yet attentive to the traditions of Spanish versification, in his poems Belli also combines a passion for communication with, paradoxically, a dedication to what cannot be directly articulated. His 1961 *¡Oh, Hada Cibernética!* (*Oh, Cybernetic Fairy!*), from which several of these selections come, is a long sequence—or perhaps a fragmentary single poem—that tessellates short perceptions in a matrix of street slang, technological idiom, and popular-magazine iconography. These emotional individual pieces combine to form a larger, "cybernetic" argument of rage against death and waste in the contemporary Third World city. A poet, translator, and journalist, Belli has taught at the Writer's Workshop at the University of Iowa; he is a professor of Hispano-American letters at the University of San Marcos, Lima.

Segregación no. 1

(a modo de un pinto primitivo culto)

Yo, mamá, mis dos hermanos
y muchos peruanitos
abrimos un hueco hondo, hondo
donde nos guarecemos,
porque arriba todo tiene dueño,
toda está cerrado con llave,
sellado firmemente,
porque arriba todo tiene reserva:
la sombra del árbol, las flores,
los frutos, el techo, las ruedas,
el agua, los lápices,
y optamos por hundirnos
en el fondo de la tierra,
más abajo que nunca,
lejos, muy lejos de los jefes,
hoy domingo,
lejos, muy lejos de los dueños
entre las patas de los animalitos,
porque arriba
hay algunos que manejan todo,
que escriben, que cantan, que bailan,
que hablan hermosamente,
y nosotros rojos de vergüenza,
tan sólo deseamos desaparecer
en pedacitititos.

1958

Segregation #1

(in the manner of a cultivated primitive painter)

I, my mother, my two brothers,
and many little Peruvians
open a hole, deep, deep,
where we take shelter
because up above everything has an owner,
everything's under lock and key,
sealed firmly,
because up above everything is reserved:
the shade of the tree, the flowers,
the fruits, the roof, the wheels,
the water, the pencils;
and we choose to sink
to the bottom of the earth,
lower than ever,
far, far away from the bosses,
today, Sunday,
far, far away from the owners,
among the legs and arms of tiny creatures,
because up above
are those who handle everything,
who write, who sing, who dance,
who speak beautifully,
and we red with shame
want only to disappear
in tiny mini pieces.

trans. Isabel Bize

Por qué me han mudado

¿Por qué me han mudado
del claustro materno
al claustro terreno,
en vez de desovarme
en agua o aire o fuego?

1962

Why Have They Moved Me

Why have they moved me
from womb
to earth
instead of spawning me
in water   air   or fire?

trans. David Tipton and Maureen Ahern

Una desconocida voz...

Una desconocida voz me dijo:
"no folgarás con Filis, no, en el prado,
si con hierros te sacan
del luminoso claustro, feto mío";
y ahora que en este albergue arisco
encuéntrome ya desde varios lustros,

An Unknown Voice...

An unknown voice told me:
"if they pull you out with forceps
from my luminous cloister, foetus,
you'll never lie with Phyllis in the meadow";
and now after three decades,
finding myself in this sullen lodging,

pregunto por qué no fui despeñado,
desde el más alto risco,
por tartamudo o cojo o manco o bizco.

1962

I wonder why
—stuttering or crippled, maimed or cross-eyed—
I was not flung from the highest peak.

trans. David Tipton and Maureen Ahern

¡Abajo las lonjas!

¡Oh Hada Cibernética!,
cuándo de un soplo asolarás las lonjas,
que cautivo me tienen,
y me libres al fin
para que yo entonces pueda
dedicarme a buscar a una mujer
dulce como el azúcar,
suave como la seda,
y comérmela en pedacitos,
y gritar después:
"¡abajo la lonja del azúcar,
abajo la lonja de la seda!"

1962

Down with the Money-Exchange

Oh Cibernetic Fairy
when with a puff will you
wither the money-exchange
that has me in its clutch,
and liberate me
for then I could
dedicate my life
to the search for a woman
sweet as sugar
smooth as silk
and eat her piece by piece
then afterwards cry
down with the sugar-mart,
down with the silk-mart!

trans. David Tipton and Maureen Ahern

Papá, mamá

Papá, mamá,
para que yo, Pocho y Mario
sigamos todo el tiempo en el linaje humano,
cuánto luchasteis vosotros
a pesar de los bajos salarios del Perú,
y tras de tanto tan solo me digo:
"venid, muerte, para que yo abandone
este linaje humano,
y nunca vuelva a él,
y de entre otros linajes escoja al fin
        una faz de risco,
        una faz de olmo,
        una faz de búho."

1962

Father, Mother

Father, Mother,
how much you struggled
despite the absurd Peruvian wages
to maintain some human dignity
for Pocho, Mario and me
yet after all this, I only say to myself:
"come death, so I can abandon
this humanity
and not return to it,
choosing in the end another lineage
        a cliff-face
        the face of an elm
        or an owl's."

trans. David Tipton and Maureen Ahern

¡Oh padres, sabedlo bien...!

¡Oh padres, sabedlo bien:
el insecto es intransmutable en hombre,
mas el hombre es transmutable en insecto!;
¿acaso no pensabais, padres míos,
cuando acá en el orbe sin querer matabais
un insecto cualquiera,

My Parents, Know It Well

My parents, know it well:
an insect cannot be transmuted into man
but a man can be transmuted into insect!
Perhaps you never thought
when here in the world, how accidentally
you killed some insect

que hallábase posado oscuramente
del bosque en el rincón más manso y lejos,
para no ser visto por los humanos
ni en el día ni en la noche,
no pensabais, pues, que pasando el tiempo
algunos de vuestro hijos
volveríanse en inermes insectos,
aun a pesar de vuestros mil esfuerzos
para que todo el tiempo
pesen y midan como los humanos?

which to avoid discovery by human-beings
either by day or night was anonymously lodged
in the most inaccessible and humble corner of the woods,
and you failed to realize that, as time passed,
some of your children
in spite of your thousand efforts
would become defenseless insects
so that they'd always measure up
and count as human-beings.

trans. David Tipton and Maureen Ahern

1962

Ernesto [Che] Guevara

ARGENTINA/CUBA
1928–1967

Born in Argentina, Che Guevara fought as a guerrilla in the Cuban Revolution. He wrote the declamatory poem included here to celebrate the impending victory of Fidel Castro's revolutionary army over Fulgencio Batista's government on January 1, 1959. After serving in Castro's communist government, Guevara returned to more immediate political activity in other parts of Latin America. He was killed at age thirty-nine while leading a guerrilla group in rural Bolivia in 1967.

Canto a Fidel

Vámonos,
ardiente profeta de la aurora,
por recónditos senderos inalámbricos
a liberar el verde caimán que tanto amas.

Vámonos,
derrotando afrentas con la frente
plena de martianas estrellas insurrectas,
juremos lograr el triunfo o encontrar la muerte.

Cuando suene el primer disparo y se despierte
en virginal asombro la manigua entera,
allí, a tu lado, serenos combatientes,
nos tendrás.

Cuando tu voz derrame hacia los cuatro vientos
reforma agraria, justicia, pan, libertad,
allí, a tu lado, con idénticos acentos,
nos tendrás.

Y cuando llegue al final de la jornada
la sanitaria operación contra el tirano,

Song to Fidel

You said the sun would rise.
Let's go
along those unmapped paths
to free the green alligator you love.

And let's go obliterating
insults with our
brows swept with dark insurgent stars.
We shall have victory or shoot past death.

At the first shot the whole jungle
will awake with fresh amazement and
there and then serene company
we'll be at your side.

When your voice quarters the four winds
reforma agraria, justice, bread, freedom,
we'll be there with identical accents
at your side.

And when the clean operation against the tyrant
ends at the end of the day

allí, a tu lado, aguardando la postrer batalla,
nos tendrás.

El día que la fiera se lama el flanco herido
donde el dardo nacionalizador le dé,
allí, a tu lado, con el corazón altivo,
nos tendrás.

No pienses que puedan menguar nuestra entereza
las decoradas pulgas armadas de regalos;
pedimos su fusil, sus balas y una peña.
Nada más.

Y si en nuestro camino se interpone el hierro,
pedimos un sudario de cubanas lágrimas
para que se cubran los guerrilleros huesos
en el tránsito a la historia americana.
Nada más.

México 1956

there and then set for the final battle
we'll be at your side.

And when the wild beast licks his wounded side
where the dart of Cuba hits him
we'll be at your side
with proud hearts.

Don't ever think our integrity can be sapped
by those decorated fleas hopping with gifts
we want their rifles, their bullets and a rock
nothing else.

And if iron stands in our way
we ask for a sheet of Cuban tears
to cover our guerrilla bones
on the journey to American history.
Nothing more.

trans. Ed Dorn and Gordon Brotherston

Enrique Lihn

CHILE

1929–

Since the publication of *La pieza oscura* (*The Dark Room*, 1963), Enrique Lihn has been acknowledged as one of the foremost experimental writers of Chile. Lihn's poems often reflect his training and expertise as a critic of visual and conceptual art. The texture and the self-referential rhetoric of his diction locate him at the vanguard of post-Freudianism in Latin American aesthetics. Lihn, who has visited at several North American universities and who directs the office of publications at the University of Santiago, is the author also of six novels.

La pieza oscura

La mixtura del aire en la pieza oscura, como si el
    cielorraso hubiera amenazado
una vaga llovizna sangrienta.
De ese licor inhalamos, la nariz sucia, símbolo de
    inocencia y de precocidad
juntos para reanudar nuestra lucha en secreto, por no
    sabíamos no ignorábamos qué causa;
juego de manos y de pies, dos veces villanos, pero
    igualmente dulces
que una primera pérdida de sangre vengada a dientes y
    uñas o para una muchacha
dulces como una primera efusión de su sangre.

Y así empezó a girar la vieja rueda —símbolo de la vida—
    la rueda que se atasca como si no volara,

The Dark Room

The air's heaviness in the dark room, as if a vague
    bloodlike
drizzle threatened to come down from the ceiling.
We inhaled some of that brew, our noses dirty, a symbol
    of children acting like grownups
to go on secretly with our struggle, for some cause we did
    and didn't know;
a game of hands and feet, twice as rough, but just as sweet
as paying back tooth and nail for the first blood drawn
    or for a young girl
sweet as the first trickle of her blood.

And that's how the old wheel—symbol of life—began to
    turn, getting stuck between one generation and
    the next

entre una y otra generación, en un abrir de ojos brillantes
    y un cerrar de ojos opacos
con un imperceptible sonido musgoso.
Centrándose en su eje, a imitación de los niños que
    rodábamos de dos en dos, con las orejas rojas—
    símbolos del pudor que saborea su ofensa—
    rabiosamente tiernos,
la rueda dio unas vueltas en falso como en una edad
    anterior a la invención de la rueda
en el sentido de las manecillas del reloj y en su
    contrasentido.
Por un momento reinó la confusión en el tiempo. Y yo
    mordí, largamente en el cuello a mi prima Isabel,
en un abrir y cerrar del ojo del que todo lo ve, como en
    una edad anterior al pecado
pues simulábamos luchar en la creencia de que esto
    hacíamos; creencia rayana en la fe como el juego en
    la verdad
y los hechos se aventuraban apenas a desmentirnos
con las orejas rojas.

Dejamos de girar por el suelo, mi primo Ángel vencedor de
    Paulina, mi hermana; yo de Isabel, envueltas ambas
ninfas en un capullo de frazadas que las hacía estornudar—
    olor a naftalina en la pelusa del fruto—.
Esas eran nuestras armas victoriosas y las suyas vencidas
    confundiéndose unas con otras a modo de nidos como
    celdas, de celdas como abrazos, de abrazos como
    grillos en los pies y en las manos.
Dejamos de girar con una rara sensación de vergüenza, sin
    conseguir formularnos otro reproche
que el de haber postulado a un éxito tan fácil.
La rueda daba ya unas vueltas perfectas, como en la época
    de su aparición en el mito, como en su edad de madera
    recién carpintereada
con un ruido de canto de gorriones medievales;
el tiempo volaba en la buena dirección. Se lo podía oír
    avanzar hacia nosotros
mucho más rápido que el reloj del comedor cuyo tic-tac se
    enardecía por romper tanto silencio.
El tiempo volaba como para arrollarnos con un ruido de
    aguas espumosas más rápidas en la proximidad de la
    rueda del molino, con alas de gorriones—símbolos
    del salvaje orden libre—con todo él por unico objeto
    desbordante
y la vida—símbolo de la rueda—se adelantaba a pasar
    tempestuosamente haciendo girar la rueda a velocidad
    acelerada, como en una molienda de tiempo,
    tempestuosa.
Yo solté a mi cautiva y caí de rodillas, como si hubiera
    envejecido de golpe, presa de dulce, de empalagoso
    pánico

as if it couldn't fly off, caught in the wink
    of bright and dim eyes
with an imperceptible, mossy sound.
Pulling into its center, imitating us, kids spinning around
    two at a time, our ears red
    —symbol of a modesty that delights in its crime—
    furiously tender,
the wheel gave a few false turns as in the age
    before the invention of the wheel
clockwise, and then counter clockwise.
For a second confusion ruled over time. I slowly bit
    into the neck of my cousin Isabel,
in the wink of the eye of he who sees everything, as in
    the age before sin
because we pretended to struggle in the belief this is what
    we were doing; a belief bordering on faith as the game
    on truth
and the facts could hardly dare to prove us wrong
with our ears red.

We stopped rolling around on the floor, my cousin Angel
    winner over my sister Pauline; and I over Isabel,
    two nymphs
wrapped up in a cocoon of blankets that made them sneeze
    —the mothball smell on a fruit's downy skin—.
Those were our victorious and their defeated weapons
    each taken for the other, like nests for cells, cells for
    hugs, hugs for chains tying down hands and feet.
We stopped rolling around, overcome by a strange
    feeling of shame, without managing to come up with
    another reproach
than the one for finding such an easy victory.
The wheel was already turning perfectly, as in the age
    it appeared in the myth, as in the day
    it was first carved in wood
with a sound of medieval sparrows' song;
time was flying in the right direction. You could hear it
    moving toward us
quicker than the dining room clock whose ticking grew
    louder to break so much silence.
Time flew as if to roll us up with a sound of foaming
    water that rushed faster near the mill's wheel, with
    sparrows' wings—symbols of savage free order—
    with itself as the only overflowing thing
and life—symbol of the wheel—moved ahead to storm by
    making the wheel turn faster and faster,
    as in a mill furiously grinding time.
I let my captive go and fell on my knees, as if I had
    suddenly grown old, seized by a sweet, cloying panic
as if I had known, beyond love in its prime
    the heart's cruelty in the fruit of love, the fruit rotting
    and then... the bloody pit, feverish and dried out.

como si hubiera conocido, más allá del amor en la flor de
su edad, la crueldad del corazón en el fruto del amor,
la corrupción del fruto y luego... el carozo sangriento,
afiebrado y seco.
¿Qué será de los niños fuimos? Alguien se precipitó a
encender la luz, más rápido que el pensamiento de las
personas mayores.
Se nos buscaba ya en el interior de la casa, en las
inmediaciones del molino: la pieza oscura como el
claro de un bosque.
Pero siempre hubo tiempo para ganárselo a los sempiternos
cazadores de niños. Cuando ellos entraron al comedor,
allí estábamos los ángeles sentados a la mesa
ojeando nuestras revistas ilustradas—los hombres a un
extremo, las mujeres al otro—
en un orden perfecto, anterior a la sangre.

En el contrasentido de las manecillas del reloj se desatascó
la rueda antes de girar y ni siquiera nosotros pudimos
encontrarnos a la vuelta del vértigo, cuando entramos
en el tiempo
como en aguas mansas, serenamente veloces;
en ellas nos dispersamos para siempre, al igual que los
restos de un mismo naufragio.
Pero una parte de mí no ha girado al compás de la rueda,
a favor de la corriente.
Nada es bastante real para un fantasma. Soy en parte ese
niño que cae de rodillas
dulcemente abrumado de imposibles presagios
y no he cumplido aún toda mi edad
ni llegaré a cumplirla como él
de una sola vez y para siempre.

1963

What has become of the children we were? Someone
hurried to turn on the light, faster than the thoughts
of grownups.
They were already looking for us inside the house,
around the mill: the room dark as a clearing in a forest.
But there was always time to win before the never quitting
child hunters got there. When they came into the
dining room there we were, angels sitting around
the table,
looking at the pictures in our magazines—men at one end,
women at the other—
in perfect order, before the bloodshed.

Going counter clockwise, the wheel broke loose before it
began turning and we couldn't even find each other
on the other side of dizziness, when we entered time
as, in calm waters, serenely quick;
we scattered ourselves forever in the waters, just like
pieces of the same shipwreck.
But part of me hasn't turned in time with the wheel,
gone along with the current.
Nothing is real enough for a ghost. Part of me is that boy
who falls down on his knees
softly crushed by unbearable omens
and I haven't come of age yet
nor will I reach it like him
once and for all.

trans. David Unger

Barro

I

Barro, rencor inagotable. Toda otra fuente termina
por ceder
a la presíon de esta materia original.
Los días del agua están contados, pero no así los días
del barro
que sustituye al agua cuando ciegan el pozo.
No así los días del barro que nos remontan al séptimo día.

De niños jugábamos con él, nada tiene de extraño que
juegue con nosotros,
los creados a imagen y semejanza suya.

Mud

I

Mud, unending malice. All other source gives way at last
to the pressure of this primal stuff.
Water? its days are numbered, but not the mud
that packs up after the well is plugged.
Not the muddy days that back us up to Creation.

We played with it as children, no wonder it plays with us,
shaped after its image and likeness.

II

God the Father, God the Son, God the Holy Ghost:
land and water, then the muck of what was in the
beginning.

II

Dios padre, Dios hijo, Dios espíritu santo:
tierra y agua; luego el barro que en el principio era.
Un solo sentimiento en el origen de todos:
este rencor inagotable.

III

Tarde o temprano volveremos a ser razonables.
Está en el orden de las cosas, nada se sabe de ellas
    mientras no las tomamos con relativa calma,
como si nada hubiera sucedido.

IV

No hay más extraño que uno. Es la apariencia de otro
    quien terminó por frecuentarnos,
por aceptar finalmente una invitacíon reiterada.
Me pareció ver a mi sombra cuando le abrí la puerta, justo
    en el momento en que íbamos a salir.
La función había comenzado. "Adelante. Adelante."
"Te estábamos esperando," dije yo y ella dijo: "No
    reconozco a los ingratos"
con un curioso temblor en la voz.

1963

A single sentiment at the start of it all:
this unending malice.

III

Sooner or later now we'll come to our senses.
It is the way of things, we don't get to know them till
    we take them more or less calmly,
as if nothing had happened.

IV

The real stranger is oneself. The looks of some other
    who ended up haunting us,
finally accepting one of many invitations.
I thought I saw my shadow when I opened the door,
    just as we were about to go out.
The party had begun. "Come in. Come in."
"We were waiting for you" I said and she said,
    "I can't bear ingratitude"
with a funny tremor in her voice.

trans. John Felstiner

Recuerdos de matrimonio

Buscábamos un subsuelo donde vivir,
cualquier lugar que no fuera una casa de huéspedes.
    El paraíso perdido
tomaba ahora su verdadero aspecto: uno de esos pequeños
    departamentos
que se arriendan por un precio todavía razonable
pero a las seis de la mañana. "Ayer, no más, lo tomó un
    matrimonio joven."
Mientras íbamos y veníamos cn la oscuridad en
    direcciones capciosas.
El hombre es un lobo para el hombre y el lobo una dueña
    de casa de pensión con los dientes cariados, húmeda
    en las axilas, dudosamente viuda.
Y allí donde el periódico nos invitaba a vivir se alzaba un
    abismo de tres pisos:
un nuevo foco de corrupción conyugal.

Mientras íbamos y veníamos en la oscuridad, más
    distantes el uno del otro a cada paso
ellos ya estaban allí, estableciendo su nido sobre una base
    sólida,
ganándose la simpatía del conserje, tan hosco con los
    extraños
como ansioso de inspirarles gratitud filial.

Memories of Marriage

We were looking for a basement to live in,
anywhere that wasn't a rooming house. Paradise lost
began to take on its true shape: one of those little flats
you can still rent for a decent price
but at six in the morning. "A young couple took it, just
    yesterday."
While we went back and forth in the dark on misleading
    streets.
Man is a wolf to man and the wolf's a landlady with rotten
    teeth, damp armpits, a dubious widow.
And there where the paper invited us to live, an abyss
    three stories deep rose up,
a new center of conjugal corruption.

While we went back and forth in the dark, farther apart
    with every step,
they were there already, building their nest on solid
    ground,
winning over the caretaker, a man as surly to strangers
as he is eager to evoke their filial gratitude.
"They haven't missed a thing. I'll bet the new elevator boy
    got a tip."
"The ideal couple." Right on time. Not a moment too
    soon.

"No se les habrá escapado nada. Seguramente el nuevo
    ascensorista recibió una propina."
"La pareja ideal." A la hora justa. En el momento oportuno.

De ellos, los invisibles, sólo alcanzábamos a sentir su
    futura presencia en un cuarto vacío:
nuestras sombras tomadas de la mano entre los primeros
    brotes del sol en el parquet,
un remanso de blanca luz nupcial.

"Pueden verlo, si quieren
pero han llegado tarde."
Se nos hacía tarde.
Se hacía tarde en todo.
Para siempre.

1963

Cementerio de Punta Arenas

Ni aun la muerte pudo igualar a estos hombres
que dan su nombre en lápidas distintas
o lo gritan al viento del sol que se los borra:
otro poco de polvo para una nueva ráfaga.
Reina aquí, junto al mar que iguala al mármol,
entre esta doble fila de obsequiosos cipreses
la paz, pero una paz que lucha por trizarse,
rompe en mil pedazos los pergaminos fúnebres
para asomar la cara de una antigua soberbia
y reírse del polvo.

Por construirse estaba esta ciudad cuando alzaron
sus hijos primogénitos otra ciudad desierta
y uno a uno ocuparon, a fondo, su lugar
como si aún pudieran disputárselo.
Cada uno en lo suyo para siempre, esperando,
tendidos los manteles, a sus hijos y nietos.

1963

Revolución

No toco la trompeta ni subo a la tribuna
De la revolución prefiero la necesidad de conversar
    entre amigos
aunque sea por las razones más débiles
hasta diletando; y soy, como se ve, un pequeño
    burgués no vergonzante
que ya en los años treinta y pico sospechaba
    que detrás del amor a los pobres
    de los sagrados corazones

As to them, the invisible ones, all we could do was
    imagine them settled one day in the empty room:
our shadows hand in hand through the first flecks of sun
    on the parquet,
a still pool of white nuptial light.

"You can see it if you want
but you got here late."
It was getting late for us.
It was getting late for everything.
For ever.

trans. John Felstiner

Cemetery in Punta Arenas

Not even death could make these men alike
who give their names to different gravestones
or shout them into the sun's wind that rubs them out:
some more dust for a fresh gust of wind.
Here, by the sea that is just like marble,
between this double row of bowing cypresses,
peace rules, a peace struggling to shatter itself,
ripping the burial parchments in a thousand pieces
to reveal the face of an ancient arrogance
and to laugh at the dust.

This city had yet to be built when its first
settlers raised still another empty city
and, one by one, they settled deep into their places
as if anyone would even try taking it away from them.
Each one forever in his own place, waiting,
the tablecloths laid out, for his sons and grandsons.

trans. David Unger

Revolution

I don't blow the trumpet or step up to the speaker's
    platform
When it comes to revolution I am more satisfied talking
    with my friends
whether or not this may be for the flimsiest of reasons
even dilettanting; and I am, as you can tell, a petty
    bourgeois though not embarrassingly so
who in the thirties already suspected that behind the love
    for poor kids in the Sacred Heart schools

se escondía una monstruosa duplicidad
y que en el cielo habría una puerta de
    servicio
para hacer el reparto de las sobras entre los
    mismos mendigos que se
    restregaban aquí abajo contra los
    flancos de la Iglesia
en ese barrio uncioso pero de cuello y
    corbata
frío de corazón ornamental
La revolución
es el nacimiento del espíritu crítico y las
    perplejidades que le duelen al
    imago en los lugares en que se
    ha completado para una tarea
    por ahora incomprensible
y en nombre de la razón la cabeza vacila
y otras cabezas caen en un cesto
y uno se siente solitario y cruel
víctima de las incalculables injusticias que
    efectivamente no se hacen esperar
    y empiezan a sumarse en el
    horizonte de lo que era de rigor
    llamar entonces la vida
y su famosa sonrisa.

lurked a monstrous hypocrisy
and that there would be a service door in heaven
for handing out scraps to the same beggars who rubbed
    against the flanks of the church down here
in that oily though prim and proper neighborhood
cold with ornamental heart
The revolution
gives birth to the critical spirit and the confusions that
    hurt its image in places where it has been carried out
    for an objective that doesn't make sense right now
and, in the name of reason, your head wavers
as other heads fall into a basket
and you feel alone and spiteful
a victim of untold wrongs that just won't be held back and
    that start to pile up on the horizon of what then was
    properly called life
and its famous smile.

trans. Jonathan Cohen

1969

Juan Gelman

ARGENTINA
1930–

Juan Gelman's poems bring an ironic intelligence and a linguistic simplicity to bear on scenes of quotidian urban reality. Born in Buenos Aires, Gelman studied chemistry at the University of Buenos Aires but abandoned his scientific studies in favor of poetry. Active in militantly leftist groups and in literary journalism, he was a founding member of the publishing house El Pan Duro (1954) and a member of the Rosa Blindata (Armored Rose) group, which in 1962 declared its commitment to "give the people the poetry they create daily." Like César Vallejo, whose poems have been a model for Gelman's compassionate meditativeness, Gelman works to find a linguistic integrity that can link his poetic vocation with his humanistic political commitments.

Los ojos

no sé quién soy o he sido sólo conozco mi desorden
pasé los años agotando obsesión tras obsesión
aprendí pocas cosas y vi cambiar al mundo
o escuché a los amantes besarse contra el mundo

Eyes

i don't know who i am or was i know only my chaos
i spent years consuming obsession on obsession
learned very little and saw the world change
or heard lovers kiss in defiance of the world

o vivir y morir por la Revolución
y nada fue más bello
que mirarles los ojos al pie de sus balazos
al final de tan corto camino

1961

Épocas

hemos debido estar gentísimos para quedarnos tan solos
lumumba usted y yo
una mañana cualquiera en medio de la historia
los senos de su mujer según recuerdo
son dos tambores desolados abiertos hacia el áfrica
o como pueblos entregados de balde al enemigo
usted medita y crece bajo el polvo
contrarias circunstancias
mataron a lumumba al héroe al gran cartero repartidor
    de buenas nuevas
como la dignidad como el honor
patricio escribe cartas
dice: es pesada la sangre que vierte la traición
dice: amen al enemigo en su cadáver odien a los amigos
    con amor
estas señales y otras estallan en su tumba lumumba gira
    en sombras
en paz con su gran congo en paz con sí como poquísimos
en paz con el pasado el presente el futuro los vientos las
    gaviotas en guerra con nosotros
no debemos huir mis pequeñitos yo nunca aprenderé
    a restar
quiero decir: a resignarme
odio tu gran cadáver lumumba ora por nosotros

1962

Historia

Estudiando la historia,
fechas, batallas, cartas escritas en la piedra,
frases célebres, próceres oliendo a santidad,
sólo percibo oscuras manos
esclavas, metalúrgicas, mineras, tejedoras,
creando el resplandor, la aventura del mundo,
se murieron y aún les crecieron las uñas.

1962

or live and die for the Revolution
and nothing was more beautiful
than looking in their eyes beside their bullet wounds
at the end of so short a road

trans. Elinor Randall and Robert Márquez

Epochs

we must have nurtured multitudes to be left so alone
on a morning like any other in the midst of history
lumumba you and i
your wife's breasts as i remember
are two disconsolate drums open to africa
or like peoples freely surrendered to the enemy
you meditate and grow beneath the dust
contrary circumstances
killed lumumba the hero the great postman bringer of
    good news
like dignity like honor
patrice also writes letters
he says: the blood that treason sheds is sluggish
he says: love your enemy in his cadaver hate your
    friends lovingly
these signs and others burst in his grave lumumba turns
    in darkness
at peace with his great congo at peace with himself as are
    very few
at peace with the past the present the future the winds the
    seagulls at war with us
we mustn't run away my little ones i'll never learn to rest
i mean: resign myself
i hate your great cadaver lumumba pray for us

trans. Elinor Randall and Robert Márquez

History

Studying history,
dates, battles, letters written on stone,
famous phrases, luminaries smelling of sanctity,
I see only dark, metallurgical,
mining, sewing, slaves' hands
creating the brilliance, the adventure of the world,
they died and their fingernails still grew.

trans. Robert Márquez

Ferreira Gullar
[José Ribamar Ferreira]

BRAZIL

1930–

Born and educated in São Joâo de Maranhão, where he worked as a disc jockey and as a journalist before moving to Rio de Janeiro, Ferreira Gullar was an early friend of Augusto and Haroldo de Campos. Although in the early 1950s Gullar was one of the Concretist writers who proposed an avant-garde aesthetic based on a sense of the graphic space of the poem, he broke from the Concretists in 1958 and proposed a neo-Concretist position which was less committed to mathematical austerity than that of the Concretists. Gullar also broke with the Campos brothers on personal terms; he became a poet, he claims, only when he gave up poetry in favor of direct political engagement.

Since 1961 Gullar's poems have addressed social issues overtly. Through dislocations and implied dramatic narratives, Gullar has struggled in his poems toward a new formal sense of "revolutionary" art. Exiled from Brazil in 1971, Gullar wrote his long poem *Poema sujo* (*Dirty Poem*, 1975) while living in Buenos Aires. He published his *Toda poesia* (*Complete Poetry*) in 1980. Several other books of poems and criticism have followed that retrospective. Gullar now lives in Rio, where he is honored as one of the Brazilian masters most influential for younger writers and theorists.

Oswald morto

Enterraram ontem em São Paulo
um anjo antropófago
de asas de folha de bananeira
(mais um nome que se mistura à nossa vegetação tropical)

As escolas e as usinas paulistas
não se detiveram
para olhar o corpo do poeta que anunciara a civilização
    do ócio
Quanto mais pressa mais vagar

O lenço em que pela última vez
assoou o nariz
era uma bandeira nacional

NOTA:
Fez sol o dia inteiro em Ipanema
Oswald de Andrade ajudou o crepúsculo
hoje domingo 24 de outubro de 1954

1954/1960

No corpo

De que vale tentar reconstruir com palavras
    o que o verão levou

Oswald Dead

Yesterday in São Paulo they buried
an anthropophagous angel
with banana-leaf wings
(one more name that blends into our tropical vegetation)

The schools and the foundries of São Paulo
didn't stop
to look at the body of the poet who had announced the
    civilization of idleness
Speed produces slowness

The hanky in which for the last time
he blew his nose
was a national flag

FOOTNOTE:
It was sunny all day long in Ipanema
Oswald de Andrade helped the sunset
today Sunday, October 24, 1954

trans. Renato Rezende

In the Body

Why try to reconstruct with words
    what the summer blew

entre nuvens e risos
junto com o jornal velho pelos ares?

O sonho na boca, o incêndio na cama,
o apelo na noite
agora são apenas esta
contração (este clarão)
de maxilar dentro do rosto.

A poesia é o presente.

1975

between clouds and laughs
through the air, with old papers?

The dream in the mouth, the fire in the bed,
the desire in the night
are now only this
contraction (this lightning)
of a jawbone within the face.

Poetry is the present.

trans. Renato Rezende

No mundo há muitas armadilhas

No mundo há muitas armadilhas
    e o que é armadilha pode ser refúgio
    e o que é refúgio pode ser armadilha

Tua janela por exemplo
    aberta para o céu
    e uma estrela a te dizer que o homem é nada
ou a manhã espumando na praia
    a bater antes de Cabral, antes de Tróia
    (há quatro séculos Tomás Bequimão
    tomou a cidade, criou uma milícia popular
    e depois foi traído, preso, enforcado)

No mundo há muitas armadilhas
    e muitas bocas a te dizer
    que a vida é pouca
    que a vida é louca
    E por que não a Bomba? te perguntam.
    Por que não a Bomba para acabar com tudo, já
    que a vida é louca?

Contudo, olhas a teu filho, o bichinho
    que não sabe
    que afoito se entranha à vida e quer
    a vida
    e busca o sol, a bola, fascinado vê
    o avião e indaga e indaga

A vida é pouca
a vida é louca
mas não há senão ela.
E não te mataste, essa é a verdade.

Estás preso à vida como numa jaula.
Estamos todos presos
nesta jaula que Gagárin foi o primeiro a ver
de fora e nos dizer: é azul.
E já o sabíamos, tanto
que não te mataste e não vais
te matar
e agüentarás até o fim.

There Are Many Traps in the World

There are many traps in the world
    and what is a trap could be a refuge
    and what is a refuge could be a trap

Your window, for instance,
    open to the sky
    and a star saying that humanity is nothing
or the morning sparkling on the beach
    waving, before Cabral, before Troy,
    (four centuries ago Tomás Bequimão
    took the city, created a people's police
    and then was betrayed, jailed and hanged)

There are many traps in the world
    and many mouths telling you
    that life is too little
    that life is too crazy
    And why not the Bomb? they ask you.
    Why not the Bomb to end it all, since
    life is crazy?

Yet, you look at your son, the kid
    who doesn't know,
    who gives himself to life and wants
    life
    and seeks the sun, the sphere, fascinated, sees
    the airplane and asks and asks

Life is little
life is crazy
but there is nothing else.
And you didn't kill yourself, that's the truth.

You're a prisoner of life as if you were in a cage.
We're all prisoners
in this cage that Gagarin saw for the first time
from above, and said: "It's blue."
And we already knew it, so well
that you didn't kill yourself and will not
kill yourself
and will endure it till the end.

O certo é que nesta jaula há os que têm
e os que não têm
há os que têm tanto que sozinhos poderiam
alimentar a cidade
e os que não têm nem para o almoço de hoje

A estrela mente
o mar sofisma. De fato,
o homem está preso à vida e precisa viver
o homem tem fome
e precisa comer
o homem tem filhos
e precisa criá-los
Há muitas armadilhas no mundo e é preciso quebrá-las.

1975

It's certain that in this cage there are those who have
and those who don't
there are those who have so much that they alone could
feed the whole city
and those who haven't enough for today's lunch

The star is a liar
the sea is a Sophist. In fact,
man is tied to life and needs to live
man is hungry
and needs to eat
man has children
who need to be raised
There are many traps in the world and they have to
be shattered.

trans. Renato Rezende

Poster

Ajuda saber que existe
em algum ponto do mundo
(na Suíça?)
uma jovem de mais ou menos
um metro e setenta de altura
com uma aurora em cabelos na cabeça
e um dorso dourado
voraz como a vida.

Ela esteve de pé
entre plantas e flores
numa dessas manhãs em que possivelmente
chovia na Guanabara
mas não lá
(na Suíça?)
onde ela posou ao sol
em biquíni
para um fotógrafo profissional.

Aqui está ela agora, impressa em cores,
como um sonho no papel,
mercadoria à venda, fata
morgana
que nos chama
por duas bocas molhadas:
uma à vista
a outra escondida
ambas fechadas (entre-
fechadas)
uma que fala (ou
falaria) e sorri

Poster

It does help to know
that somewhere in the world
(maybe in Switzerland?)
there is a young woman of about
five feet eleven inches tall
with hair like a dawn on her head
and a golden back
voracious as life.

She was standing
between plants and flowers,
one of those mornings when
possibly it was raining
in Guanabara
but not there
(in Switzerland?)
where she posed under the sun
dressed in a bikini
for a professional photographer.

Here she is now, printed in colors
like a dream printed on paper,
merchandise on sale, fata
morgana
calling us
from two wet mouths:
one in sight
the other hidden
both closed (half
closed
one that talks (or
could talk) and smiles

no meio da aurora, civil,
e a outra
calada em muitos lábios
sob o pano:
uma—boca diária
cheirando a dentifrício
e a outra, avara,
como o ouro da urina.

    Mas nada disso se sabe
se, do ventre não se ergue a vista
até o rosto onde,
por duas esferas azuis,
de entre pétalas de borboletas,
do fundo do corpo—nos fita
a escondida menina na pantera.

                Rio 1970/1975

in the middle of the morning, civilian,
and the other
silent between many lips
under the cloth: one daily mouth
smelling of dental floss
and the other, stingy
as the gold of urine.

    But we know nothing of this
if we don't lift our eyes from the hips
to the face, where,
through two blue spheres,
    between butterfly petals,
from the bottom of her body—stare at us:
the girl hidden in the panther.

               trans. Renato Rezende

Cantada

Você é mais bonita que uma bola prateada
de papel de cigarro
Você é mais bonita que uma poça dágua
límpida
num lugar escondido
Você é mais bonita que uma zebra
que um filhote de onça
que um Boeing 707 em pleno ar
Você é mais bonita que um jardim florido
em frente ao mar em Ipanema
Você é mais bonita que uma refinaria de Petrobrás
de noite
mais bonita que Ursula Andress
que o Palácio da Alvorada
mais bonita que é alvorada
que o mar azul-safira de República Dominicana

Olha,
você é tão bonita quanto o Rio de Janeiro
em maio
e quase tão bonita
quanto a Revolução Cubana

                1975

Sweet Talk

You're more beautiful than a silvery ball
of cigarette paper
You're more beautiful than a clear puddle
of water
in a secret place
You're more beautiful than a zebra
than a wildcat's cub
than a Boeing 707 in the open air
You're more beautiful than a flowery garden
along the sea in Ipanema
You're more beautiful than a Petrobrás refinery
burning at night
more beautiful than Ursula Andress
than the Alvorada, the Palace of Dawn,
more beautiful than the sunrise
than the sapphire-blue sea of the Dominican Republic

Look,
you're as beautiful as the city of Rio de Janeiro
in May
and almost as beautiful
as the Cuban Revolution

               trans. Renato Rezende

Barulho

Todo poema é feito de ar
apenas:
      a mão do poeta
      não rasga a madeira
      não fere

Noise

Every poem is made of air
and only air:
      the poet's hand
      doesn't cut timber
      doesn't wound

o metal	the metal
a pedra	the stone
não tinge de azul	doesn't dye the fingers
os dedos	blue
quando escreve manhã	when it writes morning
ou brisa	or breeze
ou blusa	or blouse
de mulher.	of a woman.

O poema	The poem
é sem matéria palpável	is without palpable matter
tudo	all
o que há nele	there is
é barulho	is noise
quando rumoreja	that goes on rustling
ao sopro da leitura.	in the breath of reading.

1980/1987   *trans. Renato Rezende*

Heberto Padilla

C U B A

1932–

In both his public life and his writing, Heberto Padilla has addressed the challenge of an intellectual in an increasingly totalitarian society. An early advocate of Castro's revolution in Cuba, Padilla worked as a journalist in Havana and as a correspondent for government-approved periodicals in London and Moscow. While living abroad Padilla came to know many international literary figures, including Sartre, Camus, Yevtushenko, and García Márquez, and he came to admire the wide range of Anglo-American poetry, especially the poems of the Modern generation.

Although Padilla held positions of some importance in the Castro regime, he became concerned about political intolerance and aesthetic restrictions in Cuban society. Officials in the regime began to regard him with suspicion. The situation reached an acrimonious climax when, even though his controversial book *Fuera del juego* (*Out of the Game*, 1966) had won the prestigious Writers' and Artists' Union Prize in 1968, Padilla was imprisoned on specious charges of espionage in 1971. He submitted a "self-criticism" confessing "counterrevolutionary sins" and apparently recanting his criticism of the Revolution. His clearly ironic, overstated tone, however, made his real position clear. Many international writers and critics, including Sartre and Julio Cortázar, protested his imprisonment and, more generally, Castro's policies with respect to intellectual freedom. (Others, including Gabriel García Márquez, acknowledged the justice of the protest but, out of public support to the declared ideals of the Revolution, refused to challenge Castro—or to support Padilla.) Although official attitudes toward artistic freedom hardened, Padilla was eventually released.

Eventually Padilla emigrated to the United States. In exile, he has consistently resisted explicit political commitments (choosing not to be involved with Cuban counterrevolutionary groups in the United States, for instance) because he fears co-optation. He refuses, as he puts it, "to carry a century" on his shoulders. In addition to many books of conceptually complex, free-ranging, meditative poems in free verse, Padilla has published several novels and a comprehensive autobiography, *Autorretrato del otro* (*Self-Portrait of the Other*, 1980).

Una pregunta a la escuela de Frankfurt

¿Qué piensa él?
¿Qué es lo que está pensando
ese hombre,
que tiembla entre un fusil y un muro?

Respondan preferiblemente
en el siguiente orden:
Horkheimer
Marcuse
Adorno.

Reordenen la pregunta
si lo creen necesario:
entre un fusil y un muro
¿qué es lo que está pensando
ese hombre que tiembla,
al alcance de un ojo, enterrado en su edad,
y sin embargo a punto de ser sacado de ella
de un empujón
que no pudo soñar jamás la madre que lo parió?

1980

A Question for the Frankfurt School

What does he think?
What is he thinking,
that man
who trembles between a rifle and a wall?

Answer preferably
in the following order:
Horkheimer
Marcuse
Adorno.

Rephrase the question
if you think it necessary:
Between a rifle and a wall
what is it that he is thinking,
that man who trembles,
within eyeshot, buried in his time
and nonetheless about to be taken from it
by a blow
that the mother who bore him
could never have dreamed of?

trans. Alastair Reid and Andrew Hurley

Autorretrato del otro

¿Son estremecimientos, náuseas,
efusiones,
o más bien esas ganas
que a veces tiene el hombre de gritar?
No lo sé. Vuelvo a escena.
Camino hacia los reflectores
como ayer,
      más veloz que una ardilla,
con mi baba de niño
y una banda tricolor en el pecho,
      protestón e irascible
            entre los colegiales.

Es que por fin
      lograron encerrarme
en el jardín barroco que tanto odié
y este brillo de ópalo
      en los ojos
me hace irreconocible.
El gladiador enano (de bronce)
que he puesto encima de la mesa
—un héroe cejijunto y habilísimo
con su arma corta y blanca—

Self-Portrait of the Other

Is it anxiety, nausea,
raptures?
Or is it just wanting
sometimes to shout out?
I don't know. I come back onstage.
I walk toward the footlights
as if toward yesterday,
      swifter than a squirrel,
with my child's drool
and a tricolor flag on my breast,
      agitator, irascible,
            among the students.

The truth is that they finally
      managed to lock me up
in that baroque garden I hated so much
and this opal gleam
      in my eyes
makes me unrecognizable.
The little gladiator (bronze)
which I have put on the table
—a scowling hero, master
of his short white blade—

y su perra enconada
      son ahora mis únicos compinches.
Pero cuando aparezca
      mi tropa de juglares
limaremos las rejas
y saldré.
¡Puertas son las que sobran!

Bajo la luna plástica
¿me he vuelto un papagayo
o un payaso de náilon
que enreda y trueca las consignas?
¿O no es cierto?
¿Es una pesadilla
que yo mismo pudiera destruir?
¿Abrir
de repente los ojos
y rodar por el sueño como un tonel
y el mundo ya mezclado con mis fermentaciones?
¿O serán estas ganas
que a veces tiene el hombre de gritar?

Las Derechas me alaban
      (ya me difamarán)
Las Izquierdas me han hecho célebre
      (¿no han empezado a alimentar sus dudas?)
Pero de todas formas
advierto que vivo entre las calles.
Voy sin gafas ahumadas.
Y no llevo bombas de tiempo en los bolsillos
ni una oreja peluda—de oso.
Ábranme paso ya
sin saludarme, por favor.
Sin hablarme.
Échense a un lado si me ven.

1980

and his snarling bitch
      are now my only buddies.
But when my troupe of jugglers
      appears
we will file through the bars
and I will break out.
Doors are things there are too many of!

Under the plastic moon
have I become a parrot
or a nylon clown
that bumbles and loses the password?
Or is it not true?
Is it a nightmare
that I myself could destroy,
opening my eyes
suddenly
and rolling through the dream in a barrel,
and the world mixed now with these seethings?
Or is it just wanting
sometimes to shout out?

The Right praises me
      (in no time they will defame me)
The Left has given me a name
      (have they not begun to have doubts?)
But at any rate
I warn you I'm alive in the streets.
I don't wear dark glasses.
And I don't carry time bombs in my pockets
or a hairy ear—a bear's.
Give me room, now.
Don't greet me, I beg you.
Don't even speak to me.
If you see me, keep to one side.

trans. Alastair Reid and Andrew Hurley

Herencias

Yo no sé si los viejos regresarán un día por el sitio
      en que uno los perdió cuando niño.
Yo no creo que sea éste el destino de un muerto; mucho
      menos de viejos cogidos por la fatiga
de nietos y de hijos. Aún cuando lo desearan
      no les sería posible regresar.
Los muertos tienen que ser perseverantes jóvenes
      deseosos de conquistar de nuevo
el gusto de la tierra y quitarse de encima
      el peso de las enfermedades que los matan.

Legacies

I don't know if the old people will return one day
      at the place we lost them when we were children.
I don't think that this is the fate of a dead man; much less
      of old people overtaken by the fatigue
of children and grandchildren. Even if they should want it,
      they couldn't come back.
The dead must be stubbornly young, wanting to conquer
      again
the taste of the earth and to push off from them
      the weight of the sicknesses that kill them.

—Los muertos son suspiros y calandrias
que cantan, hijo mío, me decía mi abuela
cuando aún tenía su pedazo de tiempo para ella
    y hasta se dedicaba a consolarme.

Los muertos más antiguos se ocupan en cavar.
    Van hacia abajo. Pesan.
No logran flotar como los jóvenes.
    Hunden el suelo donde pudieron
enterrarlos, y si fueron juntados y metidos
    en cajas de madera, muertos, en fin,
de guerra, sacados de la tumba obscena de los combates,
    ya no hay invocación que los despierte.
No existe el medio de conversar con ellos o verlos
regresar como en los tiempos en que aún no habíamos
    salido de la infancia.
Están mejor así—yo pienso—hundidos.
    Así nunca tendrán memoria, nunca tendrán
    nostalgias,
    remordimientos como nosotros.

1980

—The dead are sighs and buntings
that sing, my son, my grandmother would tell me
when she still had a piece of time to herself
    and could take the time to console me.

The longest-dead have their hands full digging.
    They sink downwards. They are heavy.
They can't manage to float like the young.
    They sink into the ground where we could bury them
and if we got them all together and put them
    into coffins, dead, finally, in war,
taken out of the obscene tomb of battles,
    still there is no invocation that can wake them.
We can never talk with them or see them
return as then when we had still not left our childhood.
They are better that way, I think—underground.
    That way they will never have memory, nostalgia,
    never have remorse, as we have.

trans. Alastair Reid and Andrew Hurley

La promesa

Hace tiempo
te había prometido muchos poemas de amor
y—ya ves—no podía escribirlos.
Estabas junto a mí
y es imposible escribir sobre lo que se tiene.
Lo que se tiene es siempre poesía.
Pero han comenzado a unirnos
cosas definitivas:
hemos vivido la misma soledad
en cuartos separados
—sin saber nada el uno del otro—,
tratando, cada uno en su sitio,
de recordar cómo eran los gestos de nuestras caras,
que de pronto se juntan con aquellas
que ya creíamos perdidas, desdibujadas,
de los primeros años.
Yo recordaba golpes en la puerta
y tu voz alarmada
y tú mis ojos soñolientos aún.
Durante mucho tiempo
me preguntabas qué cosa era la Historia.
Yo fracasaba, te daba definiciones imprecisas.
Nunca me atreví a darte un ejemplo mayor.

1991

The Promise

A while ago
I promised you many love poems
and—now you see—I couldn't write them.
You were sitting next to me
and it is impossible to write about what is just there.
What one has is always poetry.
But a few clear things
have begun to bring us together—
we have shared the same solitude
in separate rooms,
without knowing anything of each other,
trying, each in place,
to remember the looks on our faces,
which all of a sudden join those
we thought we had lost, erased
from our early years.
I remembered the knocks on the door
and your frightened voice,
and you, my eyes still filled with sleep.
For a long time
you used to ask me just what History was.
I couldn't answer, I gave vague definitions.
I never dared give you a real answer.

trans. Alastair Reid and Alexander Coleman

Gabriel Zaid

MEXICO
1934–

Gabriel Zaid's lucid, antirhetorical poems use skepticism to locate the discussion and to distance the tone. Zaid's irony fixes the poem as a locus of interpenetrating forces, a field on which political dialectics, or erotic combat, or even the shifting interpretative relation of reader to text, can be played out and examined at the same time. Since his early discursive and "mythical" work, in *Fábula de Narciso y Ariadna* (*Legend of Narcissus and Ariadne*, 1958), Zaid has pared his poems to a lean, idiomatic succinctness. His book *Cuestionario* (*Questionnaire*, 1977) collected poems written from 1951 to 1976.

Canción de seguimiento

No soy el viento ni la vela
sino el timón que vela.

No soy el agua ni el timón
sino el que canta esta canción.

No soy la voz ni la garganta
sino lo que se canta.

No sé quién soy ni lo que digo
pero voy y te sigo.

1964

Song of Pursuit

I am not the wind, nor the sail,
but the rudder that watches.

I am not the water, nor the rudder,
but he who sings this song.

I am not the voice, nor the throat,
but that which is sung.

I don't know who I am, nor what I say,
but I go following you.

trans. Mónica Hernández-Cancio

Claridad furiosa

No aceptamos lo dado, de ahí la fantasía.
Sol de mis ojos: eternidad aparte, pero mía.

Pero se da el presente aunque no estés presente.
Luz a veces a cántaros, pan de cada día.
Se dan tus pensamientos, tuyos como estos pájaros.
Se da tu soledad, tuya como tu sombra,
negra luz fulminante: bofetada del día.

1964

A Furious Clarity

We accept no givens: from here on illusion.
The light of my eyes: a world apart, but mine.

Whether you're present or not, the present is given.
At times a light pours down, our daily bread.

Thoughts are given you, yours like the birds.
Solitude is given you, yours like your shadow.
Black light shuddering at the thump of day.

trans. George McWhirter

Claustro

Entre vivir y pensar,
la puerta a medio cerrar.
Ver es ser de par en par.

1964

Cloister

Between to live and to think,
the door is ajar.
Seeing: being open wide.

trans. Mónica Hernández-Cancio

Circe

Mi patria está en tus ojos, mi deber en tus labios.
Pídeme lo que quieras menos que te abandone.
Si naufragué en tus playas, si tendido en tu arena
soy un cerdo feliz, soy tuyo, más no importa.
Soy de este sol que eres, mi solar está en ti.
Mis lauros en tu dicha, mi hacienda en tus haberes.

1964

Circe

My homeland is in your eyes, my duty on your lips.
Ask anything of me, except to leave you.
Shipwrecked, so, on your beaches, stranded on your sands,
I am a happy pig: I am yours: nothing else matters.
I belong to the sun you are; my demesne is in it.
My glory is in your joy, my home in what you have.

trans. Andrew Rosing

Práctica mortal

Subir los remos y dejarse
llevar con los ojos cerrados.
Abrir los ojos y encontrarse
vivo: se repitió el milagro.

Anda, levántate y olvida
esta ribera misteriosa
en que has desembarcado.

1969

Mortal Practice

Raise the oars, be carried
along, with eyes closed.
Open your eyes, find yourself
alive: the miracle repeats.

Go, get up, forget
this treacherous shore
where you have landed.

trans. Mónica Hernández-Cancio

Reloj del sol

Hora extraña. No es
el fin del mundo
sino el atardecer.
La realidad,
torre de Pisa,
da la hora
a punto de caer.

1969

Sundial

Weird hour It's not
the end of the world,
but it's dusk.
Reality,
the tower of Pisa,
tells the hour
on the verge of falling.

trans. Adrian Hernandez

Roque Dalton

EL SALVADOR
1935–1975

The story of Roque Dalton has become legendary in the politics of the arts in Latin America. Born in El Salvador, Dalton studied law under the Jesuits in San Salvador, in Mexico, and in Chile. In 1955 he joined the Communist Party. As a result of his political activities, Dalton was frequently imprisoned. (On one occasion, it is said, an earthquake felled the walls of the prison in which he was held under a death sentence.) Dalton lived most of his life in political exile (in Czechoslovakia, Mexico, Guatemala, and Cuba). He returned to El Salvador in 1975 as a member of the People's Revolutionary Army (ERP) and fought as a guerrilla in several revolutionary movements. In hiding near the end of his life, he had to publish his poems under several pseudonyms. Dalton was assassinated, reputedly by a member of a rival Maoist faction of the Party.

A writer of careful passion, Dalton wrote poems and essays of both criticism and theory. As a cultural critic, he is aware of the power of the dominant norm and is concerned—as James Scully describes it—to use "bourgeois culture against itself in order to hasten the exhaustion of that culture's resources and, thereby, to move beyond it." For all the militancy of his ideological commitments, Dalton writes a poetry of great generosity, beauty, and inclusiveness. He stresses that "the poet—above all the communist poet—will have to articulate all of life: the proletarian struggle, the beauty of the cathedrals left us by the Spanish colony, the wonder of the sexual act, the prophecies of the future that the great signs of the day proclaim to us." Dalton's example, both in his political work and in his poems, made him a model for other poets, including many who write a "poetry of witness." This group includes, most signally, Otto René Castillo of Guatemala and Leonel Rugama of Nicaragua.

Arte poética	*Ars Poetica*
a Raúl Castellanos	*to Raúl Castellanos*
La angustia existe.	Anguish exists.
El hombre usa sus antiguos desastres como un espejo.	Man uses his old disasters as a mirror.
Una hora apenas después del crepúsculo ese hombre recoge los hirientes residuos de su día acongojadamente los pone cerca del corazón y se hunde con un sudor de tísico aún no resignado en sus profundas habitaciones solitarias.	Barely an hour after dark that man picks up the bitter scraps of his day painfully places them next to his heart and sweating like a consumptive who still hasn't given up sinks into his deep, lonely room. Here, such a man chainsmokes
Ahí tal hombre fuma gravemente inventaría las desastrosas telerañas del techo abomina de la frescura de la flor se exilia de su misma piel asfixiante mira sus torvos pies cree que la cama es un sepulcro diario no tiene un cobre en el bolsillo tiene hambre solloza.	he concocts disastrous cobwebs on the ceiling he loathes fresh flowers his own asphyxiating skin exiles him he stares at his cold feet he believes his bed is his daily grave his pockets are empty he's hungry he sobs.

Pero los hombres los demás hombres
abren su pecho alegremente al sol
o a los asesinatos callejeros
elevan el rostro del pan desde los hornos
como una generosa bandera contra el hambre
se ríen hasta que duele el aire con los niños
llenan de pasos mínimos el vientre de las bienaventuradas
parten las piedras como frutas obstinadas en su solemnidad
cantan desnudos en el cordial vaso del agua
bromean con el mar lo toman jovialmente de los cuernos
construyen en los páramos melodiosos hogares de la luz
se embriagan como Dios anchamente
	But those men, those other men,
	gladly bare their chests to the sun
	or to murderers on the prowl
	they lift the face of bread out of ovens
	like a benevolent flag against hunger
	they laugh so hard with the children even the air hurts
	they fill with tiny footsteps the bellies of blessed women
	they split rocks like stubborn fruit in their solemnity
	naked they sing into the refreshing glass of water
	they joke around with the sea playfully taking it by
	    the horns
	they build melodious houses of light in windswept
	    wildernesses

establecen sus puños contra la desesperanza
sus fuegos vengadores contra el crimen
su amor de interminables raíces
contra la atroz guadaña del odio.

La angustia existe sí.

Como la desesperanza
el crimen
o el odio.

¿Para quién deberá ser la voz del poeta?

1963

like God they get drunk everywhere
they settle with their fists against despair
their avenging fires against crime
their love of unending roots
against the atrocious scythe of hatred.

Anguish exists, yes.

As does despair
crime
or hatred.

For whom shall the voice of the poet speak?

trans. Richard Schaaf

Buscándome líos

La noche de mi primera reunión de célula llovía
mi manera de chorrear fue muy aplaudida por cuatro
o cinco personajes del dominio de Goya
todo el mundo ahí parecía levemente aburrido
tal vez da la persecución y hasta de la tortura diariamente
    soñada.

Fundadores de confederaciones y de huelgas mostraban
cierta ronquera y me dijeron que debía
escoger un seudónimo
que me iba a tocar pagar cinco pesos al mes
que quedábamos en que todos los miércoles
y que cómo iban mis estudios
y que por hoy íbamos a leer un folleto de Lenin
y que no era necesario decir a cada momento camarada.

Cuando salimos no llovía más
mi madre me riñó por llegar tarde a casa.

1969

Looking for Trouble

The night of my first cell meeting it was pouring rain
Four or five characters out of the world of Goya
were very impressed with the way I dripped
Everyone there seemed somewhat bored
perhaps from the persecution and the daily nightmares
    of torture.

These somewhat hoarse-sounding organizers of
    labor unions
and strikes told me I'd have to
find a pseudonym
that I was going to have to pay five pesos a month
that we had to agree to do this every Wednesday
and how were my studies going
and for today we were going to read a pamphlet by Lenin
and that it wasn't necessary to say "comrade" every minute.

When we broke up the rain had stopped
Mother scolded me for coming home late.

trans. Richard Schaaf

El descanso del guerrero

Los muertos están cada día más indóciles.

Antes era fácil con ellos:
les dábamos un cuello duro una flor
loábamos sus nombres en una larga lista:
que los recintos de la patria
que las sombras notables
que el mármol monstruoso.

Soldier's Rest

The dead grow more intractable every day.

Once they were obedient:
we gave them a stiff collar a flower
we eulogized their names on an Honor Roll:
in the National Cemetery
among distinguished shades
on hideous marble.

El cadáver firmaba en pos de la memoria
iba de nuevo a filas
y marchaba al compás de nuestra vieja música.

Pero qué va
los muertos
son otros desde entonces.

Hoy se ponen irónicos
preguntan.

Me parece que caen en la cuenta
de ser cada vez más la mayoría!

1969

The corpse signed up pursuing glory
once more joined the ranks
marched to the beat of our old drum.

Wait a minute!
Since then
they have changed.

These days they grow ironic,
ask questions.

It seems to me they realize that more and more
they are the majority!

trans. Richard Schaaf

La pequeña burguesía

(Sobre una de sus manifestaciones)

Los que
en el mejor de los casos
quieren hacer la revolución
para la Historia para la lógica
para la ciencia y la naturaleza
para los libros del próximo año o el futuro
para ganar la discusión e incluso
para salir por fin en los diarios
y no simplemente
para eliminar el hambre
de los que tienen hambre
para eliminar la explotación de los explotados.

Es natural entonces
que en la práctica revolucionaria
cedan sólo ante el juicio de la Historia
de la moral el humanismo la lógica y las ciencias
los libros y los periódicos
y se nieguen a conceder la última palabra
a los hambrientos a los explotados
que tienen su propia historia de horror
su propia lógica implacable
y tendrán sus propios libros
su propia ciencia
naturaleza
y futuro

1975

The Petty Bourgeoisie

(one of its manifestations)

Those who
in most cases
want to make revolution
for History for logic
for science and nature
for next year's books or the future
to win arguments and even
to appear finally in the newspapers
and not simply
to put an end to the hunger
of those who are hungry
and the exploitation
of those who are exploited.

It is natural, then,
that in revolutionary practice
they only concede before the judgment of History
morality humanism logic science
books and newspapers
and refuse to concede the last word
to the hungry the exploited
who have their own history of horror
their own implacable logic
and who will have their own books
their own science
nature
and future

trans. Richard Schaaf

De un revolucionario a J. L. Borges

Es que para nuestro Código de Honor,
Ud. también, señor,
fue de los tantos lúcidos que agotaron la infamia.

Y en nuestro Código de Honor
el decir: "qué escritor!"
es bien pobre atenuante;
es, quizás,
otra infamia...

1975

From a Revolutionary to J. L. Borges

According to our Code of Honor,
you, too, Sir,
were one of the many clear-minded ones who made little
    of infamy.

And according to our Code of Honor,
to say "But what a Writer!"
is a lame excuse;
it is, perhaps,
another infamy...

trans. Julie Schumacher

Víctor Jara

CHILE
1935–1973

In her moving memoir *An Unfinished Song* (1984), Joan Jara reconstructs the evidence of her husband's last days, following the military overthrow of Salvador Allende's democratically elected Popular Unity government in Chile. With thousands of others detained without arrest, at first in the buildings of the Technical University and later in the Estadio Chile in central Santiago, Víctor Jara sang to sustain other people's spirits. At first he performed the songs that had made him a beloved folksinger, an icon of the Popular Front, and a representative of the New Song movement. He sang Andean and Chilean folk songs from his days as a member of the groups Quilapayún and Inti-Illimani. Later he sang the "manifiesto" he had composed on the second night of the mass detainment. Eventually his celebrity—and his singing—gave him away; members of the militia recognized him and separated him from the crowd.

A week later, his body was discovered in a corridor under the stadium. He had been beaten brutally and shot several times. The "manifiesto" survived because other prisoners in the Estadio Chile memorized the music and kept the scraps of paper on which Jara had scrawled the lyrics.

Estadio Chile

Somos cinco mil
en esta pequeña parte de la ciudad.
Somos cinco mil
Cuántos seremos en total
en las ciudades y en todo el país?
Solo aquí,
diez mil manos que siembran
y hacen andar las fábricas.

¡Cuánta humanidad
con hambre, frío, pánico, dolor,
presión moral, terror y locura!

Estadio Chile

There are five thousand of us here
in this small part of the city.
We are five thousand.
I wonder how many we are in all
in the cities and in the whole country?
Here alone
are ten thousand hands which plant seeds
and make the factories run.

How much humanity
exposed to hunger, cold, panic, pain,
moral pressure, terror and insanity?

Seis de los nuestros se perdieron
en el espacio de las estrellas.

Un muerto, un golpeado como jamás creí
se podría golpear a un ser humano.
Los otros cuatro quisieron quitarse todos los temores
uno saltando al vacío,
otro golpeándose la cabeza contra el muro,
pero todos con la mirada fija de la muerte.
¡Qué espanto causa el rostro del fascismo!
Llevan a cabo sus planes con precisión artera
sin importarles nada.
La sangre para ellos son medallas.
La matanza es acto de heroísmo.
Es este el mundo que creaste, dios mío?
Para esto tus siete días de asombro y de trabajo?
En estas cuatro murallas sólo existe un número
que no progresa,
que lentamente querrá más la muerte.

Pero de pronto me golpea la conciencia
y veo esta marea sin latido,
pero con el pulso de las máquinas
y los militares mostrando su rostro de matrona
lleno de dulzura.

Y México, Cuba y el mundo?
Que griten esta ignominia!
Somos diez mil manos menos
que no producen.
Cuántos somos en toda la Patria?
La sangre del compañero Presidente
golpea más fuerte que bombas y metrallas.
Así golpeará nuestro puño nuevamente.

¡Canto qué mal me sales
cuando tengo que cantar espanto!
Espanto como el que vivo
como el que muero, espanto.
De verme entre tanto y tantos
momentos del infinito
en que el silencio y el grito
son las metas de este canto.
Lo que veo nunca ví,
lo que he sentido y lo que siento
hará brotar el momento...

Estadio Chile, Septiembre 1973

Six of us were lost
as if into starry space.

One dead, another beaten as I could never have believed
a human being could be beaten.
The other four wanted to end their terror—
one jumping into nothingness,
another beating his head against a wall,
but all with the fixed stare of death.
What horror the face of fascism creates!
They carry out their plans with knife-like precision.
Nothing matters to them.
To them, blood equals medals,
slaughter is an act of heroism.
Oh God, is this the world that you created,
for this your seven days of wonder and work?
Within these four walls only a number exists
which does not progress,
which slowly will wish more and more for death.

But suddenly my conscience awakes
and I see that this tide has no heartbeat,
only the pulse of machines
and the military showing their midwives' faces
full of sweetness.

Let Mexico, Cuba and the world
cry out against this atrocity!
We are ten thousand hands
which can produce nothing.
How many of us in the whole country?
The blood of our President, our compañero,
will strike with more strength than bombs and
        machine guns!
So will our fist strike again!

How hard it is to sing
when I must sing of horror.
Horror which I am living,
horror which I am dying.
To see myself among so much
and so many moments of infinity
in which silence and screams
are the end of my song.
What I see, I have never seen
What I have felt and what I feel
will give birth to the moment...

trans. Joan Jara

Adélia Prado

BRAZIL

1935–

Adélia Prado teaches philosophy in the Brazilian state of Minas Gerais, where she was raised and educated. Her sense of regional identity, as well as her intense Catholicism and dedication to female spiritual identity, account for much of the characteristic verve and intensity of her poems. Her earliest work explored this combination with autobiographical and biblical narratives, and her poems since *Terra de Santa Cruz* (*Land of the Holy Cross*, 1981) have added a nationalistic strain to these concerns. Although her poems are best known for their autobiographical, spiritual, and colloquial candor, in her fiction, influenced by the example of Clarice Lispector, Prado creates worlds of cerebral magic and philosophical complexity.

Graça

O mundo é um jardim. Uma luz banha o mundo.
A limpeza do ar, os verdes depois das chuvas,
os campos vestindo a relva como o carneiro a sua lã.
A dor sem fel: uma barboleta viva espetada.
Acodem as gratas lembranças:
moças descalças, vestidos esvoaçantes,
tudo seivoso como a juventude,
insidioso prazer sem objeto.
Insisto no vício antigo—para me proteger do
    inesperado gozo.
E a mulher fela? E o homem crasso?
Em vão. Estão todos nimbados como eu.
A lata vazia, o estrume, o leproso no seu cavalo
estão resplandecentes. Nas nuvens tem um rei, um reino,
um bobo com seus berloques, um príncipe. Eu
    passeio nelas,
é sólido. O que não vejo, existindo mais que a carne.
Esta tarde inesquecível Deus me deu. Limpou meus
    olhos e vi:
como o céu, o mundo verdadeiro é pastoril.

1977

Grace

The world is a garden. A light bathes the world.
The cleanness of the air, the greens after rain,
the open country dresses in grass like the sheep in its wool.
A pain without bitterness: a live butterfly on the spit.
Wake up the tender memories:
barefoot young women, dresses fluttering,
robust with youth,
insidious joy with no reason.
I don't insist on the old addictions—to protect me from
    sudden joy.
And the woman ugly? And the man crass?
Meaningless. They are all in a fog like me.
The empty can, the manure, the leper on his horse.
They are all resplendent. On the cloud a king, a kingdom,
a jester with his fandangles, a prince. I pass them by,
they are solid. What I don't see exists more than the flesh.
God gave me this unforgettable afternoon, I rubbed my
    eyes and saw:
like the sky, the real world is pastoral.

trans. Marcia Kirinus

Sesta

O poeta tem um chapéu,
um cinto de couro,
uma camisa de malha.
O poeta é um homem comum.
Mas, quando diz:
a tarde não podia tanger
com "os bandolins e suas doces nádegas",
eu me prostro invocando:

Siesta

The poet wears a hat,
a leather belt,
a knit shirt.
The poet is a common man.
But when he says:
the afternoon can't compare
with "your bandolin and your sweet ass,"
it makes me genuflect:

me explica, ó decifrador, o mistério da vida,
me ama, homem incomum.
No oeste de Minas tem um canavial,
onde as folhas se roçam ásperas,
ásperas as folhas da cana-doce roçam-se.
Como agulhas bicando em vidro liso.
O pio das andorinhas dentro da igreja deserta.
Os trinados e as folhas cortam,
entre as canas é doce, doce e fresco,
entre os bancos da igreja.
Repouso lá e cá,
um poder em círculos me dilata,
eu danço na mão de Deus.
Na hora do encantamento,
o reverso do verso dá sua luz:
"os bandolins e suas doces nádegas",
um mistério santíssimo e inteligível.

explain to me, decipher, the mystery of life,
love me, my uncommon man.
To the west, in Minas, there's a field of sugarcane;
there the leaves rub each other roughly,
the leaves of the sugarcane scrape
like needles stippling smooth glass.
The chirping of the swallows in the deserted church.
The choir and the sharp leaves,
within the sugarcane it's sweet, fresh and sweet,
within the pews of the church.
Tranquility both here and there,
a power encircles me, and I swell,
I dance in the hand of God.
At the hour of enchantment,
the reversal of the verse illuminates:
"your bandolin and your sweet ass,"
a most holy and most common mystery.

1977

trans. Marcia Kirinus

Fluência

Eu fiz um livro, mas oh meu Deus,
não perdi a poesia.
Hoje depois da festa,
quando me levantei para fazer café,
uma densa neblina acinzentava os pastos,
as casas, as pessoas com embrulho de pão.
O fio indesmanchável da vida tecia seu curso.
Persistindo, a necessidade dos relógios,
dos descongestionanates nasais.
Meu livro sobre a mesa contraponteava exato
com os pardais, os urinóis pela metade,
o antigo e intenso desejar de um verso.
O relógio bateu sem assustar os farelos sobre a mesa.
Como antes, graças a Deus.

Fluency

I wrote a book, thank the Lord,
I didn't lose my poetic spirit.
This morning after a party,
when I woke up to make the coffee,
a dense fog silvered over the fields,
the houses, the people with bundles of bread.
Life is cloth made from a strong thread.
Its persistence governed by the clock,
the nasal decongestant.
My book, on the table, exactly counterpoints
the sparrows, the bedpan half-full,
the antiquity and intense desire of the verse.
The clock tolls without scaring the crumbs off the table.
As before, thank the Lord.

1977

trans. Marcia Kirinus

Vitral

Uma igreja voltada para o norte.
À sua esquereda um barranco,
a estrada de ferro.
O sol, a mais de meio caminho para oeste.
Tem uns meninos na sombra.
Eu estou lá com um pé apoiado sobre o dedo grande,
a mão que passei no cabelo, a um quarto de seu caminho
    até a coxa,

Stained Glass Window

A church facing north
and to its left an embankment,
a railroad.
The sun, more than half-way west.
There are some boys in the shade.
I'm there with my foot resting on my big toe.
My hand, caressing my hair, comes to rest a quarter of the
    way up my thigh,

onde vai bater e voltar, envergonhado passo de balé.
Tudo pulsando à revelia de mim,
bom como um engurgitamento não provocado do sexo.
A pura existência.

1977

where it bounces and shyly returns like a dancer's
 awkward leap.
Everything is pulsing and revealing to me,
it's as good as foreplay but not provoked by sex.
An existence this pure.

trans. Marcia Kirinus

O pelicano

Um dia vi um navio de perto.
Por muito tempo olhei-o
com a mesma gula sem pressa com que olho Jonathan:
primeiro as unhas, os dedos, seus nós.
Eu amava o navio.
Oh! eu dizia. Ah, que coisa é um navio!
Ele balançava de leve
como os sedutores meneam.
À volta de mim busquei pessoas:
olha, olha o navio
e dispus-me a falar do que não sabia
para que enfim tocasse
no onde o que não tem pés
caminha sobre a massa das águas.
Uma noite dessas, antes de me deitar
vi—como vi o navio—um sentimento.
Travada de interjeições, mutismos,
vocativos supremos balbuciei:
Ó Tu! e Ó Vos!
—a garganta doendo por chorar—
Me ocurreu que na escuridão da noite
eu estava poetizada,
um desejo supremo me queria.
Ó Misericórdia, eu disse
e pus minha boca no jorro daquele peito.
Ó amor, e me deixei afagar,
a visão esmaecendo-se,
lúcida, ilógica,
verdadeira como um navio.

1987

The Pelican

One day I saw a ship pass close by.
For a long time I stood staring
with that same unhurried greed I look at Jonathan with:
first the nails, the toes, his knuckles.
I love the ship.
Oh!, I say. Ah, this ship is a beautiful thing!
She teeters nimbly
She is the wag of the seductress
I gather everyone around me
Look, look at the ship,
and then say I don't know what I'm talking about:
because in the end it touched me,
and it walks with no feet across the mass of soft water.
One night, before I lay down,
I had—like a vision or a ship—a feeling.
The conjoining of silent interjections,
almost vocatives, stammering, I cry out:
Oh It's Thou! and Oh It's Thee!
— my throat hurts for crying—
It occurred to me in the blackness of the night
that I was being poetic,
that a greater will wants me.
Oh Mercy, I say,
and press my mouth on your pounding chest.
O love, I let you caress me,
a vision fading now,
clear, illogical,
as genuine as the ship.

trans. Marcia Kirinus

Em português

Aranha, cortiça, pérola
e mais quatro que não falo
são palavras perfeitas.
Morrer é inexcedível.
Deus não tem peso algum.
Borboleta é *atelobrob*,
um sabão no tacho fervendo.

In Portuguese

Spider, cork, pearl
and four more which I won't say:
these are perfect words.
Dying is inevitable.
God is weightless.
A butterfly is always in *transition*,
like soap in a boiling kettle.

Tomara estas estranhezas
sejam psicologismos,
corruptelas devidas
ao pecado original.
Palavras, quero-as antes como coisas.
Minha cabeça se cansa neste discurso infeliz.
Jonathan me falou:
    "Já tomou seu iogurte?"
Que doçura cobriu-me, que conforto!
As línguas são imperfeitas pra que os poemas existam
e eu pergunte donde vêm
        os insetos alados e este afeto,
        seu braço roçando o meu.

1988

God knows these are all strange things
that exist in the mind,
corruption exists because of
original sin.
Words, things I've desired before.
My mind tires of this sad oration.
Jonathan said to me:
    "Have you eaten your yogurt?"
What sweetness envelops me, what comfort!
Words are imperfect, they exist only for poems
and I ask where do
        these winged insects and this friendship come from,
        your arm brushing up against mine.

trans. Marcia Kirinus

Jorge Teillier

CHILE

1935–

Born in the rainy southern frontier of Chile, where native cultures still survive among the out-reaches of white social forms, Jorge Teillier was raised in an environment of complex political awareness. (His father, an agrarian reformer and union activist, went into exile after the coup of 1973.) In early adulthood Jorge attended the University in Santiago, and for most of his adult life he has worked as an editor for the publications office of the university. Like Pablo Neruda, Teillier as an artist acknowledges the influences of the frontier and of leftist political ideologies. Unlike Neruda, however, Teillier does not filter the perceptions of his poems through a dominant lyrical personality or through a neo-Romantic or post-Modernist or Vanguardist diction. As Teillier's poems lead Chilean poetry into post-Neruda forms, his voice modulates through themes of memory and loss, social responsibility, and natural and imaginary landscapes.

Puente en el sur

Ayer he recordado un día de claro invierno. He recordado
un puente sobre el río, un río robándole azul al cielo.
Mi amor era menos que nada en ese puente. Una naranja
hundiéndose en las aguas, una voz que no sabe a
        quién llama,
una gaviota cuyo brillo se deshizo entre los pinos.

Ayer he recordado que no ser es nadie sobre un puente
cuando el invierno sueña con la claridad de otra estación,
y se quiere ser una hoja inmóvil en el sueño del invierno,
y el amor es menos que una naranja perdiéndose en
        las aguas,
menos que una gaviota cuya luz se extingue entre los pinos.

1970

Bridge in the South

Yesterday I remembered a clear winter day. I remembered
a bridge over the river, a river stealing blue from the sky.
My love was less than nothing on that bridge. An orange
sinking into the waters, a voice that doesn't know whom
        it calls,
a gull whose gleam was undone among the pines.

Yesterday I remembered that no one is anyone on a bridge
when winter dreams with another season's clarity,
and one wants to be a leaf motionless in the dream
        of winter,
and love is less than an orange losing itself in the waters,
less than a gull whose light goes out among the pines.

trans. Carolyne Wright

Retrato de mi padre, militante comunista

En las tardes de invierno
cuando un sol equivocado busca a tientas
los aromos de primaveras perdidas,
va mi padre en su Dodge 30
por los caminos ripiados de la Frontera
hacia aldeas que parecen guijarros o perdices echadas.

O llega a través de barriales
a las reducciones de sus amigos mapuches
cuyas tierras se achican día a día,
para hablarles del tiempo en que la tierra
se multiplicará como los panes y los peces
y será de verdad para todos.

Desde hace treinta años
grita "Viva la Reforma Agraria"
o canta "La Internacional"
con su voz desafinada
en planicies barridas por el puelche,
en sindicatos o locales clandestinos,
rodeado de campesinos y obreros,
maestros primarios y estudiantes,
apenas un puñado de semillas
para que crezcan los árboles de mundos nuevos.

Honrado como una manta de Castilla
lo recuerdo defendiendo al Partido y la Revolución
sin esperar ninguna recompensa
así como Eddie Polo—su héroe de infancia—
luchaba por Perla White.

Porque su esperanza ha sido hermosa
como ciruelos florecidos para siempre
a orillas de un camino,
pido que llegue a vivir en el tiempo
que siempre ha esperado,
cuando las calles cambien de nombre
y se llamen Luis Emilio Recabarren o Elías Lafertte
(a quien conoció una lluviosa mañana de 1931 en Temuco,
cuando el Partido sólo entraban los héroes).

Que pueda cuidar siempre
los patos y las gallinas,
y vea crecer los manzanos
que ha destinado a sus nietos.

Que siga por muchos años
cantando la Marsellesa el 14 de julio
en homenaje a sus padres que llegaron de Burdeos.

Portrait of My Father, Militant Communist

On winter afternoons
when a mistaken sun gropes
for the acacia trees of lost springs,
my father drives in his 1930 Dodge
over the riprapped roads of the Frontier
toward villages that look like pebbles or flushed quail.

Or else he arrives through the mire
at the reservations of his friends the Mapuches
whose lands keep shrinking day by day,
to speak to them of the time when the earth
will be multiplied like the loaves and fishes
and will truly be for everyone.

From thirty years ago
he shouts "Long Live Agrarian Reform"
or sings the *Internationale*
in his off-key voice
upon flatlands swept by the *puelche* wind,
in clandestine labor union halls or locals,
surrounded by peasants and workers,
grade-school teachers and students,
barely a handful of seeds
from which the trees of new worlds could grow.

Honorable as a Castille cape
I remember him defending the Party and the Revolution
without hope of any recompense
just as Eddie Polo—his childhood hero—
fought for Pearl White.

Because his hope has been beautiful
as cheery trees blooming forever
at the side of a road,
I ask that he may live to see the time
he's always hoped for,
when the names of streets are changed
to Luis Emilio Recabarren or Elías Lafertte
(whom he met one rainy morning of 1931 in Temuco,
when only heroes went into the Party).

May he always be able
to raise ducks and chickens
and watch the apple trees grow
that he's destined for his grandchildren.

May he go on for many years
singing the *Marseillaise* on the 14th of July
in honor of his parents who came from Bordeaux.

Que sus días lleguen a ser tranquilos
como una laguna cuando no hay viento,
y se pueda reunir siempre con sus amigos
de cuyas bromas se ríe más que nadie,
a jugar tejo, y comer asado al palo
en el silencio interminable de los campos.

En las tardes de invierno
cuando un sol convaleciente
se asoma entre el humo de la ciudad
veo a mi padre que va por los caminos ripiados de
    la Frontera
a hablar de la Revolución y el paraíso sobre la tierra
en pueblos que parecen guijarros o perdices echadas.

1961/1971

May his days come to be peaceful
as a pool without wind,
and may he always be able to meet with his friends,
whose jokes he laughs at more than anyone,
to play horseshoes, and eat barbecue
in the interminable silence of the fields.

On winter afternoons
when a convalescent sun
appears amidst the haze of the city
I see my father who drives over the riprapped roads of
    the Frontier
to speak of the Revolution and paradise on earth
in towns that look like pebbles or flushed quail.

trans. Carolyne Wright

Sin señal de vida

¿Para qué dar señales de vida?
Apenas podría enviarte con el mozo
un mensaje en una servilleta.

Aunque no estés aquí.
Aunque estés a años sombra de distancia
te amo de repente
a las tres de la tarde,
la hora en que los locos
sueñan con ser espantapájaros vestidos de marineros
espantando nubes en los trigales.

No sé si recordarte
es un acto de desesperación o elegancia
en un mundo donde al fin
el único sacramento ha llegado a ser el suicidio.

Tal vez habría que cambiar la palanca del cruce
para que se descarrilen los trenes.
Hacer el amor
en el único Hotel del pueblo
para oír rechinar los molinos de agua
e interrumpir la siesta del teniente de carabineros
y del oficial del Registro Civil.

Si caigo preso por ebriedad o toque de queda
hazme señas de sol con tu espejo de mano
frente al cual te empolvas
como mis compañeras de tiempo de Liceo.

Y no te entretengas
en enseñarles palabras feas a los choroyes.

No Sign of Life

Why give signs of life?
I could hardly send you a message
in a napkin with the waiter.

Even though you're not here.
Even though you're shadow years distant
I love you suddenly
at three in the afternoon,
the hour at which madmen
dream of being scarecrows dressed as sailors
scaring clouds in the wheatfields.

I don't know if remembering you
is an act of despair or elegance
in a world where in the end
suicide has become the only sacrament.

Perhaps I'd have to throw the switch at the crossing
to derail the trains.
Make love
in the only Hotel in town
to hear the water mills creak
and interrupt the siestas of the state police lieutenant
and the Civil Registry clerk.

If I'm thrown in jail for drunkenness or curfew violation,
make sun signals for me with the hand mirror
in which you powder your face
like my girlfriends from High School days.

And don't amuse yourself
teaching bad words to the parrots.

Enséñales sólo a decir Papá o Centro de Madres.
Acuérdate que estamos en un tiempo donde se habla en
     voz baja,
y sorber la sopa un día de Banquete de Gala
significa soñar en voz alta.

Qué hermoso es el tiempo de la austeridad.
Las esposas cantan felices
mientras zurcen el terno único
del marido cesante.

Ya nunca más correrá sangre por las calles.
Los roedores están comiendo nuestro queso
en nombre de un futuro
donde todas las cacerolas
estarán rebosantes de sopa,
y los camiones vacilarán bajo el peso del alba.

Aprende a portarte bien
en un país donde la delación será una virtud.
Aprende a viajar en globo
y lanza por la borda todo tu lastre:
los discos de Joan Baez, Bob Dylan, los Quilapayún,
aprende de memoria los Quincheros y el 7° de Línea.
Olvida las enseñanzas del Niño de Chocolate, Gurdgieff
     o el Grupo Arica,
quema la autobiografía de Trotzki o la de Freud
a los 20 *Poemas de Amor* en edición firmada y numerada
     por el autor.

Acuérdate que no me gustan las artesanías
ni dormir en una carpa en la playa.
Y nunca te hubiese querido más
que a los suplementos deportivos de los lunes.

Y no sigas pensando en los atardeceres en los bosques.
En mi provincia prohibieron hasta el paso de los gitanos.

Y ahora
voy a pedir otro jarrito de chicha con naranja
y tú
mejor enciérrate en un convento.
Estoy leyendo *El Grito de Guerra* del Ejército de
     Salvación.
Dicen que la sífilis de nuevo será incurable
y que nuestros hijos pueden soñar en ser economistas
     o dictadores.

1985

Teach them only to say Papa or Mother's Center.
Remember we live in a time when one must speak in an
     undertone,
and to sip the soup on an Awards Banquet day
means to dream aloud.

How lovely is the time of austerity.
Wives sing happily
while they mend the only suit
of their laid-off husbands.

Never again will blood run in the streets.
Rodents are eating our cheese
in the name of a future
where all the cooking pots
will overflow with soup,
and trucks will wobble under the weight of dawn.

Learn to behave yourself
in a country where accusation will be a virtue.
Learn to travel by balloon
and toss all your ballast overboard:
the records of Joan Baez, Bob Dylan, Quilapayún,
learn by heart the Quincheros, the 7° de Linea.
Forget the teachings of the Chocolate Boy, Gurdjieff, or
     the Arica Group;
burn the autobiographies of Trotsky or of Freud
or 20 *Poems of Love* in an edition signed and numbered by
     the author.

Remember that I don't like folk art
or sleeping in a tent on the beach.
And never could I have loved you more
than the Monday sports supplements.

And don't go on thinking about afternoons in the woods.
In my district they prohibited the gypsies from even
     passing through.

And now
I'm going to order another mug of *chicha* with oranges
and you
had better shut yourself up in a convent.
I'm reading *The War Cry* of the Salvation Army.
They say that syphilis will once again be incurable
and that our children can dream of being economists
     or dictators.

trans. Carolyne Wright

Alejandra Pizarnik

In a letter to a friend, Alejandra Pizarnik described her poems as "small flames for the someone who was lost in a strange world." From the first, the intensity of Pizarnik's deeply internal voice distinguished her poems, recalling the French-language poets whom she translated, including Antonin Artaud, Henri Michaux, and Aimé Césaire. In his introduction to her first major book, *Árbol de Diana* (*Diana's Tree*, 1962), Octavio Paz noted the poems' fusion of "passionate insomnia and midday lucidity."

Although in time her poems became shorter and more obsessed with mortality, the integrity of all her work, with its desolatingly ambiguous self-knowledge and its eerie precision, is remarkable. As her friend Cristina Peri Rossi explained, "the poetry of Pizarnik moved between the horror of sterility (that 'silence' so much feared in her writings), the lack of confidence regarding the possibilities of communication with language, a fear of insanity (which is the extreme of incommunicability), and the presentiment of death." Pizarnik published her first book in Buenos Aires at age nineteen. She was thirty-six when she killed herself, in Buenos Aires, in 1972.

El despertar	*The Awakening*
a León Ostrov	*to León Ostrov*
Señor	Lord
La jaula se ha vuelto pájaro	The cage has become a bird
y se ha volado	and has flown away
y mi corazón está loco	and my heart is crazy
porque aúlla a la muerte	because it howls at death
y sonríe detrás del viento	and smiles behind the wind
a mis delirios	at my ravings
Qué haré con el miedo	What will I do with my fear
Qué haré con el miedo	What will I do with my fear
Ya no baila la luz en mi sonrisa	Light no longer dances in my smile
ni las estaciones queman palomas en mis ideas	nor do seasons burn doves in my ideas
Mis manos se han desnudado	My hands have undressed
y se han ido donde la muerte	and gone where death
enseñá a vivir a los muertos	teaches the dead to live
Señor	Lord
El aire me castiga el ser	The air punishes my body
Detrás del aire hay monstruos	Behind the air there are monsters
que beben de mi sangre	that drink my blood
Es el desastre	It is a disaster
Es la hora del vacío no vacío	It is the hour of emptiness not empty
Es el instante de poner cerrojo a los labios	It is the moment to bolt closed the lips
oír a los condenados gritar	to hear the screaming of the condemned
contemplar a cada uno de mis nombres	to study each one of my names
ahorcados en la nada	hanged by its neck in nothingness

Señor
Tengo veinte años
También mis ojos tienen veinte años
y sin embargo no dicen nada

Señor
He consumado mi vida en un instante
La última inocencia estalló
Ahora es nunca o jamás
o simplemente fue

¿Cómo no me suicido frente a un espejo
y desaparezco para reaparecer en el mar
donde un gran barco me esperaría
con las luces encendidas?

¿Cómo no me extraigo las venas
y hago con ellas una escala
para huir al otro lado de la noche?

El principio ha dado a luz el final
Todo continuará igual
Las sonrisas gastadas
El interés interesado
Las preguntas de piedra en piedra
Las gesticulaciones que remedan amor
Todo continuará igual

Pero mis brazos insisten en abrazar al mundo
porque aún no les enseñaron
que ya es demasiado tarde

Señor
Arroja los féretros de mi sangre

Recuerdo mi niñez
cuando yo era una anciana
Las flores morían en mis manos
porque la danza salvaje de la alegría
les destruía el corazón

Recuerdo las negras mañanas de sol
cuando era niña
es decir ayer
es decir hace siglos

Señor
La jaula se ha vuelto pájaro
y ha devorado mis esperanzas

Señor
La jaula se ha vuelto pájaro
Qué haré con el miedo

1958

Lord
I am twenty years old
My eyes are also twenty
yet say nothing

Lord
I have lived out my life in an instant
The last innocence shattered
Now is never or nevermore
or simply was

How is it I don't kill myself in front of a mirror
and disappear to reappear in the sea
where a great ship would await me
with its lights burning?

How is it I don't pull out my veins
and with them build a ladder
to flee to the other side of night?

The beginning has given birth to the end
Everything will remain the same
The worn-out smiles
The concerned concern
The questions of stone on stone
The grimaces that mimic love
Everything will remain the same

But my arms insist on embracing the world
because they still haven't been taught
that it's already too late

Lord
Throw the coffins out of my blood

I remember my childhood
when I was an old woman
Flowers died in my hands
because the savage dance of joy
destroyed their hearts

I remember the black mornings of sun
when I was a girl
which is to say yesterday
which is to say centuries ago

Lord
The cage has become a bird
and has devoured my hopes

Lord
The cage has become a bird
What will I do with my fear

trans. Frank Graziano and María Rosa Fort

Exilio

A Raúl Gustavo Aguirre

Esta manía de saberme ángel,
sin edad,
sin muerte en qué vivirme,
sin piedad por mi nombre
ni por mis huesos que lloran vagando.

¿Y quién no tiene un amor?
¿Y quién no goza entre amapolas?
¿Y quién no posee un fuego, una muerte,
un miedo, algo horrible,
aunque fuere con plumas,
aunque fuere con sonrisas?

Siniestro delirio amar a una sombra.
La sombra no muere.
Y mi amor
sólo abraza a lo que fluye
como lava del infierno:
una logia callada,
fantasmas en dulce erección
sacerdotes de espuma,
y sobre todo ángeles,
ángeles bellos como cuchillos
que se elevan en la noche
y devastan la esperanza.

1958

Cenizas

La noche se astilló en estrellas
mirándome alucinada
el aire arroja odio
embellecido su rostro
con música.

Pronto nos iremos

Arcano sueño
antepasado de mi sonrisa
el mundo está demacrado
y hay candado pero no llaves
y hay pavor pero no lágrimas.

¿Qué haré conmigo?

Porque a Ti te debo lo que soy

Pero no tengo mañana

Porque a Ti te...

La noche sufre.

1971

Exile

To Raúl Gustavo Aguirre

This mania of knowing I am an angel,
without age,
without a death in which to live,
without pity for my name
nor for my bones which roam around crying.

And who doesn't have a love?
And who doesn't rejoice among poppies?
And who doesn't have a fire, a death,
a fear, something awful,
even though it might be feathered,
even though it might be smiling?

Sinister delirium to love a shadow.
The shadow doesn't die.
And my love
hugs only what flows
like lava from hell:
a silent lodge,
ghosts in sweet erection,
priests made of foam,
and above all angels,
angels as beautiful as knives
that rise in the night
and devastate hope.

trans. Frank Graziano and María Rosa Fort

Ashes

The night splintered into stars
watching me dazzled
the air hurls hate
its face embellished
with music

We will go soon

Secret dream
ancestor of my smile
the world is emaciated
and there is a lock but no keys
and there is terror but no tears.

What will I do with myself?

Because to You I owe what I am

But I have no tomorrow

Because to You I...

The night suffers.

trans. Frank Graziano and María Rosa Fort

Poema para el padre

Y fue entonces
que con la lengua muerta y fría en la boca
cantó la canción que no le dejaron cantar
en este mundo de jardines obscenos y de sombras
        que venían a deshora a recordarle
        cantos de tu tiempo de muchacho
en el que no podía cantar la canción que quería cantar
la canción que no le dejaron cantar
sino a través de sus ojos azules ausentes
de su boca ausente
de su voz ausente.
Entonces, desde la torre más alta de la ausencia
su canto resonó en la opacidad de lo ocultado
en la extensión silenciosa
llena de oquedades movedizas como las palabras que
    escribo.

23 noviembre 1971/1972

Poem for the Father

And it was then
that with a dead and cold tongue in his mouth
he sang the song they didn't let him sing
in this world of obscene gardens and of shadows
        that came at the wrong time to remind him
        of songs from his boyhood
in which he couldn't sing the song he wanted to sing
the song they didn't let him sing
except through his absent blue eyes
through his absent mouth
through his absent voice.
Then from the highest tower of absence
his song echoed in the opacity of the hidden
in the silent extension
full of shifting hollows like the words I write.

trans. Frank Graziano and María Rosa Fort

Óscar Hahn

CHILE
1938–

Born in Iquique in northern Chile, Óscar Hahn now lives much of the year in Iowa City, where he is a professor of Hispanic literature and edits the *Handbook of Latin American Studies* for the U.S. Library of Congress. A painstaking writer, Hahn concentrated his early work in the volume *Arte de morir* (*The Art of Dying*, 1977, 1979, 1981), a series of concentrated lyrics that carry the elegance of Golden Age lyricism into colloquial Chilean Spanish. The author of a critical edition of the poems of Vicente Huidobro, Hahn writes poems that recall the example of Huidobro in their intensity and in their bold images distilled from the threat of technological apocalypse.

Gladiolos junto al mar

Gladiolos rojos de sangrantes plumas,
lenguas del campo, llamas olorosas,
de las olas azules, amorosas,
cartas os llegan, pálidas espumas.

Flotan sobre las alas de las brumas
epístolas de polen numerosas,
donde a las aguas piden por esposas
gladiolos rojos de sangrantes plumas.

Movidas son las olas por el viento
y el pie de los gladiolos van besando,
al son de un suave y blando movimiento.

Gladioli by the Sea

Red gladioli of bleeding feathers,
field tongues, fragrant flames,
from the blue waves, loving
epistles to you arrive, pallid foams.

Over the wings of the mist float
numerous letters of pollen,
where the waters are asked to be wed
by red gladioli of bleeding feathers.

The waves are rocked by the wind
and the foot of the gladioli go on kissing,
to the rhythm of a smooth and supple movement.

Y en cada dulce flor de sangre inerte
la muerte va con piel de sal entrando,
y entrando van las flores en la muerte.

1967

El hombre

Emergió de aguas tibias
y maternales
para viajar a heladas
aguas finales

A las aguas finales
de oscuros puertos
donde otra vez son niños
todos los muertos

1981

La muerte está sentada a los pies de mi cama

Mi cama está deshecha: sábanas en el suelo
y frazadas dispuestas a levantar el vuelo.
La muerte dice ahora que me va a hacer la cama.
Le suplico que no, que la deje deshecha.
Ella insiste y replica que esta noche es la fecha.
Se acomoda y agrega que esta noche me ama.
Le contesto que cómo voy a ponerle cuernos
a la vida. Contesta que me vaya al infierno.
La muerte está sentada a los pies de mi cama.
Esta muerte empeñosa se calentó conmigo
y quisiera dejarme más chupado que un higo.
Yo trato de espantarla con una enorme rama.
Ahora dice que quiere acostarse a mi lado
sólo para dormir, que no tenga cuidado.
Por respeto me callo que sé su mala fama.
La muerte está sentada a los pies de mi cama.

1981

Visión de Hiroshima

> arrojó sobre la triple ciudad un proyectil
> único, cargado con la potencia del universo.
> *Mamsala Purva*
> TEXTO SÁNSCRITO MILENARIO

Ojo con el ojo numeroso de la bomba,
que se desata bajo el hongo vivo.
Con el fulgor del Hombre no vidente, ojo y ojo.

And in every sweet flower of stagnant blood
with a salty foot, death goes on entering
and the flowers go on entering their death.

trans. Isabel Bize

Man

Out of waters warm
and maternal
he voyages to waters
frozen, final

To the final waters
of the dread
hidden ports whose newborn
are the dead.

trans. Sandy McKinney

Death Is Sitting at the Foot of My Bed

My bed is unmade: sheets on the floor
and blankets ready to fly out the door.
Ms. Death announces she'll make up the bed.
I beg her not to bother: just leave it like that.
She insists and replies that our date's for tonight,
snuggles down and adds that she's in love and in the mood.
I answer that I've made a promise, on the level,
not to two-time life. She says go to the Devil.
Ms. Death is sitting at the foot of my bed.
This wretched Lady Death has got the hots for me
and wants to suck me drier than a fig plucked off a tree.
I grab a big stick and try to whack her on the head.
Now she wants to lie down for a minute by my side
just to sleep a little, I need not be afraid.
From respect, I don't suggest her reputation's not so good.
Ms. Death is sitting at the foot of my bed.

trans. Sandy McKinney

Vision of Hiroshima

> launched over the triple city a unique projectile,
> charged with the potency of the universe.
> *Mamsala Purva*
> SANSKRIT MILLENARY TEXT

Eye after countless eye of the bomb
that dematerializes under the living mushroom
with an effulgence unimagined by Man, eye after eye.

Los ancianos huían decapitados por el fuego,
encallaban los ángeles en cuernos sulfúricos
decapitados por el fuego,
se varaban las vírgenes de aureola radiactiva
decapitadas por el fuego.
Todos los niños emigraban decapitados por el cielo.
No el ojo manco, no la piel tullida, no sangre
sobre la calle derretida vimos:
los amantes sorprendidos en la cópula,
petrificados por el magnésium del infierno,
los amantes inmóviles en la vía pública,
y la mujer de Lot
convertida en columna de uranio.
El hospital caliente se va por los desagües,
se va por las letrinas tu corazón helado,
se van a gatas por debajo de las camas,
se van a gatas verdes e incendiadas
que maúllan cenizas.
La vibración de las aguas hace blanquear al cuervo
y ya no puedes olvidar esa piel adherida a los muros
porque derrumbamiento beberás, leche en escombros.
Vimos las cúpulas fosforecer, los ríos
anaranjados pastar, los puentes preñados
parir en medio del silencio.
El color estridente desgarraba
el corazón de sus propios objetos:
el rojo sangre, el rosado leucemia,
el lacre llaga, enloquecidos por la fisión.
El aceite nos arrancaba los dedos de los pies,
las sillas golpeaban las ventanas
flotando en marejadas de ojos,
los edificios licuados se veían chorrear
por troncos de árboles sin cabeza,
y entre las vías lácteas y las cáscaras,
soles o cerdos luminosos
chapotear en las charcas celestes.

Por los peldaños radiactivos suben los pasos,
suben los peces quebrados por el aire fúnebre.
¿Y qué haremos con tanta ceniza?

1983

The ancient ones flee decapitated by fire,
angels are impaled on sulphurous horns
decapitated by fire,
the maidens trapped in a radioactive aureole
decapitated by fire.
The children rush out decapitated by fire.
No gouged eye, no blasted flesh, no blood
spilled in the streets is seen:
but lovers caught in the act,
petrified by hell's magnesium,
the lovers immobilized in the public way
and the wife of Lot
turned into a pillar of uranium.
The flaming hospital bubbles down the gutter,
your frozen heart down the latrine,
they creep on all fours underneath the beds,
they creep like green incinerated cats
yowling ashes.
The turbulence of the waters would turn crows white.
You will not forget that skin stuck to the wall
when you drink a fine powder, the rubble of milk.
We see the turrets glow, the rivers
inflamed, gleaming orange, the fecund bridges
give birth in the midst of silence.
Their strident color suck the life
from its own objects: the red of blood,
pink of leukemia, a glob
of sealing wax ignited and gone mad with fission.
Oil jerked us by the toes,
chairs smash windows
floating on a swell of eyes,
the melted buildings are seen raining
down the trunks of headless trees
and from the bark to the Milky Ways
suns or luminous pigs
are paddling in celestial puddles.

Up the radioactive stairs ascend the footsteps
as the shattered fish fly through the dismal air.
And what shall we do with all the ashes?

trans. Sandy McKinney

José Emilio Pacheco

MEXICO

1939–

One of the most important and versatile younger writers of contemporary Mexico, José Emilio Pacheco has published poems, fiction, plays, and literary criticism and has translated works by Oscar Wilde, Walter Benjamin, and Harold Pinter. His early poems, in *Los elementos de la noche* (*Elements of the Night*, 1963), show evidence of his early interest in film and film theory. In subsequent poems, Pacheco has worked in forms that reclaim the virtues of prose meditation and intellectual discursiveness without sacrificing the richness of his early imagery. Pacheco directs the publication offices of the National Autonomous University of Mexico. He was a Guggenheim fellow in 1970 and has taught at several universities in the United States, England, and Canada.

Alta traición

No amo mi Patria. Su fulgor abstracto
es inasible.
Pero (aunque suene mal) daría la vida
por diez lugares suyos, cierta gente,
puertos, bosques de pinos, fortalezas,
una ciudad deshecha, gris, monstruosa,
varias figuras de su historia,
montañas
(y tres o cuatro ríos).

1969

High Treason

I do not love my country. Its abstract splendour
is beyond my grasp.
But (although it sounds bad) I would give my life
for ten places in it, for certain people,
seaports, pinewoods, fortresses,
a run-down city, gray, grotesque,
various figures from its history,
mountains
(and three or four rivers).

trans. Alastair Reid

Indagación en torno del murciélago

Los murciélagos no saben una palabra de su prestigio
        literario.
Con respecto a la sangre, les gusta la indefensa de las vacas:
        útiles señoronas incapaces de fraguar un collar de ajos,
        una estaca en el pecho, un crucifijo;
pues tan sólo responden a la broma sangrienta, al beso
        impuro (trasmisor de la rabia y el derrengue, capaz de
        aniquilar al matriarcado)
mediante algún pasivo coletazo que ya no asusta ni siquiera
        a los tábanos.

Venganza por venganza, los dueños del ganado se divierten
        crucificando al bebedor como si fuera una haraña
        mariposa excesiva.
El murciélago acepta su martirio y sacraliza el acto de
        fumar el cigarrito que indecorosamente cuelgan de su
        hocico, y en vano trata de hacer creer a sus
        perseguidores que han mojado sus labios con vinagre.

Oí opinar con suficiencia que el murciélago es un ratón
        alado, un deforme, un monstruito, un mosquito
        aberrante, como aquellas hormigas un poco anómalas
        que rompen a volar cuando vienen las lluvias.

Algo sé de vampiros, aunque ignoro todo lo referente a
        los murciélagos (la pereza me impide comprobar su
        renombre en cualquier diccionario).

An Enquiry Concerning the Bat

Bats have not heard a word of their literary reputation.
Where blood is concerned, they appreciate the defense-
        lessness of cows; great useful matrons incapable of
        coming up with a garlic necklace, a stake through the
        breast, a crucifix;
all on their own they react to the bloody jest, to the
        infected kiss (carrier of rabies and hoof-rot, capable
        of wiping out the matriarchy) by means of some
        passive flick of the tail, which does not even frighten
        the horseflies.

An eye for an eye, the ranch owners amuse themselves by
        crucifying the little toper as if it were one ungainly
        butterfly too many.
The bat accepts its martyrdom and suffers the act of
        smoking a cigarette which they crudely hang from its
        snout, and tries in vain to make his persecutors
        believe they have moistened its lips with vinegar.

I have heard it claimed often enough that the bat is a
        winged mouse, a cripple, a small monster, an aberrant
        mosquito, like those slightly freakish ants which take
        suddenly to flight when the rains come.

I know something of vampires, although I know nothing
        of all the references to bats (laziness keeps me from
        checking up on their reputation in some dictionary
        or other).

Obviamente mamífero, me gusta imaginarlo como un
    reptil neolítico hechizado,
detenido en el tránsito de las escamas al plumaje,
en su ya inútil voluntad de convertirse en ave.

Por supuesto es un ángel caído, y ha prestado sus alas y su
    traje (de carnaval) a todos los demonios.

Cegatón, niega al sol y la melancolía es el rasgo que define
    su espíritu.
Arracimado habita las cavernas y de antiguo conoce los
    deleites e infiernos de la masa.

Es probable que sufra de aquel mal llamado por los
    teólogos *acidia*
—pues tanto ocio engendra hasta el nihilismo y no parece
    ilógico que gaste sus mañanas meditando en la
    profunda vacuidad del mundo,
espumando su cólera, su *rabia* ante lo que hemos hecho
    del murciélago.

Ermitaño perpetuo, vive y muere de pie y hace de cada
    cueva tu tebaida.
El hombre lo confina en el mal y lo detesta porque
    comparte la fealdad viscosa, el egoísmo, el vampirismo
    humano; recuerda nuestro origen cavernario y tiene
    una espantosa sed de sangre.

Y odia la luz
que sin embargo un día
hará que arda en cenizas la caverna.

1969

It is plainly a mammal, I like to think of it as a bewitched
    neolithic reptile, stuck somewhere along the transition
    from scales to feathers, in its already useless impulse to
    turn itself into a bird.

Of course, it is a fallen angel and has lent its wings and its
    costume (its carnival outfit) to all devils.

Short-sighted, it shuns the sun, and melancholy is the
    preponderant characteristic of its disposition.
Bunched together like fruit, it lives in caves and knows of
    old the pleasures and horrors of overcrowding.

Probably, the bat suffers from that sin known to
    theologians as *accidie*—for such laziness verges on
    nihilism, and it does not seem illogical that it should
    spend its mornings meditating on the profound
    emptiness of the world,
spouting with rabid anger at what we have made of the bat.

A perpetual hermit, it lives and dies on its feet and makes
    every cave into its hermitage.
Man imprisons it in evil and detests it because it partakes
    of a sticky ugliness, egoism, human vampirism—a
    reminder of our cave origins, with a shocking thirst
    for blood.

And it hates the light
which one day, nevertheless,
will cause its cave to be burned to ashes.

trans. Alastair Reid

Job 18, 2

¿Cuándo terminaréis con las palabras?
Nos pregunta
en el Libro de Job
Dios—o su escriba.

  Y seguimos puliendo, desgastando
  un idioma ya seco;

experimentos
—tecnológicamente deleznables—

  para que brote el agua
  en el desierto.

1969

Job 18, 2

When will you ever finish using words?
we are asked that
in the Book of Job
by God—or by his scribe.

  And we go on polishing and wearing out
  a language gone dry;

experiments
—technologically precarious—

  to make water gush
  in the desert.

trans. Alastair Reid

Límites

Todo lo que has perdido, me dijeron, es tuyo.
Y ninguna memoria recordaba que es cierto.
Estuve vivo, amé, dije palabras
que las horas borraron.
Sentí una honda piedad
por los años que faltan.

Todo lo que destruyes, me dijeron, te hiere.
Traza una cicatriz que no lava el olvido;
renace cada día dentro de ti,
desborda
esos muros de sal que no pueden cubrirte.

Todo lo que has amado, me dijeron, ha muerto.
Y no sé definirlo,
pero hay algo en el tiempo
que zarpó para siempre.
Hay rostros que ya nunca
volveré a recordar;
y hay acaso un espejo, una calle, un verano
que ya ha cubierto el eco de otra sombra baldía.

Todo lo que creíste, repitieron, es falso.
Ningún dios te protege,
sólo te ampara el viento.
Y el viento es, ya lo sabes,
una oquedad sin límite,
el ruido que hace el mundo
cuando muere un instante.

Todo lo que has perdido, concluyeron, es tuyo.
Es tu sola heredad, tu recuerdo, tu nombre.

Ya no tendrás el día
que rechazaste.
El tiempo
te ha dejado en la orilla
de esta noche
y acaso
una luz fugitiva
anegará el silencio.

1969

Boundaries

All that you have lost, they told me, is yours.
And no memory remembered that, yes, it's true.
I was alive, I loved, I uttered words
the hours erased,
I felt a profound pity
for the years to come.

All you destroy, they told me, injures you.
Traces a scar forgetfulness won't cleanse;
is born again each day within you,
spreads beyond
those salty walls unable to contain you.

All you have loved, they told me, is now dead.
And I can't describe it quite,
but there's something in time
that has sailed away forever.
There are faces now I'll never
see in my mind again;
and perhaps there's a mirror, a summer, a street
that already go under the echo of one more futile shade.

All you created, they kept repeating, is false.
No god protects you,
only the wind is your shelter.
And the wind, as well you know,
is a boundless vacancy,
the sound the world makes
when a moment dies.

All you have lost, they concluded, is your own.
Your sole estate, your memory, your name.

You won't have, now, the day
you once refused.
Time
has left you on the shore
of this night
and perhaps
a fleeting light
will drown the silence.

trans. John Frederick Nims

Homero Aridjis

MEXICO
1940–

Homero Aridjis' poems combine the erotic meditations of Octavio Paz with the mythological richness and linguistic complexity of the poets of the *Contemporáneos* generation. Born in Contepec, Michoacán, Aridjis studied journalism in Mexico City before launching his career as a poet and novelist. Since his first book, *La musa roja* (*The Red Muse*, 1958), he has published more than twenty volumes of poems and fiction.

The winner of two Guggenheim grants, Aridjis has been a visiting professor at Columbia, Indiana, and New York universities; he has also served as the Mexican ambassador to the Netherlands and Switzerland. Aridjis, who lives in Mexico City, is the president of the Group of 100, the foremost environmental organization of Mexico.

Epitafio para un poeta

Antes de que las nieblas descendieran a tu cuerpo
mucho antes del grumo de vacilación en los ojos de
    tu máscara
antes de la muerte de tus hijos primeros y de los
    bajos fondos
antes de haber equivocado la tristeza y la penuria
y el grito salvaje en el candor de un hombre
antes de haber murmurado la desolación sobre los puentes
y lo espurio de la cópula tras la ventana sin vidrios

casi cuando tus lagos eran soles
y los niños eran palabras en el aire
y los días eran la sombra de lo fácil

cuando la eternidad no era la muerte exacta que
    buscábamos
ni el polvo era más verosímil que el recuerdo
ni el dolor era nuestra crueldad de ser divinos

entonces cuando se pudo haber dicho todo impunemente
y la risa como una flor de pétalos cayendo

entonces cuando no debías más que la muerte de un poema
eras tuyo y no mío y no te había perdido

1963

Epitaph for a Poet

Before the mists descended on your body
long before hesitations clotted in the eyes of your mask
before the death of your first sons and the lower depths
before a confusion of sadness and destitution
and the savage cry in the frankness of a man
before having murmured of desolation on the bridges
and the falsity of a cupola through the window that had
    no glass

almost when your lakes were suns
and the children were words in the air
and the days were the shadow of what was easy

when eternity was not the exact death we were looking for
nor the dust more likely than memory
nor sorrow our cruelty for being divine

then when all could have been said with impunity
and laughter like a flower of petals falling

then when you owed nothing but the death of a poem
you were your own and not mine and I had not lost you

trans. John Frederick Nims

Cae la lluvia...

Cae la lluvia sobre junio
y los signos se contienen
en toda puerta que se colabora

Al fondo de ti ríen las doncellas

The Rain Is Falling...

Over the month of June the rain is falling
tokens posted
on every door that has a hand in the matter

Deep in your heart the young girls laugh

El espíritu de la mujer que ama
corre en tu cuerpo   se desnuda en las calles

No hay desengaño en este día
sólo una luz   fuego secreto
y un grito que se exorcisa adentro

En todo está el hombre
y el espíritu de la mujer que ama

La vida en los rincones
sostiene el equilibrio del mundo
con un algo de Dios que asciende de las ruinas

Los hijos del hombre hacen su universo
sobre un barco de papel que se destroza
pero la alegría no está precisamente ahí
sino en la proyección de otro universo

Nada debe detenerse
volverá septiembre y después abril
y los amigos que no acudieron esta primavera
estarán con nosotros en un invierno previsible

Así he reencontrado imágenes perdidas
hogueras muertas de otras intemperies
y lutos tardíos por bienamados yertos

Amo este tiempo
donde los perros son sagrados
y los insectos titubean en los vidrios

Te amo a ti por efímera   por susceptible al frío

La ciudad se ilumina para nuevas proezas

                                                        1963

The spirit of woman in love
runs in your flesh—takes off its clothes in the streets

No disenchantment in this day
only a brightness—secret fire
and within you a cry as of spirits laid to rest

In everything man
and the spirit of woman in love

Life in the corners
sustains the world's equilibrium
with a something of God that rises out of the ruins

The sons of man make their universe
on a paper boat that founders
yet happiness is not precisely there
but in the projection of another universe

Nothing should postpone its going
September will return and April later
and the friends that were not at our side this spring
these will be with us in a foreseeable winter

Thus I have come again on the lost images
dead bonfires from other seasons of bad weather
and mourning long delayed for the stiffened limbs
      we cherished

I love this time
when dogs are holy
and insects hesitate at the pane

I love you—you as ephemeral—as suffering the cold

The lights of the city come on for further exploits

                                          trans. John Frederick Nims

Salir de la mujer es separarse

Salir de la mujer es separarse

el cuerpo dueño de sí
lleva su novedad y es una llama

mira tu corazón ser devorado
en una bola de fuego en una nube

mira la cara lisa de la madre de piedra

mientras que bajo el sol por la montaña
la tierra es una intemperie luminosa

                                    1968

To Emerge from a Woman Is to Become Separate

To emerge from a woman is to become separate

the body its own master
wears its newness and is a flame

watch your heart being devoured
in a ball of fire in a cloud

watch the smooth face of the stone mother

while under the sun on the mountain
the earth gleams naked

                                          trans. W. S. Merwin

Descomposición con risa

le quitan las orejas
le sacan los ojos
le quitan los brazos
se llevan su pecho
la desaparecen la cabeza
le quitan el tronco
lo desaparecen completo
y se queda riendo
y sigue riendo
e invisible
ríe a lo lejos

1969

Decomposition with Laughter

they pull off his ears
they pluck out his eyes
they pull off his arms
they pry out his chest
they fade out his head
they pull out his trunk
they fade it all out
& he stays there laughing
& he keeps on laughing
invisible
laughs far away

trans. Jerome Rothenberg

Carta de México

Por estas callejuelas
ancestros invisibles
caminan con nosotros

ruidos de coches
miradas de niños
y cuerpos de muchachas
los traspasan

Impalpables y vagos
frente a puertas que ya no son
y puentes que son vacíos
los atravesamos

mientras con el sol en la cara
nosotros vamos también
hacia la transparencia

1975

Letter from Mexico

Invisible ancestors
walk with us
through these back streets

car-noises
the stares of children
young girls' bodies
cross through them

Weightless   vague
we travel through them
at doorways that no longer are
on bridges that are empty

while with the sun on our faces
we too
move toward transparency

trans. Eliot Weinberger

El poema

El poema gira sobre la cabeza de un hombre
en círculos ya próximos ya alejados

El hombre al descubrirlo trata de poseerlo
pero el poema desaparece

Con lo que el hombre puede asir
hace el poema

Lo que se le escapa
pertenece a los hombres futuros

1975

The Poem

The poem spins over the head of a man
in circles   close now   now far

The man discovers it   tries to possess it
but the poem disappears

The man makes his poem
from whatever he can grasp

That which escapes
will belong to future men

trans. Eliot Weinberger

Antonio Cisneros

PERU

1942–

The works of Antonio Cisneros bring a voice of colloquial urbanity, irony, and obliquity into Latin American poetics. A writer of great learning and of an acute lyrical self-consciousness, Cisneros has been a professor at the University of San Marcos and at the Catholic University of Lima, as well as at universities in Budapest, Southampton, Nice, and Berkeley. He has worked both as a literary journalist (editor of the influential magazine *Cuadernos*) and as a translator of contemporary British poetry.

Karl Marx died 1883 aged 65

Todavía estoy a tiempo de recordar la casa de mi tía abuela
    y ese par de grabados:
"Un caballero en la casa del sastre", "Gran desfile militar
    en Viena, 1902".
Días en que ya nada malo podía ocurrir. Todos llevaban su
    pata de conejo atada a la cintura.
Tambíen mi tía abuela—20 años y el sombrero de paja
    bajo el sol, preocupándose apenas
por mantener la boca, las piernas bien cerradas.
Eran los hombres de buena voluntad y las orejas limpias.
Sólo en el music-hall los anarquistas, locos barbados y
    envueltos en bufandas.
Qué otoños, qué veranos.
Eiffel hizo una torre que decía "hasta aquí llegó el
    hombre". Otro grabado:
"Virtud y amor y celo protegiendo a las buenas familias".
Y eso que el viejo Marx aún no cumplía los 20 años de
    edad bajo esta yerba
—gorda y erizada, conveniente a los campos de golf.
Las coronas de flores y el cajón tuvieron tres descansos al
    pie de la colina
y después fue enterrado
junto a la tumba de Molly Redgrove "bombardeada por el
    enemigo en 1940 y vuelta a construir".
Ah, el viejo Karl moliendo y derritiendo en la marmita los
    diversos metales
mientras sus hijos saltaban de las torres de Spiegel a las
    islas de Times
y su mujer hervía las cebollas y la cosa no iba y después sí
    y entonces
vino lo de Plaza Vendôme y eso de Lenin y el montón de
    revueltas y entonces
las damas temieron algo más que una mano en las nalgas y
    los caballeros pudieron sospechar
que la locomotora a vapor ya no era más el rostro de la
    felicidad universal.

"Así fue, y estoy en deuda contigo, viejo aguafiestas".

Karl Marx, Died 1883 Aged 65

I can still remember my great aunt's old house & that pair
    of etchings:
"A gentleman at the tailor's," "Great military parade in
    Vienna," 1902.
Days when nothing bad could happen. Everyone carried a
    rabbit's foot tied to their belts.
My great aunt too—20 years old in a straw hat for the sun
    scarcely worrying about more
than keeping her mouth shut & her legs closed.
The men were of goodwill & kept their noses clean.
Anarchists could only be found in the music-halls, crazy
    & bearded, wrapped in scarves.
What summers! What autumns!
Eiffel built a tower that said: "man has reached this height."
    Another etching:
"Virtue, Love & Zeal protecting decent families."
And yet it was less than twenty years since old Marx had
    been put six feet under grass—tough & stiff, fit
    only for golf-courses.
The wreaths & coffin rested 3 times at the foot of the hill
& then he was buried
next to the tomb of Molly Redgrove ("bombed by the
    enemy in 1940 & rebuilt").
And old Karl melting & grinding different metals in
    the pot
while his children jumped from the towers of Der Speigel
    to islands of The Times
& his wife boiled onions & things didn't go well & later
they did & then came the Place Vendôme & Lenin & a
    whole lot of revolts then
the ladies were scared of more than a pat on the arse &
    gentlemen suspected
that the steam-engine was no longer the symbol of
    universal happiness.

"That's the way it was & I'm in your debt, old spoilsport."

trans. Maureen Ahern and David Tipton

1968

La araña cuelga demasiado lejos de la tierra

La araña cuelga demasiado lejos de la tierra,
tiene ocho patas peludas y rápidas como las mías
y tiene mal humor y puede ser grosera como yo
y tiene un sexo y una hembra—o macho, es difícil
saberlo en las arañas—y dos o tres amigos,
desde hace algunos años
almuerza todo lo que se enreda en su tela
y su apetito es casi como el mío, aunque yo pelo
los animales antes de morderlos y soy desordenado,
la araña cuelga demasiado lejos de la tierra
y ha de morir en su redonda casa de saliva,
y yo cuelgo demasiado lejos de la tierra
pero eso me preocupa: quisiera caminar alegremente
unos cuantos kilómetros sobre los gordos pastos
antes de que me entierren,
                                        y esa será mi habilidad.

                                                        1968

The Spider Hangs Too Far from the Ground

The spider hangs too far from the ground,
has eight legs, hairy & quick like mine
& a bad temper & can be foul-mouthed like me
& has a sex & a female—or male, it's difficult
to tell with spiders—& two or three friends,
for some years now
it's dined on all enmeshed in its net
& its appetite's almost like mine, though I
skin animals before biting them & am untidy,
the spider hangs too far from the ground
& must die in its circular house of saliva,
& I hang too far from the ground
but that has me worried: I'd like to walk joyfully
for a few miles over the fat pastures
before they bury me,
                                        & that'll be my achievement.

                                                trans. William Rowe

A una dama muerta

Desde la primera vez comprendí que te iba a seguir como
        un granadero a su bandera,
entre los muertos y el torreón de las moscas—retirada en
        Verdún, 1870, por ejemplo.
                                        Así era,
la Tierra sobre el lomo del buen Atlas, terrible y necesaria,
        inevitable.
1967, la Revolución Cultural China y los quesos baratos
—fue en París donde perdí a mi amigo.
                                        Allí estabas,
gorda, desparramada y sin embargo más dura que un
        colmillo.
María era mi esposa. *You know María,*
Señoritas from Havana know a lot of things about caballeros,
Doncella cigarettes, Kingston, Jamaica.
                María Doncella,
                María Caballero,
                María Señorita,
                María Buenos Días Señor.
(Trato así de ablandar su rostro guerrero, sus incisivos, sus
        uñas convexas.
María olfateaba al enemigo desde 5 jornadas de distancia,
        era perfecta.)
María chiquita, bonita, con un cuchillo de hueso
        escondido en la media.
You know that Villa's song.
(Oh bandera torpe y pesada como un oso, hubimos de
        enterrarte para correr mejor.
María devoró las aceitunas del odre en muy pocos minutos,

To a Dead Lady

Right from the start I knew I'd follow you like a grenadier
        his banner
between the corpses & the turret of flies
                —the retreat at Verdun in 1870 for example.
You were like the earth on good Atlas' back, terrible &
        necessary, inevitable.
1967, the Chinese Cultural Revolution & cheap cheese
—in Paris where I lost my friend.
                                        There you were,
fat, splayed open, yet harder than a tusk.
María was my wife. *You know María,*
Señoritas from Havana know a lot of things about caballeros,
Doncella cigars, Kingston, Jamaica.
                María Doncella,
                María Caballero,
                María Señorita,
                María Buenos Días Señor.
(I try to mollify her warlike face, her incisors, her convex
        nails.
María smelt out the enemy from 5 days' journey away,
she was perfect.)
Nice little María with a bone knife hidden in her stocking.
You know that Villa's song.
(Oh banner listless & heavy as a bear, we had to bury you
        to make our getaway.
María devoured the olives in the wine-butt in just a few
        minutes,

y el odre fue vacío.
                    Y ahí,
sin desnudarte—María temía a los bichos y bacilos de tu
        ropa interior—
te clavamos.
                    Después, el agua hervida.)
María loves Pancho in a fantastic tower of palmeras.
Y Pancho que no sabe escoger.
Pancho partido entre la Mariguana y el Té de las Señoras.
                    (Cómo duele,
aquí junto al hígado y la última costilla voladora.
Estancia destinada a los cobardes.)
María Buenos Días Muchas Gracias said me "You are
        a bravo".
I'm sure of it.
            I'm sure.
Entre las Matanzas y el Salmo de Primera Comunión, en
        perfecto equilibrio.
Para siempre.

& the wine-butt was empty.
                    And there,
without undressing you—María feared the bugs & bacilli
        in your underclothes—
we nailed you.
                    Afterwards, the hot water.)
María loves Pancho in a fantastic tower of palmeras.
And Pancho who can't make up his mind.
Pancho torn between Marijuana & Tea with the Ladies.
 (How it hurts, here, next to the liver & the last flying rib.
Destiny of cowards.)
María Buenos Días Muchas Gracias said me "You are a bravo."
I'm sure of it.
            I'm sure.
Between the slaughtering & the Psalm at First
        Communion, in perfect equilibrium.
For ever.

trans. Maureen Ahern and David Tipton

1968

Dos soledades

I. HAMPTON COURT

Y en este patio, solo como un hongo, adónde he de mirar.
Los animales de piedra tienen los ojos abiertos sobre la
        presa enemiga
—ciudades puntiagudas y católicas ya hundidas en el río—
        hace cien lustros
se aprestan a ese ataque. Ni me ven ni me sienten.
A mediados del siglo diecinueve los últimos veleros
        descargaron el grano,
ebrios están los marinos y no pueden oírme
—las quillas de los barcos se pudren en la arena.
Nada se agita. Ni siquiera las almas de los muertos
—número considerable bajo el hacha, el dolor de costado,
        la diarrea.
Enrique El Ocho, Tomás Moro, sus siervos y mujeres
        son el aire
quieto entre las arcadas y las torres, en el fondo de un
        pozo sellado.
Y todo es testimonio de inocencia.
Por las 10,000 ventanas de los muros se escapan el león
        y el unicornio.
El Támesis cambia su viaje del Oeste al Oriente.
        Y anochece.

Loneliness

I. HAMPTON COURT

Here on this patio, lonely as a mushroom, which way
        should I look.
The stone animals watch open-eyed over the enemy prey
—spired Catholic cities now sunken in the river—for a
        hundred lustrums now
they've been ready for the attack. They don't see or
        hear me.
Around the middle of the nineteenth century
                    the last sailing ships unloaded the grain,
the mariners are drunk & can't hear me,
                    —the ship's keels rot in the sand.
Nothing stirs. Not even the souls of the dead
—a good many with the axe, the death-pain in the side,
        diarrhoea.
Henry VIII, Thomas More, their servants & women
                                are the still air
between arches & towers, at the bottom of a sealed well.
And everything is a testimony of innocence.
Through the 10,000 windows the lion & unicorn slip away
The Thames changes its voyage from West to East.
And night falls.

trans. William Rowe

II. PARIS 5^E

"Amigo, estoy leyendo sus antiguos versos en la terraza
    del Norte.
El candil parpadea.
Qué triste es ser letrado y funcionario.
Leo sobre los libres y flexibles campos del arroz: Alzo
    los ojos
y sólo puedo ver
los libros oficiales, los gastos de la provincia, las cuentas
    amarillas del Imperio."

Fue en el último verano y esa noche llegó a mi hotel de la
    calle Sommerard.
Desde hacía dos años lo esperaba.
De nuestras conversaciones apenas si recuerdo alguna cosa.
Estaba enamorado de una muchacha árabe y esa guerra
—la del zorro Dayán—le fue más dolorosa todavía.
"Sartre está viejo y no sabe lo que hace" me dijo y me
    dijo también
que Italia lo alegró con una playa sin turistas y erizos y
    aguas verdes
llenas de cuerpos gordos, brillantes, laboriosos, "Como en
    los baños de Barranco",
y una glorieta de palos construida en el 1900 y un plato
    de cangrejos.
Había dejado de fumar. Y la literatura ya no era más
    su oficio.
El candil parpadeó cuatro veces.
El silencio crecía robusto como un buey.
Y yo por salvar algo le hablé sobre mi cuarto y mis vecinos
    de Londres,
de la escocesa que fue espía en las dos guerras,
del portero, un pop singer,
y no teniendo ya nada que contarle, maldije a los ingleses
    y callé.
El candil parpadeó una vez más.
Y entonces sus palabras brillaron más que el lomo de
    algún escarabajo.
Y habló de la Gran Marcha sobre el río Azul de las aguas
    revueltas,
sobre el río Amarillo de las corrientes frías. Y nos vimos
fortaleciendo nuestros cuerpos con saltos y carreras a la
    orilla del mar,
sin música de flautas o de vinos, y sin tener
otra sabiduría que no fuesen los ojos.
Y nada tuvo la apariencia engañosa de un lago en el
    desierto.
Mas mis dioses son flacos y dudé.
Y los caballos jóvenes se perdieron atrás de la muralla,
y él se volvió esa noche al hotel de la calle Sommerard.
Así fueron las cosas.

II. PARIS 5^E

"Friend, I'm reading your old poems on the north terrace.
The oil lamp flickers.
How sad to be lettered & a clerk.
I'm reading about the free & flexible rice fields. I raise
    my eyes
& can only see
the official books, the expenses of the province, the
    yellowed accounts of the Empire."

It was last summer & that night he reached my hotel on
    Sommerard Street
I'd been waiting for him two years.
I hardly remember anything of our conversation.
He was in love with an Arab girl & that war
—the Fox Dayan's—was even more painful to him.
"Sartre is old & doesn't know what he's doing," he told
    me & also said
that Italy had made him happy with its empty beaches, sea
    urchins & green water
full of fat glistening bodies. "Like the baths at Barranco,"
a summerhouse built at the turn of the century, & a dish
    of crabs.

He'd stopped smoking. And Literature was no longer his
    trade.
The oil lamp flickered four times.
Silence grew strong as an ox.
And so to salvage something I told him about my room &
    my neighbours in London
about the Scotswoman who'd been a spy in both wars,
about the doorman, a pop singer
& having nothing more to tell him, I damned the English
    & shut up.

The oil lamp flickered again
& then his words shone brighter than some beetle's back
& he spoke of the Great March, the Blue River with its
    turgid waters
about the Yellow River & its cold currents & we imagined
toughening ourselves by running & jumping along the
    sea-shore
doing without music or wine, relying
for wisdom on our eyes only,
& none of this seemed like a mirage in the desert.
But my gods are weak & I doubted.
And the young stallions were lost behind walls
& he did not return that night to the hotel on
    Sommerard Street.
Obstinate & slow gods, trained to gnaw at my liver
    every morning.

Dioses lentos y difíciles, entrenados para morderme el
    hígado todas las mañanas.
Sus rostros son oscuros, ignorantes de la revelación.

"Amigo, estoy en la Isla que naufraga al norte del Canal y
    leo sus versos,
los campos del arroz se han llenado de muertos.
Y el candil parpadea."

1968

Their faces're dark, ignorant of revelation.

"Friend, I'm on the island that's going under north of the
    Channel
& I'm reading your poems
the rice fields are full of the dead
& the oil lamp flickers."

trans. Maureen Ahern and David Tipton

Nancy Morejón

C U B A

1944–

Nancy Morejón studied French literature and culture at the University of Havana. A journalist, theater reviewer, and essayist, she has also edited the works of Nicolás Guillén and has written widely about issues of class and race in contemporary Caribbean culture, including a book-length study of nickel miners in Nicaro, Cuba. Morejón, who lives in Havana, works for the Cuban Writers' and Artists' Union. Her poems often explore the tension between cerebral and emotional concepts of a polyvalent self. At the same time, they are poems of joy and celebration—of her family and community, of Cuba even in its cultural and economic stresses, of an African presence in the Carribbean. Alice Walker characterizes the pleasure of many of Morejón's poems: "How refreshing and almost unheard of to read the poems of a Black Woman who is at peace with her country."

Madre

Mi madre no tuvo jardín
sino islas acantiladas
flotando, bajo el sol,
en sus corales delicados.
No hubo una rama limpia
en su pupila sino muchos garrotes.
Qué tiempo aquel cuando corría, descalza,
sobre la cal de los orfelinatos
y no sabía reir
y no podía siquiera mirar el horizonte.
Ella no tuvo el aposento de marfil,
ni la sala de mimbre,
ni el vitral silencioso del trópico.
Mi madre tuvo el canto y el pañuelo
para acunar la fe de mis entrañas,
para alzar su cabeza de reina desoída
y dejarnos sus manos, como piedras preciosas,
frente a los restos fríos de enemigo.

1962

Mother

My mother had no patio garden
but rocky islands
floating in delicate corals
under the sun.
Her eyes mirrored no clear-edged branch
but countless garrotes,
What days, those days when she ran barefoot
over the whitewash of the orphanages,
and didn't laugh
or even see the horizon.
She had no ivory-inlaid bedroom,
no drawing-room with wicker chairs,
and none of that hushed tropical stained-glass.
My mother had the handkerchief and the song
to cradle my body's deepest faith,
and hold her head high,
banished queen—
She gave us her hands, like precious stones,
before the cold remains of the enemy.

trans. Kathleen Weaver

Amor, ciudad atribuída	*Love, Attributed City*

<table>
<tr><td>

al lector, compañero

aquí vuelvo a decir: el corazón de la ciudad no ha muerto
    todavía no ha de morir jamás para nosotros

ay sueño, han vuelto las mamparas
y los cabellos de los carpinteros revoloteando en la mañana
amigándose ahora con todo lo que dejo a mi paso

ahora mi corazón se hospeda en la ciudad y su aventura

la poesía viene sola con todo lo que dejo a mi paso: flor o
    demonio,
la poesía viene sola como un pájaro
                (le doy un árbol rojo)
y se posa muy fiera sobre mi cabeza, y come mi esclerótica;
pero ahora no es el alba tan sólo, no es tan sólo el
                    cantar de los pájaros
no es sólo la ciudad

aquí diré las olas de la costa y la Revolución
aquí la poesía llega con una lanza hermosa para sangrarme
    el pecho

            quién soy

quién oye el sueño de mi boca maldita
para quién hablo, qué oído dirá sí a mis palabras
la boca del poeta está llena de hormigas cada vez que
    amanece

            quién soy

el guerrillero, la loca que deambula, la medusa, la flauta
    china,
el sillón cálido, las algas, en cañón guardacosta, la angustia,
la sangre de los mártires, el óvulo de *ochún* sobre esta tierra

            quién soy

que voy de nuevo entre las calles, entre *orichas*,
entre el calor oscuro y corpulento,
entre los colegiales que declaman Martí,
entre los automóviles, entre los nichos, entre mamparas,
entre la Plaza del pueblo, entre los negros, entre
    guardacantones,
entre los parques, entre la ciudad vieja, entre el viejo
    viejo Cerro,
entre mi Catedral, entre mi puerto

aquí vuelvo a decír: amor, ciudad atribuída

              1964

</td><td>

for the reader, compañero

here I say again: the heart of the city has not yet died
for us need never die
oh dream, the summer screens return
and the carpenters' hair blowing in the morning
merging now with all I leave in the wake of my steps

my heart is lodged in the city and its adventure

freely with all I leave in my wake poetry comes:
flower or demon
poetry comes freely like a bird
                (I offer it a red tree)
and it alights fiercely on my head and eats
                   what is sclerotic in me;
but now it's not just the dawn, not just the
                   singing of birds
not just the city

here I'll tell of coastal waves and the Revolution
here poetry comes with a beautiful sword to make my
    breast bleed

            who am I

who hears the dream of my cursed youth
for whom do I speak, what ear will say yes to my words
the mouth of the poet fills with ants each time it yawns

            who am I

the guerrilla, the roving madwoman, the Medusa, a
    Chinese flute,
a warm chair, seaweed, the coast guard's cannon, anguish,
the blood of the martyrs, the ovum of *ochún* on this earth

            who am I

that I go again through the streets, among *orichas*,
through the dark and corpulent heat,
among school children reciting Martí,
among the cars, the hidden niches of the streets,
the summer screens, into the Plaza of the people
among the blacks, the *guardacantones*,
through the parks, the old city, the old, old neighborhood
    of Cerro,
and my cathedral and my port

here I say again: love, attributed city

         trans. Kathleen Weaver

</td></tr>
</table>

Notes: In the Yoruba religion in Cuba, the gods are called orichas, and the goddess of fertility is Ochún. Guardacantones were ornate stone guards, mounted on the corners of buildings as protection from carriage wheels.

Richard trajo su flauta

NO. III

el día que las dos viejas disecaron dos pájaros
    en algún sitio de un museo
regresamos vacíos deseosos de escuchar la música del siglo
la felicidad consistía en todo aquel placer de escuchar
    sometidos a la hegemonía de una magia

para mí era primera vez
primera vez
primera que reconocía un clarinete tan feroz
    tan ahumado
    caliente
gracias a abuelo Egües aquella era la llegada de una era

para nosotros la infancia revivida
    comenzada tan sólo

sólo aquel clarinete como un puente
(y la mirada cobriza de Gladys con unas cuantas libras más)

teníamos necesidad de escuchar cada soplo
el trac de la aguja embadurnada de viejo polvo

Mozart y Europa reían muy lejos
pero también nosotros bailábamos desesperadamente
al escuchar un timbal un bajo una trompeta un guiro
    una flauta

reunidos en campaña
o al escuchar los golpes de los parches nacidos de
    mismísimo fuego

era la primera vez la gran primera vez
y todo el silencio se reducía a escuchar
    a escuchar

1967

Richard Brought His Flute

NO. III

The day the two old women were dissecting two birds
in the back-room of some museum
we came home drained
wanting only to hear some jazz
happiness was all in the pleasure of listening
    held in the sway of magic

for me it was the first time
the first time
the first I ever heard a clarinet so fierce
    so smoky
    so heated
thanks to Grandfather Egües an era had begun for us
childhood revived
    and begun again

only that clarinet like a bridge
and the coppery glance of Gladys
a few pounds heavier
we hung on every breath
the dust-caked needle tracking

Mozart and Europe laughed in the far distance
while we were desperately dancing
to a kettledrum bass a trumpet
flute percussion gourd
all playing together
the drumbeats leaping out of the same fire

it was the first time the great first time
and all silence was reduced to listening

trans. Kathleen Weaver

Desilusión para Rubén Darío

               Un pavo real blanco pasa.
                        R. D.

Si pasa un pavo real por mi costado,
haré como que cuidas su figura,
sus piernas, su chasquido de patas,
su presunto caminar agobioso,
su largo cuello;

Disillusion for Rubén Darío

               A white peacock passes.
                       R. D.

If a peacock ever passes
I'll pretend I am looking at its feathers,
its legs, its crackling claws,
its vain overbearing strut,
its long neck;

pero es que hay otro pavo real que no pasa esta vez,
pavo real modernísmo,
que azora al poeta de cabellos lacios,
de traje carcomido por el salitre del océano;

pero es que hay otro pavo real no tuyo
que yo desgarro sobre el patio de mi casa imaginaria,
al que retuerzo el cuello casi con pena,
a quien creo tan azul tan azul como el azul del cielo.

1979

the fact is there's another peacock
that isn't passing now,
the peacock of modernism,
the one that startled the lank-haired poet,
his suit corroded by the salt-spray of the sea;

the fact is there's still another peacock,
not yours,
that I tear apart on the patio of my imaginary house;
I wring its neck, with grief almost—
and it seems to me so blue, so terribly blue,
like the blue of the sky.

trans. Kathleen Weaver

Octavio Armand

CUBA/U.S.A.
1946–

Octavio Armand was born into a family that was twice exiled from Cuba: by Fulgencio Batista in the 1950s and by Fidel Castro in 1960. He has lived much of his adult life in New York. Both thematically and formally, in his experimental lyrics Armand is a poet of elegant cerebral resistance to orthodoxies. He is an anthologist and the author of several books of literary essays, including *Superficies* (*Surfaces*, 1979), *Hacer la tradición* (*To Make a Tradition*, 1980), and *El bisonte de Maiux* (*The Bison of Maiux*, 1984). Armand is also an editor, famous for his generosity and acuity, with the Spanish-language journal *Escandalar*.

Braille para mano izquierda

a Carol Maier

1

El mundo no se cierra en tus ojos: allí
naces, con el peso de un labio sobre otro.
Allí todo cabe, como en una habitación cada
ves más vacía.

No estás en tus ojos. Estás aquí,
amagando la presencia. Irresistible. Como
atrapado en una estatua.

Alguien te entierra, te olvida detrás
de la torpeza.

2

Sí, la sombra es muy astuta. La estatua
sabe mucho. Pero vuelves a tocar las paredes
y los rostros, y el calor de una taza crea
el orden.

Braille for Left Hand

to Carol Maier

1

The world does not close in your eyes; there
you are born, with the weight of one lip on another.
There everything fits, as in a room that grows emptier
and emptier.

You are not in your eyes. You are here,
hinting at presence. Irresistible. As if
trapped in a statue.

Someone buries you, forgets you behind
awkwardness.

2

Yes, the shadow is astute. The statue
knows a lot. But once again you touch walls,
faces; and the warmth of a cup creates
order.

3
A tu lado, hacer palabras. Asarlas.
Pues no te has quedado en el párpado. Estás
aquí, en las manos que ningún gitano lee.

   Tócalas. Húndete, topo, entre estas
líneas; haz tu pequeño agujero; lee.

                                        1976

3
Beside you, brewing words. Braising them.
Since you have not stayed on your eyelid. You are
here, in palms no gypsy will read.

   Touch them. Tunnel between these
lines, mole; make your little space; read.

                                        trans. Carol Maier

Soneto

Yo soy un hombre sincero
Yo soy un hombre sincero
Yo soy un hombre sincero
Yo soy un hombre sincero

Yo soy un hombre sincero
Yo soy un hombre sincero
Yo soy un hombre sincero
Yo soy un hombre sincero

Yo soy un hombre sincero
Yo soy un hombre sincero
Yo soy un hombre sincero

Yo soy un hombre sincero
Yo soy un hombre sincero
Yo soy un hombre sincero

                                        1980

Sonnet

I am an honest man
I am an honest man
I am an honest man
I am an honest man

I am an honest man
I am an honest man
I am an honest man
I am an honest man

I am an honest man
I am an honest man
I am an honest man

I am an honest man
I am an honest man
I am an honest man

                                        trans. Jason Shinder

Otra poética

El ojo que mira,
¿qué mira?
La palabra que dice,
¿qué dice?
¿Adiós a dios?

Me baño en un espejo:
el cuerpo es un color
y la distancia otro.

Con letras negras:
hojas verdes.
Con letras negras:
labios rojos
como los tuyos.

Me escondo en tu respiración.
Afilo un cernícalo
hasta que vuela

Another Poetics

The eye that sees,
sees what?
The word that tells,
tells what?
Beliefs belie?

I bathe in a mirror:
my body is one color
and distance another.

With black letters:
green leaves.
With black letters:
lips red
like yours.

I hide in your breathing.
I sharpen a hawk
until it soars

y quemo la página que lees
con tus ojos que también quemo,
tus ojos negros como letras.

Tú y yo
beberemos juntos
largos sorbos
de un agua más cristalina
que la ausencia.
En una línea final serpenteante
un agua seca que sacia y no sacia.

2 marzo 1982/1986

Poema con piel

1

Comparte el temor. Repite con un labio
lo que calla el otro.
Comienza a levantar la carne una vez m
ás.
Tócate. El sudor es nuevo y la materia
no llora.
La ingle no llora, la axila no llora,
ese pie con que huyes jamás llorará.
Una vez, muy niño, inventaste un casti
llo inacabable contra el mar. ¿Recuerd
as?
Eres ese castillo, eres ese mar. Todav
ía.

2

Repite con un labio al otro. Di tu ale
gría ahora mismo como si vivieras sólo
en la punta de la lengua.
Di dolor o ceniza, lo que duele y lo q
ue duele porque ya no quema.
Di la memoria temblando como siempre e
n las raíces o la piel que deseas y no
tocas.
Di la crueldad del obsceno tonsurado y
este pánico de macho a medias que deno
minas conciencia, conciencia, concienc
ia.
Y entonces canta. Suelta las alas amar
radas en saliva. Porque a veces no est
ás solo en tu cuerpo.
Y tu cuerpo te gusta y es bueno como d
ios en medio del placer y el crimen.

and I burn the page you read
with your eyes, which I also burn,
your eyes black as letters.

You and I
will drink together
long sips
of water more crystalline
than absence.
On a final winding line
dry water for a lingering thirst.

trans. Carol Maier

Poem with Skin

1

Share fear. Repeat with one lip what
the other keeps.
Start to pick up your flesh one more
time.
Touch yourself. Sweat is new and mat
ter will not cry.
Your groin won't cry, your armpit won
't cry, that foot for fleeing will ne
ver cry.
Once, when you were very young, you b
uilt an endless castle against the se
a. Remember?
You are that castle, that sea. Still.

2

Repeat one lip with another. Speak y
our happiness right now as if you liv
ed alone on the tip of your tongue.
Speak pain or ash, what hurts and wha
t hurts because it no longer burns.
Speak memory trembling like always in
the roots or skin you want but don't
touch.
Speak the cruelty of the obscene monk
and this panic, this lukewarm macho y
ou call conscience, conscience, consc
ience.
And sing then. Loosen those wings st
uck in saliva. Because sometimes you
are not alone in your body.
And your body pleases you and is good
as god in the midst of pleasure and c
rime.

3

No hay llanto en tu boca. Pero existe.
Aunque no duela, aunque queme y no que
me existe.
Para vivir la historia en la inconsecu
encia del día.
Para reducir al tacto las fronteras qu
e berrean.
Y en el tacto, en su dolorosa plenitud,
vivir la piel con furia, júbilo.
La piel de milagrosos o vergonzosos de
talles es tuya.
Tuya día lunes seguido de día jueves.
Tuya este sábado de tres o cuatro días.
Tu boca existe para esta gozosa acepta
ción: la superficie estrictamente como
superficie: Amada en el Amado, terror
al territorio convertido en terror de
territorio.
Bienaventurada la piel, madre de dios.
La piel es infinita. El futuro está en
tu mano. El presente está en un mano.
Tu mano conoce ese pasado importuno qu
e no cabe en la memoria. Tu mano sabe,
tu piel piensa.
Abrela, toca, y el mundo será tuyo o e
l mundo serás tú.

3

There is no weeping in your mouth. B
ut it exists.
In order to live history through the
insignificance of each day.
In order to reduce bellowing borders
to touch.
And in touch, in its painful abundanc
e, to live skin furiously, jubilantly.
This skin of miraculous or shameful d
etails is yours.
Yours, Monday followed by Thursday. Y
ours this Saturday of three or four d
ays. Your month exists for this joyf
ul acceptance: surface strictly as su
rface: beloved to lover, terror of te
rritory to terror from territory.
Blessed skin, mother of god. Skin is
infinite. The future is in your han
d. The present is in your hand. You
r hand knows the nagging past that wi
ll not fit in memory. Your hand know
s, your skin thinks.
Open it, touch, and the world will be yours,
or you.

trans. Carol Maier

1984

A buen entendedor, pocas palabras

(Parábola)

En el medio del camino había una piedra
CARLOS DRUMMOND DE ANDRADE

Si en tus caminatas has movido algunas piedras
y sin saber por qué
te ha gustado más tu propia sangre
o el crimen de llevarla a solas a todas partes,
a la cama de un animal sin nombre, por ejemplo,
a su cuerpo tendido a gritos bajo el tuyo,
al altar donde un dios moribundo
te daba a beber su sangre
y tú le mordías las venas,
la herida encallecida por los siglos;
si en los huecos del camino
sabes que aún pesa aquella piedrezuela filosofal
que un día apretaste contra el cielo,
contra tu padre, contra un pájaro,
contra tu propia sangre despedazada, negra;

A Word to the Wise

(Parable)

In the middle of the road there was a stone
CARLOS DRUMMOND DE ANDRADE

If on your walks you have moved some stones
and without knowing why
you've liked your own blood better
or the crime of carrying it alone everywhere,
to the bed of a nameless animal, for example,
to its body spread screaming beneath yours,
to the altar where a dying god
let you drink his blood
and you nibbled his veins,
the wound calloused by centuries;
if in the hollow of the road
you still hold the weight of that philosophers' pebble
you once clenched against the sky,
against your father, against a bird,
against your own dark blood broken to bits;

si eres quien tú sabes,
lee esta pequeña historia:

Alguien dejó unas palabras para ti.
Se gastaron esperándote. Aquí están.
El tiempo las ha borrado.
Yo también.

Bennington, 17 diciembre 1978/1984

if you are who you know,
read this little story:

Someone left you some words.
They wore out waiting for you. Here they are.
Time has erased them.
So have I.

trans. Carol Maier

Raúl Zurita

CHILE
1951–

With the publication of *Purgatorio* (1979) Raúl Zurita was recognized as one of Chile's most dynamic and experimental younger poets. Those early poems self-consciously worked to relocate a Neruda-like cosmic consciousness of the power of the word into a contemporary landscape of enervation, mystical indirectness, and historical compromise. Zurita's second book, *Anteparaíso* (*Anteparadise*), appeared in 1982. In a multimedia convergence in the early 1980s, skywriting planes spectacularly inscribed some of the poems from that collection in the skies above New York City.

Las espejeantes playas

i. Las playas de Chile no fueron más que un apodo para las innombradas playas de Chile

ii. Chile entero no fue más que un apodo frente a las costas que entonces se llamaron playas innombradas de Chile

iii. Bautizados   hasta los sin nombres se hicieron allí un santoral sobre estas playas que recién entonces pudieron ser las innombradas costas de la patria

En que Chile no fue el nombre de las playas de Chile sino sólo unos apodos mojando esas riberas para que incluso los roqueríos fueran el bautizo que les llamó playa a nuestros hijos

iv. Nuestros hijos fueron entonces un apodo rompiéndose entre los roqueríos

v. Bautizados   ellos mismos fueron los santorales de estas costas

vi. Todos los sin nombre fueron así los amorosos hijos de la patria

The Sparkling Beaches

i. The beaches of Chile were only a nickname for the unnamed beaches of Chile

ii. All Chile was only a nickname before the coasts that were then called the unnamed beaches of Chile

iii. Baptized   there even the nameless became a calendar of the saints above those beaches that could only then be the unnamed coasts of the country

In which Chile was not the name of the beaches of Chile but only some nicknames washing those shores so that even the rookeries could be the baptism that named our children beach

iv. Our children were then a nickname breaking among the rookeries

v. Baptized   they themselves were the calendars of these coasts

vi. All the nameless were thus the beloved children of the country

En que los hijos de Chile no fueron los amorosos hijos de Chile sino un santoral revivido entre los roqueríos para que nombrados ellos mismos fuesen allí el padre que les clamaron tantos hijos

vii. Porque nosotros fuimos el padre que Chile nombró en los roqueríos

viii. Chile fue allí el amor por el que clamaban en sus gritos

ix. Entonces Chile entero fue el sueño que apodaron en la playa   aurado   esplendente   por todos estos vientos gritándoles la bautizada bendita que soñaron

1982

In which the children of Chile were not the beloved children of Chile but a calendar reborn among the rookeries so that named they themselves could be the father that so many children cried out for there

vii. For we were the father that Chile named in the rookeries

viii. Chile was there the love for which they clamored in their cries

ix. Then all Chile was the dream   golden resplendent   they nicknamed on the beach shouting to all these winds the blessed baptism they dreamt

trans. Jack Schmitt

La marcha de las cordilleras

i. Y allí comenzaron a moverse las montañas

ii. Estremecidas y blancas   ah sí blancas son las heladas cumbres de los Andes

iii. Desligándose unas de otras igual que heridas que se fueran abriendo   poco a poco   hasta que ni la nieve las curara

iv. Y entonces   erguidas   como si un pensamiento las moviese   desde los mismos nevados   desde las mismas piedras   desde los mismos vacíos   comenzaron su marcha sin ley las impresionantes cordilleras de Chile

1982

The March of the Cordilleras

i. And there the mountains began to move

ii. Shivering and white   ah yes white the freezing peaks of the Andes

iii. Separating from one another like wounds opening   little by little   until not even the snow could heal them

iv. And then   standing high   as if a thought had moved them   from the same snowy ranges   from the same stones   from the very same voids   Chile's imposing cordilleras began their lawless march

trans. Jack Schmitt

Aún abandonados florecerían

Abandonados no verían las llanuras sino sólo un vocear recorriendo los valles   alucinante   creciendo   como si un chillido les partiera Chile entero sobre sus pastos

i. Porque un crío era Chile chillando por el pasto

ii. Por eso Chile se partía   estremecido   sintiendo sus chillidos

iii. Por eso todos aguardaban   chillando   por los pastos que les enverdecieran sus penas

Even Forsaken They'd Flower

Forsaken they would not see the prairies but only a cry crossing the valleys   phantasmal   intensifying   as if all Chile were rent by a scream over its meadows

i. Because Chile was a babe bawling in the meadow

ii. That's why Chile was rent   shaken   hearing those cries

iii. That's why everyone waited   bawling for other meadows that could turn their sorrows green

Para que abandonados empiece a oírse desde los valles
el vocear de nuevos críos enverdeciéndoles sus penas y
sólo pastos miraran allí los abandonados hijos de Chile

    iv.   Porque allí podrían enverdecer las penas de
          Chile

    v.   Incluso los valles crecerían como los críos
          de una pena

    vi.   Porque todos los hijos de Chile volverían a
          tender el verdor que olvidaron del valle

Para que chillando todos los hijos de Chile se tiendan
como un verdor que les renaciera desde sus penas y allí
se les vea venir corriendo sobre estos pastos   todos
partidos de gozo cantando aún abandonados florecerían

1982

So that forsaken they could begin to hear from the valleys
the bawling of the newborn turning their sorrows green
and the forsaken children of Chile would behold only
meadows there

    iv.   For there Chile's sorrows could become green

    v.   Even the valleys would grow from pain like
          the newborn

    vi.   For all the children of Chile would again hold
          forth the greenness forgotten in the valley

So that bawling all the children of Chile can be held forth
like a greenness reborn of their sorrows and there they
could be seen running over these meadows   all beside
themselves with joy singing even forsaken they'd flower

trans. Jack Schmitt

VI

Chile está lejano y es mentira
no es cierto que alguna vez nos hayamos prometido
son espejismos los campos
y sólo cenizas quedan de los sitios públicos
Pero aunque casi todo es mentira
sé que algún día Chile entero
se levantará sólo para verte
y aunque nada exista, mis ojos te verán

1982

VI

Chile's distant and it's a lie
it's not true we've ever exchanged vows
the fields are mirages
and public places are reduced to ash
But even though almost everything's a lie
I know that someday all Chile
will arise just to see you
and even if nothing exists, my eyes will see you

trans. Jack Schmitt

Esplendor en el viento

Innarrables   todo la aldea
vio entonces
el esplendor en el viento

Barridos de luz   los pies de esa muchedumbre apenas
parecían rozar este suelo

Acercándose en pequeños grupos como si tras ellos
fuera el viento que los empujara   igual que hojas
tocados en la boca   hasta irrumpir en una sola voz
cantándose la sangre que dentro de ellos les latía

Pinchándose las cuencas de los ojos para saber si no
era un sueño el que los llevaba   mirando más arriba
desde donde salían a encontrarlos la muchedumbre de
sus hermanos   con los brazos abiertos   como si una
volada de luz arrastrara cantando hacia ellos

Splendor in the Wind

Indescribable   the entire village
then saw
the splendor in the wind

Swept by light   the feet of that multitude seemed
only to skim this ground

Approaching in small groups as if the wind were
pushing them from behind   like leaves   their
mouths inspired   and they erupted singing in a
single voice the blood that throbbed within them

Poking their eyes in order to know if it weren't
a dream carrying them   looking higher up where
multitudes of their brethren came out to meet
them with opened arms   as if drawn toward them
singing by a blinding light

PERO ESCUCHA SI TÚ NO PROVIENES DE UN BARRIO POBRE DE SANTIAGO	HEY LISTEN IF YOU'RE NOT FROM A POOR BARRIO IN SANTIAGO IT'LL
ES DIFÍCIL QUE ME ENTIENDAS TÚ NO SABRÍAS NADA DE LA VIDA QUE	BE HARD FOR YOU TO UNDERSTAND ME YOU WOULDN'T KNOW ANYTHING
LLEVAMOS MIRA ES SIN ALIENTO ES LA DEMENCIA ES HACERSE PEDAZOS	ABOUT THE LIFE WE LEAD LOOK IT'S HOPELESS IT'S INSANITY IT'S
POR APENAS UN MINUTO DE FELICIDAD	FALLING TO PIECES FOR JUST A MINUTE OF HAPPINESS

1982

trans. Jack Schmitt

Marjorie Agosín

CHILE/U.S.A.

1955–

Marjorie Agosín was born in the United States and was educated there and in Chile; she teaches at Wellesley College. In addition to four books of poems, including *Las zonas del dolor* (*Zones of Pain*, 1989) and *Brujas y algo más* (*Witches and Other Things*, 1984), she has written several volumes of essays, studies of Pablo Neruda and Violeta Parra, an anthology of Latin American women poets, and a study of the quilts sewn by womens' collectives in Chile. Agosín is a plangent spokesperson on issues of human rights in Latin America, a compassionate recorder of female experience, and a poignant voice of Latin American poetry in exile.

La danza

a Rosario Ferré

Y bailé ahogada
en el cetro azul
que flotaba entre las piernas de mi madre
y bailé en su vientre
señales ocultas que me anunciaban.

Y bailé en la cuna
con un eclipse pendular
mientras los demás mecían para mí
un destino tranquilo
quemando hojas en la llovizna
de un cuarto siempre atrás.

Pero yo bailaba
entre las piernas de mi nana-redonda
de la nana-nupcial con senos de olor
a humo
yo bailaba atrapada en su delantal
y todos los olores del cilantro
brotaron en mis pies.

Ella me cantaba:
niña baila
porque bailando te desenredarás.

The Dance

for Rosario Ferré

And I dance submerged
on the blue perch
that was floating between my mother's legs
and in her belly danced
dark signals to announce myself.

And in the cradle I danced
with a wavering eclipse
while others dangled before me
a tranquil destiny
burning leaves in the drizzle
of a room always in the back.

But I always danced
between the legs of my rounded nana
my nuptial nana with breasts smelling
of smoke
I danced caught in her apron
and all the odors of the coriander
sprang up at my feet.

She sang to me:
niña dance
because dancing will making you grow straight.

Y bailé cuando el virgo rozó en el coral
titilante de mí
y bailé cuando la sangre me despertó:
niña ven, niña álzate
mujer no dejes de bailar.
Aunque te devuelvan a medianoche
por haber jugado sin las cartas de verdad
por haber sido incauta-ilegal.

Yo bailaba yo bailaba
cuando te enterramos abuelo
y hasta la primavera se
complació en acompañarte
ese 18 de Septiembre mes
de mi nación.

Y bailo cuando te beso
y los dos nos aclaramos en la
redondez del hueco generado.

Bailé en un salvaje cristal
cuando tú me decías
baílame que así te quiero ver
bailar.

Bailé en las camas de señores respetuosos como gallinas
y como se deleitaban en la contemplación
de su vagamente erguido instrumento
mientras yo iconoclasta bailaba ausente y desde lejos.

Bailé cuando me perseguían
en las noches de azar y amenaza
por las granadas como el ron que
no acortaron mi sed...

Bailé cuando me perseguían
los celos de esa mujer
que nada pudo
por quererlo todo
y también a tí...

Bailé en otoño encima de las hojas
violé las leyes del verano
y le bailé al océano delirante macabro y azul
bailé en invierno
aquí en el norte lejano
en una casa atorada por las buenas brujas...

Bailé ventanas, bailé hongos y caracolas
bailé en Conchalí
Aguasanta y Curacaví.

And I danced when the hymen grazed the coral
quivering inside myself
and danced when blood woke me up:
niña come niña get up and
woman don't stop dancing
even if they return you at midnight
for playing with false cards
for being reckless, lawless.

I was dancing I was dancing
when we buried you Grandfather
and even the springtime was
happy to go with you
that 18th of September month
of my nation.

And I dance when I kiss you
and the two of us speak our hearts in the
roundness of the space we create.

I danced in a wild mirror
when you said
dance for me because that's how I love to see you
dance.

I danced in the beds of gentlemen respectful as hens
and how they delighted in contemplating
their somewhat lifted instrument
while I iconoclast danced absently and from far away.

I danced when they pursued me
during nights of danger and menace
because their pomegranates like rum
did not satisfy my thirst...

I danced when I was pursued
by the jealousy of that woman
who could do nothing
for coveting everything
and you included...

I danced in the autumn on top of the leaves
I violated the laws of summer
and danced to the ocean delirious macabre and blue
I danced in winter
here in the far north
in a house chock full of good magic...

I danced windows, danced mushrooms and snails
I danced in Conchalí
Aguasanta and Curacaví.

Bailé guitarras de nostalgias que nunca tuve
bailé pampa sin tamarugal
bailé a mi ciudad.

Bailé en busca de vegetales y canciones
en busca de arroz para sostener al mundo
en busca de un estacionamiento
en busca de leche y papel...

Bailé descalza nocturna y diurna
bailé palabras semánticas fónicas
dáctilas trocaicas
menudas y agudas
porque hoy yo bailo
y me alargo como una mesa redonda
donde los pies me aplauden al pasar
y hierven con ese baile parecido
al fin del mundo.

Porque si hoy es el fin del mundo
¿quién podría dejar de bailar?

I danced guitars of nostalgia that I never had
I danced the plain without groves of mesquite
I danced to my city.

I danced in search of vegetables and songs
in search of rice to nourish the world
in search of a stopping place
in search of milk and paper...

I danced barefoot nightly and daily
I danced words semantics phonics
dactyls trochaics
small and sharp
because today I am dancing
and expanding myself like a round table
where feet going by applaud me
and seethe with this dance so like
the end of the world.

Because if today is the end of the world
who would dare to stop dancing?

1984

trans. Cola Franzen

APPENDIX

POEMS BY BRAZILIAN CONCRETISTS

Pedro Xisto (1901–1987)
Décio Pignatari (1927–)
Augusto de Campos (1931–)
Ronaldo Azeredo (1937–)

The poets of the Brazilian "Concretist" movement converge from different intellectual contexts and different aesthetic/political commitments. What they share is an interest in the nature of the poem as a visual artifact, as a semiotic element deriving its power from an immediate, nonnarrative, spatialized encounter between reader and text. Their poems not only describe or represent verbal events but, as language in action, claim to occasion verbal transformations having overt political and social import. The movement built much of its theoretical strength on the semiotic formulations of the North American logician and mathematician Charles Sanders Peirce, whose "theory of signs" focused interpretative attention on the behavior of verbal signifiers in counterrelation to an aesthetic of a displaced or transcendental field of signification. In adapting Peirce for formal purposes, the Concretists paid special attention to the spacial and graphic behavior of verbal texts as signifying systems that allude to other cultural systems. (For the Campos brothers these cultural systems are often literary. For others, such informative "base systems" may be as diverse as those of political discourse, comic books, or Brazilian soap operas, about which Décio Pignatari has written a critical study.) The power of the Concretist text often emerges through the play between the concept of the poem as a static object and the track of transformation that the mind traces: between pure poetry and committed poetry, between literary and visual traditions, between representations of essence (the poem as word) and of existence. "Poetry is

the foundation of being through the word," writes Martin Heidegger, another philosophical influence on the movement.

The brothers Augusto de Campos and Haroldo de Campos, the seminal theorists of Brazilian Concretism, approach the question of the nature of the verbal artifact through their long training in the study of literary structures. The movement may be said to have begun in São Paulo in 1956, when the two brothers and Décio Pignatari published Concretist poems in their review *Noigandres* (which took its name from an enigmatic Provençal word used in Pound's *Cantos*). Haroldo, who became known as the "Cosmonaut of the Signifier" because of the range of his experiments, began work within a Joycean tradition of stream-of-consciousness indirect narrative. Like Joyce in his transition from *Ulysses* to *Finnegans Wake*, Haroldo de Campos moved from a consideration of the function of language as register of consciousness to a fascination with language as a preexistent dream universe, or textual/semiotic universe, that structures consciousness. He has pursued this syncretic and synthetic form of verbal objectivism, and both brothers have been active translators of international Ancient and Modern writings, including poetry from the Bible, Classical Chinese and Japanese texts, Provençal troubadours and that of Joyce, Mallarmé, Mayakovski, and (with Pignatari) the *Cantos* of Pound.

Plano-piloto para poesia concreta (*Pilot Plan for Concrete Poetry*) by Augusto, Haroldo, and Pignatari, originally published in *Noigandres* in 1958 and included in their *Teoria da poesia concreta* (*Theory of Concrete Poetry*, 1965), laid out the terms of the Concretist program in combative terms. Augusto continued to work more directly as a polemicist in aesthetic fields and has sought to incorporate parallel energies from musical forms (including models from works by Anton von Webern and John Cage), from the plastic arts, from the satirical and assimilative movement of *tropicalismo* (recalling the models of Raul Bopp and others), and from the theories of "anthropophagy" (recalling the example, especially, of Oswald de Andrade).

By 1958 some members of the original Concretist group diverged, on ideological and formal terms, from the original Campos positions. Ferreira Gullar broke with the Campos brothers over the issue of the math-ematical basis of Concretist forms. Gullar's alternative "neo-Concretist" period lasted only several years; direct political commitment influenced his later poems, including his major long work *Poema sujo* (*Dirty Poem*, 1975). Other poets who have elaborated Concretist positions include writers who began with a less overtly literary commitment than Haroldo and Augusto de Campos. Although Décio Pignatari was associated with the original group of 1956, his training was in the visual arts. Pignatari has pursued parallel careers in graphic advertising, cultural criticism, and semiotics. Like the works of Ronaldo Azeredo and Pedro Xisto, Pignatari's work has gradually become more fixedly visual, in the service of critical commentary on colonialism, sexual politics, and the social dialectic.

Augusto de Campos
(1957)

KEY:
vez: time, occasion
fala: speech
foz: estuary
bala: bullet
vala: trench
voz: voice

uma vez

    uma fala

      uma foz

uma vez   uma bala

  uma fala   uma voz

uma foz   uma vala

uma bala   uma vez

uma voz

  uma vala

    uma vez

Augusto de Campos
(1957)

KEY

ovo: ovum, egg
novelo: novel, plot
sol: sun
letra: letter
soletra[r]: to spell
estrela: star
terremoto: earthquake
temor: dread
morte: death
metro: subway
termo: limit
motor: motor
torto: distorted
morto: dead

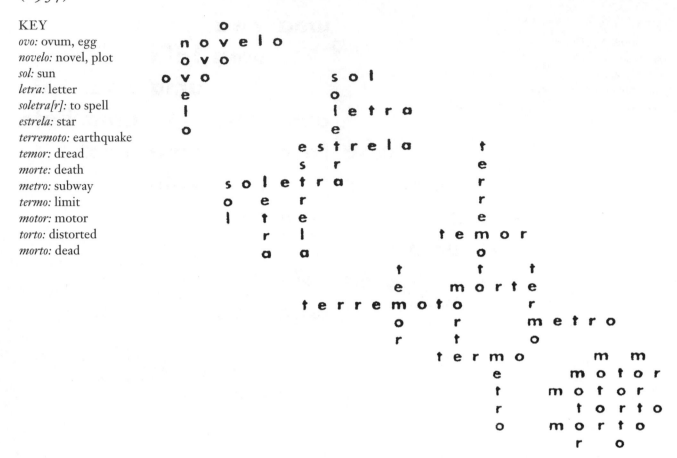

Décio Pignatari
(1958)

KEY
bebe[r]: to drink
baba[r]: to slobber
cola: glue, aerosol; tail
caco: fragment
cloaca: cloaca

beba coca cola
babe   cola
beba coca
babe cola caco
caco
cola

c l o a c a

Décio Pignatari
(1960)

KEY
organismo: organism
quer: either, or; whether or not
perdurar: to persist, endure

o organismo quer perdurar

orgasm

o organismo quer repet

o o

o organismo quer re

U

o organismo quer

o organism

Augusto de Campos
(1960)

Ronaldo Azeredo
(1964)

Labor Torpor

KEY

☐ *labor:* labor

■ *torpor:* torpor, rest

Augusto de Campos
(1965)

KEY
luxo: luxury, opulence
lixo: garbage, waste

LUXO   LUXO   LUXO   LUXO   LUXO LUXO LUXO
LUXO   LUXO   LUXO   LUXO   LUXO LUXO LUXO
LUXO   LUXO   LUXO LUXO   LUXO LUXO LUXO
LUXO   LUXO   LUXOXO   LUXO   LUXO
LUXO   LUXO   LUXO   LUXO   LUXO
LUXO   LUXO   LUXOXO   LUXO   LUXO
LUXO LUXO   LUXO   LUXO LUXO   LUXO LUXO LUXO
LUXO LUXO   LUXO   LUXO   LUXO   LUXO LUXO LUXO
LUXO LUXO   LUXO   LUXO   LUXO   LUXO LUXO LUXO

Pedro Xisto
(1966)   *Epithalamium — II.30*

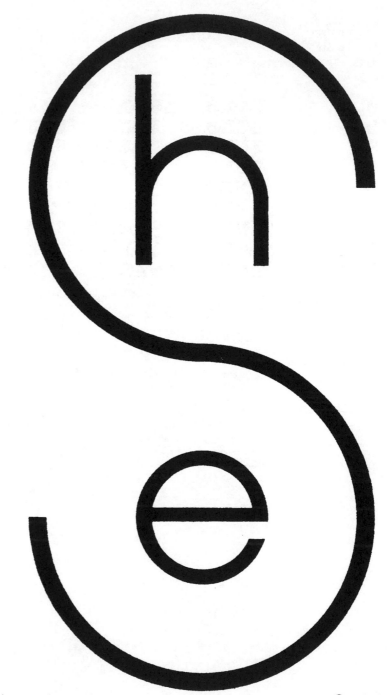

he = ele   S = serpens
& = e   h = homo
She = ela   e = eva

Pedro Xisto
(1966)   *Zen*

Augusto de Campos
(1975)

KEY
Pensa no quase amar do quasar quase humano
Think of the quasi-love of the quasi-human quasar

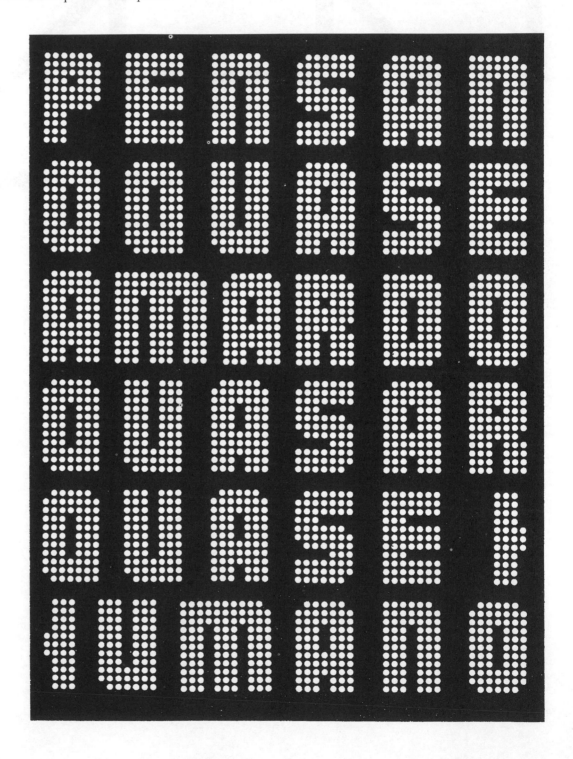

Décio Pignatari
(1981)

SELECT BIBLIOGRAPHIES

MAJOR WORKS, CHIEFLY POETRY

MARJORIE AGOSÍN

Conchalí (1980); *Brujas y algo más* (1984); *Pablo Neruda* [critical biography] (1986); *Silencio y imaginación: Metáforas de la escritura femenina* [literary criticism] (1986); *Las zonas del dolor* (1989).

DELMIRA AGUSTINI

El libro blanco (1907); *Cantos de la mañana* (1910); *Los cálices vacíos* (1913); *El rosario de Eros* (1913); *Los astros del abismo* (1924 posthum.); *Poesías completas* (1944, 1971).

CLARIBEL ALEGRÍA

Vía única (1965); *Aprendizaje* (1970); *Sobrevivo* (1978); *Cenizas de Izalco* (1982); *Nicaragua: La revolución sandinista* [cultural history] (1982); *Pueblo de Dios / Talismán / Álbum familiar* [novellas] (1990).

MÁRIO DE ANDRADE

Paulicéia desvairada (1922); *Losango Cáqui* (1926); *Primeiro andar* [stories] (1926); *Clã do jaboti* (1927); *Amor, verbo intransitivo* (1927); *Macunaíma* [novel] (1929); *Remate de Males* (1930); *Aspectos da literatura brasileira* [literary history] (1943); *Lyra Paulistana* (1946); *Contos novos* [stories] (1946 posthum.); *Cartas a Manuel Bandeira* (1958 posthum.); *Obras completas* (1944–).

OSWALD DE ANDRADE

O perfeito cozinheiro das almas deste mundo [diary-memoir] (1918- 1919); *Memórias sentimentais de João Miramar* (1923); *Serafim Ponte Grande* (1926); *Manifesto antropófago* (1928); *O rei da vela* (1937); *A morta* [drama] (1937); *Ponta de lança* (1945); *A marchas das utopias* [philosophy] (1953); *Obras completas* (1970–).

HOMERO ARIDJIS

La musa roja (1958); *Las hojas desdobladas* (1960); *La difícil ceremonia* (1963); *Antes del reino* (1963); *Mirándolo dormir* (1964).

OCTAVIO ARMAND

Horizonte no es siempre lejanía (1970); *Entre testigos* (1976); *Piel menos mía* (1976); *Como escribir con erizo* (1976); *Cosas pasan* (1977); *Superficies* [essays] (1979); *Hacer la tradición* [essays] (1980); *El bisonte de Maiux* [essays] (1984).

MANUEL BANDEIRA

A cinza de horas (1917); *Carnaval* (1919); *O ritmo dissoluto* (1924); *Libertagem* (1930); *Estrela da manhã* (1936); *Lira dos Cinquen'anos* (1940); *Belo, belo* (1948); *Mafuá do malungo* (1948); *Opus 10* (1952); *Itinerário de Pasárgada* [memoirs] (1954); *Antologia poética* (1961); *Estrela da tarde* (1963); *Preparação para a morte* (1966); *Estrela da vida inteira* (1968); *Poesia completa e prosa* (1974).

CARLOS GERMÁN BELLI

Poemas (1958); *¡Oh, Hada Cibernética!* (1961); *El pie sobre el cuello* (1964); *Por el monte abajo y otros poemas* (1970); *En* *alabanza del bolo alimenticio* (1979); *Asir la forma que se va* (1979); *Canciones y otros poemas* (1982); *Antología crítica* (1988).

MARIO BENEDETTI

Esta mañana y otros cuentos [stories] (1948); *Poemas de la oficina* (1956); *Ida y vuelta* (1958); *Montevideanos* [stories] (1959, 1961); *La tregua* [novella] (1960); *Gracias por el fuego* (1965); *Literatura uruguaya del siglo XX* [criticism] (1969); *Inventario* (1970); *Cuentos completos* (1970); *El cumpleaños de Juan Ángel* [novella] (1971).

RAUL BOPP

Cobra Norato (1931); *Urucungo* (1933); *Cobra Norato e otros poemas* (1956); *Movimentos modernistas no Brasil* [literary history] (1966); *Memórias de um embaixador* [memoirs] (1968).

JORGE LUIS BORGES

Fervor de Buenos Aires (1923); *Luna de enfrente* (1925); *Historia universal de la infamia* [stories] (1935, 1954); *Ficciones* [stories] (1944); *Otras inquisiciones (1937–1952)* [essays] (1952, 1960); *El Aleph* (1957); *El hacedor* (1960); *Antología personal* (1961); *Obra poética 1923–1967* (1967); *Elogio de la sombra* (1969); *El otro, el mismo* (1969); *El informe de Brodie* [stories] (1971); *El oro de los tigres* (1972); *Obras completas* (1974); *La rosa profunda* (1975); *La moneda de hierro* (1976); *Obra poética* (1977).

JULIA DE BURGOS

Canción de la verdad sencilla (1940); *Poemas en veinte surcos* (1940); *El mar y tú* (1954 posthum.).

JOÃO CABRAL DE MELO NETO

Pedra do sono (1942); *O engenheiro* (1945); *O cão sem plumas* (1950); *Morte e vida Severina* (1956); *Quaderna* (1960); *Dos parlamentos* (1961); *Terceira feira* (1961); *A educação pela pedra* (1966); *Poesias completas (1940–1965)* (1968); *Museu de tudo* (1976).

ERNESTO CARDENAL

La ciudad deshabitada (1946); *Proclama del conquistador* (1947); *Hora o* (1960); *Gethsemane, Kentucky* (1961); *Epigramas* (1961); *Oración por Marilyn Monroe y otros poemas* (1965); *El estrecho dudoso* (1966); *Salmos* (1969); *Homenaje a los indios americanos* (1969); *Vida en el amor* (1970); *En Cuba* (1972); *Oráculo sobre Managua* (1973); *Antología de la poesía primitiva* [anthology] (1980).

JORGE CARRERA ANDRADE

La guirnalda del silencio (1926); *Boletines de mar y tierra* (1930); *Latitudes* [essays] (1932, 1940); *El tiempo manual*

(1935); *Antología poética 1922–1939* (1940); *Micrograma* [translations of Japanese poems] (1940); *Registro del mundo* (1940); *Canto al puente de Oakland* (1941); *Lugar de origen* (1947); *Hombre planetario* (1957–1963); *Crónica de las Indias* (1965); *El alba llama a la puerta* (1965–1966).

ROSARIO CASTELLANOS

Trayectoria del polvo (1948); *Apuntes para una declaración de fe* (1948); *El rescate del mundo* (1952); *Poemas (1953–1955)* (1957); *Balún Canán* [novel] (1957); *Al pie de la letra* (1959); *Lívida luz* (1960); *Materia memorable* (1969); *Poesía no eres tú: 1952–1972* (1972); *El eterno femenino* [theater piece] (1975).

JOSÉ SANTOS CHOCANO

La selva virgen (1893, 1898); *En la aldea* (1895); *El canto del siglo* (1901); *El fin de Satán* (1901); *Poesías completas* (1902); *Cantos del Pacífico* (1904); *Alma América* (1906); *¡Fiat Lux!* (1908); *Poemas del amor doliente* (1937); *Oro de Indias* [4 vols.] (1939–1941).

ANTONIO CISNEROS

Destierro (1961); *Canto ceremonial contra un oso hormiguero* (1968); *Agua que no has de beber* (1971); *Como higuera en un campo de golf* (1972); *El libro de Dios y de los húngaros* (1978); *Crónica del Niño Jesús de Chilca* (1982).

JULIO CORTÁZAR

Bestiario [stories] (1951); *Final del juego* [novel] (1956); *Las armas secretas* (1958); *Los premios* [novel] (1960); *Historias de cronopios y de famas* [prose poems] (1962); *Rayuela* [novel] (1963) ; *Todos los fuegos el fuego* [fiction] (1966); *La vuelta al día en ochenta mundos* [fiction] (1967); *62: Modelo para armar* [fiction] (1969); *Último round* [essays] (1969); *Libro de Manuel* [novel] (1973); *Fantomas contra los vampiros multinacionales* [essays] (1975); *Pameos, meopas, y posemas* [fiction] (1984).

ALFONSO CORTÉS

Poesías (1931); *Tardes de oro* (1934); *30 poemas de Alfonso*, ed. Ernesto Cardenal (1952); *Las puertas del pasatiempo* (1967); *El poema cotidiano y otros poemas: Autobiografía* (1967); *Poesías* (1970).

JOÃO DA CRUZ E SOUSA

Tropos e fantasias [collaboration with Virgílio Várzea] (1885); *Broquéis* (1893); *Missal* [prose poems] (1893); *Evocações* [prose poems] (1898); *Faróis* (1900); *Últimos sonetos* (1905); *Obras completas* (1923–1924); *Obra completa* (1961).

PABLO ANTONIO CUADRA

Poemas nicaragüenses (1934); *Canto temporal* (1943); *La tierra prometida* (1952); *Libro de horas* (1956); *El jaguar y la luna* (1959); *Cantos de Cifar* (1960, 1971, 1979); *Siete árboles contra el atardecer* (1980).

ROQUE DALTON

La ventana en el rostro (1961); *El turno del ofendido* (1963); *Taberna y otros lugares* (1969); *Las historias prohibidas del Pulgarcito* (1974); *Poemas clandestinos* (1976 posthum.).

RUBÉN DARÍO

Epístolas y poemas (1885); *Abrojos* (1887); *Rimas* (1887); *Azul...* (1888); *Los raros* (1896); *Prosas profanas* (1896); *Cantos de vida y esperanza* (1905); *Los cisnes y otros poemas* (1905); *El canto errante* (1907); *El viaje a Nicaragua* (1909); *Poema del otoño* (1910); *Canto a la Argentina* (1914); *Obras completas* (1950–1955); *Poesías completas* (1967); *Autobiografías* (1976).

CARLOS DRUMMOND DE ANDRADE

Alguma poesia (1930); *Brejo das almas* (1934); *Sentimento do mundo* (1940); *Poesias* (1942); *Confissões de Minas* [essays] (1944); *A rosa de povo* (1944); *Claro enigma* (1951); *Fazendeiro de ar e poesia até agora* (1954); *Viola de bolso novamenta encordoada* (1955); *A vida passada a limpo* (1959).

JOSÉ MARÍA EGUREN

Simbólicas (1911); *Poesías* (1929); *Obras completas* (1974).

EUGENIO FLORIT

Doble acento 1930–1936 (1937); *Asonante final y otros poemas* (1955); *Hábito de esperanza* (1965); *Antología penúltima* (1970); *Versos pequeños: 1938–1975* (1975); *Obras completas* (1985).

JUAN GELMAN

Violín y otras cuestiones (1956); *El juego en que andamos* (1959); *Gotán* (1962); *Poemas* (1968); *Cólera buey* (1971).

ENRIQUE GONZÁLEZ MARTÍNEZ

Preludios (1903); *Silénter* (1909); *Los senderos ocultos* (1911); *La muerte del cisne* (1915); *Jardines de Francia* [translations] (1915); *Las señales furtivas* (1925); *Poemas truncos* (1935); *Bajo el signo mortal* (1942); *El nuevo Narciso* (1952); *Obras completas* (1971).

JOSÉ GOROSTIZA

Canciones para cantar en las barcas (1925); *Muerte sin fin* (1939); *Del poema frustrado* (1964); *Poesía* (1964).

ERNESTO [CHE] GUEVARA

Guerra de guerrillas [guerrilla tactics and political theory] (1961); *Che* [autobiography] (1969 posthum.); *Diario de Che en Bolivia* (1973 posthum.); *Escritos y discursos* (1977 posthum.); *Diario de Che* (1984 posthum.); *Obras completas* (1984 posthum.).

NICOLÁS GUILLÉN

Motivos de son (1930); *Sóngoro cosongo* (1931); *España* (1937); *West Indies, Ltd.* (1937); *Cantos para soldados y sones para turistas* (1937); *Sóngoro consogo y otros poemas* (1943); *El gran zoo* (1967); *Diario que a diario* (1972); *Poesías completas* (1973).

FERREIRA GULLAR

Um pouco acima do chão (1949); *A luta corporal* (1954); *Quem matou Aparecida?* (1962); *Se correr o bicho pega, se ficar o bicho come* [play] (1966); *Vanguarda e subdesenvolvimento* [essays] (1969); *Dentro da noite veloz* (1975); *Poema sujo* (1975); *Antologia poética* (1978); *Uma luz do chão* (1978); *Na verdigem do dia* (1980); *Toda poesia* (1980); *Barulhos: 1980–1987* (1988).

ÓSCAR HAHN

Esta rosa negra (1961); *Agua final* (1967); *Arte de morir* (1977, 1979, 1981); *Mal de amor* (1981).

JULIO HERRERA Y REISSIG

Los maitines de la noche (1902); *Los éxtasis de la montaña* (1904, 1907); *Los peregrinos de piedra* (1909); *La torre de las esfinges* (1909); *Obras completas* (1909–1913); *Los parques abandonados* (1919); *Las pascuas del tiempo* (1920); *Las lunas de oro* (1924); *Poesías completas y páginas en prosa* (1961).

EFRAÍN HUERTA

Absoluto amor (1935); *Línea del alba* (1936); *Poemas de guerra y esperanza* (1943); *Los hombres del alba* (1944); *La rosa primitiva* (1950); *Poesía* (1956); *Estrella en alto* (1956); *Poemas de viaje* (1957); *Para gozar tu paz* (1957); *¡Mi país, oh mi país!* (1959); *Elegía de la policía montada* (1959); *Farsa trágica del presidente que quería una isla* [play] (1961); *La raíz amarga* (1962); *El Tajín* (1963); *Antología poética* (1977); *Poesía completa* (1988).

VICENTE HUIDOBRO

Ecos del alma (1911); *Canciones en la noche* (1913); *La gruta del silencio* (1913); *Las pagodas ocultas* (1914); *Adán* (1916); *El espejo de agua* (1916); *Horizon carré* (1917); *Tour Eiffel* (1918); *Hallali, poéme de guerre* (1918); *Ecuatorial* (1918); *Poemas árticos* (1918); *Saisons choisies* (1921); *Automne régulier* (1925); *Tout á coup* (1925); *Altazor, o el viaje en paracaídas* (1931); *Ver y palpar* (1939); *El ciudadano del olvido* (1941); *Antología* (1945); *Últimos poemas* (1948 posthum.); *Obras completas* (1964).

SARA DE IBÁÑEZ

Canto (1940); *Canto a Montevideo* (1941); *Hora ciega* (1943); *Pastoral* (1948); *Artigas* (1951); *Las estaciones y otros poemas* (1957); *La batalla* (1967); *Apocalipsis 20* (1970); *Canto póstumo* (1971); *Obras completas* (1978).

JUANA DE IBARBOUROU

Las lenguas de diamante (1919); *El cántaro fresca* (1920); *Raíz salvaje* (1922); *La rosa de los vientos* (1930); *Chico Carlo* [prose] (1944); *Los sueños de Natacha* [play] (1945); *Perdida* (1950); *Azor* (1953); *Mensajes de escriba* (1953); *Dualismo* (1953); *Oro y tormenta* (1956); *La pasajera* (1967); *Obras completas* (1953, 1960, 1967).

RICARDO JAIMES FREYRE

Castalia bárbara (1899); *Tucumán en 1810* [history/cultural history] (1909); *Historia del descubrimiento de Tucumán* (1916); *Los sueños son vida* (1917); *Leyes de la versificación castellana* [literary theory] (1919); *Los conquistadores* (1928); *Poesías completas* (1957).

VÍCTOR JARA

Lyrics to Víctor Jara's poems, in Spanish and in English, are given in Joan Jara, *An Unfinished Song: The Life of Victor Jara* (1984) and in many recordings.

ROBERTO JUARRÓZ

Poesía vertical (1958, 1963, 1965, 1969, 1974, 1976, 1982, 1984, 1988).

CLAUDIA LARS

Estrellas en el pozo (1934); *La casa de vidrio* (1942); *Ciudad bajo mi voz* (1946); *Sonetos* (1947); *La canción redonda* (1947); *Donde llegan los pasos* (1955); *Escuela de pájaros* (1955); *Romances de Norte y Sur* (1956); *Tierra de infancia* (1958); *Fábula de una verdad* (1959); *Nuestro pulsante mundo* (1959); *Sobre el ángel y el hombre* (1962); *Del fino amanecer* (1967); *Apuntes* (1975); *Cartas escritas cuando crece la noche* (1975); *Póstuma* (1975).

JOSÉ LEZAMA LIMA

Muerte de Narciso (1931); *Enemigo rumor* (1941); *Aventuras sigilosas* (1945); *La fijeza* (1949); *Analecta reloj* [essays] (1953); *La expresión americana* [essays] (1957); *Dador* (1960); *Paradiso* [novel] (1966); *Poesías completas* (1970 posthum.); *Fragmentos a su imán* (1978 posthum.).

ENRIQUE LIHN

La pieza oscura (1963); *Poesía de paso* (1967); *La musiquilla de las pobres* (1969).

JORGE DE LIMA

O mundo do menino impossível (1925); *Poemas* (1927); *Novos poemas* (1929); *A túnica inconsútil* (1935); *Calunga* (1935); *A mulher obscura* (1939); *Invenção de Orfeo* (1952).

HENRIQUETA LISBOA

Enternecimento (1929); *Velário* (1936); *O menino poeta* (1943); *Montanha viva: Caraça* (1959); *Belo Horizonte bem querer* (1972); *Pausada do ser* (1982); *Obra completa* (1985).

RAMÓN LÓPEZ VELARDE

La sangre devota (1916); *Zozobra* (1919); *El minutero* (1923); *El son del corazón* (1932); *Poemas escogidos* (1935); *Obras completas* (1966).

LEOPOLDO LUGONES

Las montañas del oro (1897); *Los crepúsculos del jardín* (1905); *Lunario sentimental* (1909); *Odas seculares* (1910); *El libro fiel* (1912); *Cuentos* [stories] (1916); *El payador* (1916); *El libro de los paisajes* (1917); *Las horas doradas* (1922); *Romancero* (1924); *Poemas solariegos* (1928); *Romances de Río Seco* (1938); *Obras poéticas completas* (1948).

JOSÉ MARTÍ

Amor con amor se paga (1876); *Guatemala* (1878); *Versos libres* (1882, 1913); *Ismaelillo* (1882); *Amistad funesta* (pseud. 1885); *Versos sencillos* (1891); *Artículos desconocidos* (1930 posthum.); *Epistolario de José Martí* (1930 posthum.); *Obras del Maestro* (1900–1933); *Obras completas* (1918–1920); *Flores del destierro (versos inéditos)* (1933 posthum.); *Obras completas* (1963–1973).

CECÍLIA MEIRELES

Espectros (1919); *Nunca mais... e poemas dos poemas* (1923); *Baladas para El-Rei* (1925); *Batuque, samba e macumba* [drawings of gestures and rhythms] (1934, 1983); *Viagem* (1939); *Vaga música* (1942); *Mar absoluto* (1945); *Romanceiro da inconfidência* (1953); *Canções* (1956); *Metal rosicler* (1960); *Solombra* (1963); *Poesias completas* (1973).

GABRIELA MISTRAL

Sonetos de la muerte (1914); *Desolación* (1922); *Lecturas para mujeres* [prose] (1923); *Ternura* (1924); *La lengua de Martí* [prose] (1934); *Tala* (1938); *Lagar* (1954); *Antología* (1955); *Obras completas* (1958).

ENRIQUE MOLINA

Las cosas y el delirio (1941); *Pasiones terrestres* (1946); *Costumbres errantes o la redondez de la tierra* (1951); *Amantes antípodas* (1961); *Fuego libre* (1962); *Las bellas furias* (1966); *Hotel pájaro* (1967); *Monzón napalm* (1968); *Obra poética* (1978); *Los últimos soles* (1980).

RICARDO MOLINARI

Mundos de la madrugada (1943); *El alejado* (1943); *El huésped y la melancolía* (1946); *Unida noche* (1957); *El cielo y las alondras y las gaviotas* (1963); *Un día, el tiempo, y las nubes* [personal anthology] (1964); *Obra poética* (1978); *Obra completa* (1984).

NANCY MOREJÓN

Mutismos (1962); *Amor, ciudad atribuída* (1964); *Richard trajo su flauta* (1967); *Parajes de una época* (1979); *Poemas* (1980); *Octubre imprescindible* (1983); *Cuaderno de Granada* (1984).

ÁLVARO MUTIS

La balanza (1948); *Los elementos del desastre* (1953); *Diario de Lecumberri* [stories] (1960); *Los trabajos perdidos* (1961); *Suma de Maqroll el gaviero* [novellas] (1973); *Poesía y prosa* (1982).

PABLO NERUDA

Crepusculario (1923); *Veinte poemas de amor y una canción desesperada* (1924); *Residencia en la tierra, 1925–1931* (1933, 1935, 1947); *España en el corazón* (1937); *Canto general* [incl. *Alturas de Macchu Picchu*] (1950); *Los versos del capitán* (1953); *Odas elementales* (1954); *Nuevas odas elementales* (1956); *Tercer libro de odas* (1957); *Obras completas* (1957); *Extravagario* (1958); *Cien sonetos de amor* (1959); *Las piedras de Chile* (1961); *Plenos poderes* (1962); *Memorial de Isla Negra* [memoirs] (1964); *Arte de pájaros* (1966); *Fin del mundo* (1969); *Confieso que he vivido* [memoirs] (1974 posthum.); *Poesías escogidas* (1980 posthum.).

AMADO NERVO

Místicas (1898); *Perlas negras* (1898); *Poemas* (1901); *El éxodo y las flores del camino* (1902); *Lira heroica* (1902); *Cantos esolares* (1903); *Las voces* (1904); *Los járdines interiores* (1905); *En voz baja* (1909); *Serenidad* (1914); *Elevación* (1917); *El estanque de los lotos* (1919); *Obras completas* (1938).

EUNICE ODIO

Los elementos terrestres (1948); *El tránsito del fuego* (1957); *Pasto de sueños* (1971); *Últimos poemas* (1972); *Territorio del alba: 1946–1972* (1974 posthum.).

OLGA OROZCO

Desde lejos (1946); *Las muertes* (1951); *Los juegos peligrosos* (1962); *Museo salvaje* (1974); *Cantos a Berenice* (1977); *La noche a deriva* (1984).

JOSÉ EMILIO PACHECO

Los elementos de la noche (1963); *Poesía de paso* (1966); *Morirás lejos* [novel] (1967); *No me preguntas cómo pasa el tiempo* (1969); *Isla a la deriva* (1976).

HEBERTO PADILLA

Las rosas audaces (1948); *El justo tiempo humano* (1960); *Fuera del juego* (1966); *Por el momento* (1970); *El hombre junto al mar* (1980); *Autorretrato del otro* [autobiography] (1980); *En mi jardín pastan los héroes* [novel] (1981); *Fontana, casa de piedra* (1991).

LUIS PALÉS MATOS

Azaleas (1915); *Tuntún de pasa y grifería* (1937); *Litoral* [novel] (1949); *Poesía 1915–1956* (1957); *Poesía completa y prosa selecta* (1978).

NICANOR PARRA

Cancionero sin nombre (1937); *Nebulosa* (1950); *Poemas y antipoemas* (1954); *La cueca larga* (1958); *Versos de salón* (1962); *Ejercicios respiratorios* (1966); *La camisa de fuerza* (1968); *Canciones rusas* (1969); *Obra gruesa* (1969); *Los profesores* (1971); *Poemas de emergencia* (1972); *Artefactos* (1972); *Memorias de un ataúd* (1975); *Sermones y prédicas del Cristo de Elqui* (1977); *Nuevas sermones y prédicas del Cristo de Elqui* (1979); *Ecopoemas* (1983); *Últimos poemas* (1983); *Poemas inéditos* (1984).

VIOLETA PARRA

Poesía popular y de los Andes (1964); *Décimas: Autobiografía en versos chilenos* (1967 posthum.); *Toda Violeta Parra* (1974 posthum.); *Violeta del pueblo* (1976 posthum.).

OCTAVIO PAZ

Luna silvestre (1933); *Raíz del hombre* (1937); *Bajo tu clara sombra* (1937); *Entre la piedra y la flor* (1941); *A la orilla del mundo* (1942); *Libertad bajo palabra* (1949); *¿Águila o sol?* (1951); *Semillas para un himno* (1954); *Piedra de sol* (1957); *La estación violenta* (1958); *Libertad bajo palabra* (1935–1958); *Homenaje y profanaciones* (1960); *El laberinto de la soledad* [cultural criticism] (1961); *Salamandra 1958–1961* (1962); *Viento entero* (1965); *Blanco* (1967); *Corriente alterna* (1967); *Hacia el comienzo* (1968); *Topoemas* (1968); *Ladera este* (1969); *Posdata* (1970); *Vuelta* (1975); *Sor Juana Inés de la Cruz, o, Las trampas de la fe* (1982); *Árbol adentro* (1987).

CARLOS PELLICER

Colores en el mar (1921); *Seis, siete poemas* (1924); *Piedra de sacrificios* (1924); *Esquemas para una oda tropical* (1933); *Subordinaciones* (1948); *Práctica de vuelo* (1956); *Con palabras y fuego* (1962); *Teotihuacán y 13 de agosto* (1964); *Obras* (1977).

ALEJANDRA PIZARNIK

La tierra más ajena (1955); *La última inocencia* (1956); *Las aventuras perdidas* (1958); *Árbol de Diana* (1962); *Los trabajos y las noches* (1965); *Extracción de la piedra de la locura* (1968); *Nombres y figuras* (1969); *La condesa sangrienta* (1971); *El infierno musical* (1971); *Textos* (1971); *Poemas* (1978).

ADÉLIA PRADO

Bagagem (1976); *O coração disparado* (1978); *Salte os cachorros* (1979); *Cacos para um vitral* (1980); *Terra de Santa Cruz* (1981); *Os componentes da banda* (1984); *O pelicano* (1987).

ALFONSO REYES

El suicidio [essays] (1917); *Las vísperas de España* [cultural criticism] (1917, 1932, 1937); *El plano oblicuo* [stories] (1920); *Simpatías y diferencias* [journalism] (1921–1926); *Huellas* (1922); *Ifigenia cruel* [dramatic poem] (1924); *Romances del Río de Enero* (1933); *Cantada en la tumba de Federico García Lorca* (1937); *Capítulos de la literatura española* (1939, 1945); *La experiencia literaria* (1942); *Obra poética 1906–1952* (1952); *Parentalia* [memoirs] (1959); *Obras completas* (1955–1968), esp. vol. 10, *Contancia poética* (1958).

GONZALO ROJAS

La miseria del hombre (1948); *Contra la muerte* (1964); *Oscuro* (1977); *Del relámpago* (1978); *Trastierro* (1979); *Antología del aire: Selección* (1991).

JAIME SABINES

Horal (1950); *La señal* (1951); *Tarumba* (1956); *Recuentro de poemas* (1962); *Yuria* (1967); *Maltiempo* [prose poem] (1972).

ALFONSINA STORNI

La inquietud del rosal (1916); *Irremediablemente* (1919); *Languidez* (1920); *El mundo de siete pozos* (1934); *Mascarilla y trébol* (1938); *Obra poética* (1946, 1952); *Obras completas* (1964).

JORGE TEILLIER

Para ángeles y gorriones (1956); *El cielo cae con las hojas* (1958); *El árbol de la memoria* (1961); *Poema del país de Nunca Jamás* (1963); *Los trenes de la noche y otros poemas* (1964); *Crónica del forastero* (1968); *Muertes y maravillas* (1971); *Para un pueblo fantasma* (1978); *Cartas para reinas de otras primaveras* (1985).

JAIME TORRES BODET

Fervor (1918); *Margarita de niebla* (1927); *La educación sentimental* [novel] (1929); *Destierro* (1930); *Cripta* (1937); *Sombras* [novel] (1937); *Sonetos* (1949); *Fronteras* (1954); *Tiempo de arena* [autobiography] (1955); *Sin tregua* (1957); *Trébol de cuatro hojas* (1958); *Discursos 1941–1964* [speeches] (1965); *Obra poética* (1967).

CÉSAR VALLEJO

Los heraldos negros (1918); *Trilce* (1922); *Tungsteno* [novel] (1931); *Poemas humanos* (1939 posthum.); *España, aparta de mí este cáliz* (1940 posthum.); *Obra poética completa* (1968).

XAVIER VILLAURRUTIA

Reflejos (1926); *Nocturnos* (1931); *Nocturno mar* (1937); *Nocturno a la rosa* (1937); *Nostalgia de la muerte* (1938, 1946); *Textos y pretextos* [essays] (1940); *Invitación a la muerte* [play] (1943); *Canto a la primavera* (1948); *Poesía y teatro completos* (1953).

GABRIEL ZAID

Fábula de Narciso y Ariadna (1958); *Seguimiento* (1964); *Campo nudista* (1969); *Cuestionario: Poemas 1951–1976* (1977).

RAÚL ZURITA

Purgatorio (1979); *Selección de poemas* (1980); *Anteparaíso* (1982).

ACKNOWLEDGMENTS

Every effort has been made to ensure that permissions for all material were obtained. The editor cannot take responsibility for any errors and omissions, but would be grateful for notification and corrections. Those sources not formally acknowledged here will be included in all future editions of this book.

AGOSÍN, MARJORIE: La danza / The Dance, from *Brujas y algo mas / Witches and Other Things*, trans. Cola Franzen, Latin American Literary Review Press, copyright © 1984. Reprinted by permission of the author.

AGUSTINI, DELMIRA: Las alas, Otra estirpe, Visión, Lo inefable, La barca milagrosa, from *Poesías completas*, copyright © 1971. The Wings, trans. Elizabeth Gordon, copyright © 1993 by Elizabeth Gordon. Another Race, Vision, The Ineffable, The Miraculous Ship, trans. Karl Kirchwey, copyright © 1993 by Karl Kirchwey.

ALEGRÍA, CLARIBEL: Hacia la edad jurásica / Toward the Jurassic Age and Éramos tres / We Were Three, from *Flowers from the Volcano*, trans. Carolyn Forché, by permission of the University of Pittsburgh Press. Copyright © 1982 by Claribel Alegría and Carolyn Forché.

ANDRADE, MÁRIO DE: Inspiração, Os cortejos, Domingo, Nocturno, from *Paulicea desvairada*, copyright © 1972 by the Livraria Martins Editora, S. A. Inspiration, The Processions, Sunday, Nocturne, from *Hallucinated City*, trans. Jack E. Tomlins, copyright © 1968 by the Vanderbilt University Press. Reprinted by permission.

ANDRADE, OSWALD DE: falação, erro de português, fronteira, o hierofante, buena-dicha, plebiscito, from *Obras completas*, copyright © 1970 by Ed. Civ. Brasileiro. Babbling, Portuguese Mistake, Frontier, Hierofant, Good Luck, Election, trans. Flavia Vidal, copyright © 1994 by Flavia Vidal.

ARIDJIS, HOMERO: Epitafio para un poeta, Cae la lluvia . . ., Salir de la mujer es separarse, Decomposición con risa, Carta de México, El poema, copyright © 1975 and 1977 by Editorial Joaquín Mortiz, S. A. Reprinted by permission. Epitaph for a Poet, The Rain Is Falling, trans. John Frederick Nims, from *Sappho to Valéry: Poems in Translation*, copyright © 1990. Reprinted by permission of the University of Arkansas Press. To Emerge from a Woman Is to Become Separate, trans. W. S. Merwin, and Decomposition with Laughter, trans. Jerome Rothenberg, from *Blue Spaces*, ed. Kenneth Rexroth, copyright © 1969 by the Seabury Press. Letter from Mexico, The Poem, from *Exaltation of Light: Poems by Homero Aridjis*, trans. Eliot Weinberger, copyright © 1980 by Eliot Weinberger. Reprinted with the permission of BOA Editions, Ltd.

ARMAND, OCTAVIO: Soneto; Braille para mano izquierda; Otra poética; Poema con piel; A buen entendedor, pocas palabras: copyright © 1984 Octavio Armand. Sonnet, trans. Jason Shinder copyright © 1993 by Jason Shinder. Braille for Left Hand, Another Poetics, Poem with Skin, A Word to the Wise, from *With Dust*, trans. Carol Maier, copyright © 1984 by Logbridge-Rhodes Pub. Co. Reprinted by permission.

AZEREDO, RONALDO: concretist poem (see Appendix). By permission of the author.

BANDEIRA, MANUEL: Poética, Evocação do Recife, Rondó dos cavalinhos, Retrato, Vou-me embora pra Pasárgada, Entrevista, Boda espiritual, Mozart no céu, from *Poesia completa y prosa*, copyright © 1971 by José Olympio. By permission of the heirs of Manuel Bandeira. Poetics, Evocation of Recife, Rondeau of the Little Horses, Portrait, Off to Pasárgada, Interview, Spiritual Wedding, from *This Earth*, *That Sky*, trans. Candace Slater, Regents of the University of California and the University of California Press, copyright © 1989, reprinted by permission. Mozart in Heaven, trans. Dudley Poore, from *An Anthology of Contemporary Latin American Poetry*, ed. Dudley Fitts, copyright © 1942, 1947 by New Directions Pub. Corp. Reprinted by permission of New Directions Publishing Corp.

BELLI, CARLOS GERMÁN: Segregación no. 1, Por qué me han mudado, Una desconocida voz . . ., ¡Abajo las lonjas!, Papá, mamá, ¡Oh padres, sabedlo bien . . .!, Segregation #1, trans. Isabel Bize, copyright © 1993 by Isabel Bize. Why Have They Moved Me; An

CORTÁZAR, JULIO: Conducta de los espejos en la isla de Pascua, Historia verídica, Las líneas de la mano, Costumbres de los famas, Viajes, from *Historias de cronopios y de famas*, copyright © 1962. Reprinted by permission of the Carmen Balcells Agency, for Aurora Bernárdez. The Behavior of Mirrors on Easter Island, A Very Real Story, The Lines of the Hand, Normal Behavior of the Famas, and Travel, from *Cronopios and Famas*, trans. Paul Blackburn, copyright © 1969. Reprinted by permission of Random House, Inc.

CORTÉS, ALFONSO: La canción del espacio, La gran plegaria, from *Treinta poemas*, copyright © 1981 by Editorial Nueva Nicaragua. Space Song, Great Prayer, from *Emblems of a Season of Fury*, trans. Thomas Merton, copyright © 1963 by the Abbey of Gethsemani Inc. Reprinted by permission of New Directions Publishing Corp.

CRUZ E SOUSA, JOÃO: Antífona, Acrobata da dor, Sexta-feira Santa, Ódio sagrado, from *Obra completa*, copyright © 1961 by Ed. Aguilar. Antiphony, trans. Nancy Vieira Couto, copyright © 1993 by Nancy Vieira Couto. Acrobat of Pain, Good Friday, Sacred Hatred, trans. Flavia Vidal, copyright © 1994 by Flavia Vidal.

CUADRA, PABLO ANTONIO: El nacimiento del sol, Caballos en el lago, Manuscrito en una botella, La estrella vespertina, used by permission of Pablo Antonio Cuadra. Caballos en el lago / Horses in the Lake and Manuscrito en una botella / Manuscript in a Bottle originally appeared in *Hudson Review* 30, no. 4 (Winter 1977); La estrella verpertina / The Evening Star originally appeared in *Translation* 5 (Spring 1978). All are published in *Songs of Cifar and the Sweet Sea*, trans. Grace Schulman and Ann McCarthy de Zavala, copyright © 1979, Columbia University Press. By permission.

DALTON, ROQUE: Arte poética, Buscándome líos, El descanso del guerrero, La pequeña burguesía, De un revolucionario a J. L. Borges. Reprinted by permission of Aida Canas. Ars Poetica, Looking for Trouble, Soldier's Rest, and The Petty Bourgeoisie, trans. Richard Schaaf, from *Roque Dalton: Poems*, Curbstone Press, Willimantic, Conn., © 1984. Reprinted by permission of Alexander Taylor, editor. From a Revolutionary to J. L. Borges, trans. Julie Schumacher, copyright © 1994 by Julie Schumacher.

DARÍO, RUBÉN: Primaveral, Yo persigo una forma . . ., Era un aire suave . . ., El Cisne, Sonatina, Caracol, Lo fatal, A Roosevelt, Tarde del trópico, Nocturno, Tríptico de Nicaragua, from *Obras completas* (1950–1955), copyright © 1955. Springtime, I Seek a Form, It Was a Gentle Air, The Swan, Sonatina, Fatality, To Roosevelt, Tropical Afternoon, Nocturne, and Nicaraguan Triptych, from *Selected Poems of Rubén Darío*, trans. Lysander Kemp, copyright © 1965, University of Texas Press (stanza 11 of It Was a Gentle Air was not included in *Selected Poems*; it has been translated by Stephen Tapscott).

DRUMMOND DE ANDRADE, CARLOS: Poema de sete faces, Não se mate, Infância, Viagem na família, Resíduo, Retrato de família, Canto esponjoso, Elegia, Um boi vê os homens, No meio do caminho, used by permission of Carlos Drummond de Andrade. Seven-sided Poem, Don't Kill Yourself, Infancy, trans. Elizabeth Bishop, from *An Anthology of Twentieth-Century Brazilian Poetry*, ed. Elizabeth Bishop and Emanuel Brasil, copyright © 1972 by Wesleyan University Press, reprinted by permission of the publisher and of the distributor, University Presses of New England. Travelling as a Family, Residue, Portrait of a Family, Diminutive, Elegy, copyright © 1980 Virginia de Araújo, from Carlos Drummond de Andrade, *The Minus Sign*, trans. Virginia de Araújo (Redding Ridge, Conn.: Black Swan Books, 1981), reprinted by permission of the publisher. All rights reserved. An Ox Looks at Man, trans. Mark

Strand, from *Travelling in the Family: Selected Poems of Carlos Drummond de Andrade*, ed. Thomas Colchie, 1986. Reprinted by permission of Random House, Inc. In the Middle of the Road, from *In the Middle of the Road*, trans. John Nist, copyright © 1965. Reprinted by permission of the University of Arizona Press.

EGUREN, JOSÉ MARÍA: Las torres; Los muertos; Las niñas de luz; Peregrín, cazador de figuras: from *Obras completas*, copyright © 1974, Editorial Milla Batres. The Towers; The Dead; The Girls of the Light; Peregrin, Wandering Hunter of Faces: trans. Iver Lofving, copyright © 1993 by Iver Lofving.

FLORIT, EUGENIO: Elegia para tu ausencia, Tarde presente, Martirio de San Sebastián, from *Obra completa*, copyright © 1985. Reprinted by permission of the author. Elegy for Your Absence, The Present Evening, trans. H. R. Hays, copyright © 1943. Reprinted by permission of the Estate of H. R. Hays [Mrs. Juliette Hays]. The Martyrdom of Saint Sebastian, trans. Peter Fortunato copyright © 1993 by Peter Fortunato.

GELMAN, JUAN: Los ojos, Épocas, Historia, from *Obra poética*, copyright © 1975 by Corregidora Ediciones. Eyes, Epochs (trans. Elinor Randall and Robert Márquez), and History (trans. Robert Márquez), from *Latin American Revolutionary Poetry*, copyright © 1974 by Robert Márquez. Reprinted by permission of Monthly Review Foundation.

GONZÁLEZ MARTÍNEZ, ENRIQUE: Como hermana y hermano, Tuércele el cuello al cisne, La ventana, Dolor, Último viaje, El néctar de Ápam, from *Obras completas*, copyright © 1971. Like Sister and Brother, trans. Nancy Christoph, copyright © 1993. By permission. Wring the Swan's Neck, Pain, and Last Journey, from *An Anthology of Mexican Poetry*, ed. Octavio Paz, trans. Samuel Beckett, copyright © 1958. Reprinted by courtesy of The Beckett Estate and the Calder Educational Trust. Copyright © Indiana University Press [British commonwealth rights]. Wring the Swan's Neck, Pain, Last Journey, from *An Anthology of Mexican Poetry*, ed. Octavio Paz, trans. Samuel Beckett, copyright © 1958. Reprinted by permission of Indiana University Press [world rights except British Commonwealth but including Canada]. The Window, The Nectar of Ápam, trans. Elizabeth Gordon, copyright © 1993 by Elizabeth Gordon.

GOROSTIZA, JOSÉ: ¿Quién me compra una naranja?, Elegía, Luciérnagas, (de) *Muerte sin fin*, from *Poésia*, copyright © 1964 by the Fondo de Cultura Ecónomica. Who Will Buy Me an Orange?, Elegy, and Fireflies, selections from *Death without End*, in *Nine South American Poets*, trans. Rachel Benson, copyright © 1968 by the Las Américas Publishing Co.

GUEVARA, ERNESTO [CHE]: Canto a Fidel / Song to Fidel, from *Our Word: Guerrilla Poems from Latin America*, trans. Ed Dorn and Gordon Brotherston, copyright © 1968 by Cape Goliard. Reprinted by permission.

GUILLÉN, NICOLÁS: Pequeña oda a un negro boxeador cubano, El apellido, and Bares, from *Obra Poetica, 1922–1958*, copyright © 1985. Reprinted by permission of Letras Cubanas, Havana. Small Ode to a Black Cuban Boxer, My Last Name, from *Man-making Words: Selected Poems of Nicolás Guillén*, trans. Robert Márquez and David Arthur McMurray, copyright © 1972. Reprinted by permission of the University of Massachusetts Press. Bars, trans. Eric Orozco, copyright © 1994 by Eric Orozco.

GULLAR, FERREIRA: Oswald morto, No corpo, No mundo há muitas armadilhas, Poster, Cantada, from *Antologia poética*, copyright © 1978; Barulho, from *Barulhos, 1980–1987*, copyright © 1988.

LUGONES, LEOPOLD: Delectación morosa, La blanca soledad, Salmo pluvial, Olas grises, from *Obras poéticas completas*, copyright © 1948 Indulgence, White Solitude, Rain Psalm, Gray Waves, trans. Julie Schumacher, copyright © 1993 by Julie Schumacher.

MARTÍ, JOSÉ: Sueño despierto; Contra el verso retórico . . .; (de) *Versos sencillos*, I, IX, X, XXXVI; Dos patrias: from *Obras completas*, copyright © 1946 Ediciones Lex (La Habana). I Dream Awake; The Opposite of Ornate and Rhetorical Poetry; *Simple Verses* I, IX, X, XXXVI; Two Countries: from *José Martí: Major Poems*, bilingual edition, trans. Elinor Randall, ed. Philip S. Foner (New York: Holmes and Meier, 1982). Copyright © 1982 by Holmes and Meier Publishers, Inc. Reprinted by permission of the publisher.

MEIRELES, CECÍLIA: Retrato, Desenho, Vigília, Balada das dez bailarinas do cassino, O cavalo morto, from *Poesías completas*, copyright © 1973. Reprinted by permission of Sr. Alexandre Carlos Teixeira for the Meireles estate. Portrait, Sketch, trans. Luiz Fernández García, copyright © 1993 by Luiz Fernández García. Vigil, Ballad of the Ten Casino Dancers, and The Dead Horse, trans. James Merrill, from *An Anthology of Twentieth-Century Brazilian Poetry*, ed. Elizabeth Bishop and Emanuel Brasil, copyright © 1972 Wesleyan University Press. Reprinted by permission of the publisher and of the distributor, the University Presses of New England.

MISTRAL, GABRIELA: Decálogo del artista / Decalogue of the Artist, La casa / The House, Apegado a mí / Close to Me, La flor del Aire / The Flower of Air, Una Palabra / One Word, Una mujer / A Woman, Último árbol / Final Tree, from *Selected Poems of Gabriela Mistral*, bilingual edition, ed. and trans. Doris Dana, copyright 1971 by the Johns Hopkins University Press for the Library of Congress. By permission.

MOLINA, ENRIQUE: Mientras corren los grandes días, Como debe de ser, from *Obra poética*, copyright © 1988 by Monte Avila, C.A. As the Great Days Flow, The Way It Must Be, trans. Naomi Lindstrom, from *Toward an Image of Latin American Poetry*, ed. Frank Graziano, copyright © 1982 by Logbridge-Rhodes Pub. Co. Reprinted by kind permission of the publisher.

MOLINARI, RICARDO: Poema de la Niña Velázqueña, Oda a una larga tristeza, Pequeña oda a la melancolía, from *Páginas*, copyright © 1983 by Ed. Celtia, S. A. Reprinted by permission of the author. Poem of the Girl from Velázquez, Ode to a Long Sorrow, Little Ode to Melancholy, trans. Inés Probert, copyright © 1993 by Inés Probert.

MOREJÓN, NANCY: Madre; Amor, ciudad atribuída; Richard trajo su flauta; Desilusión para Rubén Darío: from *Poemas*, copyright © 1980 by UNAM, Mexico. Mother; Love, Attributed City; Richard Brought His Flute; Disillusion for Rubén Darío: from *Where the Island Sleeps Like a Wing*, trans. Kathleen Weaver, copyright © 1985 by The Black Scholar. Reprinted by permission of the author.

MUTIS, ÁLVARO: Amén, Canción del este, Una palabra, Sonata, from *Poesía y prosa*, copyright © 1982 by Instituto Columbiano de Cultura. Reprinted by permission of the author. Amen, East Song, A Word, Sonata, trans. Sophie Cabot Black and Maria Negroni, copyright © 1993 by Sophie Cabot Black and Maria Negroni.

NERUDA, PABLO. Copyright © Pablo Neruda and heirs of Pablo Neruda: I. -Cuerpo de mujer, VII. -Inclinado en las tardes, and XX. -Puedo escribir los versos, from *Veinte poemas de amor y un canción desesperada*, © 1924; Galope muerto, Walking around, and Explico algunas cosas, from *Residencia en la tierra*, © 1933; Algunas bestias, *Alturas de Macchu Picchu* [sections], La United Fruit Co., and América, no invoco tu nombre en vano, from *Canto General*, 1950;

Oda a la pereza, Oda a César Vallejo, from *Odas elementales*, © 1954; Oda a los calcetines, from *Nuevas odas elementales*, © 1957; Oda a la sal, from *Tercer libro de odas*, © 1957; sonnets V, XVI, and XCII, from *Cien sonetos de amor* © 1959. The editor wants to express special thanks to the representatives of the Agencia Literaria Carmen Balcells, S. A., of Barcelona, acting on behalf of the Fundación Pablo Neruda, in representation of the heirs of Pablo Neruda. Body of a Woman, Leaning into the Afternoons . . ., Tonight I Can Write . . ., from *Twenty Love Poems and a Song of Despair*, trans. W. S. Merwin, copyright © 1969 by Viking Penguin, reprinted by permission of Viking Penguin, Inc. Dead Gallop, The Heights of Macchu Picchu X, trans. John Felstiner, from John Felstiner, *Translating Neruda: The Way to Macchu Picchu*, copyright © 1982 by Stanford University Press. Reprinted by permission of the author. Walking Around, trans. Ben Belitt, from *Selected Poems of Pablo Neruda*, copyright © 1961 by Grove Press. Reprinted by permission. I'm Explaining a Few Things, The Heights of Macchu Picchu VI, trans. Nathaniel Tarn, from *Selected Poems of Pablo Neruda*, ed. Nathaniel Tarn, copyright © 1972 Delacorte Press. United Fruit Co., trans. Jack Schmitt, from *Canto General*, copyright © 1991 by the University of California Press. Reprinted by permission. America, I Do Not Call Your Name without Hope; Ode to My Socks: trans. Robert Bly, from *Selected Poems of Neruda and Vallejo*, copyright © 1971 by Beacon Press. Some Beasts, trans. James Wright, from *Selected Poems of Neruda and Vallejo*, copyright © 1971 by Beacon Press. The Heights of Macchu Picchu XII, trans. David Young, from *The Heights of Macchu Picchu*, copyright © 1987 by the Story Line Press. Reprinted by kind permission of the author. Ode to Laziness, trans. William Carlos Williams, from the magazine *New World Writing*, copyright © 1991 by William Eric Williams and Paul H. Williams. Reprinted by permission of New Directions Publishing Corp. Ode to Salt, trans. from Margaret Sayers Peden, *Selected Odes of Pablo Neruda*, copyright © 1990 by the University of California Press. Reprinted by permission. Sonnets V, XVI, and XCII, from *One Hundred Love Sonnets*, trans. Stephen Tapscott, copyright © 1986 by the University of Texas Press; Ode to César Vallejo, trans. Stephen Tapscott, copyright © 1994 by Stephen Tapscott.

NERVO, AMADO: Venganza, El dolor vencido, El don, Éxtasis, from *Obras completas*, copyright © 1938, 1981. Revenge, Sorrow Vanquished, The Gift, Ecstasy, trans. Sue Standing, copyright © 1993 by Sue Standing.

ODIO, EUNICE: Recuerdo de mi infancia privada, Creación, Carta a Carlos Pellicer, *Territorio del alba: Poemas 1946–1972*, copyright © 1972 by Ed. Universitaria Centroamericana [EDUCA]. Prólogo del tiempo que no está en sí, from *El transito del fuego*, copyright © 1957 by Ministerio de Cultura, San Salvador. Memory of My Private Childhood, trans. Suzanne Jill Levine, copyright © 1992 by Suzanne Jill Levine. Creation, Prologue to a Time That Is Not Itself, Letter to Carlos Pellicer, trans. Martha Collins, copyright © 1993 by Martha Collins.

OROZCO, OLGA: Miss Havisham, Olga Orozco, from *Las muertes*, copyright © 1951; Para hacer un talismán, from *Los juegos peligrosas*, copyright © 1962, La realidad y el deseo, from *Museo salvaje*, copyright © 1974: reprinted by kind permission of the author. Miss Havisham, Olga Orozco, To Make a Talisman, Reality and Desire, trans. Stephen Tapscott, copyright © 1993 by Stephen Tapscott.

PACHECO, JOSÉ EMILIO: Alta traición; Indagación en torno del murciélago; Job 18, 2; Límites: from *No me preguntas cómo pasa el tiempo*, copyright © 1984 by Ediciones Era, S. A. Reprinted by permission. High Treason, An Enquiry concerning the Bat, and Job

Selected Poems of Jaime Torres Bodet, trans. Sonja Karsen, copyright © 1964 by Indiana University Press.

VALLEJO, CÉSAR: Los heraldos negros, Heces, El pan nuestro, A mi hermano Miguel, Ágape, "Pienso en tu sexo," "Voy a hablar de la esperanza," Piedra negra sobre una piedra blanca, "La cólera que quiebra al hombre en niños," "Fué Domingo en las claras orejas de mi burro," "Hoy me gusta la vida mucho menos," Poema para ser leido y cantado, "Un hombre pasa con un pan al hombro," and (from *España, aparta de mí este càliz*) IX -Pequeño responso a un héroe de la República, XII -Massa, XIV -España, aparta de mí este cáliz. All poems from *Obra poética completa*, notes by Georgette Vallejo, copyright © 1968, Lima. The Black Messengers, trans. Rachel Benson, from *Nine South American Poets*, copyright © 1968 by Las Américas Pub. Co. Down to the Dregs, Our Daily Bread, To My Brother Miguel, trans. James Wright with John Knocpfle, from *Selected Poems of Neruda and Vallejo*, Beacon Press [Sixties Press imprint], copyright © 1971. Reprinted by permission. Ágape, from *César Vallejo: Selected Poems*, trans. Ed Dorn and Gordon Brotherston, copyright © 1976 by Penguin Books. Reprinted by permission of the authors. "I'm thinking of your sex," trans. Sandy McKinney, copyright © 1993 by Sandy McKinney. "I am going to talk about hope," Black Stone Lying on a White Stone, trans. Robert Bly with John Knoepfle, from *Selected Poems of Neruda and Vallejo*, Beacon Press [Sixties Press imprint], copyright © 1971. Reprinted by permission of the author. Anger, from *Collected Poems of Thomas Merton*, copyright © 1977 by the Trustees of the Merton Legacy Trust. Reprinted by permission of New Directions Publishing Corp. "It was Sunday in the fair ears of my burro"; "Today I like life much less"; Poem To Be Read and Sung; "A man walks by with a loaf of bread on his shoulder"; and (from *Spain, Take This Cup From Me*) IX. Short Prayer for a Loyalist Hero; XII. Mass; XIV. Spain, Take This Cup from Me: all from *César Vallejo: The Complete Posthumous Poetry*, trans. and ed. Clayton Eschleman and José Rubia Barcia, copyright © 1978. Permission granted by the Regents of the University of California and the University of California Press.

VILLAURRUTIA XAVIER: Nocturno de Los Ángeles, Nocturno, Poesía, Nocturno de la estatua, Nuestro amor, from *Antológia*, copyright © 1977 by Fondo Cultura Económica. Los Angeles Nocturne, trans. Rachel Benson, from *Nine South American Poets*, copyright © 1968, by Las Américas Pub. Co. Nocturne, trans. Xavier Leroux, copyright © 1993 by Xavier Leroux. Poetry, Nocturne of the Statue, trans. Dana Stangel, copyright © 1993 by Dana Stangel. Our Love, trans. Michael Surman, copyright © 1994 by Michael Surman.

XISTO PEDRO: concretist poems (see Appendix). By permission of Maria Amelia da Carvalli.

ZAID, GABRIEL: Canción de seguimiento, Claustro, Práctica mortal, Claridad furiosa, Circe, Reloj del sol, copyright © 1964, 1977, 1993. Reprinted by kind permission of the author. Song of Pursuit, Cloister, Mortal Practice, trans. Mónica Hernández-Cancio, copyright © 1993 by Mónica Hernández-Cancio. A Furious Clarity, trans. George McWhirter, copyright © 1993. Circe, trans. Andrew Rosing, copyright © 1993 by Andrew Rosing. Sundial, trans. Adrian Hernandez, copyright © 1993 by Adrian Hernandez.

ZURITA, RAÚL: Las espejeantes playas, La marcha de las cordilleras, Aún abandonados florecerían, VI, Esplendor en el viento, *Anteparaíso*, copyright © 1982. The Sparkling Beaches, The March of the Cordilleras, Even Forsaken They'd Flower, VI, Splendor in the Wind, from *Anteparadise: A Bilingual Edition*, trans. and ed. Jack Schmitt, the University of California Press, 1986. Reprinted by permission of the University of California Press and the Regents of the University of California.

INDEX OF FIRST LINES
(ORIGINAL LANGUAGE)

INDEX OF FIRST LINES
(ENGLISH)

INDEX OF AUTHORS AND TITLES